A treatise on social theory

VOLUME TWO

A treatise on social theory

VOLUME II: SUBSTANTIVE SOCIAL THEORY

W. G. Runciman, F.B.A.

FELLOW OF TRINITY COLLEGE, CAMBRIDGE

Published by the Press Syndicate of the University of Cambridge
The Pitt Building, Trumpington Street, Cambridge CB2 1RP
40 West 20th Street, New York, NY 10011–4211, USA
10 Stamford Road, Oakleigh, Melbourne 3166, Australia

First published 1989
Reprinted 1993

Printed in Great Britain at the
Athenaeum Press Ltd, Newcastle upon Tyne

British Library cataloguing in publication data

Runciman, W.G. (Walter Garrison), 1934–
A treatise on social theory.
Vol. 2: Substantive social theory
1. Sociology
I. Title
301

Library of Congress cataloguing in publication data

Runciman, W.G. (Walter Garrison), 1934–
A treatise on social theory.
Includes bibliographical references and index.
Contents: v. 1. The methodology of social theory –
v. 2. Substantive social theory.
1. Sociology – Philosophy.
2. Social sciences – Methodology.
3. Social sciences – Philosophy.
I. Title
HM15.R85 301′.01 82–4490

ISBN 0 521 24959 7 hardback
ISBN 0 521 36983 5 paperback

UP

A treatise on social theory

VOLUME I: THE METHODOLOGY OF SOCIAL THEORY

1 Introduction: the nature of social theory
2 Reportage in social theory
3 Explanation in social theory
4 Description in social theory
5 Evaluation in social theory

VOLUME II: SUBSTANTIVE SOCIAL THEORY

1 Introduction: societies as subjects for science
2 Social relations
3 Social structure
4 Social evolution

VOLUME III: APPLIED SOCIAL THEORY

1 Introduction: the case of twentieth-century England
2 The case reported
3 The case explained
4 The case described
5 The case evaluated

VOLUME II

Substantive social theory

Contents

	Preface	*page* xi
1	Introduction: societies as subjects for science	1
	What are societies made of?	1
	The dimensions of social structure	12
	Roles and systacts	20
	Mobility of persons and roles	27
	Competitive selection and social evolution	37
	Inter-societal comparisons and principles of taxonomy	48
	Conclusion	60
2	Social relations	61
	The range of variation	61
	Standard roles and routine careers	70
	Functional differentiation and the accretion of power	76
	Ranks, distances and barriers	86
	Systactic identity and collective consciousness	97
	Pervasive roles and central institutions	113
	Conclusion	121
3	Social structure	123
	Stability and dissent	123
	Reproduction, polarization and compression	138
	Systactic patterns and modes of the distribution of power	148
	Contradictions and constraints	172
	Functional alternatives (1)	182
	Functional alternatives (2)	208
	Functional alternatives (3)	244
	Inter-societal relations	266
	Conclusion	283
4	Social evolution	285
	Processes of change	285
	Regressions and catastrophes	310
	Dead-ends and turning-points	320
	Rebellions, reforms and revolutions	340
	Test cases (1)	367
	Test cases (2)	386
	Test cases (3)	411

Hegemony and decline 433
Conclusion 448

List of references 451

Index 481

Preface

This volume can be read without reference back to its predecessor. But it does assume without further argument the methodology which it was the purpose of Volume I to expound. It assumes, that is, that the reportage, explanation, description and evaluation of social events, processes and states of affairs are different activities appealing to separate criteria. Like all works of social science, it accordingly raises descriptive and evaluative questions of a kind which never arise in the sciences of nature. But the substantive theory advanced in it stands or falls according to the standards of science in general – the accuracy of the observations which it reports, and the validity of the hypotheses of cause and effect which are invoked to explain them.

I take it also as read that the purpose to which a work of sociological theory is directed is different from a work of either history or anthropology as conventionally defined, even though there is no methodological distinction to be drawn between the three. This volume is concerned neither with the detailed narrative sequences which are the stock-in-trade of the historian nor with the detailed interrelations between institutions which are the stock-in-trade of the anthropologist. It is concerned only with the two questions: first, what distinctive kinds of society – which is to say, what modes and sub-types of the distribution of the means of production, persuasion and coercion – are possible at a given stage of evolution, and second, why it is that any given society has evolved into one rather than another of the possible modes and sub-types. I well realize how irritating it will be for historians of France to see the consequence of the Revolution of 1789 treated in a few summary pages, or for anthropologists specializing in foraging or hunting societies to see the resemblances and differences between them compressed into a single oversimplified paragraph. But I hope they will accept that this is an inevitable consequence of the difference of purpose between us. It is only by classification and comparison of this deliberately schematic kind that it is possible to begin to do for the study of societies what Darwin and his successors have done for the study of species.

Even with this opening reservation, any work which draws for its examples on the whole range of societies documented in the historical and ethnographic record poses an impossible problem about the citation of references. I cannot hope to list all those which I have consulted, or even to trace the route which has led me to one small part of the available literature rather than another. All I have done is to give a reference wherever it seems to me that readers are likely to want to ask one or more of the questions 'who did you get that from?', 'what makes you so sure?', and 'where can I go for a little more detail than you have chosen to give?' Where possible, I have relied on authorities who, so far as I can judge, would be accepted as such by specialists of all schools, and the references given in the text do not fully reflect the extent of my debt to, for example, Brunt on Republican Rome, Duby on medieval Europe, Khazanov on the nomadic pastoralists of Central Asia, or Dore on Tokugawa and later Japan. But where, as for certain periods in the evolution of certain parts of Europe, I have some direct familiarity with the sources, I am uncomfortably aware of how contentious the conclusions of even the most respected authorities can be. The remarkable advances which have been made in the past few decades in our understanding of the workings and evolution of societies far apart from one another in time and place have left me with a feeling at once of gratitude to the authors without whose earlier achievements a volume like this one could not have been attempted at all and of caution about the revisions and qualifications which future research will undoubtedly require.

I have also been faced with a dilemma about the use and transliteration of sociological terms from languages other than English. To include too many is to invite a charge of pedantry. But to include too few is to compel the serious reader to take on trust interpretations which specialists might well regard as disputable. I have compromised as best I can, and where the language in question is Greek, Latin, French, German, Italian or Spanish I am reasonably confident of my judgement about the nuances carried by vernacular terms for institutions, practices and roles. But in all other languages, I have had to rely entirely on the authorities on whose writings I have drawn, and I have followed the transliteration adopted by the author in question without attempting to achieve consistency across the volume as a whole.

I have not thought it necessary to append a glossary of technical and semi-technical terms, whether English or foreign, since they are (I hope) adequately defined or interpreted in the text. But I have put in heavy type in the Index the references to them where a definition or interpretation is given, so that readers can refer back to them as and when they may need.

My particular thanks are due to Professors Ernest Gellner, Eric Hobsbawm and David Lockwood, who agreed to read the whole of the draft of this volume and whose comments have been of the greatest value. I have also been fortunate in being able to draw on the advice of friends and colleagues whose expertise in particular areas I hope I have not misused, notably Simon Keynes on Anglo-Saxon England, Nicholas Postgate on Ancient Mesopotamia, David Brading on Hispanic America and the late Sir Moses Finley on Classical Greece and Rome. Finally, I must reiterate my gratitude to the Council of my College for my continuing tenure of a Senior Research Fellowship under Title B, and to my wife, to whom the treatise as a whole is dedicated, for her unfailing understanding and support.

W.G.R.

Trinity College, Cambridge
December 1987

I

Introduction: societies as subjects for science

WHAT ARE SOCIETIES MADE OF?

§1. Sociology begins at the point at which nature evolves into culture. It is true that there is no one such point, either historically or analytically. Historically, the emergence of *Homo sapiens sapiens* even from his immediate predecessors was a process which extended over many tens of thousands of years. Analytically, the conventional definitions of man as a social animal or a tool-making animal or even, perhaps, a speech-using animal have all been undermined by what is now known of the attributes and capacities of other species. But for the purpose of sociological theory, what matters is that the long millennia of biological evolution did in the end produce a species capable of the extra-organic transmission of progressively more complex patterns of information. It is a debatable question how far a better understanding (in the explanatory sense) of how this came about would carry over into a better understanding of the workings of the many thousands of societies which have evolved since the discovery of weapons, fire, art, clothing, houses, pottery, towns, agriculture, iron, the wheel and the written word. But what is incontestably necessary is an awareness of the degree to which, at each stage, the range of forms of social institutions has been widened. The fact that we are all descended from big-forebrained, strong-fingered, bipedal-gaited, pair-bonded ancestors of what we now refer to as the Early Palaeolithic age is very much less important to the sociologist (or anthropologist or historian) than the converse fact that from those same ancestors there have evolved societies as we now know them with all the properties which are unique to man.

What, then, are human societies made of? The trivial answer that they are made of persons interacting non-randomly is trivial because it leaves unspecified those emergent properties by which both the form and the content of the interaction are defined. A substantive social theory can be formulated only in terms of concepts which stand for groups and categories of persons related to each other in certain ways and therewith for the ways in which the persons so related conceive of those relations themselves. Which such concepts are most useful depends on the merits of the theory that dictates their choice. But once the choice has been made, the explanation of any given society will involve taking the appropriate sub-set of its properties and giving a valid account of why they are as they are and not as they might have been; the description of it will involve taking the appropriate sub-set of its properties and giving an authentic account of the ways in which they are experienced by representative members of the various groups, categories and milieux of which it is composed; and the evaluation of it – so far as lies within the sociologist's as opposed to the philosopher's competence – will involve taking the appropriate sub-set of its properties and giving a coherent account of the degree to which they can be judged a good thing or a bad from the point of view of the well-being of the different groups or categories of its members as they have perceived it themselves.

In this volume, societies are conceptualized in terms of the allocation of power among their members, for the simple and sufficient reason that non-random interaction among and between the members of any and all societies necessarily implies their capacity mutually to influence each other's behaviour. Admittedly, the concept of power already has a long and uneasy history in social theory. But it remains as impossible to do without as it is difficult to define. Bertrand Russell (1938, p. 10) went so far as to suggest that power is as important a concept to social science as is the concept of energy to physical science; and although his book on the topic did nothing much to vindicate his claim, he was entirely right to make it. In what follows, I shall use *power* to stand for the capacity of persons to affect through either inducements or sanctions what is thought, felt, said or done by other persons,* subject to that capacity deriving from the possession of institutional, not personal, attributes – *institutions* being defined in turn as sets of interrelated practices whose rules, which may or may not be either explicitly formulated or universally acknowledged, apply to specifiable groups or categories of persons irrespective of those persons' choice or consent. So defined, power is everywhere and always a reciprocal relationship: A cannot have power over B without B having some power, however minimal, over A,

* Such capacity need not be 'real' – that is, it is enough to vindicate a report that a designated person has power for it to be demonstrable that it is believed, even if mistakenly, that by virtue of incumbency of a role the person's behaviour would have the effects stipulated by law or custom. This assumption is uncontentious even among theorists who differ in other respects about the definition of 'power'; but it does no harm for it to be made thoroughly explicit (as e.g. by Luhmann 1970, pp. 42–3).

even if neither is aware of its extent or of its unintended consequences. *Domination*, accordingly, obtains to the extent that one party to an institutional relationship both has and exercises more power than another. *Cooperation*, by contrast, obtains to the extent that persons within an institution, or acting on behalf of its members, pursue a joint interest with other persons irrespective of differences in power between them (if any). Capacities and actions governed by the possession of institutional as opposed to personal attributes are distinguished by the concept of *roles*, defined as positions embodying consistently recurring patterns of institutional behaviour informed by mutually shared beliefs and expectations about their incumbents' capacity directly or indirectly to influence the behaviour of each other.* *Societies*, as such, are then fully defined by the itemization of all the roles occupied by their members, the *location* of those roles is defined by reference to the dimensions of social space within which power is allocated, and *interests* are defined in terms of maintenance or augmentation of power attaching to roles in one or more of these dimensions. *Corporations*, finally, are formally, and *associations* informally, constituted collectivities of persons sharing a common interest relative to some one or more institutions but at the same time internally differentiated by roles internal to themselves. To put it summarily: the study of societies is the study of people in roles, and the study of people in roles is the study of the institutional distribution of power.

It might be objected that to analyze societies and define their constituents in this way is to presuppose that conflict of interests is 'fundamental' to human relations. But it does so only to the degree that resources being limited and their distribution unequal, all persons are thereby in either actual or potential competition with one another – a truism from which it is surely difficult for any rival observer from whatever theoretical school to dissent. To agree with it is not to endorse a Hobbesian presupposition to the effect that the 'natural' state of human society is a war of all against all. It is no more to be presupposed that cooperation for mutual advantage has somehow to be explained away as abnormal than that the quest for domination is a pathological aberration within otherwise healthy social organisms. When, how far and under what conditions domination or cooperation obtains is a matter to be settled by empirical research.

Nor does the analysis of societies in these terms presuppose that all

* It follows that roles are not merely *occupied* but also *performed* by their incumbents. But the definition is not as slipshod as this apparent confusion of metaphors may make it appear, since the location of the role entails the institutional behaviour required (in the absence of special explanation) of the incumbent, and *vice versa*.

their members are either consistently or exclusively motivated by self-interest. It would be as demonstrably mistaken to assert that all persons in all societies are concerned either to move into more powerful roles or to augment the power attaching to their existing ones as it would be to assert that the incumbents of more powerful roles are necessarily happier or more fortunate on that account. But it is because there is always a potential, if not actual, conflict of interest between them that the concept of power is fundamental to social theory. Indeed, there would still be conflicts of interest even in a society (such as does not exist) peopled entirely by altruists. To explain (or describe, or evaluate) the workings and evolution of any society it is necessary to discover how the motives and actions of those who *do* pursue their interests both influence and are influenced by the form and content of their relations of domination and cooperation among themselves and with other people. The range of variation between one society and another, vast as it is, is neither infinite nor random; and it is only as the outcome of an institutionalized competition for power that it can be explained (or, for those who wish also to do so, described and evaluated).

The aim of this volume is principally explanatory: such descriptive or evaluative conclusions as are proffered are only in passing. But this makes it all the more important that the distinction between the three should be kept firmly in mind. To agree, as I have done, with Russell that the concept of power is as fundamental to sociology as that of energy to physics is not to imply that societies ought all to be described in terms of greed, violence, ambition and Machiavellian *Realpolitik*. Some are indeed like that for those who live in them. But many others are not – whatever may be the underlying relations of domination which are misapprehended or mystified in the *Weltanschauungen* of their various component milieux. Nor do I imply that societies are either better or worse to live in because actual or potential conflicts of interest are intrinsic to them all: it is up to you whether those who regard their own well-being as improved or diminished by the exercise of power in one way rather than another should or should not be overruled on some other evaluative ground. Descriptive and evaluative questions do, inevitably, arise out of any explanation offered of how societies work and why they have evolved as they have. But the answers to them are in no way pre-empted by either the form or the content of whatever causal hypotheses about the distribution of power within them may turn out to be capable of being furnished with adequate theoretical grounding.

§2. The criterion of *membership* of a society, however, is itself problematic. Societies are not entities given in nature. Their boundaries are both fluid and tenuous, and many roles and institutions either overlap or transcend them. Nor, except incidentally, do *institutional catchment areas* – that is, regions of social space where rule-governed practices related to particular forms of power define a sub-set of roles – coincide with territorial frontiers. This may not seem so in the case of an independent autarkic *polis*, or an isolated and homogeneous lineage-group, or a nation-state with clearly defined frontiers, a common language, an autonomous government and a stable population. But no society strictly conforming to these ideal types has ever existed for any length of time, and even societies which come anywhere near it are rare enough. Once given that – subject only to the arguable exceptions of infants, hermits, psychopaths and impending suicides – persons and the groups, categories, associations and corporations which they form are always and everywhere linked to one another by institutional as well as personal relations of both domination and cooperation, the boundaries of societies need to be drawn at the points where they become either so tenuous as effectively to elude the catchment of the institutions ostensibly governing them or so weak as effectively to be governed by the institutions of another society. But the possibilities of both multiple and partial membership are in practice very wide: Chidiock Tichbourne, executed in 1586 for conspiring to kill Queen Elizabeth, was more a member of the Church of Rome than of the Kingdom of England. To point this out is not to minimize the importance of territory and population which between them encompass a variation all the way from itinerant bands of hunter-gatherers numbering less than 100 persons* among whom relations of domination are minimal to an extended polyglot empire encompassing a population of hundreds of millions held together largely by force. But the range of variation in degree and extent of societal membership can be abundantly illustrated from the writings of sociologists, anthropologists and historians: the member of a local tribal group inhabiting an area on the boundary between zones of patrilineal and matrilineal inheritance; the member of a separate ethnic and religious community in a country ruled by a colonial power; the member of a separatist commune set up within a state still exercising sovereignty over it; the member of a community of primary producers dependent upon the terms of credit and purchase accorded to them for their produce by alien merchants operating across national frontiers; the

* The lower limit on size is determined not by numbers as such but by the need for a society to be capable of reproducing itself: given a taboo on incest, a single biological family can never constitute a society.

member of a religious order answerable to both a spiritual and a temporal authority whose claims are in conflict with each other; the member of a migrant workforce having citizen rights partly in the country of temporary residence and partly in the country of origin; the member of a border settlement seeking protection from, and giving services to, both of two rival overlords between whose territory the border lies; and so on.

Moreover, societies have – like institutions – boundaries in historical time as well as in social space. Not only may people move from one role to another either within the boundaries of whatever societies they belong to or across those boundaries into another society; they may equally well stay where they are – or appear to themselves to be – and find that their societies or institutional catchment areas have so far changed around them that their roles too have changed out of recognition. Again, the range of possibilities is easily illustrated by examples: the member of a self-governing village community in a society conquered by a rival nation; the member of a traditional occupational community undermined by the effects of a technological revolution; the member of a church or sect proscribed as a result of a change of government or regime; the member of an externally identifiable ethnic or regional group embroiled in a civil war; the member of a trading outpost or commercial enclave destroyed by domestic restraint or foreign competition; the member of a military caste or profession no longer answerable to its traditional sovereign following war, decolonization or revolution; and so on.

These two considerations impose a consequential restriction on the sense in which societies can be spoken of as 'social systems'. Within the standard definition of a *system* – viz., any set of interacting variables – the assertion that societies are systems is uncontroversial. But it is not to be pre-emptively used to suggest that all social systems are self-equilibrating in the absence of exogenous disturbance. Such a presupposition is not illegitimate. But it is, or can be, doubly misleading. Not only does it have to be so construed as never to be directly testable against the evidence, but it invites the equally untestable rejoinder that social systems tend, on the contrary, to fall apart unless held together. Both assertions can in some contexts and for some purposes be construed as testable claims about some societies under some conditions. But there is as little warrant for presupposing that either cohesiveness or instability are 'the' normal state as there is for crediting either domination or cooperation with primacy over the other as 'the' general principle of social organization. It is, admittedly, right that the term 'system' should be allowed to carry some deliberate implication of continuity. Indeed, an implication of continuity is built almost by definition into the characterization of societies as such, for it is hardly more possible to conceive in sociology of an institution lasting only for a day than to conceive in psychology of an emotional state lasting only for a second. But the continuity of a society is subject to both the openness of its boundaries and the mutability of its institutions over what may be quite short periods of time.

However societies' boundaries are delineated, whether in time or in social space, there will always be borderline cases which cannot be settled by fiat. The point at which a society should or should not be treated as the same society is not a theory-neutral matter on which all rival observers will agree: it depends what they are seeking to explain (or describe or evaluate). But individual cases can, all the same, be reported initially in terms of the general concept of *differentiation*. However small the difference or slow the change between one society and another which different observers may regard as significant, they will be bound to agree that the process involved is a continuous one both logically and temporally. Just as the boundaries of a species are defined in biology by reference to the capacity of individual members to interbreed within a gene-pool, so are the boundaries of a society defined in sociology by the capacities of individual members to interact within a set of institutions – but with the all-important difference that the capacity to interact with the institutions of another society is attainable extra-organically. This therefore gives to the process of social differentiation a double mutability. Not only can a society be transformed within very much less than a single generation, but it can gain or lose individual members otherwise than through birth and death. Differentiation, therefore, is constantly proceeding both by the establishment of new systems or sub-systems of domination and cooperation and also by changes, whether endogenously or exogenously caused, of existing systems. Once given that societies are fully defined by the itemization of the roles of their members, and their boundaries delimited by the capacity of their members to interact institutionally and not simply personally, differentiation has to be analyzed in terms jointly of increasing incompatibility in interaction and of diminishing contact across social space, of which the limiting case is *fission* (i.e., the splitting of one society into two). Conversely, a society which does not merely recruit from but incorporates another may do so either by *absorption* (i.e., more by domination than cooperation) or by *fusion* (i.e., more by cooperation than by domination). No such definitions, however carefully drawn, can by themselves yield a precise and uncontroversial dividing-line between one society and the next: both absorption and fusion may be partial, or temporary, or both, and even fission may be reversible. But this need be no more serious an impediment to the classification and analysis of societies than of species.*

Once, moreover, a society has been delimited as such, the concept of *social change* can be clearly defined by reference to the axiom that societies are made of people in roles. It follows from that axiom that to speak of change either in or of any society is to speak of one or other of four things: first, movement of persons from role to role; second, movement from one location to another of persons *in* their roles; third, change in the content of roles; and fourth, the appearance of new roles into which persons have therefore to move from others or, conversely, the disappearance of existing roles from which their incumbents have therefore to move out. Since societies are constantly reproducing themselves demographically, whether by birth or immigration or both, there is always an inter- as well as intra-generational aspect to these changes, and this gives a distinctive meaning to the term *reproduction* in its sociological sense: it is the process by which new persons entering a society or institutional catchment area occupy roles which are either similarly or differently located from those occupied by their predecessors. Similarly, once change (whether inter- or intra-generational) has been defined in this way, *polarization* can be used to denote a widening, and *compression* a narrowing, of social distance between roles and therewith their incumbents, whether new or old.

§3. Before, however, it is possible to proceed to a more detailed exposition of the terms in which societies can be reported and compared, another familiar distinction needs to be elucidated. All societies – and all institutions – have a dual aspect roughly corresponding to the still more general distinction between form and content: structural and cultural. In this volume, the term *culture* will be used in two ways: first, to distinguish (as I did in my opening sentence) those features of social organization which derive from the capacity to transmit learning extra-organically; second, to refer to the content of the institutional rules (which are, of course, 'cultural' in the first sense) by which relations of domination and cooperation in human societies are governed. *Structure*, by contrast, will be used, as it generally is, to refer to the pattern as

* Cf. Darwin (1866, p. 553): 'No one can draw any clear distinction between individual differences and slight varieties; or between more plainly marked varieties and sub-species and species.'

opposed to the substance of relations of domination and cooperation, whether between persons, roles, groups, categories, associations, corporations, institutions or societies themselves.

Formally, the notions of culture and structure can be related directly to the four different kinds of social change set out in the previous section: movement of persons between roles need not entail either structural or cultural change; movement of persons in their roles is change of structure but not necessarily of culture; change in the nature and content of roles is change of culture but not necessarily of structure; and the appearance of new or disappearance of old roles is a change of both. It might therefore seem, at least in principle, that under some conditions structure and culture could vary independently from each other. But in practice they cannot. It is true that patterns of domination can be represented diagrammatically and classified in terms of a finite (but very, very large)* number of possible alternatives which may be applicable to a set of societies not only remote in time and place but also very different in culture from one another. It is also true that the same cultural rules for the allocation of power may be applicable to a set of societies in which the resulting patterns of domination are not all the same. But within any actual society, changes in structure never take place in total independence of culture, if only to the degree that structural changes must be permitted if not actually required by the institutional rules which govern the content of the roles whose location is changed; and likewise, when a group or category of persons retains its location relative to others even after the old institutional rules have changed, this is because its members have succeeded in adapting their behaviour to the new ones.

In practice, therefore, to talk of the structure of a society is to talk not merely of the formal properties of the rank-order of the roles occupied by its members but of the cultural content of the rules by which the power attaching to them is generated, preserved or modified. Observers are still free to report the structure in terms of properties of which the members of the society may themselves be unaware, and thereby to compare it with others of which 'they' are entirely ignorant. But 'their' customs and laws have first to have been understood in the primary sense – the sense, that is, in which they are social facts on the reportage of whose occurrence all rival observers can agree. Such questions as: is the dominance order transitive throughout the society? or, does the

* The number of possible 'dominance structures' for a three-person group is 2; but for an eight-person group it is already 6,880 (Coleman 1960, p. 106, citing a proof given by Davis 1954).

distribution of power follow an asymptotic curve with a long upper tail? are questions about structure rather than culture, and they are questions which will not be readily answerable by native informants unless they happen to be trained sociologists themselves. But they are not questions about structure alone.

In case this discussion seems excessively abstract for the relatively simple point which I am concerned to make, let me illustrate it with an example. There has been, and continues to be, dispute among specialists in the study of the Ancient World as to whether or not it is misleading to speak of the existence of a 'Roman middle class'. It is one of those disputes which is likely to strike the non-specialist reader as purely verbal: why not let everyone say what they mean by 'middle class' and then decide by appeal to the evidence whether the chosen definition does or does not fit the Roman case? But it is not so easy. If it were possible to consider structure separately from culture, this procedure could be followed readily enough. Of course, all observers can agree that there is a 'middle' class, structurally speaking, if the distribution of power is such that there is a distinguishable group or category of persons located somewhere between top and bottom; and since there can be shown to have been a lot of male household heads who were, structurally speaking, neither at the top nor the bottom of Ancient Roman society, it might appear simply a matter of deciding the cut-off points by fiat and classifying the borderline cases accordingly. But 'middle class' is not a theory-neutral term. Admittedly, the Romans themselves would have no difficulty in accepting its application to them: the Roman 'knights' (*equites*) were undeniably in the middle to the extent that they were non-aristocrats who nevertheless fulfilled a minimum property qualification. But closer inspection discloses a much more complex set of institutional rules governing the distribution of power in Roman society and the burdens or privileges attaching to the roles performed within it. The difficulty is not that the term 'middle class' carries, to 'us', overtones which it would be anachronistic to apply to 'them', for this is not by itself a decisive argument against its use in the proper context. It is that the institutional rules cut across the categorization which places those who were, like the *equites*, below the senatorial nobility as in 'the middle'. If power in its various forms was so distributed that *equites*, as both customarily and legally defined, were clearly intermediate in possessions, functions, privileges, opportunities and rights between a similarly clear-cut category above them and another below, then it would be at least arguable that they should be spoken of as a 'middle class'. But they were not. The distinction between slaves, freedmen and those born free, the common relation of senators and *equites* to the mode of production, the dominance of trade and commerce by the state, the importance of military as opposed to civilian roles, and the difference between Rome and the provinces all make the application of the term not only theoretically pre-emptive but even, in all but strictly delimited contexts, inaccurate as a piece of reportage. No doubt researchers still can, if they want, insist on labelling the *equites*, or indeed some wider group or category, a 'Roman middle class'. But the label cannot then pass the test of transposition *salva veritate* from one explanation (or description, or evaluation) to the next.

To insist that structure cannot be divorced from culture is not, however, to give theoretical primacy to the latter over the former. It might perhaps be argued that structure is the secondary aspect of social organization, a relationship to be inferred at a more abstract level from empirical observations of how things are actually said and done. But then it might equally well be argued that the structure of social relations as directly observed is more immediate and concrete than the institutional rules which govern them, since these are a matter of sentiments and ideas in contrast to the solid facts of actual behaviour. The truth is that neither presupposition is either necessary or helpful to the study of societies as here conceptualized. It is perfectly possible that there are topics on which there are two rival theories of which one gives priority to structure over culture and the other to culture over structure. This occurred, for example, at one time in debates among anthropologists over kinship. One school argued, put broadly, that systems of kinship are to be explained culturally as ways of conceiving of social relations, and the other that they are to be explained structurally as forms of social relations whose conceptualization is neither historically nor analytically prior to them. But there is no such debate calling to be settled one way or the other before a theory of the institutional allocation of power in human societies can be formulated and put to the test. For that purpose, the most important aspect of the relation between culture and structure is the capacity of institutions similar in structure to fulfil quite different functions and institutions similar in function to have quite different structures. For the first, the standard term is (as in biological theory) *homologues*, and for the second *analogues*, and although their application to human institutions is in some contexts controversial, there can be no dispute about the importance of the distinction to any substantive theory of social evolution deserving of the name.

THE DIMENSIONS OF SOCIAL STRUCTURE

§4. Provided, therefore, that the relevant behaviour of its members has not been misunderstood in the primary sense, the structure of a society can be reported initially in terms of the relative locations within it of groups or categories of persons sharing a common endowment (or lack) of power by virtue of their roles. But for the researcher actually to locate them requires an answer to the question how many dimensions of structure there are – or in other words, how many kinds of power. The correct answer is three – the economic, the ideological and the coercive – which, although always mutually interdependent, are never fully reducible to one another. But this distinction, obvious and familiar as it is,* is not unequivocally accepted by practising sociologists (or anthropologists or historians) of all theoretical schools. It can hardly be disputed that there *is* a distinction to be made between access to or control of the *means of production*, *means of persuasion* and *means of coercion* respectively. The more intractable arguments are over whether the three are both exhaustive and irreducible. Like so many disputes in social theory, it is often exacerbated by the intrusion of descriptive and evaluative presuppositions. But there can be genuinely explanatory disagreements over whether primacy is to be accorded to the economic 'base' over the ideological and political 'superstructure', or whether ideas and values determine the form and content of social relations independently of pre-existing economic and political institutions, or whether it is force (or the threat of it) which underlies all other relations of domination and subordination.

The conceptual distinction between economic, ideological and coercive power is already deeply entrenched in our terminology of motives, inducements and sanctions, and although it is true that the language of twentieth-century English-speaking societies has no particularly privileged status over that of others, the rationale for a three-dimensional conceptualization is in no way weakened simply because there are other societies in whose language it is not entrenched in the same way. It is enough that in any society to want money or possessions is not necessarily to want social esteem or prestige on the one hand or political or military office on the other; to want social esteem or

* It is generally held to derive from the writings of Max Weber; but since Weber, like Marx, died with his work on the topic incomplete, its interpretation will always be arguable. My choice of the terms 'means of production', 'means of persuasion', and 'means of coercion' is a conscious attempt to combine what I believe to be the most valuable insights of both Marx and Weber, although neither ever put the distinction in quite this way themselves.

prestige is not necessarily to want money or possessions on the one hand or political or military office on the other; and to want military or political office is not necessarily to want money or possessions on the one hand or social esteem or prestige on the other. Similarly, the presumptive inducements and sanctions by which power of one or other kind is defined fall into three separate and recognizable categories, whatever terms may be employed for them. To be able to grant or withhold the means of acquiring economic goods is not necessarily to be able to grant or withhold either social status or access to the means of physical coercion; and so on. There are three distinguishable families of concepts which correspond to the three dimensions of social space, and although they overlap at many points they are not interchangeable. Within the economic dimension fall the notions of endowment with and exchange, distribution and transfer of goods and/or services, whether through cash, credit or barter and whether or not within the institutional framework of the market; within the ideological dimension fall the notions of deference, exclusiveness and mutual recognition in accordance with some publicly acknowledged criterion of value, whether or not shared by all members of the institution or society within which they are acted out and whether finding expression in endogamy, commensalism, common life-styles, rituals and symbols of honour and dishonour or attributions of merit or demerit by a standard either ascribed or achieved; within the coercive dimension fall the notions of command and obedience or, on the contrary, resistance or rebellion, whether the giving of orders is directly supported by force or the visible threat of force or derives from an acknowledgement of potential access to it. It is true that not only do the three frequently overlap but they are often difficult to disentangle in practice: obedience to a ruler may be bound up with acknowledgement of ritual status, just as acknowledgement of ritual status may be bound up with a genuine belief in the efficacy of supernatural retribution; 'political' power may be exercised by the use of economic sanctions, just as ownership of the means of production may yield a monopoly of the means of coercion. But they are not synonymous with each other, which is what they would have to be shown to be for the claim to be abandoned that each corresponds to, and operates in, a separate dimension of social space.

In the same way, three categories of roles are distinguishable within the institutions which operate in each dimension; and although they often overlap, they do not by any means always coincide, which is what they would have to be shown to do for the three-dimensional framework to be invalidated. It is often said that institutional differentiation is itself found only in societies of a certain kind or beyond a certain stage of social evolution: not only does it not make sense for many of the non-market, stateless societies documented in the historical and ethnographic record to treat as distinct economic, social-cum-ideological and political-cum-military institutions – or, for that matter, law (or '*prédroit*'), kinship, religion and land-tenure – but 'their' terms for roles, sanctions and motives may well be such as deliberately to fuse them. But as with the early Sumerian *lugal* (Oates 1979, p. 25), or the *wanax* in Mycenaean Greece (Hooker 1977, p. 183), the fact that in some societies roles of the three kinds are no more than different aspects of the same institutions does not mean that it is a mistake to conceptualize social structure three-dimensionally. It means only that the culture of some societies is such that the distribution of power clusters so close to the central axis that the structure can be treated in practice as unidimensional.

The alternative line of criticism of a three-dimensional conceptualization is the claim that there is some other kind of power and therefore dimension of social structure which is not adequately embraced by it. It is a criticism which will only be as persuasive as the alternative put forward, and readers may have different views as to what, if any, form of power can least plausibly be subsumed under the threefold categorization. One which recurs from time to time in the academic literature is education (cf. e.g. Svalastoga 1965, Ch. 2). Its persuasiveness derives from the uncontentious observation that, first, knowledge is by definition a kind of power and, second, the educational institutions of all societies in which the family or household does not exclusively undertake the upbringing of children are separately visible and hierarchically ordered. But knowledge is not domination unless institutionally made so. Polymaths do not automatically hold higher institutional rank than other people simply by virtue of the fact that they have learnt things which the others have not. It is only to the extent that education qualifies or entitles those who have it to fill roles to which power of one or more of the three kinds attaches that it ranks them institutionally as opposed to merely individually. Neither it nor any other attribute which may be sought after as a means to wealth, honour or office can constitute of itself a dimension of social structure. To claim that it does is to confuse an indicator with what it is an indicator *of*.

Another suggestion is that there are four 'sources' of power rather than three because political power needs to be distinguished from military (Mann 1986, Ch. 1). But this is to confuse the different kinds of institutional power – that is, of inducements and sanctions which the incumbents of different roles can bring to bear on one another – with the different kinds of institution and forms of organization through which this is done. Political institutions are of course distinguishable from military, as they are from economic and ideological: states are not the same things as armies, markets or churches. Furthermore, the incumbents of political roles frequently command economic and ideological as well as coercive inducements and sanctions. But there is no fourth kind of power to which they have access. The 'political-cum-military', like the economic and 'social-cum-ideological', rubric covers a range of institutions and roles many of which overlap with one another. But there are still only three kinds of power and therefore, by definition, three dimensions of social structure.

There still remains the possibility that although the three dimensions of social structure are in theory distinct, the distribution of the members of a society within them is always determined in practice by one (or two) of them only – or, looked at the other way round, that one (or two) of them are merely derivative. But this is a very strong claim indeed. It is true to say that in certain societies under certain conditions the way in which power is allocated in one dimension determines the way it is allocated in the others. But to claim that any one dimension is *the* determining one is to be exposed to any single counter-example, however unusual, in which it is not. It is not difficult to find examples which will support the claim that under certain conditions the structure of a society is preponderantly influenced by its economy, its polity or (more rarely) its ideology and concomitant status-system. But a claim that any one of them is the 'ultimate' determinant can be sustained only if construed as an untestable presupposition; and what purpose will that serve in the face not merely of well-researched awkward cases but of equally plausible (or implausible) presuppositions of an opposite kind? An appeal to a mythical state of nature, in the best eighteenth-century manner, can be made just as well on behalf of any one of the three dimensions of social structure as any other. It all began (some will say) with the first assertion of property rights, the first delimitation of *meum* and *tuum* in the primeval forests. But no (will say others), it all began with the first subjugation by force or the manifest threat of force of one primitive man by another. No again (will say yet others), it all began with the first acknowledged claim to superior esteem, the first successful manifestation of what Rousseau called '*cette fureur de se distinguer*'. None of this is of the smallest help in analyzing observed societies or in constructing testable hypotheses to the effect that under specified conditions power of one kind is a lagged function of power of another. Whether, when and why the distribution of one is explicable by reference to another is not to be decided in advance.

Societies differ, however, not only in the relative importance of one or other of the three kinds of power but also in the nature of the institutional rules governing convertibility between them.* In some societies, for example, high social status can be acquired by the deliberate sacrifice of wealth, as by the *sanyasi* in the Hindu system of caste. But in others, as among the *mestizos* of rural Colombia, status can be acquired only by holding authority, at once political and economic, over other men (Reichel-Dolmatoff 1961, p. 442). In some societies, access to the means of coercion can be purchased for cash, as in most of Western Europe during the sixteenth and seventeenth centuries. But in others, as in most of Eastern Europe during the second half of the twentieth century, membership of the ruling élite is the way to economic privileges not available in the market. In some societies, status by birth is an aid to the occupancy of political-cum-military roles, but in others it is irrelevant or even disadvantageous. In some, ritual status in a religious hierarchy is fused with political-cum-military rank, but in others the two are separate to the point of incompatibility. And so on.

That there is an inherent tendency towards congruence between the three dimensions of social structure – or more generally, between all forms or aspects of ranking in human societies – has been argued by proponents of would-be general social-psychological theories of 'status crystallization' or 'cognitive dissonance'. But this is yet another question to be examined case by case. It is true that to a holder of power of one kind there will inevitably accrue power of another to the extent that the institutions of the society do provide for convertibility between them. Indeed, it is too obvious to need further comment that within any institutional catchment area, access to the means of production is likely to be of help in the acquisition of political influence and ideological hegemony, access to the means of persuasion to be of help in the acquisition of political influence and material resources, and access to the means of coercion to be of help in the acquisition of material resources and ideological hegemony. But for just this reason, it is the restraints on, and variations within, convertibility and congruence whose study is likely to shed light on the workings and evolution of societies of different kinds. Each of the three forms of power has its autonomous rules; but at the same time, each is reciprocally influenced

* Conversion can and frequently does come about through the *violation* of existing legal and/or customary rules, as when political office is won by bribery or wealth acquired by force; but if these practices are themselves institutionalized, then clearly there is a change not only in the individual attributes of the relevant members of the society but also in the location and content of the society's roles. Harrington: 'Treason doth never prosper: what's the reason? For if it prosper, none dare call it treason.'

by the other two in at least some aspects and to at least some degree. Every society has its mode of production, its mode of persuasion and its mode of coercion, and only when all three are taken into account can different societies be assigned to one or another of the range of possible alternative modes and sub-types of the distribution of power.

§5. Once it is accepted that there are three and only three dimensions of social structure, it follows logically (or if you will, geometrically) that any society can be modelled as a pyramid standing on its apex – the apex being the point of zero power in all three dimensions. Within the social space so delimited, the society's members move up or down* over the course of their lives from the vector at which they enter it on their emergence from childhood into their adult roles.† But for this model to be useful in practice in the explanation, description or evaluation of a particular society reported in terms of it, a number of qualifications have first to be entered.

(i) Persons are, strictly, the sole members of societies, since it is only they, not groups or categories or institutions, who perform the actions by which practices and therefore roles are defined. But the structure of a society is a structure of roles, not persons, and persons can occupy more than one role. Each point, therefore, which is drawn within the inverted pyramid designates an identifiable person in a specified role. But the number of such points will exceed the total adult population of the society by the number of different roles occupied by the same persons.

(ii) Distances in social space are not quantitatively measurable, and the ranking of persons according to the power attaching to their roles can only be an ordinal, not a cardinal, one. It is true that scales can in some contexts be devised which have the properties of cardinal measurement. But the place of a person in a given role on such a scale is not to be equated with his or her actual social location: it is no more at best than an indicator of one or more aspects of it.

(iii) There are aspects of power of each separate kind which may

* I assume that the metaphorical equation of more power with a higher, and less power with a lower, location in social space is uncontroversial; and even if it is not, the resulting conceptualization can be transposed *salva veritate* easily enough.

† This is not a clear-cut distinction either: persons classified as children may still be members of the labour force, or bear arms in defence of their country, or be betrothed in accordance with their status-group of origin to their future husbands or wives. Furthermore, no society's culture can be fully understood without a knowledge of its child-rearing practices. But none of this requires modification of the three-dimensional framework.

generate inconsistent rankings, even within the one dimension. Here again, there are sometimes ways in which they can be quasi-experimentally forced into a single dimension. But even if, say, the different elements of the prestige attaching to different roles in a ritual hierarchy can be tested against each other under the compulsions of a single focal ritual,* it may still be that under other conditions asymmetrical and inconsistent rankings will re-emerge. Economically, wealth or income may be inconsistent with security of entitlement to it; ideologically, symbolically valued function may be inconsistent with inherited status-group; coercively, high office may be inconsistent with military following; and so on.

(iv) Since there is an element of cooperation as well as domination in all social relationships, to portray the structure of any society in terms of inequalities of power alone would be to ignore the significance of ties of loyalty and mutual interest between vertically differentiated roles and the persons in them. As with differences in rank in incommensurable aspects of the same dimension, it will not do to say no more than that under hypothetical conditions these ties could be translated into a difference in the power attaching to otherwise similarly located roles whose incumbents in the one case do, but in the other do not, enjoy the advantage of them. Such differences are not simply properties or even functions of their roles.

(v) No structure is static. Although, like any other system, societies can be reported synchronically as they are observed at any one moment, this can be done only in the knowledge that both the structure and the culture will be different at the next. Even if new roles come into being only at longish intervals and the relative locations of the existing ones hardly change in the meantime, persons are constantly entering and leaving roles which themselves are changing as the institutions and practices of the society are, however gradually, modified.

(vi) As I have emphasized already, societies seldom have clear-cut boundaries, and institutional catchment areas frequently overlap. Although, therefore, any single person in a given role can in principle be assigned a place relative to others in the three-dimensional space of whatever society (or institutional catchment area) is under study, the role may at the same time be a function of relations of domination either external to the society or internal to a sub-system within it. The model of an inverted pyramid may, therefore, need to be supplemented by

* See e.g. Mandelbaum (1955, p. 238) for an example where the relative importance of age and kinship in determining ceremonial precedence among the Kota is decided in practice by majority support.

reference to either or both an inter-societal system within which power is unequally distributed and/or one or more intra-societal associations or corporations within which some of the society's members are ranked but to which other of its members do not belong and may not even relate at all.

(vii) Finally, allowance has to be made for the possibility that not all the incumbents of the roles whose location has been plotted are genuine – in other words, for the phenomenon of *passing*. The term is most often used in the context of racial or ethnic discrimination. But it is no less applicable in a system of castes within which a person who conceals his kinship connections and changes his name and occupation can occupy a role which would be denied him if his true social origin were known (Yalman 1960, p. 99), or in the society of Ancient Rome for which there is copious evidence of slaves passing for free, freedmen for *equites*, non-citizens for citizens and Egyptians for Greeks (Reinhold 1971), or in the societies of medieval Europe where dependent tenants might seek to pass as petty allodialists (Duby 1973, p. 238), or in early Islamic societies where converts might invent names and genealogies for themselves to avoid discrimination (Levy 1962, p. 60). Neither the structure of roles nor the institutions by which it is regulated are necessarily modified as such by the extent to which roles may be occupied under false pretences. But researchers who fail to notice when they are may, if they are not careful, find that whatever explanation, description or evaluation they put forward of the workings of the society in question will be flawed as a result.

None of these difficulties, however, constitutes an argument against either the claim that social structure is three-dimensional or the consequent interpretation of it by way of the model of an inverted pyramid. If power is of three separate, interdependent but mutually irreducible kinds, then once societies are conceptualized in terms of its allocation a three-dimensional framework is inescapable, and it must be correct to conceive of societies as inverted pyramids rather than as either triangles, diamonds, etc.,* or as unidimensional networks of inter-personal dominance. The qualifications set out in this Section do have to be acknowledged in any attempt at depicting social structure in terms of the distribution of persons in their roles as points within three-dimensional space, and they do restrict the scope of structural

* Such figures are of course perfectly valid as one kind of representation of a frequency distribution: a triangle is then the model of a society with one role at the top of a single dimension of power and an evenly increasing proportion of less and less powerful roles down to a large group or category with no power at all at the bottom.

comparison across, and sometimes even within, differences of culture. But they do not prevent the use of formal terms for the reportage of structure (such as 'narrowly stratified', 'diffuse', 'inconsistent', 'steeply graded', etc.) whose application can be agreed by rival observers across a range of culturally different societies so long as they are not taken to imply strict quantitative commensurability.

ROLES AND SYSTACTS

§6. There is still need, however, for a conceptualization of groups and/or categories of persons in their several and various roles who share a common location in one or more of the three dimensions of social structure. There are many existing standard terms for such groups and/or categories, and once societies have been conceptualized by reference to the allocation of power among their constituent roles, they can be taken to be divisible into strata, classes, cohorts, castes, estates, orders, interest-groups, ranks or whatever other such term may be found useful. But none of them will itself do to cover any and all of the others, and it is to fill this lack that I have coined the one neologism which this treatise will be found to contain – the noun *systact* (and the corresponding adjective 'systactic'). A group or category of persons in specified roles may be said to constitute a systact whenever the persons in question have, by virtue of their roles, a distinguishable and more than transiently similar location and, on that account, a common interest as defined in Section 1. The term is, therefore, applicable to any and all modes and sub-types of the distribution of power, and it makes it very much easier to report and compare the institutions of different societies without having to be pre-emptively committed to a view on such vexed theoretical questions as whether women as such can constitute a 'class', where, if at all, 'castes' are to be found outside of Hindu India, whether and, if so, how a distinction is to be drawn between 'stratified' and 'rank' societies, or what is the difference between a 'ruling class' and a 'governing élite'.

In practice, the readiest way to start in studying any particular society is to look at 'their' terms for what appear to be regarded as separate systacts by 'them'. The practising sociologist wants in the first instance to be able to report to his readers who is acquiring what from whom, who is being accorded prestige by whom and who is giving orders to whom in accordance with a pattern sufficiently consistent that the term role, as defined above, can be applied; and it will seldom take him long to pick out the *wardū*, *awilū* and *mushkēnū* of Hammurapi's Babylon, the *hippeis* and *zeugitae* of Solon's Athens, the *honestiores* and *humiliores* of the Roman Empire, the *potentes* and *mediocres* of Charlemagne's kingdom, the *thegns*, *geneats*, *ceorls*, *cottars*, *geburs* and *theows* of Anglo-Saxon England, the *noblesse d'épée*, *noblesse de robe* and *roturiers* of seventeenth-century France, the *timariots* and *zaïms* of the Ottoman Empire, the *jarls* and *things* of the Vikings, the *boyars* and *bagaïns* of the Bulgars, the *mabiis* and *kpeems* of the West African Tallensi, the *lairds*, *bonnet-lairds*, *tacksmen* and *wadsetters* of pre-industrial Scotland, the *daimyō*, *bushi*, *chōnin* and *hinin* of traditional Japan, the *señoritos*, *mayetes*, *autonomes* and *jorñaleros* of the villages of Andalusia, the *mekwannint*, *vistenya*, *tsengya* and *tayb* of Ethiopia, the *dagpo* and *yogpo* of the Nyimba region of Nepal, and so on and so forth. But the presence of terms like these is not by itself decisive. Indeed, it may sometimes raise more difficulties than it solves, as for example in the case of the ambiguous English 'yeomen',* or the shadowy Spartan *mothakes* who seem to have been boys of Helot birth foster-brothered to Spartiates, or the Spanish '*hidalgos*' whom I cited in Chapter 2 of Volume I as covering almost all families in one part of the country and almost none in another. The test is the degree to which the persons so designated can be shown to share a common location and therefore a common interest by virtue of their roles.

The easiest societies to analyze are those in which roles are clear-cut, the allocation of power in each dimension uniform and consistent, institutions unchanging and systacts marked off from each other by universally accepted legal and/or customary distinctions unambiguously expressed in 'their' terms. But no society is entirely as straightforward as this, even those where inequalities of power are minimal, and as complexity of social organization increases so do the possibilities not only of a multiplication of the criteria on which power in any dimension may be based but also of an inconsistency between one and another. What is more, not only can the same person perform several different roles, but the same role, even if designated by 'them' with terms like '*Kaiser*', '*Sultan*', '*Shah*', '*Tsar*', '*Khan*', '*Yang Dipertuan*' or '*Sapa Inca*', which appear to attribute supreme power to the incumbent, may in practice carry very different degrees of it within each dimension.

A further difficulty is that systactic, like societal, membership may be

* On whom see Wrightson (1982, p. 31): 'Freehold land tenure might therefore appear an admirable means of distinguishing the yeomanry... Unfortunately, it is a broken reed. Research has shown that many yeomen were indeed freeholders, but that many were leaseholders, many were copyholders, while some held land by a variety of tenures. Conversely, 17th-century England had many 40s freeholders who did not aspire to call themselves yeomen.'

either multiple or partial: multiple, because people perform a multiplicity of roles; and partial, because they may not wholly or consistently share all of the interests of all those clustered with them at a common location.* It is in these cases, indeed, that 'their' terms are particularly likely to be more misleading than helpful. The categories of 'lord' and 'peasant', for example, are familiar in a number of languages as denoting distinguishable groups or categories in pre-industrial societies. But they cannot be presumed to denote systacts, if only because the conflicts of interest between lord and lord or peasant and peasant will be found to outweigh those of all lords against all peasants in many more than can be dismissed as special cases. It is only when further distinctions in economic, coercive or ideological power are made within them that the institutional catchment area within which each lord's or peasant's interests lie can be sufficiently clearly demarcated for the observer to identify separate systacts which may or may not correspond to a term like, say, '*sredniak*' (middle peasant) or '*vavasour*' (vassal's vassal) already in use by 'them'.

Nor is anything gained by presupposing what it is that persons conscious of a systactic interest are actually conscious of. The possibilities range all the way from a limited interest with regard to only one of the three dimensions of social structure to a generalized awareness of relative advantage or disadvantage within a society in which the three dimensions are effectively fused. Examples of the first might be (i) the members of a small craft union concerned only with preserving a distinctive relation to the means of production in an industrializing society, (ii) the members of an association formed only to preserve the esteem traditionally accorded to their inherited rank (like Disraeli's Sir Vavasour – *sic*! – Firebrace in *Sybil*, who was modelled on

* Both these are well illustrated in the social structure of 18th-century France, which was at the same time exceptionally hierarchical and exceptionally complex. Cf. Cobban (1964, p. 21): 'To appreciate a man's real position in French society it would have been necessary to know, as well as his legal status, also his actual economic functions, the sources and extent of his wealth, his mode of life, his profession or office, his family, and during the revolution even his political affiliations. His rank on one scale might be very different from that on another. To add a final complication, the man who fell only into a single category was by no means the rule and might even have been the exception. The peasant proprietor could also be a tenant farmer for part of his land, a merchant when he bought and sold produce, or a wage-earner when he worked on someone else's land. A lawyer might be an estate manager and a merchant; he might also be a landowner, for most persons of any social standing probably owned at least some land in town or country. In rural areas the smallholders and the rural artisanate might be quite distinct or might overlap. A noble could be a local official or a judge, an army officer, an ecclesiastic, a great landed proprietor or a working smallholder.'

the actual author of *Broun's Baronetage* and *The Precedency of Honourable Baronetesses*),* or (iii) the members of an armed group or movement whose ambitions extend no further than the disruption of the existing political order to whatever degree their physical means will permit them. An example of the second might be the members of a close-knit occupational group in an Indian village persistently conscious of the impediments to social mobility in all three dimensions imposed on them by the caste system. At any one time, the importance to a society of any particular systact, and of the nature and extent of its members' awareness of their common interest, will depend not merely on its size and location but also on the degree to which the behaviour of the members of other systacts is a response to it. But over a period it will often turn out that a small and ostensibly insignificant group or category becomes, because and only because of the nature of the common interest which first binds its members together, of quite unexpected importance for the future course of social evolution, whether the minority factions of the Bedouin of seventh-century Arabia who accorded recognition to Muhammad, or the merchants and artisans of the North Italian cities of the late eleventh century who instituted the role of elective consul, or the armed retainers of tenth- and eleventh-century Japan who attached themselves to regional lords at the expense of the power of the central government, or the *baillis* who first appear in the administrative echelons of the French monarchy in the reign of Philippe Auguste.

The distinction between kinds of power, and therefore dimensions of social space, might seem to suggest that systacts should be categorized directly in accordance with it, as in Max Weber's influential distinction between *Klassen*, *Stände* and *Parteien*, or perhaps by some other trio of terms denoting even more explicitly access to or control over the means of production, persuasion and coercion respectively. But the relationships between the three are in almost all cases so complex, and the institutions which determine them in different societies so various, that a fuller and less schematic classification is necessary. In this volume, I shall use 'systact' itself more often than any other. But I shall also, and without further comment, use *order* to stand for a systact whose location is juridically defined; *estate* for a systact constitutionally entitled to separate representation in government; *class* for a systact whose members stand in a common relation to the processes of production, distribution and exchange of goods and services; *status-group* for a systact distinguished by a common value-system and life-style accorded

* I owe the example to Blake (1966), p. 219.

differential esteem; *caste* for a systact of which membership is hereditary and which has a traditional, distinctive place in the division of labour and therewith in a ritual hierarchy of purity and pollution; *faction* for a systact whose members are cooperatively organized in pursuit of a common political interest; and *age-set* for a systact of which age is a universal and sufficient criterion of membership. Where a systact of whatever type is both consistently located in all three dimensions and consistently self-reproducing over successive generations, it will be termed a *stratum*. These working definitions are not, and are not meant to be, either rigorous or exclusive.* But they are not theoretically pre-emptive, whether of explanation, description or evaluation, unless deliberately so used; and they do not presuppose that any given society has to be exclusively or even predominantly organized in accordance with the distinctions which they draw.

§7. But then how is the researcher to decide into how many systacts the society which he has chosen to study is to be divided? The answer is not given to him as a part of his initial primary understanding, however detailed, of 'their' reported roles; it has to be imposed by him in the light of an explanatory, descriptive or evaluative theory and judged by the success with which his theory can then withstand the criticisms of rival schools.

This problem, too, has a very long history, and the criteria by which different sociologists have drawn their different boundaries between one systact and another are exceedingly diverse. Adapting slightly a set of useful distinctions drawn by Ossowski (1956, p. 152), we may subdivide them first according to whether they conceptualize the social hierarchy in terms of discrete attributes (like producers vs. non-producers) or continuous variables (like income), and then according to whether (i) the attributes relate to the contribution to the society as a whole which the designated categories are held to make, or to the antagonisms between them, and (ii) the variables are simple or multiple. As soon as this has been done, it becomes apparent to what degree the ostensibly technical

* It follows from them that, to go no further afield than the societies of Europe before 1789, the Russian *sosloviye* should be rendered 'order' rather than (as is usually done) 'estate'; the English clergy were not, but the French clergy were, an estate; and the German *Stand* should sometimes be rendered 'estate' and sometimes 'status-group'. For an example which illustrates at the same time the three-dimensional character of 'aristocracy', cf. Hopkins (1983, p. 33): 'The Roman senate can best be seen, not as a separate Estate, nor even as a distinct social stratum at the top of the Roman social pyramid, but rather as the prestigious political arm of a broader class of Roman and Italian land-owners.'

choices of different researchers may be dictated not only by their explanatory, descriptive or evaluative presuppositions but also by the particular form of social organization which, even if putting forward a would-be general theory, they have predominantly in mind. The moral to be drawn, however, is not just that there is an evaluative bias to much sociological theory. It is that on any theory, there is an enormous variation in forms of social organization from a chosen sub-set of which different researchers have selected one or another as their paradigm. Attempts to impose one overriding criterion, and therefore any one number of dividing lines, on any and all societies are always and rightly resisted by sociologists of other schools, not just because their own presuppositions are different but because different societies do call for different concepts and criteria to be applied to them. Subdivision by attribute is appropriate, whatever the observer's presuppositions, where the roles of the society's members fall into clear-cut institutional areas of domination or cooperation as the case may be; and subdivision by variable is appropriate where their roles are graded along one or more fluid continua. Neither conceptualization is, or could plausibly be expected to be, privileged across the whole of the historical and ethnographic record.

It is not, therefore, surprising that attempts to force any and all societies into a common framework of two or more basically antagonistic 'classes' or, on the contrary, to impose on them a preconceived scale of measurement on which all their members can be ranked along a continuum of 'socio-economic status', have been overwhelmed by the weight of well-researched awkward cases. But there remains a difference of view between those who incline, albeit with due regard to the diversity of forms of social organization, either to a cultural in preference to a structural criterion or *vice versa*. Both schools, indeed, have a good case. On the cultural view, the dividing-lines to be drawn are those which 'they' recognize themselves to be defined by their own customs and laws: hence, they should demarcate self-classified, mutually acknowledged 'social classes', a social class being defined by one representative author of this school as 'a section or large grouping of people within a society, divided into a socially recognized and often named category possessing a common life-style and *supposedly* [author's italics] sharing similar ranges of status' (Cohen 1970, p. 229). But on the structural view, the dividing-lines to be drawn are those which the observer may well judge better than they, and in particular, those which mark barriers to mobility between one social location and the next: hence, it has been argued by a representative author of *this* school that societies should be classified in accordance with their permeability – 'permeability' being defined in terms of inverse relation to the absolute value of the correlation coefficient of paternal and filial rank – in a quasi-historical typology ranging from 'caste' societies with zero permeability to 'estate' societies with low permeability to 'class' societies with high permeability to 'egalitarian' societies with perfect permeability (Svalastoga 1965, p. 40). But once again, there is no warrant to treat either as privileged over the other. The reason for distinguishing separate systacts in the first place is that lines have to be drawn wherever the researcher finds significant differences in the power attaching to the roles of definable groups or categories of people. Whether this leads to an emphasis on culture or structure will depend on what he finds. Indeed, even where a cultural criterion seems appropriate (as, say, in a form of social organization based on strict but informal rules of commensalism and endogamy) it is pertinent to ask about the pattern of status-group distribution in social space; and even where a structural criterion seems appropriate (as, say, in a form of social organization based on legally sanctioned barriers to mobility) it is pertinent to ask about the content of the rules which give the behaviour justifying the metaphor of a physical barrier its meaning.

Nor is the answer any easier to arrive at *a priori* in studying a smaller and/or simpler society than a larger and/or more complex one. The Mbutu pygmies of the Congo are among the smaller and simpler societies in the ethnographic record and differences in power of any of the three kinds are minimal among them. But this is just what makes it difficult to draw a systactic boundary, for when differences in power do emerge they are so far constrained by the sanction of ridicule and an overt rejection of any tendency to congruence that there is no lasting division between those men who are from time to time conceded superiority in certain areas of communal activity and those who are not. Tokugawa Japan, by contrast, is a large and complex society; but its division into the basic orders of (i) nobility (including the 300-odd families of the court), (ii) the regional lords and their samurai, (iii) the peasantry, and (iv) artisans and merchants, plus priests and a subordinate caste of untouchables, is remarkably clear-cut considering that it is the product of centuries of unpredictable and often violent evolution. Nothing prevents an otherwise simpler society from having a structure which requires the researcher to divide it into a larger number of systacts than he would an otherwise more complex one. There *are* visible distinctions even among the Mbutu pygmies, fluid as they may be; and an even continuum of differences, where it is found (as, for example, in much of early medieval Germany), is not an argument against dividing a society into an ordered set of systacts with admittedly hazy boundaries. Conversely, although there may be societies in which a single distinction, such as slave vs. free or propertied vs. propertyless, is the most obviously important, there are always, on closer inspection, further distinctions to be drawn. In Classical Sparta, the principal systactic division was on any theory that between Spartiate 'Peers' (*Homoioi*) and subordinate Helots; but even aside from the position of women, the *perioikoi* of the surrounding territories and the *mothakes* whom I mentioned in Section 6, there were differences of wealth and prestige, as both Herodotus and Xenophon testify, among the Spartiates, there were 'second-class' citizens (*hypomeiones*) and declassed ones (the *tresantes* who had 'trembled' in battle), and there were Helots who rose to a kind of quasi-citizenship (the *neodamodeis*) like those whom Thucydides (v.34) reports as having fought under Brasidas in the Peloponnesian War.

It follows that comparison between societies in terms of the number of systacts of which they are held to be composed is unlikely to serve any useful theoretical purpose. The number is principally a function of the extent to which roles in a society tend to cluster in distinctly separate areas of social space. But this is not itself a function of the characteristics of those roles and the institutions within which they operate against which rival explanations of their workings and evolution can effectively be tested. There is, at the very most, a case for starting from a hypothetical fourfold division, if only because in any fairly large and complex society there are likely to be, first, a dominant élite of some kind; second, the auxiliary roles necessary for the exercise of that domination; third, a stratum of persons occupying the roles which guarantee the basic productive functions which keep the society in being; and fourth, an 'underclass' of outlaws, mendicants, vagabonds, captives, drop-outs, criminals and so forth whose roles are stigmatized by the ideology of those located above them. But for the purpose of explaining the workings and evolution of any chosen society, there are as many ways of dividing it into systacts as there are models of theories which can be validated by doing so.

MOBILITY OF PERSONS AND ROLES

§8. Even in the stablest societies, however, there are always some persons moving from one role into another, and it is only for limited periods, if ever, that roles are not changing their relative locations as well. *Social mobility* is the standard term for changes of both or either kind, and the topic is one on which there is by now a large and technically sophisticated literature. But the sophisticated techniques can be applied only to those kinds of societies and those kinds of movement across social space within them for which there are available the detailed reports on which they can operate. For the overwhelming majority of societies in the historical and ethnographic record, only the most rudimentary measurement is possible. For the purposes of this volume, therefore, it is more important to formulate a basis for simple but unambiguous comparisons between one society and another than for precise measurement of inflows and outflows between a multiplicity of roles which will hold good only for a restricted number of complex societies sharing a more or less identical culture.

The most important distinction is the one which I have emphasized already between the movement of persons between different roles and changes in the relative locations of roles as such. Conceptually, as we have seen, the distinction is clear-cut: persons may exchange roles without the location of the roles being changed, and roles can move nearer or further from each other in any or all of the three dimensions without any change of incumbents. But in practice, there is almost always a contingent connection between them. Persons can hardly go on exchanging roles on any systematic institutional basis without the distance between those roles tending to alter in the process, and the distance between roles can hardly alter to any significant degree without tending to disturb the distribution of persons among them. What is more, the inflow of new entrants into the system, whether from within or without, will never precisely match the outflow; even if there is enough room for new entrants to be accommodated within the boundaries of existing systacts, substantial changes in the relative sizes of systacts can hardly leave their relative locations entirely unchanged.

Moreover, the appearance of new and disappearance of old roles give rise to another distinction which follows directly from them but is likewise less clear-cut in practice than it may appear at first sight. This is the distinction between what is usually called 'structural' mobility on the one hand and what is sometimes called 'exchange' and sometimes 'circulation' mobility on the other – that is, between mobility caused by the creation of vacant roles which have to be filled and mobility caused by movement of persons within a fixed distribution of roles.* In the first

* There is the further complication that 'structural' mobility is also sometimes used to stand for *collective* rather than *individual mobility*, i.e. the simultaneous rise or fall of a whole group or category of persons in their roles as opposed to the rise or fall of separate persons out of their roles into higher or lower ones, whether newly created or already in existence.

case, the vacancies to be filled may be there either because of changes in the role-composition of the relevant systact or because of the rates of inflow and outflow resulting from rates of birth, death and in- or out-migration, and these cannot in practice be sifted from one another. In the second case, although exchange mobility is, formally speaking, the residue when structural mobility is subtracted from total mobility (and is, in consequence, sometimes labelled 'net' rather than either 'exchange' or 'circulation' mobility), the calculation is an artificial one. If the origins and destinations of the population under study are set out in a matrix of as many rows and columns as the society is held to have systacts, then the marginal totals will be seen to impose an inescapable arithmetical constraint on the possible rates of mobility; but the calculation cannot be interpreted as distinguishing the movement of persons between existing roles from their movement into roles which have become vacant. Indeed, it is in some contexts more plausible to regard persons as themselves creating, as they move up or down the structure, the roles which they then come to occupy.

Nor are these the only distinctions which need to be drawn before the movement upwards or downwards of persons and/or roles within the space of the inverted pyramid can be reported to the satisfaction of all rival observers. For one thing, location of origin may be taken, as I have suggested in Section 5, to be the location of a person's first adult role; but researchers with other presuppositions and purposes are free to take it as the location of the parent (normally the father) either at the moment of the person's entry or, alternatively, birth, which will have the consequence that the marginal totals for the fathers will not reflect the systactic distribution of the adult male population as it ever was at any actual moment in the society's previous history.* For another thing, some persons other than children may have only derivative or '*secondary*' rather than 'basic' rank:† many women, in particular, may have a location defined only by that of their husbands (and sometimes *vice versa*). Yet none of these distinctions poses any particular difficulty about the notion of social mobility itself, provided that they are (as they can be) sufficiently clearly defined. The difficulties which prevent the reportage of social mobility from being acceptable to researchers of all theoretical schools are, first, that its frequency is a function of the number as well as the location of dividing-lines drawn between one

* This is both because not all males are fathers and because not all fathers have only one child (and those who do, have them at different ages): see Duncan (1966) for fuller discussion in the context of occupational mobility in modern industrial societies.

† These terms were coined by Kawai (1965) reporting observations of primates but can be applied in exactly the same sense in human societies.

systact and the next; and second, that even when the chosen dividing-lines have been drawn by reference to uncontroversial institutional boundaries, the significance of movement of and between roles is a function of how far power itself is zero-sum in the given context.

This second question has been much disputed in the abstract between rival schools. But there is no need to presuppose the answer by definition, since the study of actual societies clearly shows that sometimes and in some respects power is zero-sum and at other times and in other respects it isn't, just as it sometimes is and sometimes isn't underpinned by a common consensus on its legitimacy. Consider the following pairs of hypothetical instances of collective mobility taken from each of the three dimensions of social structure. First, compare the case where a systact of agricultural tenants is forced by the pressure of population on a limited supply of land to concede to their landlords a significantly higher proportion of their total output with the case where the adoption of cooperative farming methods leaves them with a significantly higher surplus after meeting an unchanged rate of tribute or taxation: the former is a direct increase in the power of the landlords at the expense (and against the wishes) of the tenantry, but the second is a rise in the economic location of the tenantry which is independent of that of the landlords except to the degree that the ratio of shares of total output has been marginally altered in the tenantry's favour. Second, compare the case where a monarch extends patents of nobility to every single adult male householder with the case where the monarch decrees that a hitherto outcaste group is to be admitted to formal equality of status: the former directly undermines the prestige which previously accrued to the members of a more restricted aristocracy, but the latter does so, if at all, only to the degree that the total span of inequality has been marginally diminished (and perhaps to that extent resented by the marginal losers). Third, compare the case where the leaders of a revolutionary government directly usurp the functions of the administrative office-holders of the old regime with the case where they retain all office-holders in their roles on the condition that they are nominally answerable to representatives of the subordinate systacts over whom their authority extends: in the former, political power has been directly transferred from one set of hands into another, but in the latter it has merely been tempered (and perhaps more successfully legitimated) by the imposition of a marginal diminution in the social distance between governors and governed. Each instance is one of collective mobility. But within each pair, there is a qualitative difference which cannot be quantified in terms of distance moved by persons in their roles within the space enclosed by the inverted pyramid.

All these distinctions, accordingly, need to be kept in mind in any discussion of any society in which there is any change at all, whether individual or collective, in the social distance between roles and/or the persons who occupy them – which is to say, every society in the historical and ethnographic record including even the bands of hunters or gatherers within which the differentiation of adult roles corresponds to inequalities of power so small as to be almost imperceptible. The extent to which it is possible to speak of mobility rates as such, and the degree to which such rates can be calculated in terms of systactic boundaries accepted as such by all rival observers, will vary from case to case. But even where the construction of matrices and the computation of inflow and outflow tables is not remotely feasible, social mobility is taking place, by definition, wherever and whenever the distribution of economic, ideological and/or coercive power is changed. Nor should it be assumed that a claim that social mobility is or is not increasing or diminishing in a given society over a given period is more contentious without quantitative evidence than with it. Just as elaborate calculations based on censuses of population may be misleading as evidence for changes in the distribution of power, so may increasing or decreasing mobility across significant social distances be safely inferred for societies where neither the population statistics nor the vernacular terminology of roles are nearly as precise as one might wish.

§9. Any discussion of social mobility does, however, presuppose individual motivation sufficiently strong and widespread to bring it about in the first place. It is not, as I remarked already in Section 1, that all members of all societies are to be assumed to be seeking to augment the power attaching to their roles, or to move from their existing roles to another at a higher location. What Adam Smith (1776, Bk. IV, Ch. 9) called 'the natural effort of every individual to better his own condition' may in some sense be natural, but it is by no means universal. Not merely are some people in all societies indifferent to the attractions of wealth, prestige or political office (or, more often, resigned to the futility of any attempt to obtain them); there are also some to whom power accrues by ascription independently of any effort or desire of their own. But any substantive social theory will have to acknowledge that societies are as we find them more because of a desire for power among the relevant groups or categories of their members than because power accidentally accrues to people who would on the whole prefer to abdicate from the roles to which it attaches and in which they happen to find themselves. Obvious as it may be, the point is worth emphasizing because discussion of social mobility tends to be directed towards estimates of aggregate inflows and outflows and average chances of upward or downward movement, and the analysis of mobility tables (where feasible) requires that individual differences in motivation be treated as random. Not only, however, do these differences need to be reintroduced if the observed variances in mobility rates are to be fully explained (and still more so if they are to be fully described and evaluated). In addition, the mutual irreducibility of the three dimensions of social structure has to be recognized no less as it affects individual motivation than as it affects changes in the aggregate distribution of persons in their roles.

'The difference between a rich man, a celebrity and a ruler is something like this: A rich man collects cattle and hoards grain, or the money which stands for them... A ruler collects men. Grain and cattle, or money, mean nothing to him except insofar as he needs them to get hold of men... A celebrity collects a chorus of voices: All he wants is to hear them repeat his name' (Canetti 1962, p. 397). This is perhaps a rather fanciful way of putting it. But the distinction is no less distinctly enshrined in, for example, the vocabulary of the High Middle Ages and the denunciations by clerical moralists of *avaritia* as distinguished alike from *vana gloria* and from *cupiditas potentiae*. In practice, no doubt, the distinctions are likely to be blurred. People motivated by ambition are generally after as much as they can get of all three. The Homeric hero striving always to 'be best' (*aristeuein*) and 'pre-eminent above others' (*hypeirochos allōn*) may want fame and glory above all else, but he wants them as at once deriving from and expressed by the subjugation of lesser warriors and the possession of flocks and herds and honey-sweet wine about which Sarpedon expatiates to Glaucus in Book XII of the *Iliad*; and likewise, the medieval French knight gains his *recheces* through his *puissances* and further enhances his *dignetez* through both of them. But the three motives are analytically quite as distinct as the three forms of power and therefore dimensions of social structure within which their gratification is (or is not) achieved.

It is true that our traditional vocabulary of motives, rich as it is, is much better suited to descriptive and evaluative than to explanatory purposes: honour and shame, greed and avarice, vaulting ambition which o'erleaps itself, the will to power, the thirst for glory, and so on, are all terms more of literature than of social science. But they can, all the same, be put to much better use in the construction of a substantive social theory than, for example, the 'drive-states', 'appetitive behaviour', 'effector activities' and 'tension-reductions' of neo-Behaviorist psychological theory. Whatever may turn out to be the discoveries about human motives at which psychologists one day arrive, our traditional vocabulary furnishes a perfectly adequate provisional grounding for hypotheses about the causes of the modification or preservation of one rather than another set of institutions and the evolution of the society in question from one to another mode or sub-type of the distribution of power. To use again the example of Rome, the motives of the power-hungry nobles of the late Republic can be sufficiently well documented from the extant literature for the relative importance to them of wealth, prestige, and political-cum-military office to be invoked as part of the explanation of the breakdown of their inherited institutions and the unintended transition to monarchy by way of a political revolution which nevertheless left the economy and the status-system unchanged.

To some readers, there may be an initial difficulty to be overcome in treating equally seriously the desire for personal advancement in all three dimensions of social structure. Can the desire for ideological power or 'social prestige', whether secular or religious, really be accepted on an equal theoretical footing with the desire for money or possessions and for military or political office? Doesn't the word 'domination' itself carry overtones which amplify the power of property-owners and industrialists on the one side, and politicians and warlords on the other, relative to that of roles whose influence derives from honour or esteem alone? Aren't the overtones of 'honour', 'esteem' and 'prestige' merely those of outdated or peripheral aspirations for, or pretensions to, eminence of a derivative or artificial kind?* But although it may be true that the aspirations of Homeric heroes or Roman senators or medieval French knights are remote from those of the citizens of modern secular industrialized nation-states, it would be a mistake to assume for that reason that the desire for ideological power must be any more outdated or peripheral in even the most self-consciously utilitarian society than in any other. No doubt the ways in which the desire for, and acknowledgement of, social prestige finds expression will often be mutually ununderstandable in the tertiary, descriptive sense between the members of different cultures. It may be just as difficult to convey

* Admittedly, there are examples in the historical and ethnographic record where this is demonstrably so: the aristocracy of Sarawak, for example, first lost its economic and then its military power and was in consequence left with ritual status only (H. S. Morris 1980). But in 17th-century France, by contrast, political power was closely tied to prestige 'because it was remarkably hard to enforce decisions or impose sanctions except by indirect, intangible means' (Beik 1974, p. 587); cf. e.g. Lapidus (1975, p. 37) on the dependence of nineteenth-century Moroccan society on the religious prestige (*baraka*) of sultans descended from the family of the Prophet.

what Gladstone called a 'sneaking kindness for a lord'* to a mid twentieth-century Chinese cadre who venerates the personal life of Chairman Mao as 'a model for us poor peasants and lower middle peasants' (Myrdal and Kessle 1971, p. 183), as to a seventeenth-century Spanish grandee obsessed with 'purity of blood' (*limpieza del sangre*) the veneration of baseball players and movie stars by twentieth-century Americans. But the willingness to venerate and the desire to be venerated are primordial, whatever their cultural context: '*quam pulchrum est digito monstrari et diceri*: *hic est*!' ('How lovely it is to be pointed out and have it said of one "that's him!"'). These words are those of Robert de Courçon inveighing against the vanity of lecturers in the University of Paris at the beginning of the thirteenth century.† But they apply not only to countless other university lecturers but to countless other incumbents of countless other roles at countless other places and times. Locke was perhaps exaggerating when he wrote that 'the principal spring from which the actions of men take their rise, the rule they conduct them by, and the end to which they direct them, seems to be credit and reputation'.‡ But it is no more of an exaggeration than it would be to assign a similar overriding priority to the desire for access to the means of production or coercion for their own sake.

Moreover, it is equally pertinent that Locke goes on to say 'and that which at any rate they avoid as in the greatest part shame and disgrace', since in so doing he turns up the opposite side of the coin: the fear of sanctions. Here again, the fear of loss of honour or esteem may seem outdated or peripheral to readers from a modern secular industrialized nation-state.§ It is for relatively small and simple societies – the Mbutu pygmies whom I mentioned in Section 6 among them – that the use of

* The quotation is borrowed from G. M. Young's *Victorian England*, although found impossible to trace by Kitson Clark in his annotated edition (1977, p. 315 n. 24).

† Quoted by Baldwin (1970, II, p. 89 n. 92) (I owe the reference to Murray 1978, p. 229 n. 65).

‡ The quotation is cited by Macpherson (1962, p. 239 n. 1) from Locke's MS Journal as quoted in Fox Browne's biography of him.

§ This holds also, and perhaps particularly, where explicitly religious motives are at issue and the desire to acquire merit in the eyes of men is compounded by respect for the judgement of God. It is tempting to be sceptical of monkish accounts of the medieval *miles* who donates his parcel of land to the abbey *ob amorem omnipotentis dei sanctorumque apostolorum Petri et Pauli, et pro remedio animae suae atque omnium parentorum suorum* – I have taken an example almost at random from the records of Cluny (Bernard and Bruel 1880, II, p. 33) – but to be so may well be to betray, as Bloch puts it (1961, p. 84), an 'inability to lay aside the spectacles of men of the nineteenth and twentieth centuries': the fact that such donations were often made under duress does not mean that they always were.

ridicule as the principal instrument of social control has been best documented, whether it takes the form of jokes or gossip or slanging-matches or rituals of disapproval or disesteem, and whether or not the same motives are also expressed and the same functions served by such more formal practices as the denial of association and commensalism or exclusion from attendance at or participation in meetings or ceremonials. But recourse to the means of persuasion and therefore the operation of the motives which make ideological sanctions and inducements effective can be documented for larger and more modern societies* as well as for smaller and earlier ones.

It may be that in all societies there are some people so impervious to the rules of the institutions that govern them and the sanctions and inducements available to sustain them that they can hardly be counted as members of their society at all. But they cannot be other than a minority. If the entire population become anchorites, there is no mode of production; if every citizen takes the same view of government as the 'Professor' in Conrad's *The Secret Agent* (who said he was prepared to blow himself up, if arrested, by setting off a device attached permanently to his person, and was believed by the police when he said so), there is no mode of coercion; and if nobody shares standards of social worth, legitimacy or merit with anybody else, there is no mode of persuasion. But there is no society where this is so nearly the case as to undermine its analysis in terms of the rival interests of the incumbents of distinguishable roles. There are, it is true, occasional collective suicides of whole societies (albeit relatively small ones). But these do not arise from a breakdown of the society's institutions. On the contrary: collective self-destruction is made possible only by a quite exceptional degree of unity and discipline.

§10. The desire for individual mobility and the desire for the collective mobility of a systact of which the person in question may or may not be a member is, however, yet another of the distinctions which is conceptually clear-cut but not at all easy to maintain in practice. Ambitious persons who rise within a structure which they have no wish to change may still make more of a difference to it, if they succeed, than they either intended or foresaw, and collective mobility seldom if ever occurs without the leadership of one or more persons concerned to advance their personal interests as well as those of the members of the

* See e.g. Peristiany (1965) for a selection of Mediterranean societies where the avoidance of shame and disgrace is at least as compelling a motive as the fear of poverty on the one hand and violence on the other.

systact whose location they wish to raise. The difficult question of the importance of individual leaders to the systacts they represent, and thereby to large-scale collective mobility, can be left to be debated case by case. But there is a need for a theory-neutral concept in terms of which there can be reported the discrepancies between the inequalities of economic, ideological or coercive power reflected in the location of persons and their roles and the desire of those persons to see them altered for either an individual or a collective improvement as they perceive it.

For this purpose, I propose to use the term *relative deprivation*, defined as follows: a person is said to be 'relatively deprived' of X (X being a resource attaching to a role) when (i) he/she does not have X, (ii) he/she sees some other person or persons, which may include him/herself at some previous or expected time, as having X, (iii) he/she wants X, and (iv) he/she sees it as feasible that he/she should have X.* The term is, accordingly, subjective in the sense that it is used to report what 'they' feel, not what the observer predicted that they would feel, or describes them as if feeling, or holds according to some evaluative criterion that they ought to have felt. But this raises no difficulties beyond those already to be met and overcome in the primary understanding of any item or sequence of human behaviour. Why people do or don't feel relatively deprived, what it is like for them if they do, and whether they are guilty of 'false consciousness' in failing to feel it as they ought are then questions to be settled in the light of the researcher's chosen explanatory, descriptive and evaluative theories. There are many familiar reasons why relative deprivation may not be felt to a sufficient extent and degree to generate systactic consciousness and thereby an organized attempt at collective mobility. Loyalties are divided, personal interests conflict, the same persons occupy sets of different roles, communication is imperfect and the hold of customary expectations is strong. Moreover, individual mobility may be incompatible with, and even preventive of, collective: if the ablest and most ambitious members of a subordinate systact rise out of it, this may have the double effect of depriving those left behind of their potential leaders and diminishing the concern of the members of the dominant systacts at the denial of individual and/or collective mobility to the members of the subordinate ones.† But the answers to these questions

* The definition is taken from Runciman (1966), p. 10; cf. e.g. Boudon (1977). The term was originally coined by Stouffer *et al.* (1949, p. 125) and particularly influentially discussed by Merton (1957, Ch. 8).

† As Marx for one was well aware: cf. e.g. the remarks of Dunning (1971–2, pp. 417–18) on the usefulness of Marx's recognition of the significance of closure for the formation of class consciousness among Blacks in the United States in the 1960s.

are not in any way pre-empted by the reportage of the extent and degree of relative deprivation voiced by the members of different systacts in one or more of the three dimensions of social structure.

This holds, moreover, even when there is reported a pattern which may at first sight seem paradoxical. The finding which led to the initial formulation of the notion of relative deprivation was that in a branch of the American armed services where the opportunities for upward mobility were particularly poor, satisfaction with opportunities for it was greater than in a branch where they were particularly good. It can be paralleled by findings as diverse as that when a tornado struck Arkansas in the early 1960s 'those with only medium property damage were subjectively worse off than those with high property damage' (Barton 1963, p. 63) and that complaints about illiteracy in the Church in the fourteenth century increased in vehemence and frequency at just the time that the frequency of illiteracy was in fact declining (Murray 1978, pp. 292ff.). It was already expressed with a characteristically epigrammatic touch by Tocqueville when he argued that popular discontent in pre-Revolutionary France ran highest in the more fortunate parts of the country so that, as he put it, 'the French found their position insupportable just where it had improved'. But this is not to be construed as an empirical generalization, and still less as an explanatory hypothesis. It is, rather, a reminder – and an important one – that it is unwise to assume that either the frequency or the intensity of self-conscious attempts to alter the existing distribution of power are a function of either the extent or the degree of inequality which can be observed.

COMPETITIVE SELECTION AND SOCIAL EVOLUTION

§11. Within the framework so far outlined, the task of substantive social theory remains what it has always been: the construction and test of empirical hypotheses about the structure and culture of human societies sufficiently well grounded for the reported state of any one society to be explained (and/or described and/or evaluated) in retrospect in terms not invalidated by the reported state of any other. For reasons which I touched on already in Chapter 3 of Volume 1, there is no escape from the recognition that any substantive social theory is and cannot but be evolutionary. But what then follows? The failure of nineteenth-century evolutionary social theory in its several forms provides both an explanation for the subsequent reaction against evolutionism in general and a warning against some of the errors which any theory with a better chance of success will need to avoid. Such a theory will have to acknowledge that social evolution is not to be construed as a unilinear process in which one stage leads always and inevitably to the next; that there is no pre-emptive sense of 'progress' in which one society can be credited with superiority over others in its approach to some predetermined goal; that there is no direct analogy between biological and social survival; and that evaluative presuppositions are as irrelevant to the secondary, explanatory understanding of social evolution in their Marxian (or 'left-wing') as in their Spencerian (or 'right-wing') versions. The proper starting-point is, rather, the unarguable proposition that social evolution is historically continuous with biological evolution. From this it follows that, first, there must be a psycho-physiological repertory by which the range of behaviour of the human species as such is both made possible and also constrained; and second, the persistence of competition for power within human societies, and therefore the fact, as I put it in Section 1, that it is those role-incumbents who *do* pursue their systactic interests who determine how their society works and evolves, makes societies as we find them by definition the outcome of some kind of process of competitive selection.

This still leaves open the vexed question how far social evolution is not only historically continuous with biological evolution but reducible to it – that is, directly explicable in terms of natural selection. But the precise answer to it does not need to be known before the concept of competitive selection can be applied to the workings of observed societies and the structural and/or cultural changes which they undergo. It is enough to recognize that sociology is dependent on, but not therefore reducible to, psychology and ethology. It would be as implausible to presuppose that all human behaviour can be explained exclusively in 'sociobiological' terms as that it can all be explained without any reference whatever to constraints genetically imposed: the underlying mechanism must be a mutual interaction between the two.* Just how this mechanism is to be modelled and what the implications for social theory might be are matters which can safely be left to be settled by the course of future research. It is meanwhile possible – although this, too, is controversial – that some anthropological evidence may bear directly on the nature of the transition from nature to culture. Perhaps,

* From within an extensive literature, see e.g. the formulation of Richerson and Boyd (1978), p. 128: 'The "all culture" hypothesis flounders on origins and thus has difficulty reducing, even in principle, human behaviour to explanation in terms of the rest of scientific knowledge. The "all genes" hypothesis cannot accommodate the obvious fact that humans inherit at least some of their behaviour culturally.' For these authors, genes and culture are to be seen as players in a two-person variable-sum game competing to control individual phenotypes, but (as they recognize – see Boyd and Richerson 1982) such a formulation still leaves many relevant questions unresolved.

for example, the Yanomamo as reported by Chagnon (1968) provide a model for human societies in general in the period from roughly 18000 B.C. to 4000 B.C. because 'their seemingly unrelated practices of infanticide, warfare and polygyny were indeed related and mutually perpetuated each other' (Divale 1972–3, p. 224). But it is difficult to see this as material one way or another to the hypotheses about societies at a very much later stage of evolution with which the chapters to follow are concerned. The (as I believe) valid hypothesis that given the geography of Eastern Europe and the military technology of the Early Modern period, a central monarchy with a standing army was a necessary condition of survival for a politically autonomous nation-state will be neither undermined nor guaranteed by whatever discoveries may be made about the evolution of the societies of the Middle and Upper Palaeolithic.

Similarly, the problems which still attend the precise definition of the concept of 'adaptation' in the context of cultural evolution (to which I shall return in the following Section and again in Chapter 4) need not inhibit the recognition that social evolution has thus far continued, thermodynamically speaking, to run uphill. As in biological evolution, there has unquestionably been a progression towards more and more complex forms of social organization. In social evolution, this results from the interaction – or the dialectic, if you prefer – between man and his physical environment; it is, one might say, a joint property of human intelligence and natural resources. Indeed in this sense, all sociologists subscribe to one of the presuppositions of historical materialism, for it would hardly be possible to deny that the increase in usable resources has been a necessary condition of the parallel increase in organizational complexity. But it has a twofold effect: on the one hand, the newer forms progressively supersede the old; on the other, the range of forms progressively widens. Social evolution, therefore, is a history of societies tending both to diminish and to increase in variety at the same time, and there is nothing contradictory in a theory which acknowledges both. It would be no less of a mistake to deny that the survival of newer institutions is at the expense of older ones than to assert that the newer ones furnish a paradigm towards which the older are all then bound to converge.

This dual aspect of social evolution is just as well illustrated by the so-called Neolithic as by the so-called Industrial Revolution. The domestication of crops and/or livestock had, on the one hand, the effect of driving hunters and gatherers into the less hospitable and productive zones. But it did not, on the other hand, dominate them all – some survive to this day – and it did not impose a uniform pattern of roles on those societies that did conform to its technological and organizational imperatives. Similarly, the development of large-scale manufacturing industry powered by coal and steam had, on the one hand, the effect of imposing on any society that did not adopt it the eventual penalty of becoming dominated to some degree by those that did. But it did not, on the other hand, compel those that did not to follow suit, and still less did it compel those that did to modify their institutions and practices in exactly the same way as each other. Not only does the range of variation increase with the increase in complexity, but it comes to include progressively more pre-existing practices which still persist.

The history of any chosen society has, therefore, to be narrated as an evolving range of alternative modes of the distribution of power within an evolving set of constraints. The constraints are both natural and cultural, and they may or may not be visible to those affected by them: this is one of the matters about which later observers are likely to be more knowledgeable than the agents whose behaviour they are studying. It is hardly to be supposed, for example, that the individual members of the Epi-Palaeolithic communities of hunter-gatherers whom we now perceive as having evolved so intensely formalized a pattern of focal activities as to inhibit any change in the direction of domestication (Clarke 1978, p. 352) were themselves aware of it. Nor is it likely that demographic equilibrium in a 'modern' society is achieved, if it is, because and only because it was the conscious strategy of the individual parents who limited their potential fertility by marrying late (D. S. Smith, 1977). But in either event, it is demonstrable that certain institutions, roles and practices survive and that others do not. It is sometimes said that sociologists and historians (if not anthropologists) are too prone to side with the winners. But the task of substantive social theory is to analyze what has happened, not what hasn't. Later observers can report winners in the unending competition for power as winners without presupposing that their success was forseeable in advance, or experienced by them as if it had been, or morally or by any other evaluative criterion deserved by them.

§12. But what exactly is it that social selection selects? To this crucial question, there can only be one answer if the argument of this Chapter thus far is sound. But it may help to show why this is so if it is first shown why the answer is neither, at one extreme, groups as such nor, at the other, the ideas to be found in the minds of individual persons.

This is not to deny that both these answers can be framed and construed in such a way that they are true. But they will then be true only because circular. There is a sense in which Carr-Saunders (1922, p. 223) is quite entitled to claim that 'those groups practising the most advantageous customs will have an advantage in the constant struggle between adjacent groups over those that practice less advantageous customs'. But nothing is explained by saying so; and when the claim is interpreted as Carr-Saunders himself interprets it, as generating the hypothesis that societies will all adopt customs which will maximize income per head, it is demonstrably false.* Similarly, nobody can deny that the ideas conceived, transmitted and retained by individual persons survive only because they are in some sense 'satisfying', and a psychological 'struggle for satisfaction' is thus analogous to the biological 'struggle for survival' (Ruyle 1973, p. 203). But this likewise explains nothing. Even if it is widened, as it needs to be, to cover any and all of what Dawkins (1976, Ch. 11) calls 'memes', and thereby to include not merely beliefs but ideas, techniques, fashions and even tunes, the assertion that they are to be observed as we find them because of their value in satisfying those who adhere to and propagate them remains empty. To take two of Dawkins's own examples, what does it mean to say that both a belief in natural science and a belief in hell-fire are alike culturally selected for their 'appeal'? The underlying idea is that the unit of social selection must be some item, set or sequence of human thought and action which is both replicable and transmissible. But it must not be so defined that claims about the survival (or not) of such units merely commit the fallacy of affirming the consequent. The definition must be grounded in a theory capable of specifying why any designated unit does or does not survive.

It follows, given what has already been said, that the right answer to the question 'what does social selection select?' is and can only be: *practices* – functionally defined units of reciprocal action informed by the mutually recognized intentions and beliefs of designated persons about their respective capacity to influence each other's behaviour by virtue of their roles. With this answer, the danger of circularity is overcome because these roles give their incumbents by definition the capacity to influence the incumbents of other roles to whom they stand in relations of domination and/or cooperation. In other words, the theory explicitly ties the units of social selection to the underlying

* As is likewise the more recent contention that cultural evolution selects population size and density and per capita energy production (M. Harris 1971, p. 152); there are any number of societies whose members visibly forgo the further accumulation of resources at a point well within their known technological and social capabilities.

concept of power. It is because of the effects which specified practices have under specified initial conditions that the survival of those that do survive, and the modification, suppression or disappearance of those that do not, can be given an adequately grounded explanation. Because power is of three mutually irreducible kinds, the competitive advantage which a practice is hypothesized to confer on one rather than another group or category of persons in their roles may be in one, two or three of the dimensions of social structure. But this does not undermine the claim that practices, whether economic, ideological or coercive, are what social selection selects: it is immaterial to the theory what the relation between the three may be in any particular case. Sixteenth-century Inca Peru, for example, had so evolved that the interests of the royal nobility, the provincial *curacas*, the peasantry and the subordinate *yanas* were all defined in relation to a uniform hierarchy of wealth, ritual status and political-cum-military office. By contrast, in seventh-century T'ang China, the location of the hitherto more advantageously placed divisional militiamen was the outcome of a coincidental decline which was at once military (because their campaigns were unsuccessful), economic (because they lost their immunity from taxation) and social (because of a runaway inflation in the value of honours). But this difference, important as it may be to understanding a particular society's workings and evolution, poses no special theoretical difficulty. It means only that economic, ideological and coercive practices need to be carefully distinguished before the advantages which they confer on their carriers can be assessed.

I remarked already in Chapter 3 of Volume I that the agents of social change cannot themselves be understood (in the secondary, explanatory sense) as the outcome of social selection any more than the agents of genetic change as the outcome of natural selection. But just as it is the mutability of genes that enables species to adapt to their environment, so it is the flexibility of practices that enables groups or categories of persons in their roles to adapt to theirs. As in genetic evolution, *mutation* and *recombination* of practices can come about in all sorts of different and unpredictable ways. But the social theorist can and must treat the emergence of variants as random – that is, as I also argued in Chapter 3 of Volume I, not as uncaused and therefore inexplicable, but as independently caused and therefore explicable only at a different level. The roles and institutions which are the outcome of the emergence of these practices then survive, or fail to survive, to the extent that they do demonstrably confer on the roles and thereby systacts carrying them a competitive advantage in the context of the pre-existing distribution of power. What it is about them that makes them adaptive in this way has always to be argued by way of a model testable against rival hypotheses. But where the historical or ethnographic (or, it may be, archaeological) evidence permits the necessary quasi-experimental contrasts to be drawn, it will be possible for a testable and adequately grounded explanation to be framed, *post hoc*, even though the evolution of societies cannot be predicted in advance any better than can that of species.

In practice, some of the most difficult cases are those where there is no lack of evidence but there are several obviously relevant practices whose functions in conferring competitive advantage on one systact over another cannot be assigned their relative influence. A good example is furnished by the rise of a Karāva élite in Sri Lanka in the period between roughly the late sixteenth and early twentieth centuries (Roberts 1982). The example is a particularly good one because the identity of the Karāva is clear-cut and their overt competition with other groups, notably the traditionally superior Goyigama caste, is unequivocally documented for all three dimensions of structure alike. Nor can there be any doubt about their success in terms of both individual and collective upward mobility. But which of the several practices which can be shown to have worked to their advantage was decisive for that success? How can we tell what difference it would have made if a substantial number of Karāva had not adopted Catholicism under the Portuguese? Or if the Karāva had not been heavily involved in *theppan* (catamaran) fishing, which led to the formation of a class of capitalist boat-owners? Or if they had not retained their traditional caste and kin loyalties in their occupational recruitment practices? Or if under the British their leaders had not taken to sending their more talented sons to England for tertiary education and distributing philanthropic largesse in their local roles as community leaders? Although there can be no doubt that the rise of the Karāva is to be explained by reference to practices which, in their environment, the process of social selection selected, the example leaves equally little doubt that to say no more than that is to state the beginning, not the conclusion, of an adequately grounded explanation of the particular evolution which in fact took place.* But the technical problems of overdetermination, however serious an impediment to the practising sociologist, do not in any way damage the theory. The Karāva example can be used to show the need

* See the review of Roberts by Baily (1983) and rejoinder by Roberts (1985).

for alternative models of a common theory which will enable different hypotheses consistent with the evidence to be tested against one another. It cannot, however, be used to support an argument to the effect that practices are not what social selection selects.*

A different type of objection which might be made is that to identify practices as the unit of selection undervalues the sometimes decisive contribution of exceptional persons to the course of social evolution. But there is no contradiction here. We do not have to choose between a philosophical presupposition which attributes all changes in human institutions to the will of a few great men and another which sees great men as no more than the incidental vehicles for the operation of impersonal forces. The opposition is as false as that between a 'natural' state of either domination or cooperation. It is undeniable that exceptionally gifted people may make far more difference to their society's subsequent history than is implied in the bare assertion that the competitive advantage inherent in mutant or recombinant practices determines the changes in roles and institutions which then take it from one mode or sub-type of the distribution of the means of production, persuasion and coercion to another. But for the analysis of social evolution, the causes of the particular talents and temperaments of particular persons are immaterial to the analysis of the effects of the changes introduced by them. Just as the presence of certain features of a society's ecological environment – such as, say, warm water currents, or obsidian deposits, or hardwood trees, or alluvial mud-flats – may be decisive for its future evolution irrespective of how they come to be there,† so may the presence of a person who happens to be endowed with some outstanding capacity, whether for military leadership, or technological discovery, or ideological innovation. It does not matter if it is impossible (as it often is) to specify in biographical terms just how and

* Analogous examples are familiar in the study of natural selection: see e.g. E. O. Wilson's (1975, p. 29) citation of the 'group of explanations advanced by various authors for the role of cicada aggregations: they bring the sexes together for mating; they permit loud enough singing to confuse and repel predatory birds; they saturate the local predators with a superabundance of prey and thus permit the escape of much of the population. Not only are these propositions difficult to disentangle and to test in the form just given; they may all be true. If more than one is true, some method must eventually be devised to assess their relative importance.'

† A good modern example is provided by Sweden's mineral deposits, which enabled it to achieve a degree of power in seventeenth-century Europe out of all proportion to its population: not only did they furnish the material for a successful domestic arms industry, but they generated the foreign revenue with which the Elfsborg ransom could be paid to Denmark and mercenaries hired to enlarge its otherwise limited conscript army.

why the particular person who first domesticated root crops or fashioned an iron stabbing-weapon or wrote down a law code or conceived a notion of the divine right of kings or trained infantrymen to form ranks or brought wage-workers together under a single roof came to do so. What matters is whether the practices involved in such innovations confer a competitive advantage on their carriers such that their novel roles come to modify the structure and culture of the society in which they occur to the point that it evolves into a different mode or sub-type of the distribution of power.

§13. The argument sketched out in the previous Section is of such fundamental importance to the whole of this volume that it is worth devoting a little further space to the avoidance of possible misunderstandings. First of all, it needs to be emphasized that none of the terms employed is merely metaphorical, whether or not borrowed from the theory of natural selection. Practices are observable items and sequences of human behaviour informed by ascertainable intentions; the incumbents of roles do literally compete for power; the resulting movement in the location of those roles in three-dimensional social space can be empirically verified; mutations are actual changes of practices which can be specified, and recombinations are actual conjunctions of them whose effects on the roles which they redefine are likewise visible in the behaviour of the incumbents of the roles with which they interact. It would be wholly mistaken to suggest that the identification of practices as the units of social selection is merely some sort of verbal redefinition of commonsense accounts of changes from one state of a society to the next.

Second, it needs to be made clear at the outset that social selection, like natural, operates at more than one level. Individual role-incumbents compete with one another both in seeking to maintain or augment the power attaching to their existing roles and in seeking to move into higher-located ones; systacts are collective competitors for improved access to the means of production, persuasion and coercion within their institutional catchment areas; and societies themselves are in competition with one another both where each is in pursuit of the same external resources and where one is seeking directly to dominate the other, economically, ideologically, coercively or all three. But neither societies nor institutions nor systacts nor roles nor the individual incumbents of roles are what the process of selection is selecting. Selective pressure may come to bear at any or all levels, and may originate from outside the society in question as well as within. Its object, however, is always the same. Social evolution comes about because practices (like genes) give roles (like organisms) advantages in competition for power (like competition for reproductive capacity) through being thereby attributes of systacts (like groups) and societies (like species). Like genes, practices are selected not for their own attributes as such, but as attributes of their carriers. There may or may not, according to context, be a direct correspondence between their own defining characteristics and the nature of the competitive advantage which they confer. In social, as in biological, evolution, the higher-level attributes can explain the competitive advantages which determine the course to be taken. But they have in their turn to be explained by the mutation or recombination of the practices which, like genes, are available to be selected for their function in bestowing the higher-level attributes on their carriers.

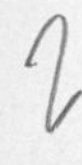

Third, and as a further consequence of the multiplicity of levels at which selection operates, the concept of a practice need not and should not be too tightly defined. The proper criterion is always the functional one. This is not simply a concession forced on us by our ignorance of human psychology by comparison with our understanding of molecular biology. On the contrary: if, as we now know, the agents of biological variation are chromosomal segments or regions of DNA which code for polypeptides determining characteristics observable at the phenotypic level, then there can be as many equally acceptable definitions of 'gene' as there are functions at one or other level which it is invoked to explain (Kitcher 1982, pp. 354–6). Likewise with 'practice'. The items and sequences of behaviour of which practices consist can, if thought useful, be broken down into separate actions. But there will be no more of a direct correspondence between these actions and the attributes of the roles defined by the practices they constitute which confer competitive advantage on them than there is between nucleotide substitutions and the phenotypical attributes which confer competitive advantage on organisms.

Fourth, the valid analogies, of which there are several, between social and natural selection need to be seen as just that – analogies and nothing more. We have, at least by implication, seen already that evolution of societies, as of species, arises from changes which, although random at one level, are the effects of ascertainable causes at a different one; that in social, as in natural, selection the possibility of variation is literally infinite (with interaction between role-incumbents corresponding to sexual interaction in biology); that social selection does not, any more than natural selection, require that competition should always be to the literal extinction of the less advantaged; and that since practices interact in complex ways, just as genes do, recombination can be a more powerful generator of novelty than mutation. What is more, there are three further parallels which can equally legitimately be drawn. First, considerations of social mobility are of equivalent importance in social selection to considerations of population genetics in natural selection: the distribution of persons among roles over successive generations within societies needs to be modelled as precisely as it can, just as do gene frequencies over successive generations within species. Second, there correspond to considerations of theoretical ecology in the study of natural selection considerations of theoretical sociology in social selection – 'sociology' here standing for the study of why, in a given context, one attribute of a role rather than another confers economic, ideological or coercive advantage. And third, in the explanation of natural and social selection alike, an equally significant part may be played by the physical migration of individuals and groups from one environment to another. Taken together, all these give grounds to expect that the study of social evolution can be both clarified and supported by occasional reference to the methods and discoveries of evolutionary biology. But none of them is an argument for the reducibility of sociological to biological theory. Sociological theory has to stand on its own foundations, however close the two may be in certain aspects of their mode of reasoning.

This said, it might be asked where exactly the originality of the theory which I am advancing resides. After all, Marx has been claimed already (by Engels among others) to have done for the study of societies what Darwin did for the study of species; and if his notion of conflict between economic classes is qualified by Weber's rider that the independent effects of ideological and political conflict have also to be admitted, what more am I adding to that? But it should not take much reflection to see that the answer is: a very great deal. It is not merely that neither Marx nor Weber (nor anyone else) has addressed the question of precisely what is competitively selected, and how, in the course of the continuing conflicts out of which new forms of society evolve. Nor is it merely that Marx's basic concept of a dialectic between successive pairs of opposing classes has to be rejected as unequivocally as Weber's basic concept of rationalization. More important still, neither Marx nor Weber nor anyone else has seen how to integrate the idea of social evolution, once shorn of evaluative and teleological presuppositions, with a conceptualization of societies and their constituents which enables the outcome of the continuous competition for power to be rigorously explained in terms of it. It is true that the idea of social evolution as such is long familiar, and this volume can fairly be said to be another attempt at a task at which earlier and more gifted sociologists have failed. But without the rejection of the presuppositions which misled them, and the reconceptualization of the issues in a form which none of them envisaged, they could never have hoped to succeed.

This is not to deny that many of the accounts to be given in the chapters to follow of the workings and evolution of specific societies could equally well be accommodated within a Marxian, Weberian or for that matter a commonsense historical framework. But the purpose of this volume is not simply to put forward a set of particular hypotheses of cause and effect relating to one or another chosen society. As I emphasized in Chapter 3 of Volume I, a theory which furnishes hypotheses of cause and effect with an adequate grounding does so by showing not that, but why, they hold good. The test of this one, therefore, as of any other, is whether it can not only establish the reasons for which the particular hypotheses about chosen societies are valid but also generate others by which the theory itself will be further extended and tested; and if it is successful, it will incorporate what was valid in earlier evolutionary theories as cases of its own. The fundamental insight on which it rests is that the evolution of any and all societies from one mode or sub-type of the distribution of power to another depends on the practices which the process of social selection has selected and, given the institutional context, the functions they have been selected *for*.

INTER-SOCIETAL COMPARISONS AND PRINCIPLES OF TAXONOMY

§14. How, then, are the thousands of different societies in the historical and ethnographic record to be classified and compared for the purpose of testing and extending this theory? There can be no question that they do have to be classified. Arid and scholastic as exercises in taxonomy can be, any substantive theory presupposes a taxonomy and any taxonomy is only as good or bad as the theory which gives it its rationale. Nor can labels for different societies be theory-neutrally assigned. It may, perhaps, be agreed among all rival observers that two or more societies share the common institutional characteristics of, say, chattel slavery or parliamentary elections or a hereditary nobility, provided that nothing more is implied than that it has been reported of all of them that the incumbents of designated roles own people as things, vote candidates into membership of a legislative assembly or inherit superior ascriptive status at birth. But it is another matter entirely to jump from this to talk of 'slave', 'democratic' or 'feudal' societies and thereby to pre-empt a judgement about the importance of these roles in explaining how these societies function and evolve (or what they are like to live in or whether they are good or bad). To say, for example, that twentieth-century Britain is a liberal-democratic-capitalist society is to imply both that it differs from other actual or possible ideologically 'liberal', politically 'democratic', or economically 'capitalist' societies and that the particular institutional combination which gives it this label is the key to understanding its structure and culture alike.

Now it evidently follows from the argument of this chapter thus far that societies will have to be classified in terms of their mode of the distribution of power – which is to say, their particular articulation of modes of production, persuasion and coercion. The resulting polynomials, like 'liberal-democratic-capitalist', will carry both a 'Linnaean' rationale whereby synchronic distinctions from other societies can be drawn and a 'Darwinian' rationale whereby places are assigned in a presumptive evolutionary sequence. This is, emphatically, not to imply that societies when so classified will lend themselves either to lawlike synchronic generalizations or to unilinear evolutionary sequences. Indeed, it is in the nature of a process of evolution through competitive selection of mutant or recombinant practices that it will not generate regularities which could be enshrined in laws of any kind. But any label used to designate a society chosen for discussion must always have this twofold rationale. Otherwise, there can be no way of modelling in testable form any theory which claims to explain how societies function or why they have evolved as they have.

To assign two or more societies to the same mode of production, persuasion or coercion is, however, to presuppose that those of their roles which determine these can be equated despite the other differences in structure and culture between them; and this is something about which it is all too easy to make a mistake. Yet however difficult it may be to avoid misreportage of an observed role, the test is always the same: is the relative power attaching to it in the different societies equal, and is it defined by functionally analogous economic, ideological or coercive practices and the sanctions and inducements that go with them? Often enough, inter-societal equivalence of roles is unproblematic. Rival observers can no more plausibly dispute that a medieval Islamic *wahil tujjar*, or merchant's representative in an alien country, is the same as an Archaic Greek *proxenos*, or a Catalan *justicia* the same as a Roman *defensor pacis*, than that Charlemagne's *missi dominici* were the same as Ashoka's *dhāmma-mahāmāttas*. Similarly, the role of 'casual wage-labourer' applies no less unquestionably to the Roman building workers referred to in Cicero's letters or to the refugees from a devastated area reported in a capitulary of Charles the Bald as hiring themselves out as grape-pickers than it does to the landless villagers of medieval England for whose services other villagers competed with manorial lords at harvest time* or the dockers and stevedores of Mayhew's London. But there are three dangers. The first is that ostensibly similar roles may rest on dissimilar practices; the second is that the sources themselves may assume too readily that the practices are similar when they are not; and the third is – paradoxically, perhaps – that the sources may strive not too little, but too much, after precision.

Consider, for example, the role of 'vassal', to which I shall be returning several times in the chapters to follow. It is abundantly documented in contexts where there is no reason to doubt that the intentions or beliefs of the parties are as reported and the role of 'vassal' is clearly recognized and understood by 'them'. But even within the same cultural tradition, the role of the twelfth-century vassal as reported by Galbert de Bruges is not that of the vassal whose homage to King Pepin in 757 is reported in the *Annales regni Francorum*, and still less is he the vassal whose homage to the seigneur of Vitry on 6 July 1789 is reported in the departmental archives of that part of the province of Burgundy.† The practice whereby someone voluntarily makes himself 'the man of another man' has a history of its own extending back to the forms of commendation practised in Merovingian Gaul and forward until long after the societies of Europe ceased under any plausible taxonomy to be 'feudal'. The role of 'vassal' is defined not just by the application of the term to the practice of commendation, but by the relative privileges and duties of the vassal on the one side and the lord to whom he commends himself on the other. Nor is the temptation to assimilate medieval European vassals and their lords to ostensibly similar roles in other cultures any less dangerous. It has often been done in relation to one or another African kingdom. Thus, the Ganda *batongole* held land granted as a benefice from his *kabaka* in return for the performance of special services, and the Rwanda institution of

* This, as it happens, is not directly reported in the documentary sources, but can be semi-deductively inferred from the injunctions in the bye-laws recorded in court rolls (Postan 1972, p. 148).

† These three examples are all borrowed from documents reproduced by Boutruche (1959, pp. 332–48: 'Les rites vassaliques').

ubuhake involved personal, contractual obligations of service in return for maintenance and protection on the European model. But the *batongole*'s special relationship to the *kabaka* was in the context of a centralized royal authority administered through territorial chiefs from whose jurisdiction the *batongole* was exempted; and the relationships involved in the Rwanda *ubuhake* were not those of lord to vassal but of patron to client in the context, again, of a centralized administrative system.* The roles may look the same, and a theory of 'feudalism' may be being advanced which requires that they should be so. But they aren't.

The same difficulty may be present, moreover, even where the role in question is both culturally and structurally distinctive. Consider the example of a 'king'. It is not just that there are borderline cases, like the 'kinglets' (*reguli*) of the smaller German tribes or the *xinesi* of the Texan Indians whom their chronicler, Fray Casañas, called 'like petty kings'. Nor is it just that, as I have remarked already, the powers of the incumbent of a single topmost role may be different between one and another of the three dimensions of social structure. It is that in addition the cultural content of the role differs between one society and the next. For example: are those, like the Merovingian kings, who do not claim divine descent, to be equated with those, like the Saxon kings, who do? if Julius Caesar in Rome or Enrico Dandalo in Venice had accepted the crowns which were offered them would they have been 'kings' in the same sense as Louis XIV or Henry VIII? did Agathocles, tyrant of Sicily, really become a 'king' just by calling himself one in imitation of the Hellenistic monarchs? and weren't the Roman emperors kings even though they were never called such?† None of these questions can be answered with a simple yes or no. The role is equivalent only if both the practices which define it and the relative power attaching to it are sufficiently similar: a 'constitutional' monarch is not, properly speaking, a monarch at all. Admittedly, some kings are stronger than others and even very weak kings can still be kings. But the Japanese 'emperor'

* Both these examples are taken from Steinhart (1967), who dismisses still more curtly a number of other attributions of 'feudalism' to African societies. Cf. Law 1977, pp. 108–10, on 'the "fief" system' in the Oyo kingdom: chiefs who were patrons (*babas* – literally, fathers) of provincial towns were entitled to a share of the tribute which they handed over annually to the *Alafin*; but they were not vassals, they did not hold land, they were not obliged to perform military service, and they were closely watched by 'little fathers' (*baba kekere*) appointed by the Alafin from among his palace slaves.

† Cf. Appian's Preface to his *History*. Although the emperors were never *reges* to their Latin-speaking subjects, they were *basileis* to their Greek-speaking ones: even Augustus was so referred to in an epigram (F. Millar 1977, p. 613 n. 19).

(*tennō*) was no more a real king after the establishment of the shogunate than were the kings of England after the so-called 'Glorious Revolution' of 1688.

The danger that the sources may fail to distinguish the differences in the practices which underlie the same ostensibly similar roles is well illustrated by the example of 'patrons' and 'clients'. The difficulty is not just that a Roman *patronus* may not be doing at all the same things as an Italian *padrone* or a French *patron*. It is that even within a working definition accepted by all theoretical schools, there is still a risk of wrongly equating different roles and the practices defining them. Suppose that 'clientage' is defined as a relationship of mutual benefit which holds in any or all the three dimensions of structure between the client and a superior to whom the client accepts that he owes specified duties and from whom he expects to receive specified favours in return. So far, so good. Nothing has been said to prevent all rival observers from agreeing how to recognize an instance when they see one. But without some more detailed specification of the content of the mutual expectations of patron and client, the term could be inaccurately applied to different societies whose institutions were in fact quite different in kind. It is not the exact nature of the favours done or duties performed which needs to be spelt out: these can well vary within the role. It is the extent to which the expectations underlying the practices involved are to be understood in the primary sense as cooperative or antagonistic. The observer may find the same pattern of regular attendance on the 'patron' by the 'client', the same deferential modes of address, the same consistent support in elections or law-suits or feuds, perhaps even the same quasi-familial images of father/son relationships in which both parties expound to the visiting fieldworker the dictionary meaning of their own vernacular term for the role. But it is still possible that in one case the defining sanction in the minds of both 'patron' and 'client' is a degree of coercive, ideological or economic domination which is wholly absent in the other, where the deference is merely symbolic, the 'patron' feels no less dependent on the 'client' than the other way round and both think of themselves as cooperating in defence of their mutual interests against their common opponents. Even within the common culture of twentieth-century Mediterranean societies, the role of a Lebanese *za'im* whose power over his clients is based on physical force (M. Johnson 1977, p. 211) is very different from the role of a Maltese landowner whose power over his tenants and retainers is based on economic inducements and sanctions in the context of a 'long-term, personal, moral relation' (Boissevain 1977, p. 89).

Finally, there is the third danger – that the vernacular term for a distinctive role may, far from being too unreflectingly applied in the sources, be applied after too *much* reflection. For the study of periods and milieux no longer accessible for participant-observation, it might seem that the most reliable sources would be the accounts of 'a few good observers who tried to elaborate a theory of the society in which they lived' – as Mousnier (1979, p. 4) puts it in choosing Loyseau, Domat, Saint-Simon and Barnave as guides to the changing perceptions of the French *ancien régime* by those who lived through its several phases. But those perceptions, and the terms in which they are handed down to us, are a function of purposes and presuppositions of their own. Even where these are not overtly evaluative – as in Saint-Simon's case they unashamedly are – the underlying observations of roles and practices on which the account is based are likely to have to be, as it were, disinterred from the implicit but nonetheless pre-emptive explanatory and/or descriptive and/or evaluative theory. Thus Domat's sociology, for example, is at the same time partly theological and partly jurisprudential (Voeltzel 1936); and this makes it hardly less problematic accurately to reconstruct from his works the systactic structure of later seventeenth-century France than, for example, to reconstruct Crusader 'serfdom' in the Levant from the few brief and probably idealized chapters of Jean d'Ibelin which refer to it (Prawer 1980, p. 203).* Even where the author's purpose is, or appears to be, strictly sociological, there is a risk that his chosen designation of roles and practices may be more contentious than it seems. No sociologist studying eleventh-century English society can be other than grateful for the survival of the anonymous manual of estate management known as the *Rectitudines Singularum Personarum* (Leibermann 1903, pp. 444–53). No sociologist studying seventeenth-century English society can be other than grateful for Gregory King's decision to draw up *A Scheme of Income and Expense of the several Families of England Calculated for the Year 1688* (Thirsk and Cooper 1972, pp. 780–1). But it would be most unwise to equate King's 'Cottagers' with either the '*Kotsetlas*' (or '*Cottarii*') of the *Rectitudines* or the 'Paupers' with whom he places them himself for the purpose of his own scheme. Indeed, it may even be easier for the latter-day sociologist to be satisfied about the precise nature of a role whose apparently anomalous designation is left to speak for itself in the contemporary sources without any attempt at theoretical refinement.

* Not that legal texts ought always to be interpreted as idealizations: cf. Udovitch (1970, p. 4) on the confirmation of the sociological content of medieval Islamic legal texts by the evidence of the documents of the Cairo Geniza.

The Archaic Greek *dēmiourgos* is a role which, puzzlingly at first sight, includes prophets, doctors, builders, minstrels and heralds in the *Odyssey*, but by the Classical period designates either magistrates on the one hand or artisans on the other. But it may very well be that the apparent anomaly can be better accounted for (Murakawa 1959; Jeffrey 1973–4; Quiller 1980) for the very reason that the literary as well as the epigraphic sources make no attempt at elaboration or commentary.

There are, accordingly, at least some roles which can uncontentiously be reported as occurring in otherwise very different societies; and where this is so, it follows that to that extent the two or more societies cannot but share at least one small component of the polynomial label which would exhaustively define them. But this is no more than the start of the construction of a taxonomy which will assign the societies to their appropriate 'Linnaean' and 'Darwinian' place. It may be that a large number of roles in all three dimensions are common to the societies which are being compared: there are the slaves, the electors, the nobles and whoever else whose reciprocal influence on each other is a function of the same mutually acknowledged practices and the same relative difference of location. But this is not yet by any means enough to licence the inference that they share a common mode of the distribution of power. For that, the equivalent roles have to combine to make up functionally equivalent institutions – or in other words, the institutions have to be analogous to, although not necessarily homologous with, each other.

§15. As with equivalence of roles, equivalence of institutions is sometimes and for some purposes unproblematic. If a large industrial corporation in twentieth-century Britain is compared to one in Sweden, or Japan, or the United States, there is no difficulty in recognizing the same roles of shareholders, directors, managers and wage-workers, and no doubt that in broad terms the relationships between them are homologous in form as well as analogous in function. But even then, the practices which define these roles are by no means identical, and more detailed analysis will quickly disclose significant differences which need to be reported and explained in their turn.

This holds no less at earlier than at later evolutionary stages. Corvée labour, for example, is an institution which can be documented in apparently homologous form across a wide range of pre-industrial societies, whether the work in question is irrigation, or building, or the repair of bridges or fortifications, or the tilling or harvesting of noble, Church or state lands. But neither the underlying practices nor the resulting functions need be the same. It is one thing to help bring in the harvest on the demesne of a feudal lord or to help drag to the regional or imperial capital the stone with which monumental buildings are to be constructed. It is quite another to help in stocking the communal storehouse or collecting the produce to be offered at the shrine of the local deity. The critical difference is not in the nature of the work, or even in the relative social distance between labourers and supervisors. It is in the element of domination or cooperation in the underlying practices and in the function thereby performed. The Trobriand Islanders brought together under the orders of their headman to help build a canoe (Malinowski 1922, pp. 113–20) are the incumbents of very different roles from, say, the *neaniskoi* in the cleruchies of Ptolemaic Egypt gathering their assigned quantities of crops under the orders of a royal official (Hunt and Edgar 1934, no. 412).

A direct transition within the same society from one function of corvée labour and therefore one mode of the distribution of power to another can clearly be seen in the instructive example of the contrast between Inca and pre-Inca Peru (Murra 1980, Chs. 2, 5). Before the *Tahuantinsuyu* (the Inca conquest state), it was already traditional for agricultural and building work to be carried out by the communal efforts of the able-bodied population of a lineage-group (*ayllu*). The beneficiary of the work done, who might be a regional or valley lord linked initially by kinship to those whose corvée contribution he was entitled to receive, was always expected to feed the workers, to provide them with maize beer, and to donate seed or cuttings as necessary. The amounts of work exacted by corvée appear to have been precisely calculated, whether the work was building a house for a newly married couple, irrigating or terracing previously uncultivated land belonging to the ethnic group, or making the maize beer needed for libations to the local gods. But all of it was performed within an institutional context of reciprocity – what one of the Spanish chroniclers explicitly called 'the law of brotherhood'. After the Inca conquest, the same ostensibly identical practices were continued. But now, the institutional context was quite different. Under the *Tahuantinsuyu*, all land was deemed the property of the state (whether the Crown or the cult of the Sun). Although corvée duties for the state were so organized as not to interfere with the routines of the *ayllu*, and the custom whereby the sponsors of the work provided food and beer for the workers was scrupulously retained, the ostensibly similar roles conceal a quite different set of intentions underlain by a belief in sanctions of a quite different kind. The *Tahuantinsuyu* was not just the *ayllu* system writ large. The surplus crops stored in the state warehouses were not for communal redistribution; the assignment of lands to the Sun was something much more than the cultivation of a special field to provide chicha beer for the local deity; and the respect accorded to the traditions of the *ayllu* went hand-in-hand with a ready willingness to use the means of coercion against any community or ethnic group which sought to resist the will of the king. The able-bodied adults going to work singing in their best clothes and with food and beer provided to them free were still 'performing corvée duties' within the same apparently uncontroversial dictionary definition. But institutionally, there had evolved a different mode of the distribution of power.

Given a three-dimensional structure, it follows that the terms in which institutions are reported will by definition carry an implicit reference to three ideal types of society in which one form of power pervades the entire society to the exclusion of the other two. It is true that no such society is actually to be found in the historical and ethnographic record. But the theoretical possibility furnishes the basis for inter-societal comparison of institutions and the typology which they generate. The idea of a mode of production which determines who is in a position to acquire what from whom implies the ideal type of a society in which all institutions are held together by a 'cash nexus', all roles relate to a capacity to pay or be paid for goods and services, and all systacts are therefore classes or fractions of classes whose members' power, or lack of it, derives from the relation of their roles to the processes of production, distribution and exchange. The idea of a mode of persuasion which determines who is in a position to be accorded deference by whom implies the ideal type of a society in which all institutions are held together by mutual ascription of prestige, all roles relate to location on a common ideological scale of esteem or derogation, and all systacts are therefore self-differentiating and mutually acknowledged status-groups. The idea of a mode of coercion which determines who is in a position to give orders to whom implies the ideal type of a society in which all institutions are held together by force or the threat of force, all roles relate to possession of or access to the means of exercising force, and all systacts are therefore gangs, parties, factions or armies. Even though, in practice, institutions are held together by inducements and sanctions of all three kinds, it is still in terms of the ratio of each to each, as well as the relative locations of their constituent roles, that they need to be compared between one society and another.

Out of these comparisons, there comes a range of distinctive and largely familiar combinations whose place in a 'Linnaean' grid of mutually exclusive possibilities corresponds to a place along a 'Darwinian' sequence within which, as the amount of power available to be allocated among roles increases, the range of possibilities widens within a simultaneously evolving range of constraints. The distinctive combinations which are held to constitute separate modes of the distribution of power do, of course, embrace a variety of sub-types, and these again have both their 'Linnaean' and their 'Darwinian' rationale: the common categorization of Britain, Sweden, Japan and the United States as 'liberal-democratic-capitalist' does not, as I have already implied, mean that their institutions are anywhere near identical. On the contrary, it is no less remarkable that they should reproduce the common mode through such dissimilar but functionally equivalent institutions than that they should have evolved into it by way of such different economic, social-cum-ideological and political-cum-military histories. But the criterion of classification according to mode of production, persuasion and coercion remains the same.

§16. How far, then, should classification be taken along these lines? Ultimately, no doubt, to the point where every society, like every plant or animal species, has its own 'Linnaean' polynomial and its own 'Darwinian' niche. Although it is possible in theory that two distinct societies, like two different species, should have evolved identical characteristics, the probability is infinitesimal. Conceivably, among the many hundreds of *poleis* of Classical Greece there might be two with indistinguishable practices, roles and institutions – the same ruling council of household heads with fixed and unalienable allotments of land, the same code of civil and criminal sanctions, the same religious cults, and the same hierarchy of ritual status including the same denial of rights to women and younger men. But even here, where the possibility of direct imitation is reinforced by similarities in both ecological and cultural environment, there are in every reported case some differences, slight as they may be, in what the members of the *poleis* themselves called their '*nomima*'. Even the smallest and simplest societies differ from one another in practices which relate to their methods of food procurement, their patterns of residence, their exchanges of prestige goods, their degree of role-specialization, their religious beliefs, their emphasis or otherwise on relations of kinship, and their preference for immediate or deferred returns for their labour. All these have implications for the roles by which they are defined and all have, if their structure and culture are to be explained, to be traced to the competitive advantage bestowed on their carriers. But it would be absurd to suggest that these differences amount to alternative modes of the distribution of power. They are differences within them, not of them. On any theory, the resemblances among the different hunter-gatherers or the different *poleis* are greater than any between any pair drawn from each category – to say nothing of contrasts with societies at an altogether later 'Darwinian' stage.

For the purpose of framing a workable taxonomy of modes of production, persuasion and coercion, therefore, the question to ask is not how many different roles are reported for any given set of societies chosen for comparative study, but how many different ways there are in which the institutions which they constitute can and do determine the allocation of economic, ideological and coercive power. And the answer will turn out to be: not all that many. Vast as the range of practices and roles may be, the range of institutions which can be distinguished by this criterion is much, much narrower. The ways in which the different incumbents of different roles may perform them is infinitely variable. But the ways in which they can combine to form institutions which produce and reproduce a society sufficiently stable to have a mode of the distribution of power which calls for a label are not.

The hunter-gatherers and even the *poleis* are, it might be objected, still too short of free-floating resources for any great variation to be possible at the institutional level. But consider the societies which have evolved beyond this stage to the level of the great agricultural states and empires, with their large landholdings, extensive commercial networks, well-staffed bureaucracies, well-equipped armies, established churches and entrenched doctrines of secular or sacred legitimacy. The differences between them in both structure and culture are enormous, ranging from Imperial Rome to Ottoman Turkey to Petrine Russia to Sung China to Inca Peru to the Baltic territories of the Teutonic Knights and yet others whom we shall meet in the chapters to follow. Yet all the same, how many different institutional means did they have at their disposal for maintaining their different structures and cultures intact?

Here is a list which does not claim to be totally rigorous or exhaustive, but which does embrace, at least in outline, the range of institutional variants reported in the historical and ethnographic record. In the mode of production, it covers (i) serfdom, (ii) tenancy (including share-cropping and service tenancy), (iii) peasant production by autonomous cultivators, (iv) debtor–creditor relations (including both peonage and 'putting-out' systems), (v) indentured or corvée labour, (vi) division of labour by status-group or caste, with ritual exchange of produce and services, (vii) wage-labour and (viii) slavery. In the mode of persuasion, it covers (i) a ritual hierarchy of purity and pollution, (ii) hereditary kingly/noble/commoner status, (iii) hierarchy in the literal sense of a rank-order based on allegiance to or participation in the sacred, (iv) ethnicity, ascribed by birth, (v) an age-set ranking in which prestige is automatically accorded to elders, (vi) genealogical ranking according to actual or fictive proximity to a king, chief or lineage head, (vii) attribution of prestige according to the functional value conventionally accorded to occupational roles, and (viii) a charismatic rank-order according to exemplary personality and achievement. In the mode of coercion it covers (i) a conscript army at the disposal of the ruler, (ii) a warrior aristocracy which, together with its servants, holds a monopoly of weapons, (iii) a republican magistracy and civilian militia, (iv) decentralization of sovereignty among local magnates, (v) a servile administrative and military apparatus answerable directly to the monarchy, (vi) a corps of professionals voluntarily recruited (including by purchase) into administrative and political roles, and (vii) the hiring of aliens for pay.

It goes without saying that a list of this kind still leaves us a long way away from a workable taxonomy. But that is precisely because instead of generating automatically a 'Linnaean' grid of $8 \times 8 \times 7 = 448$ boxes it both permits a number of empirically practicable overlaps and disallows a number of logically possible combinations. The way to construct a workable taxonomy is neither to list every single different economic, ideological and coercive role and thereby generate as many modes of the distribution of power as societies. But nor is it to construct a schematic list of theoretical possibilities and define modes of the distribution of power *a priori* in the hope of fitting the societies in the historical and ethnographic record to them. It is to examine the range of reported societies at the given 'Darwinian' stage from the viewpoint of seeking 'Linnaean' variants in the means, such as I have listed them, by which they maintain a reproducible mode of production, persuasion and coercion. It will then become clear not only that there are often resemblances sufficient to outweigh the differences, but also that relatively few of the differences explain so much about the distribution of power as to qualify as candidates for a distinctive mode. There is no need to impose Procrustean categories which lop off any structural or cultural characteristics which are inconvenient for a theory which claims regularities at a level of generality where they do not in fact exist. But nor is there any need to take account of differences in practices and roles which do unquestionably exist but which, as it is put by Leach (1961,

p. 4), are as irrelevant to the understanding of social structure as a classification of butterflies according to their colour to the understanding of the anatomical structure of lepidoptera.

CONCLUSION

§17. This, then, is the basis on which a theory of social relations, social structure and social evolution will be constructed in the chapters to follow. Moreover, the sequence in which these topics are to be covered is itself a function of the argument thus far. First comes a discussion of roles as the basic constituents by whose itemization societies are defined and whose location within the three dimensions of social structure makes it possible to identify the distinctive groups or categories of persons in their roles for which I have coined the term 'systact'. This is then followed by a discussion of social structure as such, which is seen in terms of the composition of, and relations between, systacts and the possibilities and constraints which determine the range of institutional variation across the multifarious societies whose modes of production, persuasion and coercion are documented in the historical and ethnographic record. Finally, the variation between societies in both structure and culture is analysed historically and the process whereby societies evolve from one mode or sub-type of the distribution of power to the next is traced to the competitive selection of the practices which bestow economic, ideological or coercive advantage on the roles and systacts which carry them.

This outline can hardly fail to attract the gibe that it presages the kind of social theory which consists of history without the dates and anthropology without the details. But it is a gibe which I willingly accept. The arguments of this volume depend neither on a precise narration of sequences of actions and events nor on a close specification of the content of microsociological behaviour. But they are, all the same, about societies (and wider and narrower institutional catchment areas) as actually observed and reported, and not 'Society' in the abstract. In Volume III, when they are tested against the evidence for a single society over a relatively short period of years, it will be necessary to specify both dates and details. But a general substantive theory of social relations, social structure and social evolution can hardly hope to succeed in its aim unless the level of analysis at which it operates is, indeed, general.

2
Social relations

THE RANGE OF VARIATION

§1. To say that societies are fully defined by the itemization of their constituent roles is not to say that there is, as it were, a periodic table of 'atomic' roles. This is not only because cultural evolution, unlike chemical, is open-ended. It is also because the practices by which roles are in turn defined are not themselves tied to those roles in any determinate form. Not only are practices, not roles, the units of social selection, but the same role may be enacted through any one of several different sets of practices and the same practice may be an integral part of several different roles. As an example, consider again the role of a monarch. As I have already pointed out, monarchs, despite being invested with titles suggestive of supreme power, may possess markedly different degrees of it in the three different dimensions of social structure. But even if the role carries ultimate title to all of the society's material resources, unchallenged ideological supremacy at the summit of an ascriptive hierarchy of deference, and total control over the means of coercion, the nature of the practices involved may vary widely from case to case. In the economic dimension, the domination of the monarch may be exercised through many different forms of rent, or taxation, or tribute and the practices related to them; in the ideological dimension, it may be exercised through many different ritual practices, whether sacred or secular; in the coercive dimension, it may be exercised through the practices of many different possible agencies of control, whether explicitly political and military or para-military and whether relying on formal or informal means of compulsion. As always, it depends on the whole institutional context within which the role and the practices defining it are observed to function.

What is more, it is no less important to remember that the role must operate not only consistently but, as it were, convincingly so. The particular incumbent may even, if successfully 'passing', be an out-and-out charlatan without the role itself being compromised. Nor, as I have emphasized also, need the inducements and sanctions on which the role rests be real in the sense that they could be guaranteed to be effective: it is enough that they should be believed in by the persons whose relations to one another are determined by the role as they define it to themselves. But there is still the risk that the observer may misunderstand the role in the primary sense and misreport it in spite, or perhaps because, of the consistency of the practices attaching to it. Thus, the very persistence and regularity of rituals of obedience to a monarch may tempt the visiting fieldworker into the mistaken inference that the intentions and beliefs of the participants constitute the concession of a total monopoly of legitimate authority to the monarchy. But it could well be prudent to look out for evidence of other behaviour, which, given its context, would have to be accepted by all rival observers as showing that the rituals of obedience are symbolic only, and that the powers ceremonially attributed to the monarch are in fact exercised by the incumbents of other proprietorial, governmental and/or sacerdotal roles.

Furthermore, allowance has to be made for the possibility that a role may be created, or virtually so, by the behaviour of its prospective incumbent. Again, the behaviour in question needs to be seen in its institutional context. People cannot create roles for themselves to occupy at will just by a declaration of intent. But under the appropriate circumstances, a declaration of intent may then elicit the responses which do indeed bring the role into being.* An entrepreneur can create the role for himself by persuading enough people to lend him money and enough to work for him for wages. A shaman can create the role for himself by persuading enough people that his powers of divination are sufficient for them to be willing to entrust themselves to his guidance and acknowledge his prestige.† A warlord can create the role for himself by persuading enough people that under his generalship an army can be mobilized which will be able to win control of the region.‡ The starting-

* In some contexts, the declaration of intent will not create a wholly new role but reformulate the content of an existing one. Thus Agathocles, whom I cited in Section 13 of Chapter 1, could proclaim himself king because he effectively was one already, just as Leovigild, king of the Visigoths from 568 to 586, could take to sitting on a throne (Thompson 1963–4, p. 5) only by virtue of already possessing the power which the practice both symbolized and reinforced.

† Thus Eliade (1970, p. 7) aptly characterizes shamans as 'privileged adherents' who may equally well be recruited by heredity or by self-proclaimed vocation.

‡ Cf. e.g. Eberhard (1957) and Elvin (1973, p. 174) on the abortive career of the twelfth-century Chinese industrialist Wang Ko, who successfully mobilized his own workmen to attack the local officials and their troops but was then deserted by them and subsequently executed.

point for the reportage of a society's distribution of power is still the set of roles listed by 'them' in answer to the questions who is (institutionally speaking) in a position to acquire what from whom, who to be accorded prestige by whom and who to give orders to whom. But not only may the roles so listed exclude significant variations within the range ostensibly covered by the vernacular terms, or fail to take account of the extent to which an inherited terminology has been overtaken by changes still conceptualized from within it. They may also fail to allow for the emergence of mutant or recombinant practices which form the basis for roles whose possibility is simply not envisaged by 'them' until after the event.

§2. What, then, is the maximum and minimum of power which can attach to any actual role? In the economic dimension, the ideal-typical range extends all the way from the pauper who is totally without property or access to the means of acquiring it to the monopolist of the whole of a society's means of production. But in practice, no group or category of a society's members is ever absolutely destitute except under conditions of famine which cannot in the nature of things be permanent; and even if there is a role to which there attaches title to all and every type of property, ownership or control of at least some part of it will still remain in the hands of the incumbents of subordinate roles. In the ideological dimension, the ideal-typical range extends all the way from the pariah or outcaste to the quasi-divine embodiment of the source of all honour and prestige. But in practice, not even the members of the lowliest status-group are denied all value by their fellow-citizens except in cases of stigmatization so extreme as to license genocide* which are, like famine, necessarily temporary; and even if there is a single dominant role at the summit of an ascriptive hierarchy of deference, it cannot be such as to reduce all other roles to a common level of untouchability. In the coercive dimension, the ideal-typical range extends all the way from the rightless chattel to the all-powerful despot. But in practice, even slaves have, unless actually being put to death, some minimal counter-sanctions against their masters; and even despots depend on at least some other members of the societies over which they rule to make their supposedly unlimited coercive capacity effective. Large as the total span of social distance may be, it is compressed in even the least egalitarian societies well within the ideal-typical extremes of

* I use this term to cover by extension not merely the extermination of a stigmatized ethnic or national group or category but also the working to death of captives, or the use of slaves or prisoners as sacrificial victims.

total powerlessness at the apex of the inverted pyramid and total power at some unlimited distance above it.

Once again, a few examples will serve to indicate the actual range of variation across the historical and ethnographic record:

(i) In the economic dimension, there are societies so far from the extreme of unbridled market forces (as exemplified by, say, the United States during the period labelled by Hofstadter (1948, Ch. 7) 'The Spoilsmen: an Age of Cynicism') that inequalities in wealth and the means to acquiring it are almost non-existent in them. Among the !Kung Bushmen, ecological constraints and a cultural rule of strict generosity combine to make it impossible for there to emerge a role entitling the incumbent to anything more than limited and transient control over food, water, weapons and personal possessions (E. M. Thomas 1959); and there is in addition an institutionalized mechanism of sharing with putatively consanguineous relatives (*hxaro* relationships: cf. Wiessner 1982) which continually redistributes goods between family groups. It is true that the *n!ores*, or blocks of land round water-holes, are each collectively owned by a resident group (Lee 1979, Chs. 3 and 12). But their exploitation is not denied to neighbouring groups; and although descent from a long line of *n!ore* owners is of value in strengthening claims to leadership, the role of leader carries no title to wealth. However influential !Kung leaders may be, 'they never translate this into more wealth or more leisure time than other group members have' (*ibid.*, p. 345).

(ii) In the ideological dimension, there are societies so far from the extreme exemplified by, say, France in the reign of Louis XIV that it can be said that in them any claim to superior prestige is self-defeating, simply because the culture is such that the very notion of a role carrying inherently superior status invites the counter-sanction of ridicule. The Mbuti Pygmies, whom I cited in Section 7 of Chapter 1, do, like many other similar societies, accord a certain respect to age as such (Turnbull 1965, p. 302), but they consistently deny it to the practitioners even of highly valued skills: all that is accorded to them is some conditional praise for individual performance.

(iii) In the coercive dimension, there are societies so far from the extreme of despotism exemplified by, say, Ancient Dahomey (Herskovits 1938, Pt 5) that it can even be said of them, as it has been of the Rwala Bedouin (Lankaster 1981, p. 96) , that 'political power does not exist'. This, to be sure, is so only in the sense that a sheikh's ability to invoke the sanction of force depends on his deployment of his wealth and his status as a 'good man' (*rajul tayyib*). But the Bedouin still furnish a good example of a society where the topmost role, although well above the apex of the inverted pyramid in both the economic and the ideological dimensions, is very much closer to it in the coercive.

In the same way, it is possible also to document the range of variation in the degree to which cooperative* practices are constitutive of any itemized role. Again, the role in question may under certain conditions be brought into being by a declaration of intent, and there is thus the difficulty that the line cannot be drawn precisely between the creation of an informal bond and the emergence of an acknowledged institution. For example, the 'companionship' (*hetaireia*) of age-peers in Archaic Greece hovers somewhere between a transient association between two or more young men in search of fame and plunder and an established transitional role within a male-dominated agrarian society of independent households in which there are too few vacancies for the role of household head to absorb all the would-be incumbents. But this is a borderline difficulty of an innocuous kind. There is a risk of misreportage only if it is presupposed that an informal relation between like-minded people is institutional to an extent that it is not – as, for example, in the case of the 'Blue' and 'Green' circus cliques of Constantinople.†

Perhaps the closest approximation to the ideal type of a cooperative relation explicitly and exclusively formed to further a mutual joint interest is 'brotherhood-in-arms', such as that sworn under contract by two English esquires in the church of St Martin at Harfleur on 12 July 1421 '*pour acroistre et augmenter lamour et fraternite*' between them and, more specifically, to go hostage for each other in the event of capture and ransom or, alternatively, to pool any spoils of war (text printed by McFarlane 1963, pp. 309–10). It is, admittedly more in the nature of a private insurance arrangement than of the type of *coniuratio* which, if actively and successfully prosecuted, could significantly modify the existing systactic structure.‡ But, as with 'stock-friends' among nomadic pastoralists or the 'friendly societies' of early industrial

* Cooperation may, where it occurs, be against the members of other groups or categories perceived as separate but equal rather than either superiors or inferiors, as in societies which are 'plural' in the sense first given to that term by J. S. Furnivall – that is, societies where the ring is held, as it were, by an external power under whose domination equilibrium is preserved between separate and mutually visible subsystems which compete economically, socially and politically with one another (M. G. Smith 1965, pp. viii–xiii).

† See Cameron (1976) for the evidence that 'these few hundred sports fans' (p. 80), although more than merely that, nevertheless did not amount to serious factions in the way that, by contrast, the eleventh-century guilds did.

‡ Such, for example, as the partially successful rent strikes by tenants of the bishopric of Worcester in the fourteenth century (Dyer 1968), or the 'secession' of the Roman plebs in 287 B.C. which led to the creation of the role of *tribunus plebis*.

capitalism, it formally enshrines the recognition of the advantage to be gained by an explicit commitment to further the interests of the incumbents of similarly located roles in a way which none could do in isolation. Like *hetaireia*, brotherhood-in-arms was particularly adaptive for young men who had been born into the higher levels of a status-conscious warrior society but lacked either substantial means of their own or a powerful patron committed to furthering their interests. But roles of this nature can be documented at all levels in all sorts of society. They are not confined either to any particular systactic structure or to any particular evolutionary stage. They disappear only at the ideal-typical extreme of non-cooperation where all relations are vertical relations of domination and subordination.*

§3. Viewed historically, the range of possible roles cannot but presuppose an evolutionary sequence. Without armies, there can be no generals but only leaders of war-bands; without markets, there can be no bankers but only treasurers or guardians of goods and spoils; without churches, there can be no ministers or priests but only preachers or mystagogues. It can hardly be disputed by theorists of any rival school that once the practice of craft specialization had evolved among the societies of the Aegean in the third millennium B.C. it 'produced not merely a few new roles and occupations, but a whole new field of roles, and the very concept of occupation itself' (Renfrew 1972, p. 362), or that the same process was repeated in North-west France in the second half of the eleventh century A.D. when '*pour la première fois en Europe, une opération artisanale prit la forme d'un ensemble complexe où le travail se divisait entre plusieurs "métiers"*' (Duby 1973, p. 268). But to emphasize in this way the unquestionable importance of the emergence of roles (and thus incipient systacts) bound up with the division and specialization of labour is not to presuppose what caused it, or what it was like for those involved, or whether it was a good thing or a bad from their (or any other) point of view.

There is, however, a sub-category of roles brought into being by deliberate design. Some roles are directly imposed on prospective incumbents, willing or unwilling, by the incumbents of other, dominant roles. The extreme case is the 'scapegoat' where that term is used not simply in the sense resting literally on the 'supposed possibility of

* Such a society would be a 'tyranny' in the classical sense, in which not only is power concentrated in the hands of the tyrant and his agents, but any cooperation whatever between persons either similarly or dissimilarly located is conspiratorial by definition. The parallel with the ideal type of the modern 'totalitarian' regime is familiar (cf. e.g. the account of Hitler's Germany given by Neumann 1942).

transferring our bodily and mental ailments to another who will bear them for us' (Frazer 1914, p.v.), but in the extended sense of the stigmatization of a group or category which is thereby not only downgraded in the ideological dimension but stripped of economic and coercive power as well.* It is thus an example which all rival observers can accept of a role which is, as it were, both artificial and real. Indeed, the same holds for the widely reported phenomenon of 'role-reversal', where a short-term, factitious exchange of incumbents within an unchanged structure of dominant and subordinate roles is deliberately effected and self-consciously acted out. Here again, however difficult the selection of the constituent practices may be to explain (or the resulting behaviour to describe or evaluate), there can be no dispute about the fact that slaves are (play-) acting like masters, the young like the old, women like men, or low-caste Indian villagers like high-caste ones.

A further complication is that although symmetrical reversals of roles are normally strictly ritualized, and it is central to the ritual that the reversal should be temporary, in other contexts an artificially created role may be a case of permanent, forced individual or even collective mobility. Those Chinese who were denounced during Mao Zedong's 'Cultural Revolution' of the 1960s as 'capitalist roaders' or 'hidden counter-revolutionaries' were not only forced out of the roles which they had previously occupied but at the same time stigmatized by reference to an ascriptive criterion of status which had hitherto been irrelevant to the way in which they were treated by their fellow-members of Chinese society.† More generally, indeed, it can be said that the existence of ascriptive status-groups at any location depends upon the collective definition of a distinguishable systact in terms of attributes whose relevance to the social structure is culturally imposed. To take the most widespread example of all, the location of women cannot be analyzed in purely structural terms: relations between men and women

* Strictly, two qualifications need to be added: first, an already virtually powerless group or category may still be scapegoated to the ultimate point of 'sacrificial' killing (cf. e.g. Wyatt-Brown 1982, pp. 433–4, on the function of groundless panics about slave insurrection and subsequent quasi-judicial execution for the periodic reinforcement of white Southern ideology and mores); and second, a scapegoat role is sometimes quite compatible with the exercise of considerable political power (cf. e.g. Hopkins 1978, p. 173, on court eunuchs).

† There is an interesting contrast here with the attitude of the authorities during the French Revolution to '*çi-devant*' nobles. In China, not only the wives but even the infant children of men denounced as counter-revolutionary were tainted by the association (Butterfield 1981, Ch. 5); but in France, there was an ideological conflict in the culture between guilt by association and the notion of individual responsibility, so that although 13- or 14-year-old children of noble parents might be arrested they were unlikely to be convicted (Higonnet 1981, pp. 160–5).

are role-relations because and only because the culture of the society in question has made them so,* whether by law or custom.

Finally, there is the need for any itemization of a society's roles to take account of the possibility that a role may be evolving within, so to speak, the vernacular term for it. I have cited already from Archaic Greece the puzzling change in the meaning of *dēmiourgos*, and the same set of societies offers an example of a term for a role which appears to have been almost continually changing as progressively greater power attached to it: *aisymnētēs*. When it first appears, in the *Odyssey* (VIII. 258), it denotes merely the umpire chosen to supervise the games organized for Odysseus's benefit by the Phaeacians. But by the time of Aristotle (*Politics* 1285a), it stands for an elected dictator chosen, in the case which Aristotle has particularly in mind, to fight off a rival faction driven into exile. The transition cannot, unfortunately, be documented precisely from the surviving sources, since the *aisymnētai* who occur in them do not have the practices which constitute their roles reported in sufficient detail. But it is evident that the term was retained all the way through a transition very similar to that followed by the North Italian cities in the late Middle Ages, where the role of an elective consul whose power was carefully circumscribed in both extent and duration evolved through that of *podestà* into that of a dictatorial *signore* (Waley 1969, p. 231). Despite the terminological continuity, therefore, it would be as much of a misunderstanding in the primary sense to assimilate a Homeric to a Classical *aisymnētēs* as a North Italian consul to a *signore*.

§4. Roles vary also in the degree to which the practices which define them belong in one, two or all three dimensions of structure. But this is not in itself a determinant of their location. A role which is purely economic, ideological or coercive may or may not at the same time assign its incumbent a higher or lower rank in the other two dimensions: once again, structural questions cannot be divorced from cultural. In one society, a 'holy man' whose position is determined by his ideological purity and the life-style that goes with it may rank low in both the economic and the coercive dimensions as a necessary condition of his high prestige, just as, conversely, certain highly lucrative occupations may be lucrative precisely because they are derogating. But the culture

* Here, the further distinction needs to be drawn between domination of women by men within and between structurally separate units: for an extreme example of the first, see the account of the Pukhtun of Swat given by Lindholm (1982); for an extreme example of the second, see the account of the Bena Bena of the New Guinea Highlands given by Langness (1977).

of another not wholly dissimilar society may be such that holiness is no bar to riches or, conversely, riches – however got – no bar to honour and esteem. Moreover, a role defined by practices of all three kinds may rank much higher in one society than another. Here, 'monarch' is no longer a good example since the role carries a structural implication by definition (unless, for that very reason, it is qualified by a term such as 'constitutional'). But consider the role of a professional military commander – one, that is, who is neither a mercenary nor a militiaman but a paid, full-time, publicly acknowledged head of a body of permanent, properly armed and fully trained troops. The role is relatively highly located in all three dimensions: it entitles the incumbent to relatively substantial remuneration, it confers on him relatively superior esteem and it gives him some relatively effective control of a significant fraction of the society's means of coercion. But his location is also a function of the position of the army as a corporation within the society as a whole.

The range of variation here can be well illustrated by contrasting the army of Sung China with that of Wilhelmine Germany. The Sung Chinese army was a large one – 1¼ million men in the mid eleventh century – equipped with the formidable Chinese crossbow and commanded by experienced professionals. But military roles never carried the same prestige as roles in the other two major departments of state. The examination system by which officials were recruited created a landholding systact of successful graduates who explicitly looked down on the profession of arms and were in any case determined to forestall the possibility of local commanders mounting the kind of armed rebellion which had destroyed the T'ang. In late nineteenth- and early twentieth-century Germany, on the other hand, the prestige of the military was such that the army was the dominant corporation in the state and its commanders the dominant systact. The professionalization of command dating back to the reforms of Scharnhorst and Gneisenau culminated under Bismarck and Moltke in a system in which a dedicated and victorious military élite, predominantly but not exclusively of aristocratic origin and retaining its connections with the land, enjoyed a degree of power which the German counterparts of the Confucian civilian officials of Sung China were powerless to diminish or resist.*

* See McNeill (1983), pp. 33–41 and 242–56, and the references there cited. As a descriptive touch, it is quite impossible to imagine the Kaiser ever saying, as the Sung emperor Kao-tsung is reported to have done, 'what makes me happy is not that Ch'i has been defeated, but that the generals have obeyed orders' (Dawson 1972, p. 165).

STANDARD ROLES AND ROUTINE CAREERS

§5. There are no cultural universals in the sense of identical institutions or even roles found in all human societies. But there are some universal practices and thus properties of roles: there is, for example, no known society which has 'completely lacked leadership, the setting of a course of action followed by others' (Fried 1967, p. 82). Moreover in each dimension of structure there are fundamental practices which relate directly to presumptive inducements and sanctions and thereby roles of one or other of the three mutually irreducible kinds.

The fundamental economic practice is the exchange of goods or services. 'Economic' needs strictly to be put in inverted commas, since to say that exchanges of goods take place in all societies is not to say that those societies have institutions which amount to an 'economy', and still less to pre-empt any solution to the protracted theoretical debate about the distinguishing characteristics of 'primitive' economic behaviour. But even in those societies where exchanges are most remote from the ideal type of market exchanges between agents each pursuing the maximization of profit, transactions can be observed between persons who have the power to give or withhold goods or services to or from one another in accordance with some institutionally acknowledged rule of reciprocity. It would, of course, be a misunderstanding in the primary sense to equate the exchange of gifts with buying and selling in a market. But even in the case of a pure exchange of gifts – and in some contexts, all the more so – there is a potential for differences of advantage between donor and donee; and this in turn implies the possibility of institutionally differentiated 'economic' roles.

Likewise, there is no society in which there are no relationships between persons one of whom is deferring (however reluctantly) to the other's social standing. The criterion by reference to which there arises the mutually acknowledged difference in social esteem may be one of many kinds. It may, indeed, be economic and/or coercive; or the ideology of the society may set a value on ritual expertise, or seniority, or wisdom (whether sacred or secular), or pedigree.* But there is always some such attribute on which a value is collectively set, just as there are in all societies some 'individuals who are more or less looked down upon', whether 'persons suffering from physical or mental disability, idlers who are good for nothing, widowers who have not married again

* I use this term to cover not merely the inheritance of parental rank by children but the widely observed convention that – to paraphrase Goody (1962, p. 382 n.1) – the longer the line the stronger the claim.

and therefore have no one to help them in their work, braggarts who bore the others, etc.' (Landtman 1938, p. 9). Individual differences of this nature are, to be sure, far from generating castes, ranks, nobilities or clear-cut status-groups of any kind. But the possibility of roles embodying differences of power in the ideological dimension is latent in the intentions and beliefs constitutive of 'deference actions' (Shils 1968, p. 117) even of the most rudimentary kind.

The same holds also in the coercive dimension. However far a society may still have to evolve before the emergence of law, a police force, an army and a set of specialized, permanent, centralized, non-kin governmental roles, the possibility of recourse to force, and therewith the threat of it, is universal. Where the use of physical sanctions is restricted to individual or familial retaliation for an offence, it is obviously premature to talk of a role by virtue of the incumbency of which the action in question is performed. Even, indeed, where there is an institutionalized procedure for dealing with disputes, it may well be that they are not a reinforcement of, but a substitute for, coercion at the individual level: among the foodgathering Chenchu of Andhra Pradesh, for example, as they were then studied in the 1940s, 'If a duped husband feels strong enough, he is likely to beat up his rival, but a weak man may appeal to the older men of his own group and ask them to intervene with the leading men of the culprit's group' (Fürer-Haimendorf 1967, p. 20). But the substitution is still a substitution for the physical restraint of an offender against institutional norms.* It is true that differences in physical strength, which are of course universal, do not in themselves generate differentiation of roles; victory in a fight between one member of a society and another need not thereby institutionalize the location of the victor. But wherever the recourse to force, or the threat of it, is bound up with an appeal to an acknowledged practice, the relationship of the offender to the fellow-members of the society concerned carries the potential for the emergence of 'political' roles.

§6. Some standard roles, however, determine not only the present but the future location of their incumbents: they are not merely roles but

* Cf. e.g. the Kapauku Papuans among whom 'social control is not based upon compulsion', but dangerous criminals are nevertheless killed and culprits beaten or shot with an arrow through the thigh if they refuse the chance to fight back or run away (Pospisil 1963, p. 48). Similarly, Schapera (1956, p. 87) remarks of the South African Bergdama that although there are no legislative or judicial roles and arbitration by elders is not binding, nevertheless a communal decision that an offender is to be thrashed, expelled or put to death 'is reached casually round the camp fire, and if necessary the younger men are then told to enforce it'.

careers. 'Career' is, in English, a nineteenth-century word (just as 'careerist' is a twentieth-century one). But the notion that a role may embody expectations about the future as well as intentions and beliefs constitutive of practices acted out in the present extends all the way from a simple agricultural village dominated by 'elders' who, as the term implies, occupy that role strictly by virtue of their age,* to a complex industrial society in which the division and specialization of labour has so far evolved that occupational roles are characterized by a whole succession of admissions, qualifications, exclusions and promotions of the kind that gives 'career' its dictionary meaning.

The most straightforward cases are those where there is a precise vernacular term for a role defined by practices entailing both qualification for entry and emergence after a concluding rite of passage into a new and superior role. For example, the Athenian 'ephebes' were 18-year-old male citizens who spent a year doing military training and a further year on garrison duty, attended certain required public ceremonies, wore special dress, and at the end of their training were presented as part of a formal rite of passage with their spears and shields.† But there are many other roles to which age-grading is less directly but still significantly relevant: it has correctly been remarked, for example, of the familiar occupational designation 'clerk' in twentieth-century Britain that it 'does not define a meaningful reality in stratification terms' in view of the 'diverse routes to clerical work and diverse destinations from it' (Stewart *et al.* 1980, p. 113). In this, as in other such cases, the same vernacular term covers what are really two or more different roles. Indeed, in the limiting case of ritual trainees the ostensible role is purely simulated: the university graduate recruited for a senior executive role who does a two-week stint in the mail room of the bank can no more accurately be reported to be a 'mail clerk' than the regimental officer observed serving his men on Christmas Day a 'mess-room waiter'.

At the same time, the career prospects which attach directly to a role need to be distinguished from the personal characteristics of different

* See e.g. Bradbury (1969, p. 18) on the villages of the nineteenth-century Benin kingdom where ideally, at any rate, all males passed from the youth to the adult to the elder (*edion*) age-grades, the *edion* 'were the repository of the land, laws, rights and reputation of the village', and the assembly of *edion* was presided over by the oldest man.

† See Pollux, *Onomasticon* VIII.10.5. Later, under the Roman Empire, *ephēbaia* became private, civilian and self-elective, thus furnishing yet another example of the evolution of a role through the mutation or recombination of the practices defining it within an unchanged vernacular term.

incumbents which may further their individual upward mobility. The practice of *apprenticeship*, for example, which is to be found across a wide range of different societies, may involve a process of competitive selection whereby only the ablest and most industrious entrants are admitted into the superior role, or it may operate in a manner tantamount to age-grading whereby only but all those persons who spend the necessary period in training are thereby deemed to be qualified,* or it may carry an entrance fee which thereby restricts it exclusively to the children of the well-to-do.† The initial report of the society in question must, therefore, specify not only the presence or absence of standard roles but also the extent to which their incumbency is institutionally dictated by practices of this kind. Analogous to closed apprenticeship are, for example, a *cursus honorum* whereby certain political roles are occupied only by incumbents who have previously held other qualifying offices, or inheritance customs whereby property is known to have to pass strictly to persons standing in predetermined relationships to the testator. In cases like these, it is more than that entry into certain roles is barred to certain groups or categories such as, say, women or non-citizens or persons of designated ethnic origin. It is that certain roles are defined by practices which dictate not only the relations of their incumbents to the incumbents of others but also their incumbency (or not) of other future roles.

Sometimes, this aspect of a role is explicitly recognized in the vernacular term for it – for example, the French '*dauphin*'. But usually, there is a career or age-grade aspect to a number of standard roles such that some but not all the members of the resulting systact are purely transitional occupants. Thus, in many of the so-called 'liberal professions' of modern industrial societies there is an element of age-grading which persists after the period of formal apprenticeship: not merely is there a premium on experience (as convincingly explained by theorists of market economies since Adam Smith and before), but seniority itself may carry a further prestige of its own. Or in societies

* There are also cases where an age-grade element is deliberately introduced into a pre-existing method of training as a matter of policy: see e.g. Dore (1962) on its use in the schools of Tokugawa Japan to cope with the problem of abler but lower-ranking samurai sons, or Marsh (1961, p. 187) on its effect in equalizing the chances of promotion for men from official and commoner families once they had been admitted into the Chinese bureaucracy.

† This of course is a relative matter: the importance of apprenticeship in eighteenth-century England, for example, was that despite its costs it was '*much less expensive*' (author's italics) than the traditional vocational training of the ancient professions (Holmes 1982, p. 15).

which have the institution of slavery there may be practices whereby slaves can expect as a matter of course to be manumitted on the death of their owners or when they have accumulated sufficient capital to be able to buy their freedom. It may or may not be guaranteed that every slave, or even domestic slave, becomes a freedman, any more than that every medical student becomes a Fellow of the Royal College of Physicians. But the distribution of power at any one time is already to some degree determined by how far standard roles are not only roles but also careers.

§7. Many roles – and careers – are standard not only in being found at a similar location in a wide range of different societies but also in being *composite* to a similar degree – that is, defined by practices already relevant to power of all three kinds. A 'chief' for example, even if less powerful than a 'monarch', still commands inducements and sanctions in all three dimensions: it is typical of chiefdom as reported for a wide range of societies that any incumbent of the role will (i) be accorded prestige as enjoying an intimate association with gods or ancestral spirits, (ii) be entitled to tribute or tithes and preferential access to, or use of, crops or game or women or corvée labour, and (iii) be entrusted with the right to judge or arbitrate in intra-societal disputes and to mobilize and command the means of coercion needed for internal control and external warfare. Similarly, the members of a subordinate Indian *jāti*, or 'sub-caste', who are located on a ritual scale of purity and pollution defined by the culture and ideology of Hinduism, are at the same time tied in both to the division of labour and corresponding economic rewards and to the distribution of coercive power. To say this is not to pre-empt the explanation (or description or evaluation) of the Indian system of caste: specialists are not, and perhaps never will be, in agreement about the relative importance within it of economic, ideological and coercive sanctions. It is, however, to say that the standard roles are all three-dimensional ones.

There is often a difficulty in that the vernacular terms for composite roles are uncontroversial but – perhaps for that very reason – particularly imprecise. Thus, for example, any report of the structure and culture of Classical Roman society will include reference to the existence of a category of 'nobles' who, although internally differentiated and often at odds with one another, all occupied a recognized common location. But the role of 'noble' is never explicitly defined in any of the documentary sources which have come down to us. The answer has to be elicited from them by quasi-deductive inferences licencing the conclusion that by the second century B.C. the traditional distinction between 'patricians' and 'plebeians' had evolved into a distinction which effectively marked off a patrician-cum-plebeian nobility not totally closed to outsiders but recruited predominantly by descent (Brunt 1982). But it would be as much of a mistake to leave it at that as in the case of the Indian *jāti*. For nobles were at the same time so far tied in to the system of recruitment to political careers that Cicero (*Letters to Atticus* IV.8A.2) could complain that a rich noble could presume from birth on a consulship irrespective of ability, and a *déclassé* noble could reasonably hope for a subvention to maintain the economic position deemed appropriate to his rank (Tacitus, *Annals* XIII.34). Once again, we are dealing with a composite role the essence of which is that its incumbents were virtually guaranteed a consistent location in all three dimensions.*

The cases where a standard composite role (or career) is defined by the power (or lack of power) attaching to it in all three dimensions have, however, to be distinguished from those where it is defined by reference to one only, and the location of its incumbents in the other two is variable not because (as in the example of the Sung Chinese and Wilhelmine German armies) the location of the relevant corporation is different, but because the role is explicitly accorded or denied privileges of the other two kinds. For example, a merchant in Anglo-Saxon England, who travelled about the kingdom with his own private retinue, and could look forward to attaining noble rank if he made three successful journeys across the sea,† was very differently located from his no less affluent counterpart in Tokugawa Japan, whose career prospects never extended to promotion to noble rank and who remained, however prosperous, at the mercy of his political superiors. Both occupy a standard role defined by homologous economic practices. But they are very dissimilarly located in both the other dimensions relative to the other roles and systacts in their respective societies.

* Descriptively, the accounts of Juvenal and, later, Ammianus Marcellinus vividly convey the feel of the quite extraordinary arrogance of the Roman nobility towards their inferiors. In other societies, too, there have been aristocrats far removed from their fellow-citizens in possessions, pride of birth and political influence alike. But where else were free but humble clients *so* insultingly degraded by their noble patrons? As Auerbach (1957, p. 48) comments on Ammianus's description (XXVIII.4) of a nobleman turning his head aside 'like a threatening bull' from a client trying to kiss him and offering his knees or hands instead: 'What a gesture!'.

† The evidence on which these inferences are based is first, a law of King Alfred (Liebermann 1903, s.v. Alfred c34) and second, a fragment now attributed to Archbishop Wulfstan (*ibid.*, p. 458 (*Textus Roffensis*)).

At the furthest extreme from standard three-dimensional roles are composite roles which are not merely structurally inconsistent but culturally paradoxical, in the sense that they combine two disparate and even contradictory attributes. The warrior-bishops of medieval Europe, the slave-generals of the Ottoman armies, the half-proletarian half-peasant artisan-serfs of nineteenth-century Russia (Esper 1981), or the caste of craft specialists among the Marghi of the Western Sudan who are both high-prestige iron-smelters and low-prestige corpse-carriers (Vaughan 1970) are all as it were extremely non-standard, and there are some composite roles such as the Old Babylonian *naditum* which are so far non-standard as to be unique.* But although they thereby complicate inter-societal comparisons based on contrasting the structural locations of culturally similar roles or careers, they do not on that account (*pace* Gelb) defy primary understanding. Even if the combination of practices is unique, the practices themselves are not. However exotic, no role or career in any society is such that it cannot be theory-neutrally reported by reference to the practices defining it and thereby located in relation to the others with which its incumbents interact.

FUNCTIONAL DIFFERENTIATION AND THE ACCRETION OF POWER

§8. Itemization of roles requires, however, not merely the identification of their constituent practices and their location relative to others in each of the three dimensions, but also some assessment of the overall amount of power available for allocation in the society as a whole. There are no quantitative measures except for certain limited aspects, and even then only for societies of certain types: any attempt to place different societies along a single continuum even of economic power as measured by, say, gross domestic product or real income per head will yield at best a very approximate indicator of their capacity either to dominate one another or to generate further growth in free-floating resources from within themselves. But whatever the difficulties of measurement, observers of all theoretical schools will be bound to agree that there are large and

* See R. Harris (1963): a *naditum* combined the roles of nun and merchant, and was associated with a temple compound but with personal property rights in her own cash and real estate. Gelb (1972, p. 4) goes so far as to say that 'The uniquely "capitalistic" development of the *naditum* institution at Sippar is beyond my comprehension, as it seems beyond anything that can be connected with the aims and activities of cloisters and monasteries of all times'; but that is no reason to suppose that the recording angel would not endorse the accuracy of the cuneiform sources. Cf. E. C. Stone (1982) for the institution as it functioned at Nippur.

significant differences between societies in the total amount of economic, ideological and coercive resources at the disposal of their members, and that these differences cannot but be relevant to both the structural and the cultural differences between them. Most of what has been written on the relation between total resources and differentiation of roles has been addressed to the division of labour.* But it would be a mistake to concentrate on its economic aspects alone. The emergence of priests, intellectuals and artists as full-time specialists, as likewise of bodyguards, policemen and soldiers, is no less important than that of bankers, wage-labourers and entrepreneurs; and conversely, the significance of *non*-specialization needs equally to be understood in relation to the accretion of power in all three dimensions.† Although the emergence of differentiated roles is not linked in any consistent pattern to an increase in resources, a minimal accretion of power is a necessary condition of specialization, and *vice versa*. It is true that specialization begins at a stage where resources are still very limited: in New Guinea, for example, even though the societies in question do not have institutions which could conceivably be labelled economy, church or state, 'there are shrine priests, hunt leaders, advisers to the headman, youth leaders, war party leaders often with special titles signifying their offices' (Cohen 1978, p. 53). But, as we have already seen, such roles are likely to be not only relatively powerless but relatively impermanent. The person who performs the focal rituals, or organizes the raiding parties, or takes charge of the periodic distribution of communal produce is likely for most of the time to lead much the same life and perform much the same tasks as everyone else, and division of labour is likely to be by sex and age rather than occupation (let alone career). What is more, not only

* It is, however, worth noting in passing how much discussion of the division of labour has been pre-empted by evaluative presuppositions, whether in agreement with Adam Smith's panegyric in the opening chapter of *The Wealth of Nations* ('the division of labour, which occasions, in a well-governed society, that universal opulence which extends itself to the lowest ranks of the people', etc.) or on the contrary with Marx's praise, in *Capital*, of Smith's 'master' Adam Ferguson as the first author clearly to expound its *ill*-effects.

† Cf. e.g. Humphreys (1978, p. 252) on Classical Athens: 'It seems that it was only in the later 5th century that specialisation developed in Athens to a point where different occupations began to be perceived as blocs in the society and not merely as isolated or part-time skills. The earlier assumption – which remained influential – had been that all citizens performed all roles in turn, moving from one context to another. This free circulation of persons through the roles belonging to different interaction contexts, on the implicit assumption that the appropriate norms and values would be respected in each case, prevented the development of an explicit, institutionalized hierarchy of roles and functions, and left the question of their ranking to subsist unresolved.'

may the total amount of resources available be insufficient to provide the basis for full-time, central, specialist, governmental roles, but the nature of the resources may in any case make them difficult to accumulate for the benefit of the incumbents of dominant roles once instituted: as Gluckman remarks, 'One cannot build a palace with grass and mud, and if the only foods are grains, milk and meat, one cannot live much above the standard of ordinary men.'*

There is, accordingly, a pattern of a kind in the relation between functional differentiation and total resources, although it cannot be expressed in quantitative terms and would not in any case show a consistent correlation all the way from the hunting and gathering bands to the large industrialized nation-states. It is, if nothing more, plausible to expect not only the number of roles per person to decrease as the total number of roles increases but, at the same time, the distance between roles to widen. This is not to say that relatively undifferentiated societies are not sometimes more powerful than more highly differentiated ones: a particularly striking example is furnished by the Mongol conquest of Sung China, in which a simply structured but aggressively motivated society of nomadic warriors overran within two generations a populous, complex, highly differentiated society of professional armies, expert administrators, affluent merchants, and largely commercialized agricultural and artisan producers. The point is rather that itemization of roles has always to take account of the differences between societies in the total resources available to them. This means, in practice, that the degree of specialization has if possible to be specified in the sense both of variety of functions and of extent of multiple or exclusive incumbency of more or less specialized roles.

Of particular theoretical interest in this context is the category of roles intermediate between the part-time specializations of societies with a minimum of power available for distribution and the complex hierarchies of large and relatively advanced societies where roles can carry a virtual monopoly of power within a given institution. These are the so-called 'big-men', the essence of whose role is, as it is put by Sahlins (1974, p. 139), that they must 'personally construct their power over others' in contrast to the chieftainships 'properly so-called' whose incumbents 'come *to* power'. The power in question is of a qualitatively different order from that of the leaders of hunting and gathering bands. The successful 'big-man' has accumulated significant wealth, he is equalled in prestige only by other big-men with whom he is in

* Quoted from Gluckman (1960) by Goody (1971, p. 32 n.23).

competition, and he commands a following which extends well beyond his immediate kin. But his power is inherently constrained by the impossibility of accruing further resources to attach to his role. It rests on his ability to continue to provide what his followers expect from him, and if he fails to do so he has no other inducement or sanction by which to retain them; they can simply transfer their allegiance to someone else. The requirement to be generous with the surplus produce accumulated by his physical and organizational efforts is not in itself what marks the role off from that of chieftainship proper. But the 'big-man' never reaches the stage at which his role enables him to levy tribute or taxes, to command a professional administrative staff, or to be accorded permanent ascriptive status independently of his own charismatic appeal.

The societies where 'big-men' (or 'centre-men' or 'men of renown' or some other equivalent term) are, as it were, classically reported are those of Western Melanesia, to which I shall be returning in both Chapter 3 and Chapter 4. But the same intermediate stage between minimal differentiation and full-time specialization is also reported for societies as remote from Melanesia as, for example, the nomadic cattle-herding Borana of East Africa (Dahl 1979, pp. 278–9), or for that matter Homer's Ithaca. Even if it cannot be accepted as an accurate piece of historical ethnography, the *Odyssey* gives an account of a society whose details must be presumed to have been largely recognizable to 'Homer's' audience, and it exemplifies precisely the difference between personal leadership and chiefdom 'properly so-called'. Odysseus's role is that of *basileus*. But the maintenance of a *basileus*'s power depends on his personal prowess. In Odysseus's absence, Ithaca is in a state of virtual anarchy. His father, Laertes, lives away on his farm 'unable to rule *iphi*, by might' (Finley 1956, p. 95), just like an ousted Anuak headman (Gluckman 1965, p. 125) who has had to retire to the village of his maternal kin where he has kept a separate set of gardens. Odysseus's son, Telemachus, has no body of officials or subordinates who can sustain him as regent or *dauphin*: even when he wants to assemble a ship's crew, he has to depend on those of his contemporaries who are also his friends (*Odyssey* III.363). The 'people' of Ithaca are neither citizens nor subjects, and they are neither conscripted nor taxed. The rival *basileis* who are the suitors for the hand of Odysseus's presumed widow are seeking her hand as the means to legitimate one of them as, so to speak, *the* 'big-man', rather than simply fighting it out among themselves. But when Odysseus returns, he has to fight to re-establish his own former pre-eminence. It is true that the *Odyssey*'s plot depends on Odysseus's twenty-year absence. But it still provides an example from a wholly different time and place of a role at exactly the same evolutionary stage as can be observed in Melanesia, among the Borana, and even in early Iceland. Here, the '*godi*', although his role was literally that of 'priest', depended on 'men who were ready in the last resort to fight on his side. The number and quality of his followers would depend on tradition, in his family and theirs, but particularly, because of the element of choice in the contract, on his personal popularity' (Foote and Wilson 1970, p. 134).*

§9. Once this stage of evolution has been passed, and there have emerged dominant roles whose incumbents exercise much more effective power over much larger numbers of people, a whole new terminology of institutions is called for. We are now in the world of states, armies, churches and commercial (if not yet industrial) enterprises, and therewith of administrators increasingly likely to be not only more specialized in what they do but to do it as a career. It is controversial in what sense and in what contexts these roles should be termed either 'professional' or 'bureaucratic'.† But their presence marks a change that is equally critical whichever the dimension in which the power of the ruler or rulers is delegated to the specialists concerned.

Economically, the most important contrast is between societies which do and do not have a permanent, central agency for the collection of taxes. There are, to be sure, other ways in which a ruler or government may be provided with surplus resources in cash or kind, whether

* Homologous relationships are reported also at local or community level within societies which have long since evolved into more complex modes: thus, for example, Chandavarkar (1981, p. 612) remarks of the role of the 'jobber' in the mill districts of early twentieth-century Bombay that 'Since his strength derived from the social and commercial ties he established with his workers, he had to remain receptive to their needs and responsive to their demands.'

† However debatable it may be as an explanatory term, the descriptive overtones of 'bureaucracy' do seem to transcend all times and places. The primordial 'bureaucrats' of Mesopotamia and Egypt have, unfortunately, left no literary memorials: at most, there are a few general statements of bureaucratic norms (O'Connor 1983, p. 191). But by the time of the later Roman Empire, there is an almost ideal-typical description in the *de Magistratibus Populi Romani* of John Lydus, whose relatively fast promotion to the 'cornicularian dignity' (III.9) still took, despite his jumping his probationary period through being the protégé of the praetorian prefect, no less than 40 years! A. H. M. Jones (1964, II, Ch. 16), who cites John Lydus several times, conveys a vivid picture of conservatism, sinecures, corruption, ritualism, promotion by seniority, unnecessary form-filling, over-recruitment, inter-departmental jealousy, immovability of incompetents, delegation of real work to juniors, and extravagant and often bogus holidays.

internally by prestation or liturgy or externally by extortion or plunder. But they are qualitatively different from taxation properly so-called; and one of the necessary conditions of a system of taxation is the existence of roles whose incumbents are agents for its collection. As with the recruitment of labour by middlemen or *locatores*, tax-collection may be farmed out to independent entrepreneurs not directly subordinate to the governing authorities. Nor need tax-collectors be full-time specialists: the function may be performed as part of an ecclesiastical or military role. But there is a difference in kind, not merely degree, between kings dependent on the revenues of their own domains, supplemented by cash commutation of personal services, use (and abuse) of personal credit, and personal patronage of trading and mercantile activities, and heads of state whose revenues are systematically collected from the groups or categories liable to taxation by the incumbents of specialized, permanent, public, institutionally recognized roles.

There is a similar difference of kind in the coercive dimension between societies with and without public law. 'Law' itself is, or can be, a contentious theoretical term. Not only is it debatable how exactly it should be distinguished from custom and '*prédroit*' (L. Gernet 1968, Pt 3, Ch. 1), but it may be a mistake to infer from the existence of codes like Hammurapi's or those of the Anglo-Saxon or Lombard kings that effective coercive sanctions are available to the rulers whose laws they are. This, however, serves only to reinforce the point that the presence of specialist, central agents whose roles empower them to enforce the sanctions is critical. Thus, for example, the *reth* of the Shilluk of the Upper Nile was the sole recognized hereditary mediator in intra-societal disputes; but he had no means of enforcing his authority and any attempt to do so merely resulted in weakening it (Howell 1952, p. 106; Evans-Pritchard 1962, p. 73). Yet even among so relatively 'primitive' a society as the German tribes as reported by Tacitus, there is *ius coercendi* in the hands of the priests and *principes* are sent out with a large supporting retinue to administer *iura* in the villages (*Germania* 11, 12). It is at this point that the trick has, so to speak, been turned and there has come into being a new set of roles and therewith the specialization of functions which both reflect and reinforce a significant accretion of power.

The same holds in the ideological dimension. Again, the difference is between the personal prestige of a leader of opinion whose following can melt away overnight and the institutionalized status attaching to a sacred office whose incumbent can thereby call on the services of the incumbents of permanent, specialist, subordinate roles. An example of a purely religious kind (although with political consequences) is the 'bureaucratization' of the Delphic oracle, which gave it its unique position in the culture of Classical Greece. More commonly, however, the expansion of specialist roles is bound up with the sacred legitimation of secular power: there is a conscious need for specialist practitioners who will perform the ceremonials by which the coercive sanctions at the ruler's disposal may be buttressed by ideological ones.* Sometimes, this is achieved by the direct and deliberate application of the coercive sanctions themselves, as when Gustavus Vasa, who had been viewed initially as a usurper and was at odds with the Pope, established his legitimacy simply by taking control of the Church in Sweden '"out of the plenitude of our royal power"' (Roberts 1968, p. 116). But specialized roles are both a symptom and a cause of a significant accretion of power in this dimension, too. Nor is this only in relatively simpler or earlier societies, or in societies which have retained monarchical or ecclesiastical institutions: in the Soviet Union in the post-Stalinist period, ritualization was deliberately instituted on a large scale for the purpose of reinforcing the legitimacy of the regime through the recruitment both of 'commissioners' to plan the new ceremonials and 'masters of ceremony' to perform them (C. Lane 1981, pp. 47–9, 51).

There is, however, another aspect to the differentiation of roles to which there attaches increasing power. As it does, so does there arise the possibility that their incumbents will use that power to promote their own upward mobility outwith and in defiance of the institutional rules. The conditions and consequences of this will be a recurring theme in Chapters 3 and 4. But even for the initial purpose of itemizing the roles in question, the terms of recruitment may have to be taken into account no less than the nature of the fiscal, legal, or ritual practices by which the roles themselves are defined. In particular, the deliberate use of otherwise low-ranking persons in highly placed roles as a safeguard against disobedience or usurpation is well documented in examples ranging from the Roman emperors' freedmen to Charlemagne's former serf Archbishop Ebo of Rheims to the *ministeriales* of the Salian kings to the eunuchs at the courts of the Abbasid caliphs in Baghdad (Ayalon

* Conversely, there may emerge 'carriers of models of cultural and social order – be they Jewish prophets and priests, the Greek philosophers, the Chinese literati, the Hindu Brahmins, the Buddhist Sanga or the Islamic Ulema' (Eisenstadt 1981, p. 160) whose role involves the institutionalization of the perception of the *tension* between ideology and politics – a role whose power derives from the great intellectual innovations of what Eisenstadt, following Jaspers, calls the 'Axial Age'.

1975, p. 50) or the Ming emperors in Peking (J. Gernet 1982, pp. 406–7) to the secretaries of the grand princes of fourteenth-century Moscow (Hellie 1982, p. 462). The device is not always successful even from the standpoint of the rulers' immediate interests. But to the extent that it is, the rank of the low-born incumbent of the highly located role is 'secondary' rank in the technical sense. The nearest approach to the ideal type is to be found in Islamic societies, where the pervasiveness of patron–client relations means that the would-be rebellious *mawlā** has no choice but to transfer his allegiance from one superior to another: he cannot redeploy the power attaching to his role to set up on his own. But Islamic societies also furnish the limiting case in which the practice becomes self-defeating: the Egyptian Mamluks, bought as slaves and trained as soldiers with no loyalty except to their masters, became in the end, as Weber aptly put it, benefice-holders (*Pfründer*) with *Herrschaft* over their own nominal *Herrscher* (1956, II, p. 595). The paradox is readily explicable, since once the means of coercion are in the hands of subordinates, then whatever their origins their loyalty will be conditional on the satisfaction of their interests, and the only defence of their masters against mutiny or desertion will be personal ascendency and a proven capacity to achieve further military success. Secondary rank may, accordingly, not always be quite what it seems, and it may be a serious mistake to report the distribution of power as though *ministeriales*, *radcnihts*, *administradores*, *baillis*, palatine guards, party apparatchiks and civil servants generally are wholly dependent upon, and answerable to, the superiors who have assigned them their roles.

§10. The same is true of corporations. Armies, churches and industrial or commercial enterprises may be ostensibly performing their specialized tasks under the control of the incumbents of governmental roles. But just as individual servants may use their secondary rank to usurp the power attaching to their roles, so may corporations use the power which accrues to them from their functions virtually – or even actually – to secede from the society to which they belong. This can happen even in relatively homogeneous and peaceful societies, and in societies already divided by regional, national and ethnic hostility it can lead (as for example in the Austro-Hungarian Empire) to a pluralism so extreme as to pose a perennial political problem for the governing élite.

Institutional isolation, however, need not lead to fission. Nor need

* Who might be either servile or free, but even if a converted non-Arab rather than a manumitted slave would still be in a *walā* relationship with an Arab patron (Pipes 1981, p. 108).

autonomy be tantamount to subversion. Functional differentiation may result in the performance of specialized tasks by so-called 'total institutions' (Goffman 1961, p. 16) such as monasteries, asylums or prisons, whose inmates have little or no contact with the wider society of which they are nominally members and whose governors exercise a more or less unfettered domination over them. But it does not follow that they are, so to speak, societies outside of their society rather than within it. They may or may not be. The Brazilian *Casa-Grande*, as vividly described by Freyre (1963, Chs. 4 and 5) was, as he says, at once fortress, chapel, school, workshop, house of charity, harem, convent, hospital and bank. But its master was not a robber baron or ungovernable *caudillo*. On the contrary, he was a loyal son of the Church and subject of the State, and there was no conflict between him and his superiors over the way in which he exercised the power attaching to his role. When, on the other hand, in tenth-century Italy local magnates acquired the right to build their own *castelli*, levy their own tolls, and contract with their own tenants the terms on which they would not only work but fight for them, this was the kind of sub-systematic differentiation which soon becomes tantamount to fission; by the mid-tenth century, the 'kingship' of Italy was a role only in name.*

For that matter, monasteries themselves may perform their function either in overt opposition to the society from which they originate or as an integral part of a division of labour between the *laboratores* who work, the *bellatores* who fight and the *oratores* who pray. The 'holy men' who joined the great monastic communities of late Roman Egypt were self-proclaimed antagonists of the pagan society from which they removed themselves in order, as the *Life* of St Anthony puts it, to 'create the heavenly *politeia*' in the desert (epigraph to Chitty 1966) and they periodically re-emerged into the wider society in order to destroy old temples and terrorize 'idolatrous' town-dwellers. By contrast, the Benedictine abbeys of medieval England were so far integrated into their society as to be the archetypal exemplars of the institution of manorialism itself (Kosminsky 1956, p. 171). Likewise, those who fight, no less than those who pray, may constitute an autonomous corporation amounting to a separate society, like Werner of Urslingen's 'Great Company' which rampaged about central Italy in the summer of 1342,

* Fission of this kind may, however, facilitate reunification in the longer term: when China split up into ten or more rival states after the fall of the T'ang, the provincial system was fragmented into units too small to be viable, with the paradoxical consequence that it was thereby made easier for the Sung to re-establish the local prefectural system after 960 (Twitchett and Wright 1973, p. 34).

or Pancho Villa's *División del Norte* which with its accompanying women and children advanced like a 'folk migration' (Quirk 1960, p. 243, quoted by Wolf 1971, p. 36) on Mexico City in 1914. But again, they may or may not be a threat to the existing order. Armies sometimes overturn the governments which have recruited them or hired them or otherwise brought them into being, but they may also disband quietly enough or, if retained in peacetime, maintain their corporate autonomy without disturbing the existing mode of the distribution of power.

There is, however, one particularly important form in which functional differentiation and the accretion of power are so linked that wherever it occurs, social relations are different in kind: *urbanization*. Viewed geographically, the residential concentration of persons for the performance of roles not otherwise feasible is no more than a special case of differentiation by region. The aggregation of merchants, administrators and artisans within a fortified settlement is simply a more intensive instance of the geographical specialization which assigns trades or crafts to particular villages or regions, whether forcibly (as, for example, under the Mongols or Inca) or spontaneously in response to market opportunities. But viewed sociologically, urbanization is a special case of differentiation by corporation: towns or cities are semi-autonomous, internally differentiated concentrations of specialized roles which may stand in any one of a whole range of varying relations to the other component institutions of the society in question, including other towns or cities within it.

There is an extensive literature on urbanization, and the contrasts between the *poleis* and *ethnē* of Classical Greece, between the medieval city as a centre of production and the ancient city as a centre of consumption, and between the politically autonomous cities of Western Europe and the politically subordinate cities of Islam and the Far East, have all passed into the common corpus of historical knowledge. But for the purposes of sociological theory, the important point is that a town or city is not to be analyzed as 'a social entity *sui generis*' but as 'an institutional expression of power' (Abrams 1978, pp. 9, 25). The relevance to it of contrasts like these is not to do with degree of residential concentration as such, but with the accretion and distribution of power, the evolution of novel economic, ideological and coercive roles and changes in the relations of domination and cooperation which obtain between the incumbents of those roles and others, whether in the town or city itself, in its social and geographical hinterland, or in the other institutions of the society as a whole. The mutual relation between specialization and the accretion of resources is here exemplified particularly clearly. Large-scale residential concentration is only possible at all where the persons so concentrated, whether their roles are themselves directly productive or not, have the capacity to procure goods and services which cannot be generated or performed on a household or family basis. But once this minimal condition is fulfilled, the scope for variation in both structure and culture is very wide. At one extreme, there are dispersed communities loosely attached to a ceremonial, administrative or market centre which is in turn dominated by a regional or even imperial capital. At the other, there are tightly knit, strongly defended, well-endowed municipalities dominating their surrounding *contado* and so far economically, ideologically and coercively independent of the empire, kingdom, republic or principality to which they are nominally subject that fission has *de facto*, if not also *de jure*, taken place almost by the mere occurrence of their foundation.

RANKS, DISTANCES AND BARRIERS

§11. Even in societies where total resources are small and differences in power are minimal, to identify a role is to place it relatively higher or lower than at least one other to which its incumbent relates by virtue of the practices defining it; and this cannot but invite the question: how far are they apart? I have stressed that to interpret the distribution of power by way of the model of societies as inverted pyramids is not to presuppose quantitative commensurability between them. But no satisfactory explanation (or description or evaluation) of the mode of the distribution of power of any society can be advanced without some criterion whereby it can be established which roles outrank which. Given a workable operational definition, certain measurements can, so far as the evidence permits, be accepted as accurate by all rival observers. Differences in wages or salaries, or orders of precedence in face-to-face ritual contexts, or number of soldiers in an army or followers in a retinue are all matters of fact which could in principle be checked against the recording angel's archives. But their usefulness is only as indicators. On no theory are these what power actually *is*.

It is, no doubt, possible in principle to assign a precise relative location to any two persons in their respective roles, simply in the sense that if a quasi-experimental *crise révélatrice* could somehow be contrived it would furnish the necessary demonstration. Economically, A has more power than B if, when the chips are down, A's role enables A to buy out B and not B to buy out A; ideologically, A has more power than B if, when claims to precedence are challenged, A's role enables A to secure deference from B and not B from A; coercively, A has more power than B if, when both sides come to blows, A's role enables A to force B to do A's bidding and not B to force A. But in practice, such experimental engineering is never feasible, and even if it were, then (as I implied already in Section 5 of Chapter 1) it would have to be endlessly repeated in order to make sure that every aspect of what may well be a constantly shifting relationship had been taken into account. This is of no help whatever to the practising sociologist who needs to choose the techniques and criteria of measurement that will yield the observations best suited to testing hypotheses about how societies of different kinds function and why they have evolved into the mode and sub-type of the distribution of the means of production, persuasion and coercion which they have.

Economic inequalities are, at first sight, straightforward to the extent that it is possible to express them in monetary terms. But even in a sophisticated market society, it is impossible to grade all roles and their incumbents along a unidimensional scale of income and wealth. It is true that assets, both tangible and intangible, can in principle be assigned a market value, that expectations of income can be capitalized and discounted to net present value, that receipts in kind can be assessed at whatever the recipient would be willing to pay for them, and that disutilities directly attaching to sources of income can likewise be deducted at a value determined by what the person concerned would pay to be rid of them. But it would still be seriously misleading to present the results of such an exercise as a ranking of persons in their roles in a cardinal order of economic power. To know how much money a person has is not to know what goods and services he or she can command by virtue of the relevant role, and still less to know to what extent and in what ways that role conditions or constrains his or her relations to the incumbents of others. There are rules which govern the uses to which economic resources can be put, there are capacities and potentialities for their acquisition which are unequally distributed but cannot be quantified, there are unpredictable fluctuations in market values even of readily marketable goods and services, and there are communal or collective benefits to which no monetary value can be assigned at all. These difficulties do not constitute a reason for neglecting to measure differences in income and/or wealth which attach to occupational or other roles in societies where the market so functions as to make them measurable. But they do amount to a reason to be sceptical of differences in income and wealth as indicating by themselves the distance between economic roles.

The recognition that distances between roles or systacts are a matter not just of attributes but of relationships might seem to be more readily accommodated where the relationships are in the ideological dimension, if only because 'social distance' in this sense has since Bogardus (1925) been operationally defined in terms of the degree of intimacy which a person at a higher location is willing to permit a person at a lower one. But quite apart from the technical problem that people behave inconsistently with what they say (Lapière 1934), a refusal of commensalism, intermarriage or other forms of close association may reflect hostility between equals rather than ideological domination of inferiors by superiors. This difficulty can be circumvented by explicitly asking the members of the society how they rank themselves and each other in order of social prestige, and in the case of occupational roles this has been shown to produce remarkably consistent replies across a whole range of industrial societies as well as in sub-cultural groups within them.* But it is open to question how far these replies can be interpreted as the reflection of an internalized scale of values to which the respondents genuinely subscribe: they may simply be acknowledging the desirability of a role without expressing their approbation or avowing their recognition of a widely held scale of values which they personally repudiate. This need not undermine the observer's report of the distribution of power, since deference is still deference when accorded unwillingly;† but it may well undermine the interpretation of the nature of the power attaching to the ostensibly prestigious role. Nor can reliance be any more unquestionably placed on the attribution of prestige that may appear to be implied in the title by which the role is designated. An honorific-sounding designation like 'Excellency' or 'Highness' may indeed reflect the exceptional prestige attaching to the role of ambassador or prince. But there are cases where high-sounding titles are vacuous or even self-defeating. The late Roman *magnificentissimi* and *gloriosissimi*, like the Byzantine *panhypersebasti* and *pansebastohypertati*, are as much an illustration of the point that roles

* In the absence of sample surveys it is impossible to tell whether the same was true of societies earlier than the twentieth century. But there is no need to dismiss out of hand the literary evidence of contemporary observers who appear to have thought so: cf. Norman (1958, p. 80) on the 'descending scale of occupational prestige from goldsmith, shoemaker, builder, weaver to hawker and oilseller' which can be quasi-deductively inferred for fourth-century Antioch from the writings of Libanius.

† There is also the possibility that deference may be accorded *hypocritically* – that is, willingly but without conviction. But this, like the phenomenon of 'passing', does not undermine the identification of the role to which, in the particular case, the deference is merely simulated (nor need the use of the concept of hypocrisy in this context be pre-emptive of a value-judgement – that, as always, is up to you).

cannot be created simply by declaration of intent as they are an example of an innovation in terminology reflecting a significant shift in the distribution of power.

When it comes to power of the kind which rests either directly or indirectly on coercive sanctions, the difficulty of measurement arises chiefly from the familiar paradox that such power is apt to be most useful when least used. This is not only because manipulation, propaganda, bribery or patronage may be a more effective instrument in the hands of rulers than force. It is also because the threat of force, or even the hint of a willingness to use it, may be more effective too. When, in the agitation which led up to the passing of the Reform Bill of 1832, Earl Grey told a deputation led by Francis Place that any disturbances would be put down by military force, he probably believed what he said and was probably believed to believe it (Perkin 1969, p. 368). But with an army of no more than eleven thousand men to call on, how relieved he must have been that it was never put to the test! Organization, tactics and morale are weapons no less than swords and guns, and the power of neither rulers nor over-mighty subjects can be assessed simply from an inventory of military resources. Moreover, there are many societies, not all of them 'modern', where the subjects (or at least the male ones) are armed against their rulers not literally with a weapon but instead, or also, with a vote. The distribution of political power is at the same time the distribution of access to the means of coercion and the distribution of entitlement to influence collective decisions as to how those means are to be used. Here too, measurement is feasible only in very broad terms. Within a common category of 'free', an Athenian citizen-farmer holding office by lot, putting proposals of his choosing to a sovereign assembly, serving with pay as a volunteer juryman, and voting his betters into exile by scratching their names on a potsherd was significantly more advantageously located than a Roman one living too far away to cast his vote more than seldom if at all,* excluded from any possibility of office-holding himself, and able only marginally to influence the election of one rather than another candidate for magistracy under an electoral system both heavily weighted and easy to manipulate. But there is no quantitative scale of political power on which they can be placed.

None of this is a reason not to make cardinal measurements where they can be made or test an observed institutional hierarchy of roles for the formal properties of a rank-order. I remarked at the end of

* MacMullen (1980, p. 455) estimates a turn-out of perhaps 2% of those eligible. There are no statistics of this kind in the sources, but the inference can be quasi-deductively drawn from the size of the area where voting took place.

Section 5 of Chapter 1 that terms such as 'narrowly stratified', 'diffuse', 'inconsistent' or 'steeply graded' can be applied by rival observers of all theoretical schools, and however much they may dispute the interpretation of the results they will not deny that they have been furnished with additional relevant information about the relative ranking of, and distance between, roles and their incumbents. Indeed, to appreciate the value of measurement it is enough merely to reflect how thankful we should be if only we *could* apply the techniques now available to us to societies now lost to us for the purpose. Consider yet again the example of Ancient Rome. Many facts about its structure can be reconstructed to the satisfaction of rival observers from the surviving literary, juristic, epigraphic and archaeological evidence. But how much better could explanatory hypotheses about that structure be framed and tested if we could plot a frequency distribution of personal incomes, or construct a Bogardus scale for the attitudes of freeborn Roman citizens to freedmen, slaves, provincials and foreigners, or calculate a Gini coefficient and Lorenz curve showing the imbalance of voting power in the centuriate and tribal assemblies, or construct a log-linear model of odds ratios specifying the association between father's juridical status, birth cohort and son's juridical status!

§12. The discussion of roles has now, in a sense, come full circle. The researcher who approaches a chosen society without presuppositions as to why it is as it is, or what it is like for its members to live in, or how far it is a good or bad one will have begun by inferring what he can about its structure and culture from what 'they' tell him are the differentiated groups and categories of roles which are more or less powerful in relation to others. He will not, however, assume without further enquiry that their answers to his questions license either semi- or quasi-deductive inferences adequate by themselves to yield a three-dimensional model of the relative location of all the itemized roles. This is not only because even the most careful native informants may misreport their institutions and practices,* and even the most experienced observers fail to ask all the questions they should.† It is also

* Anachronism is a frequent problem here: in seventeenth-century England, for example, the forms of land-tenure still meticulously reported in the manorial records and other documents are far less significant to the systactic location of the occupant than the total amount of land, however held, under his control and his associated 'gentility' and life-style (Campbell 1942, Ch. 4).

† A memorable example of how primary misunderstanding can result is given by Rattray (1923, p. 84). When, after living for many years among the Ashanti, he asked why he had not been told that the Queen Mother used to outrank the King, he

because the vernacular terms, however accurately applied, will not comprehend all the relevant aspects of how people in their distinguishable roles behave, institutionally speaking, towards one another.* From this arises the need for indicators by which differences of power can to some degree be measured and compared. But the indicators in their turn are no more to be taken fully to represent what they indicate than are the vernacular terms. It is as a glossary on 'their' terms for their own social relations that indicators of the economic, ideological and coercive sanctions and inducements attaching to itemized roles are to be construed.

The danger of relying too uncritically on the vernacular terms is not, on the other hand, an argument for scepticism. It may be that no society has a comprehensive vocabulary of roles whose dictionary meanings are enough by themselves to locate all of them as precisely as could be done by a trained sociologist with the aid of ancillary empirical research. But it is also true to say that there is no society in which major institutional differences of power are not also reflected in 'their' vocabulary of practices and roles. Nowhere in the historical and ethnographic record is there a society whose language does not embody some sort of notion of rank or distance as applicable to social relations between the more and less powerful of its members, whether in relation to seniority, leadership, wealth, actual or fictive pedigree, ritual prestige, access to means of coercion, or rights over land or property of other kinds. There are differently ranked roles in every known society, however minimally they are differentiated and however fleetingly their incumbents perform them; and it is noticeable how quickly, once differentiation increases, the vernacular terminology reflects it. Nor is it only the terminology for roles at the top and bottom which proliferates (often, to be sure, with evaluative† rather than sociological connotations). It is striking also how

received the reply that 'The white man never asked us this; you have dealings with and recognize only the men; we supposed the European considered women of no account, and we know you do not recognize them as we have always done.'

* There is a particular likelihood that systactic distinctions will be blurred when roles are categorized by native informants from the top down. Sir Thomas Wilson (Thirsk and Cooper 1972, pp. 751–7), like Gregory King, was much more concerned with differentiations within the nobility of seventeenth-century England than within the common people, just as was the Persian King Ardeshir who, according to Jahiz of Basra (Levy 1962, p. 69) indiscriminately lumped all 'cultivators, menials etc.' into the lowest of the four categories into which he divided his subjects but was careful to rank second and third 'religious leaders and guardians of the fire-temples' and 'physicians, scribes and astrologers' respectively.

† Notably in Rome, where the equation of poverty with ignobility was as consistent and explicit as the assimilation of nobility to virtue (Yavetz 1965). But the sources are, of course, heavily biassed: it must be likely that if the opinions of the voiceless *plebs*

soon, and how widely, intermediate systacts are explicitly distinguished as such, whether as *mesoi politai*, *mediocres*, 'middling sort', *couche moyenne*, *clase media* or *Mittelstand*, or as the Anglo-Saxon *half fre* who are paralleled not only by the Lombard *aldii* or the *lidi* of the ninth-century polyptych of St Germain-des-Prés but by the Chinese *pu-ch'u* or *k'o-nu* (Pulleyblank 1958, p. 210) and the Fulani *dimajai* (Hill 1976, p. 404). However many supplementary observations may be needed before the distribution of power can be sufficiently accurately reported for the explanation of it to begin, there is always some such set of explicit distinctions made by 'them' which corresponds to differences in power of a more than transient kind.

Sometimes, indeed, these distinctions are so very clear-cut that they constitute a rank-order with hardly any need for supplementary observations at all. The domination of the Spartan Helots by the Spartiate 'Peers', even though complicated, as we have seen, by some downwardly mobile *tresantes* and *hypomeiones* and some upwardly mobile *neodamodeis*, is one such example. So is the society of early Anglo-Saxon England, where an intermediate systact of formally free *ceorls* with their access to royal justice, their hide or so of land, their right (and duty) to bear arms, and their own groups of household dependents stood midway between the nobility on one side and slaves, whether by birth, purchase or capture, on the other. It is true that such very clear-cut structures are found only where the society is relatively static. Nor should the categories of census-takers or law-makers be any more readily taken at face value than those of ordinary speech. The 'social classes' of the Registrar-General are just as artificial an imposition on the pattern of roles in twentieth-century British society as either the categories of the Soviet census (where there is a deliberate bias against 'unproductive' labour combined with a concealment of roles in the political *apparat*) on twentieth-century Russian society or the elaborate wergilds of the laws of King Ine on the society of seventh-century Wessex. But just because there are quasi-sociological terms used by some of the members of a given society which cannot be taken at face-value, it does not follow that there are no others which can.

There are also societies where orders or estates embracing a diversity of persons widely distant from each other in wealth and/or social prestige and/or political influence are defined by a vernacular terminology which all observers are bound to accept. The impoverished

sordida could be accurately sampled, it would turn out that many of them consciously rejected the values of their 'betters', much as many manual workers in mid twentieth-century Britain have been shown to do (Young and Willmott 1956).

Spanish *hidalgo* 'eating black bread under the genealogical tree', or the petty member of the Polish *szlachta* with his landholding one millionth the size of the estates of the Radziwills, or the eighteenth-century French nobleman to be found working as a muleteer or gamekeeper or in a *dépôt de mendicité* (Carré 1920, p. 130) all nonetheless occupy a rank as unarguable to the latter-day historian as to their own contemporaries. No doubt there is, in these cases, a risk of misreportage if account is not taken both of the occupancy of multiple roles by the members of a heterogeneous order of 'nobility' and of the span between the highest and lowest roles which its members can occupy without forfeiting membership. But the juridical definition is not to be dismissed as meaningless simply because it is less important to the workings and evolution of the society than the pattern of roles which cuts across it.

There is, accordingly, an enormous amount of evidence in the historical and ethnographic record which can and should be accepted without further comment as ranking roles already itemized in vernacular terms. Moreover, it amounts to a solid body of common sociological knowledge shared uncontroversially between the members of the society under study and the academic researchers studying it. There is a sense in which native informants all know at least approximately where they stand, and no rival observer can dispute it unless he doubts that they are truthful and of sound mind. Whatever the risks of overinterpreting what 'they' say on the one hand, and the limitations of would-be quantitative measurement of social distance on the other, sociologists of all theoretical schools can broadly agree with Touraine (1965, p. 157) that '*Chacun de nous s'adapte à une certaine hiérarchie sociale suffisamment au moins pour reconnaître quand il s'élève ou quand il descend socialement.*'

§13. But to have ranked a society's principal roles relative to one another and measured (so far as may be possible) the distance between them is still not to have reported all that is needed before its workings and evolution can start to be explained. It is not just a matter of adding a narrative account of the emergence of the practices which define the itemized roles. There needs also to be established (i) how far the itemized roles are open to all the society's members, (ii) how far the incumbents of any itemized role can maintain themselves in it at their own discretion, and (iii) how far incumbency carries an institutional entitlement (a) to determine or influence the selection of the next incumbent or (b) to transmit all or part of the power attaching to it to the incumbent of some other role.

The range of answers to these questions is very wide, but once again not unmanageably so. Obvious though it may be, it is worth emphasizing both that all societies have to have mechanisms of some kind whereby successors move into vacated roles and that there are certain purely numerical constraints which operate on any such mechanism. Some roles, to be sure, may not need to be refilled at all. They may have been abolished (as both monarchy and slavery have sometimes been*); they may have lost their function (like certain traditional occupations overtaken by technological or ideological changes, such as blacksmiths and witch-doctors); or they may have been abandoned as soon as more attractive alternatives are available (like resident domestic service). But as long as the society continues in being at all there are at least some, both dominant and subordinate, for which replacements have to be found, whether by inheritance, election, appointment, coercion (or seizure), lottery (or divination), accession by age-grade, or allocation through a job market; while at the same time, there will always be more potential incumbents for the available roles than makes it possible for every member of the society to spend an equal proportion of his or her adult lifetime in every different role. Admittedly, there are societies (notably pioneer societies†) so open as to have almost no institutional rules for succession to either dominant or subordinate roles, just as there are societies (notably age-set societies) where roles are occupied strictly in rotation. But even so, there are no societies where succession is literally random, except to the extent that selection by lot is itself deliberately institutionalized; and there are no societies, even if organized around age-sets, where every adult member, female as well as male, shares equally in the incumbency of all differently located roles.

At the opposite extreme, a society in which entry to all roles but one is closed to everyone from the moment of birth is conceivable in theory. But no such has ever been reported, or ever will. Even in the systems of caste reported for Indian village communities there is some scope for individual and collective mobility and some differentiation within *jāti*. There are, however, roles in many societies which are defined by a limitation on entry: an aristocracy by birth is a caste by definition if, as claimed for example of early eighteenth-century France, its members

* Not that formal abolition is always to be equated with actual elimination: the Russian Revolution abolished tsardom but not, as events were to prove, autocracy, and the ostensibly manumitted *libertos* of nineteenth-century Portuguese East Africa remained subject to their masters to the same degree despite the proclamation of emancipation (see the comment of the British consul in Mozambique quoted by Lovejoy 1983, p. 228; and on the French *engagés*, cf. Shepherd 1980, p. 78).

† Or pioneer regions or communities within settled societies, like, for example, parts of Warwickshire in medieval England (Hilton 1975).

are strictly confined in their choice of career to the '*mestier de la guerre pour lequel ils sont nés*' (*mémoire* of 1702 quoted by Bercé 1974, I, p. 131). Conversely, the role of *novus homo* in the Roman Republic was defined in part by a restriction whereby the topmost political office was the almost but not quite total prerogative of men whose forebears had held high office too. Similar restrictions may, for that matter, define subordinate roles within societies whose higher ranks are, by contrast, relatively more open: thus in fifteenth- and sixteenth-century Japan, butchers, tanners and leather-workers were all outcastes (*Eta*) whose activities, although much in demand by competing military lords, were at the same time ideologically defined as polluting (J. Price 1966, p. 2). Where roles are closed off in ways like these, it is likely that passing will frequently be attempted, and if the attempt is successful it must follow that not even the most diligent observer will be able to detect and report it.* But it may, on the other hand, happen that its frequency is such as visibly to erode the conventional restrictions on entry. Where this is so, the definition of the ostensibly restricted role will have to be modified accordingly: thus, in sixteenth- and seventeenth-century Poland, the juridical barriers restricting entry to the order of nobility could be breached by any aspiring outsider who was able and willing to '*mener un train de vie propre à la noblesse*' (Dworzaczek 1977, p. 161) – which many could and did.

In the same way, the relative certainty of tenure attaching to the incumbency of a role may be just as significant a defining characteristic of it in the lower ranks of a society as in the higher. The Japanese *Eta* were lowly placed outcastes; but (like the Tibetan *Ragyappo*, or the Indian *Harijan*) they were assured of a place in the division of labour, and they were less heavily taxed than the peasantry. In thirteenth-century England, men of unfree status were both tied to their holdings and justiciable by their lords, and the inescapability of their condition was both in legal theory and in actual practice a defining characteristic of the role of 'serf'; but they might also enjoy a near-total customary security of heritable tenure (Hatcher 1981, p. 10) sufficient to protect them against the rack-renting which their lords might otherwise have practised during times of steeply rising land-values. At higher systactic

* For present-day Japan, Kitahara (1974, p. 59, as quoted by Hane 1982, pp. 147–8) claims that 'Not a few people have gotten ahead in the world by escaping from the *buraku* and blending into society at large by concealing their family origin and background. There are those, not only in the sports and entertainment fields but in political, financial and academic circles, whose names, if known, would strain people's credulity.'

levels, it is broadly (but by no means universally) true to say that the more powerful a role, the more security of tenure is a matter of licence rather than compulsion. Kings usually try to stay on their thrones (even though some have chosen to abdicate), just as slaves usually choose freedom if it is offered them (even though some have been known to refuse*); but kings are likely to have more choice in the matter than slaves. Accordingly, it is important to distinguish the role of a 'dictator' like Cincinnatus, whose position at the head of the Roman state was strictly temporary – sixteen days in 450 B.C. – from that of one like General Stroessner, whose location at the head of the twentieth-century Paraguayan state is permanent subject only to the possibility of forcible removal or assassination. But wherever the role in question may happen to be located, the distinction needs to be drawn between an incumbency which is more or less nearly lifelong and one which varies as a function of the incumbent's own choice, temperament and circumstances.

The power to transmit a role at will is not, strictly speaking, an attribute of that role as such: a monarch who can choose his or her heir may be no more powerful in any other respect than one who cannot. Yet on no theory can it be irrelevant to the distribution of power whether, for example, a Renaissance captain can hand over his private army to his son (or, as quite often happened, his son-in-law), or whether a marcher lord can treat his fiefdom as hereditary even though it supposedly reverts to his sovereign on his death, or whether senior party members in a one-party state can effectively guarantee that membership will be open to their children or other protégés or nominees. The range of variation here is from roles whose incumbents are replaced strictly in rotation or by lot, like the Athenian magistracies (other than generalships),† and roles where the incumbent is at liberty to choose anyone at all as successor, like a Roman emperor who could adopt a wholly fictional 'Caesar' as his heir (and arrange if necessary for the elimination of rival claimants). When little power attaches to the role, the difference is by definition less important. But there is, all the same, a significant range from a society whose subordinate members are free to transmit such small possessions, titles or offices as they may have to

* For example, those gypsies who preferred to flee across the border from Bukovina into Moldavia, where slavery persisted, after the secularization of monastic lands by Joseph II in 1785 (Blum 1978, p. 44).

† Always remembering that those eligible were only male citizens over thirty years old.

one where there are rules of inheritance or appointment which, as in the extreme case of slavery, deny the right even to make over personal possessions to a child or to influence the child's treatment in any way.

SYSTACTIC IDENTITY AND COLLECTIVE CONSCIOUSNESS

§14. How, then, do systacts come to form out of sets of more or less similarly located roles? The question is both historical and analytical. Historically, groups or categories of persons who share a common location by virtue of their roles have come together through the competitive selection of the practices defining them, and the process may have been fast or slow, planned or unplanned, smooth or uneven. But analytically, there are many fewer systacts than roles, and there needs to be specified the nature and extent of the common interest which ties any particular sets of them together.

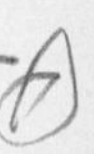

The question of identity of interests needs, however, to be kept separate from the further question whether the members of a distinguishable systact do or do not cooperate actively out of a shared sense of relative deprivation in safeguarding or furthering their common interests against whatever competitors for power they perceive as above, below or equal to but separate from them. The transition from (in Marx's terms) *an sich* to *für sich*, or from 'quasi-group' to 'interest-group' (Dahrendorf 1959, p. 182), or from 'awareness' to 'consciousness' (Lloyd 1966, p. 57), depends not merely on the location of their roles but on the extent, magnitude and intensity of their sense of relative deprivation and the nature of their opportunities for acting on it. What is more, collective action frequently arises out of vertical rather than horizontal cooperation, and horizontal cooperation is in any case not a sufficient condition of systact formation:* clubs, fraternities, secret societies,† Islamic *turuq*,‡ and Cypriot *omadhes*§ are all interest-

* Cooperative action can, however, be a *symptom* of incipient systact formation, as for example in the murder of Count Sigehard of Burghausen in 1104 by *ministeriales* of several different lords (Leyser 1968, p. 25).

† Although by now a standard sociological term, 'secret society' is not a rendering of a literal equivalent, but a British neologism probably coined early in the nineteenth century with Freemasonry in mind (Dunstheimer 1972, p. 23 n.l).

‡ Literally, 'paths' (to knowledge of God): 'orders' in a similar sense to monastic orders or brotherhoods, but with political overtones, is perhaps the nearest rendering.

§ These are teams of armed men pledged to secrecy and placed at the disposal of a chosen leader: see Sant Cassia (1983) who defines an *omadha* as 'an ego-centred coalition of a non-corporate character' (p. 121).

groups of a kind, but they are, as it were, more *für sich* than *an sich* – they can and often do serve systactic interests of varying kinds,* but they should not be taken to constitute systacts in themselves.

Analytically, the decisive criteria for systactic identity are four. First, the roles grouped together must embody a common interest independently of the individual interests of their incumbents (which will often be a function of their simultaneous incumbency of other roles): thus, for example, it will be a mistake to attribute a systactic identity to intellectuals if the groups or categories so labelled share a common economic location, social prestige and/or political allegiance only by virtue of a conjunction of individual circumstances and attitudes.† Second, the common interest in question must be substantively as well as formally distinctive: thus, it will be a mistake to attribute a systactic identity to slaves, even where they are juridically defined as an order and share a common interest in gaining their freedom, if they stand in different and mutually antagonistic relations to the means of production, range in status from outcastes to members of the courtly élite, and serve as senior administrators or generals as well as forced labourers in chain-gangs. Third, the common interest must be common to a more than negligible number of persons in their similarly located roles (unless, as in the limiting case of monarchy itself, the power attaching to the role is in inverse proportion to the number of incumbents): thus, it will be a mistake to attribute systactic identity to wage-labourers if there are only a handful of landless migrants who occasionally contract to sell their labour for cash in a society where the adult workforce is overwhelmingly employed on other terms.‡ And fourth, the common interest must not be overridden by simultaneous conflicts of interest which can, as we have seen, occur between roles which may be very similarly located in all three dimensions of structure, but are at the same time tied cooperatively to others above or below them.

* Thus, the secret societies of nineteenth-century China functioned to mobilize opposition to the central government and its local officials, whereas their contemporary West African counterparts such as the Ngura and Aro *okonko* functioned to promote the interests of the dominant slaveowners, traders and village and lineage heads.

† Thus Lapidus (1984, p. 130) characterizes the Islamic clerisy (*ulama*) as 'not a separate class but a body of people belonging to every social level'. On the other hand, intellectuals may constitute a coherent status-group even though they do not share common economic or political interests: cf., e.g., Annan (1984, pp. 5–7) on those of late Victorian Britain.

‡ There are, of course, borderline cases: for example, the 'moneyers' of the early Middle Ages were a self-consciously powerful group (or category) because and for as long as money was scarce (Lopez 1953, p. 43), but it must be debatable whether they should be assigned a systactic identity or not.

Historically, the emergence of a recognizable systact across the analytical boundary of pre- or non-institutional groupings can come about in ways which range all the way from deliberate imposition to spontaneous coalescence. A good example of the first is the Russian 'Table of Ranks' of 1722, by which Peter the Great sought – albeit with only limited success* – to establish merit rather than birth as the basis of selection for government office. A good example of the second is the start of combination against their employers by the wage-earners of eighteenth-century England, such as the Newcastle keelmen and the London weavers (Rudé 1964, Ch. 4). Whatever the form it takes, however, whichever the dimension of social structure in which the relevant practices have arisen, and whether the speed of evolution is almost instantaneous or almost imperceptibly gradual, the process is always two-sided. Systacts are formed within a pre-existing set of roles which is modified by the emergence of mutant or recombinant practices, and their location is a function both of what the incumbents of the novel roles do and of how the incumbents of other roles respond to what they regard them as doing in relation to the means of production, persuasion or coercion as the case may be.

An example which usefully illustrates not only the two aspects of systact formation but also the interrelation between the three dimensions of social structure is the emergence of a distinctive *Kleinbürgertum* in the towns of late pre-industrial Germany (Friedrichs 1978). The change which precipitated it was the combination of a sudden contraction in demand (and thus an increase in indirect costs per unit of production) with the possibility of developing export markets. There was thus for the incumbents of both the *Verlager*'s and the craftsman's role not only the opportunity but the motive to move to a putting-out system in which the *Verlager* supplied the credit and the craftsman gained indirect access to the export market which he was not equipped to exploit on his own. The indebtedness of the craftsmen to the *Verlager* became more or less permanent; their chances of individual mobility diminished; their sense of relative deprivation was exacerbated; they drew increasingly close to wage-earners in economic location while all the more reluctant to assimilate to them in 'culture' (*Bildung*); and their roles thus evolved into what was later to form the distinctive urban lower-middle stratum

* It has been claimed that its only effect on the systactic structure apart from some marginal assistance to sons of the clergy was to reinforce prevailing attitudes where it coincided with them (Hassell 1970, p. 294). Perhaps the most successful of such attempts was Solon's division of the citizens of Athens into four classes differentiated by wealth in 594 B.C., but the reliability of the historical tradition is open to question.

of German society as a whole. Notice, however, that this evolution was not solely economic. If it had been, then the once independent craftsmen would have joined the proletariat rather than formed a new and distinctive systact which later fused with other, adjacent roles. But no less distinctive to it were, first, the retention of its members' political roles as citizens, and second, their retention of an ideology of respectability (*Ehrbarkeit*). Moreover, the example at the same time illustrates the point that collective consciousness has to be analyzed separately from systact formation '*an sich*'. Elsewhere, as in Switzerland, different selective pressures caused the *Verlagssystem* to be accompanied by quite different forms of ideology and political organization.

§15. Where, or if, a clearly demarcated, externally acknowledged, stable, self-reproducing systact can be identified in a distinctive area of social space, it can be reported to the satisfaction of all rival observers in terms of a number of straightforward attributes such as size, turnover, average income of individuals or household heads, degree of endogamy, legal privileges or liabilities allowed to or imposed on its members, and so forth. But there are few such to be found. Here or there in the historical and ethnographic record, there may be reported a homogeneous category of smallholding allodialists, an exclusive sacerdotal élite, a distinctive class of tied or servile labourers, a closed occupational caste, or a strictly differentiated age-set which comes close to the ideal type; and where there is, the explanation of the society's workings (if not its evolution) will be easier to that extent. Usually, however, detailed itemization of the pattern of roles will disclose hazy systactic boundaries, cross-cutting membership of conflicting roles, inter-dimensional inconsistency, internal sub-systemic differentiation, and uncertain perceptions on the part of the incumbents of other roles and systacts.

In this context, the dictum that roles are a matter of relations as well as attributes has a particular force. In all societies, whatever their structure or culture, there are practices of two kinds which determine to some degree the relations between the incumbents of different roles and the extent to which domination or cooperation obtains between them. The first are those engendered by geographical and thereby social contiguity; the second are those engendered by kinship, whether actual or fictive. They permit very wide variations, both separately and in their own interrelations with one another. But – like relations of domination and cooperation generally – they are neither infinite nor random, and the forms which they take are critical to the transition from roles separately itemized to systactic identity and thence (if that is what happens) to a sense of relative deprivation which finds outlet in collective action.

It may seem redundant to point to the importance of ties between neighbours (or fellow-members of itinerant bands of hunter-gatherers or nomadic pastoralists). But contiguity can create conflict as well as identity of interests. Cooperation among landholding villagers both in the organization and performance of agricultural tasks and in mutual defence against landlords or the agents of central government can be abundantly documented in both the historical and the ethnographic record. But so can the hostility engendered when land – especially good land – is in short supply and each landholder sees his neighbour's interests as in zero-sum conflict with his own. Nor does this apply only at the level of petty proprietors and subordinate tenants. The Mexican *hacendados*, for example, were divided in their interests precisely to the extent that physical contiguity, instead of uniting them against encroaching squatters or surrounding free Indian villages, brought them into conflict with one another: given their mode of production, their economic interest lay almost self-evidently in expanding at each other's expense in order to wipe out the threat of competition (Mörner 1973, p. 192, citing Florescano 1971, pp. 140–1).* Again, therefore, common location of roles is not to be translated directly and unquestioningly into identity of systactic interest.

Kinship (or quasi-kinship) likewise stands in a highly variable relation to the distribution of power. At one extreme, relations of domination are defined directly in its terms, so that junior or lesser kin have a common systactic interest against seniors† or chiefs or lineage heads; at the other, kinship is what gives seniors and juniors within the same household or village or district their common interest against either separate equals (as particularly in feuds) or alien overlords (as particularly under colonialism) or simply against the dominant systact within their particular society. The limiting case is a society where, as

* The consequences should not be exaggerated, however. A detailed study of the Guadalajara region has shown that although 'landowners both private and communal simply invaded and encroached upon each other's land with dizzying frequency', still 'The pushing and pulling over boundaries, the judicial arguments between and among haciendas and communal peasant villages... are... not incompatible with the view that haciendas were basically stable in the amounts of land they held after 1700 or so, and were not aggressively expanding in the late-colonial period' (Van Young 1981, pp. 338, 295).

† It is a vexed question how far juniors in an age-set system are to be viewed as a subordinate class; but the difference is largely verbal since if all juniors become seniors the class is transitional only, whereas if they do not then it is not, after all, an age-set system (cf. Meillassoux 1981, pp. 78–9, commenting on Rey 1975).

in the Israeli *kibbutzim*, the influence of parenthood on social organization is deliberately reduced to a minimum (Bar-Yosef 1959). But there is no society in which relations of both domination and cooperation are not to some degree constituted by kinship roles, sociologically defined; and there are many in which it is in both aspects pervasive, wide-ranging and (in the genealogical sense) deep, from the traditional five 'mournings' of the Chinese patriarchal clans through the Lombards' reckoning of '*omnis parentilla usque in septimum geniculum*' (Beyerle 1947, p. 48 = *Edictus Rothari*, c. 153) to the twelve generations of the Tiv to the twenty or more calculated by the Northern Somalis.

Even in societies where kinship is hardly reckoned beyond the nuclear family, there still operate the two forms of power inherent in all kinship relations: control of the roles which children (and, very often, women) may occupy and control of the definition of kinship itself. In medieval Europe, for example, kinship fluctuated in importance relative both to vassalage and to regional loyalties, and in the case of France it combined with territorial ambitions of geographically contiguous families and local patron–client networks to turn dynastic cohesion into internecine hostility and from that into would-be fission from the slowly emerging nation-state. What is more, it is possible for quasi-kin practices to be deliberately and anachronistically grafted onto local ties as a counterweight to the fusion of geographical contiguity with aristocratic lordship. This is what appears – contrary to what many specialists previously assumed – to have taken place in Ancient Greece (Roussel 1976). Elements of 'tribal' organization and terminology were later incorporated into societies which, at the time when they first entered the territories to which they gave their names,* had not been 'tribal' at all. The range of possible permutations is, accordingly, very wide. But in relation to systact formation, there are at the same time four constraints which operate the whole way across it.

(i) Kin practices, although they may define roles of which those concerned in them are fully aware, may not be sufficiently relevant to relations of either domination or cooperation to count even as a borderline case. In some West African societies, for example, descent lines may be so far subordinate to locally based cult or work groups or political assemblies that they 'serve only as mental representations which, in certain ritual or quasi-ritual situations, unify symbolically a fragmented and dispersed universe of kin' (Jackson 1977, p. 43).

(ii) If relations of domination are entirely bound up with relations of

* Or, in some cases, from which they took them (Gschnitzer 1955).

kinship and contiguity, then there can be no systactic identity, let alone collective consciousness, among the members of different such groupings who are, nevertheless, similarly ranked. The Scottish clans are a clear instance. The impoverished cognatic descendant of an eponymous Mackintosh was not the fellow-member of a common systact with a similarly impoverished descendant of an eponymous Macleod, not just because there might well be a running feud between them but because they did not and could not have a common interest within the institutions which furnished the context of their roles. They might, to be sure, have a *latent* common interest in the sense that under other circumstances their similar location might override their dependence on their chiefs. But that is another matter.

(iii) Where contiguity is sufficiently impeded, not only collective consciousness but even systactic identity can be ruled out by simple force of circumstance. It is obvious that a necessary condition of collective consciousness is some minimal physical communication between the incumbents of roles similarly located in social space. But it can also happen that groups or categories similarly located are so tenuously attached to the institutions of their society (as opposed to their immediate locality) that they cannot be said to have a common interest at all. The near-servile deportees on the plantations of Southern Mexico under the regime of Porfirio Díaz failed to constitute a systact not because, like Scottish clansmen, their loyalties were vertical rather than horizontal – on the contrary, they were notoriously brutally treated by their employers – but because the plantations to which they were confined were effectively 'total' institutions in Goffman's sense. They had, accordingly, 'no corporate identity, no tradition of protest, no freedom of manoeuvre, and no clear point of reference' (Knight 1980, p. 26). Not merely, when the time came, did they not play any more part in the Mexican Revolution than did the privileged *acasillados*,* but their roles were not such that they should conceive of so doing. No doubt they would all have like to return to the communities from which they had been deported. But they did not otherwise have a definable common interest to be conscious of.

(iv) There are cases where systactic identity is ruled out because of the transience of incumbency of roles at a common location. Vagrants, drifters, casuals and downwardly mobile 'skidders' (Wilensky and Edwards 1959) may well have no common interest even if at some one

* Katz (1974, pp. 44–5): this example could accordingly be added to those which I cited in Section 10 of Chapter 1 as cases where the pattern of relative deprivation in relation to the location of the persons concerned is an S-shaped curve.

given moment they all occupy roles located very close to the apex of the inverted pyramid, simply because they do not stay where they are, either sociologically or geographically, for long enough. But it is not only rapidity of turnover which can make this so. There are also cases where the incumbency of the roles is not only too transient but at the same time too feeble for systactic identity. A good example is provided by the *Mudéjares* – the Spanish Muslims overtaken by the Reconquest whose leaders withdrew to areas still under Muslim control and left them, until their sudden and final expulsion, at the mercy of a Christian society which veered ambivalently between seeking to absorb and to eliminate them (Boswell 1977). They had – or so it could be argued – a latent common interest in preserving what they could of their declining wealth, their status as tolerated heretics and their political rights as a subject minority. But their systactic identity was being constantly eroded by a joint process of assimilation to the Christian society of which they were part and emigration to Muslim areas. By the time of their final removal, those who remained were scarcely aware of their common culture. They were, to be sure, still a recognizable group and category of persons, since it was as such that they were expelled. But they could barely, if at all, be counted as a systact, and they would not long have continued even as a group or category. Like some of the examples which I gave in Section 2 of Chapter 1, they illustrate the way in which, once a traditional corporate structure has dissolved under exogenous pressure, people can find their roles and therewith their systactic identity disappearing, as it were, under their own feet.

§16. At this point, we are again confronted with the question which I raised in Section 7 of Chapter 1: how many systacts does a given society have? I said then that the question is not theory-neutral; and indeed, latent interests and embryonic systact formation are often better indicators of the practices whose selection will determine the future course of social evolution than the manifest divisions between large and compact groups or categories by which the observer may have been more immediately impressed. But at the same time, there are gaps and boundaries which so clearly delimit a particular area of social space that unless one or more of the countervailing conditions listed in the previous section applies, attribution of systactic identity follows almost automatically.

It can, however, happen that there is only one group or category of similarly located roles in a society for which the necessary conditions of systactic identity hold. This then creates the apparent paradox of a one-systact society, which looks like a contradiction in terms to the extent that all social relations are reciprocal and any rank-order requires that there are at least two definable categories of which the second is ranked below the first. The paradox is, however, only apparent. A one-systact society does indeed contain two – or, in practice, many more than two – groups or categories of persons in similarly located roles. Its distinguishing feature, however, is that for one or another of the reasons set out in Section 14 the incumbents of the subordinate roles lack the necessary degree of common interest with others similarly located. Societies of this kind may, for that reason, be more difficult to explain (or describe or evaluate). But there is nothing anomalous about them. Classical Rome, as we have seen, was a society dominated by a stratum with a near-monopoly of both agricultural and urban land, an unassailable social prestige, and an almost total hold over the principal political-cum-military offices, and its collective consciousness was correspondingly well entrenched. But below it, there were no similarly distinctive classes, status-groups or factions – let alone strata – identifiable in the same way as such.

The most remarkable feature of the structure of Ancient Rome was not the size of the gap between top and bottom. There were very marked inequalities between the relatively rich and the abjectly poor, between the well- (or at least free-) born and the low-born or servile, and between citizens and non-citizens (both slave and free). But common class interests were undermined by the common relation to the means of production of servile workers and free; common status-group interests were undermined by the steady upward mobility through the structure of freedmen and their sons; and common political interests were undermined by relations of dependence which tied citizen clients to senatorial patrons. Within the complex gradation of roles, there were of course groups and categories who not only had, and knew that they had, a common interest of some sort but sometimes acted in pursuit of it. The *equites*, for example, sometimes tried to exploit their monopoly of seats in the *repetundae* courts before which their senatorial opponents might be brought to trial, and the guilds (*collegia*) sometimes sought recognition of the right to bring together and represent local constituencies of artisans or craftsmen. But what we are observing here is the formation not of systacts so much as of *coalitions* – that is, associations temporarily formed for a common economic, ideological or coercive purpose between incumbents of roles which are not necessarily located together.* These coalitions were formed within a society characterized not only by large differences of power but by a high intensity of conflict between higher and lower roles. But the need for them arose precisely because below the single dominant stratum the structure was so imprecise and so ubiquitously cross-cut by linkages and antagonisms, both horizontal and vertical, of non-systactic kinds. Nothing illustrates this better than the so-called 'Roman Revolution' itself which, if 'revolution' is defined in terms of the overthrow of a dominant by a subordinate systact in pursuit of a new social order, was not a revolution at all. The change in the mode of the distribution of power which it brought about was the fall of the Republic and therewith the surrender of *libertas* by the hitherto dominant systact to an absolute monarch. But there was no transfer of power from the top down, and no consequential change in the mode of production:† there was merely the forcible replacement of one section of the nobility and its clients by another.

The obvious example of a two-systact society is Sparta, which, like Rome, I have cited more than once already. Despite the qualifications which need to be made about intermediate roles and internal differentiation within the categories of Spartiate and Helot, the division is so clearly fundamental to the distribution of power that any alternative or additional categorization of Spartan society has to start from it. Another example is traditional Rwanda and the dichotomy within it between superior Tutsi and inferior Hutu (Maquet 1961); and there are many cases of relatively simple communities within a more complex total society where there is one self-evident dividing line, as in the villages of colonial New England which consisted of farmers on the one side and labourers on the other (Main 1967, p. 112) with women holding secondary rank deriving from the male household head. The idea of a single critical division is familiar particularly in the context of the dichotomies between master and slave, lord and serf, bourgeois and proletarian. But the point of these is that they are, indeed, theoretical. Marx himself never denied the existence of 'intermediate' classes. His claim was not that there is only one dividing-line to be drawn within a 'capitalist' or any other type of society, but that one particular dividing-

* Coalitions might, indeed, shade over into *conspiracies* like that of Catiline, in which the incumbents of a variety of roles (including some slaves) were united simply by a shared personal interest in the overthrow of the existing regime.

† It could, however, be argued that the Principate modified the economic as well as the political and military roles of the citizenry to the extent that citizens were compelled to become tied tenants (*coloni*) as the supply of slaves (who were only to a limited extent recruited by breeding) declined.

line (and that defined in relation to the mode of production) is overwhelmingly important to the explanation of the current workings and future evolution of societies at given stages. In practice, there are very few societies where a two-systact structure is maintained intact for any length of time. Not only does the diversity of roles in even relatively simple societies make it unlikely (to say nothing of the chances of inconsistent rankings in the three separate dimensions of structure), but the existence of a single dividing-line between two and only two clearly distinguishable systacts is itself likely to invite attempts to break it down – as in Rwanda (Codere 1962) it spectacularly did.

As an example of a three-systact society, I have already cited early Anglo-Saxon England. It is true that the salience of the division between earls, *ceorls* and slaves may in part be a function of the paucity of the sources: already by the time of the Laws of Ine, the structure of Wessex, at any rate, is visibly more complicated and the gradations of rank among formally free landholders are further cross-cut by a corporate ecclesiastical hierarchy. But there is nothing inherently implausible in the supposition that in the first generations following their arrival in Britain, the Anglo-Saxons were a relatively undifferentiated people who were led by a warrior nobility and at the same time absorbed into their households servile dependents drawn from the indigenous population which they had subjugated or displaced. The difficulty in finding examples of self-evidently three-systact societies is not that it is inherently unlikely, but that, as where there are only two, the more clear-cut the structure the more impermanent it is likely to be.* A division into 'upper', 'middle' and 'lower' is familiar enough: I have commented already in Section 12 on the frequency with which a 'middle' rank of some kind is explicitly distinguished by a vernacular term. But, as I also remarked, this is apt to be in a context of increasing differentiation, and the accretion of power available for distribution between a now so designated 'upper', 'middle' and 'lower' group or category will also have generated the possibility of further differentiation within the three. Thus, the Spanish *clase media* of the nineteenth century was designated as such at the same time as the roles which constituted it were being progressively differentiated from those of the so-called *clases acomodadas* – the emerging *haute bourgeoisie* who were

* An interesting and unusual example, to which I shall return in Chapter 3, is the Jesuit state in Paraguay, where the converted Guarané Indians in the 'reductions' formed a middle stratum between the Jesuits above them and the Negro slaves below them; but it was still a part of the Spanish Colonial empire, to whose rulers the Jesuits were subject in their turn.

moving steadily closer to the dominant élite and away from the ill-paid, politically discontented and socially marginal members of the *clase media*, who were left behind in a 'calvary of keeping up appearances by means of "double employment"' (R. Carr 1982, p. 287).

Differentiation of this kind is, moreover, often compounded by structural inconsistencies between the three dimensions. The German *Mittelstand*, for example, has its English counterpart in the late nineteenth- and early twentieth-century 'middle class' whose members, as G. K. Chesterton was to remark in his *Autobiography*, were so distinctively 'in the middle' as to be no more likely 'to drop an aitch than to pick up a title'. But, as many commentators then and since have observed, the English 'middle class', however distinctive as a status-group, never constituted a distinctive political faction in the way that the German *Mittelstand* did;* and a threefold division in any case ignores the gulf separating the 'respectable' working class from unskilled, un- or under-employed, near-destitute and criminal. There are, accordingly, contexts in which *a* threefold division of a society will force itself on all rival observers; but there are very few societies of which it can plausibly be reported that they consist of three systacts only. There can, for example, be no dispute that French society in 1789 was divided into three and only three estates or that the division was directly relevant to the outbreak of the French Revolution. But it was relevant to the outbreak of the Revolution precisely because, as events were to show, it no longer corresponded – if it ever had† – to the other divisions within the overall systactic structure.

A division into four systacts is, as I have earlier suggested, more plausible in a wide variety of cases. There is an élite, however modest; there is an 'underclass', however small; and in between, there is not only a body of productive labourers (who may, of course, be significantly differentiated among themselves) but also some group or category of administrators, supervisors, clerics, advisers or managers who are, however, subordinate in turn to the élite. But by the stage at which functional differentiation and the accretion of power have made these

* Not that explicitly political consciousness was wholly unknown to the English middle class: as remarked by Brewer (1982, p. 230) of Wilkite radicalism, 'It is the pseudo-Masonic societies, the lodges and trading clubs which link the economic and social to the political aspirations of the middling sort.' But collective organization along these lines was coalition- rather than systact-based, and the Wilkite coalition was very short-lived.

† The clergy had always been internally differentiated just as much as the nobility and the *tiers état*: indeed, they reproduced within themselves many of the systactic conflicts of the wider society, as corporations so often do (Hutt 1957).

broad distinctions apparent, there will also have arisen the possibility of further internal differentiation. Moreover, these further dividing-lines will, in turn, be cross-cut by regional, sexual and ethnic differences, membership of corporate sub-systems, and variable degrees of consistency across semi-autonomous ecclesiastical and military hierarchies. Consider English society in the later Middle Ages. A fourfold distinction can be drawn clearly enough: there are the great magnates and bishops owing allegiance to no lord but the King; there are the bailiffs, burgesses, notaries, priests, clerks, sheriffs and other ancillary supervisors and officials; there are the dependent cultivators and artisans; and there are the landless vagrants, the paupers, brigands, beggars, mountebanks and outlaws. But to leave the itemization of roles at that would be to leave out much that any researcher with a theoretical purpose in view would need reported as well. It is not just that those listed would have to be assigned a corporate or associational as well as a societal location. Account has also to be taken of traders, mercenaries, moneylenders, small proprietors, shopkeepers, tinminers ('tinners', as they were known, who were exempted from tax and removed from pleas of villein), goldsmiths, aldermen, yeomen and domestic servants of varying rank and function none of whom fit at all neatly into a simple fourfold division.

It is, therefore, hardly surprising that societies should be difficult to divide both clearly and comprehensively into any particular number of systacts, even if certain well-demarcated strata are discernible within them. They are much more likely to appear as a 'vertical mosaic' – the metaphor applied by John Porter (1969) to twentieth-century Canada, where a multi-layered structure of roles is cross-cut by intricate ethnic, regional and religious in addition to corporate and associational differentiation. It is true that under either endogenous or exogenous pressure, societies can sometimes disclose widening rifts between systacts which had earlier appeared to grade into one another along an even continuum. But there is then the risk that the observer may be mistaking an ephemeral coalition of interests for an enduring feature of the structure.* If we revert to the model of the inverted pyramid, then with the single exception of age-set societies there is no reason to expect

* It can, however, happen that an initial coalition of interests between adjacent roles leads to a subsequent conflict between differentiated systacts: thus, in the *bonnes villes* of sixteenth-century France, there was a split between merchants and office-holders as a direct consequence of the earlier success of the office-holders in ministering to, and profiting from, the merchants' needs for their services (B. Chevalier 1983, Ch. 6) – the office-holders became 'noble' while the merchants remained 'honourable' only.

to find clear-cut dividing-lines forming a series of parallel planes. Instead, there are likely to be clusters of roles which only here and there share a distinctive area of three-dimensional space, and which even then may be occupied by persons who simultaneously occupy other roles elsewhere.

In any case, to divide a society into a fixed number of systacts is at best to report a distribution of power among the incumbents of its itemized roles which happens to be particularly clear-cut as observed at one particular time. It is true that where the culture is static and the structural division is into mutually acknowledged, self-perpetuating strata between which mobility is restricted to a minimum, it will be only the incumbency of roles which is changing, not the distribution of power between them. But no society, however stratified, is totally immune to demographic pressures which are bound to influence, if not the rate of individual mobility between strata, at least their relative size and thereby, perhaps, the social distance between them; and even in 'traditional' societies where roles are normally refilled by persons born into adjacent locations, there is likely to be a flow of hypogamous and hypergamous women* who take a secondary rank above or below their stratum of origin. Indeed where, as over most of Africa, rates of endogamy are minimal and the practice of the dowry is replaced by the practice of bridewealth, not only will the formation of strata be inhibited but even that of classes (Goody 1976, Ch. 8).

§17. The further transition from systact formation to collective action can be said to have occurred, broadly speaking, when a significant proportion of the members of a defined group or category are observed to act by virtue of their roles in pursuit of the maintenance or enhancement of the power attaching to them and, therefore, of the location of the systact which they form. It is not necessary for all, or even a majority of, the individual members of the systact to take action or even to approve of it, provided that whatever action *is* taken is taken on their behalf. Thus, many members of an industrial workforce may refuse to take part in a collective withdrawal of labour by which, if it succeeds, their economic location will be improved; many members of an aspiring status-group may disapprove of their spokesmen's explicit claims to higher prestige although their own prestige will rise if those

* Or, more rarely, men: deliberate male hypergamy is reported in, for example, Hawaii where a person 'usually but not exclusively a male' wanting to claim high status and thereby political position had either to advance appropriate genealogical claims or to select a high-status spouse (Earle 1978, pp. 174–5).

claims are accepted; and many non-combatants in a civil war will gain political influence or autonomy if the war is won by activists who have taken to arms on behalf of the faction to which they belong. It does not matter how many members of the same systact would not, if questioned, even articulate a conscious sense of relative deprivation, let alone determination to act on it. The critical condition is that the behaviour observed should be directed to some modification of the existing mode of the distribution of power by which the common interest which makes the systact a systact would be advanced.

On the other hand, there are certain conditions under which attribution of collective consciousness would be mistaken despite the appearance of collective action. Thus, it would be wrong to report a coalition of systact members in pursuit of individual upward mobility as systactic action. Nor, even if collective action is both intense and widespread, can cases be counted where those acting are being manipulated for other purposes from without. This does not exclude leadership by members of other systacts: indeed it is something of a commonplace that peasant rebellions are apt to be bourgeois-led.* But if, for example, a peasant community is being manipulated by a local *caudillo* or *cacique* who has no intention of redressing the peasantry's grievances and seeks only to bring pressure to bear on the central government for his own advantage, it must be a misreportage to speak of the peasantry as acting out of collective consciousness of their systactic interest. And finally, the membership of the systact must be relatively stable, not so much in the sense that rates of inflow and outflow need be particularly low as in the sense that incumbency of roles within the systact must not be too short-term. To revert to the example of management trainees within a corporate hierarchy: they may agitate or petition for improved conditions for themselves and the workers whose roles and therefore interests they are for the moment sharing, but they cannot be said to share a collective consciousness with them.

The necessary and sufficient conditions of collective consciousness are, however, often met in one or more areas within the total pattern even of a very complex society's roles. As an example, consider the *lower* 'middle class' in England in the late nineteenth and early twentieth century. It is a particularly good example because its undeniable identity

* This is not, however, to imply that a generalization could be sustained to the effect that peasants are incapable of autonomous systactic action: rebellion aside, the peasantry of Lower Austria, for example, in the late nineteenth and early twentieth century formed their own mass-membership pressure group (the *Niederösterreichischer Bauernbund*) and dominated the *Christlichsozial* party at all levels of its leadership (G. Lewis 1978).

can be, and is, very differently interpreted by theorists of rival schools. For a start, the term 'class' is, strictly, a misnomer, since the roles which at that time clustered so closely together in a distinctive space below the professional and managerial classes and above the upper working class differed in their relation to the means of production – small urban proprietors on the one hand and junior clerical employees on the other.* But the changes which took place in English society after 1870 imposed not only a common economic location on both,† but also a common social status and a common political interest. Their status location is abundantly documented in novels, reminiscences, academic or journalistic studies, and journals such as *The Office*, *The Clerk's Journal* or *The Clerk's Gazette*. Their political location derived not merely from an innate conservatism but also from an ideology of 'jingoism' which, although found at all levels of late Victorian English society, was particularly 'manifest, visible and widespread' here (R. N. Price 1977, p. 91). Thus despite, or even because of, the rapidity of social change in England as a whole, this particular systact can be seen not only to have shared a distinctive location acknowledged no less from within than from without, but also to have articulated among its members a particularly keen sense of relative deprivation – to whatever little long-term effect on the distribution of power which gave rise to it.

In the majority of cases, accordingly, the observer's initial report will be of a distribution of roles and their incumbents, of which some will be very visibly located at a distinctive level but others will occupy only an indeterminate and sparsely populated area of social space. Yet the rarity of clearly demarcated and collectively conscious systacts whose relative location is explicitly laid down by strict institutional rules is not so much of a difficulty in the way of explaining the workings and evolution of different societies as it may appear. For just as it is only those people who *do* pursue their interests whose actions can explain the

* For theorists for whom relations to the means of production are the paramount criterion, there should be added to 'what is conventionally defined as the petty bourgeoisie' – small businessmen, independent small professionals and craftsmen, self-employed intellectuals and agricultural smallholders – 'persons unaccounted for by the census, the self-employed in illegal activities' (D. L. Johnson 1982, p. 200). But these are in a highly discrepant status-group – unless and for as long as they are successfully passing as 'respectable'.

† Both were exposed to the 'full force of the market', the first 'over sales, competition and interest rates', while the second 'were particularly poorly organized within the labour market' (Crossick 1977, p. 14) at a time when the influx of potential recruits had increased in consequence of the Education Act of 1870 and the economy was going into a downturn. For the difference from the world of the mid Victorian 'counting house', see Lockwood (1958, Ch. 1).

distribution of power, so it is only those roles which *do* have the potential for systact formation and collective consciousness that can explain changes (or the successful prevention of changes) in a society's mode of production, persuasion and coercion. They are the carriers of the practices which, given the continuing competition for power, social selection selects. No large and complex society can in practice be defined completely by an itemization of every single one of its roles. But there is no need to make the attempt. Just as the question for the practising sociologist to ask is not 'How many systacts are there?' but 'Have I missed any out?', so is the criterion for the itemization of roles not 'Have I missed any out?' but 'Have I missed any out to which there attach systactic identity, collective consciousness and a sense of relative deprivation which might find outlet in collective action?'

PERVASIVE ROLES AND CENTRAL INSTITUTIONS

§18. Once a society's principal roles have been itemized and such systacts as they may constitute identified, its structure and culture can be so reported as will enable rival theorists to test their conflicting explanations of how it works and what has caused it to evolve as it has, their conflicting descriptions of what it is like for its members to live in, and their conflicting evaluations of whether it is better or worse from their own point of view than it might have been. But in many instances, there will almost be forced upon observers of all theoretical schools certain initial conclusions about its structure and culture. These conclusions are, broadly speaking, to the effect that there is one institution, or perhaps one set of practices observable in several institutions, which is self-evidently central to the pattern of social relations as a whole. To point it out need not be to presuppose the validity of any chosen theory of the society's workings and evolution (although of course it may): it can be to say no more than that no observer can fail to be struck by the pervasiveness of the practices and roles connected with – as it might be – slavery, or pawnship, or the *hacienda*, or the Party, or the 'cash nexus', or the 'web of kinship', or the large industrial corporation, or the Mafia, or the bureaucracy, or the Church.

Consider pawnship, for example, as it has been observed in a number of the matrilineal societies of central Africa. It is not found in all of them. But where it is, every member of the society is affected by it, since the roles of both pawn and pawn-owner are matrilineally transmitted, anyone is liable to be pawned at any time, and the same person can simultaneously occupy the roles both of pawn and pawn-owner. The system is such, therefore, that it can be said of it that 'There is so much to be gained by working it well, by under-writing one another's claims to pawns, by milking one's owner, and by pleasing one's pawns, that everyone is involved in it up to the neck' (M. Douglas 1974, p. 303). Theoretically, it may or may not be the case that the function of pawnship is to moderate the otherwise disruptive claims of matrilineal kinsmen in societies of small autonomous villages lacking a strong central judiciary, that the latent *Weltanschauung* underlying it makes the experience of those involved qualitatively different from that of the members of other matrilineal societies organized in small autonomous villages where pawnship is unknown, or that the apparent general interest in making it work well means that they are better off in their own terms with it than without it.* But no rival observer could fail to agree that it did pervade Lele society at the time in question.

Or consider further the Mexican *hacienda*. To many observers, it was up to 1910 the dominant social and political, as well as economic, institution of the society (cf. McBride 1923, pp. 40–1, 81). By this they tended to mean not only that the *hacendados* constituted the most powerful group or category in Mexican society, but that their outlook and mores were anachronistically 'feudal' and that it would therefore be a thoroughly good thing if their excessively large holdings of cultivable land were redistributed among small *rancheros* and Indian villagers forthwith. Now these implications are not only pre-emptive but, as further research has shown, highly questionable. Many *hacendados* were heavily in debt, and some owed money to their resident peons rather than the other way round.† Many *haciendas* were sold either to the Church or for disposal into smaller lots; most depended on wage-labour, rather than the labour of service tenants; much *hacienda* land was let out to rent-payers or sharecroppers; many *hacendados* were so far from being 'feudal' in outlook that they were either simple rentiers on the one hand or highly commercialized wheat-farmers, cane-growers or stock-breeders on the other; and in some parts of the country they were not dominant at all, since 'removal of the Indians from their land and

* See for example McSheffrey (1983, pp. 362–3), who cites the testimony of Brodie Cruickshank, *Eighteen Years on the Gold Coast of Africa* (London, 1853), for the conclusion that the condition of pawns in the nineteenth century became increasingly assimilated to that of slaves as interest rates came to range between 50% and 100%.

† Cf. Brading (1978, p. 26) on 'the paradox of peons "bound" not through debt, but through fear of losing unpaid wages' – their employer being, it might well be, unable even to pay his annuity or mortgage debt to a local ecclesiastical institution.

communities would have been contrary to the economic interests of the most powerful class in the province: the Spanish merchants' (Waterbury 1975, pp. 420–1). Yet for all that, it is not inaccurate to report the *hacienda* as the central institution of Mexican society. Even though the power of the *hacendados* was less than it has often been made out to be and (as we have seen) their individual interests often conflicted, social relations in what was still a predominantly agrarian society did revolve around the *haciendas*: the Indian villagers, the merchants of the provincial towns, the clergy, the politicians, the migrant day-labourers, the army officers and the dirt-farming smallholders all stood to them in relations of domination and cooperation of one kind or another no less than did their resident peons, their rent-paying tenants, their sharecropping '*medieros*', or the squatters on the outer fringes of their imperfectly policed estates.

In many societies, there is no central institution whose constituent roles are anywhere nearly pervasive throughout. As the example of the Mexican *hacienda* shows, an institution which is unarguably central in many or even most regions may be peripheral in another;* and there are often large groups or categories of persons whose relations with one another are conducted wholly outwith the range of institutions which pervade those of their fellow-citizens elsewhere. Moreover, there are many societies where institutions which will turn out to be central at a later stage of evolution coexist for some time with a still pervasive set of roles which will seem peripheral only with hindsight. The urban merchants of tenth- and eleventh-century North Italy may have been precursors of the dominant bourgeoisies of the independent city-states of the twelfth and thirteenth centuries. But it would be a mistake to fail to see that in the earlier period, their relations with both the rest of their society and each other were set in a context in which the central institutions and pervasive roles still depended on the ownership of land (Wickham 1981, pp. 91–2).

On the other hand, it can also happen that roles are more rather than less pervasive than they appear at first sight. Slavery, for example, can pervade a set of institutions to an extent which goes beyond the mere number of slaves or the degree of their subordination: in Classical Rome, slavery was a matter not just of the powerlessness of the majority of the agricultural and domestic labour force, but of the conceptions of work, status and discipline which informed the relations of the dominant stratum with their free – and freed – fellow citizens as well. Whether

* The same holds for the institution of the manor in medieval Europe: cf. Postan (1972, pp. 97–9) for England and James (1982, pp. 195–6) for France.

the centrality of an institution in this sense is at the same time a clue to the stability (or otherwise) of the society is a question which can only be settled on other grounds. But the initial itemization of roles needs not only to specify their structural location but also to take account of the extent to which some of them may, culturally speaking, permeate the rest.

§19. In some cases, moreover, this permeation is such that a whole society can be reported as characterized by the involvement of its pervasive roles in one structural dimension at the expense of the other two. It may be that its religious institutions are central and its economic and political relations pervaded by ideological practices; or it may be so extensively commercialized that even ideological and political relations between its members are pervaded by market practices; or it may be so riven by factionalism and violence that its economic and ideological roles are pervaded by coercive practices.

Where ideological sanctions are pervasive, they may be either religious or secular or some combination of the two. But the most obvious example is the Indian system of caste where, for all the significance of differences in land tenure and access to the means of coercion, generations of observers have been struck by the pervasiveness of the ideology of birth, ritual purity and prescribed social contact and the pattern of social relations which it engenders. I have remarked already that specialists are in disagreement over the relative importance of ideological, economic and coercive sanctions in preserving the culture and structure of village India. But whether or not the ideology is, as it were, base rather than superstructure, whether or not there underlies the self-images of Indian villagers a latent *Weltanschauung* wholly antithetical to Western notions of equality, and whether or not the *jajmani* system is a good thing for the landless as well as the landowners,* any report of the structure and culture of a traditional Indian village will have to acknowledge that the intentions and beliefs which inform its practices and institutions are permeated by a distinctive conception of hierarchy. These practices and institutions have,

* There is a parallel here with Central African pawnship in that such judgements as Epstein's (1967, p. 250) that 'Since Indian villagers, landowners and landless alike, were all subject to the hazards of the climate and the environment, they were all prepared to participate in a system which offered all of them at least the minimum necessities of life, except in times of extreme crop failure and general famine', are perfectly compatible with a comment such as that of Alavi (1973, p. 54) that the system is not reciprocal when land is short and 'ties of economic dependence and political domination are now stronger despite the erosion of the ritual relationships'.

admittedly, their economic and political aspects. But, as Dumont (1970, p. 105) says of *jajmani* relations, 'whilst directly religious and "economic" prestations are mingled together, this takes place within the prescribed order, the religious order'.

Perhaps the best example of a society permeated by economic rather than ideological or coercive sanctions is eighteenth-century England, of which it has been said (McKendrick 1982, p. 13) that 'consumer behaviour was so rampant and the acceptance of commercial attitudes so pervasive that no one in the future should doubt that the first of the world's consumer societies had unmistakably emerged by 1800'.* It was not just foreign observers who were struck by it, but the English themselves: Defoe is perhaps their most prolific and eloquent native spokesman, but he is one among many. No observer seeking to itemize the society's roles could fail to notice not merely the extent to which new ones deriving from commercial practices had come into being since the end of the seventeenth century but also the extent to which existing ones were being commercialized and their incumbents coming to occupy a new, commercial role in addition to a pre-existing one. Thus, a noble landowner might invest in cutting a canal or laying a turnpike or underwriting an insurance risk while his younger brother – unlike his Continental counterpart – went directly into trade,† and both would, like many of their social inferiors, be active buyers and sellers of stocks and shares. Beneath them and their like was an expanding, diversifying and increasingly prospering middle class ranging from the affluent bankers, high-feed attorneys and profit-hungry slave-traders down through the 'anthill of petty-traders, horse-dealers, builders, innkeepers and manufacturers who excelled in turning a penny for themselves: men prepared to work hard, adapt to the ups and downs of the market, put their irons in many fires and drive hard bargains' (R. Porter 1982, p. 94) to the small craftsmen and shopkeepers enmeshed in the outer reaches of the network of credit extending from the metropolis into the shires (Holderness 1975–6); and beneath them again was a swelling body of wage-earners competing for work within an increasingly specialized labour market. The subservience to Mammon of the proverbial 'nation of shopkeepers' does not, of course, mean that either

* Or before: Thirsk (1978, p. 106) is prepared to talk of 'the growth of a consumer society' in England as early as the late seventeenth century.

† It is true that by the latter part of the century, French nobles too were *dérogés* only if they entered *commerce de détail* and many of them played a considerable part in the *poussée industrielle* (Chaussinand-Nogaret 1976, pp. 129, 150); but no observer (so far as I am aware) has ever maintained that the French nobility was *more* commercially minded in 1780 than the English.

coercive or ideological sanctions had withered away. Eighteenth-century England was still a society dominated in the dimension of prestige by a hereditary aristocracy to which deference was freely accorded and entry eagerly sought, and the use of violence by the agents of the state against the rebellious or deviant among its subjects is as readily observable as their recourse to bribery and corruption. But the reference to Mammon is not a purely descriptive gloss to be qualified with an 'it was as if' or an 'as it were'. The society *was* permeated with commercial attitudes to a very much greater extent than could be inferred just from a ranking of persons and their roles in order of income and wealth.

For a society where roles deriving from coercive sanctions are pervasive, one of the best examples is once again late Republican Rome. The stratum which dominated it did so, as we have seen, across the institutional board. But it is impossible not to be struck by the extent to which the power which its members wielded rested on their ability to use force – and, it might be added, their lack of inhibition about doing so. It is not merely that their numerous slaves were systematically chained and beaten* and the several slave revolts put down with ruthless ferocity, or that arbitrary power of life and death was wielded by magistrates over their fellow-citizens. It is rather that the ostensible protection of the law was in practice available only to the strong: the traditional maxim *vim vi repellere licet* meant a great deal more than that the law-abiding citizen had the right of self-defence (Lintott 1968). The only protection against armed gangs roaming the streets in the service of one patron was the protection of another; in the countryside, landowners could arm their slaves for murder or kidnap with impunity; the collection of taxes from rural freeholders was carried out by physical extortion against which appeal to a provincial governor was futile; and where a private plaintiff sought to take a stronger defendant to court he had to look to his own means of coercion for the purpose – there is no evidence that the praetors ever used their servants to do it (Kelly 1966, pp. 8–11). In their dealings alike with their inferiors, their superiors and their equals, formally free Romans enacted roles as pervasively informed by the sanction of violence as eighteenth-century Englishmen's roles were informed by the sanction of loss instead of gain or Indian villagers' roles informed by the sanctions of an ideology of purity and pollution.

* This remark is not invalidated by the *humanitas* shown by, say, Cicero or the younger Pliny to their favoured household slaves, or by the conditions enjoyed by commercial slaves earning their manumission: the penalities were always there, and they were unhesitatingly used (for a celebrated case where every single slave in the household was executed following the murder by one of them of their master, a praefect of the city, see Tacitus, *Annals* XIV.42–5).

None of these observations licences an inference to the classification of these societies as 'caste', 'market' or 'slave' societies respectively, if by that is meant that the ideology of purity and pollution, the commercialization of social relations, or the forcible subjection of the greater part of the civilian workforce can be invoked to explain without further argument why the whole set of their institutions is as it is reported to be. But there are many societies of which all rival observers will be bound to report that they are characterized by pervasive roles defined by practices which rest on one of the three kinds of inducement or sanction rather than another, even if that in itself tells us nothing about why those practices were selected at the expense of others during the course of the society's earlier evolution.

§20. We are now at the frontier between the reportage of a society's structure and culture which observers of all theoretical schools could in principle check against the recording angel's archives and the explanation of how it functions and why it has evolved as it has. Any itemization of its roles and specification of its institutions implies, to be sure, an initial categorization of it as being of one kind rather than another; but this can be transposed *salva veritate* into whatever terms may be required for the purpose of framing and testing a chosen explanation (or description or evaluation) of it. The frontier is likely to be crossed, however, almost as soon as one society's institutions are contrasted with another's. Theory-neutrality can still be preserved if the researcher says no more to his readers than that both are characterized – to repeat my same examples – by chattel slaves or mercenary armies or parliamentary elections or a hereditary nobility. But what if, say, in one society the slaves are all in the army and none on the land while in the next they are all on the land and none in the army? Or if in one the nobility are all supporters of the government and in the next they are all its opponents?

It is for this reason that any serious comparison of two or more societies by reference to their central institutions leads directly into consideration of analogues and homologues. Counterfactual hypotheses are implicit even where they are not overtly framed, for to say that any practice, role or institution does or does not have the same function in one society as in another is to make a claim about what would or would not be the case if one or more antecedent conditions had been other than they were. To say that in Classical Rome, in contrast to Ottoman Turkey, slaves were used to work the land while a citizen army fought wars of conquest is already to imply that the pattern is not fortuitous;

and to say, for example, that in twentieth-century America class is the analogue of caste in the allocation of persons to occupational roles whereas race is the homologue of caste in assigning persons to roles in a hierarchy of ritual purity and pollution is to make an explicit claim of institutional cause and effect.

The same is also true where similar but not identical roles are reported for different societies. Consider for example the role of *caudillo*, defined as the leader or patron of an armed following of clients whose power rests on his ability to reward his followers by either exploiting or upsurping the power of the central government. The role is by no means peculiar to the Latin American societies to which it is most often applied. A petty nobleman in seventeenth-century France leading a local peasant *jacquerie* in an attack on the hated collectors of the salt-tax fits it almost as well. Yet it might be misleading to designate him a *caudillo*, not so much because the descriptive overtones seem out of place – a Mexican *vaquero* in his tight trousers, wide sombrero and bullet-stuffed bandolier would not be all that incongruous in the world of the Three Musketeers – as because there is an implied pre-emption of a functional explanation. Homologous groups can be found in many different institutional contexts: private armies, adolescent gangs, and bands of criminals or bandits are all homologues of the *caudillo* and his following. But *caudillismo* is a characteristically Latin American phenomenon because of the circumstances of the period between the achievement of independence from Spain (or, in the case of Brazil, Portugal) and the subsequent re-establishment of central authority in the hands of urban élites able to mobilize the necessary economic, ideological and coercive resources for the purpose. Hence the deliberately pre-emptive definition of *caudillismo* given by Silvert (1968, p. 347): 'a personalistic, quasi-military government of provincial origin and economic interest serving a function of loose national integration in periods of decay and withdrawal of effective central authority'. This makes explicit the implication of function and thereby points deliberately to the analogue not of local rebels against the tax-gatherer so much as of magnates to whom a monarchy with limited resources concedes local autonomy in return for acknowledgement of its national legitimacy – a topic to which I shall be returning more than once in Chapters 3 and 4.

The final moral to be drawn, however, before structural and cultural alternatives are analyzed as such and modes of the distribution of power distinguished from one another, is the relative narrowness of the range of possible institutional variation. Whatever may be the variants which can correctly be identified as analogues or homologues of the *caudillo* and his following, the number of possible candidates is not large. On one side, the limiting case is the secessionist leader who severs his tie to the central institutions of the society altogether. On the other, it is the local *cacique* or 'boss' who retains his following only by integrating his role into central institutions now powerful enough to force that concession from him. In between, there are many permutations on the relation of patron to client through which the *caudillo*'s power is expressed and sustained. But once given a society whose central government is, from whatever causes, weak, there are not that many ways in which 'loose national integration' can be maintained at all. There are federal roles, like that of the *tagos* in Ancient Thessaly, who was periodically elected to the headship of a loose, segmentary state dominated by large local landowners directly controlling their own tied labour force; there are ceremonial roles, like that of the Japanese emperor (*tennō*) under the shoguns, who was retained as the ideological focus of national legitimacy while the means of coercion were wielded as necessary against semi-autonomous regional *daimyō* by the shoguns themselves; there are plenipotentiary roles, like those of the *missi dominici* and the *dhāmma-mahāmāttas*, who both represented the ruler in outlying territories which he could not hope to visit regularly himself; and there are roles more directly analogous to that of *caudillo* under 'feudal' monarchies where, as in Germany under the Ottonians, the vassals became stronger than the king* rather than, as in England under William I or Sicily under Roger II, the other way round. But to the question 'how many ways are there of integrating a society whose central authority is in a condition of withdrawal or decay?', the number of answers cannot be many. The one given for any particular society should not be pre-empted in the initial report of its structure and culture. But the converse is that when it *does* come to comparison and contrast with other societies, the limited number of possible analogues and/or homologues will drastically limit the range of relevantly similar roles.

CONCLUSION

§21. In this chapter, there have been set out the terms in which the pattern of social relations observed in any and all societies can be so reported as to test and extend the theory of competitive selection of practices which it is the purpose of this volume to advance. These

* A state of affairs compounded later by the pervasive practice of multiple vassalage, which in Germany (unlike England and France) 'was allowed to pursue unchecked its destructive course' (Ganshof 1952, p. 95).

reports will, therefore, be chosen with that purpose explicitly in view. They will present the structure of the societies cited as a structure of roles and their incumbents whose different locations reflect and perpetuate both the conflicts of interest and the potential for cooperation between them; they will isolate the practices hypothesized as adaptive for one or more designated roles and systacts which carry them; they will disregard any feature of structure or culture which does not relate to the distribution of the means of production, persuasion and coercion and thus to the mechanisms which bring about – or, as it may be, inhibit – social change; and they will categorize the institutions of different societies in terms of the range of alternative possible combinations constitutive of distinctive modes and sub-types of the overall distribution of power.

3
Social structure

STABILITY AND DISSENT

§1. To ask of any reported society 'How does it work?' is to presuppose that the pattern of its constituent roles is stable enough for it to be categorized at all. But stability is a relative matter. Societies are not only sets of itemized roles, but systems of social relations in motion. Quite apart from the continual entry of native-born children, if not also of immigrants, into their roles, and losses by death or emigration, it is hardly plausible to suppose that there has ever been, or ever will be, a society or institutional catchment area in which no single person is trying to alter in any way the existing distribution of power. But there are very different degrees of instability. At one extreme, there are societies so stable that even a participant-observer who spent a lifetime in the field would see no significant difference in either their itemized roles and the practices defining them or in their rates of social mobility. At the other extreme, there are societies where a few days' visit would be enough to reveal not only the location and content of their itemized roles but also the distribution of their incumbents to be in continuous turmoil. The question 'how do societies work?' is not, therefore, to be construed as 'what keeps them stable within their given mode and sub-type?' so much as 'what keeps them no more unstable than they are?'

It follows from the distinction between forms of change drawn in Section 2 of Chapter 1 that the attempts of societies' members to bring about changes and the instability resulting from their attempts are of four broadly distinguishable kinds. Individual mobility alone, whether achieved through individual effort or through institutional arrangements such as rotation of offices or selection by lot, has, as we have seen, only an indirect effect on either the structure or the culture. There are, accordingly, societies where despite continuous, widespread and even dramatically long-distance rises and falls of persons between roles, the composition of systacts and the distances between them remain virtually unchanged: a good example is Korea, which remained remarkably stable in this sense over the whole period from 1392 to 1910 despite periodic invasion and violent turnover in the membership of the governing élite (Henderson 1968, Chs. 1 and 2).* The struggle for individual mobility may be so intense and so widespread as to amount to near-continuous civil war. But the resulting changes are in, not of, the society: the competitors for power accept the existing institutions and practices, and both structure and culture remain intact.†

Relatively less stable, and more commonly found in practice, are those societies where individual mobility (whether peaceable or violent) is combined with collective – that is, where roles and thereby systacts are changing their relative locations concomitantly with the movement of persons between roles. In a society where individual mobility is readily feasible, the two are virtually bound to reinforce one another. If there is a sudden rise in the wealth, social standing and political influence of, say, yeomen or merchants or soldiers, this is likely of itself to attract the incumbents of other roles to attempt to join the ranks of the yeomen, merchants or soldiers. But it is impossible for roles to move, and their incumbents with them, independently of any significant changes of other kinds. The nearest to an ideal-typical example is 'Sanskritization' (Srinivas 1952, p. 30) in traditional Indian society – that is, a collective rise in the ritual hierarchy of purity and pollution on the part of a *jāti* whose members have deliberately adopted for the purpose the practices of their superiors.‡ But it can happen also, and with not much more of a concomitant increase in individual mobility, in societies where the dominant institutions are caste-like only in a tenuous sense: thus, the attorneys of eighteenth-century England, who, although an individual attorney might be a 'gentleman', were until the middle of

* The qualification should, however, be added that the invasions did significantly reduce the number of slaves in the society: the mass emancipations made possible in the consequent disturbances appear not to have been more than partly reversed by re-enslavement (sources cited by Patterson 1982, p. 289).

† This kind of instability thus corresponds to the second of the two kinds of *stasis* distinguished by Aristotle (*Politics* 1301b), where dissent is not directed against the system, but the dissenters merely wish to gain control of it themselves – with, in some cases, the further aim of making some mild constitutional changes, or perhaps creating a new, or abolishing an old, governmental role (*archē*): a good modern example is the French 'revolution' of 1830 (Pinkney 1972).

‡ Whether this will be enough without some concomitant change of occupational roles is, however, debatable: Bopegamage and Kulahalli (1971, p. 131) argue that 'Since the prestige of occupation is fixed, a caste cannot rise in the hierarchy unless it loosens itself from the ritually low occupation.'

the century treated virtually as lackeys, came to insist so successfully on the collective respectability of which they felt relatively deprived that by 1814 a character in one of Maria Edgeworth's novels could be made to say 'There are no such things as attorneys now in England, they are all turned into solicitors and agents' (Robson 1959, p. 152 n. 1).

Cultural evolution can, however, occur without either individual or collective mobility, whether by gradual diffusion or deliberate imposition of mutant or recombinant practices, in such a way as will change the content of roles without at the same time changing the location either of the roles themselves or of their present incumbents. One of the most striking examples is Japan after the Meiji Restoration of 1868. It is true that the goal of forced modernization was not attained without some disruption of the previous order; the samurai did not accept the surrender of their traditional function until after the defeat of the Satsuma Rebellion of 1877, and the Land Tax of 1873 aroused violent discontent among the peasantry. Furthermore, the introduction of universal compulsory education in 1890, together with an increase in the number of 'white-collar' occupational roles, did promote individual mobility to the point that social distinctions came increasingly to depend on achievement rather than ascription (Norbeck 1970, p. 176). But it seems agreed among specialists that given the magnitude of the cultural changes which the Meiji government succeeded in bringing about, the structural changes in the traditional social hierarchy were minimal, from the ex-*daimyō* at the top through the now demilitarized samurai, the urban commercial class, the peasantry in the villages and the outcastes (*burakumin*) at the bottom – with women at all levels remaining economically, socially and politically subordinate to men.

It follows, accordingly, that there is a six-stage continuum along which societies can in principle be ranged. At one end are societies so totally stable that their members never move from their initial adult roles, which are both identically located to those of their parents and defined by identical practices. Next come societies where people move up or down from role to role and enter adulthood in roles (or careers) which may be very differently located from those of their parents, but the practices defining the roles remain the same. Next come societies where roles are in addition changing their relative location and taking their existing incumbents with them, but with so minimal a mutation or recombination of practices that the culture remains virtually the same. Next come societies where novel roles are emerging and existing ones disappearing, but the movement of persons from one role to another is lateral only. Next come societies where cultural change is accompanied by individual mobility between the roles but the structure is otherwise unchanged. Next, and at the other end, are societies where both structural and cultural changes are occurring simultaneously. These distinctions are, admittedly, ideal-typical: the force of 'in principle' is that few if any societies can in practice be assigned a place along the continuum, since quite apart from the difficulty of defining what is to count as a significant extent or degree of instability, the same society may be undergoing changes of different kinds in its different parts, both institutional and geographical. Analytically, however, the distinctions are both precise and exhaustive, and thereby furnish a framework within which hypotheses about the stability or otherwise of whatever societies are chosen for study can be modelled in testable form.

Moreover, these distinctions relate directly to the notion of adaptation entailed by a theory which links social evolution to the competitive selection of practices. Where a society is totally stable, it follows that its practices are adaptive for all its constituent roles in their relations both with each other and with their common environment. Under these conditions, individual mobility is a joint function of genetic endowment, psychological motivation and the demographic pressures imposed by fertility (or immigration) on the one hand and availability of roles at chosen locations on the other. A modicum of collective mobility may likewise occur, as in the example of 'Sanskritization', without the emergence of any mutant or recombinant practices. But when there does come about a cultural change and roles appear, disappear or are more or less rapidly modified out of recognition, then it is essential not only to identify the practices responsible for the change but also to establish for what carriers they are adaptive. If the answer is that they are adaptive only for those already dominant within their own institutional areas, then the change will be of the kind to be labelled (if it is sufficiently radical) 'revolution from above'.* But where mutant or recombinant practices emerge which are adaptive for subordinate roles and systacts, there will follow an evolution to a different mode (or at least sub-type) of the distribution of power which is 'revolutionary' in the conventional sense, and the resulting movement of persons and roles will be of the

* Which may, as in the Russian case (to which Stalin himself applied the phrase), be the sequel to a revolution from below: cf. the characterization by E. H. Carr (1971, p. 445) of the forced industrialization which Stalin carried out as 'an economic revolution directed by the political initiative and decisions of a ruling group' – a designation which holds equally for Meiji Japan, however different the ideology of the two 'ruling groups' in question. As early as 1799 (Rosenberg 1958, p. 161) a Prussian minister talking to a French *chargé d'affaires* predicted that in his country revolution would come about 'from above'.

kind amounting to a both structural and cultural transformation of the society as a whole.

§2. It is quickly apparent from even a cursory glance at the historical and ethnographic record that stability correlates only fitfully with either the size or the complexity of societies, or with their degree of structural inequality, whether measured by total span of social distance or by the size of the gaps between particular systacts in the space enclosed by the inverted pyramid. Nor is there any consistent correlation with either the extent or the degree to which social relations within and between their constituent roles are based on cooperation rather than domination. It may be true to say that in some small and simple societies stability is assured by the combined constraints of a harsh environment and the close cooperation between its members which the environment more or less requires.* But this is because cooperative practices are, in the particular context, adaptive for all roles: it is equally easy to point to cases like the Ik (Turnbull 1972) where a change in the environment generates both a less cooperative culture and a less egalitarian structure. Moreover, if the argument thus far is well grounded, we should expect to find homologous practices and institutions which in some contexts promote stability and in others the opposite. Consider the purchase of office, of which the classic example is the French '*paulette*', and its English homologue, the purchase of army commissions. Both were initially adaptive for the purchasers and the vendors alike, but both in the end gave rise to conflicts of interest which led to their abolition. Yet their obvious analogue – the Classical Greek institution of *liturgies*, whereby civic duties, including the fitting-out of warships as well as payments for celebrations and festivals, were performed by leading citizens at their own expense under pressure of public opinion and in pursuit of social prestige – was likewise adaptive for the incumbents of both liturgical and governmental roles only for as long as the initial conditions remained unchanged. Only in societies with no effective

* Apposite examples are to be found among South American Indian societies such as the Pilaga, Sharente or Tupino among whom the chief has not only to be materially generous but daily to 'gratify the people of his group with an edifying discourse' stressing the values of peace, harmony and honesty (Clastres 1977, p. 23, citing Steward 1949, p. 343). It is, however, as well to be reminded also that even among the most cooperative hunter-gatherers there are persons who 'desire to hoard rather than share, to marry in, to be lazy and freeload, to try and lord it over others, to be sullen and isolate themselves, or to be quick to argue and fight' (Leacock and Lee 1982, p. 9; cf. E. M. Thomas 1959, p. 183, on 'the normal strains and jealousies of Bushmen'), and that violence is by no means unknown (Lee 1979, p. 398, estimates the !Kung murder rate at 29·3 per 100,000 person-years).

means of imposing regular capital or income taxes on the rich, an ideology of patriotism common to rich and poor citizens alike, and a political system in which the rich could not wholly ignore public opinion could it continue to survive. When the *poleis* were all subordinated to the Roman Empire and that empire was effectively bureaucratized, liturgies became increasingly assimilated to compulsory taxation,* and the change was, as Finley (1973, p. 153) puts it, not 'another brutal innovation by the military absolutism of the Late Empire' but 'the irresistible end of a long development'.

The complex relation of stability to dissent is nowhere better illustrated than in the analogues and homologues of the institution of slavery. It is safe to assume, as I have remarked already, that with few exceptions no slave assents to his or her condition. But not only is slavery sometimes more stable than some of its less coercive analogues, but some of its homologues are much less stable than others. In Classical Athens, which depended on slaves for the performance of tasks ranging from silver-mining to arms manufacture to monumental stone-carving to agricultural labour to domestic service to police work to the keeping of public archives, there is no evidence for any attempted uprising or any concerted refusal to carry out any of these tasks, whereas in societies employing wage-workers or (in the countryside) dependent but formally free tenants the frequency of strikes, stoppages and revolts is abundantly documented. Yet there are societies in which uninhibited recourse to coercion fails to prevent rebellion (in Rome, ten legions were needed to put down Spartacus and his followers in 73 B.C.); and slaves used to perform identical functions can be a cause of stability in one society but instability in another. Contrast, for example, the success of the Ottoman institution of the *devshirme*, whereby young Christian slaves from the conquered territories were taken to be reared as professional soldiers in the Sultan's service, with the self-defeating use of slave soldiers (*achikunda*) by the Portuguese in East Africa in the early nineteenth century. The Ottoman slave soldiers performed their function as an integral part of a successful conquest state. But the more successful of the *achikunda* at once used their position to escape from their masters and set up on their own (Lovejoy 1983, pp. 228–9). It is true that once Ottoman expansion ceased, the systact of 'Janissaries' began to use the

* Roman Egypt is particularly well documented in the surviving papyri, which report a range of responses all the way from 'pillars of local society' who undertook liturgies from which they were legally exempt to refugees who absconded as soon as they even suspected that they were about to be nominated by the *epistratēgos* (N. Lewis 1983, pp. 177–84).

power attaching to their roles to the detriment of the central government (Inalcik 1973, p. 51). But this in turn furnishes an excellent example of how the same practices can confer a different competitive advantage on their carriers if the institutional environment has changed in a way which alters their function.

Slavery also serves to illustrate the difference which can be made by practices related to social mobility. The terms of manumission and the conditions and frequency of its use vary almost as much across the range of societies where slavery is reported as do the forms of the relation between masters and slaves itself. There is no rate of manumission which is optimal for stability. Where it is virtually nil, as in Athens for all categories of slaves and in Rome for those working on the land,* the apparent effect may be either resigned acquiescence (as in the Athenian case) or desperate revolt (as in the Roman). Athenian slaves did, admittedly, run away *en masse* when the opportunity arose in the Peloponnesian War (Thucydides VII.27.5), but there was never an Athenian Spartacus. Yet Rome also offers a striking illustration of the stabilizing effects of large-scale manumission in the non-agricultural sector of its economy. For reasons which the sources do not enable us to reconstruct, the practice of manumission and thereby the creation of a substantial population of freedmen with full citizen rights was established well before the period of the Republic's spectacular expansion by conquest. When, therefore, there was a large influx of slaves among whom were some of the ablest and most industrious members of the working population, the possibility of manumission, whether by purchase, gift or testamentary disposition,† together with their realization of its possibility, had a twofold stabilizing effect. First, it encouraged them in the dutiful performance of the tasks assigned to them; second, it steadily fed into the free population a group or category which did not, as I have already pointed out, constitute a separate systact with its own collective consciousness but rather an aggregate of dissimilarly located persons whose common interest was only in the system itself which had enabled them to achieve their varying degrees

* The exceptions are insignificant, although it is true that a few slaves were manumitted in Athens (including the celebrated banker Pasion) and a few agricultural slaves were manumitted in Rome (Treggiari 1969, pp. 106–10).

† I exclude as an emergency measure offers of manumission made to slaves who are enlisted for the defence of the state in time of war – as happened not only in Greece and Rome but during the War of American Independence, among other cases. In the same category belong offers of liberty to slaves of the enemy, as made for example by the Ostrogothic king Totila to those armed by Tullianus to fight with the Byzantines (Procopius VII.6.13), or by both sides during the *stasis* in Corcyra (Thucydides III.73).

of individual mobility. It is, however, equally easy to point to cases where the prospect of freedom has the opposite effect of heightening the sense of relative deprivation among slaves more impatient for what they now see as a more easily attainable goal: a good example is furnished by the spontaneous mass desertion of slaves from their masters in the Western Sudan in the early years of the twentieth century (Roberts and Klein 1980).

All of these examples serve to confirm that the explanation of social stability is to be sought in practices whose function will vary according to the wider institutional context; and the precise distribution of power among the society's itemized roles may only become visible when put quasi-experimentally to the test. Indeed, the dilemma which this poses could be said to be at least as familiar already to rulers as to sociologists. Rulers have often hesitated between repression and tolerance in the knowledge that only with hindsight will they be able to tell whether their choice was the right one. Was Thrasybulus of Miletus giving good advice when he told his fellow-tyrant Periander of Corinth to cut down all the leading citizens like so many tall ears of corn (Herodotus V.92)? Or would he have done better to be like the oligarchs of Rhodes, whose practices were such as to lead the geographer Strabo to call the Rhodians 'people-caring' (*dēmokēdeis*) although not 'people-ruled' (*dēmokratoumenoi*)?* Perhaps the shrewdest tactic is a minimal but regular measure of economic benevolence combined with a readiness to use the means of coercion where benevolence fails.† There is no way of predicting the answer in advance, and the academic observer is no more likely to guess right than the practising politician. But that is not a reason for supposing that the answer, when it *can* be framed and tested in retrospect, will tell in any way against the theory of competitive selection of practices. On the contrary: it is with hindsight and only with hindsight that quasi-experimental contrasts will reveal which practices functioned to the advantage of which roles and systacts carrying them.

* Strabo XIV.12.5 (who, however, exaggerates the power of the Rhodian magistrates: see O'Neil 1981).

† Eighteenth-century England is a good example of a society where a tradition of modest but obligatory charity among the rich (Mingay 1963, p. 275), coupled with a chronic fear of rioting by the 'lower orders' (Coats 1976, p. 110), functioned at least to some degree to keep dissent under control in the face of an increasing number of poor: remarkably, Parliament saw no need for a police force on the Continental model, even after the Gordon riots (Christie 1985, p. 35). Cf. L. Stone 1972, p. 77; '...the English propertied classes realized very early on that the financial cost of poor relief was a small price to pay for the domestic tranquillity and social deference that resulted'.

§3. There is at the same time a subjective aspect to all this, since institutional instability is, among other things, a function of the extent to which particular incumbents of subordinate roles are disposed to a sense of relative deprivation sufficiently intense that they seek either to modify the practices which define their roles or to escape from them altogether. But whatever may be the influences which dispose some persons to be more or less dissatisfied than others with the existing mode of the distribution of power and their location in it, their feelings are, methodologically speaking, only an intervening variable in the competitive selection of practices. The fact that only some and not other incumbents of similarly located roles will be the carriers of systactic consciousness and the leaders, spokesmen or organizers of collective movements of protest can be taken as read. What is equally incontestable, but much more directly relevant to the argument of this Chapter, is that societies differ widely in the degree to which their mode of the distribution of power is accepted by the members of their subordinate as well as dominant systacts as legitimate. It is perfectly possible for stability to be achieved by a dominant systact which makes no attempt whatever to secure the cooperation of subordinate systacts or roles. But equally, there are societies which are demonstrably stabler than they would otherwise be because their ideology is such as to reconcile, or at least help to reconcile, the incumbents of subordinate roles to their location.*

The merit of any chosen doctrine of legitimacy as a doctrine is, to be sure, a philosophical, not a sociological, matter: whether a regime is morally entitled to claim legitimacy is a question to which the answer will depend on your own evaluative presuppositions and the inferences you draw from them. But if the members of the society themselves subscribe to evaluative presuppositions from which it follows that their rulers are legitimate in their eyes, then the practices thereby generated and sustained may be of critical importance to the society's workings

* This holds equally whether the ideology in question is conservative or revolutionary: for example, a number of observers of twentieth-century Mexico in the aftermath of the establishment of the communal *ejidos* have commented on the way in which the rural poor were given the gratifying sense that '*la terre est à eux*' (F. Chevalier 1966, p. 747; cf. Huizer and Stavenhagen 1974, p. 58) despite the fact that their material circumstances had not significantly improved; cf. e.g. Heath (1973, p. 75) on the popularity of agrarian reform and nationalization of the mines in Bolivia in the aftermath of the revolution of 1953, even though '...it is beyond dispute that most of the mineworkers' initial economic and social gains from the revolution have proved illusory or transient' (Whitehead 1981, p. 313).

and evolution. Priests* (or priestesses), propagandists, *literati*, holders of ritual or ceremonial offices and acknowledged religious or secular authorities on tradition and custom† not only occupy roles which have their own location in the social structure but also influence, by virtue of the practices defining their roles, the location of others. The particular functions of these practices need, as always, to be studied case by case. But two general points are worth making. First, ideological evolution is irreversible not just in the sense that the clock can never literally be put back, but in the further sense that once a doctrine has been challenged any subsequent version has to incorporate some response to that fact: to no society, whatever its culture, can there not be applied the maxim of al-Ghazali that a condition of carrying a traditionalist faith is that the carrier should not know that he is a traditionalist. Second, where the power of a dominant systact *is* credited with legitimacy by those subject to it, this may well be a consequence of the successful exercise of that power itself in the form of what is sometimes called 'ideological hegemony' – that is, restriction of the conditions which would make an effective challenge to its legitimacy possible.‡ From neither of these considerations does it follow that the theory of competitive selection of practices has to be modified. But it does follow that the process of

* There may also be significant variation in the degree of respect accorded to priestly roles even within the same culture: see e.g. Boxer (1969, pp. 242–3) on the 'singularly privileged position in Portuguese society' of ordained priests resulting from the uniquely 'sacerdotal and sacro-magical aspects' of Portuguese Catholicism.

† The vexed question how to distinguish 'religious' from 'secular' ideology is immaterial to the argument here. It makes no difference to anything said in this volume whether religion is so defined as to include Buddhism, Confucianism and Marxism, or whether 'atheistic religion' is construed as a contradiction in terms (cf. Weber's apt reference to the Confucianism of the Chinese *literati* as '*Die religiose* (*oder wenn man will: irreligiose*) *Standesethik dieser Schicht*' (1922, I, p. 239)).

‡ That this state of affairs is itself a cultural universal, or virtually so, is a central contention of the so-called 'critical theory' of the Frankfurt School, with the further complication that it is linked by them to an epistemology which denies the logical separation of explanation from evaluation. But for the purposes of this volume, it does not matter what view of the legitimacy of their society its members would take in an 'ideal speech situation' – if, indeed, that can be specified without circularity. The claim that ideological hegemony is being exercised rests, as the authors of the Frankfurt School themselves accept, on the presupposition that a causal relation can be established to the satisfaction of all rival observers (cf. Geuss 1981, Ch. 3 §3); and to the extent that recognition that this is so brings an acknowledged improvement in the well-being of those who have come to it by reading works of critical theory (or in any other way), it can be accepted by all observers as an 'improvement' in the non-preemptive sense in which, as I argued in Chapter 5 of Volume I, such evaluative terms can be let stand in works of sociology as well as of moral or political philosophy.

selection works differently in this context from where economic or coercive practices are the principal objects of selection.

It would, however, be a mistake to view the function of dominant ideological roles and their defining practices simply in terms of their capacity to reconcile the incumbents of subordinate roles to the location at which they find themselves. In the first place, once legitimacy is explicitly claimed by, or on behalf of, a dominant systact this in itself invites counter-argument to the effect either that the ideology is inadequate or that although the ideology is adequate the members of the dominant systact are inadequately living up to it: in medieval Europe, the apparent ideological hegemony of the Church, far from ensuring cultural consensus and structural stability, gave rise both to intense disagreement about the nature of political legitimacy and to frequent invocation of the proclaimed criteria for it against rulers and their agents themselves. In the second place, stability may be more successfully achieved where the dominant systact proclaims no doctrine of legitimacy at all: in Republican Rome and the *poleis* of Classical Greece, no attempt was made to justify the authority of rulers beyond *de facto* tenure of office and common interest in the 'safety of the commonwealth' (Aristotle *Politics* 1276b),* and ideological roles were a vehicle of communal patriotism rather than the other way round.† The distribution and use of a society's means of persuasion may be no less important to its workings and evolution than the distribution and use of its means of either production or coercion. But the degree to which they are concentrated in the hands of the incumbents of dominant roles whose interest lies in preserving the *status quo* should not be presupposed to correlate with their success in doing so.

As, therefore, in the case of all practices, ideological innovation succeeds or fails not simply through its psychological attraction to the incumbents of the roles by which the mutation will be carried but by its function in the context of the pre-existing distribution of economic and coercive as well as ideological power. Consider the history of attitudes to slavery. Specialists of all schools are agreed that its legitimacy was never seriously questioned in the Ancient World and that the advent of

good

* Finley's puzzlement at this difference between the Ancient World and the Middle Ages (1983, pp. 131–2) is adequately answered by Eisenstadt's emphasis (above, p. 82, n. *) on the emergence of ideological roles which in the European case, required the evolution from paganism to Christianity.

† It is true that the Roman élite manipulated their sacerdotal functions in the service of their political interests (Taylor 1949, Ch. 3); but this was an aspect of competition for office-holding, not of vindication of their title to rule.

Christianity, although it may have helped to incline some individual slaveowners to manumit their slaves out of piety, made little or no difference to the way in which the institution was viewed.* There were, to be sure, critics of the way in which it operated in practice. Stoic philosophers argued against cruelty towards slaves, just as Dominican friars were later to condemn the brutality of their treatment during the Atlantic slave-trade. But Verlinden (1977, p. 15) is able to cite only one single author between the Sophists and the Abolitionists who queried slavery as natural. Yet it would be wrong to conclude that ideas about its legitimacy made no difference to its eventual replacement. A novel doctrine about the legitimacy of an institution succeeds or fails in reinforcing or undermining it in no different a way from a technical discovery which may or may not be put to economic use or a mutation in the form of political or military organization which may or may not come to permeate the existing mode of coercion. The nineteenth-century Abolitionists would not have succeeded as and when they did without a conjunction of ideological, economic and coercive sanctions not hitherto available to slavery's opponents, and as always the three were, although interrelated, not wholly reducible to one another.†

It is also true that there are many societies which are stabler than, so to speak, they have reason to be because novel institutions and roles which they could in theory have evolved were inconceivable to their members at the time. Ideologically, the notion of a secular monarch whose role at the top of a hierarchy of social prestige owed nothing to a 'supernatural radiance' shared with the Gods (Oppenheim 1977, p. 206) was inconceivable in Ancient Mesopotamia; economically, the notion of a systact of wage-earners linked to corporate enterprises through contracts extending for the duration of its members' working lives‡ was inconceivable in Classical Rome; politically, the notion that

* In Islamic societies, by contrast, manumission (coupled with conversion) was an act of personal piety and social virtue not merely permitted but encouraged by the Quran. But this is not to say – as pointed out by Cooper (1981) for the Muslim slaveowners of the East African coast – that there were not strong prudential reasons for them to avoid the perpetuation of a self-reproducing stratum denied any hope of further integration into their society.

† This claim has of course to be tested against the evidence. But the irreducibility of ideological to economic and/or political causes can be convincingly demonstrated by reference to the case of Jamaican society between 1787 and 1834: see Turner (1982) on the influence of the Baptist and Methodist missionaries both on their local congregations and on domestic opinion in England.

‡ The qualification is important, because there were substantial numbers of wage-earners (*mercenarii*) who were casually or seasonally employed not just as porters, builders, entertainers and field-labourers but even in the mines (see Crook 1967,

subjects of the realm should play any role in directing its institutions was 'unthought of by princes and unthinkable to impartial and articulate observers' (Shennan 1974, p. 30) in Early Modern Europe. In this sense, therefore, it may well be true to say that the members of these societies whose interests would have been advanced by the realization of these undreamt-of options were in a state of false systactic consciousness. But the relevance of such counterfactual hypotheses to the theory of social selection is the same as that of hypotheses about the part played in the abolition of slavery or any other institution by ideas about its legitimacy. Any set of institutions and practices, however long hallowed by tradition, is potentially vulnerable: the novel doctrine by which the deference hitherto accorded to them is undermined may be adaptive for either or both or neither the economic and/or political interests of the relevant systact. But the answer always lies in the mutant or recombinant practices defining the roles of the carriers and their relation to the pre-existing distribution of power.

§4. If, accordingly, the question is asked 'what kinds of societies are – relatively – stablest?', the answer must be first, that it is not a matter of the mode of the distribution of power as such; second, that even a widespread sense of relative deprivation among incumbents of subordinate roles is by no means always destabilizing; and third, that no society remains stable for ever. The stablest societies are those which are both protected against exogenous competitive pressure and so firmly constrained either by unquestioned custom or the preponderant power of a dominant systact (or both) that there is never a conjunction of motive and opportunity sufficient for a mutation or recombination of practices to bring about a change in the mode of production, persuasion or coercion. But these conditions hold only for a finite period. No society remains totally isolated from exogenous pressure, not even the peoples of the New Guinea Highlands who believed, until the first Australian gold prospectors appeared in their midst in the 1930s, that they were the only human beings in the world; and even the most unchanging societies on record are the product of an antecedent evolution which has made them what they are when first reported in the historical or ethnographic record.

This does not mean, however, that stability, where observed, has somehow to be explained away as an abnormality any more than that systactic conflicts and changes from one mode of the distribution of

pp. 198–203) – which makes the complete lack of the 'modern' connotations of wage-labour all the more striking.

power to another are to be viewed as abnormalities within a fundamental tendency towards equilibrium. Once societies are seen as the outcome of a process of the competitive selection of practices, neither is any more inherently problematic than the other. It is not difficult, as we shall see, to explain why some societies of hunters and gatherers, or of nomadic pastoralists, have been as exceptionally stable as they have; and although the exponential acceleration in the rate of social evolution since the 'dawn of civilization' is plain to see, it is possible to specify conditions under which, had they obtained, the world would still be divided between a Roman and a Chinese empire, an 'Indian' America, an aboriginal Australia and an Africa of semi-permanent tribes and states oscillating in a sort of perpetual Brownian motion. Of course there is always conflict: as I said in the opening paragraph of this Chapter, there is always someone trying to alter in some way the existing distribution of power. But it is equally a matter of course that conflicts can be resolved, tensions relaxed, rivalries contained, institutions re-established, and traditions upheld.

In any case, some societies are stable for the simple reason that their rulers have the determination as well as the power to see to it that their practices remain as they are. Here, Sparta is the proverbial example. It is true that its two-systact system did in the end break down, for reasons to be analyzed further in Chapter 4. But the practices by which the Helots were kept in subjection* proved adaptive for the Spartiates over a period of many generations. Another near-proverbial example is the Venetian Republic. Although in the end it lost its independence to Napoleon's troops, it had by then for centuries been the envy of foreign observers for a stability consciously contrived and deliberately sustained. Admittedly, the careful system of interlocking councils and overlapping ballots by which the holders of high office came to exercise the power attaching to their roles was not a guarantee against the possibility of change: it was by a hairsbreadth that the Republic did not forcibly evolve into a *signoria* through the attempted *coup d'état* by Marco Querini and Bajamonte Tiepolo in 1310 or Doge Marino Falier's abortive plot of 1355. Nor did the mode of production remain unchanged (as we shall later see). But Venice does, nevertheless, deserve its reputation as an example of the relative stability which can be achieved, given certain initial ecological and sociological conditions, by a dominant systact whose members are collectively conscious of a need

* It is possible that some of these practices were of a more purely ritual character than the sources suggest (Ducat 1971); but that does not diminish their function in maintaining the stability of the system.

to preserve it. Indeed, a similar degree of stability can even be maintained where cooperation is minimal, provided that the rival contenders for the topmost roles are committed to the existing institutions. In Haiti, for example, despite continuous banditry as well as a succession of assassinations and *coups*, the structure and culture stayed virtually unchanged from independence until the American intervention. There was throughout the nineteenth century an autonomous but impoverished Creole-speaking peasantry in the countryside and a French-speaking middle class of petty traders, rentiers and officials in the towns; and the turnover within the élite was largely a function of conflicts between mulattoes and *noiristes* (Nicholls 1979, Chs. 3 and 4).*

Even much larger and more powerful societies than these may remain relatively stable over remarkably long periods. The standard example is China. But two important qualifications need to be made. The first is that despite an exceptional degree of structural stability, there were major changes of culture from the militarism of the T'ang through the commercialism of the Sung to the near-authoritarianism of the Ming. The second is that although until the Taiping Revolt of the mid nineteenth century organized dissent was rebellious rather than revolutionary, this should not be allowed to obscure such structural changes as did take place as warriors, merchants, monks, landlords, officials, moneylenders, court eunuchs, tied tenants, smallholders, smugglers and bandits collectively rose or fell relative to others quite apart from whatever the rates of individual mobility from one role to another may have been. It has still to be explained why Chinese society was as stable as it was over so long a period without more profound and extensive changes in its modes of production, persuasion and coercion. But the example serves equally to point the moral that stability is always a relative matter. China's institutions were by no means static, despite an equipoise in the distribution of power among competing roles and systacts in which dissent was either channelled into purely individual mobility or held cyclically in check by countervailing economic, ideological and/or coercive power.

* The same can be true where the forcible replacement of the dominant stratum is from outside. In sixth-century Italy, it made no difference to the social structure whether Goths replaced Byzantines or Byzantines Goths, and the attitude of the people of Naples is nicely described by Procopius (V.8.32) when he puts into the mouth of two of them the remark that 'it is great foolishness not to comply in every way with the wishes of whoever is going to be lord (*kyrios*); but if the outcome is uncertain...'.

REPRODUCTION, POLARIZATION AND COMPRESSION

§5. Since even the stablest societies are, nevertheless, systems of social relations in motion, there is always a comparison to be drawn between their structure at any one time and a time either before or after; and since the incumbents of existing roles are constantly being replaced by new entrants into either these same roles or new ones created by, or brought into being for, them, the readiest way in which to make the comparison is in terms of rates and distances of inter-generational social mobility. 'Reproduction' in this context does not need to be interpreted strictly in terms of a comparison between the location of the first adult roles of new entrants and that of their fathers at the time of their own entry into their first adult roles. Apart from the question whether fathers should be chosen as the reference point, account has also to be taken both of possible intra-generational mobility by the fathers and/or the children and of the immigration of members of other societies whose parents' location in their society of origin is irrelevant.* Moreover, even if this is the most informative comparison to make, it cannot be quasi-deductively inferred from it that the society as a whole has been either polarized or compressed. But it is always worth asking of any society to what extent, for any given systact at any given moment, its members are located higher or lower than their parents were; and the answer, as always, is to be sought in the practices which so function as to alter the structure in the one direction or the other.

From what has been said, it will be evident already that there is no one tendency which should be presupposed to be normal. But on any theory, there are certain constraints which will keep the degree of either polarization or compression well within their ideal-typical limits. Structurally, the ratio of the number of roles potentially available at any given level to the number of potential incumbents born at other locations will determine the maximum rate of mobility, both inter- and intra-generational.† Even rulers determined not only to promote the children

* The Jesuits in Paraguay again offer an interesting and unusual example. Neither the Jesuits themselves at the top of the structure nor the Negro slaves at the bottom of it were demographically self-reproducing; but the Indians in the middle were, to the point that population growth led to the fission of several 'reductions' (Mörner 1953, p. 164).

† Differential fertility may also determine the *minimum* rate: here, a good example is medieval Europe, where despite an ideology of fixed orders and the functions ascribed to them the continuing performance of those functions – particularly those performed by a celibate clergy – required a considerable amount of inter-generational mobility (Herlihy 1972–3, p. 626).

of the incumbents of lower-ranked roles and demote the children of the incumbents of higher-ranked ones but also to narrow the span between the roles themselves will still find a substantial proportion of the society's total roles filled by persons of the same systactic origin. To be sure, the attempt can be made to correct this by deliberate manipulation of the structure. But it will be effective only if a drastic modification of the culture is brought about as well.

Such modifications are by no means impossible. All landlords can be dispossessed, all monasteries dissolved, all capitalists expropriated, all bureaucracies abolished, all armies disbanded, all nobles disinherited, all cadres demoted, all slaves manumitted, all outcastes legitimized, all paupers enriched, all serfs liberated, all non-citizens enfranchised and all captives pardoned. But it may be at just such times that the governing élite will succeed in its aims, if it does, because and only because the society's central institutions are left to be administered by the same experienced incumbents of the same virtually unaltered roles. Or changes in one direction at one systactic level may have to be mirrored by changes in the opposite direction at another, whether the ostensible aim is compression or polarization: for example, a policy of giving industrial workers control over decisions affecting the enterprise where they work may simultaneously strengthen the superordinate bureaucracy needed to enforce the diminution of the power attaching to traditional managerial roles. It still should not be presupposed that a high and constant *reproduction ratio** between one generation and the next is the norm from which any deviation calls for special explanation. But there can never, in practice, be a society whose reproduction ratio is nil.

The effect of any chosen practices on the extent and degree of polarization or compression has, accordingly, to be assessed by reference not only to the competitive advantage which they confer on their carriers but also to the different forms of social mobility which they promote or retard. Where there is a change of culture only, neither polarization nor compression will occur unless individual mobility is on such a scale that the resulting change in the relative size of the different systacts is enough by itself to generate a degree of collective mobility.† But changes of

* The term is, in my view, best defined as the proportion of the members of a society who, at any given time, occupy roles whose systactic rank is the same as that of the roles occupied at the date of their birth by their fathers. But this definition – which specialists will recognize as a measure of absolute mobility (or inflow) rather than relative mobility (or outflow) – can be modified *salva veritate* as may be required.

† A good example is the 'Time of the Wandering Bandits' in mid seventeenth-century China. So many soldiers were unpaid and so many peasants unable to meet the taxes out of which the soldiers' pay needed to be found that both were driven to banditry

culture can also result in increased rates of 'exchange' rather than 'structural' mobility which neither compress nor polarize the systactic structure as such. If, say, the introduction of market practices into an agricultural society puts competitive pressure on landowners to switch from manorial autarky to export sales, this may result in the downward mobility of those least willing or able to adapt to the change in their roles and the replacement of themselves (or their sons) by their former subordinates (or *their* sons); but the location of the now commercialized systact of landowners may well remain exactly what it was. Indeed, even a change which collectively downgrades the whole of a traditional élite and replaces it with the whole of a hitherto subordinate systact may leave the social distance between the two the same as it was before their locations were reversed.* In other words, reproduction ratios can vary quite independently of any concomitant widening or narrowing of social distance between the roles occupied by the second generation of incumbents.

For either polarization or compression to approach their ideal-typical limits, cultural and structural instability have both to combine to the same effect. But even then, the mobility generated may be either individual or collective. Early Modern Russia offers a good illustration of both. When Ivan IV sought to strengthen his power over his subjects, he killed or dispossessed many thousands of the old nobility of *boyars* and princes of the blood and replaced them by a new systact of *pomeshchiki* – men of lower rank who were awarded temporary landholdings in proportion to the importance of the services which they were required to perform in return.† The result was at the same time a widening of social distance between the role of the tsar and those of his servants and an acceleration in the rate of individual mobility as the sons of peasants, petty nobles and soldiers rose to fill the vacancies left by the virtual destruction of the traditional élite. But the practices which

in such numbers as to become a threat first to the government of their localities and then to the dynasty itself.

* As often, a particularly apt quasi-experimental example can be found at the local rather than the societal level: Robben (1982) shows how the palm-grove owners of a Brazilian coastal village were displaced as the dominant systact controlling both raft-fishing and patronage as soon as tourists became the patrons of the hitherto poor fishermen who, once enabled to acquire motorboats on credit, took over both the fishing market and political relations with the municipal factions of the wider society.

† Not that the innovation was his – the earliest *pomest'e* grant in North-east Russia was before 1328 (Hellie 1971, p. 26), which makes it all the better an illustration of the competitive selection of a practice whose delayed impact on the evolution of the society as a whole could not have been predicted in advance.

defined the roles of the *pomeshchiki* did not serve merely to stabilize the system by removing the threat of a boyar revolt. They also brought about a collective downward mobility of the peasantry in the direction of serfdom, since the new service nobility had to be supported by a systact of dependent cultivators at a time when the economy in general was suffering from the combined effects of declining productivity and protracted warfare. Individual peasants had, therefore, every reason to try to escape, both geographically and sociologically, to areas where less burdensome practices might be imposed on them, while rival landlords had every reason to try to prevent them (or, in the case of the very large monastic or secular landlords, to offer more attractive terms to the peasants of the smaller *pomeshchiki*). The response of Ivan IV and his successors was progressively to limit the freedom of movement traditionally accorded to the peasantry to the point that it was finally denied them altogether. Even those who were successfully established elsewhere might be forcibly returned to their original lords (Blum 1961, Ch. 14). Over a period of perhaps two or three generations, Russian society underwent an evolution which illustrates not only the way in which the mutation of practices gives rise to both individual and collective mobility, but also how that mobility may polarize the society in one area of social space while simultaneously compressing it in another.

Patterns of social reproduction can, therefore, be very various, despite the demographic constraints which act on them. But within those constraints, it is always possible to relate an observed divergence from a more or less consistent reproduction ratio to the mutation (or recombination) of practices and thereby emergence of novel roles which has brought it about. Thus, the introduction of market practices has often brought about an initial polarization by widening the distance between rich and poor and thereby enabling the rich to transmit to their chosen heirs relatively greater economic power than they themselves had at the time of their own entry into their adult roles; and conversely, in societies where redistribution of a 'big-man's' accumulated wealth is a condition of his continued occupancy of the role, his sons can attain a similar location only if they are able to re-enact from scratch, as it were, their father's career.* Yet a similar set of practices can produce quite

* Dahl's account of the Borana is again apt in showing in the case of a pastoral society how 'the dependence on household labour for herd management, and the ecological advantages of herd dispersion in themselves place a limit on accumulation by one single herd-owner, and to opportunities of transferring capital from one generation to the next in a non-egalitarian manner' (1979, p. 274).

opposite effects on the structure of different societies. Thus, the organization of the adult male population for warfare has often polarized the societies where it occurs – so much so, indeed, that theories have been constructed on the basis of attributing to it the origins of social stratification as such. But there are also cases where its effect has been to narrow the distance between the topmost roles and the general body of adult male citizens. The so-called 'hoplite revolution' in Archaic Greece (and, with certain important differences, early Rome*), by increasing the dependence of the societies concerned on armoured infantrymen rather than noble 'Homeric'-style champions, gave members of these emergent systacts a measure of coercive power which their fathers and grandfathers had been denied. There is, however, no incompatibility. Nothing requires that if organization for warfare polarizes the structure of one society it therefore cannot compress that of another. It all depends on what systactic interest is served by the competitive advantage which the mutant practices confer on the novel roles which carry them.

§6. Where, therefore, mobility is at issue, roles have to be seen both *intra*-generationally as careers which determine in part the future location of their incumbents and *inter*-generationally as potential openings for subsequent incumbents whom the present incumbents may or may not – as discussed in Section 13 of Chapter 2 – be entitled to select. This means that the model in terms of which the relevant functional hypotheses are to be framed is not so much one of vectors in three-dimensional space as one of vacancies waiting to be filled from a pool of recruits initially distributed among different systacts of origin. Moreover, the variables which these hypotheses will have to accommodate will include not only the current distribution of power among roles but the relative fertility of the members of different systacts and the capacity of educational institutions, whether formal or informal, to determine the relative outflow ratios from one systact to another.

For reasons sufficiently expounded already, the precise calculations which this implies can be made for very few of the societies on record. But given a few tolerably well-estimated demographic parameters, the effects of an observed set of practices over a few generations can be

* The sources for the evolution of the Roman Republic are tantalizingly inadequate: it is at least possible that the *plebs* was initially *infra classem* (i.e. did *not* serve in the legions) and that Servius Tullius created the *comitia centuriata* in order to check the expansion of the army of *clientes* of the great patrician houses and, to a lesser extent, non-patrician senators (Momigliano 1975).

demonstrated convincingly enough. Economically, for example, in a society where wealth consists predominantly in land, its distribution will to a significant degree be a joint function of rules of inheritance and family size.* Ideologically, in societies where the nominal status of a hereditary aristocracy is transmitted to all sons by their fathers, high fertility will dilute its value to the point where the distance between the aristocracy and their immediate inferiors will have virtually disappeared. Politically, in societies where eligibility for office is determined by birth, reproduction ratios will be high unless differential fertility rates either create openings having to be filled by 'new men' or force excess children of office-holders into subordinate and/or extra-political roles. It is still possible for demographic effects to be nullified by overriding cultural influences. In a society where all systacts are castes, their relative sizes could change enormously between one generation and the next but their relative location remain as it was. Conversely, in a society where positive discrimination is being enforced to the limit, no child of high-ranking parents will be allowed to remain at his or her location of birth. But more commonly, reproduction ratios find their own level within the limits set by the numbers of births and of vacancies at each systactic level.

A significant difference can, however, still be made by formal practices of education and recruitment, even if not as much as would-be reformers have sometimes supposed.† In estimating reproduction ratios, it is important to remember that they are a function of the number of systacts as well as the rate of outflow from location of birth. But with this reservation, it is possible to compare the relative influence in different societies of institutions consciously designed to channel children of lower-ranking parents into higher-ranking roles or *vice versa*. In industrial societies, educational institutions are so linked to the division and specialization of labour as to make it as implausible to expect to find a strict caste-like reproduction as to find rates of exchange mobility at or close to the theoretical maximum: variation is more apparent in the relative size and internal composition of employment categories than in the rates of individual inter-generational mobility from one to another. But in pre-industrial societies, the range of

* Thus, not only will primogeniture tend to concentrate landholdings (as in England) and the *retrait lignager* to keep them dispersed (as in France), but the effects of partible inheritance will be compounded where combined with polygyny (as in several parts of Africa).

† See Boudon (1973) for a formal demonstration of the constraints which operate over time even in would-be meritocratic industrial societies whose educational institutions are designed to promote equality of opportunity.

variation is wider. The rates themselves are lower at the maximum than in industrial societies, simply because there are far fewer vacancies in non-manual employments (even if skilled artisans as well as petty traders are defined as 'middle class'). But some are very much more caste-like then others, and the consequences of different reproduction ratios over several generations may bear directly on the course of the society's evolution.

Consider from this point of view the case of the *ancien régime* in France. It was, as we have already seen, a highly stratified society. But there was, in the middle and upper ranks, considerable multiple membership of cross-cutting roles and considerable individual social mobility. What is more, because of the importance of social status and the ideological sanctions on which it rested, much of that mobility was – as it often is where differential esteem is accorded ascriptively from birth* – long term. It was thus a perfectly feasible goal alike for the newly *anoblis* to envisage their grandsons rising to full recognition as members of the Second Estate and the newly prosperous yeoman-like *laboureurs* to envisage their grandsons entering the systact of local *seigneurs* – to say nothing of the vacancies to be filled in commerce, the law and the Church. Even, therefore, in so rigidly hierarchical a society, reproduction ratios were never as high as the ideological emphasis on status by birth might lead one to expect; and it is arguable that this not only moderated the pressures for social change in the seventeenth century but intensified them in the eighteenth, when a number of the channels of mobility came, for a variety of reasons, to be blocked, and the sense of relative deprivation among the families excluded from the roles to which they aspired was heightened accordingly.

§7. Neither polarization nor compression can, however, continue indefinitely, or even for more than a few generations, whether brought about by collective mobility over a large enough distance or by individual mobility at a sufficiently high rate. Reproduction ratios will always tend upwards rather than downwards. This is not simply because the joint influence of upbringing and education in assigning children to adult roles close to their parents' location is likely to be stronger than the

* This holds in particular for *ethnic* stratification which can, indeed, be defined in terms of ascriptive criteria (which may or may not involve distinguishable physical as well as social attributes) denying legitimate status mobility to the incumbents of the relevant roles who are therefore faced with the choice of individual mobility by 'passing' (Runciman 1971–2, p. 499) or collective mobility either by 'Sanskritization' or by collective organization directed toward changing the culture (as in the case of some Indian *harijan* and some Japanese *burakumin*).

impetus given to individual mobility by psychological and genetic influences. Nor is it even because cultural changes are seldom drastic enough to sustain high rates of collective mobility for more than a limited period. Reproduction ratios tend upwards because an increase in rates of inter-generational mobility, whether individual or collective and whether 'structural' or 'exchange', is necessarily self-defeating. Once the initial polarization or compression has come about, the children of subsequent generations enter their adult roles from a starting-point determined by the previous mobility of their parents. It follows that the only alternative to a higher reproduction ratio is an actual reversal of the previous trend whereby a polarization is recompressed or a compression repolarized. Hence the paradox of 'permanent revolution': once previously subordinate systacts have been raised as high as they can and as many of those born into them promoted individually into higher-ranked systacts as there is room for, what is to be done about *their* children?

In this context, the relation of inter-generational mobility rates to the number of systacts and the distance between them is critical to the significance of reproduction ratios. To invoke the notion of reproduction in explaining (or describing or evaluating) a society's workings and evolution presupposes that the rates of mobility which define it are across a distance which takes the people who traverse it into roles more than marginally higher or lower than those of their parents. But if the effect of such mobility over one generation is to compress those distances, reproduction ratios in the second generation are to that degree less significant; whereas if its effect is, on the contrary, to polarize them, then the equivalent mobility in the second generation will be to that degree more difficult to achieve.

Consider what may, at first sight, seem a rather far-fetched comparison between two societies both of whose reproduction ratios can be shown to be low compared to societies in other ways like them: twentieth-century Sweden and tenth/eleventh-century (pre-Conquest) England. If we assume the fourfold systactic division which I have said can serve as a reasonably uncontentious starting-point for all but the simplest societies, then twentieth-century Sweden turns out to have a fairly open élite, a high rate of inter-generational mobility between manual and non-manual occupational roles,* and an underclass whose membership is only to a limited extent a function of birth. Now for totally different reasons, the same can plausibly be said of tenth/

* See Erikson *et al.* (1979, 1982, 1983) for comparisons of social 'fluidity' as well as mobility in Sweden with England and France.

eleventh-century England. Its élite was expanding and open from below to men not born into it; there was considerable movement both ways from one generation to the next between the prosperous 'middle class' of burgesses, reeves, *radcnihts*, petty *thegns*, *liberi homines* (i.e. 'sokemen'), or thriving *ceorls* and both the *thegns* above them and the dependent cultivators below; the dependent cultivators could either rise from their location at birth into the 'middle class' or descend into the 'underclass' of slaves or outlaws; and movement was to all appearances considerable both into the underclass, as the sons of dependent cultivators fell into slavery or lost their means of livelihood, and out of it, as manumission or the opportunities offered by raids and wars enabled the sons of slaves or outlaws to rise to formal freedom.* Both societies, therefore, can plausibly be credited with relatively low reproduction ratios. But whereas in twentieth-century Sweden this is because inter-systactic distances have been steadily *diminishing*, in tenth/eleventh-century England it was because they had been steadily *widening* as a strengthened monarchy and Church expanded their apparatus of auxiliaries, an increasingly active land market created opportunities for enrichment as well as of falling into penury, and endemic violence in a society where slavery was still an established institution generated both enslavement and manumission not only inter- but intra-generationally. Even, therefore, if precise calculations are feasible and rival observers can all agree that reproduction ratios are virtually identical, their effects on the workings and evolution of the societies to which they apply may be of opposite kinds.

These effects can, moreover, become not merely anomalous but frustrating when rulers seek to change the structure in ways which turn out to involve irreconcilable objectives. They may, if they so decide, forcibly proscribe or drive into exile the members of groups or categories to whom they are opposed; they may remove what they see as barriers to the promotion of their friends; they may dismantle corporations within which internal stratification has hitherto perpetuated succession from fathers to sons; they may abolish existing rules of inheritance of property, status and office and replace them with new ones; and they may drastically modify the practices of education and recruitment whereby children born at different locations are channelled into their adult roles. But the dilemma of 'permanent revolution' applies no less to regimes to which the notion of revolution is anathema. Any deliberate change of mode is an attempt to create a structure and

* See Runciman (1984), where such evidence as there is for all this is summarized.

culture which, once created, should by definition be let be thereafter. For rulers committed to compression, this creates the paradox that the children of parents who were upwardly mobile from their own location of origin have either to be deliberately demoted (which cannot but be regarded as unfair) or to be allowed to retain such advantages as their parents' location may bring them (which cannot but be regarded as licencing the entrenchment of privilege). For rulers committed to polarization, it creates the paradox that once the desired amount of mobility has taken place, the only way to renew the same possibilities for the children of the first generation is to abolish some of the very advantages or disadvantages which have been deliberately allowed to accrue to their parents: the proverbial example is Andrew Carnegie, who favoured 100% inheritance taxes in order that the sons of men who had, like himself, risen from rags to riches should enter their adult roles at a systactic level corresponding to their *grand*fathers' location. Judgements of this nature are, to be sure, evaluative, and whether these dilemmas of policy concern you one way or the other depends on the moral or political philosophy to which you happen to subscribe. But that they exist as dilemmas of policy is a matter of sociological fact which bears directly on the changes which do or do not take place within any given society over two or three generations and the feelings of relative deprivation to which those changes (or the lack of them) may give rise.

The concept of a society's reproduction ratio, therefore, although defined by reference to notional figures in an artificially constructed inter-generational mobility matrix, is of theoretical significance for two reasons. Not merely can it provide a measure of structural change; it can also underwrite the categorization of societies in terms of their mode and sub-type of the distribution of power by specifying the minimum degree of continuity which has to hold between one generation and the next. The notion of reproduction thus links the notion of stability directly to the two topics to be considered next: first, the shared structural patterns of roles which, at any given stage of cultural evolution, place different societies in a common 'Linnaean' category; and second, the constraints or contradictions which, in the absence of exogenous pressure, either inhibit or necessitate a change amounting to an evolution from one 'Darwinian' category to the next. Only then can a general account be offered of how the practices which define the roles constitutive of different societies assign them to their respective modes and sub-types of the distribution of power.

SYSTACTIC PATTERNS AND MODES OF THE DISTRIBUTION OF POWER

§8. However remote the goal of an exhaustive and rigorous typology in which every reported society has its own distinctive polynomial, the criteria by which societies cannot but be contrasted with one another on sight are by now clear enough. Structurally, they differ in terms of the relative numbers of, and distances between, their constituent roles and the rates of mobility between them; culturally, they differ in terms of the source and nature of the forms of economic, ideological or coercive power whose distribution among differently located roles makes the structure what it is. But beyond this, the necessary distinctions cannot be developed theory-neutrally. Sensible as it is to start by asking of a society not 'is it feudal?' or 'is it capitalist?' but 'is there a fusion of benefice and vassalage?' or 'is there a free market in both labour and commodities?', the purpose of such ostensibly down-to-earth questions is, all the same, to lead on to more ambitious ones. It is on their backs, as it were, that hypotheses framed in terms such as 'feudalism' and 'capitalism' will, if vindicated, not only furnish the explanation of the particular society's workings and evolution with an adequate theoretical grounding but also justify its assignation to its taxonomic place.

It should also be clear by now that although practices are the units of social selection, it is in terms not of practices but of institutions and the modes of production, persuasion and coercion defined by them that any taxonomy will have to be framed. It is, no doubt, feasible to mark off any and all societies (or institutional catchment areas) where, say, vassalage, or clientage, or corvée labour or any other pervasive-looking roles are to be found from any and all where they are not. But this, as we have already seen, is to ignore the very different functions which homologous practices may perform in allocating power between the nominally dominant and subordinate roles.* An instructive example (to which I shall return in Chapter 4) is the practice of sharecropping, which has been assumed to have a regressive function in the societies where it persists alike by Marxian theorists for whom it is as residue of 'feudal' exploitation, and by neo-classical theorists for whom it is an 'irrational' impediment to the maximization of productivity. Both these views,

* What is more, there are cases where the formal relationship is largely or even totally redundant: when, for example, the Italian city-states incorporated the practice of feudal investiture into their dealings with their *condottiere*, 'The condottiere feudatories were not expected to serve by virtue of their new feudal status, and still continued to fight on the basis of a separate contractual system' (Mallett 1974, p. 92).

however, are equally misleading (Robertson 1980): the institutional contexts in which sharecropping persists range all the way from large *latifundia* where the number of would-be tenants relative to the available land works unequivocally to the landlord's advantage through co-operative sharing of risk in village communities exposed to the possibility of natural disaster, to the dependence of elderly and childless landowners on young, able-bodied tenants without whose labour they could not even feed themselves.

At the same time, classification in terms of institutions can and should be carried out with tacit reference to the evolutionary background. We have seen that although there is no consistent correlation between functional differentiation and the total amount of power available for distribution, nevertheless a certain accumulation of resources is a necessary condition of the emergence of novel roles and institutions and the consequent evolution of societies from one to another mode. It is as economic, ideological and coercive resources increase that institutional diversification gathers pace and a 'Darwinian' process analogous to speciation generates a progressively wider 'Linnaean' range of unmistakably dissimilar forms. This diversification is, as I emphasized in Section 11 of Chapter 1, simultaneously accompanied by an increasing pressure for standardization as the adaptive characteristics of some but not other mutant and recombinant practices take effect on the relations between their carriers and the incumbents of the other roles institutionally tied to them: not only are certain of the logically possible institutional combinations impossible in practice, but the exogenous pressure exerted by relatively more powerful societies becomes increasingly inescapable. Yet for all the constraints which limit the range of variation, there can be no question that the number of different societies having to be assigned to more and more different categories of structure and culture has steadily increased since the long millennia when hunting, foraging and gathering was the only way of life known to the human species. The number of possible modes of production, persuasion and coercion may, as I have argued, be relatively small. But the number of variant sub-types is very much larger.

§9. Given the connection between the evolution of new modes and the expansion of resources which makes them possible, it is not surprising that classification is least contentious for societies in the 'hunter-gatherer' mode where the power available to be distributed among different roles is minimal. It is debatable to what extent it is safe to draw from reports of such societies by nineteenth- and twentieth-century observers semi-deductive inferences about their previous history and the exogenous pressures exerted by societies at a more 'advanced' level with which they have been in contact. But there is no dispute among specialists that there are striking similarities in the roles and practices of hunting and gathering societies extending all the way from the Arctic to the tropical rain forests to the Andaman Islands to the Kalahari Desert. Economically, they are alike in the pervasiveness of 'generalized reciprocity'* and the mutual acknowledgement of equal access to communal resources. Ideologically, they are alike in conceding prestige only to skill, seniority or claims to purely ritual precedence. Politically, they are alike in the regulation of disputes and enforcement of collective decisions resting on informal leadership rather than formal title to the exercise of coercive sanctions.† For all the reported differences between distinguishable sub-types in technology, ritual, part-time division of labour, and relation of co-residence to kinship, all are demonstrably alike in the very limited amount of the power attaching to any role.

There is, accordingly, an obvious rationale for distinguishing as a separate mode those societies where such power as attaches to superordinate roles is not so much *limited* as *dissipated*, as with the Melanesian and other 'big-men' and the Homeric *basileis*. This mode includes among its sub-types some (but by no means all) segmentary lineage systems, of which the Mandari of the Southern Sudan (Buxton 1958) are a good example. Here, the '*Mar*' is a hereditary chief who presides over a council of elders, is credited with spiritual qualities enabling him to mediate with the supernatural, and draws on the labour of numerous clients and wives; but his role at the same time requires him to supply his people with food, shelter or implements on request, and his continued incumbency of it depends on his pleasing his retainers and keeping the cooperation of the council elders and heads of collateral lineages. The Shilluk of the Upper Nile, whose *reth* only weakened his authority if he tried too hard to enforce it, belong in this category too, as do those nomadic pastoralists whose leaders, rich, prestigious and militarily successful as they may be, will, as in the case

* This should not, however, be presupposed to be motivated by altruism alone: as emphasized by Sahlins (1965, p. 186), 'Generalized reciprocity often consists of specific obligations to render certain goods to certain kinsmen (kinship dues) rather than altruistic assistance.'

† There may be a role which can plausibly be labelled 'headman', as among the Ainu (Watanabe 1972, p. 461). But although the Ainu headmen were local leaders drawn from core groups of male patrilineal kinsmen, they were formally recognized as superior only in ceremonial contexts (particularly the important winter bear ceremony).

of the Rwala Bedouin, lose their political power altogether if their attempt to mobilize coercive sanctions arouses the hostility of their followers. Where, indeed, the society's capital resources are entirely in the form of mobile herds rather than stored-up produce, disgruntled followers can remove not merely the labour which they contribute but a significant share of the total wealth. The *sardar* in Iranian Baluchistan (Salzman 1978, p. 135), even if he was somehow able to enlist the loyalty of a personal military following, could not coerce fellow-tribesmen who had only to remove their camels and tents whenever they chose.

Societies where power is liable to be dissipated almost as soon as it has accumulated need, however, to be distinguished in turn from those where it is not *dissipated* so much as *shared*. This does not mean that their structure is egalitarian or their culture cooperative. Their distinguishing characteristic is rather that although there may be quite substantial resources available within them, there are no economic, ideological or coercive roles to which there attaches a monopoly of power because there is a group or category among whose members the monopoly is effectively parcelled out. Typically, they will be adult male household heads, whether living in the kraals of the East African Nuer, the long-houses of the Daflas of the North-east Indian frontier, or the yurts of the Kirghiz of the Central Asian Pamirs. They may occupy the same structural location because they hold roughly the same amounts of land or moveable property, because they belong to mutually antagonistic but equally matched descent-groups, because they form a recognized age-set, because they all share in the collective decisions of a council of warriors, or any combination of these. They may have dependent clients, kinsmen or slaves, and these roles may be reproduced from one generation to the next with little or no prospect of mobility.* They may engage in raiding, piracy or warfare under the leadership of chiefs or *duces*, and they may concede authority to mediators or go-betweens in their quarrels or feuds among themselves. But although effective sanctions may be concentrated in the hands of a dominant systact (or even stratum), no single member of that systact can aspire to a role to which there attaches a more than marginally or temporarily larger share of the power available to it.

The transition to statehood, if and when it comes, may be very rapid.

* The Daflas differ strikingly in this respect from their more settled Apa Tani neighbours, who, although they have no political role more powerful than that of representatives appointed to negotiate at village level on behalf of their individual exogamous clans, recognize private property in land and accord prestige on the basis of it (Fürer-Haimendorf 1967, p. 81).

Herodotus (I. 96–100) tells the story of Deioces the Mede who, having made a personal bodyguard a condition of accepting leadership, then used it to transform the role of arbitrator into that of tyrant, and Tacitus tells the story of Maroboduus, a German *rex* of noble *genus* (*Germania* 42) who, despite the subsequently fatal unpopularity which he incurred (*Annals* II. 44), did briefly establish something like an empire which he governed from something like a palace. But the transition involves the creation of a hitherto non-existent institutional apparatus. Before it happens, there is simply no scope for such conceptions as royal, state or church title to all the land of the community as such, or acknowledgement of some single sacred source of aristocratic or ecclesiastical prestige, or command over the services of warriors by right of conscription rather than personal following. This does not rule out significant differences between sub-types in both structure and culture: societies at this level may be relatively poor or prosperous, relatively warlike or peaceable, relatively ritualistic or pragmatic. But they have in common a selection of practices from a set characterized by the absence of a basis for domination by any single role of the institutions of the society as a whole.

§10. As the power available to be distributed accumulates further, there are an increasing number of societies which fall along a continuum of gradually increasing complexity rather than into one or other of a clearly demarcated range of sub-types within a precisely delimited mode. At this stage of evolution, coercive sanctions are likely to be more significant than either economic or ideological. However many intermediate variants there may be, there is a clear difference of mode between societies which, although they have evolved military and administrative roles that go beyond the authority excercised by hunt- or war-leaders, ritual specialists, elders, elected or appointed arbitrators or senior kinsmen, still fall short of what can plausibly be labelled statehood, and societies dominated by the incumbents of central, specialized roles who have institutionally privileged access to the means of coercion. This is not to say that an accumulation of economic resources is not also a necessary part of the process, whether brought about by trade, metallurgy, piracy, exploitation of fishing grounds, introduction of new crops, or a shift from pastoralism to arable farming. But it comes about in societies which may, in terms of production, consist of horticulturalists or nomadic pastoralists or settled (or semi-settled) agriculturalists or any combination of these. The crucial transition is from *semi-* to *proto-statehood* (Runciman 1982, pp.

352–6) – that is, from the existence of specialized political roles which fall short of an effective monopoly of the means of coercion to the existence of potentially permanent institutions of government properly so called.

So defined, semi-states may include societies of both the second and third of the modes distinguished in the previous section. But they also include societies at this level of resources where power is neither dissipated nor shared so much as *obstructed* at a point just short of statehood. A good example is furnished by the chiefdoms of traditional Hawaii. The Hawaiian 'chiefs' were altogether more powerful than Melanesian 'big-men' or Borana *abba olas* or Archaic Greek *basileis* or heads of balanced segmentary lineages or *sheikhs* of nomadic Bedouin: they enjoyed precisely the access to tribute, the command of an administrative staff and the entitlement to ascriptive status independent of personal charisma which these others all lack. But they never were able to advance beyond that point. They never became kings in the full, monarchical sense. As Sahlins (1974, p. 148) puts it, they had not 'broken structurally' with their people. Their roles were ideologically constrained within an institutional framework of kinship; they were – for geographical as well as political reasons – unable to bring the means of coercion effectively to bear at any distance from the centre; and they were never able to organize the exaction of tribute on a scale adequate to sustain a bureaucracy which could then continue to exact it.

The rulers of semi-states may find their ambitions obstructed equally effectively by uncontrollable subjects, as in Hawaii or among the Alur (Southall 1957, Ch. 9; Winans 1962), or by adjacent rivals, as with early Anglo-Saxon 'kings' like Oswine of Northumbria (Bede, *Ecclesiastical History* III.14), or the 'kings' of the fortified mountain-top camps of Madagascar whose little semi-states were as numerous as they were fragile (Maurice Bloch 1977, p. 113). But for the purpose of assigning them their place in a Linnaean-cum-Darwinian taxonomy, it does not matter which: the distinguishing feature is that their topmost political roles do not quite amount to rulership. This may seem to imply that the distinction is teleological, which in one sense it is. But the practices which obstruct the transition to statehood do not merely account for these societies' failure to be other than they are; they also explain their workings in their own distinctive mode.

From this stage on, the range of possibilities starts to widen further again. Whatever the interrelation between the cumulation of economic, ideological and coercive resources, it is no longer a question of how a usable surplus of power can attach to any superordinate role at all but of how the surplus, now that it exists, is institutionally distributed and applied. Nor does it matter for the purpose of taxonomy whether the transition to statehood was 'primary' or 'secondary' (i.e. endogenously evolved, or only in response to exogenous pressure). If a society is a state, this means that even if the incumbents of the specialized, central governmental roles are forcibly displaced, their roles are filled by others, not abolished; a set of self-reproducing institutions channels to them a sufficient proportion of the society's economic resources for them to be full-time specialists in their roles; and their roles are sufficiently acknowledged as legitimate for them to function on a permanent basis even if some individual incumbents are denied legitimacy. Notice also that once this is the case, there arises the possibility of structural inequalities as extreme as any in their impact on the incumbents of subordinate roles. There can now attach to the topmost roles the power not merely to carry out summary execution, imprisonment or expulsion, but also to distribute or redistribute economic resources at will and to grant or impose honorific or stigmatizing titles and life-styles on noble or outcaste systacts.

A further defining characteristic of this qualitative difference is, however, the novel possibility of rebellion or even revolution. There are now free-floating resources in all three dimensions which are actually or potentially available to be appropriated by the relatively deprived incumbents of hitherto subordinate roles. As we have seen, competition for power can take place even in large and complex societies through individual mobility alone; and as we have also seen, attempts at collective mobility, however intensely motivated by a sense of relative deprivation, may result only in an uneasy equipoise which leaves the structure and culture unloved but unchanged. But now the threat – as it is seen by the incumbents of the dominant roles – is not merely the disaffection of junior kinsmen or domestic slaves or clients or retainers but the countervailing power of mercenaries, *ministeriales*, tenants, vassals, sectarian clergy, slave-gangs, merchant capitalists, specialist craftsmen, tax-farmers, local chiefs or headmen or emirs and any and all other groups or categories whose roles might enable them to mount a systactic challenge to the existing structure and culture. For that reason, ideological sanctions now tend to assume a relatively greater importance. It is true that not every successful aspirant to monarchical power feels the need, as Marc Bloch (1924, p. 68) puts it of Pepin in 751, '*de colorer son usurpation d'une sorte de prestige religieux*', or, like the local rulers of South-east Asia colonized by Indian traders, to be ritually inducted into the *Kshatriya* caste. But the emergence of states is, nevertheless, accompanied not merely by the more effective appropriation of an economic surplus and the more effective organization of the means of coercion but also by the emergence of doctrines and practices of legality, nationhood and nobility.

§11. Any choice of categories for more detailed consideration can be vindicated only by the scope and validity of the hypotheses which they generate. There are, however, several modes of the distribution of power at this stage of evolution which can be clearly distinguished in terms of their pervasive roles and central institutions over and above the simple 'patrimonial' proto-states where the incumbents of the presumptively permanent central administrative and military roles still stand, in accordance with Max Weber's definition, in a purely personal relation to the *Herr* – the chief, king, generalissimo or tyrant – whom they serve.

In the first such mode, the central distinction is between the roles of *citizen* and non-citizen, whether or not some or all non-citizens are slaves* and whether or not an urban centre dominates a surrounding rural hinterland. The concentration of power in the hands of arms-bearing household heads united by allegiance to a common civic ideology and a common set of political institutions holds no less for twelfth-century Cremona, or Lucca, or Pisa, or Siena than for Spartiates, *perioikoi* and Helots or for Athenians, metics and slaves. The distinguishing characteristic of the citizens, whatever their relation to their subordinate cultivators, is that they constitute a state militia. Control of the means of coercion does not rest with autonomous households or aristocratic specialists or hired professionals. The function of this militia need not, to be sure, be purely defensive: its members may engage in deliberately offensive wars, or in overseas raiding and piracy, or (as with the Swiss mountain cantons as well as many of the Greek *poleis*) hire themselves out as mercenaries abroad. But if the offensive wars are regularly won, as in the case of Rome, then a change of mode becomes inevitable. The pressures which, in Rome, selected the practices constitutive of an absolutist mode will be analyzed in Section 31 of Chapter 4. But whatever precisely caused the change, the role of citizen was not and could not be any longer central.

In the second mode, by contrast, the central distinction is between

* It follows that slavery defines not a mode but a sub-type, with helotry or tied tenancy seen as functionally equivalent alternatives, rather than slavery defining a mode and helotry or tied tenancy merely seen as sub-types of a 'slave' mode of production (and persuasion and coercion) – which they demonstrably are not.

the roles of *warrior* and subject – the 'subjects' being members of formally free but subordinate systacts exploited and/or protected through a monopoly of the means of coercion in the hands of full-time professionals. The ideology is now that of conquest, often legitimated as a holy war or *jihād*, and the extraction of the economic surplus is by way of tribute or booty rather than rent or tax (and still less, as in the 'citizen' mode, liturgy). The thirteenth-century Mongols and the Teutonic Knights belong to this category no less than the first Islamic caliphates or, equally, the Sokoto Caliphate of the early nineteenth century where 'under the guise of pursuing the *jihād*, slave raiding and war were institutionalised into a coercive system for the mobilization of labour and for the redistribution of peasant output' (Lovejoy 1978, p. 348). As with 'citizen' societies, it is a mode which cannot survive its own success if that success involves territorial expansion beyond certain limits: the evolution from the early Islamic state to the Abbasid Caliphate is no less a transition of kind than that from the Rome of Cincinnatus to that of Augustus. But societies in this category can maintain a more or less permanent symbiosis with their subject communities. Warlike nomadic pastoralists can, like the Mongols, draw tribute from settled agriculturalists without adopting their practices and institutions, and predator states like the West African Gonja can inflict periodic razzias on stateless neighbours from whom they extract booty in the form of slaves who can then be sold in exchange for the horses, guns and powder with which further slaves can be acquired.*

In the third mode, into which societies of either of the first two may evolve, the central distinction is between a *bureaucracy* in the service of a ruler and the general body of subjects or citizens, including those performing military service, over whom the agents of the central government have the power to levy tax. These societies are often empires – a term which is not itself very precise but may be taken to imply an effective monopoly of the means of coercion extending over territories and communities not otherwise directly integrated into the institutions of the central state. But this is not a defining characteristic. The decisive difference is that the bureaucracy is no longer 'patrimonial' in Weber's sense. Those who staff it are not the companions, kinsmen

* An unusual sub-type where a warrior society reproduced itself by the capture and sale of slaves but without the institutions and practices of a centralized state is the West African Aro, whom we fleetingly met in Section 14 of Chapter 2 and whose manipulation of commercial alliances and a religious oracle within a loosely structured federation of villages enabled them to procure slaves both for export and for internal use either for productive labour or for seizure by the oracle (Lovejoy 1983, pp. 82–3).

or *therapontes* of their chief, but servants of the state of which he (or occasionally she) is the head. After late Rome, Sung China is perhaps the most obvious example, the more so because of the contrast with what preceded it. T'ang China falls in a transitional category, dominated as it was by a military aristocracy supported by revenues drawn from precisely allocated plots of land held for life by peasant households conditionally on payment of tax in the form of cereals or cloth or corvée labour. But the system proved unworkable. Not only did the 'method of equitable distribution of land' (*chün-t'ien-fa*) collapse under the pressure of peasant vagrancy, official corruption and usurpation by the rich, but the power of the central government passed to the regional commanders of large armies now manned by professional soldiers with the predictable consequence of a rebellion which the government was too weak to resist. It can, no doubt, be debated how far the rebellion of An Lu-Shan in the mid eighth century was inevitable. But only when order was re-established under the Sung did Chinese society come to be solidly based on a new much enlarged bureaucracy of 'scholar-gentry' who drew the tax revenues of the state partly from the countryside but partly also from commerce, and whose determination not to repeat the fatal mistake of the T'ang led them (as I remarked in Section 4 of Chapter 2) deliberately and, in the end, no less fatally to restrict the army's autonomy and prestige.

This mode does, however, also include among its sub-types the strong monarchical societies of Early Modern Europe as they emerged from decentralization, anarchy, rebellion or civil war similar to that which engulfed the T'ang.* It is true that many of these monarchies were 'absolute' more in their ideology than their practice, not least the France of Louis XIV where the splendours of Versailles and the cult of the *roi soleil* were a manifestation not merely of the power attaching to the monarchical role but of the need to make it seem greater than it really was. It is also true that all of them required some form of compromise between the ruler and the potentially overmighty among his subjects, whether by incorporating them into a service nobility, absorbing them into the largely ceremonial routines of the court, circumscribing them by reliance on *ministeriales* or eunuchs loyal to the

* This accords with the categorization of Eisenstadt (1969, p. 11) who includes the 'West, Central and East European states, from the fall of the feudal systems through the Age of Absolutism' among what he calls 'the centralized historical bureaucratic empires or states'; but his list is too all-embracing, including as it does societies which underwent changes in the mode of the distribution of power too radical not to require a distinction of kind to be drawn.

Crown, or redirecting their energies and resources abroad. But whatever the practices adopted and roles thereby evolved, the relation of the several sub-types to a common 'absolutist' mode is clear and distinctive enough. Similarly, whatever reservations are appropriate about the relative 'absolutism' of the power of the shoguns of Tokugawa Japan over the regional *daimyō*, there can be no doubt of the success of Odo, Toyotomi and Tokugawa in unifying a society rent for generations by outbreaks of civil war into a centralized state with a standing army, a salaried bureaucracy, a monopoly of artillery and coinage, and a highly efficient national network of police informers reminiscent of the spies of the Abbasid caliphs and the Ming emperors of China. Indeed, it is significant that the vernacular role which Toyotomi Hideyoshi deliberately adopted for himself was that of 'regent' (*kampaku*), which added to the military powers of a shogun authority over the court nobility, temples and shrines, and entitlement to act on behalf of the emperor 'in all aspects of national governance' (Osamu 1982, p. 350).

The fourth mode covers those societies which are, by contrast, genuinely *feudal*. As here used, the term is neither restricted to the narrow sense of central institutions constituted by a fusion of benefice and vassalage nor extended to the all-embracing sense in which any form of domination of unarmed cultivators by military landholders can be so labelled. For the purposes of this volume, it is to be construed in the sense of decentralization of power in the hands of local magnates who directly appropriate the economic surplus produced by dependent cultivators. It accordingly includes not only late Lombard Italy, post-Jagellonian Poland, post-Mongol, pre-Safavid Iran and Latin America in the period following independence. It also includes the Roman Empire in the West after the central government had lost its hold over the large aristocratic landowners, and the Byzantine Empire in the East after the 'Collapse' (Ostrogorsky 1968, Ch. 7 §4) which culminated in the fall of Constantinople to the Venetians and Crusaders in April 1204. The central institution of a feudal society in this sense *may* be a fusion of benefice and vassalage, and it *may* in such cases be the grant of land in return for military or other services which precipitates the loss of power from the ruler to the magnates. But just as vassalage can in other contexts so function as to strengthen the monarchy rather than weaken it, so can grants of land be made to officials without undermining the power attaching to the royal role: in traditional Tibet, for example, 'land is granted as salary by an absolute ruler who demands unrestricted obedience and who can resume the land at will' (Carrascó 1959, p. 208).

The critical difference in the feudal mode of the distribution of power lies in the success of the magnates in interposing themselves between the central government and the dependent cultivators. Economically, the difference is between tax payments to the state and rent payments to the magnates. Ideologically, it is between the supremacy of a monarch whose agents derive their legitimacy only from him and the dominance of magnates whose prestige derives, on the contrary, from their virtual independence of royal patronage. Coercively, it is between the answerability of free men to no authority other than the king and an obligation to serve in the retinue of a magnate with his own manorial (or ecclesiastical) court who may even march against the royal army itself. A 'feudal' monarchy is still a monarchy; but in contrast to an 'absolutist' one, the magnates defer to the king only because of the military leadership which he provides, the lands or entitlements to revenue which he bestows, and the national unity which he symbolizes.

A fifth mode covers those societies of which, unlike any of the preceding four (or, for that matter, the patrimonial proto-states), it is plausible to say that the dominant systact is, as it were, in the middle. The qualification is necessary because in structural terms it is obviously contradictory to say that a group or category located in the middle of the space enclosed by the inverted pyramid is at the same time dominant – that is, located by definition at the top of it. But to put it this way is to point the crucial distinction between societies in the 'citizen' mode, where a citizen oligarchy is indeed the dominant systact, and *bourgeois* societies in which the ostensible institutions of absolutism coexist with a gentry or merchant aristocracy sufficiently powerful for the label of 'absolutism' not to apply. The prime example, although by no means the only one, is seventeenth-century England. For all the debates about how the 'Great Rebellion' came about and whether it was a civil war, a bourgeois revolution, or both, specialists are not in disagreement that the Stuart monarchs failed to achieve their intended control over Parliament. Seventeenth-century England can be classified neither as a Polish-type feudalism nor as a French-type absolutism. Its systactic structure was one in which a national (or in some of its regions supra-national) monarchical state was compelled to accommodate a systact of increasingly commercialized gentry secure in their control of local government, their hold through Parliament on the finances of the central government, their preservation of chartered liberties, their independence (if they so chose) of the patronage of the Court and their capacity, in the last resort, to resist by recourse to the militia.

This sort of dominance from below the top is equally well exemplified under a different form of government by the Dutch United Provinces in the same period, where the institutions of a strong, rich nation-state with an exceptionally powerful navy and an effective system of social welfare were headed only by a stadholder and a so-called 'Grand Pensionary'. But there are other sub-types too, both earlier and later. Earlier, the cities of the German Hansa – although they explicitly called themselves a *confederatio* rather than a *universitas*, *collegium* or *societas* (source quoted by Dollinger 1970, p. 412) – formed a merchant-dominated society which was, however, still part of the Holy Roman Empire and owed much of its relative stability to the military strength and ideological prestige of the Teutonic Knights. Later, the newly emancipated United States of America formed a society characterized not only by an explicitly anti-monarchical ideology but by a constitution deliberately framed to curtail the powers of the executive in the interests of an intermediate systact of yeoman farmers and commercial gentry. There are, it is true, societies belonging to other modes in which a commercial or merchant class enjoys a high degree of autonomy, wealth and prestige. In many Islamic societies, for example, urban traders in alliance with the clerisy, or overlapping with them through simultaneous incumbency of economic and ideological roles, were powerful enough to defend their interests through their capacity to 'manipulate the juridico-religious agencies to their own advantage' (Stambouli and Zghal 1976, p. 18). But (as these authors, who are writing specifically about the pre-colonial Maghreb, are themselves at pains to stress) the means of coercion were still controlled by an army drawn from the adjacent rural tribesmen. Similarly, in Sung China, although merchants were tolerated and even encouraged in a context where commercial activity was rapidly increasing and local élites were simply 'the rich' (McKnight 1971, p. 6), there was no question that they enjoyed their privileges at the discretionary power of the emperor and the central bureaucracy, not the other way round.

§12. These five broad categories between the hunter-gatherers, stateless pastoralists and tribal or communal semi-states on the one hand and industrial or industrializing nation-states on the other still do not exhaust the 'Linnaean' range of possible modes at this 'Darwinian' evolutionary stage. But the other alternatives are genuine hybrids – genuine, that is, in that their central institutions and pervasive roles are a stable combination drawn from several modes of production, persuasion and coercion of which none is so far dominant that they can be classified as a sub-type of it. Compare in this respect Anglo-Saxon

England as it was under Edward the Confessor with Babylonia as it was under Hammurapi. It goes without saying that both their antecedent and their subsequent evolution followed markedly divergent paths and that there are fundamental differences between them in both ecology and culture. Ecologically, the greater part of Mesopotamia is desert and the organization of agricultural production was therefore dependent on irrigation, whereas in wet, wooded England it was the problem of clearing and ploughing which needed to be solved. Culturally, the difference between Mesopotamian religion and Christianity extends not merely to their theological content but to the ideological implications for their respective practices defining the relation of sacred to secular power. Yet the similarities in their economic, social-cum-ideological and political-cum-military institutions and the interrelations between them so far outweigh the differences that they cannot but be assigned the same common hybrid mode, however labelled, of the distribution of power.

The functioning of these institutions will be discussed in more detail in Section 27. But for a start, notice that the two societies are alike in the reasons for which they cannot be fitted into any one of the five modes previously listed. There was slavery in both, and the Babylonian *wardū* and Anglo-Saxon *theows* are similar in the functions they performed as well as the locations they occupied. But the relation between citizens and non-citizens was central to neither society in the sense in which it was to Classical Athens or Rome (or Sparta or the North Italian city-states): the dominance of the monarchy and the church was much more important. Yet neither can be labelled 'absolutist': their bureaucracies were minimal, and they depended on local landholders and village communities for the performance of the administrative functions which held them together. This, on the other hand, is not to say either that power was decentralized to the point of feudalism or that their warrior nobilities constituted the dominant institution of the state: in both, the monarch had the power to levy tax and the performance of military service was a duty to the Crown. Nor, lastly, would it be possible to assign either to the category of societies dominated by an emergent bourgeoisie: in both, there were towns, merchants with high status, some wage-labour, and an active market in land-leases and money-lending, but these sectors of the economy were nevertheless subordinated to a state and church dependent for the resources supporting them on the extraction of an agricultural surplus from a range of dependent cultivators.

There was, accordingly, in neither society a set of pervasive roles or a central institution which might provide an obvious basis for defining a distinctive mode. Yet the same systactic pattern of roles was common to both. Both monarchies were strong not because of the coercive power directly available to them but because both combined ideological legitimacy with a system of authority embracing local lordships (whether ecclesiastical or lay) and local kin-based, partly self-governing village communities which provided taxes, soldiers, corvée labour and prestations in kind. Moreover, there is an obvious parallel between Hammurapi's Code and the laws promulgated by the Anglo-Saxon kings, both of which testify not so much to sanctions strictly enforced as to the wish of the ruler to proclaim his status by laying down a set of idealized norms of social control. Below the monarch, there was in both societies a range of formally free persons in roles extending from the higher nobility with direct access to the king down to humbler cultivators working a minimal landholding with the help of their families and liable to periodic military service or guard duty. The Babylonian *awilū*, like the Anglo-Saxon *ceorls*, are admittedly an ambiguous category. But this is because the order of the juridically free did in fact, like some of the later European 'nobilities', cover a wide social distance in both cases. Below them in turn were the semi-servile and the slaves (who in both societies were likely to have been captured in battle), and the vagabonds and lordless men (in Babylonia, the *hapirū* who are persuasively rendered by Bottéro (1954) as 'refugees').

The precise distribution of landholdings and relation between ownership and occupancy is a matter of some dispute among specialists on Anglo-Saxon England, and of still more among specialists on Ancient Mesopotamia (where the predominance of temple records in the cuneiform sources at one stage led researchers to the mistaken inference that private landholding was non-existent). Likewise, the evidence on trade and commerce is, for both societies, not nearly as full as would be necessary for comprehensive reportage of volumes, prices and mechanisms of distribution and exchange. Yet it seems clear that in both societies the church (or temple) was a large landholder in its own right which at the same time performed a limited redistributive function,* that some land was the property of the king worked by his own direct dependents, that there was nevertheless an active land market, that debt was frequently an insuperable problem for smaller landholders, and that cooperative farming arrangements at village level coexisted with large

* Again, this has been much overstated by some Mesopotamian specialists: see Powell (1978, p. 139) for a judicious summary statement on the function of the temple as *Wiederverteilungswirtschaft*.

estates worked under the supervision of bailiffs or overseers. It also seems clear that in both societies the merchants, although subject to regulations of various kinds, still operated as private capitalists* who were free to invest their profits in land, that wage-labour was not purely intermittent or seasonal, that purchase and loan transactions were sophisticatedly calculated and strictly administered, and that artisan production for sale for cash was quite extensive.

The one significant role in Babylonian society (apart from that of *naditum*) to which there is no parallel in Anglo-Saxon England is that of the *mushkēnū*, who appear to have been a systact of royal dependents performing certain fairly onerous obligations in return for holdings of land (Speiser 1958) and to have been required (as the literal meaning of the term suggests) to prostrate themselves in the ritual gesture of *proskynesis* (Diakonoff 1982, p. 28 n. 56 and p. 74 n. 236). But in both societies, rank in the hierarchy of social prestige was closely related to the nature of the task performed. The Babylonian *ilkumahum* corresponds to the privileged royal servant who ministers directly to the royal household (Edward's steersman and goldsmith were both rewarded with grants of land); other craftsmen and servants in both cases had lower status and more onerous obligations; in both societies, such servants were clearly distinguished from those liable to military service and from slaves; and in both societies there is a common category of professional entertainers – the Babylonian *aluzinnū* seem to correspond precisely to the cupbearers, jesters and musicians reported in the Anglo-Saxon sources.

§13. Once beyond this stage of evolution, we start to approach the practices, roles, institutions and societies of the 'modern' world. Modernity as such is a concept which can have no place in an explanatory theory: all societies were once modern, just as the society within which this treatise is being written will one day be ancient. But 'modernity' can serve as an abbreviation to encapsulate the qualitative difference which, on any theory, separates the societies discussed in the previous section from the nineteenth-century world of industrializing nation-states. Economically, it is a world not only of steam-engines, spinning-jennies and electric telegraphs, but of classes of wage-labourers confronting their employers in the relation of vendors of labour-power to owners or controllers of the means of industrial as well as agricultural production. Ideologically, it is a world not only of secular

* Leemans (1950, Ch. 6) effectively demonstrates the independence of the Babylonian *tamkarum* from the royal economy.

rationalism and doctrines of individual rights, but of increasingly well-educated status-groups choosing among competing value-systems and aligning themselves with institutions which define in very different ways the criteria of social prestige and their own relation to them. Politically, it is a world not only of mass parties and expanding franchises, but of the mobilization of the entire population for what will later come to be called 'total' wars. Perhaps it is plausible to suggest that just as coercive power tended to be more important in the transition to statehood, and ideological power thereafter, so in the nineteenth century did economic power become more important than either. But as always, the relation between the three dimensions is one of dependence, not reducibility, and the priority of one over the others is not to be presupposed in advance.

Among the industrial (or industrializing) societies of the twentieth century, the most familiar distinction is between those classified as *capitalist* on the one side and *socialist* on the other. But if these terms are defined exclusively by reference to ownership of the means of production, the distinction is less useful than if it is widened to include an ideological and a political criterion as well as an economic one. This is not to question the significance of the difference between a society in which the means of industrial production are in the hands of the incumbents of governmental roles and one in which they are in the hands of the incumbents of entrepreneurial roles interacting through the institution of the market. But not only may it happen that a more 'left-wing' regime (such as the mid twentieth-century Swedish) holds a smaller proportion of the society's fixed assets than a more 'right-wing' one (such as the mid twentieth-century South African); it may also happen that a capitalist state, although it leaves ownership to the market, exercises a degree of control over the workings of the economy fully comparable to that exercised by a socialist state (as in Britain during the First World War under Lloyd George). It is true that even if the economy is considered in isolation, there remain (as we shall see) institutional differences overriding the tendency of capitalist governments to become involved both as employers and as planners and the tendency of socialist governments to allow decentralization of management and payment by incentive. But the reason for which the differences are more important than the resemblances is that they are directly related to both of the other dimensions of power. In socialist societies, a single party with its bureaucracy directs the economy in accordance with an ideology explicitly inimical to private ownership of the means of production. In capitalist societies, rival parties compete for votes as rival companies compete for consumers of their products and services, and the ideology is as hostile to one-party rule as it is to a command economy.

In any case, a three-dimensional criterion is essential in order to accommodate those societies which combine the rule of a single party or faction with a capitalist economy and an ideology which is no more liberal than socialist but rather nationalist (and, it may be, racist). For these societies, the nearest to a standard term is *authoritarian*. It is a matter of dispute among specialists whether a society such as Nazi Germany should be regarded as exemplifying a 'fascist' sub-type of this mode, or whether 'authoritarian' societies should be categorically distinguished from 'fascist' as being at least to some degree 'pluralist' (Linz 1970, p. 255) rather than 'totalitarian'. But if the criteria which I have just given are accepted (and the test, as always, is in the validity of the explanations to which the definition leads), the difference is one of degree rather than kind. Hitler's Germany is the totalitarian sub-type of the authoritarian mode, as is Stalin's Russia of the socialist. Franco's Spain, by contrast, was relatively more open: the Falange never held a monopoly of the means of coercion, recruitment into the governing élite was from quite a wide range of systactic origins, and the ostensibly dictatorial role of '*caudillo*' was exercised with a cautious regard for other institutional interests. It is true that during the Second World War, a 'totalitarian mobilization' and penetration of 'all sections of society' by the single party was undoubtedly sought; but it was not fully achieved (Maravall 1978, p. 6). Likewise, Japan from 1940 to 1945 is labelled by some authors 'fascist' (e.g. Moore 1967, pp. 304–5); but the party never dominated the state, and others therefore prefer some such label as 'wartime state monopoly capitalism' (Taguchi 1968, p. 468).

The authoritarian mode has sometimes been argued (by Marx, among others) to be intrinsically short-lived, or at best transitional. But although this is true of many cases, it is not of them all. Germany, Italy and Japan went to war and lost it: they were not – or at least, not yet – undermined by internal contradictions. Nor does the failure of Francoism to outlive Franco mean that an authoritarian mode might not have been continued in Spain (with or without direct intervention by the army) or might not re-evolve. Nor is the rapid turnover of the incumbents of governmental roles in some Latin American societies in the authoritarian mode evidence for its inherent instability – any more, it might be said, than the sometimes even more rapid turnover of Roman emperors. It is quite true that the authoritarian mode is sometimes a response to internal or external crisis, and that it may then be more appropriate to speak of authoritarian 'situations' than authoritarian 'regimes' (Linz 1973, p. 235). But there is no contradiction between practices which sustain single-party control of the means of production and persuasion, and practices which keep private ownership of the means of production within a free market in labour and commodities. Perhaps the most striking example is Mexico, where in the aftermath of the events of 1910–20 power passed to a single party whose revolutionary rhetoric was successfully combined with the active encouragement of capitalist practices. Notwithstanding oil nationalization and the *ejido* system of communal landownership, the practices, roles and institutions of a capitalist industrial society were all preserved, including strikes by formally free wage-workers, strong independent employers' associations, and the determination of economic policies by market forces to an extent arguably greater than in multi-party electoral systems (Casanova 1970, pp. 15, 51, 143). Nor, indeed, does anything prevent an authoritarian regime from permitting if not encouraging practices which confer competitive advantage on workers at the expense of shareholders, villagers at the expense of latifundists, or low-status ethnic groups at the expense of high-status ones.

Can there, then, be industrial societies which combine a centrally planned economy with a multi-party system? No such has yet evolved. But it might be a mistake to assume that the necessary practices and roles could not be combined within a reproducible mode. Suppose, for example, that a Swedish government were to implement an extreme form of the 'Meidner proposals' whereby the means of production all come to be owned by trusts controlled by trade unions whose heads are directly involved in the formulation of successive five-year plans which determine investment, prices and wages. Managers would then cease to be entrepreneurs, rentiers would become pensioners of the state, and trade unions would no longer bargain locally with autonomous employers but become 'transmission-belts', in Lenin's celebrated phrase, for the dissemination of central policy. But would this necessarily prevent the continuing alternation in office of rival parties within a liberal-democratic ideology of free competition for educational places and thereby occupational roles, including the roles of the governing élite?

There is also a theoretical possibility of yet a further kind. Thus far in this Section, the modes of production and coercion have been taken as dominant. But what if the mode of persuasion is given priority? One or more Islamic societies could well evolve in such a way that the roles and institutions of industrial capitalism are subordinated to the roles of autonomous mullahs whose parliament licenses only those practices which are deemed compatible with the principles of the Quran and are thereby capable of securing the ideological commitment of a community of believers – the *umma* – for whom the sanction of public opinion is binding. *Pace* Weber, there is nothing in Islam which need inhibit the rational pursuit of profit. Although the role of merchant may have an elective affinity with Islamic doctrine which is lacking to the role of entrepreneur, the first is well capable of evolving into the second.* An orthodox Islamic industrial society might restrict the workings of the banking system (because of the Quran's injunctions against usury), impose high income and capital taxes (the traditional *khums* and *zakat*) on the owners of the means of production for the support of the ulemate, the army and the urban poor, and maintain controls on the free workings of the labour and commodity markets in the furtherance of ideological as distinct from economic objectives. But need that modify the distinctiveness of a mode of the distribution of power whose most important characteristic is a pervasive ideology as vehemently hostile to socialism on the one side as to liberal democracy on the other?

That particular box in the Linnaean grid is for the moment empty, as is the category of 'multi-party socialism'. But there is one industrial society which, whatever is about to happen to it in the future, has maintained for more than a generation in the mid twentieth century a mode of the distribution of power falling outside any of the categories which I have so far put forward. That society is South Africa. It could by no conceivable stretch be labelled socialist. But nor could it be labelled either capitalist or authoritarian. It is not capitalist because the mode of production has been dominated by a structural principle which goes directly against that of a free market – strict ethnic discrimination coercively enforced and underpinned by a strongly held ideology purporting to legitimate it. It is not authoritarian because within the dominant white population politics and the law have continued to be practised through the institutions of parliamentary liberalism. The structure cannot but be potentially unstable because of the formidable demographic imbalance between the white and non-white populations. But it has shown itself sufficiently capable of reproduction to refute any hypothesis to the effect that industrialization must dissolve barriers of status and therefore class based on ethnicity. Quite the contrary: these

* As, to give a specific example, in the career of Ahmed Kayama (b. 1928) in Iran, which vividly exemplifies intra-generational mobility 'from bazaar-type trade right into the heart of the modern sector of an industrial economy and the beginnings of a vertically-integrated business' (Graham 1978, p. 48).

practices can be so adapted by their carriers that they function to preserve and even to widen the pre-existing inequalities in the distribution of power (cf. Blumer 1965).

I defer until later any further speculation about possible modes and sub-types into which the industrial societies of the future might evolve. But the conclusion already to be drawn is the same as at each of the earlier stages in the expansion of the economic, ideological and coercive resources available to be allocated among competing roles and systacts. The range of variation widens, but within a set of constraints which rules out many of the institutional combinations which might appear to be logically possible. The result is a world in which observable differences in modes of the distribution of power are at the same time much less than the enormous flexibility of practices might seem to imply and much more than was ever envisaged by nineteenth- or early twentieth-century theorists of evolution, whether Comte, Marx, Spencer, Durkheim or Weber.

§14. It is, however, worth remarking (if only in parenthesis) that if the purpose of a classification of societies is descriptive or evaluative rather than explanatory a quite different set of distinctions will need to have been drawn. Descriptively, different modes of the distribution of power only partially correspond with differences in the *Weltanschauungen* through which the respresentative members of different systacts and milieux interpret their own experience of their roles to themselves; and evaluatively, there is even less likelihood of correspondence between modes of the distribution of power and states of society which significantly augment or diminish the well-being, as their members themselves perceive it, of groups or categories sharing a common location. This volume, as I have said, is principally concerned with explaining the workings and evolution of societies of different kinds, and only incidentally with conveying what it was like to live in them or assessing whether they were better or worse for those who did than they might have been. But there are two descriptive contrasts which are implicit already in much of the discussion thus far and will inevitably recur, if only incidentally, in what follows. The first is between those societies (or milieux within them) whose *Weltanschauung* is self-consciously egalitarian and those where marked differences of power, however much they may be disliked, are taken for granted. The second is between those whose *Weltanschauung* embodies a conscious recognition of change from, or rupture with, the past and those where traditional attitudes and mores are unquestioned.

The first contrast is familiar alike from accounts such as Tocqueville's of the transition from 'feudal' to 'democratic' manners exemplified in the American and French Revolutions and from accounts such as Dumont's (1970) of the gulf which separates the presuppositions underlying the Indian conception of hierarchy from those of the European tradition of rationalism, individualism and the rights of man. But it is a contrast which can be no less well documented in terms of similarities between societies which are in other respects almost totally dissimilar. Thus, fully to understand in the tertiary, descriptive sense the institutions and practices of the nineteenth- and twentieth-century United States, it is necessary to acquire a feel for the caste-like assumptions which underlay the attitudes of white-skinned Americans to their black-skinned fellow-citizens and which generated the 'American Dilemma', as Gunnar Myrdal (1944) called it, whereby a self-righteously anti-'feudal' repudiation of inherited status could coexist with a categorical denial of equality to persons whose distinguishing characteristic was as little the fault of themselves as the descent of King George the Third from King George the Second. At the same time, the strident egalitarianism among (white) Americans which led Bryce (1910, II, p. 813) to comment in 1893 that 'there is no rank in America; that is to say, no external and recognised stamp, marking one man as entitled to any social privileges or to deference and respect from others' can itself be paralleled descriptively from a society as different in other ways as Rome in the first century A.D.: in Petronius's *Satyricon* (CXVII. 11–12), there is a memorably vivid depiction of Corax, the hired porter, whose determination to remind his employers that he is as good a man as they is at least as insistent as that of any latter-day counterpart whom Lord Bryce might have encountered on the quayside when disembarking in New York.

The same holds at the opposite extreme where the arbitrary power of an autocratic ruler is inescapably present in the *Weltanschauung* of those subject to it. Compare from this point of view the Soviet Union under Stalin with England under Henry VIII. Under no explanatory rubric will these two societies be assigned the same polynomial label. But how strikingly, even sinisterly, alike they are from the point of view of the people who lived in them! To read the *Lisle Letters* and Sir Francis Bryan's all too sensible warning to Lord Lisle to 'keep all things secreter than you have been used', for 'there is nothing done or spoken but it is with speed knowen in the Court' is to be irresistibly reminded of the atmosphere of fear, treachery and suspicion conveyed by a description of life under Stalin like Nadezhda Mandelstam's *Hope Against Hope*.

Adequately to convey to the reader what it is like to be under the constant threat of arrest, deportation and execution, to be unable to tell which acquaintance or colleague may be an informer or a spy, to witness the obsessional paranoia of the ruler being directed against people wholly innocent of the charges made against them, and to know that your livelihood and career and those of your family or friends may depend on your willingness to compromise your most deeply held principles requires the invocation of concepts which will generate categories cutting directly across those of 'feudalism', 'absolutism', 'socialism' and the rest. Indeed, from the viewpoint of the participants there may well be the further irony that they themselves perceive the practice of terror to be irrelevant to the workings and evolution of institutions which, to the best of their belief, would answer as well or better to the ruler's ostensible aims without it.

The second descriptive contrast – between traditionalist and self-consciously innovative societies – calls likewise for concepts which will correlate with explanatory categories only in passing. It is true that to invoke, for example, 'Confucianism' – whether literally or metaphorically – to describe the sense of rightness held to attach to an unchanging hierarchical order legitimated by the inherently superior virtue of its élite carries the further implication that the pervasiveness of this sense of rightness itself explains, at least in part, the remarkable stability of the system. But it can equally happen that the subjective experience of the members of a strongly traditionalist society fails to reflect changes which are going on without their sensing it. An *ancien régime* is only *ancien* with hindsight: to those who live under it, it is 'the' *régime*, whether they like it or not, and there is no reason to expect that even the most perspicacious of them will detect beneath the seemingly unchanging surface of custom and precedent the mutant or recombinant practices by which the traditional structure and culture are being imperceptibly undermined. Indeed, it is hardly possible to describe authentically what it was like to live in a strongly traditionalist society without conveying to the reader the way in which the dominant habits of thought and action precluded the serious consideration of alternatives.

The resulting categories, accordingly, will correlate neither with the stage of evolution which the societies in question have reached nor with the particular content of their inherited and hitherto unquestioned ideologies. It may be that there is a sense in which the idea of deliberate progress achieved at the conscious expense of tradition is a creation of the secular rationalism of the European Enlightenment: certainly, the shift from recollections of a golden age located in the mythologized past to visions of utopia located in the prophesied future has been exhaustively documented by historians of ideas. But a sense that times are and ought to be changing and that the old order is deservedly giving way to the new is by no means unique to the 'modern' West. Nor, conversely, is a sense of commitment to inherited institutions confined to societies which have never consciously questioned their institutions in the past. A revolutionary ideology can harden into an orthodoxy no less dogmatic than a conservative one. It is, for example, perfectly possible to envisage the Soviet Union becoming as traditionalist – descriptively speaking – within the ideology of Marxism-Leninism as China ever was within the ideology of Confucianism. The idea of a stable hierarchy legitimated by the Mandate of Heaven may command no more unquestioning or long-lasting an adherence than the idea of a society of 'non-antagonistic classes' in which the hierarchy is legitimated by the claim that the rulers represent the interests of the proletariat whose collective expropriation of their previous exploiters marks the final stage in the dialectic of history.

There is also a further and final reason for which both contrasts cut across the categories generated by an explanatory theory. The sense which people have of what their societies are like is often a function of their own conscious invocation of a parallel with other societies remote in both time and place – an invocation which will be no less potent if the supposed facts on which it rests are inaccurate to the point of fiction. If, to revert to an example from Volume I, the members of a society feel that they are living through a renaissance, they *are* living through a renaissance and their society has, from this aspect, to be bracketed with others of which the same is true. It follows that a full account of any society – full, that is, in that it not only reports and explains but also describes it – will have to categorize it by reference to a set of concepts which will not only supplement but may well conflict with its categorization for the purpose of explanation. If, in the remainder of this volume, that is left largely implicit, it is not because it is not as proper or interesting a sociological exercise. It is because, first, descriptions of the *Weltanschauungen* which two or more societies, or milieux within them, are held to have in common cannot be summarized as briefly as they would have to be without compromising their authenticity; and second, my own priority in this volume is to advance an explanatory theory of the workings and evolution of societies to the description of which I have nothing particular to add.

CONTRADICTIONS AND CONSTRAINTS

§15. I have stressed that to categorize a society at all is to credit it with the minimal stability implicit in the notion of a reproducible set of roles, and therefore institutions, which continues to be there for rival observers to observe. But this does not exclude the possibility of its reported roles and institutions being such that observers of all theoretical schools can predict without adducing any further evidence either or both that it cannot long remain as it is and/or that certain changes of mode or sub-type are impossible for it. For the first, I shall use the term *contradiction*, and for the second, *constraint*.

'Contradiction' has a particular meaning within Marxian social theory – viz., the incompatibility of a given mode of production with a set of social relations joined to, but lagging behind, it. But contradictions within a given society's total set of roles and institutions can be identified without presupposing that their outcome will be explicable exclusively by reference to incompatibilities among their practices which answer to the Marxian definition. Likewise, although there are constraints specified by Marxian theory which rule out certain logically possible transitions from one mode of production to another, there is no need to presuppose that they are the only ones which preclude societies from evolving into categories ostensibly open to them. Notice, moreover, that on any theory constraints and contradictions are opposite sides of the same coin. To say that the coexistence of two or more observed institutions can only be temporary is to say that there is at least one sub-type of the mode to which the society in which they coexist has been assigned which is only a transitional option for any other society in which the same contradiction evolves.

Contradictions may be due (i) to an incompatibility between practices simultaneously required by the conflicting objectives of rulers, (ii) to constraints imposed by the systactic structure as such, or (iii) to a conjunction of practices which are bound, in their common context, to undermine the competitive advantages attaching to each other.

(i) The objectives of rulers may conflict with one another whether they know it or not, and the incompatibility may be either cultural or (as we saw in the discussion of polarization and compression in Section 7) structural. The ruler of a state created out of the conquest by nomadic pastoralists of sedentary agriculturalists may or may not be aware of the contradiction between his need to regulate and centralize the polity and his need to preserve the independence and privileges of the supporters on whom his power still depends (Khazanov 1984, p. 284). Lycurgus (if he existed) may or may not have been aware of the contradiction between his disesteem for the institution of the family and consequent willingness to see estates devised away from natural heirs and his desire to preserve the number of Spartiates, which led in the end to an unequal concentration of land among progressively fewer citizens (Hooker 1980, p. 143). The rulers of post-colonial Kenya may or may not have been aware of the contradiction between their need to maintain political stability by providing employment in the public sector and their dependence on revenue limited by the attainable rate of real output (Kitching 1980, p. 247). Sometimes, it is true, there may turn out to be a way of maintaining stability for longer than at first seemed feasible: thus, the dilemma facing the Kenyan government could at least temporarily be resolved by external borrowing. But eventually something has to give – that is, one or other of the contradictory sets of practices has to be modified if not abandoned entirely.

(ii) A good example of constraints and thereby contradictions imposed by the systactic structure as such is the society of seventeenth-century France. There has been much debate among specialists over how far resistance to the central government was spontaneously popular and based on the grievances of the peasantry as a class and how far it was regional rather than populist and tacitly encouraged, if not actually led, by the provincial nobility. But there is no dispute that first, there *was* a '*provincialisme populaire et un fonds antifiscal commun à toute la société*' (Bercé 1974, p. 676), and second, the provincial nobility *did* wish to preserve their autonomy, and with it '*les moyens et les occasions d'exercer la protection seigneuriale*' (*ibid.*, p. 682). But the role of *seigneur* derived its legitimacy from the very monarchy which the nobility sought to resist. It was not that they could not conceive of the possibility of an alternative: they were perfectly well aware of the existence of republican governments. It was rather that their own dominant location depended, as they could see for themselves, on a monarchy no longer 'feudal' whose interests were, accordingly, in conflict with their own. Indeed, a parallel dilemma confronted those rebels against the existing systactic structure who were not merely rebellious but revolutionary in their practices and aims: the Ormists of Bordeaux were doomed to failure because they could not defeat the monarchy without an alliance with the *Parlement* and could not defeat the *Parlement* without an alliance with the monarchy (Westrich 1979, p. 134). In the event, these contradictions were resolved by the victory of the monarchy, but one which depended on leaving a not insignificant amount of power with local corporations and on coming to an accommodation with both the nobility and the Church.

(iii) By contrast, Republican Rome offers an example where the contradictions resulting from the success of a citizen army in conquering alien territories do not seem to have been perceived by any of those involved at the time. To Sallust – and indeed to all the ancient authors – the fall of the Republic was a morality tale of corruption through avarice and ambition. But although it is true that the rival ambitions of individual members of the ruling stratum did, for reasons to be analyzed more fully in Chapter 4, destroy the institutions which had made them possible, this was not because of the fact of their individual motivation. It was because, as Marx saw, 'the preservation of the ancient community implies the destruction of the conditions on which it rests' (1964, p. 93). The more successful the *assidui* who manned the legions in maintaining the supremacy of Rome in Italy and beyond, the more they undermined their role as a relatively equal, propertied citizen militia. Admittedly, Tiberius Gracchus was explicitly motivated to introduce his attempted reforms by his dismay at the replacement of smallholdings by slave-worked estates through the impoverishment of the soldiers whom the increasing frequency and duration of campaigns deprived of their ability to maintain them. But there was 'an inherent contradiction in the Gracchan objective of increasing the number of Rome's peasant soldiers, when it was soldiering that did much to destroy the peasantry' (Brunt 1971 a, p. 92). It was inevitable that the cycle of war, booty (including slaves) and further war would require the armies to call first on propertyless Roman *proletarii* and then on Italians, and that the best agricultural land would come to be increasingly taken over by large proprietors, who would have to be forcibly dispossessed if discharged veterans were to be re-established successfully as freeholding farmers.

These three types of contradiction are not mutually exclusive. But the examples given serve to show that there are societies belonging in quite different modes of the distribution of power whose structure at a given time can be seen almost at a glance to be unworkable for more than a limited period. It does not follow that the outcome can be predicted in advance. But with hindsight, theorists of all schools can be brought to agree that one or another of the roles and institutions concomitantly observed had to lose out in the inescapable competition between the practices defining them.

§16. A special case of contradictions and related constraints is the occurrence of *cycles* – a cycle being defined as a change which results in due course in the return of the system to its initial state. The idea is long familiar in social theory, whether in the classical conception of a transition from tyranny through oligarchy to democracy and from there back to tyranny again, or in Ibn Khaldun's view of Islamic societies as alternating between rule by cohesive, egalitarian, warlike enthusiasts from the desert and rule by effete, bureaucratic, hierarchical intriguers in the towns. Indeed, it has its almost proverbial models in each of the three dimensions of social structure: economically, the cycle from boom to slump to boom; ideologically, the cycle from charisma to its routinization to the re-emergence of a new charismatic leader preaching a return to purity of doctrine and conduct; coercively, the cycle from conquest to retreat to a yet more determined effort at reconquest. But no useful sociological generalizations can be sustained in these terms. The classical *poleis* did not, as it turned out, conform to the classical cycle; Ibn Khaldun's view of Islamic societies fails against the awkward counter-example of the Ottoman Turks; booms and slumps can be smoothed out under certain conditions; not all ideological routinization generates a new charismatic movement; not every defeat of an expansionist state sets it on a policy of determined *revanchisme*. Cycles do occur. But where they do, it is because and only because a society's practices and thereby roles generate a contradiction which forces a change which runs up against a constraint which then compels the system to revert to the (once again contradictory) state in which it was initially observed.

Consider as an example the cycle from egalitarianism to hierarchy and back again among the Kachin as explained by Friedman (1975). His account is explicitly Marxian, but the sense in which he takes conditions of production to be determinant 'in the last instance' (p. 164) is not likely to be contested, at least in this context, by theorists of rival schools. The key to the cycle is demographic growth in an environment where productivity per head cannot be expanded in parallel – a state of affairs familiar from many times and places, but which in this instance generates a distinctively contradictory pattern of its own. The growth of population has the effect of translating lineage segmentation into local segmentation, and the practice of exchanging prestige goods generates both variations in brideprice and competition in the giving of community feasts. Land, however, is communally owned; and thus the structure becomes that of a conical clan within which competitive advantage is conferred by practices of tribute and corveé and chiefly surpluses are supplemented by the output of slaves. But this inevitable polarization goes no less inevitably into reverse as the increasing demand for surplus labour and continuing population growth comes up against the ecological barrier of the fallow cycle: the high yields available in Upper Burma are critically dependent on maintaining the fertility of the soil. The result is feuding, increasing indebtedness, ecological degradation and declining productivity per head. Revolts break out, prestige goods are devalued, and the recently evolved social ranks are suppressed. The cycle from egalitarianism (*gumlao*) to hierarchy (*gumsa*) back to *gumlao* is complete. What is more, the experience of the Kachin groups which descended from the highlands into the plains of Assam provides one of those nice quasi-experimental contrasts which the historical and ethnographic record throws up now and again to gladden the heart of the general theorist: in the plains, the same contradictions led not to a reversion to the original egalitarian structure but to the evolution of small, class-based states.

Here, as we have seen elsewhere, the neatness of the example is thanks in part to its modest local scale. But it is paralleled *modo grosso* by China, where a set of practices which generated both rising agricultural productivity and rising population led, in the absence of a change in the mode of production, to an inescapable contradiction between the requirements of the state, if it was to retain its effective monopoly of the means of coercion, and the institutions of Chinese rural society. It is a matter of continuing debate why China did not, as in theory it could have, evolve out of what one specialist calls its 'high-level equilibrium trap' (Elvin 1973, Ch. 17) into industrialization. But given that it did not, and that the periodic checks to population growth through plague and famine could not by themselves preserve the traditional order intact, it was inevitable that there should be a crisis every time the constraints on further increases in productivity per head were reached. These crises could only be resolved by an outbreak of violence and the restoration under a new mandate of the old institutional forms. Restoration was not, as I have pointed out already in Section 4, accomplished without some changes of both structure and culture; but the cyclical pattern is as unmistakable as in the case of the Kachin.

Nor are such cycles confined to pre-industrial societies. Among capitalist industrial societies there are examples enough of booms followed by slumps followed by booms which sometimes, at least, do follow the lines predicted by both Marxian and neo-classical theorists; and among socialist industrial societies, there are at least some no less inevitable-seeming cycles of a predominantly political rather than a predominantly economic kind. Consider the example of Poland between the end of Stalinism and the imposition of martial law by General Jaruzelski in December 1981.* Poland is distinctive among the societies of Eastern Europe for, among other things, an intense nationalism and an accompanying resentment of a government perceived as alien. But both Gomulka after 1956 and Gierek after 1970 enjoyed periods of stability. The cycle which repeated itself under both of them was generated not by their lack of legitimacy but by contradictions in all three dimensions of structure between their stated aims and the means necessary to achieve them. Economically, the contradiction was between a commitment to higher living standards for the population as a whole and a commitment to managerial practices which ruled out the possibility of generating the necessary increases in agricultural and industrial productivity. Ideologically, the contradiction was between the continuing ascription of prestige to traditionally high-ranking occupational roles and the claim of the Polish United Worker's Party to embody values justifying the 'leading role' of its members. Politically, the contradiction was between government ostensibly by, or at least on behalf of, the working class and effective domination by a core of 'old guard' party activists.

None of these contradictions was necessarily incapable of resolution within what would still be a sub-type of the socialist mode of the distribution of power. But in the Polish case, their resolution was decisively constrained by the police and security apparatus controlled by the Party. Economically, the regime was unable to use its control of the means of production to change radically the organization, deployment and remuneration of the workforce. Ideologically, it was unable to use its control of the means of persuasion to alter the party line in a direction which might win the commitment of the population at large. Politically, it was unable to use its control of the means of coercion to impose on its own members and supporters a system of open elections to party posts and thus the possibility of a 'loyal opposition'. It was therefore inevitable that the cycle of apparent concessions, mounting relative deprivation, spontaneous resistance, and re-establishment of Party control should be repeated – in the knowledge that the Soviet Union would never allow the emergence of roles by which power of the Party would be undermined.

These three examples are deliberately taken from very different parts of the historical and ethnographic record, and they could easily be paralleled by others at each evolutionary stage. But there is a further

* I am here summarizing an analysis expounded at greater length elsewhere (Runciman 1985).

general point to be made, which is well illustrated by contrasting the example of the Kachin with that of the Poles. The Kachin example might seem to suggest that the absence of exogenous pressure is a necessary condition of the continuance of the cycle: in an environment where they were in direct contact with more powerful neighbours, would the Kachin not have been compelled either to break out of the cycle from semi- into proto-statehood or else to resign themselves to either fusion or absorption as the case might be? But the Polish example suggests the opposite: a necessary condition of the continuance of *their* cycle is the exogenous influence of the Soviet Union. As Parkin (1972, p. 62 n. 16) remarks, to put the question of comparative stability in its proper form requires us to 'think away the Red Army'. Accordingly, the distinction between endogenous changes (or the lack of them) and 'secondary' changes provoked, encouraged or imposed by contact with other societies should not be presupposed to determine whether an observed contradiction will result in an evolution from one mode of the distribution of power to another or in a cyclical regression in the face of an inescapable constraint. As always, it depends on the context within which one rather than another practice is adaptive for one rather than another systact or role.

§17. In societies in the 'hunter-gatherer' mode, it cannot be claimed that there are any characteristic contradictions, if by that is meant, in accordance with the definition given above, that the societies in question cannot in consequence remain as they are. There are, to be sure, contradictions in the sense of personal conflicts of interest, and Leacock and Lee, whom I quoted in Section 2, use the term in that sense. But they readily concede that foraging societies have persisted for hundreds and even thousands of years, not only in isolated ecological niches but also in symbiotic equilibrium with neighbouring agriculturalists (1982, p. 13). Similarly, although some Marxian theorists have claimed to detect inherent contradictions in nomadic pastoral societies between 'the domestic framework of productive work and the community conditions of reproduction' (Lefébure 1979, p. 9), it is indisputable that some nomadic pastoralists have reproduced their institutions unchanged over centuries despite their contacts with the agriculturalists on whom they depend for grain. There is, however, no need to fall back on the horns of the false dilemma between the presuppositions of a dialectical materialism for which change is always the norm and a functionalism for which it is always the exception. Some hunters, some foragers and some pastoralists maintain their structure and culture unchanged over many generations and would, under certain conditions, continue to do so indefinitely. But it is also true that these conditions include practices which prevent individual conflicts of interest from generating contradictions such as would be bound to lead either to a cycle of crisis and restoration or to an evolution to a different mode of the distribution of power. In foraging societies, equilibrium is maintained by, among other things, infanticide and the deliberate spacing of children; in nomadic pastoral societies, it is maintained by, among other things, fission on the part of dissident households. Conflicts of interest in these societies do not of themselves require a change in the mode of the distribution of power or lead to contradictions as here defined: or, in other words, they are not fundamental for the simple reason that they can be, and often are, headed off in advance.

It is, however, at the stage of evolution when free-floating resources become available on a significant scale that characteristic contradictions arise between practices old and new. Where economic and/or ideological and/or coercive resources accumulate beyond the customary powers attaching to a pre-existing set of roles, those roles have to adapt one way or the other to accomodate them. It is true that no mutant or recombinant practice need be selected at the expense of another if the extra resources are dissipated in such a way as to leave the relative locations of the pre-existing roles unchanged. If the 'big-man' can retain his position only by giving his newly won surplus away to his dependents, or the *basileus* can retain his augmented prestige only by continually renewed exhibitions of prowess, or the victorious *sheikh* can retain his warriors only for as long as they choose not to desert him for a neighbouring rival, then no change in the mode of the distribution of power need arise. Further, given constraints of the kinds already discussed, an apparent change of mode may be only the first stage of a predictable cycle. The petty kings descending from their hill-forts in Madagascar to extract protection-rents from the surrounding peasants, or the Hawaiian chiefs trying but failing to achieve the 'structural break' with their people which will turn them into heads of states, are forced back into their pre-existing roles until such time as one of them can command resources so much more substantial as to amount to a difference of kind. But in many other instances equally remote from one another in both time and place, an accumulation of resources, however caused, can be seen to require one practice or another to give way and one or more novel roles to emerge. This is the process which underlies the formation of states in those cases where it is primary rather than secondary. The extra means of production, persuasion and coercion which are now available to be appropriated may be the outcome of a number of different and sometimes complex interactions between trade, population growth, technological innovation, a rise in communal – if not yet 'civic' – consciousness, a shift from stock-rearing to agriculture and so forth. But there comes a point at which mutant practices are visibly selected for their competitive advantage and one or more of the pre-existing roles visibly overwhelmed.

The same holds equally when it comes to the contradictions characteristic of the societies of Western Europe after the disintegration of the Roman Empire in the West. It is not that there is a necessary contradiction between the institutions of any and all societies in the feudal mode. On the contrary, an entirely plausible model can be constructed in which the central monarchy remains weak, ideological hegemony rests with the Church, manorial landholders, both ecclesiastical and lay, dissipate or thesaurize the surpluses extracted by rent and corvée, population is kept stable by war and disease, and military superiority depends on defensive stone-built castles and highly trained mounted knights. As we shall see in more detail in Section 22, the central institutions of such a society are well capable of reproducing themselves under certain specifiable conditions. But those conditions never held in Western Europe. The institutional contradiction, when it came, was not resolved, as in Chinese society, by a cyclical reversion to the *status quo*, but by an evolution to yet another mode of the distribution of power.

Once the need for defence against marauding Magyars, Saracens and Vikings was over, how could societies with expanding populations, increasingly prosperous towns, improved communications between centre and periphery, legitimate monarchies, and a proven capacity for the raising of tax fail to generate an irreconcilable conflict between pressures for a recentralization of power on the one hand and the fission of autonomous principalities (or citizen republics) on the other? As it turned out, the resolution took the form of a recentralization which followed a loss of power by the local magnates alike economically (as productivity per head collapsed), ideologically (as churchmen and monarchs in cooperation denied them their title to wield the means of coercion as they chose), and coercively (as they succumbed both to monarchical force – including artillery – on one side and to well-equipped urban militias on the other). Like the evolution of Rome from citizen-state to absolute monarchy, the evolution of France from feudal to absolute monarchy was a process initially set in train by the impossibility of a stable reproduction of the existing systactic structure.

Once at the stage of the capitalist industrial societies, the notion of a characteristic contradiction is thoroughly familiar in the form of the Marxian hypothesis of a revolutionary polarization between the owners of the means of production and the vendors of labour-power resulting from the contradiction between forces and relations of production. The particular hypothesis has been invalidated in its original form. But the diagnosis of a contradiction was not wholly incorrect. Marx and Engels were right in seeing that something had to give. The surprise (as it would have been to them) was that the selection of mutant practices took a form which they had only fleetingly anticipated. Instead of a relentless polarization between proletariat and bourgeoisie, there have evolved roles and institutions in all capitalist industrial societies which have at the same time complicated the systactic structure and decreased both the relative size and the relative impoverishment of the working class. Yet at the same time, the characteristic contradiction which remains is between practices selected as productive of resources and practices selected as redistributive of them. How serious it may be, how far it can be resolved by an ideology of free competition and universal suffrage in a multi-party system, and what will be its long-term consequences are questions about which rival theorists cannot yet hope to agree. But, as always, a definitive answer can as confidently be expected to emerge with hindsight as a prediction made now can be expected to fail.

In socialist industrial societies, finally, the characteristic contradiction is between the practices sustaining a single-party state and centrally planned economy and those implied by the nominal abolition of class antagonisms in the interests of workers and peasants. In the Polish case, there is, as I argued in the previous Section, the constraint imposed by the Soviet Union whose exogenous pressure generates a cycle of revolt and repression rather than an evolution resulting from the selection of one set of practices at the expense of another. But traces of the same contradiction are visible in the Soviet Union itself, where, although there have not been the same collectively conscious manifestations of relative deprivation as in Poland and elsewhere, the same dilemma of reconciling central control with popular participation remains unresolved. Again, it is too early to say either when or how this will lead to a change in the mode of the distribution of power. But there is a potential for instability and thereby a context in which mutant or recombinant practices might modify the existing systactic structure, whether change was being sought by the governing élite or not.

FUNCTIONAL ALTERNATIVES (1)

§18. How then, after all this long preamble, do societies of different kinds actually work – which is to say, what is it that causes (or at any rate permits) their constituent practices, roles and institutions to cohere and reproduce themselves sufficiently for them to be assigned their taxonomic place? Some, as we know, do not. Some are in a condition of obviously ephemeral stability; some are undergoing a rapid and perhaps violent transition to a different mode of the distribution of power; some are literally being destroyed under the observer's eyes. But most are, at any one time, stable enough to be assigned their place in a presumptive taxonomy with both a 'Linnaean' and a 'Darwinian' rationale. To ask how they work is neither to favour questions about function at the expense of questions about origin nor to favour evidence of harmony at the expense of evidence of discord. Nor is it to presuppose that institutional catchment areas coincide with geographical frontiers. It is merely to recognize that where relative stability is observed and reported, it has, no less than conflict and change, to be explained. This can only be done by showing which of the given society's practices, roles and institutions so function as to preserve the existing mode of the distribution of power; and for hypotheses to that effect to be validated, there will have to be drawn appropriate quasi-experimental contrasts to analogous and homologous practices, roles and institutions either in other societies or in the same society at other times.

Critical to the possibility of such contrasts is the flexibility of practices which, as I remarked in Section 12 of Chapter 1, enables the incumbents of an existing role to adapt to a change in their environment in the same way as the mutability of genes enables the members of a species to adapt to a change in theirs. But there is more to this flexibility than the evident capacity of human agents to modify the practices which define their roles and thereby their economic, social-cum-ideological and political-cum-military institutions. In the first place, it extends to the capacity of roles actually to reverse their existing institutional function. In the second place, it extends to the capacity of roles defined by practices in one dimension to perform functions in another, and that not only through a single person's occupying a second role but also through the adaptation of the role itself.* This multiple flexibility has

* Such adaptation can, moreover, take either of two different forms: thus, the incumbent of a subordinate role can be used to perform an additional function, as for example when the Ottonian Henry II employed his chaplain for a military reconnaissance in the Carinthian Alps (Leyser 1981, p. 726); or a dominant role can

the consequence of making the explanation of the coherence (if such it is) of the roles itemizing any chosen society in one way easier and in another more difficult: easier, in that it makes it less problematic to account for the persistence of a mode of the distribution of power through what would otherwise be fundamental cultural and structural changes; more difficult, in that it makes it more problematic to identify the particular practices whose function is decisive for a relative stability which may in addition vary between one geographical and/or institutional area and the next.

It might be objected at this point that I have excluded altogether the possibility that a society may be in a state neither of stability nor of change (whether unidirectional or cyclical) but of chronic and uncontrollable *in*stability – if you like, of 'consistent chaos'. What does it mean to talk about institutional functions and coherence of roles in a context not merely of contradiction between incompatible practices but of anarchy, confusion and civil war? Rome during the death throes of the Republic, Arabia during the first and second *fitnahs*, Catalonia in the early years of the eleventh century, England in the reign of King Stephen, Japan after the fall of the Ashikaga Shogunate or Russia in the 'Time of Troubles' of the early seventeenth century could all, among many others, be cited as examples of times and places at which previously established institutions ceased to work at all. But the breakdown of a system is not to be equated with its negation. A society in chaos may not be possible to assign to a given mode of the distribution of power. But it shortly will be unless it ceases to exist; and it will cease to exist only in cases of extermination or dispersal. Reportage of a society in chaos is still reportage in terms of a displacement of old roles by new ones which are both symptoms and causes of it, whether economic (thieves, beggars, black marketeers), ideological (iconoclasts, heretics, millennarians) or coercive (usurpers, gangsters, warlords). However long a period of anarchy and confusion may persist, and however unpredictable may be its eventual outcome, the society in question will still be definable by the itemization of the roles which its members occupy, and the answer to the question how it works will still lie in the function of the practices which define those roles.

On the other hand, this often cannot be done without reference to the pressure exercised by another society, and that pressure can operate in what may at first sight seem paradoxical ways. It is not merely that it

be deliberately adapted to additional functions by its incumbent, as for example when Merovingian bishops organized famine relief and the ransoming of captives out of their own private funds (James 1982, pp. 54–5).

may, so to speak, be powerful without being real: an external threat, even if conjured up purely for the purpose by Machiavellian rulers, can function (and often has) to stifle the expression of relative deprivation at home. It is also that the same exogenous pressure can in some contexts preserve and in others undermine the practices and institutions of the society subject to it. A colonial government holding the ring between rival ethnic and religious communities in a 'plural' society may, on the one hand, be preventing the outbreak of civil war or may, on the other, be unwittingly fostering an independence movement whose success will result in a total fission of the rival communities. A society of nomadic pastoralists intermittently preying on the inhabitants of a settled agricultural region insufficiently well defended by the agents of their own central government may be preserving a long-standing symbiotic pattern of social relations, or it may be on the brink of provoking unsuccessful resistance followed by headlong dispersal. A multinational trading company may be helping to smooth the transition to autonomous economic growth and therewith political stability in a newly emergent 'third-world' state, or it may be so far heightening the sense of relative deprivation among those who feel excluded from the benefits which it brings as to touch off an attempted revolution. But all this can be accommodated perfectly well within the general theory of the competitive selection of practices. As always, the apparent paradox of similar causes producing dissimilar effects dissolves when the function of exogenous practices for different roles and systacts within the society affected is analyzed by reference to their conflicting interests in the context of the pre-existing distribution of power.

However unstable a society may be, therefore, however fluid its boundaries, however ramshackle its institutions, however confused its pattern of social relations, and however powerful the alien influences at whose mercy it lies, the question 'how does it work?' has still to be answered in terms of the functions of identifiable practices and thereby roles. It is true that there is always the danger that the existing mode of the distribution of power may have been inaccurately reported in the first place. Particularly when a society is, for the moment, in chaos, it may be difficult for participants and observers alike to be sure that they are correctly understanding in the primary sense what is going on between the incumbents of imperfectly articulated roles. To revert to the example of commendation and vassalage, the different senses in which a man may be making himself 'the man of another man' need not be a function simply of changes in the institutional context such as took place between early Merovingian Gaul and the last days of a vestigial pre-Revolutionary 'feudalism'. It can also result from an ambiguity dictated precisely by the anarchy which is driving hitherto independent allodialists to offer their independence in return for the promise of protection on terms which may be fluid, uncertain and temporary. But the possibility that roles apparently reported in the sources during a period of confusion and disorder were not in fact there to be explained at all should not be thought to imply that whatever pattern of roles the recording angel *would* confirm is therefore inexplicable.

§19. At the level of minimal resources – which is to say, among the hunters, the simple pastoralists and the itinerant foraging bands – the possibilities of variation are so far constrained that the question of functional alternatives arises only to a very limited degree. The cultural differences between them may, as I noted in Section 9, be quite marked, but not in ways which can so significantly augment the amount of power available for redistribution that evolution to a novel mode is bound to follow. If, however, the comparisons are extended to cover all the different kinds of societies which, in 'Darwinian' terms, can be classified as 'pre-state', then it becomes necessary to account for the reproduction of altogether more widely different alternative institutions. As we have seen, power may be dissipated or shared rather than simply limited, and its accumulation in specialist roles may be obstructed rather than simply dissipated or shared. These differences of mode are not accidental, and their explanation makes it not merely possible but necessary to elaborate and refine the very broad categories introduced in Section 9: the ways in which power can be dissipated, shared and obstructed need to be related to the nature of the competitive advantage which the relevant practices confer (or not) on the roles and systacts which carry them.

Let me accordingly go back to the 'big-men', whose roles are constituted by practices which require them constantly to rebuild their power. The dissipation of that power is not to be explained by the modesty or altruism of the incumbents of the role. The Melanesian big-man is no less ambitious, proud and egotistical than the Homeric *basileus*. He would if he could command a larger following, marry more wives, have a larger store of pigs, vegetables and shells to dispense to kinsmen, dependents or allies, and be more widely renowned than he is for his bravery, his generosity and his rhetorical skills. But he cannot. In contrast to the Polynesian 'paramount', he cannot command a following of thousands but only (at most) of hundreds; he is not the head of a conical clan but only of one among many unranked segmentary units defined by neighbourhood and/or kinship; he is not credited with *mana* by virtue of divine descent; he controls no body of professional soldiers, envoys, ceremonial attendants or supervisors of the stores; and he is economically more dependent for his position on his followers than they on him (Sahlins 1962–3, p. 297). He may try his best to modify the practices which define his role in such a way as to compound the power he has accumulated by his efforts. But if he tries to extract more from his followers than he gives in return, they will desert him; if he tries to claim sacred status, they will ridicule him; and if he tries to bully them, they will – in at least some reported cases – kill him.*

The nature of the constraints, both sociological and ecological, which limit the power attaching to 'big-man' roles varies in different contexts. Among the Borana, the ambitious and successful herd-owner is constrained by (i) his dependence on the labour of a household whose numbers cannot, even with (as in Melanesia) polygamy, be expanded beyond a certain point, (ii) the difficulty of accumulating a surplus of meat and milk without inhibiting the physical mobility of the herd, (iii) the ecological advantages of herd dispersion, and (iv) the lack of less ecologically vulnerable investment opportunities. The practice of redistribution of food to poorer dependents (often carried out secretly, so that the recipient should not be cast in the role of client) functions as at once an insurance, an adjustment to the difficulty of storage, and a tacit purchase of influence (Dahl 1979, pp. 274, 278). Among the nomadic patrilineal tribes of Baluchistan, by contrast, the power of the *sardar* whom we met in Section 9 is constrained by the absence not of alternative investment opportunities so much as of a differentiated sedentary population: where the *baluch* are in systematic institutional contact with local cultivators (*shahri*) geographically tied to their source of irrigation, the relations between them are articulated through a ruler (*hakom*) entitled not only to extract taxes from both *shahri* and *baluch*, but to command tithes from the *shahri* and military service from the *baluch* (Salzman 1978, p. 132). For as long as the initial conditions hold, the *sardar* can no more turn his role into that of a *hakom* than the Melanesian big-man can turn his into that of a Polynesian paramount. It is because the practices constituting rulership, as opposed to leadership, function in the interests neither of the leader (who cannot make them stick) nor of his followers (who have nothing to gain from

* Assassination or even desertion is, however, rare: Meggitt (1971, p. 193) claims that Sahlins exaggerates the likelihood of big-men losing their followers and that a survey of the literature shows that in most Melanesian societies 'they maintain their position by being the most efficient entrepreneurs or managers in their local communities'.

them) that 'big-man' roles persist. Social relations within societies of this mode are by no means totally cooperative, any more than they are among egalitarian foraging bands such as the !Kung. But they are not therefore unstable.

The same is true for societies in the mode where a limited fund of power is shared rather than dissipated. In those where the topmost roles are those of a collegiate magistracy, or a council of 'elders'* or a 'lodge' of selected chiefs like that which the Cheyenne and other Indian tribes of the American High Plains set up for the summer months (Eggan 1966, p. 53), the power attaching to them may be further constrained by restrictions on individual tenure. Thus, Aristotle's reference to the danger of tyranny inherent in the Archaic Greek type of magistracy (*Politics* 1310b) is well illustrated by a surviving inscription of the seventh century B.C. from Dreros in Crete which expressly forbids a *kosmos* who has occupied the role for the statutory period of a year to do so again until ten years later (Meiggs and Lewis 1969, pp. 2–3). Roles of this kind frequently emerge as part of a transition from semi- to proto-statehood, and the dangers against which collegiality and/or limitations on tenure (or succession by inheritance) are intended to offer protection are often real enough. But collegiate, non-hereditary roles can sometimes persist within a stable set of institutions even if the social distance between top and bottom is quite large and rivalry between competing residential and/or kinship units quite intense. Among the still pastoral Kirghiz, political roles within an agnatic kinship system 'are achieved by those senior members of the relevant kinship group who can gain the unanimous consent of the membership on the basis of certain prescribed personality attributes' (Shahrani 1978, p. 245). There is, admittedly, a central government to whom they are answerable. But a chief (*khan*), local descent-group head (*be*) or patrilineage-group head (*aqsaqal*), acting either individually or in concert, is empowered to mediate in all local disputes. These office-holders tend to be rich men in a society where the *khan*'s household unit (*oey*) owns 16,000 sheep and goats and 4,000 yaks while the poorest 70 *oey* out of a total of 333 own no animals of any kind at all. But there is an institutionalized system of dispersion of herds from rich *oey* to poor along kinship lines which functions both to spread the ecological risks to which the herds are exposed and to inhibit the sedentarization of the poorer *oey*.

* 'Elders' being used here to designate not literal seniors so much as autonomous representatives of households or local or kin groups of which they are the head, like the Lapp *sii͗* dâ-ised (Vorren and Manker 1962, p. 144), or the 'great commoners' of the Nyakusa (G. Wilson 1937, p. 34).

Inegalitarian as it may be, the system is stable by virtue of a combination of practices which involve at once a sharing of political power, a redistribution of economic resources, and an ideological limit on differences of social prestige.

Pure age-set systems – systems, that is, where all and only coevals have equal power or lack of it – involve a sharing of power in the different sense that every (male) person who lives long enough is guaranteed a turn; and this pattern of roles is standardly contrasted with that of segmentary lineage systems where social distance is between lineages of different size and seniority in the genealogical sense. The contrast is strikingly exemplified in the ethnographic literature on the Eastern and Western Nilotes (Southall 1970), and there is no doubt that these societies demonstrate the analogous functions of two distinct alternative sets of practices at a common evolutionary stage. The range of variation is, however, wider than this contrast by itself would suggest. Segmentary lineage systems are compatible with a degree of stratification which separates one at least temporarily dominant lineage group from the rest; and an age-set system like that of Benin is compatible with the role of a king (*oba*) who appoints his own patrimonial retainers into a hierarchy of ranks seen by the elders of the capital themselves as analogous to the age-grades of the villages. It would, therefore, be a mistake to hypothesize that age-sets, any more than segmentary lineages, preclude the possibility of statehood. The hypothesis to be tested is rather that age-sets will function in the absence of exogenous influence in ways which, despite the tensions which are inevitably engendered, are adequate to maintain one or more distinctive sub-types which will reproduce themselves stably over successive generations.

Critical to the functioning and reproduction of age-set roles is the strength of ideological rather than economic or coercive sanctions. Young men of fighting age, even if not engaged in warfare as such, cannot be disciplined by force if they are jointly determined to resist. The elders may, as among the Samburu (Spencer 1965, p. 184), have the ultimate sanction of an 'unshakeable belief in the curse' but even so, its too ready use becomes self-defeating, and 'real prestige among the elders is obtained by not resorting to it in the interests of better relations between men, especially within the clan' (*ibid.*, p. 209). The stability of the system derives from an ideology of respect (*nkanyit*) which contains the hostility of young men towards polygamous elders until such time as they succeed to their roles. The mode of production is typically but not exclusively pastoral, and the domestic units reproduce themselves from one generation to the next through exchanges of women and transfers of cattle.

Conflicts of interest may arise within age-sets as well as between them, and may indeed not be confined to the age-sets. An interesting quasi-experimental contrast is provided by the Turkana neighbours of the Samburu, among whom conflicts arise within families rather than between age-sets, since not only is the age of marriage younger but bridewealth is heavier. What is more, this difference in their practices has the further consequence that whereas the ideology of the Samburu tolerates adultery and divorce, the Turkana disapprove of adultery as much as they do of murder. But these and other variations between different East African pastoralists, including the actual number of age-sets (cf. Gulliver 1953 for the Jie or Dyson-Hudson 1966 for the Karimojong), confirm not the instability of age-set systems but, on the contrary, the flexibility of their constituent practices in adapting to changes in the ecological and/or sociological context. Contact with neighbouring societies may well result in their absorption or fusion and a consequent change in the mode of the distribution of power. But for as long as demographic and climatic pressures can be released through migration or fission, there is no inherent contradiction in the homologous practices and roles which characterize the pastoral or semi-pastoral age-set societies in the ethnographic record.

By contrast, those societies whose evolution is held at the semi-state level because of the obstructions, whether internal or external, which stand in the way of the occupants of would-be governmental roles, are meta-stable only. Examples are reported from many different times and places where semi-states headed by military chieftains have 'maintained an oscillatory pattern of encroachment and retrenchment with their contiguous neighbours', as it is put by Schaedel (1978, p. 290) about the southern and central highlands of Peru from the late thirteenth century until the time of the Inca ascendancy. I have already cited the petty kings of the middle Anglo-Saxon period in England as well as their nineteenth-century Madagascan counterparts who descended from their fortified mountain-tops to exact protection-rent from the cultivators in the valleys only to be driven back again under pressure from adjacent rivals. The list can be extended at least as far back as the early Sumerian city-states whose leaders occasionally 'succeeded in uniting a number of such cities into larger coalitions, but these seldom survived for long' (Oates 1979, p. 24), and at least as far forward as the early fourteenth century in the Valley of Mexico, where the power vacuum created by the decline of the previous Toltec state 'was filled by a score of small, autonomous, internally unstable and mutually hostile political domains' (i.e. semi-states), of which two finally emerged as dominant by the end of the century (Brumfiel 1983, p. 266).

If and when one or other of several such societies competing for supremacy secures a lasting advantage over the rest, the role of the victorious chieftain will evolve into that of a monarch, and his followers, dependents and kinsmen will become his subjects. But the evolution to a new mode need not require the disappearance of the previous practices of kinship or clientage; it need only involve a change in their function. Thus, a society of nomadic pastoralists which establishes permanent relations of domination over one or more societies of sedentary agriculturalists may well retain its same internal pattern of roles, but its 'tribal aristocracy' now becomes both a governing élite and a dominant class which extracts a surplus from the subordinate agriculturalists not as booty but as tribute. Indeed, it can even happen that the new pattern of roles comes about through the deliberate adaptation of homologous practices to their altered context. After the formation of the Inca state, this was done, as we saw in Section 14 of Chapter 1, with corvée labour; and at the same time, the subordinate *yanaconas*, who appear to have been non-servile dependents similar to the Old Babylonian *mushkēnū*, were treated by the now dominant Incas 'as retainers of the crown' (Murra 1980, p. 101) whose relation of clientage to their traditional superiors was transferred – with varying success (Schaedel 1978, pp. 310–11) – to their new rulers.

The institutional differences, accordingly, between one sub-type even of a relatively simple mode and another are not just differences in their customary practices. They are also differences in the functioning of homologous roles in different contexts. The range of possible variation is of course constrained by the level of economic, ideological and coercive resources available. But it is important to remember that, as I remarked in Section 10, extremes of social distance between the highest and the lowest roles in the three-dimensional space of the inverted pyramid become possible very early in the 'Darwinian' sequence of modes. From this standpoint, the evolutionary shift from the egalitarian foragers, hunters and pastoralists to even the simplest of states is more radical than any either before or since.

§20. Once the evolution to statehood has come about, there emerges clearly the distinction outlined in Section 11 between the 'patrimonial' mode where the incumbents of governmental roles are still the personal dependents or followers or retainers or quasi-kinsmen of a monarchical ruler, the 'citizen' mode in which all formally free adult males can participate either directly or indirectly in government, and the 'warrior' mode dominated by a self-perpetuating aristocracy and supported by tribute or plunder rather than prestation, liturgy, tax or rent.

Patrimonial roles and relations can, as Weber emphasized, be adapted to function even in societies which have grown in territory and resources to the point of being classified as empires. Indeed, the persistence of patrimonial roles and practices can help to explain the workings of societies whose institutions are very different in other ways, from Pharaonic Egypt to early modern France. But at the level of power with which this Section is concerned, the central institution of the patrimonial state or proto-state is the set of administrative roles whose incumbents are at once culturally attached to the monarchy and structurally separated from the rest of the subject population. For societies of this type to work – that is, for the ruler's own role to be sustainable by successive incumbents – three conditions are necessary: (i) economically, the ruler must be able to remunerate his staff in cash or kind from a surplus produced by others than themselves, (ii) ideologically, there must be what Weber called an *Einverständisgemeinschaft* between the ruler and his subjects sufficient to legitimate his role, and (iii) politically, the ruler's police or soldiers must have a near-monopoly of the means of coercion within the territory over which he rules. These conditions are, however, fulfilled across a wide range in both time and place, from the tyrannies of Greece and Sicily to the kingdoms of Central Africa to the principalities and counties which emerged in North-western Europe after the collapse of the Carolingian empire to the medieval Italian *signorie* where 'the state came to be regarded almost as the personal property of the ruling family' (Hyde 1973, p. 152).

It is true that none of these societies was very long-lived. But it is possible to specify conditions under which they would have been. If the inter-societal balance of power of all three kinds remains constant, a Greek tyranny or African kingdom or early medieval European principality or Italian *signoria* is well capable of reproducing itself over successive generations with its structure and culture unchanged. Indeed, if the geographical context is such that the relative deprivation of overmighty subjects can most easily be assuaged by fission, then the stability of the system is all the better assured. This may or may not be what the ruler wanted: the forced removal of populations by Sicilian tyrants was a deliberate decision of policy, whereas the secession of Toro from Nyoro through the disloyalty of the king's ostensible representative (B. Taylor 1962, p. 43) was not at all what the king had in mind. But secession, emigration or colonization can serve just as well as deliberate expulsion or exile to leave the patrimonial ruler secure in his role and confident of the succession to it of a son or kinsman or other nominee.

Several sub-types of the patrimonial mode can be distinguished. The citing of tyrannies may seem to imply that the stability of a patrimonial proto-state is critically dependent on the judicious use of force, as in Herodotus's anecdote about Periander of Corinth. But it need not be, unless a 'tyranny' has been defined as a state entirely lacking in legitimacy in the eyes of the subject population. Indeed, it is noticeable how far the Archaic Greek tyrants took pains to give their power an appearance, at least, of ideological legitimacy. Herodotus also recounts both the 'very silly trick', as he himself calls it, by which Peisistratus dressed up a tall woman to look like the goddess Athene bringing him home to Athens (I.60), and the extraordinary lengths to which Cleisthenes of Sicyon was prepared to go in persuading the Thebans to disinter the remains of the legendary hero Melanippus for reburial in place of a shrine dedicated to the Argive Adrastus (V.97). Patrimonial rulers often rely on the personal loyalty of their retainers or bodyguards. But such ties are notoriously fragile when a ruler of forceful character is replaced by a weaker one. More effective practices and roles include, for example, the slave constabulary commanded by one of the king's sons in the Central African Kingdom of Kuba (Vansina 1978, p. 363) or, alternatively, the myths of semi-divine descent vindicated by victory in war such as enabled some (but not all) of the early Germanic kings to hold their *comitatus* – their followings of more or less noble warriors – together on a permanent basis.

At this stage, the role of bodyguard has evolved into that of soldier or policeman, and that of companion into that of courtier.* The part-time specialists in war, ritual and economic management become a systact of permanent officials responsible to the ruler and rewarded by him on a regular basis. As we have seen, the incumbents of the new roles may be recruited from near-equals whose loyalty rests on comradeship or consanguinity or from inferiors whose loyalty rests on dependence and gratitude, or from some of each. But whatever the previous functions of the roles which they come to occupy, these roles now combine a personal, private dependence on the patrimonial ruler with an impersonal power over his subjects. This holds equally for the incumbents of the subordinate magistracies (*timai*) in Peisistratus's Athens, the palace officials and provincial chiefs of the Nyoro kings, and the seneschals, constables, butlers, chamberlains and secretaries of the eleventh-century Capetians as they slowly but steadily re-established the institutions of monarchical government in Northern France.

* Cf. the remarks of Steinhart (1978, p. 143) on the Ankole *Mugabe* and on the parallel with early medieval European kingships (pp. 146–7).

The ideological inducements and sanctions on which patrimonial rulers depend may also be provided in a number of alternative institutional forms. Where ritual and political practices are fused within a single role, the 'divine king', like the Egyptian pharaoh,* commands obedience in both dimensions of power together. In Sumeria, the 'lord' (*en*) who appears in the earliest cuneiform texts seems to have held both ideological and coercive power, but subsequently to have been displaced into a purely priestly role by the '*lugal*', who was generally the son of a rich landowner able to draw on his father's retainers and appointed by the assembly of elders for a limited period (Jacobsen 1957, pp. 138–9). Only as a result of more or less continuous warfare did the *lugal* evolve thereafter into a king whose role combined ritual and magical with judicial and military functions. In Greece, by contrast, where the *basileis* of the Archaic semi-states had originally combined military leadership, adjudication of disputes and the performance of collective rituals, it was only very much later, and then only in Macedonia, that '*basileus*' came to designate a kingly role in the full sense:† the religious functions attaching to it remained separate under both the tyrannies and the magistracies which marked the emergence of statehood. When ideological roles are institutionally distinct from political, there is always the possibility that their incumbents may be tempted to take sides against the patrimonial ruler. But there is usually an identity of interests, often reinforced by substantial economic rewards,‡ between priests and kings. In post-Carolingian Europe, as in the African kingdoms, the normal relationship between the incumbents of the topmost ideological and coercive roles was one of mutual support which, fragile as the coalition might be, rested on a mutal recognition of the benefits of cooperation in all three dimensions of structure.

Indeed, *pre*-Carolingian – i.e., Merovingian – Gaul shows how a subtype of the patrimonial mode can evolve in which ideological roles function to sustain political stability after the collapse of a strong central state. By the late sixth century, the dominant role in the *civitates* corresponding to the old tribal territories into which the country was

* Unfortunately, there are not the literary or archaeological sources which would make it possible for specialists to reconstruct the evolution to statehood: by the time of the three main groups of texts which proclaim the royal divinity, the relation of history to myth is irrecoverable (Kemp 1983, pp. 71–6).

† When Herodotus reports the accession of Perdiccas to the 'tyranny' (VIII.137), he speaks of it as having been 'acquired' (*ktēsamenos*), thus clearly implying the difference between semi-statehood and a properly monarchical role which is there to be occupied.

‡ For the Nyoro, see Perlman (1970, p. 147), who reports an evident generosity in the tolls allocated by kings to their rainmakers.

effectively divided was that of bishop. According to Gregory of Tours, in his *History of the Franks* (VI.46), Chilperic I kept complaining that wealth, power and respect had all fallen into the hands of the Church and the bishops. This, no doubt, was a petulant exaggeration. Bishops like Gregory were never going to usurp or make redundant the role of king: at most, they might side with their parishioners in resisting the royal tax-collectors. But it is true that within their *civitates* they did, as I mentioned in passing in Section 18, operate a semi-independent system of patrimonial administration even though they did not themselves control, or seek to control, the means of coercion. The explanation is partly historical: the collapse of the Roman state had left a vacuum which the Merovingians had not been able adequately to fill. But it is also functional: the bishops had 'the control of the cultic and moral activity of the people of their *civitas*' (Wood 1977, p. 24) together with the substantial incomes which this entailed. Whether the readiness of their parishioners to believe in the efficacy of divine intervention on their behalf was quite as it is presented in Gregory's *History* is one of those matters about which it is difficult if not impossible to decide at this distance without access to the recording angel's archives.* But their use of relics to exhibit the value of their personal standing with God in winning supernatural protection for their *civitates* (Brown 1971b, p. 15) offers a striking parallel to the hero-cults of the emerging proto-states, both magistracies and tyrannies, of Archaic Greece. Their power was, to be sure, circumscribed. They had to compete for it not only with kings and their courtiers but with the more influential landowners and merchants, and even on occasion with rival holy men. But despite these conflicts of interest, the practices by which their roles were defined functioned to sustain, not weaken, the patrimonial mode of the distribution of power.

Two other sub-types of the patrimonial mode call for separate mention – the patrimonial 'empire' and the 'federal' state held together by a patrimonial ruler. A patrimonial empire is (*pace* Weber) something of a contradiction in terms, if it implies the conquest of a wider territory

* Descriptively, however, there can be no doubt about the contrast with the *Weltanschauung* of a fifth-century bishop like Sidonius Apollinaris. As always, where description is at issue, the contrast cannot be fully conveyed without citing the sources at length. But the flavour of Sidonius's, as opposed to Gregory's, conception of the pastoral role is nicely captured by Brown (1971a, p. 130): '...frank memories of good dinners, of martyrs' vigils that had ended, in the cool of the morning, with a *fête champêtre*, of spacious private libraries stocked with the classics, where the Fathers of the Church were tucked away discreetly at the women's end' – a description which can be authenticated word for word from Sidonius's letters.

than the ruler and his retainers can hope to control directly. But the Carolingian empire is the obvious case in point. It was an achievement which, for all the conflicting interpretations it has received (Bullogh 1970), seems agreed among specialists to have depended on the exceptional personal qualities of Charlemagne himself. Yet even if Charlemagne had been succeeded by a son whose skills and energies matched his own, the institutions necessary to reproduce his domination of the territories bequeathed to him did not exist. The dynastic disputes which determined the lines along which Louis the Pious's inheritance disintegrated were more the symptom than the cause of the instability which followed on his father's death. Charlemagne's host, however triumphantly victorious over Lombards, Saxons and Avars, was not a standing army; his court was not a government; his *missi dominici* were not *intendants*; his secretariat was not a chancery; his counts were his subjects only in name. The ideology of kingship and the revival of the Roman imperial tradition were real enough, but the allegiance to the royal person remained conditional. The dramatic expansion of Charlemagne's power beyond the normal limits of a patrimonial society depended on his sharing the rewards of conquest with followers without whose cooperation his role would be irrecoverably diminished. Carolingian vassalage was very different from that of the Anglo-Norman kings. The Austrasian aristocrats who received the reward of their support in land and offices were thereby created not benefice-holders or provincial governors but near-autonomous princes. A cyclical regression was just as inevitable after Charlemagne's death as it had been in India after the death of Ashoka in 232 B.C.

Patrimonial-cum-federal states, by contrast, are borderline cases not simply because the idea of federation is at least partly inconsistent with the idea of personal domination but because a federation is often no more than an unstable coalition between semi- or proto-states whose leaders are unwilling to surrender their autonomy to one another except on a strictly temporary basis. Nonetheless, a society can successfully combine the two for long enough to count as a distinctive sub-type. Several of the early Germanic kings whom we meet in the pages of Caesar, Tacitus or Ammianus Marcellinus owed their position to successful leadership of a federation of *gentes*, *pagi*, or *nationes*,* and

* The most complex structure reported in the sources is that of the Alamannic confederacy headed by two *reges* 'higher in power' under whom were five separate *reges* 'next in power' who in turn were each the superiors of ten lesser *regales* and a 'large following drawn from various nations' (Ammianus Marcellinus XVI.12.23–6); but it must be possible that these were roles which lapsed in time of peace.

their societies did not necessarily lapse back into anarchy after their deaths or retirements or, on the contrary, evolve into unified monarchical states. Indeed, it may be that their roles were preserved by exogenous pressure, since it was to the Romans' interest that otherwise unstable tribes should be fused into larger entities over whom a single ruler could be relied upon to have permanent authority (Wallace-Hadrill 1971, p. 17).

One of the most interesting examples, however, is the early Thessalian confederacy, which I mentioned in passing in Section 20 of Chapter 2. Here, a particular combination of geographical and sociological pressures sustained a distinctive federal kingship for a remarkably long time.* The separate 'tetrads' were each dominated by a noble systact whose estates were worked by serf-like '*penestai*', and the system is to that extent reminiscent of medieval Europe. But the relation between tetrarchs and their elected king (*tagos*) was not that of vassalage; and although the tetrads may have originated by fission from a single semi- or proto-state established at the time of the so-called Dorian invasions, they had not been ceded benefices in return for their obligations of service. They served a monarch whose personal officials they were and whom they followed in war as commanding the Thessalians as a whole: the *tagos* Cineas who appears in Herodotus (V.63) as a '*basileus*' is a king who is leading his personal troop of cavalry to the support of the Peisistratids in accordance with a pre-existing alliance between the Thessalians and Athenians. The constitution under which the *tagos* held power is attributed by Aristotle to an ostensibly historical Aleuas the Red whom modern scholars have tended to dismiss as legendary. But whatever the origin of the role, it was a kingship which was at once patrimonial and federal and which survived the occasional periods of interregnum, or *atagia*, which followed the death of an existing incumbent.

Interregna, indeed, are often the crucial test of the permanence of the kingly role and thus of the society's evolution from proto-statehood to statehood proper. A patrimonial state cannot be said to be functioning stably as such if the death of the ruler plunges it back into anarchy. But there are, on the other hand, societies where even after a lapse of several years a successor may move into the vacant role without an institutional disturbance. The Lombards, at an early stage of their occupation of Italy, decided 'by common consent' (Paul the Deacon, *History of the Lombards* III.16) that Authari should succeed to the kingship after an

* This account is drawn almost entirely from Larsen (1968, pp. 12–26), but differs slightly in interpretation.

interregnum of ten years, and he was then succeeded in turn by the Duke of Turin whom his widow chose – after consultation with the '*prudentes*' – as her consort. Moreover, when the interregnum was ended, the dukes explicitly recognized Authari's need for the wherewithal to support his personal officers and attendants, and (if Paul the Deacon is to be believed) gave up half of their own possessions for the purpose.

Later on, it is true, the relationship of the Lombard nobility to their king was to turn out less patrimonial than feudal. The residual practices of centralized government inherited from the Roman Empire died out, local landowners assumed direct control of their own armed retainers, and in the end, in the post-Carolingian period, Lombard counts became nominal vassals of the King of Italy. But at the time of the late sixth-century interregnum, the Lombards were a stable, patrimonial state whose officials, even though they lacked the power to maintain the Roman tax system, were able to advise, adjudicate and administer on the king's behalf and would appear to have preserved their roles in the wings, as it were, when there was no king for them to be answerable to. Indeed, there are even examples where an interregnum marks not a period of regression towards semi-statehood or anarchy but a deliberate institutional device to prevent it. Direct inheritance from the king to his eldest son is by no means the universal or even modal practice among patrimonial states, and in a number of African kingdoms, as with the Lombards after Authari's death, the king's widow (or sometimes sister) might exercise a decisive influence.* Once *a* method of succession has been institutionalized, there is no inherent contradiction which prevents a patrimonial state from reproducing itself even if the powers of the king fall well short of absolutism and the allegiance of his more powerful subjects continues, in their minds at least, to be conditional on his performing his role to their satisfaction.

§21. When we turn to societies in the mode whose defining characteristic is the central distinction between citizens and non-citizens, the range of alternative sub-types widens again. As I remarked already in Section 11, the distinction is equally central to the Greek *poleis* and to the North Italian towns of the twelfth and thirteenth centuries which, even if conscious of recreating in some sense a classical past, differed not only quantitatively but qualitatively from them in their mode of production. The difference between towns which were ritual

* Alternatively, royal officials like the Soga 'client-chiefs' (*bakungu*) might perform this function (Fallers 1965, p. 128).

and administrative centres of consumption and towns which were centres of production and commerce is on any theory crucial to their subsequent evolution. The *poleis*, as we shall see in Section 12 of Chapter 4, were an evolutionary dead-end, whereas the North European towns were the institutional carriers of the practices of mercantile capitalism with all the long-term consequences which that turned out to imply. Yet the role of citizen is as crucial to the explanation of the workings of the one as of the other. In both, homologous political practices were sustained by functionally analogous economic ones; and for all the cultural difference between an ideology derived from Christianity and one derived from pagan doctrine, in this dimension of structure too an analogous function was performed by ritual practices carried by professional religious roles.

It might be objected that even in Classical Greece, the differences between the practices of different citizen-states were so wide, and the Greeks themselves so very conscious of them, that to bracket all *poleis* together in a common mode of the distribution of power is to override institutional variants which are fundamental to their workings. Do not Athens and Sparta stand at opposite poles of a continuum from oligarchic militarism to participatory democracy? Yet for all the difference in outlook, mores and systactic structure, the answer to the question 'how did it work?' is basically the same. It is true that the Spartiate 'Peers' were a warrior élite *par excellence*, trained from boyhood as soldiers and wholly emancipated from production of the agricultural surplus on which the functioning of the state depended. But they were not an aristocracy. They did not, like Islamic emirs or Teutonic knights, command personal followings of social inferiors who were, nevertheless, formally free; their two joint kings, although of superior status by birth, were not located at the top of a graded hierarchy of nobility and gentry; they did not extort either rent or tribute individually from either the Helots or the *perioikoi* but, on the contrary, were denied the right to accumulate more than a minimum of personal wealth and required as a condition of citizenship to contribute regularly to their common 'messes' (*syssitia*). In Sparta, no less than in Athens or Pisa or Iceland, the central institutions rest on the practices which define the role of citizen.* Politically, power is shared among adult males qualifying as citizens; economically, the wealth extracted from the labour of non-citizens is redistributed through some form of

* Cf. Finley (1975, p. 175): 'The Spartan governmental machinery had its peculiarities to be sure, but not a single feature of significance other than the kings that can legitimately be called unique among the Greeks.'

liturgy rather than tax;* and ideologically, equality of status in mutually acknowledged among, but only among, the citizen body.†

Within this mode, there is a range of sub-types among which the span of social distance within the citizen body varies between a 'democratic' and an 'oligarchic' extreme. Even in Sparta, as we saw earlier, there were differences of all three kinds within the systact of Spartiates, and many Greek *poleis* were dominated by leading families and their clients even if their constitutions exposed the heads of them to the sanctions of periodic scrutiny, loss of office, or ostracism. In the North Italian towns, there was a constant tension between the *magnati* and the *popolo* (P. J. Jones 1965, p. 77), and the *consorterie* of leading families and their clients continued to exist side by side with the institutions of communal government. No less than in Archaic and Classical Greece, the possibility of an evolution to tyranny was never totally blocked, even by the most carefully contrived constraints on the power attaching to elective governmental roles. It is true that in Athens, once democracy was established, there seems not to have been any prospect of a tyranny, just as in Rome the overthrow of the early monarchy seems to have achieved its objective once and for all. But conflicts of economic interest between richer and poorer citizens remained endemic, and the distinction of status which marked off the gentleman proprietor who worked on his land only if he chose from the smallholder who starved if he didn't remained fundamental (de Ste Croix 1981, Ch. 3, §ii).

Furthermore, the citizen body corresponds no more closely to the ideal type of a republic of equals in rural than in urban societies within this mode. The Icelandic '*bondi*', for all his pride in his right to bear arms and to participate in the *thing*, might still find himself working not his own land but that of a large proprietor (*leilendingr*: Musset 1951, p.

* In the strict sense, liturgies are voluntary. But in practice, powerful ideological (and sometimes coercive) sanctions are brought to bear on the recalcitrant; in Nuremberg, for example, until as late as the mid-sixteenth century, the annual *Losung* still functioned as a quasi-liturgical contribution which was thought to legitimate the privileges of the rich in the eyes of their poorer fellow-citizens (Strauss 1976, pp. 90–1). For a vivid descriptive account of the resentment of a rich merchant (Francesco di Marco Datini) at having to pay a *prestanza*, see Origo (1963, pp. 140–6).

† Some of the most eloquent testimony to this equality comes from the pejorative descriptions of contemporary observers who disapproved of it. No doubt such observers tend to exaggerate in the light of their own presuppositions. But Bishop Otto of Freising's diatribe in his *Gesta Frederici Imperatoris* against 'honourable positions' being given 'even to workers in the low mechanical trades' (Waitz 1912, p. 116) is as authentic a tribute to the relative egalitarianism of the North Italian towns as the disapproval of 'demagogues' practising vulgar trades in the Athenian literary sources or Cicero's contemptuous references to an electorate which included artisans and shopkeepers 'and suchlike dregs' (*pro Flacco* VIII.18).

97), just as a '*république syndicaliste*' like thirteenth-century Montpellier was at the same time '*fortement hierarchisée*' under a dominant mercantile systact (Sautel 1955, p. 349). Yet in every case, the central institutions revolve around practices which define the economic, ideological and coercive power of citizens as against non-citizens. The relations of production may be quite widely dissimilar not only with regard to the roles of the servile, enserfed, helot or sharecropping cultivators but also in the location of intermediate groups like metics or *perioikoi*. Likewise, the chances of mobility (if any) from either subordinate or intermediate systacts into the citizen body may vary widely between one sub-type and another. But these diverse practices all function to sustain a citizen monopoly of the means of coercion, the extraction of surplus produce from subordinate cultivators, and an ideology at once patriotic and anti-monarchical.

A partially deviant sub-type, which I have cited already for its distinctive institutional characteristics, is Rome from 287 B.C. to the time of the Gracchi – that is, to the time at which the contradictions generated by its successes in war within a citizen mode set off the internal violence which was to lead in the end to the evolution of the Principate. These distinctive characteristics are well known: that Roman society in the period was politically oligarchic, ideologically hierarchical, and economically exploitative even within the body of adult male citizens is not denied by specialists of any theoretical school. What is more, the vertical ties between patron and client remained pervasive, albeit in modified forms, throughout the transition. Yet despite all this, the central institutions of the society guaranteed the rights of citizens not only to protection (within the city) against the arbitrary power of magistrates but also to a say in the choice of these magistrates themselves. These rights had been won not by the exercise of countervailing economic, and still less ideological, power but by the threat of secession by men under arms on whose service the safety of the city depended. Oligarchic as the Roman constitution was, the ordinary citizen could have some occasional influence on the choice between rival contenders for office; he did benefit to some degree from the rewards of conquest; he did have the occasional chance to help deny a victorious *imperator* a triumph, or accuse him of misappropriation of booty; he did enjoy the formal freedom and the social prestige attaching to it which marked him off from foreigners and slaves; and he did have the option of changing sides, or at any rate patrons, in the civil wars between rival factions which brought the Republic down. The enormous social distance between the most and the least advantaged citizens in all three dimensions of structure does not alter the facts that they were still citizens, not subjects, serfs, slaves or (merely) kinsmen, and that the functioning of the system depended on their being so.* Indeed, if a test is called for, it is decisively furnished by the so-called 'Social' War which broke out in 91 B.C. This was not a class conflict. It was not about land, but about relative deprivation of citizenship, and it was only won, after much unnecessary bloodshed, by the concession to the Latins and loyal Italian allies of what the Senate had refused to grant when it had been sought by constitutional means.

Republican Rome is an extreme case. No other 'citizen' society on record was dominated to the same degree by so highly privileged a minority within the total body of enfranchised arms-bearing males. But in none of them was the structure ever compressed to the point that all citizens were identically located. Even at the very beginning of settlement in Iceland, where the original immigrants had no previous inheritances of land to differentiate them, distinctions of birth and relations of clientship were present nonetheless, and debtor–creditor relationships soon developed (Foote and Wilson 1970, pp. 62, 86); and even at the foundation of the pilgrim colony at Plymouth, Massachusetts, there was an initial differentiation between pilgrims and 'strangers' or 'particulars', and as new land was opened up those more concerned to enrich themselves than were their fellows moved away from the original settlement and did so (Demos 1970, pp. 6, 11). In the mountain cantons of Switzerland, the communities which came together in 1291 to form the historic *Eidgenossenschaft* were internally dominated by powerful families (Steinberg 1976, p. 13), and the autonomy which they were to preserve was still part of a broader pattern of differently located inter- and intra-societal roles: thus, the Raetian *Landfriedensbündnis* of 1395 was not a charter of peasant liberty, but only a guarantee to maintain a structure in which lords and free peasants were conceded their separate systactic identity (Barber 1974, pp. 38–9). These are all societies well beyond the level of resources at which the total span of social distance between roles occupied by adult males is, or could be, constrained to the point of equality of power. This said, they may be significantly more or less inegalitarian in both culture and structure, quite apart from variations in their modes of production, persuasion and coercion and the articulation between them. Athens is indeed institutionally different from Sparta, as is Milan from Genoa,

* The legal distinction between *honestiores* and *humiliores*, which marked a systactic differentiation between first- and second-class citizens (Garnsey 1970), was, symptomatically, an innovation of the Principate.

and no medieval commune is the same as any Greek *polis*. But these are still sub-types within a mode of the distribution of power whose distinguishing characteristic is the set of practices defining the role of citizen and the central economic, social-cum-ideological and political-cum-military institutions which go with it.

§22. Societies at this same approximate level of resources which fall to be assigned to the 'warrior' mode are particularly well exemplified within the Islamic world. But they are by no means exclusively so. An early European instance is reported almost in passing by Tacitus. If his account of them (*Germania* 30–1) is accurate, the warriors of the Chatti had by his time already ceased to be involved in productive activity at all, and were supported entirely by the labour of the rest of the population in the intervals between one war and the next. Tacitus's picture of fierce but indolent parasites with neither land (*ager*) nor occupation (*cura*) of their own is probably exaggerated for literary effect (cf. *ibid.*, 15). But it does suggest that as early as the first century A.D. the *comitatus* may, in some North European societies, have been in the process of forming a systact detached from any economic function other than the seizure of booty in war itself (Thompson 1965, p. 52). This kind of embryonic aristocracy holding a monopoly of the means of coercion resembles the *basileis* of Homeric Greece in outlook and mores, but with the difference that there is now a set of institutionalized roles for the public enforcement of law; and it resembles the warrior aristocracies of the feudal mode in Europe, but with the difference that it does not consist of politically autonomous landholders who extract rent from their own tied tenants. The 'king', if such he is, rules not through his personal functionaries or kinsmen but as head of an élite now systactically distinct from the general body of their fellow-members of the *gens*; these warriors are neither the full age-set of able-bodied males nor the haphazardly recruited war-band but the sons of nobles who tend to fight on horseback rather than on foot;* and their wealth comes not from liturgies, taxes or rents but from booty or tribute extracted from unarmed cultivators on demand.

The reason for which Islam furnishes such exemplary instances of societies dominated by a warrior élite is not the ideology of the *jihād* as

* The correlation of aristocracy and cavalry is familiar all the way from Archaic Greece (Aristotle, *Politics* 1289b, 35–40) to nineteenth-century Africa (Goody 1971, pp. 36–7); in North-west Europe, the fighting man *par excellence* has become a mounted knight by the time of Richer's *History of France* in the late tenth century (Contamine 1984, p. 31).

such, since that ideology is present equally in Islamic societies which belong to either the patrimonial or the absolutist mode. Yet ever since the first Muslim state as it evolved in the period immediately following Muhammad's death, there has been a tension – if not an outright contradiction – between the functional requisites of centralized administration and the ideology of government as the regulation of society in accordance with the precepts of the Quran. The Abbasid caliphs, whether or not as 'heterodox' or 'extremist' as sometimes portrayed (Cahen 1963), were able, until they lost control of the means of coercion to their own armies, to maintain the institutions of an absolutist state. But between their fall and the rise of the 'gunpowder' empires of Ottoman Turkey, Safavid Persia and Mughal India, the Near East was divided between more or less permanent emirates whose nominal allegiance to a common Islamic 'way' (*Shari'a*) carried no more implication of political unity than the common 'Hellenism' of the mutually antagonistic Greek *poleis*. These emirs were not, like their North-west European contemporaries, vassals or delegates or conditional office-holders. Nor, on the other hand, were they patrimonial kings whose relations to their servants and subjects were those of a patriarchal household writ large. Nor were they chief magistrates of citizen republics. They were the commanders of a warrior élite permanently garrisoned in capital towns; and although they allowed autonomy to both merchants and clerics under their protection, they still ruled through their monopoly of the means of coercion and drew their revenues from the labour of a formally free, fellow-Muslim peasantry.

A characteristic feature of societies in this mode is mobility, both geographical and social. All such warrior élites offer opportunities to outsiders whose fighting abilities are sufficient to earn them entry, and it was not impossible for an impoverished or dispossessed peasant, particularly if he could pass as a Turk (Hodgson 1974, II, p. 103), to turn soldier and recoup his fortunes through plunder or even rise to the role of emir. But such careers are equally possible in societies whose armies are not themselves the central institution of the state. More significant for the workings of the Islamic emirates were the practices by which the economic surpluses were extracted from the peasantry. The *iqta* – the land-grant to individual officers – is the homologue of the European fief. But there are critical differences in function. The *iqta* did not bring into being a self-reproducing class of rural landowners living off their rents. Indeed, it served to blur rather than sharpen the distinction between rent, tax and tribute. Under a strong government which could appropriate any surplus for itself, it functioned more like tax; under a weak one which could not, it functioned more like rent. But it usually channelled the agricultural (and to a lesser extent pastoral) surpluses to the support, first, of the warriors of the garrison towns, second, of the *ulama*, and third, of the urban poor, and it did so in the form more of tribute than either tax or rent. There was also, to be sure, a merchant class whose social prestige was sanctioned by the example of the Prophet himself and whose wealth was drawn partly from land and partly from trade. But it never constituted a bourgeoisie on the North-west European model.* The pervasive roles were military roles, the dominant systact owed its position to coercive sanctions, and the subordinate cultivators, juridically free and ideologically equal as they might be, were protected only by custom and patronage, if at all, against the surrender of any surplus beyond subsistence level.

The institutions of the Islamic warrior societies of the period of the European 'Middle Ages' were, to some degree, mirrored in those of their military opponents, notably the Spain of the *Reconquista*. Medieval Spain was regionally very diverse, and it was evolving fast, both institutionally and geographically. But for a period, after the Reconquest was under way and before the institutions of Castile had assumed the form out of which an absolutist mode was to evolve, the Spanish kings were heads of warrior élites united by the common ideology of a righteous war against the infidel and supported by Muslim booty and tribute. The warriors owed their service to the king neither as patrimonial servants nor as beneficed vassals but as tax-exempt *caballeros* wealthy enough to maintain their own horses and equipment, to whom in turn free commoners might commend themselves in a relation of *behetria* reminiscent of the Islamic *mawlā* relation between patrons and clients. What is more, the *caballeros* could be either *hidalgos* defined by noble birth or *caballeros villanos* – non-noble town-dwelling knights who, together with any co-resident *hidalgos*, constituted 'an urban patriciate of a military nature sharply contrasting with the mercantile aristocracies of the great cities of Europe from Lombardy to Flanders' (Lourie 1966, p. 65). In these frontier towns, the effective ruler was a noble who, like an Islamic emir, organized its defence at the head of a following of cavalry or foot-soldiers according to their means, and the

* A convincing test is furnished by comparing Islamic with Italian city-states: an Islamic one like the island of Qays in the Persian Gulf remained piratical, not mercantile, while Amalfi came to be dominated by a mercantile patriciate with extensive interests in international politics as well as international trade.

whole *Extremadura* was dominated by *caballeros villanos* living off stock-raising and booty in cattle and slaves (Lacarra 1963, pp. 211–12). To be sure, this state of affairs only lasted for as long as the infidels were still there to be crusaded against. But the subsequent evolution of Spanish society is only explicable as a consequence of the Reconquest, and it was only after several generations that its pervasive roles were not those of societies organized for more or less permanent holy war.

Nor is it only in conflict with Islam that there evolved Christian societies in the 'warrior' mode. On the north-east frontier of Europe from the mid twelfth century, a holy war was likewise waged against the recalcitrant pagan tribes and semi-states of the Baltic littoral. These semi-states were mostly ruled by a '*knes*' who, like an Archaic Greek *basileus*, might command a strong following of retainers and kinsmen, but was not yet a patrimonial monarch like his Polish, Swedish or Danish counterparts. At first, the 'Northern Crusade' was conducted within the existing institutions of Church and State. But it came increasingly to be conducted by military-cum-monastic orders, and in due course the Teutonic Knights, whose principal field of operations was diverted from Palestine after the fall of Acre in 1291, came to constitute an autonomous society administered with purely nominal regard for the suzerainty of either emperors or popes. In contrast to the Jesuits in Paraguay, on the one hand, or the great Spanish military orders of Santiago, Calatrava and Alcantara on the other, they were both an exclusive military élite and the heads of a centralized territorial government. They were unique not only in the practices which defined their roles but in the efficiency with which they functioned over a period of more than two centuries. Despite the lack of statistics by which to measure the performance of their economy, 'the evidence of land-purchases, castle- and church-building, loans and campaigning suggests that it was doing very well' (Christiansen 1980, p. 199). We have, accordingly, yet another sub-type of the warrior-aristocratic mode capable of reproducing itself over successive generations for as long as the same initial conditions hold.* They were not, to be sure, demographically self-reproducing; their continuity depended on a sufficient supply of recruits to the role of 'knight-brother' willing to dedicate their lives to the Order and to accept the practices, both military and monastic, which it imposed. But these practices were as well adapted to the Knights' administrative as to their crusading functions: 'the Teutonic Knights had few problems' (Urban 1973,

* Which by the first half of the fifteenth century they had ceased to do: for a vivid description of the Order in its decline, see Burleigh (1984).

p. 530). Succession to the role of Grand Master was not bedevilled by dynastic loyalities or ambitions; the systact of officers bound by vows of obedience was at least as reliable as either patrimonial servants or salaried officials, let alone beneficed vassals; and the lower ranks of the administration were staffed by sisters and lesser brethren bound by the same rules and customs and motivated by the same creed.

The Teutonic Knights, like the Islamic emirs, furnished protection alike for the clerics of the true faith and for the urban merchants. Burghers were settled in each newly acquired *Kommende* where market and customs dues could be levied for the benefit of the Order, and the Grand Master exercised an authority over his towns 'greater than that of any other territorial ruler' (Dollinger 1970, p. 91). Nor could there emerge, any more than in the emirates, a stratum of autonomous landowners living off serfs or the labour of tenants tied to the soil. There were a few such, but only in Livonia were there either knights or bishops with their own estates on a sufficient scale to emancipate them to any significant degree from the central control of the Grand Master in Marienburg. As in Islam, the indigenous peasantry, once they accepted the faith, might retain their freedom of movement, their property rights and their access to public law (although some were subject to the jurisdiction of local lords). But they did not bear arms, and they had no political influence beyond the village assemblies of male household heads: no more than in Islam did membership of a common faith protect them from exploitation.

Yet another sub-type of the warrior mode, in which the ideology of conquest is based neither on Christianity nor on Islam, is exemplified by the Mongols following their unification as a single state under Chinghis Khan. The structure of their society is, unfortunately, a matter of some dispute among specialists. On one view, the Mongol state would appear to have been a patrimonial monarchy in which the administration was entrusted to the Khan's 'friends' (*nüxüt*), and the *arat* – the nomadic rank and file – were excluded from control over the herds and their pastures which constituted the means of production (Krader 1978, pp. 96ff.). On another, which is (to me, at least) more convincing, the achievement of Chinghis Khan was not so much to create a personal entourage as to break down the old tribal divisions among the warrior aristocracy; although the aristocracy had control of the distribution of pastures, they did not deprive the rank and file of the ownership of their own stock from which, indeed, they were required to pay dues in kind for the benefit of the poor (Khazanov 1984, pp. 233ff.). For the purposes of this Chapter, however, the more important point is that for as long as the Mongols continued to expand by conquest while maintaining the institutions of nomadic pastoralism, their society continued to function as a warrior aristocracy living off booty and tribute from sedentary agriculturalists. Only where they themselves became sedentary did they evolve into a monarchy with an embryonic (or assimilated) bureaucracy and a tax-based mode of extraction of the agricultural surpluses.

A decisive test is furnished by the contrast between the Mongols who overran China and the so-called Golden Horde – the Khanate which dominated Southern Russia until broken up in its turn by Timur. In China the Mongols, while retaining their separate identity both ethnically and juridically, ruled as one of a succession of imperial dynasties; although they allowed much of North China to revert to pasture, abolished the Sung examination system and introduced the practice of tax-farming by groups of Central Asian Muslim merchants reminiscent of the Roman *publicani*, they adapted their roles to the existing mode of the distribution of power more than the other way round. But the Golden Horde remained a nomadic warrior aristocracy for over two hundred years. Like the Teutonic Knights, they established towns in the conquered territories and encouraged trade. But they remained based in the Caspian Steppes, they drew the agricultural surpluses of the conquered territories as booty, they regularly exported slaves, and they treated the Russian princedoms as vassal states from which tribute could be extracted on demand by force of arms.

Finally, there belong also in this mode the independent armies amounting to a separate society, like Werner of Urslingen's 'Great Company' which I cited in Section 10 of Chapter 2 or the Catalan Company of 10,000 men and perhaps 20,000 camp followers formed after the Peace of Caltabellota in 1302 who succeeded in constituting themselves an autonomous principality which lasted more than two generations. These are, admittedly, borderline cases, since they do not reproduce themselves in their original form – nor are they envisaged by their members as so doing – any longer than the period of exceptional conflict and disorder which brought them into being. But for as long as these conditions obtain, they function in much the same way as any other society in the warrior mode. The dominant role is that of captain or generalissimo; the means of coercion are in the hands of the officer systact and deployed with the help of retainers, men-at-arms and attendant foot-soldiers; the economic resources which support them are acquired through booty or plunder or (at its most acceptable) requisition; and whatever protection they give to merchants or clerics can be withdrawn at will. It is implausible to envisage on any hypothesis conditions in which 'companies' at this level of power could reproduce themselves indefinitely as independent states. Sooner or later, they will have either to evolve into, or be absorbed by, a larger and more powerful society of a different sub-type or model. But they can be durable enough for the question 'how do they work?' to have to be answered by reference to as distinctive a set of roles as is reported for any of the sub-types of either the 'patrimonial' or the 'citizen' modes.

FUNCTIONAL ALTERNATIVES (2)

§23. From what was said in Section 11, it will be clear that the question 'how do "feudal" societies work?' is to be answered with 'feudal' taken in its broader, but not its all-embracing, sense, and that a fusion of benefice and vassalage – 'feudalism', that is, in its narrow sense – may or may not be the central institution. The defining characteristic of the feudal mode is decentralization of the means of coercion into the hands of local landholders. But there must still be a central source of legitimacy. Feudalism is not separatism or anarchy, although it may evolve into either or both. Nor should the decentralization of power be presupposed to require any particular relation between magnates and their dependent cultivators: serfdom, which is sometimes treated as the natural if not inevitable corollary, is only one functional alternative among several. The point is rather that the magnates' dependents must in some way, of which serfdom is the most obvious, be 'theirs'. The two questions about the systactic structure to be resolved, therefore, are first, what are the practices which sustain a decentralization of power to the magnates without progressively destroying it? and second, what are the practices which inhibit successful resistance to the magnates from below?

This formulation may look like an attempt to bypass the question of whether or not 'feudalism' is a distinctive mode of production which as such determines the political and ideological 'superstructure'. But if the argument of this Chapter so far is sound, it follows that feudalism is of course a distinctive mode of production, but is at the same time a distinctive mode of persuasion and coercion. This mode of production has to be based on agriculture, since the independence of the magnates would be impossible without their control over the land and its cultivators; and the extraction of the surplus therefore takes the characteristic form of rent, whether in cash, produce or labour.*

* The practice of wage-labour is not ruled out: a Mexican squatter or a fugutive Ottoman *reaya*, no less than an English cottager, may be selling his labour-power to

Intermittent plunder at one extreme or arms-length purchase at the other would be practices equally incompatible with long-term territorial control. Landlords may shift from demesne cultivation to tenancy and back again (Harvey 1983); they may market the surplus produce directly through agents, or store it on their own autarkic manors; and they may permit or refuse their dependent cultivators a greater or lesser degree of formal freedom. But landlords they remain. It is true that decentralization of power is not peculiar to feudal societies – we have seen it already as a defining characteristic of segmentary lineage systems, and it is found even in capitalist industrial societies to the extent that large corporations operate in the commodity and labour markets under often remote and tenuous control by the agents of the state. But 'feudal' can only be used of industrial corporations as a descriptive metaphor (or a pejorative value-judgement). No industrial society of whatever mode or sub-type can be decentralized to the degree that feudal societies are. Its much higher level of resources will require a much closer interdependence of roles and institutions both within the economy and under the state.

It follows that the internal conflicts which have to be contained in feudal societies will be of a quite distinctive kind. These conflicts are now between systacts fully conscious of their collective interests. The magnates may or may not be a hereditary aristocracy; they may be more or less internally differentiated in wealth, prestige and the size and strength of their military followings; and their relations to one another may be more or less cooperative or antagonistic. But they form a stratum whose interests must be preserved both against the central government and its agents on the one hand and against the dependent cultivators on the other, and the nature of the conflict is quite different in the two cases. The conflict between magnates and cultivators is a *class* conflict: the cultivators are trying to maintain or wrest back control over the means of production and the magnates are trying to extract from them the optimum surplus.* But the conflict between the magnates and the state is a *political* conflict: in a feudal monarchy the king is himself one lord among many with his own domain and his own dependent cultivators, and even where the state is linked to urban commercial interests the conflict with the magnates is over the means of coercion

the manorial lord or *hacendado* or *ayan* for cash payments – but not in a free national or even regional labour market.

* This does not mean that they necessarily try to keep them at subsistence level: it often furthers the interests of landlords to have more rather than less prosperous tenants, and on occasion to encourage them to purchase their freedom from villeinage.

rather than of production. There is, moreover, a conflict over the means of persuasion in which the state and the dependent cultivators will, under certain conditions, cooperate. If the legitimacy of the regime itself is threatened by a movement from below, the central government and the magnates will form a coalition to protect their common interest; and conversely, if both magnates and peasants have a common interest in questioning the legitimacy of the regime, or at least the authority of its agents, they will form a coalition under the banner of regionalism (and perhaps religion). But where the central government is more concerned with curbing the excesses of the magnates – 'baronial gangsterism', as it is sometimes called, or near-anarchic *caudillaje* – then it is to its interest to cooperate with the dependent cultivators under the auspices of the Church to promote an organized peace.

A final and no less important characteristic of societies in the feudal mode is that there cuts across all three lines of conflict the actual or potential conflict between urban and rural interests as such. Towns which, whatever the reasons for which they were founded, establish more than a limited degree of autonomy cannot but disturb the stable, or at least meta-stable, distribution of power between rulers, magnates and peasants. But it would be a mistake to suppose that their mere existence creates a contradiction within the system. The magnates themselves may reside in the town rather than the countryside (this is one of the striking differences between Byzantium and North-west Europe, as later between Japan and Eastern Europe); towns may generate tolls, rents, market dues and other revenues to the advantage of magnates as well as or instead of the central government; and the merchants, craftsmen, notaries and clergy of the towns may serve the interests of the magnates as much as or more than they weaken or undermine them.

Stability of a feudal society over several generations requires high reproduction ratios among both magnates and dependent cultivators, not least because the heritability of land originally granted as a benefice is precisely what marks the decentralization of power. If the incumbents of the benefice can be rotated at the ruler's discretion, like the early Ottoman *timars* (Beldiceanu 1980, p. 753) or the *iqta* in a strong Islamic state, then however ruthlessly they exploit their dependent cultivators (all the more, perhaps, because their tenure is short and they are more concerned with plunder than rent), these will not be 'their' men in the feudal sense. Equally, if the sons of dependent cultivators are not somehow required to enter their fathers' roles, the power of the magnates cannot but be diminished. It will not matter if a few sons whose labour is surplus to the magnates' requirements leave the territory of their birth for artisan employment, or mercenary service, or colonization of frontier territories elsewhere. But in feudal societies, large-scale geographical and social mobility can only be both symptom and cause of an imminent change in the mode of the distribution of power. The reproduction ratios do not need to be quite so low that the two principal systacts become castes: apart from the replacements made necessary by the deaths in internecine violence between rival *thegns*, barons, *ayans*, *dynatoi*, *caudillos* or *daimyō*, changes of ownership of magnate estates through purchase, hypergamy or usurpation need involve no disturbance to either the structure or the culture. Nor does it matter if the ranks of the dependent cultivators are replenished from the sons of slaves on the one hand or petty allodialists on the other. What does matter is that cultivators hitherto tied to the soil should not be free to seek higher wages as and where they choose (as happened in late fourteenth- and early fifteenth-century England) or to move at will into roles within either increasingly autonomous towns or an increasingly powerful central state.

What, then, are the practices which will sustain a feudal mode of the distribution of power? Between the central government and the magnates, there must be some reciprocally acknowledged tie, whether the respective roles are formalized as those of lord and vassal or are simply those of sovereign and subject, and whether the nominal sovereign is king, generalissimo or president. I have remarked already on the inherent contradiction between the rival claims of monarch and magnates once their common territory is at peace, productivity is rising, and population, both rural and urban, is growing: a coalition, although it may confirm the magnates' hold over their dependent cultivators, can under these conditions last only on the monarchy's terms. But if the magnates have a common national interest in the retention of the monarch in his role of head of state; if they are at the same time strong enough as an estate to curb or frustrate any incipient tendency to absolutism; if the cavalry service for which they are equipped and trained has not been superseded as the dominant arm of warfare; if they are not dependent on urban agents outside their control for the marketing of their agricultural surpluses; and if their dependent cultivators can neither resist (they have no weapons or access to them), flee (there is too little unoccupied cultivable land for them to flee to), or find other employment (there is virtually none); then, for as long as these conditions hold, the society in question can be predicted to reproduce itself very much as the ideal-typical model of a feudal society sketched out in Section 17.

The society which most nearly approximates to this model is

sixteenth-century Poland. It was not then apparent what would be the consequences of a weak monarchy for Poland's treatment at the hands of other and militarily more powerful societies. The power of veto which the Diet enjoyed over the Crown secured the nobility what they saw as their rights without depriving them of its benefits in symbolizing and reinforcing national unity. Their heavy cavalry was to all appearances a match for any likely opposition. The higher nobility on their large, isolated estates exported their surpluses through Danzig and controlled a near-autarkic manorial-type economy (including the *propinacja* – the local inn at which peasants bought their alcohol for the profit of their lords); the middle and lower nobility sold their surpluses locally and imitated the upper nobility's life-style as best they could (Kula 1976, p. 123).* Urban influence was negligible and corvée labour could be extracted from the peasantry at will. The profits from the sale of surpluses were spent not on improvements to productivity but on imported luxuries. In due course the mode of production, like the mode of coercion, was to be overtaken by mutant practices and novel roles which penetrated the system from outside. But if the inter-societal context had stayed as it was in the sixteenth century, the old roles could have reproduced themselves unchanged from one generation to the next; and they would have done so not because the respective roles of monarch and magnates were defined by a fusion of benefice and vassalage but, on the contrary, because the magnates were virtually in the position of conceding sovereignty (and the military resources underpinning it) back to the Crown.†

By contrast, the society outside of Europe whose institutions most strikingly recall the Western European sub-type of feudalism is one whose earlier evolution seems fully to confirm its relative instability. The resemblances between Europe from the collapse of the Carolingian empire to the emergence of the early modern monarchies and Japan from the late twelfth-century Kamakura Shogunate of Minamoto-no-

* Kula also makes the point that Polish noblemen had no alternative careers open to them. In the absolutist monarchies, there were roles to be filled in the army, the administration and the judiciary. 'But in Poland there was practically no standing army, nor a permanent state administration, nor a professional judiciary, and to engage in manufacturing or commerce entailed the risk of demeaning one's noble status and bringing "ignominy" upon oneself' (*ibid.*, p. 147).

† A remarkably close analogue, to which I shall return in Chapter 4, is Iran between the Mongols and the Safavids, when the Seljuk *iqta* evolved into the *suyurghal* – a heritable grant of land carrying title to its tax revenue. 'The lords of large *suyurghals* were more or less independent rulers over their own territories; they were, however, obliged to play an active part in the military operations of their sovereign' (Fragner 1986, p. 510).

Yoritomo to the Tokugawa unification in the early seventeenth century have long been familiar to Western scholars, and by none more forcibly summarized than Marc Bloch (1961, p. 446). But once given the resemblances, the differences are striking too. The practices defining the relation of lord to vassal in Japan were by no means the same as in Europe: not only was the power attaching to the two roles more one-sidedly in favour of the lord, but the chain of vassalage descended not from the emperor but from the shogun. Nor is it easy to say at what point in Japanese history the decentralization of the means of coercion had become a self-reproducing 'feudal' system as opposed to an anarchic rejection of central authority amounting to near-permanent civil war. In consequence, there has been much debate among specialists about whether it is useful under any definition to speak of a Japanese feudalism at all. If, however, its constituent roles and the practices which define them are examined from the perspective of this Chapter, it is clear that Japanese society should indeed be assigned to the feudal mode for a part of the period in question, albeit to a sub-type reminiscent more of Latin America in the heyday of *caudillaje* than of post-Jagellonian Poland.

Initially, Minamoto-no-Yoritomo held his power to dispense benefices carrying rights to revenue from land grants (*shōen*) within the legal institutions of a patrimonial monarchy. But in the thirteenth century, as military roles came to displace civilian, subordinate officials and their vassals increasingly usurped proprietary rights over the *shōen* and the roles of the dependent cultivators became increasingly defined by the practices of personal servitude. In the Ashikaga Shogunate which emerged from the anarchy of the mid fourteenth century, the local governors (*shugo*) became a systact of magnates who held, under the shogun, *seigneurie banale* over their territories. But not all military retainers were their vassals, and not more than a fraction of the land under their jurisdiction was held by them in benefice. Concentration into compact domains in the hands of *daimyō* who commanded sub-infeudated vassals in their own right took place only after a further round of fighting in which the system as it had been under Minamoto-no-Yoritomo disappeared completely. Now, for a few decades, Japanese society functioned through a throughgoing decentralization of the means of coercion and control of the dependent cultivators by armed retainers of the magnates whose relation to them, even if not identical to European vassalage, was both closely homologous in structure and closely analogous in function. But civil war broke out yet again, and when it ended it was through the cumulative success of Odo Nobunaga,

Toyotomi Hideyoshi and Tokugawa Ieyasu in re-establishing a distinctive sub-type of the absolutist mode. This absolutism was, admittedly, qualified in several ways (as we shall see in Section 26 of Chapter 4), and it incorporated many practices inherited from the previous era. But it was an absolutism nonetheless.

The Japanese case, accordingly, although it confirms the function which the practices of benefice and vassalage can serve in a system of decentralized power, confirms also the contradiction inherent in a decentralization resulting less from the initial strength of local magnates than from the weakness of the central state. The sixteenth-century *daimyō* were neither Polish *szlachta* manipulating the monarch's role to their own advantage nor post-Carolingian counts whose delegated power was exploited by them up to, if not beyond, the limits which the royal *prévôts* and *baillis* were seeking to impose. They functioned, in that period, much more like Latin American *caudillos* than either. Like the *caudillos*, their power over their territories had been acquired by usurpation of the means of coercion rather than either production or persuasion. They were not cooperating with each other to preserve their power against that of the shogun, but competing with each other in an attempt to maximize it relative both to the shogun and to each other. The differences in culture are of course large:* nineteenth- and early twentieth-century Latin America shared with contemporary Europe and the United States a whole range of institutions and practices inconceivable in sixteenth-century Japan, from multinational business corporations to presidential elections. But the structures are interestingly similar both in the pattern of social relations and in the nature of the instability inherent in them.

The case of Mexico (to which I shall also return in Chapter 4) is particularly instructive, not because its regional *caudillos* stood in the same relation to the central government and the peasantry as the *daimyō*, but because Porfirio Díaz, who for the first twenty years after his seizure of power in 1876 had all the appearance of a Mexican Tokugawa, turned out to be the precursor of a revolution and civil war out of which a new sub-type of the authoritarian mode evolved only after a resurgence of *caudillaje*. This resurgence took a number of different forms dictated by

* Although not the differences in military organization and technology. Just as in Mexico in 1916, Pancho Villa's cavalry charges were decimated by the machine guns of the better-disciplined troops of the Constitutionalist army, so had Odo Nobunaga's deployment of musketeers trained to fire in succession from behind screens of pointed stakes decimated the Takeda cavalry: J. W. Hall (1970, p. 138) suggests that the musket hastened the unification of Japan by several decades.

the very different ecological and sociological contexts and histories of Mexico's different regions. But its regional diversity was no greater than that of sixteenth-century Japan or, for that matter, seventeenth-century France. As in both France and Japan, it was this very diversity which helped to preserve a temporary balance of power between a central government unable to impose its authority to the extent that it wished and local magnates unable, and indeed unwilling, to secede altogether from their common nation-state. It is true that the Mexican *haciendas* are nc more analogous to the castle-towns of the Japanese *daimyō* than to the estates of the French nobility. Few *hacendados*, even if they also occupied a political role, aspired to regional monopoly of the means of coercion, and where a would-be rebel against the central government returned to his *hacienda* it was more likely to be a symbolic gesture of defiance than a prelude to mobilization of armed revolt (cf. Bazant 1977, p. 44, on Vincente Guerrero in 1830). But it is no less true of Mexico between 1910 and 1920 than Japan in the mid sixteenth or France in the mid seventeenth century that the local magnates, although they did not wish actually to secede from a society to whose central governmental roles they still conceded ideological legitimacy based on nationhood, had effectively taken the power attaching to those roles into their own hands.

Within this sub-type of the feudal mode, there could be, and often was, class conflict of the same kind as between European peasants and seigneurs. Whether Mexican peasants attached themselves to one or another *caudillo* against the central government or sought to exploit the antagonism between the two to gain advantage for themselves depended on local circumstances. Zapata's followers in Morelos fighting for the restoration of village lands under the banner of Our Lady of Guadalupe were as different from Villa's freebooting cowboys from Chihuahua as either from the 'Red Battalions' of urban workers in Mexico City (J. Meyer 1970) who sided with the eventually victorious Constitutionalists. But this was feudalism on the Japanese as opposed to the Polish model. Local magnates maintained their location relative to both state and peasantry, but only for so long as no incumbents of central governmental roles were able to mobilize sufficient resources to regain a society-wide monopoly of the means of coercion.

If there is any single characteristic institution whose function is central to the workings of a feudal mode, it is the late Roman *patrocinium*,* which exemplifies in almost ideal-typical form the functional

* For which the *locus classicus* is Salvian, *De Gubernatore Dei* (v.43), where he laments the plight of peasants in Gaul 'who are driven to flight by the tax-collectors and

connection between the practices governing the relations between the magnates and monarchy on one side and magnates and peasantry on the other. As Wickham comments (1984, pp. 17–18), there was nothing new about relations of private patronage in the late Roman Empire; but the significance of what Salvian reports of fifth-century Gaul is that peasants as well as landlords now had a systactic interest in feudal relations based economically on rent rather than absolutist relations based economically on tax. The magnates now realized that their interests would be better served by displacing the state than by exploiting it, and so in the same evolutionary shift the dependent cultivators became not the state's dependents but theirs. In Gaul, this mutation of practices was part of the response of the dominant systact to the whole process of the fall of the Western Empire and its replacement by barbarian kingdoms commanding too few resources to be able to transcend the constraints of the patrimonial mode.* In the Eastern Empire, on the other hand, although there is ample evidence for the same pressures for smaller men to place themselves under the protection of magnates as a means of escape from tax, the institutions of central authority remained in place. Only very much later, when *pronoia* grants became virtually heritable, a few large landholders secured total immunities, petty allodialists were increasingly impoverished and the central government came to depend militarily on large bodies of mercenaries which it could barely afford, is there any case for assigning Byzantium to the 'feudal' mode; and even then, as I shall argue in a little more detail in Chapter 4, it is more plausible to explain the period following the reign of Basil II in terms of oscillation within an absolutist mode than evolution to a feudal one.

The number of times and places at which one sub-type or another of the feudal mode has evolved is, obviously enough, a matter of historical contingency. It is possible to specify antecedent events, processes and states of affairs which might have occurred but didn't, and would, if they had, have prevented the decentralization of power in late Lombard Italy, post-Jagellonian Poland, post-Ashikaga Japan, post-colonial Latin America, the later Ottoman Empire, post-Carolingian Europe and post-Mongol, pre-Safavid Iran. But this only makes it all the more striking that, with one partial exception, nowhere in Africa is there a

abandon their little holdings because they cannot retain them, and seek out the estates of great men and become the tenants of the rich' (A. H. M. Jones 1964, II, p. 775).

* Although it is true that the Merovingians did not, as we saw in Section 20, abandon taxation altogether (cf. Goffart 1982).

reported example. We have seen already (in Section 13 of Chapter 1) that despite instances where benefices may be granted in return for services, the pervasive roles are those of patron and client rather than lord and vassal. Similarly, although there are numerous cases of attempts to wrest local autonomy from central government – Lloyd (1965, p. 71) remarks that 'The majority of African Kingdoms have been riven by secessionist tendencies' – they are attempts at fission from patrimonial states. This, however, becomes less surprising than it may at first appear when we remember that African societies lacked not only the wheel but the plough* and that land was always in plentiful supply. The consequences were twofold. First, local chiefs or lineage heads were not territorial magnates;† second, dependent cultivators were neither serfs‡ nor peons but junior kinsmen or slaves. The various African kingdoms differed widely from one another in size, stability, mode of recruitment into governmental roles, rules of kinship, ideology (royal vs. local cults), means of coercion, and nature and scope of rights held by kings, chiefs or lineage heads over both land and people (including functions performed by slaves). Rival descent-groups as well as local chiefs might contend for greater power, ruling dynasties might be replaced through rebellion or conquest, and even large and powerful states like Oyo might collapse through internal conflicts. But a 'feudal' mode as I have defined it is nowhere found.

§24. As I first remarked in the course of Section 11, in those societies where the role of vassalage is pervasive, the practices which define the relation of lord and vassal can function not to weaken the central authority of the state or proto-state but to strengthen it. Where, accordingly, statehood is fully achieved, the vassal's role can become the analogue, and perhaps even the prototype, of the roles of the professional

* Except for Ethiopia – which is the one exceptional case for which there are reported the same institutions of both lay and clerical landlordism as in medieval Europe (Goody 1971, pp. 30–1; 1976, pp. 110–11).

† Cf. Peel (1983, p. 45) on Ijeshaland: '...it is profoundly misleading to call its chiefs an "aristocracy" or a "nobility" or an "upper class", with the implication that here we have a social formation akin to European feudalism...In Ijẹsha, the main productive resource, land, was virtually a free good; the claim of *obas* and chiefs to be "owners of the land" (*onile*) meant that they claimed the allegiance of the people who worked a territory, but, as we have seen, they had to work at winning and holding that allegiance.'

‡ The nearest parallel known to me is the institution of *botlhanka* among the BaTawana, which is clearly 'comparable to hereditary serfdom' (Tlou 1977, p. 369), although 'to some extent, their masters accorded them the treatment enjoyed by the master's own children' (*ibid.*).

bureaucrats, service nobility, or venal office-holders who staff the administrative echelons of societies in the absolutist mode. 'Absolutist' remains a slightly uneasy term. Not only do all the societies so classified fall far short of totalitarian control, but their resources were in some cases little greater than those available to a 'feudal' monarch.* How can William I of England, with his handful of tenants-in-chief and their subordinate knights and auxiliary foot-soldiers, be placed alongside the Emperor Diocletian with an army half a million strong or Louis XIV with up to 300,000 or even 400,000 men in the field in the War of the Spanish Succession? But resources are of value to the incumbents of the roles to which there attaches control of them in proportion to the relative power attaching to the other roles over which domination is sought. England in 1086 *was* a centralized state, whatever might subsequently happen in the reign of King Stephen, and it owed its strength to the ability of a conquering and now more than patrimonial monarch both to impose and to adapt a set of practices which in other contexts had served the interests of magnates at the expense of those of kings.

More powerful still was Norman Sicily under Roger II. His father, like William the Conqueror in England, had granted extensive territories to his followers as fiefs. But no more than in William's case had this involved a decentralization of the means of coercion. He retained full powers of jurisdiction within a framework of Roman law; he allowed no private castles; he supplemented his military resources with mercenaries;† his *curia* was 'not a restriction on the king but an emanation of the royal will' (Mack Smith 1968, p. 28); he supplemented the revenues from his own large demesne with taxation; he inherited and exploited a sound and sophisticated Muslim coinage (as William the Conqueror had an Anglo-Saxon one); and he employed an experienced Greek and/or Muslim bureaucracy. It is this last which particularly distinguishes his administration from that of the Norman or even the Plantagenet kings of England. As Maitland and others have remarked, even under Edward I the whole government of the realm could be assembled together in the persons of perhaps three dozen people.‡

* Not that the size of the territory over which the ruler exercises nominal sovereignty is a reliable indicator of the power attaching to his role: the directives laid down by the German principalities in the form of *Landes-* and *Polizeiordnungen* in the seventeenth and eighteenth centuries were much more effective in changing attitudes and behaviour at the local level than those laid down by the Tsars (Raeff 1983).

† Which was Norman practice generally (D. C. Douglas 1967, pp. 6–7).

‡ The patrimonial nature of many of the practices still characteristic of the English monarchy under Henry I can be inferred from the *Constitutio Domus Regis* of 1135/6 (White 1948).

Twelfth-century Sicily was, at least briefly, an absolutist society in the standard sense of the term, complete with ideological trappings just as splendid as Louis XIV's and an even tighter hold over the Church. Yet Norman Sicily and Norman England are both borderline cases. Just as the test of the evolution of a society to statehood is whether its novel political roles can outlast a crisis of succession, so is the test of evolution from a patrimonial to an absolutist mode the independence of the society's central institutions from the personal attributes of the particular caliph, emperor, shogun, sultan, shah, Sapa Inca or king. Norman Sicily had not fully evolved into absolutism for as long as the adaptation of the practices of vassalage and benefice to the functions of a centralized administration depended on an exceptional ruler whose successors would be unable to prevent the magnates from reverting to their feudal roles.

A 'centralized feudal system' (as Crawcour 1961, p. 342, and Morishima 1982, p. 80, designate Tokugawa Japan) is, therefore, still a contradiction in terms, whatever the sub-type in question. The Japanese *daimyō* did, admittedly, enjoy considerable autonomy within their domains, but – as Crawcour himself points out elsewhere (1974, p. 119) – they did not own their own territories or even castles, and they had to submit to periods of enforced residence in the imperial capital by which they were no less tightly tied than Louis XIV's courtiers at Versailles. The decisive transition to absolutism comes about when (i) there is a standing army independent of levy or scutage strong enough to repress either magnate or peasant rebellion, (ii) governmental resources are not merely feudal rents or aids but regular taxes adequate to support the enlarged military and administrative apparatus on a permanent basis, and (iii) there is an ideology of rulership sufficiently pervasive for the legitimacy of the regime not to be challenged even though policies carried out by its agents in its name may, on occasion, be violently opposed.

There is a range of different institutions and roles whereby these functions have been successfully performed in different contexts. But once again, the number of possible sub-types is not unmanageably large, and many of the practices on which the stability of absolutism depends are reported for societies widely separate in both time and place. I have already commented on the use of slaves, freedmen, low-born *ministeriales* and eunuchs as servants and administrators. Similarly, it is not surprising to find parallels in the court ceremonials and religious rituals by which different absolutist rulers have sought to enhance their prestige, or in the widespread adoption of the practice of tax-farming, whether by curial *procuratores* and *susceptores* in the later Roman Empire, Islamic *iqta*-holders, the Central Asian merchants who collected taxes for the Mongol rulers of China, or the *fermiers-généraux* of eighteenth-century France. But the workings of absolutist societies will not be adequately explained simply by listing practices common to most or even all of them. These practices could function very differently in different contexts – just as vassalage could strengthen a feudal monarchy or weaken it, so might tax-farming either strengthen an absolutist monarchy or weaken it by degenerating into parasitic forms of what Weber called 'prebendalism'. What is more, absolutist institutions were everywhere the conscious creations of rulers well aware of the systactic opposition which they had had to overcome. This applies no less to Pachacuti, the creator of the Inca *Tahuantinsuyu*, or to al-Mansur and his brother and predecessor al-Saffah, than it does to Tokugawa Ieyasu or Peter the Great or Louis XIV. The degree to which their various regimes approximated to the ideal type of a service nobility, a professional mandarinate, or an administration of office-holders by purchase, or combined them in a particular institutional mix of their own, depends not on the inherent efficacy of any one set of practices as such, but on the function that one set of practices rather than another performed in the context of the pre-existing systactic structure.

§25. Let me start from venality of offices as practised by the French monarchy, which has been extensively studied by Mousnier (1945) and others and seems agreed among specialists to have fulfilled the double function of raising much-needed money and providing a channel of upward social mobility for regional bourgeois and minor nobility. Its history is sufficiently chequered to imply that it was not wholly or consistently a stabilizing influence. It was denounced at the meeting of the Estates-General in 1614–15, and temporarily abolished in 1618. When restored, it brought into being a self-reproducing systact of office-holders who, although tied as a status-group to the monarchy, were at the same time non-productive as a class and resistant as a faction to the *intendants* who by the middle of the century represented the monarchy in virtually every province or *généralité*. Yet it was clearly a (if not the) central institution of an absolutist state which fulfilled all three of the conditions necessary for the permanent subordination of the magnates and their *fidèles*. The venal *officiers* were the analogues of the Russian *pomeshchiki*, with the difference that the magnates had not, like the *boyars*, been killed or dispossessed. But that difference was not as critical as it would otherwise have been. The revenues raised by the sale of offices, when added to the *taille* from which the nobility were exempt, could finance wars against the Huguenots or, later, other European societies; and these wars diverted the magnates from *caudillaje* or civil war into the pursuit of glory in a national standing army on behalf of a monarchy whose ideology enhanced their prestige.

The resulting distribution of power was by no means wholly in the monarchy's interest. The *intendants* often cooperated with local magnates; the tax-farmers simultaneously occupied the role of *officiers* and thereby profited not only from the share of the *taille* which they kept for themselves but from the high rates of interest at which they lent back to the government money which ought to have been its own; the central administrators, even in the heyday of Colbert, saw their roles at least as much in patrimonial as in bureaucratic terms (Dessert and Journet 1975); neither fiscal nor judicial practices were uniform from one region to another; the loyalty of military and naval commanders was often suspect; and the *parlements* frequently used their powers to obstruct the declared intentions of the central government. What is more, the mounting costs of warfare imposed a level of taxation which not only perpetuated the risk of local revolts but was often beyond the physical capacity of the countryside. Yet there can be no question that the system did in fact work: there was no regression to a feudal decentralization of sovereignty after the last great outbreak of *caudillaje* in the *Fronde*. However short of funds the government was, the interests of the financiers were tied to those of the state (D. Parker 1983, pp. 101–2). The magnates could neither take over the state nor exploit it on their own terms. There were no serious local rebellions after 1675. The urban poor were forcibly detained and subjected to a regime of 'labour, prayers and floggings' (Ranum 1968, p. 243, quoted by D. Parker 1983, p. 81). The army, now supplemented by mercenaries and police, was well able to maintain internal order even in the aftermath of defeat in the field at the hands of foreign powers. The legitimacy of Louis XIV was never questioned. For all the resistance to central authority and resentment of the venal office-holders, and for all the abuses by individual incumbents of the power attaching to their roles, the sale of offices, the farming of taxes and the recruitment of magnate families into the national army did preserve a stable absolutist state whose eventual overthrow as the unintended consequence of a *révolte nobiliaire* was in circumstances wholly different from those of the Wars of Religion and the *Fronde*.

In Russia, the service nobility was if anything more closely bound to the monarchy under Peter the Great than were the *noblesse d'épée* and *noblesse de robe* under Louis XIV. If the *pomeshchiki* were the analogues of the venal *officiers*,* they were also the homologues of the vassals of a strong 'feudal' monarch. The obedience demanded from them was categorical. Although by the end of the seventeenth century the heritability of the *pomestye* had made them indistinguishable from allodial *votchina* (Blum 1961, p. 183), this in no way weakened the link between landholding and the obligation of service, whether civilian or military, from the age of fourteen. Only after 1762 was the obligation relaxed by allowing for voluntary retirement at a relatively early age, so that although the principle of service was maintained, 'The Russian noble was no longer "enserfed" to the state' (de Madariaga 1981, p. 89). But even so, this implied no decentralization of power to local magnates. All it did was to create the class and status-group of gentlemanly rentiers descriptively familiar to all readers of nineteenth-century Russian novels. The army, which grew steadily in size, continued as in France to be officered by the nobility. Tax revenues likewise were steadily raised as the costs of war and administration mounted. Peasant revolts were forcibly suppressed. Although the lack of a clear-cut law of succession raised the danger of rival contenders as heirs to the throne, the legitimacy of the monarchy as such was never questioned.

The most striking institutional difference between France and Russia, apart from that between a service nobility and a venal bureaucracy, lay within the mode of production. In both societies, the state was financed by taxation levied on the agricultural surplus. But in Russia, the primary producers were not wage-labourers, tenants, sharecroppers or petty allodialists. They were serfs,† whether bound to private landlords, the Church, the monarchy or the state itself. Yet the difference did not, as in the late Roman Empire in the West, lead to a decline of tax at the expense of rent. The collection of tax was, to be sure, inefficient in the sense that much of the revenue theoretically due to the treasury never reached it. But it was not significantly more so than in France: Prussia was, in this as in other respects, more efficient than either. Serfdom did

* And, it might be added, of the clergy as used by the Habsburgs in seventeenth-century Austria; but as Anderson (1974, p. 310) rightly points out, 'no matter how astute, priests could never be functionally equivalent to *officiers* or *pomeshchiki* as building-blocks of Absolutism'.

† Except for the half-million or so *odnodvortsy* – free smallholders who were, however, obliged to perform militia service and are thus both analogues and homologues of the *agrarii milites* of medieval Saxony, the 'soldier-farmers' (Elvin 1973, p. 37) of T'ang China, the 'soldier-peasantry' (Anderson 1974, p. 180) planted by Charles XI of Sweden on specially allotted lands in the mid seventeenth century, or the Prussian freemen who had originally been invested by the Teutonic Knights with small estates from which military services had to be rendered (Carsten 1953, pp. 160–1).

not lead to feudalism because the Russian nobility, like the French *officiers* and unlike the Polish *szlachta*, used the powers attaching to their roles in support of, not in opposition to, the state. The tsars and the nobility cooperated in the subjection of the peasantry who, once tied to the land (or to a factory or workshop), could be exploited for the support of their proprietors and the central government alike. Individual landowners might still, like individual *hacendados* in Mexico, be in near-continuous conflict with one another: even in the reign of Catherine the Great, landlords kept trained bands of serfs reminiscent of the late Roman *bucellarii* (literally, 'biscuit-eaters') who were used to wage private wars against their masters' neighbours (Dukes 1967, p. 19). But unlike the large senatorial landowners of Gaul in the last decades of the Roman Empire in the West, the Russian nobility still needed the state both as the guarantor of their domination over their serfs and as the means of their own advancement in its service. At the same time, therefore, as it was the analogue of the venal bureaucracy of France, it was functionally tied to relations of production in which, unlike France, market practices were of minimal significance. There was a trend during the eighteenth century away from labour services (*barshchina*) towards payments in cash (*obrok*) – which Catherine the Great disapproved of – and wage-labour was increasingly employed in industry. But the central institution remained serfdom, and the collection of the poll tax operated within it. The serfowners responsible for meeting the amounts assessed recognized, as did the tsars, that it was in their joint interest to see that the peasantry had the capacity to pay. Over most of the country (the exception being Little Russia, where perhaps as many as a quarter of serfs were landless), the allocation of tax was passed down to the village commune (the *mir*), thus integrating into the system the richer serfs who determined the apportionment of the obligations among the effective tax-units.

Prussia, as I have said, stands in contrast to both Russia and France as a model of efficient – or at least much less inefficient – absolutism. Its structure was held together, like Russia's, by a service nobility dominating an enserfed peasantry. But Prussia's nobles at the same time performed roles much closer to those of a professional bureaucracy. The Prussian nobility was never a *noblesse de robe*, and those commoners whom the 'Sergeant King', Frederick William I, appointed privy councillors in the mid seventeenth century acquired estates and intermarried with the local nobility (Carsten 1953, p. 259): a more accurate term for the German counterparts of the French *officiers* is *nobilitierten* or *briefadligen Beamten* (Malettke 1980, p. 23). But both the ennobled officials who served Frederick William I and the self-reproducing nobles who served Frederick the Great* were integrated not merely, as in France and Russia, into a standing army but also into a bureaucracy which, although brought into being to serve the needs of the army, came to function increasingly independently of it.

By the end of the reign of Frederick William I, the *Generalkriegscommissariat* had extended its area of control to embrace taxation, municipal government, the financing of trade and manufacturing, and the guilds. Junkers who might otherwise have been the focus of resistance to the monarchy in the provincial Estates were offered careers within a corporation which reproduced – as the Teutonic Order had done – the systactic structure of the society as a whole. Within that corporation, roles were never sinecures; nobles entered the civil service by way of the universities and secured their particular appointments by examination. Nor did Junker sons have the option of careers in the Church; the Protestant pastors were exclusively of commoner origin. It is arguable that it was Prussia's relative poverty which made the creation of this noble bureaucracy possible at all. If Frederick William I had had to contend with rich local magnates, large ecclesiastical landlords, prosperous merchant towns, and a nobility whose incomes would be drastically reduced if they entered the service of the state, Prussian absolutism might have evolved into the same sub-type as that of Louis XIV. But in the event, Frederick the Great came to exercise as much power as either Louis XIV or Catherine the Great through institutions and practices different from either the French or the Russian. It is true that by the end of the eighteenth century, the structure of Prussian society showed unmistakable signs of strain. The Prussian army's shattering defeat by Napoleon at Jena in 1806 was to require it to be rebuilt on the basis of a quite different mode of production, which permitted the Junkers to evolve as agricultural capitalists while continuing to perform their traditional military functions. But Prussian absolutism did, all the same, work as well as or better than either Russian or French, and has to be assigned to a distinctive sub-type of its own.

The apparent paradox of a professional civil service emerging from within a stratum of warrior nobles points an obvious contrast to the

* A descriptive touch which nicely conveys the attitude of Frederick the Great is his apparent convinction that any officer whose name he couldn't remember couldn't be noble – with the consequent danger that the officer might lose his commission (Goodwin 1967, pp. 91–2). Commoners were commissioned when necessary in wartime, but in peacetime were either retired or transferred to the artillery or to garrison duty: in this, the policy of Frederick William I had been the same.

society where a professional bureaucracy first evolved in something approaching ideal-typical form. The Chinese mandarinate has long been recognized as unique. But its uniqueness lies not simply in the competitive examination system which was, in any case, tempered by the continuance of practices of recommendation and patronage, but in the subordination of military to civilian institutions under the Sung. I have remarked already on the irony that the determination of the Sung emperors not to risk another rebellion like that of An-Lu-Shan exposed them to still more damaging defeat at the hands of the Jürchen and Mongols. But internally, the enlarged bureaucracy of successful candidates located in provincial towns and supported by agricultural surpluses produced by tenant labour functioned to sustain the central state no less effectively than a service nobility or a systact of office-holders by purchase. Indeed, it resembled a service nobility in that its reproduction ratio was quite high,* and the investment which ambitious ambitious families committed to the promotion of aspiring sons gave it something of the character of office-holding by purchase. Even at its largest, however, it was a tiny proportion of the total population, and just as the Russian system had to rely on incorporating the *mir*, so did the Chinese have to rely on the institutions of village self-government – with the difference that the Chinese villagers were not serfs and that relations of kinship were uniquely strong as well as pervasive among them.

The use of village institutions to apportion taxes, levy recruits, organize the repair of bridges and fortifications, and maintain internal order is familiar from a wide range of agricultural societies. But in China, the local patrilineages (particularly in the South) were more powerful, and the villages more independent of the central government, than in any other agricultural society ruled by an absolute monarchy. Although in theory all land belonged to the emperor, the Sung abandoned the pretence that this implied direct intervention to adjust the size and distribution of holdings: the government's policies were directed rather to increasing agricultural production (Golas 1980, pp. 299, 310). The strength of kinship ties is sometimes invoked to help explain the fact that a society in which there was an active commodity

* The examination lists of 1148 and 1246 show that some 40% of successful doctoral candidates were the sons, grandsons or great-grandsons of civil servants (Kracke 1953, p. 69) – a figure interestingly close to the 33% of Roman consuls under the Principate who were the sons, grandsons or great-grandsons of consuls (Hopkins 1983, p. 135). Reproduction ratios of this order are likely – other things equal – to be both low enough for institutional stability and high enough for flexibility without giving rise to a too widespread or intense sense of relative deprivation among the excluded.

market, credit networks were highly developed, the role of the private entrepreneur was accorded relatively high prestige (legitimated by a Neo-Confucian philosophy of profit),* neither slavery nor serfdom (although they existed) were pervasive, the idea of a permanent labour-force paid money wages out of tax revenue was familiar from the eleventh century onwards, and a steadily increasing proportion of government revenue came from state monopolies and levies on commerce, still failed to evolve the institutions and practices of advanced financial, commercial and industrial capitalism. But for the purpose of this Chapter, Sung China has to be counted as yet another distinctive sub-type of the absolutist mode. That it failed to evolve otherwise than it did is no more a demonstration of internal contradictions than is its failure to resist the Mongol invaders. It is true that in due course the Ming emperors introduced practices much closer to the ideal type of absolutism, if by that is implied more intrusive surveillance of, and more direct interference in, the day-to-day lives of their subjects. But the Sung emperors were absolute monarchs. There was no decentralization of sovereignty to autonomous magnates. Neither the local élites nor the urban merchants threatened the emperors' legitimacy. I cited earlier (in Section 4 of Chapter 2) the Emperor Kao-tsung's plaintive surprise that his generals should have obeyed his orders. But this was a symptom of the army's alienation from, not its domination of, the institutions of the central government. The internal stability of the society is as well explained, in the context of a commercialized mode of production and a Confucian ideology of legitimacy, by the subordination of the military to the civilian bureaucracy as is the stability of Prussian society by the subordination of the civilian to the military bureaucracy in the context of the dynastic legitimacy of the Hohenzollerns and the retention of a mode of production based on serfdom.

This does not yet, however, exhaust the range of institutional alternatives for the successful functioning of an absolutist state. We have seen that in many patrimonial states the ruler employs permanent, full-time, specialist administrators deliberately drawn from an inferior systact of origin, and the practice is one which continues in a number of fully-fledged absolutist societies – including Ming China, where the power of the court eunuchs increased at the direct expense of that of the

* Lo (1969, pp. 60–2): the government itself needed their services, particularly during the period of extensive naval construction (p. 77), and was therefore careful not to alienate them, although in due course, under pressure of increasingly onerous exactions, it did.

mandarins. The difficulties are obvious enough: insubordination or even mutiny, the hostility of freeborn notables, potential shortage of new recruits, and problems of remuneration and training. Yet it is possible to specify the conditions under which an absolutism organized around this set of practices and institutions could remain stable. Slavery can take many forms and perform many functions, and although there can be no dispute that the slaves recruited by the caliphs and sultans of Islamic societies were, indeed, the property of their masters, the relationship was tempered to a considerable degree by personal loyalties. Roles of patron and client analogous to the lordship and vassalage of Western Europe were pervasive throughout Islam, and the literary sources are full of anecdotes testifying to the strength of *istina* (a term deriving from a verb which had come to mean 'to foster a person's career') between slave soldiers (*ghilmān*) or civilian secretaries (*kuttāb*) and their masters or patrons (Mottahedeh 1980, Ch. 2).

Like European vassalage, Islamic practices of clientage sometimes functioned as analogues of weakened ties of kinship, and the emphasis on loyalty in the literary sources may also, as with vassalage, be a symptom of the frequency with which it was disregarded in practice. But their advantages to would-be absolutist rulers were clearly seen by them. They were a means by which the patrimonial relations of the household and camp could be adapted to the government of territories conquered in the name not of a dynasty but of a creed. If the slave soldiers were 'bodyguards writ large' (Crone 1980, p. 84), the scholarly Iranian *mawāli* who staffed the *diwans* of the caliphs were, likewise, not a mandarinate but a personal secretariat whose roles were extended to perform the functions of as many separate administrative departments as the ruler wished. It might be objected that for all the pomp and splendour of the court of Harun-al-Rashid, the collapse of the Abbasid caliphate demonstrates the underlying weakness of institutions which, as in the empires of Ashoka and Charlemagne, rested on practices arguably more patrimonial than absolutist. In Baghdad, moreover, the problem of succession to the caliph's role and the difficulty of controlling outlying provinces were compounded by the increasing disposition of the Turkish soldiery to acknowledge no authority but their own. But these same institutions and practices were to emerge some three centuries later in an Islamic society which unmistakably transcended the limits of patrimonialism: Ottoman Turkey.

Although (as we shall see in Chapter 4) the stability of Ottoman absolutism depended on the continued *jihād* against the infidels of Christian Europe, the failure to take Vienna in 1529 and again in 1623 hardly disqualifies Ottoman Turkey from being assigned to the absolutist mode. Its systactic structure proved capable of reproducing itself with little alteration of its central institutions and no serious challenge from the incumbents of subordinate roles. Economically, the extraction of tax from unarmed cultivators was effected without the intermediacy of local magnates and at rates which may well have compared favourably with the dues and services previously exacted by the Christian landlords of the Balkan peninsula. Ideologically, the tension between the secular authority and the *ulama*'s demands for adherence to the Islamic ideal was resolved by a tacit concordat which put Sufism in the position almost of an established church: Sunni orthodoxy, far from undermining the legitimacy of the sultans in their quasi-caliphal role, was applied with remarkable success to creating a sense of unity among the population at large (Gibb and Bowen 1957, I/II, pp. 78–9). The use of slaves as soldiers and administrators was refined by the *devshirme*, on whose success I commented already in Section 2; and the servile Janissaries, who fought as infantry, were supplemented by free Muslim cavalry (*sipahis*) supported from the yield of lands assigned to them in return for their military service. Moreover, the problem of succession was successfully overcome: although the succession of a weak or incompetent heir did allow power to pass to the Grand Vizier, the sultan's role as such remained intact. The Janissaries did, admittedly, later usurp privileges to which they could never have aspired under Mehmet the Conqueror, and even deposed individual viziers and sultans. But until the late eighteenth century, the systactic structure continued to reproduce itself without any change of culture or structure amounting to an evolution to a different mode of the distribution of power.

If the functional alternatives for the administration of an absolutist monarchy are a venal bureaucracy, a service nobility, a professional mandarinate, and a corps of specialized slaves, late imperial Rome fits none of them. But this is not because less power attached to a Roman emperor's role than to that of a French king, a Russian tsar, a Chinese emperor or an Ottoman sultan. It is because late Rome combined institutions and practices from all four sub-types of absolutism so far discussed. Until the collapse in the West, a large standing army and an elaborate bureaucracy were supported by taxes levied on the agricultural surplus* whose collection, extortionate, regressive and cumbersome as

* Taxes of other kinds were levied too; but the only one which was not paid directly or indirectly by the peasantry – Constantine's *collatio lustralis* levied in gold on all

it might be, was regularly maintained despite an increase in immunities and the periodic remission of arrears. There were frequent civil wars as rival pretenders sought, with the support of their own armies, to claim the imperial role for themselves. But the role itself remained there to be fought for; and in the East, with its long tradition of veneration for monarchy, legitimate successors were seldom challenged. The flight of peasant *coloni* from their landlords was, to be sure, a perennial problem. But peasant revolts were, if anything, less of a threat than in seventeenth-century Russia, China or France.

If there was a single institutional principle which underlay the economic and governmental practices of the Roman Empire, it was that its priorities were, like those of the Ottoman Empire until its decline, military. The Republic had been built on conquest, and when the institutions of a citizen-state gave way to those of an absolute monarchy, military appointments and careers were still those which principally integrated the provincial gentry and the upwardly mobile peasant recruits into the distribution of honours and rewards. The remarkable recovery of the late third century which culminated in the reforms of Diocletian depended on 'men whose rise to power was as spectacular and well merited as was that of Napoleon's marshals' (Brown 1971a, p. 26). It is true that civilian *dignitates* were more often filled by recommendation and patronage than on proven merit, that the administration and civil service were permeated with influence and bribery, and that the senatorial aristocracy of the West became, as the correspondence of Symmachus confirms no less eloquently than Ammianus's history,* increasingly concerned with the retention of status and *otium* rather than active service to the state. But for as long as local magnates derived their privileges from the continuing strength of the state, exercised their patronage over their tenants from within the framework of imperial law, evaded but did not actually displace the imperial tax-collectors, and sought advancement for their sons of a kind which depended on imperial power, the absolutist mode reproduced itself from one generation to the next.

Because the Empire in the West did, in the end, give way and its tax revenues prove inadequate to sustain an army capable of policing a frontier more than twice as long as that of the Eastern Empire, it is

negotiatores – burdensome as it was on those who had to pay it, yielded only about 5% of total imperial revenue (A. H. M. Jones 1964, I, p. 465; II, p. 872).

* See particularly Ammianus's diatribe at XIV.6 (introduced with the questionable claim that he is '*nusquam a veritate sponte sua digressurus*').

tempting to exaggerate the prior symptoms of internal weakness. But the mixture of inherited practices over which Diocletian's successors ruled enabled the society to reproduce itself for another five generations before the conventional date for the extinction of the Western Empire in 476. Barbarian pressure, plague, internal warfare, limited agricultural productivity, poor communications (except by sea), and unproductive expenditure on an expanding clergy and bureaucracy still did not disclose any inherent contradiction in the systactic structure. The senatorial aristocracy did function to some degree as a service nobility; the provincial gentry did supply a kind of mandarinate; the emperors, although less reliant on slaves and freedmen than in the days of the Principate, still commanded a range of servile employees from the eunuch chamberlains (*cubicularii*) to the *mancipi* in the imperial factories and mint; and the sale of offices (particularly provincial governorships), although it cannot be said to have benefited the imperial treasury in the manner of the French *paulette*, still testifies to a similar readiness by aspirants to riches, rank and political influence to bid against one another to achieve them. The later Roman Empire thus offers the example of a working absolutism which held together a remarkably large territory for a remarkably long period by means of a set of institutions which is distinctive precisely by combining all four of those which, in their ideal-typical forms, define the major functional alternatives open to societies of this mode.

There are still a number of societies not yet mentioned at all, or touched on only in passing, which would need to be included in a complete list of sub-types of monarchical absolutism. The Inca *Tahuantinsuyu*, with its uniform hierarchy of wealth, ceremonial status and political power, its tightly organized local communities, its taxation in the form of corvée labour and its state-owned surpluses of foodstuffs and woollen goods held in its ubiquitous storehouses, is one of them; but it was so soon overtaken by the Spanish Conquest that its stability has to remain open to question, particularly since the arrival of the Spaniards had been preceded by an eight-year conflict over the succession. Another is Mughal India, where a largely alien military stratum of city-dwelling *mansabdars* were rotated in short-term *jagirs* analogous to the Ottoman *timars* and supported by taxes in cash or kind which, under Akbar, took a third of the output of the indigenous cultivators. But few Hindus held *mansabs*, and despite Raja Todar Mal's brief incumbency of the role of prime minister (*vakil*), the Hindu population was never assimilated into the Muslim state. Although the Mughal bureaucracy was sufficiently 'vast and complex a machine' not to depend on the ruler in person (Wolpert 1977, p. 168), factional rivalry and internecine warfare were endemic until the whole society was taken over, like the *Tahuantinsuyu* by the Spaniards, by the British. Another example is nineteenth-century Afghanistan under the 'Iron' Amir 'Abd al-Rahman Khan, who instituted a 'highly centralized form of absolutist government to an extent that neither his predecessors nor his successors were able to emulate' (Kakar 1979, p. xx); but he was able to do so only by courtesy of Britain and Russia and thanks to continuing British subsidies in money and arms. Yet another example, which is distinctive in its critical dependence on an ideology of sacred kingship which secured the devotion of the 'sea-people' (*orang laut*) who both crewed the ruler's fleet and formed a counterweight to the semi-autonomous nobility (*orang kaya*), is the seventeenth-century Malaccan kingdom of Johor; but its dependence on that ideology was illustrated only too well by the assassination of the ruler in 1699 from which the kingdom never fully recovered (Andaya 1975, p. 191) and after which the *orang laut* reverted to their traditional nomadic sea-life. All these have, therefore, to be categorized alongside Norman Sicily and Norman England as borderline cases, not because they had not evolved roles defined by the practices on which absolutism rests, but because those practices were still constrained within patrimonial institutions dependent on the personal attributes of individual kings. Yet, for that very reason, they demonstrate all the more clearly that absolutism is a distinctive mode of the distribution of power with its own 'Linnaean' and 'Darwinian' rationale.

§26. When we turn to those societies at the same approximate level of resources which did not evolve into absolute monarchies, we are faced with the paradox to which I referred in Section 11 of domination from, as it were, the middle. But then this means no more than that politically, the society is an oligarchy rather than a monarchy; ideologically, the highly located traditional status-groups do not consistently outrank the 'new men'; and economically, there is a financial and/or commercial and/or proto-industrial* class which overlaps, even if it does not altogether dominate, the class of landowning magnates. Nor do any of these distinguishing characteristics imply that the central government is

* This term is used not to carry any presupposition about the influence of rural craft production on the evolution of industrial capitalism, but only to allow for the contribution made by mining, brewing, shipbuilding and textiles, in particular, to the evolution of entrepreneurial roles in societies still far below the levels of per capita output made possible by the exploitation of industrial technology.

therefore less powerful than it might otherwise be. A merchant patriciate may be just as well able to control internal dissent and to wage an aggressive foreign policy* as a monarchy like that of Peter the Great or Louis XIV. The difference is rather that in societies in this mode, there is likely to be both more cooperation between mercantile and governmental roles and also more devolution of power to highly located economic, rather than military, roles.

For all its ambiguities, the term 'bourgeois' is as hard to do without now as the term 'feudal' was earlier. It cannot be defined as a set of occupational roles – merchants, financiers, shopkeepers, notaries and so forth – not only because they stand in different relations to the means of production but because even within each of these occupations there are large distances between the most and the least highly located in all three dimensions of structure. The systactic boundary is one which embraces all but only those roles whose economic location gives their incumbents both social prestige† and political influence. But unlike the free adult males of the 'citizen' societies discussed in Section 21, these 'bourgeois' are not a militia. On the contrary, they form a consistently *un*warlike systact whose profits may be taxed to fund the conscript or mercenary armies which protect and expand their society's territory and trade, but who do not themselves engage (except, perhaps, in times of national emergency) in the profession of arms. To say that they are a ruling class whose executive committee is the state is an exaggeration only to the extent that there remain other high-ranking roles whose incumbents they need to persuade to cooperate with them. They do not dominate the army, the landowning magnates or – if there is one – the court by the exercise of the power which attaches to their roles so much as by using that power in the service of what is perceived by the army, magnates and court as a common interest.

The distinctiveness of societies in this category can be brought out clearly if they are directly contrasted with the oligarchic Roman sub-type of the 'citizen' mode. Like them, Rome was governed by a small number of rich men; its economic institutions, like theirs, rested on private property and market exchange; and its social élite was likewise open, although perhaps less so than theirs, to able and ambitious men who did not inherit noble status at birth. But by no stretch could it

* Cf. Wallerstein's observation (1980, p. 60) that the Dutch state in the seventeenth century, far from being weak, was 'the *only* state in Europe with enough internal and external strength such that its need for mercantilist policies was minimal'.

† Not that they are necessarily indifferent to the attractions of a quasi-aristocratic life-style: the Regents of the Dutch Republic often used their profits to buy land which carried the right to 'historic seals or escutcheons' (C. H. Wilson 1968, p. 48).

plausibly be claimed to work in the same way. There is not merely the difference that the Roman élite was intensely militaristic and that conquest abroad was mirrored in private violence at home. There is also the pervasiveness of agricultural and domestic slavery relative to the limited and intermittent use of wage-labour; and although slavery can function within a much more sophisticated set of capitalistic financial and commercial practices than the Roman, the Romans cannot be said to have used the labour of their slaves for profit except in the limited sense that they bought them as cheaply, sold them as dearly, and supported them as inexpensively as they knew how.

More important still, there was no Roman bourgeoisie as here defined at all. The wealth of the *equites* was based, like that of the senators, on land, and those of them who became tax-farmers (*publicani*) had to provide the treasury with security in the form of substantial estates. The entrepreneurs, merchants and traders reported in the sources seem to have been mainly provincials or freedmen. Senators as well as *equites* might have business interests, and a rich noble might keep a squad of slave builders and architects to rebuild collapsed or burned-down houses bought from their owners at knock-down prices (Plutarch, *Crassus* II.4–5). But this involved no change in the mode of the distribution of power. The enormous influx of wealth in the period which followed the defeat of Carthage gave rise to a range of novel roles, from antique-dealer to speculative property-developer. But it was an influx into a pre-existing set of institutions both ideologically and politically impervious to the kind of thoroughgoing commercialization which, as we have seen, permeated the society of Hanoverian England.

It is in its political institutions that Hanoverian England is most reminiscent of the later Roman Republic. In both societies, the sons of a homogeneous landowning nobility and gentry competed for office under an electoral system which, although both unrepresentative and manipulable, was altogether different from appointment by an absolute monarch.* But whereas in Rome, the function of money in politics was limited to personal loans and the bribery of voters, in England, although loans and bribes had their uses too, commercial and financial interests were integral to the composition of factions and the mobilization of electoral support. I have commented already on the direct involvement of English noblemen in commercial ventures, which although it never

* England was, to be sure, a monarchy with its hereditary House of Lords as well as its elected House of Commons. But the Commons controlled the purse-strings, and the monarchy did not control the Commons. Nor did inheritance of title carry entitlement to political office.

extended to retail trade* went far beyond what can be documented for the Roman Senate; and unlike Rome, private moneylending was supplemented by investment in government stock.† As the National Debt grew, it not only drew in steadily more investors but involved the government directly in the maintenance of the credit of the Bank of England on which, in turn, the country's commercial prosperity depended. There may have been little to choose between the two societies in the practice of venality. But in England, it extended down into the boroughs and parishes from a central government which not only financed its patronage by the systematic deployment of secret funds but deliberately delegated to local interests functions of a kind inconceivable in Rome. England's diminutive army was raised by recruiting officers, 'themselves small businessmen, often pocketing £5 for every soldier who took the King's shilling' (R. Porter 1982, p. 135), whereas the Roman *assidui* had answered the call to arms directly, whether as volunteers hoping for booty or, later, under compulsion (W. V. Harris 1979, p. 101). Nor could it possibly be said of Rome, as it can of England, that just as politicians (and particularly radical politicians) used methods derived from the world of business, so 'the tradesman and entrepreneur treated politics as a commodity whose purchase could bring him profit' (Brewer 1982, p. 238). However close the similarities in life-style and mores between a Hanoverian English and a Republican Roman nobleman, the latter could no more conceive of a government whose policies were dictated by his society's commercial interests than of a society the members of whose government saw nothing derogating in the open pursuit of commercial profit as opposed to the rewards of governorship or the spoils of war.

The distinctiveness of English institutions and practices is an issue of perennial controversy among specialists, and there is no doubt a risk – particularly for a member of the same society educated in its history as written in the first half of the twentieth century – of exaggerating the special character of primogeniture, the common law, the parliamentary tradition, the yeomanry, the justices of the peace, the lack of a standing army, and so on. But there can be no question that monarchical absolutism had failed; that the size of the central bureaucracy and the

* Perhaps more important, on the other hand, was the difference that in England social mobility was possible *from* the role of retail trader into the nobility, even if the total number of cases was small and the process might take more than a generation (Perkin 1969, p. 60).

† Which extended down the social structure to smaller owners, tradesmen, craftsmen and artisans in and around London as well as to spinsters and widows (Dickson 1967, Ch. 11: 'Public Creditors in England').

peacetime army were both small by comparison with other societies at a similar level of resources; that the younger sons of noble families did move into professional roles (even if these were largely limited to fighting, pleading and preaching); that the systact of yeomen, however hard to define, was both distinguishable and prosperous; and that English society was a great deal more mobile, both socially and geographically,* than the model of a 'traditional' agrarian society in which landlords, dependent servants, smallholders and village craftsmen succeed one another in unvarying accordance with inherited custom. By the mid eighteenth century, the mode of production had so far evolved in the direction of wage-labour that perhaps as many as half of all English families were in receipt of money wages. As small-scale industry grew from the early seventeenth century onwards, it not only reduced the dependence of adult males on seasonal agricultural employment but enabled increasing numbers of women and children to contribute to the family budgets (Clay 1984, p. 31). Direct taxation was low.† It was the excisemen, not the tax-gatherers, who were the objects of popular execration, and businessmen paid nothing on their profits. Pitt did introduce an income tax as a wartime measure in 1797, but even the costly and unsuccessful war against the American Colonies was almost half financed by borrowing. There had always been an active land market, even if less so and later in some parts of the country than others (Hyams 1970), and although many large estates were consolidated in the course of the eighteenth century, many new men bought land and many established families sold it (Speck 1977, pp. 70–4).

The proliferation of commercial roles and commercialization of existing ones which accompanied all this did, predictably enough, give rise to as many complaints as panegyrics in the contemporary sources. Moralists were as quick to denounce the propensity of the 'middling sort' and 'lower orders' to ape their betters as advertisers and manufacturers were quick to exploit them, and the evidence for a rising sense of relative deprivation among the poor is as easy to document as the evidence for rising output and the wider diffusion of consumer goods. But this was within a mode of the distribution of power which was never seriously threatened on that account. These were not the

* There was a significant age-set aspect to this mobility: apart from migrants seeking their fortunes and permanent vagrants, servants and apprentices typically left home in their teens and worked on annual wage-contracts until they married (Wrightson 1982, p. 42).

† The contrast with France is again instructive: indirect taxes on consumption were much higher in England and direct taxes much higher in France, where the agricultural producers bore the heaviest burden.

practices which later and for other reasons were to disturb the mutual reinforcement of profitable commerce, parliamentary oligarchy, and an established Church which was as closely, not to say comfortably, integrated into the prevailing ideology of hierarchy as any of the society's secular institutions, whether political or economic.

The evolution of Dutch society differed at many points from that of England, and the course and pattern of antagonism between contending factions and its relation to conflicting religious doctrines and international rivalries is as peculiar to the one as to the other. But they are alike in the self-sustaining feedback between coercive, ideological and economic practices which enabled both to function as commercially minded, anti-absolutist oligarchies with a common view of the economic functions of the state. No doubt the success of the Amsterdam *Wisselbank*, like that of the Dutch East India Company, owed much to an inter-societal balance of power which allowed Holland a predominance which could at any time have been undermined by a shift of alliances. But for as long as it was not, trade and finance each benefited the other, and the far-flung overseas contacts of the Dutch merchants made the *Wisselbank* uniquely attractive to investors in both the strength of its deposits and the negotiability of its bills. It seems, indeed, to be agreed among specialists that the prosperity of the Dutch in the seventeenth century owed much to a unique combination of geographical with sociological causes. Fishery encouraged shipbuilding and shipbuilding encouraged overseas trading; Protestant immigration from the South encouraged artisan production in the cities which in turn encouraged further immigration; the shift of the Eastern spice trade to Amsterdam from Antwerp coincided with the shift of the sea lanes to the Cape route; the systematic drainage of a soil unsuited to arable farming combined with a growing population encouraged intensive cultivation of industrial crops and the import of cheap grain. But these opportunities could not have been exploited as they were without a skilled labour-force, commercial confidence, some provision of welfare for the urban poor, the use of a strong currency to hire mercenaries as well as to import grain, the political dominance of Holland over the rest of the United Provinces, and the ideological dominance of Arminian humanism over Calvinist extremism. It is impossible, even with hindsight, to disentangle the relative influence of each of these mutually reinforcing institutions and practices. But there can be no doubt that they *were* mutually reinforcing. Indeed, the self-reproducing capacity of the systactic structure was demonstrated by its passing the same test as those less complex and powerful societies in which, like the Lombards, an interregnum turned out to be negotiable without any change in the mode of the distribution of power. There were two periods in which the role of stadholder was without an incumbent and its functions were performed, to the extent that they were, by the Grand Pensionary, but in neither case was the stability of the society materially disturbed.

It is true that for all the solidity of the upper-middle class which constituted the politically dominant systact, there did survive in Holland aristocratic, or at least quasi-aristocratic, roles and practices. Yet despite the 'seals and escutcheons', the tendency towards closure among the élite and a shift from entrepreneurial to rentier roles never went so far as, by contrast, in Venice. For all its remarkable stability, Venice, like Holland, evolved from a patrimonial through a citizen to a bourgeois mode. A comparison between the seventeenth-century élites of Amsterdam and Venice (Burke 1974) shows clearly that in the almost totally closed, predominantly rentier and much more lineage-conscious society of Venice, the economic roles of the patriciate were subordinated to a markedly greater degree to considerations of birth. Admittedly, Venice remained as far as Holland from monarchical absolutism. Moreover, its shopkeepers, guild masters and master craftsmen were no less favourably treated than their Dutch counterparts, and the skills and techniques of the Venetian financiers could still rival those of Amsterdam. But the crucial difference was in social mobility rather than systactic structure. There was no equivalent in Holland to the 'Golden Book' in which the Venetian nobility registered their sons at birth (as the *cittadini* by birth registered theirs in a 'silver' one). In the end, this restriction on mobility functioned so well as to lead to a regression to whose causes and consequences I shall return in Chapter 4. But the mode of production remained commercial, the ideology remained civic and the profits of trade were still used to hire the mercenaries on whom the safety of the republic depended. Descriptively, it may seem to be stretching the indispensable term 'bourgeois' too far to bracket Rembrandt's sanctimonious-looking *Goldweigher* with Longhi's masked noblemen dallying and intriguing at Carnival time. But explanatorily, their respective societies are still sub-types within a common mode.

If eighteenth-century Venice is the most 'aristocratic' of pre-industrial 'bourgeois' societies, the most 'democratic' is the United States of America as it was in the early years of the nineteenth century. Its remarkable evolution poses both of the difficulties which make controversial the delineation of societal frontiers. Its speed of social change was such that 'men who, as children, had heard the war-whoop of the Cherokee in the Carolina backwoods lived to hear the guns at

Vicksburg' (Cash 1960, pp. 10–11), and the regional diversity of its institutions was such that a Yankee merchant, a Southern planter and a Western homesteader not only inhabited institutional catchment areas totally separate from one another but so far differed from one another in outlook and mores as to belong, in cultural terms, to different worlds. Yet it *was*, after the Constitution of 1789, a single society, albeit federally constituted, and for all the anti-oligarchic rhetoric which inspired the 'jostling crowd of clod-hoppers and mechanics' (Thistlethwaite 1955, p. 126) who came to the White House to celebrate the inauguration of Andrew Jackson as President in 1829, it was – except in the short-lived Utopian communities of Fourierite or Owenite inspiration – a society as inimical to socialism as to aristocracy.

Politically, near-universal adult male suffrage made impossible the oligarchic manipulation of place and patronage which had characterized Hanoverian England; but although factions were therefore formed from the bottom up rather than the top down, they never functioned to undermine a systactic structure in which the principal dividing line within each region or locality remained that between rich and poor. Ideologically, a strident resentment of inherited privilege did not prevent acceptance of the legitimacy of differentiation based on the successful accumulation of land, money and (in the South) slaves within a single generation. Economically, the common opposition of small farmers and artisans to merchant capitalists and big-money banks did not alter the fact that their mode of production was unequivocally commercial. The vivid description of American society given by an immigrant in 1836 is only mildly exaggerated: 'Business is the very soul of an American... it is as if all America were one gigantic workshop, over the entrance of which there is the stirring inscription, "No admission here, except on business"' (quoted by Hofstadter 1948, p. 57). The Yankee merchant, the Southern planter and the Western homesteader were dedicated alike to the pursuit of profit,* and their objections to big banks were objections not to financial capitalism as such but to the terms on which credit was available for the furtherance of their own small enterprises. It was still – for a little while – a society of farms and townships, country stores, log cabins and artisan enterprises. But its pervasive roles were capitalistic through and through; and as it evolved – with astonishing speed – the institutions and roles of an

* Tocqueville saw this as clearly as so much else: in his chapter 'That Almost All the Americans follow Industrial Callings', he comments that 'In democracies nothing is more great or more brilliant than commerce', that Americans are 'all more or less engaged in productive industry', and that most American farmers 'make agriculture itself a trade' (1889, II, pp. 141–3).

industrial economy, the adaptation of these roles was to make the United States as nearly the exemplary type of an industrial as it had been of a pre-industrial capitalist society.

§27. There remain to be considered the societies at this level of resources which were classified in Section 12 as 'hybrids' – that is, not as transitional cases but as a category whose distinctive mixture of institutions and practices not found together elsewhere will be stable over several generations in the absence of exogenous pressure. I commented there on the striking resemblances between the institutions of late Anglo-Saxon England and those of Babylonia at the time of Hammurapi, and if we now ask not only what homologous practices they share but how far these practices can be shown to perform analogous functions, it will become apparent that we are indeed dealing with a stable as well as distinctive mode of the distribution of power.

We have seen that neither of these two societies can be assigned to a 'feudal', 'absolutist' or 'bourgeois' any more than to a 'warrior' or a 'citizen' mode. But to classify them by exclusion is not to explain how the practices defining their constituent roles enabled them to function as they did. The relative strength of their monarchies is one part of the answer. The kings' writ did run over the whole society, whatever might be the resistance or uncertainty at the frontiers. But in the absence of a corps of *intendants* and a standing royal army,* cooperation with the other large landholders, whether ecclesiastical or lay, was essential. It is true that by the end of the Anglo-Saxon period, the royal household of chamberlains, butlers and lesser attendants had developed to the point of what one specialist is prepared to call a 'crude but powerful bureaucracy' and 'something like a chancery' (John 1982, p. 176), just as the correspondence of Hammurapi documents a range of royal servants and officials which goes well beyond the personal entourage of a patrimonial king. But Edward the Confessor was no less dependent on the cooperation of bishops, *thegns* and local hundreds and wapentakes than Hammurapi on that of temple priests, holders of 'eternal' (non-royal) land (*eqlum durum*) and local village communities.

At the same time, however, the power attaching to the roles of the landholders and officials depended on their integration into the institutions which provided tax and labour services to the king. The late Anglo-Saxon prelates, with their own dependent tenants and their

* Cnut's 'housecarls', who may even have numbered as many as 3,000 men (although Kirby 1967, p. 125, doubts it), were something more than a bodyguard, but still a corps of household troops rather than a national standing army.

incomes from tithes and 'scot', were, with the *thegns* of the shires and the royal officials, part of a unified élite whose interests were tied to the successful maintenance of royal influence and prestige. In those parts of the country where there were no royal *burhs* and the system of hundred, borough and shire courts could not be imposed, it is the *thegns* and mass-priests who are taken for granted in the sources as the agents of central authority. Similarly, in Hammurapi's Babylonia, although the temples had their own substantial estates with their own dependent labourers and craftsmen, their administrators reported to the king (Ḍiakonoff 1982, p. 71, n. 230), and the sources convey (so far as I can judge at second hand) the same impression of a unified ecclesiastical-cum-royal élite. Furthermore, however far both societies may have been from absolutisms with complex bureaucracies, large permanent armies, and highly developed systems of direct and indirect taxation, in both the royal authority extended sufficiently far down the structure to create political roles at the local level. The roles of the superior *villani* and petty *thegns* of Anglo-Saxon England who served as the lesser agents of royal or ecclesiastical power and were liable to periodic military or auxiliary service are precisely matched by those of the Babylonian *ba-irū* or *redū* (Landsberger 1955) who were ranked with the formally free *awilū* rather than the *mushkēnū* and whose tenure of their modest landholdings was likewise conditional on periodic military or auxiliary service.

Within this framework of political-cum-military institutions, the mode of production in both societies was likewise an amalgam. In both, taxation was supplemented by the performance of labour services,* tenancy was supplemented by slavery, renders in kind were supplemented by sales for profit, and redistribution of land by inheritance was supplemented by market disposals. In both, royal and ecclesiastical land was extensive, but coexisted with allodial estates. In both, dues to the Church (or temple) were paid as well as taxes to the king. In both, long-distance trade was in the hands of private capitalists operating for profit. In both, the less fortunate cultivators risked debt, impoverishment and thereby slavery (although in both enslavement might subsequently be reversed).† In both, the large landholders had the advantage of being

* The emphasis on 'bridgework' in the Anglo-Saxon sources is paralleled by the emphasis on the upkeep of canals in Hammurapi's letters.

† For Babylonia, see the relevant sections of Hammurapi's law-code (Driver and Miles 1952); for late Anglo-Saxon England, see the manumission of the family whose 'heads had been taken for their food in the evil days' (Whitelock 1979, p. 610).

better protected against human or natural calamity, but cooperation at village level gave smaller landholders some similar benefits.* In both, the importance of kinship relations in landholding appears to have declined† as internal differentiation between *ceorls/awilū* increased and the land market became more active.‡ In both, a wife's dowry was hers to bequeath in due course to her children.§

There is only one difference, for which the explanation is partly sociological and partly ecological, which perhaps marks off the structure of late Anglo-Saxon rural society as a different sub-type of this hybrid mode, and that is incipient manorialism. As the late Anglo-Saxon kings extended their power more effectively down to the level of the shire and hundred, they – like Hammurapi – concerned themselves directly with the collection of tax, the performance of military duties, and the administration of justice at village level. But they also relied increasingly on local lords for the maintenance of order (to the point that a law of Athelstan presumes that every man has a lord); and the estates of such lords, for which distinctively manorial practices are reported as early as the laws of Ine, were in some parts of the country, at least, reminiscent of the fully-fledged manorialism of the thirteenth century. The first manorial court reported in the sources is a grant of sake and soke to the Archbishop of York in a charter of 956, but it may merely be the earliest which happens to survive (Finberg 1974, p. 230). This whole development is a matter of some dispute among specialists (Aston 1958), and however much a forerunner of later developments the estate pictured in the *Rectitudines Singularum Personarum* may be, there is no

* As Whitelock remarks (1979, p. 97) of a bishop of Winchester's ability to restock 70 hides 'stripped bare by heathen men', what *ceorl* could afford to restock his own few acres? But, as with the *awilū* in the village communities of Hammurapi's Babylonia, 'the major agrarian unit was...the community of *ceorls*, the effective leaders of the village community over so much of England, who took a corporate responsibility for the ploughing, sowing and probably the reaping and harvesting, though the balance of loss and gain remained intensely personal to the individual holder of the land' (Loyn 1962, p. 157).

† Diakonoff (1982, p. 38 n. 91) goes so far as to say that 'In the Old Babylonian period of Mesopotamia, at a time of a strong rise in commodity production and money relations, the family communal structures of the farming population are barely observable.'

‡ Including an active leasing market: for Babylonia, see Diakonoff (1982, p. 76 n. 242); for late Anglo-Saxon England, see Lennard (1959, pp. 164–5).

§ For Babylonia, see again the relevant sections of Hammurapi's laws; for late Anglo-Saxon England, see the bequest to a daughter of 'the estate which was bought with her mother's gold' in a will reproduced by Whitelock (1930, p. 54, ll.25–6). On the 'recognised instability' of Anglo-Saxon marriages, see Lancaster (1958, p. 246).

suggestion of feudalism. The large landlords of Wessex were not the king's vassals, they did not hold benefices, they did not build castles to be manned by their own troops, the obligation of military service was directly to the king, and the unit of tax assessment for the levying of the *geld* was the village, not the manor. But there is, all the same, no role in Babylonian society corresponding to the late Anglo-Saxon *landhlaford* or *landrica*, who took a share of the fines imposed on the men of his estate and had – in theory, at least, according to a law of Edgar – the right to deprive a persistently defaulting tenant (*geneatmann*) of not only his property but his life.

In Mesopotamia, the mode of production is similarly complex. In the Ur-III period, prior to the strengthening of the monarchy, both the royal estates and those of other latifundists had been worked by *gurush*, who were semi-servile labourers (Gelb 1972, p. 88, is prepared to call them 'serfs') strongly reminiscent of the Anglo-Saxon *geburs* of the *Rectitudines*. In the Old Babylonian period, the royal estates were worked by an inferior category of *mushkēnum* called *ishakkū* who appear to have been the slightly less servile equivalents of the *gurush*. Accordingly, it may not be inappropriate to call these estates 'manorial': not only was demesne land cultivated by tied labourers for the benefit of the Crown, but tenant land was allocated to other workers and craftsmen in return for services to be rendered. But nowhere in Babylonia were there non-royal estates corresponding to the late Anglo-Saxon where a lord much more remote from royal authority managed through his reeves a differentiated community of *geneats*, *geburs* and smallholding *kotsetlas* as well as slaves.

Yet this single institutional difference can by no stretch be claimed to amount to an alternative mode of the distribution of power. The manorialism of later Anglo-Saxon England was, in the practices which it imposed on the *kotsetlas* and *geburs*, a function of population pressure on a limited supply of arable land, and its Babylonian analogue was the increase in debt in the village communities. In both societies, large landholders increasingly rose, and small ones increasingly declined. The difference was that the ascendant manorialist, as it were, of Hammurapi's Babylonia was likely to be a usurious merchant (see Klengel 1973 on Balmunamche), whereas in late Anglo-Saxon England he was more likely to be a *rusticus* who had accumulated the five hides of land which, according to a text now attributed to Archbishop Wulfstan, carried him to the role and title of *thegn* (Liebermann 1903, I, pp. 456–8). But in neither case was this a symptom of any inherent contradiction in the total set of institutions and practices. Indeed, it could plausibly be argued that, on the contrary, the scope for upward mobility in both societies was such as to assuage rather than exacerbate the sense of relative deprivation among the more ambitious of the potential recruits to their respective élites.

Where the mode of production is overwhelmingly based on agriculture, it is inevitable that the great majority of the population will enter adult roles similarly located to those of their parents. But this still leaves room, as in both these societies, for enslavement and manumission at the bottom as well as promotion and demotion at the top. Both had a small, semi-hereditary class of merchants and another of craftsmen, and in both smaller landholders could become larger ones (and larger ones smaller ones). The combination of a moderately flexible market in land (including some fief-like tenancies conditional on specialist services), a strong religious-cum-monarchical ideology* and a system of government permitting some autonomy at village level constituted a stably self-reproducing mode of the distribution of power for which, precisely because of the diversity of practices combined, there is no standard sociological term.

It might be objected that both of these societies were, in the event, rather short-lived: the sack of Babylon by the Hittites was as decisive as the Battle of Hastings. But although their continuing internal stability has to that extent to be taken on trust, the unquestionable fact remains that both succumbed to pressure from without, not from within. Both attracted the attention of predators from outside their boundaries not so much because they were weak as because they were rich.† Whether or not they would ever have been able to strengthen their armies sufficiently to defeat any and all of their several invaders is irrelevant to their common membership of a distinctive mode of the distribution of power well capable of reproduction over successive generations if left alone to do so.

* I have remarked already in Section 3 on the 'supernatural radiance' attributed to Mesopotamian monarchs; but the impression made on contemporaries by the spectacular coronation of King Edgar in Bath in 973 suggests that by then the Anglo-Saxon monarchs were not too far behind in this dimension either.

† Cf. Sawyer (1965, p. 145): 'It was the wealth of England, not the inadequacy of the English defences, that tempted so many continental adventurers to come here in search of loot and tribute.'

FUNCTIONAL ALTERNATIVES (3)

§28. It becomes no easier, as we move from the pre-industrial to the 'modern' world, to pinpoint the moment at which the evolution of a society from one mode or even sub-type to another can be said to have occurred. It is true that in 1945 Germany made the transition from fascism to liberalism in its Western and to socialism in its Eastern half no less abruptly than Rome made the transition from citizen republic to absolute monarchy in 27 B.C. But there is no conceivable way of dating the transition of English society to capitalist liberal democracy. Indeed, some of the practices and roles which between them assign England to this mode can be traced back through the Middle Ages to before the Norman Conquest, when, as we have just seen, there was already an active land market, some wage-labour, a small mercantile bourgeoisie and a sector of commodity production for profit. But however long and complex the sequence which lies behind it, and however debatable, therefore, the point at which a capitalist liberal democracy can be said to have evolved, there can be no argument about its being a distinctive and novel mode. For the purposes of this Chapter, the question then is: which of its constituent roles explain the degree of stability which the several sub-types of the mode can, by now, be seen to have achieved?

Much of the literature on this topic is tendentious and polemical. But whatever the evaluative presuppositions of rival observers from different theoretical schools, the answer still lies in the mutal reinforcement of the economic, ideological and coercive practices which function to preserve the allocation of power among the roles and systacts which industrialization has brought into being. There is clearly some sort of elective affinity between a free market in labour and commodities, a belief in open competition and equality before the law, and an electoral system in which most if not all adults have votes. But equally clearly, the three sets of institutions have not always walked hand-in-hand down the road from medievalism to modernity. In industrial societies where the central institution is the market, the pervasive economic roles are evidently those of the owners of the means of industrial production on the one hand and the vendors of labour-power on the other. But given the equally evident conflicts of systactic interest which this generates, selective pressure must somewhere be counteracting them.

For all the visible inequalities of power of all three kinds and the sense of relative deprivation which they generate, liberal-democratic-capitalist industrial societies seem, at the very least, no less well able to reproduce themselves than industrial societies of any other mode. Indeed, this much is tacitly conceded even by committed adherents of the theory which predicts an inevitable, if eventual, transition to public ownership of the means of production and government by a single party legitimated by its claim to represent the interests of the working class.* The market functions to distribute goods and services in an unequal pattern which nevertheless subjects institutional concentrations of power to the continuing possibility of competition. Occupational roles are allocated through an educational system which promotes at least some upward mobility among the abler or more fortunate children of the incumbents of lower-ranking roles and at least some downward mobility among the less able or fortunate children of the higher-ranking. The dominant ideology of free competition and formal equality before the law is propagated through institutions controlled by interests favourable to the continuance of the system, and reinforced by appeals to national self-interest.† Competitive elections to political office permit an alternation of factions which channels popular discontent without threatening the political institutions themselves. Taxation of incomes and profits permits some provision of collective goods and services and some transfer of individual benefits to the underclass disadvantaged by the workings of the market. The administrative and technical systact brought into being as industrialization proceeds identifies its interests more with than against the institutions from which it draws its rewards. Indirect ownership of the means of production comes to be diffused to some degree through insurance and pension funds as well as personal holdings of property, but the means of coercion are retained under central government control. Trade unions formed to advance the interests of the vendors of their labour-power operate for that purpose within the existing set of economic institutions rather than seeking actively to overturn it.

All this is thoroughly familiar to observers of all theoretical schools, however much they may disagree about the relative importance of one practice or another to the institutions of Britain or the United States or any other society within this mode. Indeed, what is striking is the initial diversity among the range of societies which do nonetheless all belong to it. The United States, which is perhaps closest to the ideal type,

* Cf. e.g. Westergaard and Resler (1975, Part 5: 'Acquiescence and Dissent: Responses to Inequality').

† There is a parallel worth noticing between support for conservative and nationalist parties by working-class electors in capitalist societies and support of Sunni orthodoxy by servants, artisans and soldiers in pre-industrial Islamic societies: in each case the double function is served of legitimating differentiation both from foreigners (or infidels) and from liberal (or Shiite) bourgeoisies.

furnishes, as we have just seen, a context peculiarly favourable to the practices carried by the roles out of which evolved the institutions of liberal-democratic capitalism. But this only makes the resemblances between it and, for example, Australia all the more remarkable. Despite large differences of geography, climate, ideology, political history and manner and timing of industrialization, Australia by the mid twentieth century had evolved into a sub-type very close to the United States (Mayer 1967). There is still ample room for institutional variation: late twentieth-century Japan is at least as different from the late twentieth-century United States as was mid eighteenth-century France from mid eighteenth-century Russia. But no observer could seek to deny that the function of its central institutions is equally the maintenance and reproduction of a stable liberal-democratic-capitalist system.

This holds as much when the structure is viewed from below as from above. All capitalist societies evolve 'trade union' roles in one form or another, even if against strong initial resistance. But quite apart from contingent differences in the nature and degree of legal and customary recognition accorded to them by their governments, unions differ widely in both structure and function. In Japan, whose uniqueness in this respect has been extensively studied by both Japanese and Western observers, the system of industrial relations evolved within a set of traditional practices of a strongly paternalist kind. Indeed, the practices defining the *oyabun-koyabun* institution (Ishino 1953) explicitly extended a homologue of the relations of sons to fathers into apprenticeship in work, clientage in politics, and gang membership in the world of professional crime. As unions began to organize, employers to compete for labour, strikes to increase in frequency, and social reformers to press for improvements in working conditions, there evolved the distinctive two-tier system of Japanese industry in which large firms offered selected employees career-long security and extensive welfare benefits, while smaller firms and a network of sub-contractors operated on a high turnover of less well-remunerated and less well-organized casual and temporary workers (including a much higher proportion of women).* The unions, which were made illegal in 1938 but revived after the defeat of 1945, are predominantly enterprise unions. Their penetration of the labour-force correlates strikingly with company size (Galenson and Odaka 1976); and the annual 'Spring Offensive' for improved wages

* Steven (1983, p. 43), who presents the inverse relationship between dependence on sub-contracting and size of firm in 1971, also points out that a retirement age of 55 in large firms helps to promote the reproduction of the class of small proprietors (p. 85).

and conditions is organized by leaders thoroughly committed to the existing system.

There is disagreement among specialists as to how far this system can continue unchanged under pressure of increasing competition for workers among rival firms, intensified demand for collective welfare provision as a right, and a diminished respect among younger workers for the traditions of paternalism itself (Cole 1979). But whether or not industrial relations in Japan will therefore evolve towards a 'Western' sub-type – or, perhaps, the other way round (Dore 1974) – its relevance to the argument of this Chapter is the same. Japanese practices in this institutional area, while homologous with their practices in others, have conferred competitive advantage on roles very different from those which emerged in the industrial capitalist societies of the West. But they have functioned no less effectively since 1945 to reproduce an unequivocally liberal-democratic-capitalist industrial system. Admittedly, this system would, for reasons to be given in Chapter 4, have evolved very differently if Japan had won the Second World War instead of losing it. But this does not alter the fact that in the circumstances which actually obtained after 1945 its distinctive practices performed the function which they did.

Cutting across the variation among capitalist industrial societies in the relations between organized labour and its employers is the variation in the collective consciousness of subordinate systacts and the extent and degree of relative deprivation articulated by their members. If strikes are taken as an indicator, there is a pattern which can convincingly be related both to structural characteristics of the more and less strike-prone industries (plant size, social isolation and other such variables) and to differences in the culture of the labour movements in different societies.* But it would be difficult to argue that systactic consciousness, whether expressed in this or other forms, has significantly altered the overall distribution of power between roles located higher or lower within the inverted pyramid. In those industries where trade unions are strong, the attitudes and behaviour of their members can be demonstrably influenced both by the aims and tactics of their leaders and by contingent events which heighten their sense of relative deprivation: in England, for example, there have been several periods of exceptional militancy in the course of the twentieth century to date – first in the 1910s, then in the 1920s and then again in the 1970s. But they have not affected the systactic structure of English (or British) society

* On France, see Gallie (1978, 1983), and on Italy, Low-Beer (1978).

as a whole. Labour militancy in all capitalist industrial societies has been important as a cause (and sometimes a symptom) of changes in the distribution of power both between skilled and unskilled manual workers and between higher-paid manual and lower-paid non-manual workers. But it has never – so far – been a decisive influence on the mode of the distribution of power as such.

The society which comes nearest to constituting an exception is Sweden, which evolved into a distinctive sub-type of the liberal-democratic-capitalist mode during the 1930s and 1940s as the role of its trade union leaders became more and more closely integrated into the institutions of the state. But this, far from being caused by the collective action of a systact relatively deprived of political power, was the result of cooperation between the L.O. (the central union organization), the S.A.F. (the employers' confederation) and the Social Democratic government in the course of which the ideology of the L.O. became progressively less militant.* The concentration of power in a highly centralized trade union structure and a system of collective bargaining in which the state was directly a party to periodic negotiations at national level meant that concessions sought by the L.O. on behalf of its members could be granted in return for concessions sought by the state (which was itself a large employer). This 'historical compromise', as it came to be designated, marked a shift in the distribution of power in Swedish society in favour of the systact of wage-earners which remained stable for a generation. But it did not abolish intra-systactic conflicts of interest (Korpi 1983, p. 48), any more than it altered the characteristic practices by which either workers' or employers' roles were defined; and it led in due course to a cyclical reaction in which the pattern of industrial relations came more to resemble that observed in other European capitalist societies (Lash 1984).

There is, accordingly, a wide range of sub-types of liberal-democratic-capitalist industrial society, whose differences in 'unionateness', systactic consciousness, inequality of remuneration, provision of welfare, rates of social mobility, and degree of involvement by government in the regulation of industry need to be accounted for by comparative analysis of their variant practices and their functions. But the variations are all on the theme of the central institution of the market. There is, to be

* An alternative hypothesis to account for the Swedish pattern of industrial relations has been advanced by Ingham (1974), who attributes it to features of the infrastructure – high industrial concentration, low technical complexity and high product specialization. But as shown by Jackson and Sisson (1976), the influence of the infrastructure was marginal to the behaviour of the employers, which was determined rather by Sweden's late and rapid industrialization and the conjunction of political and economic events which led to the coalition of interests just summarized.

sure, a tendency in capitalist societies for the proportion of the gross national product expended by the state to rise from what it was in the earlier stages of industrialization, whether it is expended in weapons or welfare or some fluctuating combination of both. But this has yet to make a difference to the stable reproduction of the mutually sustaining institutions of a market economy, a liberal democratic polity, and an ideology of freedom (in, if you wish, its 'bourgeois' sense).

§29. When the pervasive roles and central institutions of capitalist industrial societies are contrasted with those of socialist ones, it is immediately obvious not only that analogous functions are performed by institutions very different in structure but also that homologues persist although their function is now changed. In the allocation of economic resources, the central plan is the analogue of the market. Ideologically, legitimation of the Party's 'leading role' by the doctrine that it represents the interests of the proletariat is the analogue of legitimation of liberal democracy by the doctrine of equal opportunity. Politically, the recruitment to governmental roles by appointment within the Party (the *nomenklatura*) is the analogue of competitive election within and between rival parties. The outcome is thus a mixture of consciously intended differences and half-acknowledged similarities in the practices by which 'socialist' roles are defined. The relative location of the class of wage-workers is not markedly different,* with or without an apparatus of semi-autonomous workers' councils and a greater or lesser equalization of pay and prestige between manual and clerical roles. The hegemonic ideology does not do away with intellectual dissent altogether. Control of the means of coercion continues to attach to the roles of the senior members of the Party and army. Social mobility may be artificially promoted either for an initial generation or by periodic campaigns of positive discrimination, but thereafter reverts to a broadly similar pattern to capitalist societies at the same stage of industrial and technological development. At the same time, homologous practices survive or re-emerge in the economy (albeit the market is 'black'), in the educational system (albeit academic standards are subordinated to ideological), and in the network of political coalitions characteristic alike of multiple and of single party systems.

It would, however, be a mistake to infer from this that capitalist and

* Schurmann (1968, p. 308) presents in diagrammatic form the changes in command relationships in Chinese industrial management between 1949 and 1961, from 'political-military administration' to 'one-man management' to 'effective leadership' to 'independent operational authority', in all of which the workers are – as they are bound to be – at the bottom.

socialist societies could usefully be categorized as sub-types of a common 'industrial' mode of the distribution of power. It is true that even under Stalin the Soviet Union never fully exemplified the ideal type in which the economy is totally controlled from the centre, the political apparatus extends into every association as well as corporation, and the ideology of socialism is unequivocally accepted by the incumbents of all roles. But it is equally true that even where the regime relaxes central planning, curbs the activities of the police, and permits a degree of cultural dissent, the central institution remains the bureaucracy, and it is only by an analysis of its practices and functions that the workings of Soviet society can be properly understood. The literature on this topic is hardly less voluminous or polemical than that on the practices and functions of the market in capitalist societies, and theorists of rival schools disagree strongly over whether the bureaucracy is to be viewed as a quasi-proprietary class whose power derives from control of the means of production or as a service class which merely administers the control exercised by a ruling élite. But on either view, the relation of the bureaucracy to the industrial workforce is categorically different from that of the employers – whether private entrepeneurs, institutional shareholders or the state – in capitalist industrial societies.

Soviet workers do still sell their labour for wages, but with two differences which critically modify the nature of the role. The first and more obvious is that they are selling to a purchaser who controls not only the price but also the supply of labour (to say nothing of the price and availability of the consumer goods which money incomes can buy). The second and less obvious is that since there is no able-bodied worker who is legitimately unemployed,* there are no unemployment benefits, and the choice of employment with which workers are confronted is a choice between occupational roles whose rewards and conditions are administratively set (Fehér *et al.* 1983, p. 73). This state of affairs is, of course, very differently described and evaluated by observers with different presuppositions. But it is just as fundamental a difference from capitalist industrial societies as the political difference between competition for office within a single party and competition between two parties or more; and the two differences taken together define the bureaucracy which serves (and overlaps with) the Party as a systact clearly located above the industrial workforce in all three dimensions of structure. Whether the reproduction ratio of the Party itself is so high

* There is, to be sure, an underclass: but it is one of criminals, delinquents and alcoholics (Connor 1972), not of beggars, casuals or underemployed or 'sweated' labour forced to accept market rates.

as to make it a stratum permeable only when a lack of sufficient children of existing incumbents creates vacant roles for others to fill is a matter largely determined by the governing élite, with consequences which may or may not be intended.* But there is no reason to suppose that the stability of the system depends on some optimal rate of upward mobility. It is likely enough that feelings of relative deprivation will be exacerbated by what can be seen as a form of transmission of hereditary privilege. But the single Party remains in sole control of the means of coercion; the centrally planned economy, however much or little autonomy it may concede to the workforce as consumers, is fully capable of sustaining growth in real output per head without reverting to a capitalist mode of production; and the bureaucracy, relatively privileged as its members may be, does have 'an ideological commitment which conditions its activity' (D. Lane 1976, p. 42).

The Soviet Union does not have to be taken as the paradigm of socialism any more than the United States of capitalism. But even where a socialist society is deliberately structured in such a way as to avoid what is seen as the excessive centralism of the Soviet model, the function of the pervasive roles and central institutions remains the same. The most distinctive sub-type is Yugoslavia. Its evolution since 1945 has been conditioned by circumstances unique to it of which the two most important are the ethnic and regional divisions within it and the personality and career of Tito. But the practices instituted under the rubric of 'workers' self-management' did not thereby modify the distribution of power as between the industrial workforce and the Party apparatus. By giving workers more influence at plant level the governing élite diminished the power attaching to the role of manager, and by allowing market forces to determine to some degree the price of both labour and consumer goods it widened the range of economic differentiation between different groups and categories of workers. But it did not undermine the coercive control or the ideological hegemony of the Party, which retained an unfettered capacity to decide to what extent market forces should influence the allocation of labour and resources.† Indeed, it is because and only because that capacity was retained through practices adaptive for the party apparatus that the

* Poland in the 1970s is an interesting case. A vigorous attempt was made to increase the representation of industrial workers in the Party; but some 60% of members who left or were dismissed from the Party between 1976 and 1978 were working-class recruits (Woodall 1982, pp. 132, 198).

† Cf. Nove (1983, p. 134): 'In real-life Yugoslavia the workers' councils' powers are limited by state regulations (including regulation of prices) and by political intervention through the so-called League of Communists (i.e. the party).'

society could reproduce itself after Tito's death within the same mode.

The other socialist society whose structure has been deliberately manipulated by its governing élite away from what are seen as the failings of the Soviet system is China. It is still too early for any firm conclusions to be drawn from it for the purposes of comparative sociological theory, not only because its economy is still predominantly agricultural but because of the twists and reversals which have characterized the policies of the regime both during the lifetime of Mao Zedong and since his death. Yet for all the difficulties facing specialists seeking to analyze the causes and consequences of the 'Cultural Revolution', there is no disagreement among them either that China's initial revolution was the outcome of a coalition between guerrillas and peasantry or that Mao was concerned to avoid the creation of a privileged 'new class'. To that extent, therefore, China offers as close an approximation to an experimental test as history is likely to provide, since if so determined and so powerful a leader was unable to create a structure and culture closer to his vision of the ideal type of socialism than in fact he was, it must be likely – to put it no more strongly – that the constraints were insuperable.

Mao's dilemma was twofold: first, the need to compromise between 'red' and 'expert' qualifications for the incumbency of dominant roles; second, the related need to compromise between positive discrimination by social origin (*chushen*) and admission to the relevant role (*chengfen*) of committed supporters of the regime irrespective of 'bad class' bourgeois or landlord origin. Whatever the policy chosen, its implementation had to depend no less than in the Yugoslav (or the Soviet) case on a concentration of power at the top sufficient to overrule what would otherwise be the outcome of conflicts of interest at a lower level. Indeed, many observers have seen in Mao's role as Chairman a replication of the role of an exceptionally powerful emperor under the old regime. But whether or not such a concentration of power in a single topmost role is a necessary condition of the imposition of radical equality of power of all three kinds among the rest of the society's roles, is it possible for a socialist society to reproduce the institutions which Mao sought to create to the point that it has to be counted a new and stable mode of the distribution of power?

It might be argued that the *chengfen* problem is purely transitional. It is, after all, only a matter of time before there is no member of society left who was born under the old regime, and the view that revolutionary attitudes matter more than outdated class distinctions was already being expressed by Deng Xiaoping and tacitly endorsed by Mao at the Eighth Congress of the Party in 1956 (Schram 1984, pp. 34–5). Mao, as we know, changed his mind, and unleashed a campaign against the old landlord and bourgeois classes reminiscent of the corresponding phase of the French Revolution not only in the ferocity with which reactionaries were hunted but in the irony that many of the hunters were of the same systactic origin. But he also realized that, as he put it with the Soviet Union in mind (*ibid.*, p. 41), 'the bourgeoisie can be born anew'. Even when there are no 'reactionary elements' left, the bureaucracy will seek to defend its privileges, the children of intellectuals will do better in competition for educational places, some party cadres will simulate revolutionary attitudes out of personal ambition, peasants will be less productive under a 'brigade' than under an 'enterprise' system, and positive discrimination in favour of workers and peasants and their children will still not guarantee that the incumbents of dominant roles are both 'red' and 'expert' – or even either.

The use of ideological hegemony to reaffirm the class struggle can, therefore, hardly fail to generate 'opportunism, sycophancy, patronage, avoidance of activists, and privatisation' (Shirk 1984, p. 66).* This may – depending on your values – be an acceptable cost. But it limits the effectiveness of the cooperation which the regime is seeking. Income differentials can be narrowed, reproduction of status-groups can be broken by ensuring that education and occupation are no longer correlated, and forced geographical mobility can be used both to re-educate the children of intellectuals and to create vacant urban roles for the children of peasants to fill. But the requisite practices can only be imposed by a numerous bureaucratic (or military) apparatus whose roles carry power of a kind which marks them off as a systact privileged – however humble their origins and modest their incomes and life-styles – far above those on whom their decisions are imposed with the force of coercive and ideological sanctions combined.

The fact that Mao's policies were reversed after his death does not mean either that the reversal was inevitable or that a 'functionalist' theory of stratification is thereby proved. If nothing else, it must be possible that there will evolve a continuing cycle whereby the regime will alternately equalize and restratify occupational roles.† But equally, the

* Reportage in these evaluatively pre-emptive terms is by inference from interviews with *émigrés* in Hong Kong, and may need to be discounted to some extent on that account (Oksenberg 1970, pp. 304–6).

† Skinner and Winckler (1969, p. 410) detect already before the Cultural Revolution a three-dimensional cycle in the policies of the regime towards the peasantry from 'exhortation to coercion and then to remuneration', with a corresponding cycle in the

Chinese case cannot be used to argue for the evolution of a distinctive new mode, as opposed to sub-type, of the distribution of power. The practices constitutive of the roles on which the stability of the system depends are those which make the Party, as their carrier, the central institution of Chinese society, and it is a party which, however different its policies from those of the Communist Party of the Soviet Union, draws its legitimacy from the same ideology and exercises its authority through the same coercive sanctions.

The number of socialist societies which have come into existence since 1917, and particularly in Eastern Europe since 1945, provides a basis for comparisons in terms both of the social distance between occupational roles which persists after abolition of private ownership of the means of production and of rates of social mobility between them (see e.g. Kolosi and Wnuk-Lipínski 1983). But it is in the second generation that the distribution of power between roles and the movement of young adults into them needs to be observed. All that can safely be said is that at the present stage of evolution, the differences between societies in which a single party holds power in the name of a proleterian ideology and controls the economy either directly by command or by devolution within a central plan differ in their practices and institutions to an extent which amounts to sub-types of a common mode, but not to variants so marked as to undermine the applicability of the initial definition.

No doubt it is possible that, over successive generations, the practices of socialist societies will come increasingly to resemble those of capitalist societies – rewards by incentive, political office by election, free access to the means of persuasion for critics of the regime, and transmission of educational advantages and therefore preferential access to high-ranked roles from parents to children. But it does not follow that their function will thereby be changed. Those of their members who share a common economic location do so through their relation not to the means of production but to a politically determined allocation of rewards. Those who rank equally in social prestige do so not as a status-group of consumers practising a distinctive life-style, but in relation to an order of prestige determined by ideology of the ruling party. Those who have institutional access to the political, administrative and military apparatus which controls the means of coercion have it not through resources in votes or money but through recruitment into the roles to which such access attaches by choice of the governing élite. However wide the

response of the peasants themselves 'from a tentative enthusiasm through disillusion to a calculative indifference'.

variation between socialist societies (or within the same ones over a period), and whatever the labels polemically attached to each others' institutions by their propagandists or spokesmen, their differences are all within a common mode of the distribution of power.

§30. The same holds for the authoritarian mode. Whatever the other differences between them, societies which combine the rule of a single party or faction with a capitalist economy and a nationalist ideology can reproduce themselves in as stable a form as can either capitalist liberal democracies or single-party socialist states. It is true that the reproduction of the system may be problematic to the extent that succession to the topmost role is uncertain. A charismatic head of state in the Weberian sense, who combines in his or her person the source and agency of authority and is legitimated by successive plebiscites, creates a potential instability for that very reason, even if those who own the means of production and those who control the means of coercion are both committed to the existing structure and culture. But as we have seen in a range of different societies already, disputes over succession, however protracted and violent, do not necessarily force a change in the mode of the distribution of power. Nor are the societies where the authoritarian mode has evolved in response to either internal contradictions or external pressures necessarily backward or peripheral societies of illiterate peasants and weak bourgeoisies. In twentieth-century Europe, this may, to some degree, be true of Greece, Portugal or Spain. But it is not of Germany or Italy, and even in twentieth-century Latin America it cannot plausibly be argued of Argentina or Chile.

Distasteful as the ideologies of authoritarian societies may be to readers whose evaluative presuppositions are of either a socialist or a liberal-democratic kind, the effectiveness of nationalist (and, in the case of German fascism, racist) propaganda is undeniable. The ruling élite needs to be united, and its control of the means of persuasion needs to be so deployed that it is seen to be bringing benefits in the way of economic growth, social welfare and improving educational standards. But once these conditions are fulfilled, there is nothing inherently unstable about authoritarian practices and roles. In some contexts, the army can be seen to function as an analogue of the middle class in effecting a 'demobilization' of subordinate systacts (Germani 1978, p. 74). But it is also possible for the two to function in coalition rather than as alternatives; and there is also the institutional variant of a fusion of military with business roles either in nationalized industries or in the private sector.* Further, there is a range of functional alternatives in the relations of the army to the party. In Hitler's Germany, the Nazi party was the central institution and it was in the role of head of the party that Hitler took over the state; in Franco's Spain, by contrast, it was Franco in the role of head of state who took over the party (Carr and Fusi 1979, p. 25). Or again, the regime may, as in Brazil after 1964, retain the institutional forms of parliamentary representation, but so contrive the outcome of elections between approved contenders that they function to give quasi-plebiscitary legitimation to the regime (Cammack 1982, p. 11). If there is any one sub-type which can be argued to be inherently unstable, it is only the military junta which fails to evolve a dominant presidential role whose incumbent can be legitimated as such (Philip 1984, p. 10).

Within this mode, the most interesting sub-types are not those nearest to the ideal type of totalitarianism but, on the contrary, those which most nearly exemplify the apparent paradox of 'left-wing' authoritarianism, whether in its Mexican form under the presidency of Cárdenas after 1934, its Peronist form in Argentina, or in the 'military radicalism' of Peru between 1960 and 1976. There is, as I have remarked already, no necessary constraint which prevents an authoritarian regime from furthering the interests of lower-ranked systacts. The potential contradiction, however, lies in the dependence of the governing élite on the cooperation of the more privileged systacts immediately below it. Perón had no more difficulty in using his control of the means of persuasion to present himself as the friend and protector of the 'humble' worker while implementing a policy of generous wage increases than the Peruvian radicals had in implementing an anti-oligarchic land reform which they believed to be in the popular interest. But how are the relatively highly located opponents of these policies to be held in check when they have not, as under a socialist mode, been stripped of the power attaching to their roles or, as under a liberal-democratic mode, been afforded the opportunity to secure a re-distribution of power in their favour by parliamentary means? In Argentina, the use of organized trade-union protest to further working-class demands carried the inevitable risk of provoking a *coup d'état* (O'Donnell 1976, pp. 202–3); and in Peru, the continuance of working-class opposition after the initial reforms at a time when the electoral 'Left' was still weak left the governing élite similarly exposed to the

* Cf. Martins (1971, p. 71) on the 'directorships craze' among the military in Salazar's Portugal.

dangerous opposition of systacts whose members doubted its capacity for counter-insurgency (Philip 1978, pp. 163–4).

Given this need for authoritarian societies to avoid the formation of systactic coalitions whose demands may prove impossible either to meet or to resist, it follows that the function of the pervasive roles of patron and client will be critical even when the society has evolved beyond the stage where only rural *caciques* or *mafiosi* can deliver the votes of otherwise uninformed and unorganized electors. Where there is universal suffrage but not the institution of liberal-democratic competition for votes, the practices of political clientelism must continue to be adaptive for both patron and client roles. Nor need the agents and propagandists of the ruling faction be directly involved: it may be the local bureaucracy whose patronage is exercised in promoting the interests of relatively disadvantaged systacts in return for electoral support. Further, it is possible for economic rather than political pressures to unite systacts which would under other conditions be opposed to one another: thus, hyperinflation may unite producers – industrialists and unionized workers – against rentiers and salaried professionals, and this may work to the advantage of the authoritarian regime.* Admittedly, no such regime can be stable which depends entirely on conditions which are – or are held to be – an emergency. If vertical coalitions are formed only in response to appeals for unity in the face of economic crisis, or threats from the 'enemy within', or demands for resistance to the interference of an alien government, they are likely to disintegrate once the crisis is overcome, the internal enemy crushed, and the alien government put in its place. But vertical ties which are partly cooperative, although between roles very unequally located, can sometimes function all the more effectively in the aftermath of emergency, as the example of Mexico in the 1920s clearly shows.

Whatever interpretation is placed on the events of 1910 to 1920 – to which I shall return in Section 19 of Chapter 4 – the stability which Mexico achieved after the assassination of Carranza and the election to the presidency of Obregón rested on the patronage of a governing élite which held an effective monopoly of the means of coercion. This patronage was extended both geographically into the territory of the local *caciques* and institutionally through the army, the remnants of the Church, the trade unions, the growing industrial bourgeoisie, and the

* See Maier (1978) for a comparative discussion of 'Coalitions of Inflation' in which he stresses both that traditional class alignments continue to be important in determining political outcomes (p. 67) and that the interests of different roles under different inflationary conditions are often far from clear (p. 62).

dominant *Partido Revolucionario Institutional* (P.R.I.). It is true that the old, 'feudal' style of *caudillismo* died out; the *caciques* became progressively *embourgeoisés*; the army became increasingly professionalized; and the systactic consciousness of wage-workers was reflected in a steady increase in the incidence of strikes. But local politicians still performed in their 'modernized' roles as 'reform intermediaries offering their services to peasants in return for organizational and electoral support' (Buve 1980, p. 244); the federation to which two-thirds of unionized workers belonged retained its close links with the P.R.I.; the government's control over central finance, energy, and transport gave it extensive power of patronage in the private sector which it had no inhibitions about using; the professional soldiers were required to be P.R.I. members; social welfare was administered according to clientelistic rather than bureaucratic patterns and norms (Poitras 1973); and the P.R.I., whose organization extended throughout the electorate an increasingly tight network of patronage at local level, never tolerated more than a token presence by a rival party. Whatever their other disagreements, there is (so far as I can discover) no dispute among specialists about the paternalistic and clientelistic character of the roles which sustained post-Revolutionary Mexico in a new sub-type of what was still an unmistakably authoritarian mode of the distribution of power.

§31. These alternatives do not, as we know, by any means exhaust the institutional possibilities open to the societies of the late twentieth century whose modes of production, persuasion and coercion can draw on the hugely expanded resources which industrialization makes available (always provided that the resources are not dissipated by excessive population growth, unproductive investment, ethnic or regional fragmentation, or civil or international war). There is not very much for the sociological theorist to say about these possibilities for the simple reason that it is much too soon: guesses, however well informed, to the effect that one random mutation or recombination of practices rather than another presages an impending change of mode or sub-type are no substitute for explanation with hindsight. Yet for the purposes of this Chapter, there may be some theoretical interest in a few hypothetical suggestions, even if the modes or sub-types envisaged have not yet turned out to be realized, and may never do so. I have chosen four: first, a hypothetically 'fascist' Japan undefeated in the Second World War; second, a hypothetical liberal-democratic but (in its mode of production) socialist society for which Sweden might furnish the model; third, a hypothetical industrialized Islamic society for which Iran might furnish the model; and fourth, a hypothetical South Africa freed of the constraints imposed by inter-societal pressure and the demographic imbalance between ethnic groups.

(i) Suppose it is correct to say that Japan, if it had not gone to war, would have maintained from 1940 onwards a fascist sub-type of the authoritarian mode within which its industrial growth would have proceeded at much the same rate as it has done within the imported institutions of liberal democracy. What then? That there would have been many points of stress within the systactic structure goes without saying. It is safe to predict that there would have been underground political factions, proscribed associations of industrial workers, and escapist religious sects. But where would have been the contradictions requiring a change of mode? If anything, there are more of them – or of something approaching them – under a liberal-democratic mode where the promise of growth has to be reconciled with the promise of full employment, the ideology of equal opportunity has to be reconciled with the visible entrenchment of privilege, and the appearance of a competitive party system has to be reconciled with the manifest exclusion of any seriously threatening alternative.

Under a fascist regime, the pervasive practices which define the vertical relations between dominant and subordinate roles in Japanese society would have been still more adaptive for their carriers than they have shown themselves to be under liberal democracy.* The unquestioned legitimacy of the emperor would have enabled the incumbents of the most powerful political roles to be reshuffled or deposed without compromising the institutions by which they had initially been promoted into them. The industrial combines (*zaibatsu*) would have continued to prosper (as they in fact did in the Second World War). The conflict of interests between the military, industrial and (dwindling) agrarian élites would not have weakened their cooperation in the face of any perceived threat from below, against which para-military force would have been unhesitatingly deployed. The two-tier labour market would have continued to tie the interests of the best-trained industrial workers to their enterprises rather than to their class; a controlled influx of labour from the countryside into the

* There is some disagreement among specialists about just how strong was the cultural tradition of consensus and hierarchy inherited from the Tokugawa era. But many different observers have been struck by it: see e.g. Nakane (1970, pp. 143–4) on the meaning attached by Japanese as opposed to Americans to the concept of 'democracy', and (from a different theoretical perspective) Steven (1983, Ch. 7) on intra-party relations in post-war Japanese politics.

towns would have provided a pool of unskilled recruits for expanding industry without an accompanying risk of union-organized unrest; women, casuals and small sub-contractors would have continued to bear the brunt of economic recession; appeals to patriotic sentiment would have been used to direct discontent against the country's trading partners and rivals; the *burakumin* would have remained in their ghettoes, perhaps supplemented by other stigmatized groups or categories such as immigrant Koreans; status-group endogamy, promotion by age-sets, and the tradition of family loyalty would have continued to inhibit strong feelings of relative deprivation; and – not least – the close integration of the police into neighbourhood communities would have ensured the use of coercive sanctions against political deviants as well as criminals. Nor would rates of social mobility either have stayed so low (aside from the *burakumin*) as to create a dangerous pool of frustrated malcontents or have risen so high as to have a destabilizing effect on a structure pervaded by hierarchic practices and doctrines: selection for lifetime careers through a mixture of patronage and competitive examination would have staffed the bureaucracy without any risk of the unintended surplus of persons over roles which has been observed in both socialist and capitalist industrialized societies of the so-called Third World.

No doubt some of this is debatable. But is there anything palpably implausible about it? As I shall argue in more detail in Section 33 of Chapter 4, there are no theoretical grounds for hypothesizing that the internal effects of Japan's 'revolution from above' were such as to make an evolution to either socialism or liberal democracy inevitable or even likely. It may be that under a fascist regime, xenophobia and militarism would, in the end, have been bound to lead to overexpansion and thereby defeat. But that is an argument of a different kind.

(ii) There is perhaps a stronger case for the suggestion that despite my remarks in Section 13, 'liberal-democratic socialism' is not a realizable mode. I say this not because state (or collective) ownership of the means of production is logically incompatible with competitive elections for political office, but because the combination has failed to evolve in the society whose systactic structure is most favourable to it: Sweden is still a capitalist society. This is not a decisive objection if it rests on the accidents of personalities and policies. There may be any number of contingent reasons for which the intentions of the incumbents of governmental roles to collectivize ownership of the means of production might be thwarted, discarded, watered down or indefinitely postponed. But the objection is strengthened by observation of what has taken place in Sweden since the heyday of the joint domination of the Social Democratic Party and the L.O. which, as I noted in Section 28, evolved out of the particular industrial and political circumstances of the 1930s.

The 'Meidner proposals' for progressive acquisition of a controlling interest in private companies by trade union funds were unanimously endorsed at the L.O.'s Annual Congress in 1976.* But that was at a time when the 'Solidary Wage Policy' was sustained by the L.O.'s domination of the trade unions as a whole, and the government's welfare and employment legislation appeared to give them not only a high measure of security but also considerable powers to influence the management of individual enterprises. Subsequently, however, a reaction among the electorate against the Social Democrats, the apparent breakdown of the 'Swedish Model' in the face of the same competitive pressures as confronted the rest of the industrialized societies of the West, and an increasingly fragmented labour market, all combined to suggest that the evolution towards a novel mode of the distribution of power was being reversed. In particular, the unions themselves, on whose active support such an evolution would depend, seemed increasingly to be seeking to exploit the forces of the market rather than to abolish them. The large and powerful Metalworkers' Union broke with centralized bargaining in 1983 in pursuit – with the support, and under the initiative, of the Metal Employers' Association – of higher differentials. The private-sector, white-collar workers' federation (the P.T.K.) began to distance itself explicitly from both the L.O.† and the Social Democrats. Some white-collar union members came out in overt opposition to the Meidner proposals. There was, and perhaps still is, a strong ideological commitment among trade union members as a whole to the principles underlying the 'solidary' policy (Scase 1977, Chs. 4–6; cf. Wright 1985, Ch. 7). But it has failed to inhibit the pursuit of competitive advantage by groups and categories of wage- and salary-earners differently located in the market, or to generate a collective commitment to indefinite continuation of centralized wage bargaining.

Suppose, then, that it does turn out that Sweden evolves away from rather than towards the mode of the distribution of power envisaged by

* With the rider that 'over-centralisation and bureaucratisation' were explicitly to be avoided (Gill 1983–4, p. 50).

† Lash (1985, p. 225) argues convincingly against Himmelstrand *et al.* (1982) that joint negotiation by the L.O. and P.T.K. was a symptom not of unity but of the independent strength of the P.T.K., which could no longer be assumed to fall in behind decisions reached by the L.O.

the more radical of its Social Democrats. Will that conclusively demonstrate the unworkability of such a mode? Or might there be other pressures by which practices could be selected which would lead to it, or other institutional variants by which an alternative sub-type of it could be sustained? It would be rash to offer a categorical answer. All that can safely be said is that if there is an inherent contradiction in the structure which it implies, it lies in an incompatibility between the practices necessary for the functioning of a competitive electoral system and the practices necessary for the trade unions to function as agencies of central economic decisions (H.-G. Myrdal 1980, pp. 63–4). Centralization of ownership would not do away with either inter- or intra-systactic conflicts of interest in the labour market. If, therefore, members of a union federated under a national body with the authority to discipline it were to see their economic interests being undermined as a result of its decisions, their sense of relative deprivation would be likely to find expression in attempts to have those decisions modified or reversed by exercising the power which attaches to their roles as electors. Rivalry at the polls would, accordingly, not be rivalry between factions seeking to control the incumbency of governmental roles for purposes which presupposed the maintenance of the existing institutions. It would be rivalry between parties of which at least one would base its appeal on a willingness to alter the existing institutions in the systactic interest of those who had voted it in.

(iii) No such problem, on the other hand, would be likely to arise in an Islamic society where the means of coercion are in the hands of a systact all of whose members are recruited from religious roles and share a common commitment to the ideology whose prescriptions it is their acknowledged obligation to enforce. Such a society should perhaps be labelled a 'hierocracy', rather than a 'theocracy', particularly in the context of 'Twelver' Shiism where, until the appearance of the Hidden Imam and the true reign of God upon earth, the holders of political power are, at best, jurists and interpreters with an interim mandate to uphold the *Shari'a* through their role of collective viceroy (*niyabat-i-'amma*).* There may, at any one time, be a privileged *ayatollah* ('sign

* Mahdism, where a ruler claims actually to be the living 'Imam of the Age', is by contrast a true theocracy; but it rests in practice on charismatic legitimacy with all the potential for instability which that involves (cf. Dekmejian and Wirszomski 1972) – as did the interesting pre-industrial variant of the fourteenth-century Sarbadar 'dynasty' (or more accurately, succession of chiefs) where no leader claimed Mahdihood but the society was ruled by militant Sufis in the expectation of the Mahdi's imminent coming (Arjomand 1979, p. 77).

of god') or *mari-i-taqlid* ('source of emulation') to whose role there attaches sufficient ideological power for his political decisions to be accepted as binding; and if there is not, there may have to be an alternation of rival factions within the governing élite. But in either case, the mode of persuasion remains the same. Could not, then, the legitimacy of the 'guardianship of the jurists' (*wilayat al-faqih*) be at once Islamic and nationalist without the contradictions between the two which confronted both Kemal Ataturk and his successors in Turkey and the Pahlevi shahs in Iran?

Economically, a predominantly mercantile capitalism in the Islamic tradition is fully compatible with an industrial economy in which the means of production are controlled partly by the state and partly by private entrepreneurs, with the option (also traditional in Islamic societies) of using the labour of members of other, non-Islamic societies for selected ancillary roles. There is no difficulty in recruiting and training an army and police which can, as necessary, curb or support the urban militia which is the homologue of the traditional *futuwwah*. Islamic institutions of higher education can so function as to turn out not merely obscurantist mullahs but a trained bureaucracy paid from tax revenues and fully capable of administering the governmental institutions of an industrial society. The exclusion of women from any other than domestic roles, however alien to both liberal-democratic and socialist ideology, is unlikely to impair the functioning of the system beyond the possible loss of talented potential incumbents for certain professional roles. There might, no doubt, continue to be violent changes of regime of the kind long familiar in the societies of Islam; but such changes need not imply any inherent contradiction in the distinctive mode of the distribution of power.

(iv) Finally, then, consider further the industrial society in whose distinctive mode of the distribution of power ideology has been no less unquestionably important, but in a very different way. South Africa, as I stressed in Section 13, has always been potentially unstable on account of the demographic imbalance between a dominant white minority comprising under 20% of the total population and a subordinate majority increasing at an equal or higher rate (unless the minority's reproduction rate were to be augmented by net immigration or, conceivably, reclassification of Coloureds as White). But suppose (and the supposition is not unrealistic) that diseases introduced by white settlers had had something of the effect on the Bantu peoples that they had on the Hottentots of the Cape (or the American Indians). Would there then have been anything to threaten the continuing reproduction of a capitalist economy* drawing on the wage-labour of a disenfranchised systact whose nominally temporary residence in urban areas was ideologically justified by reference to incumbency of roles in tribal 'homelands'? Once it is assumed that numbers pose no threat and exogenous pressure is negligible, only three conditions are necessary for continuing stability. First, the means of coercion have to remain under monopoly control of the white minority; second, there must be no ideological divisions or reversals within the white minority sufficient to undermine the legitimacy of the system to themselves; and third, the economy has to continue to grow sufficiently both to sustain the apparatus of coercion and to offer relatively higher incomes to the African workers than are available to them outside it. But there is no inherent contradiction in this set of institutions and practices. Why can a system of ethnic stratification maintained by force within an otherwise market-run economy by an internally democratic *Herrenvolk* not constitute a distinctive and stable mode of the distribution of power in an industrial society?

The actual systactic structure of late twentieth-century South Africa is well documented but complex, and it is a matter of debate among specialists how far there has evolved under pressure of industrialization an urban African bourgeoisie and proletariat whose relative location at a lower level of power is both homologous and analogous to that of their white counterparts. But there can be little doubt that some of the practices which define the internal structure of roles in the African population have functioned indirectly to reinforce the effect of those which define their relation to the dominant minority. Not only has vertical social distance in all three dimensions perpetuated internal conflict of interests, but African hostility has often been directed against Indian traders and Coloured boss workers who, in turn, would for the most part prefer to try to maintain their systactic location under white rather than African rule.† It is true that there have been

* It is true that the state's ownership of means of production through its Industrial Development Corporation grew in the period from its formation in 1940 to the point that by 1971 it could be said that South Africa was practising a state capitalism unparalleled in any other major capitalist society (Adam 1971, p. 29), and that there is a strong streak of anti-capitalism running through the ideology of Afrikanerdom. But the I.D.C. functions like any other capitalist corporation within the ethnically stratified labour market, and the anti-capitalism of the *reddingsdaad* movement was not an attack on capitalism as a mode of production but on the exclusion from it (in favour of 'Anglo-Jewish' interests) of the *volk* (O'Meara 1983, p. 163).

† See Adam (1971, p. 109), arguing – rightly, in my view – against the claim of van den Bergh (1965, p. 68) that 'Political consciousness militates against ethnic particularism.'

ideological conflicts not only between Afrikaners and other whites but also between 'hard-line' (*verkrampte*) and 'soft-line' (*verligte*) Afrikaners. But their differences have been those of tactics rather than principle. In the generation after the National Party came to power in 1948, only a handful of whites advocated universal suffrage (and therefore black majority rule), and non-Afrikaner members of the proletariat and lower middle class tended to be as strong supporters of the National Party as their Afrikaner counterparts. More prosperous and liberally inclined opponents of the system (or their children) have tended simply to emigrate.

It might, perhaps, be argued that South Africa is a deviant case because it is one of those where the catchment area of its central institutions is both broader and narrower than that defined by its political geography. It cannot be called a 'settler' society, because it is the indigenous territory of the Afrikaner nation no less than of the Coloureds or the various African tribal, linguistic or national groupings who have long inhabited it. But (it might fairly be said) the white minority has imposed its domination on an alien set of peoples whose roles are defined by a form of 'colonial' dependence no different from what it would be if the minority were members or agents of an expansionist metropolitan society somewhere overseas. An urban African proletarian in the Cape, or the Transvaal, or Natal is not merely one of many wage-earning employees of a white-owned industrial or commercial corporation (or of a white domestic employer). He or she is at the same time a member both of a designated tribal grouping with a designated 'homeland' and of a segregated residential community (or, in the case of domestic servants, a white household) outside of that homeland where he or she is denied citizen rights. Yet although it is true that urban Africans are members of South African society in a very different sense from the dominant white minority, it is the institutional catchment area controlled by the dominant white minority which defines their subordinate roles. If colonialism, it is internal colonialism. However hostile to the institutions into which they have been integrated by a combination of economic inducements and coercive sanctions, the Africans of South Africa are members of the same society as the white minority, and that society has, therefore, to be accorded its distinctive mode of the distribution of power. How long it will last I make no attempt to predict. But it does, for the time being, share sufficient similarities with colonial societies properly so called to lead appropriately to the discussion of societies whose central institutions are as they are because and only because of the pressures exerted by other ones.

INTER-SOCIETAL RELATIONS

§32. As it happens, there is scarcely a single one – if that – of the societies which I have so far cited from the historical and ethnographic record whose structure and culture can be fully explained without any reference whatever to the influence of any other. That influence may, as I pointed out in Section 17, preserve or it may undermine the practices of the society in question. It may be exercised through relations of either domination or cooperation, and it may involve economic, ideological or coercive inducements or sanctions. It may be limited to the haphazard and peripheral incursions of traders, raiders or missionaries. It may involve self-reproducing institutional enclaves such as industrial corporations, military bases or ecclesiastical foundations. It may operate at a distance through the roles of consuls, ambassadors, advisers or 'political agents', or it may amount to so close and direct an exercise of power that the institutional catchment areas of the two societies become virtually coterminous.

In order to explain how much difference these influences make to the workings of the institutions of the two (or more) societies between which they are exercised, the relevant practices have as always to be identified together with the roles and systacts which carry them. But there is an obvious difference between those cases where the incumbents of the relevant roles in the less powerful society are responding to pressures from the more powerful society imposed on them against their will, and those where adoption of the roles of the less powerful society is the outcome of conscious and willing imitation of the practices of the more powerful. Inducements can be just as powerful as sanctions in accounting for the results of exogenous pressure, whether in, say, an eighteenth-century Scottish landlord's adoption of English forms of tenancy or in the adoption by the government of an industrializing nation-state of the late twentieth century of the forms of investment in, and management of, manufacturing industry which are seen to have promoted the fastest economic growth elsewhere. It is true that such imitation, although voluntary, may still be reluctant. The Scottish landlord may resent his perceived need to model his role on that of his English counterparts, and the government of the industrializing nation-state may feel driven to what it holds to be a dangerously premature expansion of indigenous manufacturing capacity by the fear of domination by multinational corporations whose prices and terms it will not be strong enough to resist. But these institutional modifications are, nevertheless, quite different from those forced on a weak or defeated regime which has no alternative but to submit.

Yet the effect on the societies in question cannot be predicted simply from the motives and attitudes of those of their members who are, whether eagerly or reluctantly, modifying the practices defining their existing roles or seeking to modify those of the other society. Indeed, the history of inter-societal relations is full of apparent paradoxes which dissolve only when the mode of the distribution of power within which the modification is attempted is seen for what it is. Thus, for example, at the time when European domination of Africa appeared to be at its height and it was the policy of the colonizing powers that the institution of slavery should be abolished, it turned out that the implementation of that policy was directly dependent on the cooperation of a systact of traditional chiefs who, in many of the societies in question, were themselves the largest slaveowners (M. A. Klein 1978, p. 599). Similarly, at the time when it appeared that Spanish domination of Central America was virtually complete and it was the policy of the Spaniards to cajole or coerce the indigenous Indians into surrendering their labour to Spanish merchants and landlords, it was in the weakest of the conquered societies – the Maya – that ownership of the means of production remained (with the exception of salt and stockrearing) entirely in Indian hands (Farriss 1984, Ch. 1): precisely because the Yucatan peninsula was so poor, the Spaniards had no incentive to do more than to extract from the indigenous Indians enough of the surplus produce from their plots to meet the Spaniards' needs.* Nor should such apparent paradoxes be read as symptoms of any inherent contradiction in the relationship. The mode of the distribution of power through which it is preserved may be just as stable as where the relation is one of either unstinting cooperation on the one hand or unrestrained domination on the other – or a combination of the two.

Economic, ideological and coercive power are no less interdependent between than within societies. Economic inducements and sanctions are unlikely to succeed in the longer term unless backed by force; ideological inducements and sanctions are unlikely to be effective except where the hegemonic society is visibly more successful and the example which it sets is one of economic and military as well as cultural achievement; coercive inducements and sanctions are unlikely to sustain a stable relation of dependency without some acquiescence, if no more, in their ancillary benefits. Even in its mid-Victorian heyday of

* Cf. Greishaber (1980, pp. 261–2) on the Bolivian *altiplano*.

apparently effortless ease, Britain's 'mere influence' rested on the threefold combination of 'the cutting edge of trade, the seductive force of literature and of the useful arts, and upon the ultimate sanction of the navy whose arm did bind the restless wave' (Gallagher 1982, p. 99) – a combination which was uniquely efficacious for as long, but only for as long, as all three advantages held. But it is still possible to single out certain practices which under specifiable circumstances will sustain a stable relationship of inter-societal dependence. Or rather: it is possible to single out certain practices which, if flexibly adapted and subtly combined, will so function as to keep the relationship stabler than it would otherwise be.

Of all economic relationships between different societies, the stablest have been those between hunter-gatherers and agriculturalists where produce is exchanged to mutual advantage without any attempt being made by either side either to dominate the other or to extend the cooperation, such as it is, more widely. But it is equally possible for stable relationships to be established where an exchange of goods and services, even if on very unequal terms, persists in the perceived interest of the incumbents of the dominant roles, and novel self-reproducing institutions evolve in consequence. In the three-way Atlantic trade of the sixteenth and seventeenth centuries, African rulers became slave-dealers who sold subjects as captives in exchange for manufactured goods from Britain, which then imported sugar from the plantations of the Caribbean to which those slaves had been transported in British ships.* These relations were, of course, cooperative only between traders and rulers: they depended on the exploitation of defenceless people by the carriers of the interlocking practices who benefited jointly from that exploitation and were in a position to impose its continuance through command of the necessary means of coercion. But, as in any market, there can also be patterns of inter-societal exchange which, although they leave the richest relatively richer than the poorest, still leave the poorest richer than they were.

Analysis of this variant is to some extent hampered by disagreements over the different but related question whether economically advanced societies necessarily depend for their prosperity on the exploitation of weaker ones. But the answer cannot be a categorical affirmative for two reasons. First, the most advanced societies – those in which capitalism emerged and then triumphed – did not gain their initial advantage at the

* The total pattern of trade of which these exchanges were a part was much more complex (Frank 1978, pp. 219–31), but it seems agreed among specialists that the key to its high profitability was the cheapness of slaves.

expense of the weaker* so much as use their relative strength once they had acquired it to extend their influence overseas. Second, there is in any case more advantage to be gained, given a distribution of skills and natural resources which requires even rich countries to look outside their own borders, in exchanges with other rich countries than with poor ones: 'the advanced world is its own market' (J. A. Hall 1985, p.227). On the other hand, an unequal but stable symbiotic relationship is perfectly possible where a richer society imports raw materials from a poorer one and exports to it in return manufactured goods which are paid for out of such profit as has been earned (and would not be otherwise) on the raw materials. The influences which prevent such relationships from reproducing themselves for more than a limited number of years are not so much economic as ideological and political. The weaker society has no means of increasing its economic power in the international market, and the economic interests of its dominant systacts are likely to be tied to those of its trading partner. The risk is that the awareness of this will provoke the opposition of indigenous groups who not only feel relatively deprived of the benefits of the relationship but also see in it a threat to their cultural and political independence.

This risk is particularly well illustrated by late twentieth-century Iran under Mohammed Reza Shah, whose underestimation of the strength of the opposition of the *ulama* cost him his role. But it is equally true, for example, of early twentieth-century Mexico. Mexico's northern provinces, in particular, benefited greatly from American investment which, unequal as the relationship was, bestowed some of the fruits of economic growth on miners, cowboys and railway workers as well as bankers, traders and commercially minded *hacendados*; but political leaders had always to ensure that they were capable of mobilizing nationalist sentiment behind them in their dealings with the United States. Without doubt, an economically dominant society can reproduce its dominance through local bourgeoisies who are successively recruited into that role and maintain their collective identity as a class. But such continuance is conditional not only on the terms of trade but on a degree of recourse to the means of coercion. There is an evident parallel between inter-societal and intra-societal division of labour, and wage-workers may stand in the same relation as a class to the owners of the means of production whether or not those owners are members of the

* This is not to say that they did not exploit the weaker from the earliest phase of contact, but only that the volume of transactions with them was insignificant by comparison with the volume of internal transactions on which their superior wealth was based (O'Brien 1984).

same society. But if the relation is across a societal frontier, it will on that very account require some form of ancillary support if it is to be stably maintained.

The same is true of ideological hegemony. Its importance in inter-societal relations is not to be underrated: both Christianity and Islam demonstrate equally forcibly the capacity of alien practices and doctrines to influence the systactic structure of societies which might at first have appeared impervious to them. But it is another matter for hegemony to continue to be exercised by the dominant society over successive generations through ideological influence alone. The most effective practices, broadly speaking, are those where the superior prestige of the dominant society is sustained not only by a consistent and strongly held ideology which legitimates that prestige but also by the visible evidence of a pattern of consumption and conduct perceived as enviable for its own sake. Nehru, for one, testified explicitly to the 'psychological triumph of the British in India' which rested on the successful persuasion of the educated members of the indigenous population of the benefits of 'respectability' of life-style as defined by the ideology of the colonizers (1958, p. 264, quoted by Stavrianos 1981, p. 477); and the same can be documented both for the influence of French culture in territories colonized by France and for the influence of American culture in independent ex-colonial societies dominated by American economic corporations. But the influence is likely to fade, for two reasons: either the practices of the dominant society are adopted and accepted and the new styles and attitudes are reproduced without need of further external example, or they continue to be resisted and their prospective carriers succumb to the pressures exerted by other systacts.

Exogenous ideological pressure continues to operate strongly over successive generations only when the inspirational source is – paradoxically – less rather than more closely attached to economic and coercive institutions, and it is not an alien society which is perceived as the influence but a more or less disembodied creed. The Roman Catholic Church continues to exert ideological hegemony across a range of remote societies precisely because, among other conditions, the answer to Stalin's celebrated question 'How many divisions has the Pope?' is 'None'. Likewise, an Islamic counterpart, whether Sunni *mufti*, Shiite *ayatollah* or self-proclaimed Mahdi, is less likely to continue to dominate the practices of the faithful in societies remote from his own if he is identified with its national politics as well as its religious doctrines.

It is much the same with domination by force alone. There can be no doubt of its efficacy when one society is able and willing to bring overwhelmingly superior means of coercion to bear. But it can be much less effective if it has to be repeatedly invoked against determined opposition. Just as its use internally is often more effective as a threat which is only sometimes carried out, so is its use in maintaining the institutions of a weaker society in a form which suits the interests of a stronger. Roman legions against the Achaean League, British gunboats in Alexandria or Buenos Aires, or Soviet tanks in Hungary or Czechoslovakia are all more likely to achieve that purpose if they are believed to be available to act in support of the puppet governments of client states than if they are part of a permanent occupying force whose continuous engagement in active repression both mobilizes and unifies a national movement of resistance.

This dilemma is no easier to resolve where the dominant society also offers economic inducements and sanctions in the form of bilateral trade agreements or aid programmes, or ideological inducements and sanctions in the form of cultural missions or propaganda campaigns. For these will merely defeat their intended purpose if they are visibly seen to depend for success on being imposed at the point of a sword or a gun. There may be no immediate answer to superior military technology if coupled with the willingness and ability to use it to best effect. But over a longer period, technology can spread by imitation, diffusion or purchase; and even if it does not, it may stimulate defensive countermeasures which make it much less effective than it at first appeared to be. It can hardly be doubted that, for example, Portugal won its overseas empire because and only because of a superiority in 'guns and sails' (Cipolla 1965), or that the Ottomans' conquest of Egypt in 1517 was due to their use of field artillery which the Mamluks despised as unworthy of cavalrymen (Hodgson 1974, II, p. 419). But unless absorption (or fusion) is total, even the most decisive defeat in battle does not necessarily bring about a lasting subordination of the loser's institutions to those of the winner or an irreversible transformation of the loser's mode of the distribution of power.

The only general conclusion is the by now familiar one that between, as within, societies a stable distribution of power depends on the degree of advantage conferred by mutant or recombinant practices on carriers who adopt them in the context of an initial distribution which may favour the dominant role, institution or society only for the shorter term. In inter-societal relations, the critical carriers are those in the subordinate society whose reproduction at the same location depends on maintaining cooperation with the rulers of the more powerful society at the same time as domination over the subordinate systacts within their own. The initial impact of a much more powerful society can often be so violent as not merely to weaken but to shatter the institutions of the less powerful and to force an almost instantaneous change in its modes of production, persuasion and coercion alike. But long-term relations of dependency are less often found and less easily explained. If there is a proverbial example, it is China, whose perennial influence over client societies on its borders was (and is) sustained by its own economic resources, its unshakeable conviction of its own legitimacy, and its capacity to discipline recalcitrant tributaries by force of arms. But even here – as with its internal structure – the stability is cyclical at best. The mere fact that the relation *is* inter-societal renders it less likely to reproduce itself unchanged than to lead either to a successful assertion or reassertion of independence by the subordinate society or to a further exercise of power of one, two or all three kinds by the dominant society which absorbs the institutions of the subordinate society into the same catchment area as its own.

§33. At that point, where imperialism has fully succeeded, there are no longer any inter-societal relations: the institutions of the absorbed society have become regional institutions of the absorbing one, as '*tota Italia*' became part of Rome or the Baltic states part of the Soviet Union. Domination is a matter of degree between, as within, societies, and semi-autonomous institutions are often allowed to remain as a conscious preference on the imperialists' part. The maxim that 'Refusals to annex are no proof of reluctance to control' (Gallagher and Robinson 1982, p. 4) can be construed as directing attention not only to the strength of inter-societal pressures which are not exclusively or even directly coercive, but also to the possibility that such pressures may be just as decisive for the survival, modification or abolition of traditional practices as an absorption which results from outright conquest (or surrender under threat).

There is, however, a distinction to be drawn between two forms of colonization. The organized intrusion of one society into the territory of another may be either an attempt to control it for the purposes of the home society or, on the contrary, an attempt by the colonists to escape from the institutional catchment area of the home society and set up an independent society of their own. The distinction, like so many others, is not exclusive: Rhodesia during virtually the whole of the period when it was so called is a notable example of confusion amounting to conflict between the two objectives, which resulted in a long and uneasy oscillation of power between settler interests and the Colonial Office (Blake 1977, Chs. 11–13). But the Puritan pilgrims who disembarked from the *Mayflower* in 1620 are at the opposite pole from General Sir Charles Napier's incursion into Sind ('*Peccavi*') in 1842, and the great wave of 'colonization' in the eighth century B.C. which established Greek settlements all the way from Spain to the Crimea is likewise at the opposite pole from the 'colonization' of the Pacific Islands by England, France, Germany and the United States in the later years of the nineteenth century A.D.

Yet the nature of the institutions and practices established by the 'colonists' and their reciprocal effect on those of the society into which they have intruded cannot be explained in terms of this feature of the relationship alone, any more than (as we have seen) from the degree to which the relation is one of domination or cooperation. The *Mayflower* pilgrims may have hoped to preserve a separate, stable, self-reproducing society whose relations with the indigenous population of Massachusetts were restricted to a minimum of peaceful trade; but they were drawn willy-nilly into expansion and warfare. The British in nineteenth-century India may have hoped to impose a chosen set of practices directly on the indigenous population through a combination of trade, religious and cultural conversion, and force; but they had in the event to work through native élites whose systactic location they were bound to preserve as a necessary condition of sustaining their own domination. There is a pattern of a kind to be discerned in the structure of colonial relations as these extend from the first preliminary contact between would-be autonomous settlers and cooperative (or at least indifferent) indigenes through the emergence of the roles of proconsuls, viceroys, or governors-general able to draw on whatever resources they need from their home governments in order to impose that government's domination against either native or settler resistance. But it is a pattern of wide cultural variation within a set of structural constraints which are themselves variable to a considerable degree.

Let us start from the enclaves. Alien communities settled permanently on the territory of a host society have a history extending back at least as far as the Sumerian merchants whose distinctive architecture and pottery have enabled archaeologists to infer their presence in North-eastern Syria in the fourth millennium B.C. The standard form of the relationship with the host society is one of cautious cooperation for mutual advantage for which Naucratis in Egypt furnishes an early, well-studied, and almost ideal-typical model (J. Boardman 1980, pp. 118–33). A merchant community drawn from many different parts of the Greek world enjoyed a collective monopoly of trade with Egypt under the authority of its own overseers (*prostatai tou emporiou*) on its own substantial site with its own houses, warehouses and sanctuaries adjoining a native Egyptian population. But all this was subject to the permission of the rulers of a powerful state whose admission of foreigners was on conditions that suited themselves. It was not, therefore, a 'colony' in either sense,* and still less was it a 'treaty port' like the 69 which, by 1920, dotted the Chinese coast and interior, where resident Europeans enjoyed not merely exemption from direct taxation and the right of consular jurisdiction, but the right to station their own troops, staff their own bureaucracy, and take Chinese to law in their own courts. It was, rather, like Canton *before* the opening-up of China to the Western powers (Austin and Vidal-Naquet 1977, p. 235): neither party to the relationship is dominant, and their internal systactic structure is of equally little mutual concern.

Permanent enclaves of this kind are, however, relatively rare. It is more normal to find that the colony, of whichever kind, either increases its power to the point of dominating the host society or else is subordinated to, if not actually destroyed by, it. This second alternative, where it occurs, removes the case from consideration altogether, like the ill-fated Scottish colony at Darien whose short history Macaulay narrated to such effect. But the first creates the possibility of a stable relationship in which the domination of the colonizing society – whether this means the colonists themselves independently of their society of origin or the government of the society of origin itself – is exercised in a manner which still falls short of absorption. There are four main sub-types: first, the *minimalist* model, where the dominant colonial community or corporation is reproduced only by immigration; second, the model of *indirect rule* through local élites who retain not only the forms but the substance of power; third, the *planter* model, where a dominant systact still institutionally related to a society of origin is demographically self-reproducing; and fourth, the *vice-regal* model, where the society of origin of the original colonists is directly represented by the presence of its appointed agents in governmental roles. The four are not exclusive and there are many transitional and borderline cases. But they define between them the range of possible institutional variation.

* The same holds for military as opposed to commercial enclaves: for example, 'the establishment of English enclaves in America was the final phase of the Elizabethan struggle with Spain. Some of the earliest attempts to establish English "colonies" such as that of Sir Humphrey Gilbert in 1570 were efforts to set up self-sufficient military outposts from which more vigorous attacks on the Spanish empire could be launched' (Lang 1975, pp. 110–11).

The most nearly ideal-typical example of the minimalist model is that of the Jesuits in Paraguay where, as we have seen already, the society's reproduction was dependent on the immigration of successive new recruits into the colonizing élite while the subordinate indigenes reproduced themselves demographically to the point of outgrowing the institutional catchment area which the Jesuits were able to control. But a homologous case – for an initial period, at least – is Ptolemaic Egypt, where after the death of Alexander the Great, a colonizing élite of exclusively Greek origin maintained its domination over the indigenous population through the entry into strictly personal service with the monarch of immigrants drawn by the familiar threefold lure of '*Reichtum*, *Macht und Ansehen*' (Habicht 1958, p. 7). This state of affairs was, however, temporary, partly for structural and partly for cultural reasons. Structurally, it could only last for as long as there was, in Habicht's words, no '*standische Element*' – that is, the 'friends' of the king did not become a self-reproducing systact transmitting property and privilege from fathers to sons in the way that could not, of course, even arise with the celibate Jesuits. Culturally, it could only last for as long as the king had not established the legitimacy of his rule (*ibid*., p. 15). Gradually, therefore, as the society reproduced itself over successive generations, the Greeks became an indigenous élite recruited from Egypt rather than Greece. This departure from the original minimalist model did not by itself generate an insoluble contradiction. But the system became increasingly unstable as continuing exclusion of Egyptians from governmental roles (and from the *gymnasia* in which distinctively Greek practices and life-styles were preserved and transmitted), together with continuing exploitation of subordinate Egyptians by dominant Greeks, provoked a mounting sense of relative deprivation which the Greeks were less and less able either to remedy or to suppress.*

The most nearly ideal-typical example of indirect rule is furnished by the princely states in India after 1858. Descriptively, the institutions and practices of the small, extravagant, ill-run, archaic state of Dewas Senior have been immortalized in E. M. Forster's *The Hill of Devi*, which vividly conveys the flavour of life in a court whose expenditures on elaborate and often comically incompetent rituals and pageantries

* Cf. Walbank (1981, p. 119): 'Since the flow of Greek and Macedonian immigrants had long ago dried up, the King and his court felt themselves weakened and hence were led to make repeated concessions to the temples and to publish amenities (euphemistically termed "benefactions" (*philanthrōpa*)) for the peasantry. But these very concessions reduced their ability to raise adequate revenues for the future and so still further weakened the government; it was a vicious circle.'

contrasted as starkly with the administrative standards of the Government of India on the one hand as with the abject poverty of its subordinate peasantry on the other. Dewas is not to be taken as representative of them all, and Forster's account is not that of an academic researcher. But so extreme a case is revealing precisely because, as Forster saw, even the most irritatingly inadequate native ruler could maintain his independence on suffrance for as long as his imperial masters were unwilling, and his 'feudal' subjects unable, to displace him. 'Feudal' is the term applied not only by Forster but also by Nehru to the princely states in the loose sense that their rulers 'can exalt and depress their own subjects at will, regard the State reserve as their private property, promulgate a constitution one day and ignore it the next' (quoted from *Abinger Harvest* by Das 1977, p. 12). But the rulers themselves did see their relation to the British Crown as a kind of feudatory one. The function of indirect rule, accordingly, was to unite the interests of the princes and the Government of India in preserving a maximum of independence for the princes, who could thereby be relied upon to do what they could to repress any upsurge of nationalist sentiment within their territories. The exasperation to which a ruler like the Maharajah of Dewas drove the British is testimony as much to the convenience of the practices of indirect rule when it worked as they wished as it is to the instability inherent in the possibility of succession to the princely role of incumbents legitimated not by appointment but by descent and therefore immune to the normal inducements and sanctions of imperial rule.

For a near-approximation to the ideal type of a 'planter' society, we need to go no further than the Caribbean islands with which the descriptive overtones of the term are chiefly associated. Descriptively, Edward Long's romanticized but not wholly imperceptive *History of Jamaica*, published in 1774, is in its different way as close to a classic source as Forster's *Hill of Devi* for princely India: there are the rich, arrogant, intemperate, hospitable, quarrelsome planters lolling on the verandahs of their spacious houses, ministered to by their dozens of domestic slaves, riding intermittently out to oversee the slave gangs in the canefields, and relying for recruitment into the roles of clerk, manager, lawyer and surveyor on canny, frugal and industrious immigrant Scotsmen. It had not always been as easy a life as Long's picture suggests, and it was not to remain so for very much longer. But the particular circumstances of the mid eighteenth century gave the Jamaican planters a singularly advantageous combination of economic prosperity, political autonomy and ideological self-confidence. The local merchants had so far lost control of the sugar trade that their role effectively degenerated to that of factor (Pares 1960, p. 33); the commission system (K. G. Davies 1952) functioned in favour of the larger planters who came to dominate the local House of Assembly; the introduction of tea-drinking into England as a regular habit sustained the demand for sugar; the supply of slaves was adequate to overcome the high mortality of those who worked in the canefields; and the absentee landlords and merchants to whom the local planters were in debt were a sufficiently powerful parliamentary interest in London not only to influence prices but also to check the political interference which governments in London might seek to exercise over their colonists. The Governor, although he might be under instructions from London to prohibit the passing of measures too much in the planters' interests, could neither dictate to a bureaucracy staffed by farmers who had bid for their offices to absentee holders nor suborn an assembly of rich freeholders whose privileges had been guaranteed in return for its agreement to the annual remittance of a fixed amount of revenue to the Crown (Metcalf 1965).

The 'vice-regal' model, finally, is perhaps best exemplified in the societies of Spanish America in the brief period following the conquests. Over the seventeenth century, there developed an increasing conflict of interest between the colonial bureaucracies and the Spanish Crown in which the distribution of power shifted steadily in favour of the colonial bureaucracies and the landowners and merchants whom they served. But it is a remarkable feature of the Spanish conquests in America, in contrast to those of the English, that not only was the Crown determined to prevent the emergence of an uncontrollable systact of local magnates, but the *conquistadores* themselves had no such ambitions of their own. Ideology had much to do with it. Pizarro and Cortes saw themselves as agents of the Spanish Crown and the Catholic Church: they 'came to the New World to acquire the resources to re-enter the old one with enhanced status and prestige' (Lang 1975, p. 11). But the *conquistadores* were in any case 'not men dominated by feudal ambitions. They were first and foremost entrepreneurs and merchants' (MacLeod 1973, p. 374). When, therefore, royal officials took over the government of the New World on behalf of Charles V, it was not necessary for them to overcome by force the resistance of a 'plantocracy' with separatist inclinations and would-be autonomous governmental institutions. It is true that there did not attach to the role of viceroy anything like a monopoly of power. But that was less because of the intransigence of local *encomenderos* to whom the Crown had conceded rights to Indian labour than because many of the viceroy's subordinate officials themselves had direct access to the King or the Council of the Indies. The towns, far from being the focus of dissident settler interests, were established in the name of the Crown and governed by *corregidores* who, although they frequently exploited the role at the expense of the Indian communities subject to them, occupied it only for a limited term of years and had no control over the appointment of their successors. The instability of the system had more to do with the relative weakness of Spain itself in the inter-societal competitions and conflicts of the late sixteenth and seventeenth centuries than with any inherent contradiction in the relations between a strong Church and State and a colonial society whose élites could do more to improve their location by working within the institutions imposed on them than against them.

The history of imperialism is a topic as vast as it is contentious, and it is contentious not only because of the difficulties of drawing quasi-experimental contrasts which will disentangle inter- from intra-societal influences, but also because of the risk that the contrasts will be distorted by the value-judgements of researchers predisposed to assign praise or blame to the beneficent or pernicious influence (as they see it) of colonizing societies over the colonized. But from the perspective of this volume, that influence has to be analyzed no differently from any other which may determine what practices are selected within any chosen society and why it has therefore evolved into one rather than another mode. Imperialism, in other words, is not, any more than industrialism, a mode of the distribution of power. It is, rather, a pattern of social relations capable of generating competitive pressures which may cause either or both the colonized and colonizing society to evolve into one rather than another mode or sub-type. Whether the story is one of the diffusion of democratic political institutions, cultural enlightenment, and economic progress marred by occasional lapses into violence and exploitation, or, on the contrary, it is a story of brutal conquests, insensitive imposition of alien norms, and unscrupulous extraction of wealth barely if ever redeemed by occasional concern for the well-being of the indigenous population, is up to you. But it is a story which fits the theory of competitive selection of practices just as well as if the incumbents of the dominant roles were – which by definition they could not be – drawn by origin from the subordinate society instead of the dominant one.

§34. One final point about inter-societal relations needs to be made before this Chapter can be brought to a close. It is a fact of human history acknowledged, even if deplored, by observers of all theoretical schools that the institutional links between one society and another have both spread and tightened to the point that by the second half of the twentieth century there has come into being a single system to which they all relate in some way and to some degree. The last of the hidden cities, undiscovered islands, fugitive communities and lost tribes which until recently lay unvisited by explorers and untouched by any knowledge of the practices of the wider world are now open to the gaze of the company prospector, the academic fieldworker, the development agent, the television cameraman and the package tourist. In the process, there has evolved a global hierarchy of more and less powerful societies whose relations to one another have therefore to be reported and explained in much the same terms as those used to report and explain the relations between their own constituent systacts. There are the same sorts of inequalities in economic bargaining power, in ideological and cultural hegemony, and in political influence underwritten by force. There are the same sorts of aspirations and frustrations felt by those relatively deprived of the share of total resources which they consider their due. There are the same sorts of countervailing associations and corporations seeking a redistribution of power in their favour. And there are the same sorts of strategies and techniques available to the more advantageously located in their determination – if such it is – to maintain the practices and institutions of the *status quo*.

This being so, every society now extant which is fully defined by the itemization of all the roles which its members occupy must have an ascertainable rank in a global hierarchy of power. In practice, it is neither feasible nor necessary for the sociological theorist to draw up such a rank-order before advancing hypotheses about the workings and evolution of whatever societies may have been chosen for study. But where an institution is as it is in some significant respect because and only because the global distribution of power is as it is, then clearly the society in question has to that extent to be assigned its rank. This applies no less when the society is at the top than when it is at the bottom. The notion of exploitation of the weaker by the stronger – which in this context carries no descriptive or evaluative overtones – is likely to explain at least as much about the practices and institutions of the exploiting as of the exploited society. How, on any theory, could the functioning of England's institutions in the eighteenth and nineteenth centuries be explained without reference to its status as – for the moment – the most powerful society seeking to exert that power beyond its own geographical and institutional boundaries? In earlier centuries, when the system is still far from global, inter-societal hierarchies can only be local, even if the locality embraces what is, to 'them', the limits of the *orbis terrarum*. But by the time that Portugal, and then Holland, and then England, and then the United States have come to extend their influence quite literally round the world, explanation of the workings of their domestic institutions leads as unavoidably and directly to the institutions of Calicut, or Tahiti, or Hawaii or Johor as the other way round.

The existence of an inter-societal hierarchy can, moreover, be just as important when the societies in question are approximately equal in resources as when one is manifestly more powerful than the other. In these circumstances, they may either compete or cooperate (or, again, evolve a mixture of the two). Where they cooperate, the critical motive may well be a common fear of domination by some other society perceived as more powerful than either of them; but it may equally well be a positive desire to secure the joint gain in economic, ideological or coercive resources which some form of (at the minimum) 'acephalous consociation' (M. G. Smith 1971, p. 95), or alliance, or federation or (ultimately) union may bring. Among the 700 or so *poleis* of Ancient Greece, inter-societal relations ranged all the way from short-term defensive symmachies, periodic common ceremonies at shared cult-centres, and trading relations formalized by *proxenoi* residing on each other's territory through reciprocal rights of marriage, land-purchase and citizenship to thoroughgoing federations (*sympoliteiai*) or so-called 'leagues' in which one partner had in fact become so far dominant that membership on the part of the less powerful *poleis* was voluntary only in name. Which variant was adopted at a particular time and place, and how stable or otherwise it might prove to be, depended more on particular conjunctures of political circumstance than on institutional analogues and homologues of the kind from which a useful inference might be drawn for the benefit of comparative sociological theory. But the bewildering shifts from one form of association to another, the sudden reversals of alliances, the alternating fusions and fissions, the cycles of enmity and friendship, and the bursts of imperial ascendancy and withdrawal are a reminder that where no marked inequalities in power exist between the members of a closed multi-societal system, the pattern of domination and subordination may be just as fluid as the systactic pattern within a society where strongly antagonistic communities are so closely located that a near-anarchic cycle of hostilities and truces becomes a stable pattern of its own.

For the comparative analysis of social structure, however, the cases which can most usefully be studied are neither those of inter-societal anarchy on the one hand nor those of war to the finish on the other, but those in which a society's institutions and practices are as they are in response to the pervasive threat of sanctions or offer of inducements by one or more other societies whose location in the global or quasi-global system gives them the capacity so to do. It is, no doubt, conceivable that a single overwhelmingly powerful society will one day come to absorb all the rest into a unified world empire, or – less implausibly – come to dominate the major centres of population and resources to such a degree that the societies which remain outside its direct control are nevertheless in the sort of peripheral relation to it as were the remoter German tribes to the Roman Empire or the remoter African tribes to the British. But for the time being, at any rate (however long that may be), inter-societal relations are predominantly between more and less powerful nation-states. These nation-states may be either more or less dominated by an exceptionally powerful society such as the Soviet Union or the United States, and may either rise or fall quite sharply relative to one another in the global ranking. But the great majority of them are sufficiently well endowed with independent economic, ideological and coercive resources to be able to retain their juridical autonomy under any readily foreseeable circumstances short of the aftermath of full-scale nuclear war.

Within this global ranking as it has evolved since the European voyages of discovery first set the process of economic, ideological and political integration into motion, there have been cases of stability no less striking than the reversals of rank-order by which the process has been sometimes dramatically punctuated. Of the first, the almost proverbial example is Ottoman Turkey during its long years as the 'sick man of Europe'. Of the second, the almost proverbial example is Prussia, whose evolution from a modest little Electorate on the sandy shores of the Baltic into the international power by which German unification was achieved is the more remarkable because it was achieved without the benefits of extra-European imperialism. It hardly needs saying that the explanation of these differences lies more in the historical contingencies of victory or defeat in war, diplomatic or dynastic alliances and reversals of alliances, and unforeseeable shifts in technology, trade and population than to any inherent advantages in collective psychology which predetermine some societies to succeed and others to fail. But at the same time, it is the responses to these contingencies, once they have occurred, which determine success or failure in inter-societal competition. Moreover, these responses are in turn determined not merely by individual decisions of policy but by the characteristics of the society's existing institutions which confer advantages on the carriers of some practices rather than others. The response of Japan to the intrusion of the societies of the West was made possible by a set of institutions whose relative importance is a matter of continuing debate among specialists but whose latent potential for successful 'modernization' – to which I shall return in Chapter 4 – is by now beyond dispute. Conversely, where a society like nineteenth- and early twentieth-century Turkey,* or more recently some of the societies of Latin America or sub-Saharan Africa, remain in a relation of continuing subordination within the global order, it is not simply because of their relative lack of resources. It is also because of practices which cause their responses to be adaptive for their dominant systacts but not, as in the Japanese case, advantageous at the same time for the society as a whole in competition with others.

The analogues and homologues which the inter-societal system offers to the internal structure and workings of its constituent members must not, however, be used to argue that it can be analyzed as if it were itself a society writ large. It is sometimes discussed as though the inter-societal division of labour were such that societies could be assimilated to classes or even castes (Mazrui 1977, Ch. 1) which perform their differentiated functions within a distribution of power that assigns to the dominant a bourgeois and/or brahminical and to the subordinate a proletarian and/or untouchable role. But this can only be a descriptive metaphor. To the representative member of the less powerful societies of the so-called Third World, it may well be that it is as if he or she is held down in a subordinate systact which more powerful societies not only employ for the menial tasks of primary production but stigmatize as inferior within a set of cultural and 'racial' values and restrain by political intervention underwritten if necessary by military force. But to take the metaphor literally would be to deny the juridical autonomy of the member states of the United Nations. Their rulers can accurately be reported as such whatever the difference in the relative power of the societies over which they exercise their dominant roles. They may feel, in their negotiations with the representatives of more powerful societies, as if they were trade union leaders bargaining for higher wages for their members or spokesmen for ethnic groups seeking recognition as status

* Not that the rulers of Turkey failed to exploit conflicts of interest between the more powerful societies to their own advantage. But they did so from a position of weakness: the dismemberment of the Ottoman Empire was retarded rather than its subordination being reversed.

equals from their traditional superiors or commanders of dissident factions fighting for such political autonomy as they can. But that is not what their roles in fact are. However intrusive the influences which draw the members of weaker societies into the institutional catchment area of stronger ones, they are drawing them across a boundary which does not exist where the relation is not 'neo'-colonial but colonial in the proper sense.

To end this Chapter on that note is not to weaken the emphasis which I placed in Section 2 of Chapter 1 on the extent to which societal membership can be both multiple and partial. The Liberian employee of a late twentieth-century multinational corporation controlled from New York may be just as tenuously attached to the institutions of the society of which he remains a citizen as a fourteenth-century Norwegian fisherman whose livelihood is entirely bound up with the terms for his produce offered to him annually by a Hanseatic merchant and whose relation to the Norwegian monarchy of which he is nominally the subject is one of purely symbolic loyalty if not of total indifference. But there was a Kingdom of Norway, just as there is a Republic of Liberia. Although the existence of nation-states does not guarantee that the roles of their members are exclusively or even predominantly defined within the catchment area of their own institutions, that in turn does not alter the fact that the juridical frontier is also an institutional boundary in social space whose existence all rival observers are bound to accept. Whether inter- or intra-societal pressures are more important to the selection of practices, and thereby evolution of roles, within any given catchment area where the institutions of two or more societies overlap is a question to be decided case by case within the range of possibilities which this concluding group of sections has outlined.

CONCLUSION

§35. This Chapter has set out in deliberately general terms how the various institutions, roles and practices characteristic of distinguishable kinds of societies function to keep them in being as self-reproducing systems whose distinctive modes and sub-types of production, persuasion and coercion can remain stable over several generations in the absence of exogenous pressure. But the 'Linnaean' aspect of social selection can never be kept wholly separate from the 'Darwinian', as the examples cited have already shown. Competition for power never goes into total abeyance. At any moment, even the most secure-looking equilibrium may be upset by a mutation or recombination of practices which, whether consciously promoted by their carriers as a purposive innovation or scarcely recognized by them as marking any significant change in their customary behaviour, turn out to have consequences for the structure and culture of their society whose importance neither they nor anyone else could have predicted at the time.

4
Social evolution

PROCESSES OF CHANGE

§1. The fact that social evolution comes about through competitive selection of practices does not mean that the 'great engines' of human history – war, trade, religion, population growth, division and specialization of labour, and geographical and technological discovery – are any less important to it than they have traditionally been held to be. But it is because of their influence on the nature and degree of the advantages conferred by mutant or recombinant practices on their carriers that war, trade and the rest generate, sustain or dissolve modes and sub-types of the distribution of power. Indeed, their often contradictory effects cannot be fully explained unless these advantages are analyzed in detail. Wars sometimes promote and sometimes retard economic development; trade sometimes follows the flag and sometimes is followed by it; a new sacred or secular creed, or technique of production, or form of administrative organisation may displace or be displaced by pre-existing social-cum-ideological, economic, or political-cum-military institutions; and population growth has sometimes preceded, sometimes accompanied, and sometimes followed a change in the mode of the distribution of power. Which occurs, and why, depends on the institutional context within which war, trade and the rest promote new roles or modify old ones. The eventual outcome is contingent not only on the random events by which conflicts between contending factions, armies, classes, churches, status-groups, communities and nations are decided but also on the initial distribution of power when the conflict began.

This emphasis on happenstance must not, as I have insisted throughout, be read as a denial that human history is a sequence of causes and effects. Often, moreover, the effects are consciously planned by agents who have correctly seen that their interests will be served thereby, and in this sense it would be palpably inappropriate to speak of, say, the Meiji Restoration, or the *Code Napoléon*, or the conquests of Alexander the Great as coming about 'by accident'. But the success of (some) rulers in moulding (some) institutions to their purposes is no more an argument against the theory of social selection through the random mutation or recombination of practices than the success of (some) stockbreeders in raising (some) beefier cattle or (some) speedier horses is an argument against the theory of natural selection through the random mutation or recombination of genes. The explanation of a change from one mode or sub-type of the distribution of power to another does not lie in the deliberate intention, if such it was, to bring it about. It lies in the reasons for which the intention came to be successfully implemented – which, in any case, most are not.

To revert to the examples which I cited in Section 6 of Chapter 1: the Bedouin factions who acknowledged Muhammed, the consuls of the medieval North Italian towns, the tenth- and eleventh-century Japanese *bushi*, and the *baillis* of Philippe Auguste were all, no doubt, using their novel roles to further their interests as they saw them. But the importance for the evolution of their societies of the mutant or recombinant practices carried by those roles was not just a function of the intensity of their incumbents' sense of relative deprivation. Nor does it matter whether or not one or other of them may have guessed that their roles would so function as in due course to bring about a significant and irreversible social change. Given the initial conditions, it is the practices themselves which are 'the' causes of the change, not the state of mind of those performing the actions which constitute them. It is a truism of sociology that unintended consequences make more difference to the future evolution of institutions and societies than intended ones, and if the consequences *are* the intended ones it is not because they were intended but because of the function which the roles whose incumbents had conceived the intentions performed within the pre-existing mode and sub-type of the distribution of power.

The first question to be asked, therefore, when a novel role is observed is not what conscious policy (if any) lies behind its emergence but what systactic interest it turns out to serve. Consider the example of wage-labour, whose importance to social evolution is not disputed by theorists of any rival school. It is a role whose incumbents may well adopt it deliberately because they perceive it as better (or less badly) serving their individual economic interests than any alternative available to them. But it does not follow that the emergence of the role, even on a substantial scale, will necessarily lead to the formation of a systact (or two) collectively conscious of a common interest, and still less does it follow that the interest served by its emergence is that of the wage-earners rather than the employers.

The practice of wage-payment is both older and more widespread than is sometimes supposed. I have cited already the casual building-workers of Classical Rome, the itinerant grape-pickers of Carolingian France, and the landless labourers of the villages of medieval England, and there are any number of examples in the historical and ethnographic record where the role of vendor of the labour inherent in one's person is reported, to use Marx's phrase, residing in the pores of the old society without altering the mode of production. Indeed, sometimes wage-labour is so far alien to the existing institutions of a society that it is only members of other societies, or other communities within the same society, who enter the role at all: in the Ivory Coast, young men would work as wage-labourers only in regions other than their own, since to do so for fellow-Africans in their home territories was held to be demeaning (Ancey *et al.* 1974, p. 23, quoted by Iliffe 1983, p. 55). But where wage-labour does spread pervasively throughout the society, the recruits into the novel role may be of very diverse societal and systactic origins, ranging from immigrants to emancipated bondsmen to impoverished smallholders or artisans to dependent women and children. The decisive condition is the advantage conferred on their employers as well as (and usually more than) themselves within the pre-existing distribution of power, and this may equally well be a highly stratified structure which enables tributary labour to be commuted for cash or, on the contrary, a mode of production bound up with lineage roles in which land- or stock-holding elders oblige younger men to take up wage-labour in order to save the bridewealth necessary for marriage to women whom the elders control. As always, no empirical generalization is possible at this level. The explanation of the change of mode rests on the identification with hindsight of the advantages to either or both wage-workers and capitalists which adoption of the practice turned out to bring.

The same holds where it can be seen with hindsight that the decisive advantage lay not in a mutant practice but in the recombination of existing ones. Let me revert once again, from this standpoint, to the example of Holland after the revolt from Spanish rule in 1572. In Section 26 of Chapter 3, I cited some of the mutually reinforcing practices which combined to sustain a level of prosperity out of all apparent proportion to the size of the society, its natural resources and its military strength relative to that of France and Spain. This prosperity was not achieved easily: 'The Dutch did not acquire their awesome financial power in a day' (G. Parker 1974, p. 573). But in so far as there was a single key to its acquisition, it 'lay in the fact that the chief investors ran the government' (*ibid.*, p. 572) – or in other words, in an overlap in the incumbency of the roles which carried the economic and coercive practices most important for the furtherance of the interests of the dominant systact. The effect was that the delegates to the Estates not only raised large sums of cash through the sale of annuities but cooperated in reducing the costs of servicing them even though this was against their interests in their roles as investors. The confidence of both domestic and foreign investors was, as always in financial markets, self-reinforcing. Lenders were readily forthcoming, redeemable government debentures traded regularly at a premium, and interest rates were the lowest in Europe. The contrast with royal profligacy, rapacious tax-farming, periodic bankruptcy and pervasive tax-evasion in neighbouring France could hardly be more striking.

In any but the smallest and simplest societies, the sequence of events through which mutant or recombinant practices come to alter the mode of the distribution of power is likely to be too complex, even if detailed evidence is to hand, for the interaction of causes and effects to be precisely traceable. But that does not invalidate the claim that it was the practices hypothesized to be decisive which did set under way the sequence of events which led to the outcome finally observed. Consider as an example, this time from the ideological dimension, the spread of Protestantism in sixteenth-century France. Its consequence was an 'alarming convergence of religious and aristocratic protest' which created 'a combined movement of formidable power' (Elliott 1969, p. 95). But the process is extraordinarily difficult to unravel. There was no obvious systactic interest which impelled half the French aristocracy to abandon and half to retain their allegiance to Rome. Some conversions were genuinely religious, others overtly political. Condé himself might not have been converted at all had he not fallen ill in 1558. 'Fashion and example played an important part' (*ibid.*, p. 97). Calvin and Beza were astute and successful in their recruitment of pastors from among the aristocratic familes. Unemployed nobles '*nés pour le mestier de la guerre*' saw in the Protestant cause the prospects of a soldierly career. Regional loyalties helped to make Protestantism a focus of opposition to the monarchy. Yet whatever the intricacies of the process of conversion, they do not need to be unravelled in detail before it can be hypothesized that Protestantism was adaptive for the political interests of those who took up its practices and doctrines. Indeed, not the least of its strengths was the institutional overlap between the organization of the Huguenot churches and the patron–client networks of the Protestant nobility. If the final outcome for the Protestants was defeat and exile, it was by no means a foregone conclusion; and if Condé had succeeded, French society would have evolved very differently from the way in which it did under Louis XIV. Competitive selection of practices is no less demonstrably at work because it is impossible to say with certainty exactly how the Huguenots came as near to victory as they did or why exactly they were, in the event, defeated.

These examples should not, on the other hand, be taken to imply that the process by which practices are selected is exclusively or even normally one of a competition between carriers of which the winning systact (if such it is) is thereby able to impose the practice in question on the society as a whole. The process can equally well be one of cooperation across systactic boundaries in pursuit of a limited joint advantage. In these cases, there is more to it than the need for some minimal cooperation for any role to be institutionalized at all: it is not just that landlords need tenants, priests need congregations and generals need troops. It is that the mutation or recombination of practices takes place within two separate systacts as a complementary process. A hoplite revolution comes about not just because there has evolved the role of heavy-armed foot-soldier but because the previously dominant élite modifies its own military practices and acquiesces in a diminution of the power attaching to *its* roles; an absolute monarchy succeeds in curbing the power of territorial magnates not just because there are potential recruits, whether civilian or military, who cannot be bribed or coerced into placing themselves under magnate protection but because the monarchy enters into a direct relation with them which may cover any or all of the provision of land or weapons, right of access to royal justice and entry into a status-order legitimated by service to the Crown. This does not necessarily make it a mistake to attribute systactic consciousness and an articulated sense of relative deprivation to the subordinate group or category whose interests the process can be seen to have furthered. But it is a warning against any assumption that classes, status-groups, orders, factions, castes or estates improve their location to the extent that they do because and only because they have achieved the transition from '*an sich*' to '*für sich*'.

The classic example, in view of Marx's own preoccupation with it, is the changing location of the wage-earning class within English society as it evolved over the course of the nineteenth century. It is not in dispute between rival theorists that significant upward collective mobility took place or that it was accompanied by a significant degree of collective consciousness: real wages rose, trade unions became stronger, increasing social recognition was accorded to the 'respectable' working class, and the franchise was extended to cover an increasing number of adult male manual workers. But these advances were not achieved by a direct confrontation between proletariat and bourgeoisie from which zero-sum gains were won by the former at the latter's expense. Nor did the efforts of either industrial or political organizers unify the proletariat (any more than the bourgeoisie) into a single systact sharing a common economic, social and political location. The Reform Act of 1832, which is conventionally held to be a watershed, may partly have been a response to fears of revolution. But it was also a response to a coalition of 'ultra' Tories and bourgeois freeholders who respectively secured from it an increased representation of the landowning interest and independent representation of the towns (Kumar 1983, pp. 26–30).

Nor is it accidental that much of the subsequent legislation favourable to working-class interests was supported by factions within either the commercial and industrial bourgeoisie or the county landowners. The enactment of legislation giving effective recognition to the trade unions by Disraeli's administration of 1875 is neither paradoxical nor unique. One version of the story attributes the relative lack of clear-cut class conflict to the favoured location of the 'aristocracy of labour' whose higher earnings enabled them not only to adopt a more respectable lifestyle but to pay as much as a shilling a week in union dues in the cause of restrictions on the entry of outsiders into their roles. But this 'aristocracy' cannot on close inspection (Harrison and Zeitlin 1985) be given clear-cut systactic boundaries any more than can the proletariat generally; and in any case, it is often craftsmen and artisans who are the most active members of radical factions. None of this undermines the initial observations that collective upward mobility was achieved by large fractions of the urban working class and that it was achieved in part through a heightened sense of relative deprivation which found expression in the pursuit of identifiable systactic interests. Otherwise, indeed, there could hardly have evolved either a Labour Party or a Trades Union Congress such as came to play their acknowledged part – of which more in Volume III – in the history of twentieth-century Britain. But nor could they have done so without the active cooperation of the incumbents of other and more powerful roles who did not see the interests of the systact (or coalition) to which they belonged as being prejudiced thereby.

§2. It still remains, however, to be considered in closer detail in what exactly *adaptation* consists. I have spoken in earlier chapters of the adaptation of roles to changes in their environment, whether sociological or ecological, as if its reported occurrence was unproblematical, at least within the theory being advanced in this volume. But if practices, not roles, are the units of competitive selection, it has to be shown exactly how the process of adaptation comes about; and if power, not survival, is the criterion of success, it has to be shown exactly how success is to be assessed to the satisfaction of rival observers from all theoretical schools.

The first stage in the process of social change is when a role, or a set of complementary roles, comes under pressure from some source either within or outside of the society or institutional catchment area concerned – 'pressure' being a physical metaphor whose literal meaning is a threat to the power attaching to the given role but which needs to be extended to cover the effect that a potential 'vacuum' of power can have in providing opportunities for the members of existing roles to augment the power which attaches to them. Now precisely because it is not the role itself that is the unit of selection, an adaptive response to the threat (or opportunity) may take the form either of a mutation within a still recognizably similar set of practices which constitutes the role or of a displacement and recombination of the previous set which amounts to a reconstitution of the role in another form. To illustrate the process at work and at the same time test the notion of adaptation against some already familiar evidence, let me return to three of the societies which I have discussed already: late Republican Rome, early modern Russia and post-Meiji Japan. For all the differences between them, they demonstrate as effectively as each other that although selective pressure may originate either from within the society in question or from outside it, in neither event is it the society as such which is to be taken to adapt to the pressure (or fail to). Adaptation, where it occurs, is by the roles which are the carriers of the practices. It is they whose competitive advantages are initially changed, and only when that initial process has been correctly analyzed will any concomitant change in the power of the society as a whole in relation to other societies be explicable.

In Section 15 of Chapter 3, late Republican Rome was offered as an example of a contradiction between the practices which had initially sustained it as an oligarchic, militaristic citizen-state and those which resulted from its spectacular expansion by conquest. It was, however, by no means inevitable that the contradiction should be resolved by evolution to an absolutism of the particular sub-type which Augustus successfully imposed. Nor can that evolution be explained by a claim that absolutism was adaptive for Roman society as a whole: from no theoretical standpoint can it be held to have been either a necessary or a sufficient condition of successful resistance to exogenous pressure. Nor was the critical mutation and recombination of practices that which had shifted the mode of production away from peasant proprietorship towards slave-worked *latifundia*. Such a shift could in theory have been quite compatible with the maintenance of republican institutions and the employment of freeborn citizens as career soldiers, or urban craftsmen, or shopkeepers, or casual wage-workers, or pioneers settled on hitherto uncultivated land, or simply civilian clients of the great patrician houses – Cicero's 'men of slender means and no jobs of whom plenty are always available to respectable and generous patrons' (*Pro Murena* XXIV). The practices which in fact brought the Republic down were those that defined the relation of discharged veterans to their commanders. Once they no longer had their own smallholdings to return to (and after Marius, there was no longer a property qualification for service in the legions), they looked either to their patrons or to the state for means of support. But the state was not in a position to provide it. It was to individual generals that the legionaries had to look for donatives, or a share of booty, or resettlement on confiscated land.

Once the murder of Tiberius Gracchus had unleashed a continuing and seemingly unbreakable sequence of political vendettas between rival factions, there was at the same time more opportunity for discharged veterans to employ their skills by enlisting in the service of their chosen general (who might in any case have refused to disband the troops legally assigned to him for a supposedly limited period) and less opportunity for stable employment in a civilian economy disrupted by near-permanent civil war. The irony is that neither Marius nor Sulla nor Lepidus nor Catiline nor any other disgruntled faction-leader, power-hungry general, defeated ex-candidate or would-be neo-Gracchus ever sought to change the mode of the distribution of power: they were not trying to recreate the role of king any more than to abolish the roles of the Republican magistrates. But the unintended consequence of their actions was that a decisive competitive advantage was bound to accrue to a role to which there could attach the power to bind to the state, rather than to individual commanders, the soldiers on whose loyalty the stability of the society by now depended.

Augustus, having emerged victorious over his rivals, achieved this economically by massive hand-outs from his own resources supplemented by taxation, coercively by tight control of appointments to military commands, and ideologically by insistence on an oath of loyalty to his own person. Later, it is true, the succession came to be fought for by rival claimants backed by their own legions. But it was succession to the monarchical role for which they were, by then, fighting: republican institutions were never to be restored. This irreversible evolution from a citizen to an absolutist mode was not, as I pointed out in Section 16 of Chapter 2, a revolution: the 'violent transference of power and property' (Syme 1939, p. viii) was not from one systact to another but from one set of members of the dominant stratum to another supplemented by some upward individual mobility by provincials into the ranks of the senatorial nobility. But it was, nonetheless, a resolution of the contradictions generated by expansion within a 'citizen' mode through a political evolution effected by practices of which one exceptionally gifted and fortunate commander was the partly deliberate and partly unconscious carrier.

To contrast the evolution to absolutism of early modern Russia with that of Republican Rome is to bring out two major differences: first, the forcible displacement of a previously dominant stratum which was necessary to effect it; second, the change in the mode of production which was necessary to sustain it. We have seen already that Russia's transition to the tsarist sub-type of absolutism required the destruction of the systact of *boyars* and the recruitment of a new service nobility of *pomeshchiks*, and it is easy to see the advantages which this new role conferred not only on its incumbents but on the tsar whose power they strengthened. But, as we have also seen, the practice whereby tenure was conditional on actual performance of service gave way over the course of the seventeenth century to an assimilation of *pomestye* to *votchina*, which was formally enshrined in an imperial decree of 1714. For whom, then, was the institution of the *pomestye* adaptive?

Like the west European fief, the Byzantine *pronoia*, the Islamic *iqta*, the Ottoman *timar* and the Mughal *jagir*, the *pomestye* could function either to strengthen the ruler against the magnates or the magnates against the ruler; and once heritability was conceded, the continuing loyalty intended to be secured thereby might instead turn to intransigent separatism. In the Russian case, the concession of heritability did not lead to feudalization: uniquely (Blum 1961, p. 188), the connection between landholding and service to the state was preserved throughout and beyond the evolution of absolutism. But it was not because of the advantage conferred on the role of tsar so much as on the roles of the reconstituted nobility; and on no interpretation can this be claimed to have been adaptive for the society as a whole. The cooperation of the nobility was secured less by the prestige which attached to a successful military or administrative career than by the direct control of the output of heritable estates worked by enserfed labourers denied their freedom of movement; and when, in the nineteenth century, the tsars sought to implement reforms which seemed to them and their advisers in the interests of the society as a whole, they were much less well able to do so than the post-Meiji rulers of what had been a relatively less 'absolutist' and more residually 'feudal' Japan.

In this sense, accordingly, it might seem plausible to argue not only that the Meiji Restoration *was* adaptive for Japanese society as a whole but that it has therefore to be explained in those terms. After all, its intended purpose was to enable Japan to catch up with the more powerful societies of the West, and it succeeded. By comparison with Russia, Japan's industrialization prior to the First World War was not only much more thoroughgoing but much less dependent on foreign capital, and it was Japan's defeat of Russia in 1904 which signalled to the world that Western hegemony was no longer what it had been when Commodore Perry sailed into Edo Bay in 1853. But the adaptation to exogenous pressure was by and for the rulers of Japan, not their subjects. For many of their subjects, the changes of practices and therefore roles were both under compulsion and against their interests as they saw them. However much specialists in Japanese history may disagree about the extent to which the samurai cooperated in their transformation into industrial managers or the peasants maintained or increased their output of rice in response to inducements rather than sanctions, there is no dispute about the social distance between dominant and subordinate roles. If evaluation is at issue, it may or may not be demonstrable that the first generation or two of the Japanese proletariat suffered more from industrialization than their counterparts in the mills of nineteenth-century England. But to explain it in terms of adaptation *by them* would be to take a symptom for a cause. The 'success' is the success of those who had retained the power of the Tokugawa élite and carried through the modernization of their society without surrendering it.

But what (it might be objected) if exogenous pressure is such as to force the entire society into a drastic transformation of both structure and culture if it is to survive at all? Is not this the kind of adaptation to a changed environment for which a homeostatic model of self-equilibration of the total system is the appropriate one? To these questions, the answer is that although any adjustment of a society's practices in response to external threat (or opportunity) is – given that its institutions are all to some degree interdependent – self-equilibrating by definition, the concept has no explanatory value in this context. It merely restates the question why self-equilibration takes place as and where it does.

As an extreme example of the need for drastic adaptation in response to overwhelming exogenous pressure, consider the responses of the North American Indians of the Great Lakes and St Lawrence and Hudson basins to the arrival of the English and French. The Europeans brought with them to societies wholly unprepared for them firearms, disease, Christianity and a voracious demand for beaver pelts. Such was the competition between English and French settlers on the one side and the different Indian societies on the other that the pressure was intense on all the Indian societies not only to switch from horticulture to fur-trapping but to discard their traditional ritual practices and to engage in progressively fiercer warfare with one another. Kinship roles, which were pervasive among them all, underwent radical changes of function. Smaller family units set off to find their own hunting territories; men left their families for longer and longer periods; prisoners taken in wars with other tribes were adopted as replacements for those killed; and kin-based leagues like the Iroquois became semi-states in which war rather than ritual dictated the allocation of power among the quasi-governmental roles.* Some, like the Huron, gained initially from European contact only to be later destroyed by smallpox and defeat in war. Some migrated. Some survived by siding with the English against the French, or *vice versa*. It explains nothing to say that those that did survive did so by successful adaptation of the society as a whole to its changed environment. The adaptation, where it occurred, was by the carriers of mutant or recombinant practices which enabled *them* to retain the economic, ideological or coercive power which attached to their roles

* Much of this is usefully summarized by Wolf (1982, Ch. 6), who does not, however, cite the study by Martin (1979) of the ideological response of the Micmac who (in Martin's view) were enabled to participate vigorously in the fur trade because and only because they blamed the beavers for the epidemics brought by the Europeans and were thereby freed from their traditional inhibitions about killing them.

and thus ensure that their institutional catchment area was not, as it were, swamped by the power of the European intruders or a rival Indian society in league with them.

What is more, the notion of homeostatic adaptation by the society as a whole ignores the concomitant costs of changes as drastic as these. 'Cost' here has nothing to do with value-judgements about whether the change is for the better or the worse: if you regard the fur-trade as wicked, the intensified warfare as deplorable, the Christian missionaries as hypocritical and exploitative, and the French and English settlers as predatory and callous, that is irrelevant to the assessment of the causes of the change in the mode of distribution of power. In a substantive theory of social selection, 'costs' are diminutions of the power attaching to the roles in question, and the roles may be either those of the members of subordinate systacts at whose expense the incumbents of the dominant roles successfully adopt the mutant or recombinant practices or those of the apparent winners who maintain their systactic location for a period only to fall victim to longer-term consequences by which their interests are undermined. The stablility re-established after the evolution to Augustan absolutism, or Russian serfdom, or Japanese industrialization 'from above', or North American fur-trading under European dominance may have done more than depress the location of subordinate roles and systacts. It may also have generated a heightened sense of relative deprivation among their successive incumbents which might find collective expression at some later date when other mutant or recombinant practices had emerged of which the Roman legionaries, the Russian serfs, the Japanese proletarians or the impoverished Indian horticulturalists could turn out to be carriers to their own advantage in their own turn.

§3. What then of the notion of social evolution itself? Evolution is more than qualitative change: it is change in some definable direction. But it must not be equated with progress in either of the two senses to which it was tied by nineteenth-century evolutionary sociologists who, for all the other irreconcilable differences between them, shared an unquestioned presupposition that evolution was not only change for the better but change in the direction of a predetermined goal. Only when both these presuppositions have been discarded without trace is it possible to construct a theory of social evolution properly analogous, but not reducible, to the theory of the evolution of species by natural selection.

There is, to be sure, nothing to prevent practising sociologists from defining a change in a society's practices and institutions as for the better (or worse) by whatever criterion they choose. But the change in question will be no better explained if they do. Even a theory which holds that human history is the working-out of a master plan designed by an all-wise deity still leaves its protagonists with the task of formulating hypotheses about the causes of the Fall of Rome, the Industrial Revolution and the rest which are testable against the evidence of the historical and ethnographic record. The more insidious presupposition is that, as one of Spencer's commentators puts (and endorses) it, 'Social evolution, in any precise sense, is only appropriate when we really are justified in assuming that a particular outcome is necessary' (Peel 1971, p. 257). But this is simply not so. Evolution is, by definition, movement away from rather than towards. With hindsight, no doubt, it can be seen as change towards whatever has in fact evolved thus far. There can be no dispute that the industrial societies of the nineteenth and twentieth centuries exhibit a heterogeneity of roles and a complexity of organization which far transcends that of the hunting and gathering bands. Nor can it be doubted that they stand at the end of a sequence from less to more heterogeneity and complexity which, even if randomly initiated and sporadically interrupted, proceeds nonetheless via identifiable causes to demonstrable effects. But it is not a teleological seqeuence determined by properties of the end-state. Given the potential for variation in social behaviour inherent in the biological inheritance of the human species, the interaction in their roles of the members of different systacts and societies with their environment and each other will inevitably confer selective advantages on some rather than others because of the function of the practices which constitute their roles in the pre-existing distribution of the means of production, persuasion and coercion. But there is no final *dénouement*, and no purpose at work other than the motives and plans of the individual agents who are seeking changes which they can only to a limited extent either control or foresee.

The major shifts of mode in which this process periodically results come about only when there is a displacement of previous institutions sufficiently radical for it to be evident that the society's structure and culture have now to be differently explained. Where the shift is gradual and, as often, initially confined to a limited geographical or institutional area, it is possible for different modes of production, persuasion and coercion alike to coexist within the boundaries of what is nevertheless a single society. In such contexts, it is the articulation (to use the Marxian term) of the different modes which needs to be analyzed correctly. We have seen already that the same institution or role may perform a very different function in different societies; and likewise when, within the same society, institutions and roles characteristic of different modes are found together, their mutual interaction may produce very different outcomes. In particular, it is essential to distinguish the genuine hybrid, whose capacity for stable reproduction depends on the mutually reinforcing effect of practices that in other contexts would be competitive with one another, from the transitional society in which the mutant or recombinant practices confer an advantage on their carriers that sooner or later compels the practices which constituted the hitherto pervasive roles and central institutions to give way.

To illustrate in more detail how the competitive selection of practices generates an evolutionary shift which the agents who are its carriers cannot possibly have planned in advance, let me revert to the example of the 'hoplite revolution' in Archaic Greece (Salmon 1977; cf. Cartledge 1977, pp. 21–4). Clearly, the mere fact that new forms of body-armour have been devised and manufactured which give a decisive advantage to infantrymen fighting in close formation need not by itself bring about any change in the systactic structure. But in the conditions which obtained at the time, rising population, accompanied and reinforced by a switch from stock-rearing to arable farming (Snodgrass 1980, pp. 35–6), brought about near-continuous warfare among emerging proto-states in close geographical proximity. There was thus a need for more troops at the same time as there were more potential recruits from outside the dominant aristocratic families motivated to fight in defence of their own homes and farms. If, at that stage, they had been content with the unequal distribution of power between the aristocracies and themselves, it would still have been possible for the change in armour and tactics to have made no further difference. But there is evidence in the literary sources for a mounting sense of relative deprivation among smaller proprietors whose modest but increasing wealth was not matched by a corresponding political influence or social prestige.* In Hesiod's Boeotia, the smallholder wronged by the verdict of corrupt *basileis* could only hope that supernatural misfortune would overtake them in punishment (*Works and Days*, lines 219–24). But in Corinth under the government of the Bacchiad clan, there were enough

* It may be relevant to cite as a descriptive touch the sentiment which Plato later put into Socrates' mouth on behalf of a poor, fit, sunburnt, hoplite fighting alongside a fat, pampered, rich one: 'people like that are only so rich because the poor are too cowardly to have a go at them' (*Republic* 556d).

discontented arms-bearing subjects for them to be able to mount the necessary support for a successful *coup d'état* by an ambitious usurper.

There is no suggestion in all this that the first non-aristocratic hoplites were consciously seeking a redistribution of power in their favour as a consequence of a new style of warfare. There is no trace in the sources of any organized secession such as that which led to the creation of the role of *tribunus plebis* in Rome. Nor, equally, was the hoplite role deliberately created by would-be tyrants of aristocratic origin. Hoplite organization was a necessary condition of tyranny, not the other way round. The mutant practices which emerged in the wake of a technical innovation created a new political-cum-military role which gave the arms-bearing citizen-farmer of non-aristocratic origin a common systactic interest against both the aristocratic clans or clientèles on the one side and the propertyless labourers, vagrants and dependents on the other. That the resulting 'revolution' should more often lead initially to tyranny than to oligarchy is simply a reflection of the lack of collective systactic consciousness among a group or category which had yet to formulate its own constitutional demands or put forward its own spokesmen or leaders. But once it did, tyranny became the exception rather than the rule,* and the way was open for the evolution of the *poleis* of the Classical period. For all the differences between them, these *poleis* varied only as sub-types of a common mode whose defining characteristic was, as we have already seen, the domination by an adult male militia of a non-combatant, non-citizen and more or less servile workforce within a consciously anti-monarchical ideology of local patriotism.

If unpredictable innovations leading in this way to unforeseeable institutional changes are particularly favourable examples against which to test the theory of competitive selection of practices, it might be objected that a more exacting test is furnished by societies where a change of mode does *not* result despite overt and conscious competition between contending systacts whose members are fully aware of what is at stake. But the theory stands up against examples of this kind equally well. An obvious case is Byzantium over the centuries between the reign of Heraclius and the collapse, under exogenous pressure, in 1204. Interpretation of the period is controversial among specialists not least

* Except in Sicily, where tyranny survived longer for reasons which continue to be disputed among specialists: the extent to which it is to be explained by exogenous pressure from neighbouring Carthage rather than internal *stasis* is hard to disentangle, but given the combination of the two there were, as Finley (1968, p. 76) says of Syracuse, 'many who were ready to accept the strong-man appeal'.

because of the limitations of the sources for certain important processes and events. But the changes in Byzantium's central institutions can be better explained as an oscillation between a stronger and weaker absolutism in response to the exigencies of personality and circumstance than as a progressive decline from a strong monarchy drawing troops and taxes from formally free allodialists* to a decentralization of power into the hands of magnates who not only dominate their own dependent peasantry but enjoy both fiscal and juridical immunity for themselves. There was, during the eleventh century in particular, a fierce struggle for power between the military and bureaucratic factions within the aristocracy (*to stratiōtikon* vs. *to politikon*). But the great families were anti-imperial rather than separatist (Vryonis 1959, p. 162): they sought influence within, not independence of, the institutions of monarchy. Immunities were granted at various times and for various reasons, but they were rarely total except for members of the imperial family or 'a few highly favoured monasteries' (Angold 1984, p. 68; cf. Svoronos 1966, p. 15). Peasants frequently placed themselves under the patronage of powerful landlords in order to be protected from extortionate tax-collectors, but the state never surrendered its juridical rights or its right to levy troops. There was no *seigneurie banale* (Patlagean 1975, p. 1389).

Pronoias were, admittedly, granted in the twelfth century by the Comneni. But the number attested in the sources before the collapse of 1204 is fairly small; and in any case, they can be interpreted as a device to secure cheap troops and integrate the magnates into the institutions of the state rather than a forced concession of the means of coercion in localities where the magnates were strong and the emperor weak.† It is true that the power of the state declined after the death of Basil II in 1025, when the story becomes one of incompetent rulers, falling population, court intrigue, ethnic divisions in the provinces, and the unreliability of foreign mercenaries. But it was a decline within the same

* A non-specialist can comment only at his own peril on the quality of the sources. But I find it difficult to see that the seventh-century 'Farmer's Law' (Ashburner 1910, 1912) can sustain all the inferences drawn from it by Ostrogorsky (1968, pp. 135–7). If there were communities of freeholding peasants (*georgoi*) paying taxes directly to the state, they will only have been on the sort of newly colonized territory that, as Ostrogorsky concedes, the 'Farmer's Law' has evidently in view.

† Herrin (1975) documents the failure of the central government to maintain its power in the theme of Hellas and Peloponnesos in the late twelfth century, but shows that although 'both military and civilian authorities transformed their appointed roles', the ecclesiastical administration (within which roles were occupied for longer) continued to function as before: in a manner reminiscent of Merovingian Gaul, churchmen filled the political vacuum (pp. 225, 258).

mode of the distribution of power. After a good deal of to-and-fro, the only main systactic change was that the location of the military aristocracy was higher at the end of it than the beginning. Practices which might, in other contexts, have led to the evolution of different central institutions led in the Byzantine case to an oscillation which was neither the cyclical outcome of irreconcilable contradictions nor the achievement by the governing élite of a stable equilibrium on its own terms. It was a reflection of a balance of power between monarchs and magnates within which mutant or recombinant practices functioned partly to the advantage of the one and partly to that of the other. In a context such as this, the theory of competitive selection explains the survival – however improbable it may have seemed at the time – of traditional institutions just as well as it does a cumulative evolution which brings about an irresistible shift of mode.

§4. There is, however, a different route which evolution can follow: *fission*. Sometimes, as we have seen, a society divides into two in an amoeba-like fashion without any change in the mode of the distribution of power in either. But at other times, fission is the consequence of the localized appearance of mutant or recombinant practices and thereby novel roles and institutions which are so far incompatible with those of the rest of the society that the members of the dominant systact in the anomalous area come to feel that they have no choice but to secede.

A familiar and intensively studied example is the nineteenth-century United States of America. We have noticed already that the Yankee merchant, the Southern planter and the Western homesteader occupied totally different institutional as well as geographical worlds. But it was the South which seceded. Whether or not secession could have been avoided by the adoption of different political tactics, specialists of all schools seem agreed that slavery was, in broad terms, the reason for it. But it became so only because of a divergence between the institutions of North and South much more radical than would have been conceivable to the makers of the Constitution of 1789 or, indeed, predictable by reference to differences of culture or structure (Pessen 1980): for all their differences in outlook, climate, ecology, population density, urbanization, railroad mileage, commercial productivity and above all racial balance, both were prosperous, capitalist, stratified, still predominantly rural oligarchies neither of which permitted social mobility into their élites of their Black members. The imbalance between them was that less than 2% of the population of the North was Black (and relatively few of these slaves) whereas one-third of the population of the South was Black (and of these only 5% were free). In this context, the evolution of slave-worked plantations as opposed to family farms and wage-worked industry led to a conflict of political and ideological interests out of all proportion to a difference in wealth which was as yet by no means overwhelmingly in favour of the North. It was not that in the colonial period the Yankee merchants dissociated themselves from slavery as an institution, but that their interest in slaves was as commodities rather than labourers: they 'entered with zest' (Franklin 1967, p. 103) the lucrative three-way trade. But ecology, the cotton gin and England's seemingly insatiable demand for as much cotton as the planters could grow tied the Southern economy to slavery within a political framework which explicitly conceded to the Southern states 'dominion of property' on their own terms.

Both the profitability of the slave plantations and the degree of brutality characteristic of the relations between masters and slaves are strenuously debated among specialists of rival schools. But there is no reason to suppose that there were any internal contradictions in the structure and culture of the South which would render the 'peculiar institution' inherently unstable. The large plantations, where slaves were most highly concentrated, were profitable enough; the ideology of the slaveowners was impervious to abolitionist argument; the means of coercion were firmly in White hands; and systematic breeding guaranteed the demographic reproduction of the system even after the supply of imported Africans began to be checked at source. What had seemed to the constitution-makers of the 1780s a matter of local difference which was not to be allowed to stand in the way of a common commitment against the threat of social upheaval led to an evolution of institutions so divergent that there was no alternative between secession from and suppression by the North.

The example of the American South serves also as a reminder of the further point that societal boundaries are never to be taken as given: social evolution takes place within institutional catchment areas whose connections and overlaps are themselves affected by it and may or may not coincide with frontiers established by custom or law. Scotland is for this purpose an even more illuminating example, since it had been a relatively homogeneous, albeit violent, society in the later Middle Ages, yet became, after its formal unification with the English Crown, more deeply divided between Highlands and Lowlands than ever. As late as Johnson's and Boswell's 'Highland jaunt' in the 1770s – a generation, that is, after the Battle of Culloden – Johnson could still speak of the 'Southern inhabitants' of Scotland as knowing no more of the condition of the Highlands and Islands than of Borneo or Sumatra. Yet this would have been no more predictable at the time when James VI of Scotland became James I of England than would have been the American Civil War at the time when George Washington became President of the United States.

In Scotland, two increasingly divergent modes of the distribution of power evolved on either side of a line which was not only geographical but linguistic. The systactic structure of Highland society in the fifteenth century had not been markedly different from Lowland: 'It is an old platitude to state that the Highlands were organized in clans, but it is more difficult to define the practical differences between their society and that of the late medieval Lowlander' (Smout 1969, p. 41).* But as the Lowlands evolved in the direction of relative commercial prosperity, firmer government (backed by a more professional soldiery), slightly more efficient farming methods and the emergence of a class of merchants and burgesses in increasingly populous towns, Highland society was left with the clan as its central institution in an ecological environment as conducive to poverty as to lawlessness. Where the vertical tie of chief to clansman (fictitious as it might be) continued to be pervasive, the interest of the chiefs lay more in the number of men on whom they could call than in the profitability of their lands, and the interest of the clansmen lay more in the strength of their claim to subsistence than in their potential for horizontal alliance with their fellow-crofters elsewhere. Economically, the threat of crop-failure and starvation reinforced the dependence of tenants on the benevolence of their chiefs; coercively, the continuance of raids and feuds reinforced the military roles of chiefs and clansmen alike; ideologically, the traditional deference on which the chiefs were able to draw was reinforced by the continuance of pagan beliefs in supernatural influence. In one sense, there could be no dispute that the mid eighteenth-century Highlands were a part, and an inescapably subordinate part, of the United Kingdom of Great Britain and Northern Ireland. But what did that mean to a Gaelic-speaking, cattle-stealing, war-making clansman in a distant Highland glen whose chief still had the power to assign him his land, arrange his marriage and order him to his death in battle? The evolution of Scottish society is explicable only by reference to separate institutional catchment areas which, even if actual fission was out of the question after 1745, differed so markedly in the selective pressures at

* Cf. *ibid.*, p. 43: 'James VI legislated against anarchy in the two areas as though they were an identical problem, and Privy Council referred to both Highlanders and Lowlanders quite indiscriminately as "clannit".'

work within them that their practices and therefore their constituent roles were far less like one another than those of many pairs of juridically autonomous societies much more remote from one another in both time and place.

§5. It follows from all this that the question 'what causes social evolution?' can be a good deal more difficult to answer in practice than it may have appeared in Chapter 1. Invocation of the notion of competitive selection of practices is entirely valid as far as it goes. But it leaves it to be specified just how the selection comes about, and in just what sense, therefore, the various processes by which it does are 'the' causes of any particular shift from one mode or sub-type of the distribution of power to the next. To be sure, the emergence of mutant or recombinant practices is always critical. But they emerge in a context of initial conditions which are themselves changing, so that the competitive advantage which they at first confer may not merely be modified but subsequently disappear altogether. What is more, a novel role may equally plausibly be explicable by reference to an anterior event, process or state of affairs which was of itself contingently sufficient. Thus, in the example which I used in Section 3, the 'hoplite revolution' in Archaic Greece could be said to have been caused either by the design of the body-armour which made disciplined infantrymen standing shoulder to shoulder the most effective fighting force or by the rise in population which intensified the warfare in which the adoption of hoplite tactics was adaptive for the rulers of proto-states unwilling to surrender their independence or expose their newly assarted ploughlands to annual plunder and destruction. In the evolution of these societies, the role of hoplite was crucial because and only because certain practices which it carried were, in that particular context, characteristics of it on which the pressures of competitive selection came to bear.

The capacity of the same practices to produce dissimilar and even contradictory effects in different anterior conditions is, accordingly, a perennial difficulty. But the solution lies in every case in establishing what it is that a selected practice has been selected *for*. From this perspective, the example of sharecropping, whose institutional context, as we saw in Section 8 of Chapter 2, ranges all the way from the exploitative *latifundium* through the cooperative village community to the dependence of incapacitated landowners on able-bodied tenants, is a particularly instructive one. The practice can be defined straightforwardly enough: an owner of cultivable land agrees to make it available to a supplier of labour in return for a fixed proportion of the output. The terms of the contract may, however, vary in a number of significant details – the size of the landlord's share, the degree of supervision by the landlord, the obligation (or not) to provide seed, tools and draught animals, the timing of payments, the option of renewal, and so on – so that the role of 'sharecropper' is not to be assumed to be identical across time and place even before its different functions are examined. The critical question is: what competitive advantage attaches to its defining practices? And the answer depends on the initial distribution of power between the 'landlord' and 'tenant' roles.

Where land is scarce and labour plentiful, then it is hardly surprising to find that sharecropping contracts are weighted in the landlord's favour, often with further duties on the tenant's part; and if it is preferred to either rent or wage-labour by the landlord, it may be because of the nature of the crop (and perhaps the related need for supervision), the protection which it gives against inflation, or even, as Marc Bloch suggested of French landlords of the *petit bourgeois* type, for the satisfaction of a tie involving personal deference (1966, p. 148). Where, on the other hand, it is labour which for one reason or another is at a premium, able-bodied young men may cultivate a number of fields as sharecropping tenants for landlords who cannot do so for themselves, and sharecropping may be a transitional stage on the way to outright inheritance or possession. In between, where neither role is dominant (and, it may be, the same persons simultaneously occupy both landlord and tenant roles), sharecropping on freely negotiated terms can persist because it is a mutually advantageous device for the pooling of risk.* Moreover, sharecropping also illustrates the selective advantage which may accrue from recombination rather than mutation. Where the landlord is dominant and has access to liquidity which the tenant lacks, he may combine the letting of the land with money lending, thus forcing the sharecropper into a role both homologous and analogous to debt-peonage. Conversely where, as among the Ethiopian Amhara, sharecroppers are often young men who will one day have fields of their own and very few farmers are landless (Hoben 1973, p. 9), combination with the practices of clientage may enable the tenant to secure favourable terms as a condition of political support for the landlord/patron.† The

* A persuasive analysis of its advantages to both roles in an Indian context is given by Bliss and Stern (1982, §§3.2, 5.2) – including the possibility that legal restrictions on tenancy may encourage sharecropping because it can pass as wage-labour (p. 131).

† *Ibid.*, p. 138: 'Tenancy arrangements between an ordinary man and a man of power and authority may have a "political" as well as an economic dimension. The tenant may be the landlord's "follower", visiting him often with small gifts of liquor, beer or livestock, escorting him on journeys and attending church festivals in his retinue. In

incidence of sharecropping, accordingly, can be explained only in terms of the functions performed in different contexts by different variants of a common practice; and these variants can in turn be explained only in terms of the pre-existing distribution of power.

But if a straightforward-looking practice like sharecropping can be selected for a variety of functions which it performs for its carriers and which thereby explain its persistence, so can it function as an evolutionary agent because of different advantages which it may confer in different contexts on what may not have seemed at first sight the more powerful role. Comparison of exploitative sharecropping systems – where, that is, the landlord is in much the stronger bargaining position – shows that the pattern of systactic interests and the sense of relative deprivation to which they give rise may create a context in which institutional evolution comes in the end to favour the previously disadvantaged. Paige (1975) offers a general argument to the effect that decentralized sharecropping systems, particularly where irrigated rice as opposed to cotton is the crop, 'are likely to create a homogeneous landless peasantry with strong incentives for collective action and intense pressure for group solidarity' (p. 62). This statement perhaps needs more qualification than Paige himself gives it. Robertson, in the paper already cited, gives the example of the Kelantan plain in Malaysia where half the population of smallholding farmers both own and sharecrop and 'the advantages [in pooling risk and maximizing land-use] of alternative land/labour contracts are well-known and frequently discussed' (1980, p. 424). But Paige has in mind systems where, as in Southern Vietnam prior to the victory of the North, large absentee landlords extract through local agents crop-shares and interest-payments which are negotiated on terms highly favourable to the landlords because of the competition among landless peasants whose only hope of individual mobility is through gambling (1975, p. 316). The sequence of events by which the landlord class was in due course dispossessed involved, to be sure, exogenous influences: it did not arise directly from the systactic consciousness of the peasantry. But Paige convincingly argues that in the Mekong delta, both the landlord class and the landless peasantry were equally firmly constrained by economic institutions to which they had no alternative. The landlords were as little able to invest

this as in any patron–client tie in Dega Darnot, the landlord gains honor and support while the tenant expects help in court, or protection and an occasional gift. The share of the crop is sometimes less than the customary amount when the "political" aspect of the relationship is predominant. This is particularly true when the field held by the tenant is at a great distance from the landlord's residential parish.'

their capital differently as the peasantry to withdraw their labour, and a zero-sum conflict over crop-shares and land-rights meant that the pressure for collective action characteristic of decentralized rice sharecropping was channelled towards forcible resistance. It was not that the practice of sharecropping was somehow itself turned to the advantage of the landless peasantry, but that given the overall distribution of the means of production, persuasion and coercion, it generated a sense of relative deprivation and related practices of political cooperation among them which turned out to be of decisive advantage when, with outside help, their conflict with the landlords took a revolutionary form.

It is not, however, only as a prelude to revolutionary violence that sharecropping can function as the agent of an evolution in the peasantry's favour. In Central Mexico in the early twentieth century, where the number of *peones acasillados* on the *haciendas* declined as the less well-irrigated lands were increasingly let out to sharecroppers (Brading 1978, pp. 205–6), the process was seen by some observers as a transition to the subdivision of the great estates into independent smallholdings. As Brading points out, the possible effect of market forces on bringing this about was overtaken by the outbreak of the Mexican Revolution, and the evolution of the agrarian institutions of Mexico after 1920 has to be sought in coercive and (to some degree) ideological pressures as much as in economic. But just as sharecropping can be the agent of its own dissolution in a context of acute land shortage, landlord inflexibility and a crop whose cultivation favours systactic cooperation among the cultivators, so can it in a context where self-interested reformism on the landlords' part favours a trend towards either outright sales (if landlords' liquidity is low) or intensified capital investment and wage-labour (if landlords' liquidity is high). The moral to be drawn, once again, is that to understand how sharecropping can function either to dissolve or to preserve the institutions and mode of the distribution of power of which the roles which it defines are a part, it is necessary to analyze the interaction between the level at which selective pressure comes most strongly to bear and the features of a changing context which confer different advantages on one or another of the carriers of the practice at different times.

§6. With that all-important caveat in mind, it may be worth recapitulating the definition of the subject-matter of this volume as I outlined it in Chapter 1. I said there that the study of societies is the study of people in roles, and the study of people in roles the study of the institutional allocation of power; and since power is of three irreducible but interdependent kinds, societies can be modelled as catchment areas of three-dimensional space in which roles are vectors whose relative location is determined by the rules of the institutions made up of them. But this schematic picture has to be qualified still further, since it must allow both for the complications of social mobility and for the continuous operation of selective pressure at more than one simultaneous level.

We have seen already that the reproduction ratios of different systacts can themselves promote or retard a society's evolution in the direction of one rather than another mode or sub-type. But 'structural' mobility, whether involving movement of persons into newly created roles or movement of persons in their roles to a different location along one or more of the three axes of social space, can itself be an agent of evolution. Practices are carried in a double sense. Not merely are they continued in being by the performance of roles by their incumbents, but if those incumbents are at the same time socially mobile, the practices which define their roles are functioning in a changing context which may shift the competitive advantage which they confer from one role (or systact) to another.

For example: the growth in population which appears to have taken place in North-west Europe in the post-Carolingian period contributed to the evolution of a new mode of the distribution of power partly by increasing the number of dependent cultivators available to competing local lords and partly by creating a need and opportunity for new administrative and mercantile roles at the local centres of power.* But it could not be said that the net increase in entrants into adult roles resulting from higher fertility and lower mortality was itself 'the' cause of a change in the mode of the distribution of power or even of economic growth. The change occurred because and only because of the interaction between social mobility and a set of institutions in which competitive advantage was changing in favour of an emerging seignorial systact with a monopoly of the means of coercion. Only then could there evolve a mode in which semi- or proto-states based on warfare and plunder gave way to weakly centralized kingdoms or principalities legitimated by the Church, in which warfare was directed outwards (Duby 1984, Ch. 12) and the landholding warrior systact was supported

* Cf., e.g., Musset (1959, p. 298) on the *chapelains ducaux* and *trésoriers épiscopaux* whose roles enabled them to acquire land, stone houses and seignorial rights and to become barons or bishops' vassals; and on the geographical flow from villages and small towns of recruits to the roles of artisan, notary and government tenant – 'careers where skill counted for more than capital', see Herlihy (1972–3, p. 646).

by a surplus generated partly from the labour of an enserfed peasantry and partly by trade and artisan production.

The inverted pyramid can, accordingly, still be taken as the model for social structure. But the roles which define any actual society have to be seen not just as either vectors or vacancies but also as moving points which cluster together at various and shifting locations and which, moreover, have the properties that they can not only increase up to any number at the same location but be occupied by persons moving from other points whether or not they are at the same time in movement themselves. Numbers, as such, can be either a strength or a weakness. Inspection of the structure tells nothing by itself about whether size confers competitive advantage. Indeed, it is possible that, as in the sharecropping example, an increase in the number of landless labourers in a society where cultivable land is in short supply may at the same time weaken them economically, strengthen them coercively and divide them ideologically.

When, therefore, we move from studying the workings of a society's institutions with a view to discovering what are the practices and roles which keep it as relatively stable as it is to studying the selective pressures which are causing it to evolve in whatever direction it happens to be going, it is all the more clearly impossible to divorce structure from culture. The structure has still to be modelled as such if the theory of competitive selection is to be interpreted in testable form. But there need, as it were, to be superimposed on the pattern of systactic size and location and social mobility the institutional ties between role and role and the nature of the rules which govern them. Only then will it be possible to relate the changes in structure observed over a given period to the pressures (or opportunities) which determine what practices are selected for what advantages which they confer on what roles.

Enough has (I hope) now been said in general terms about the processes whereby social evolution comes about before the theory of competitive selection of practices can be more stringently tested against the historical and ethnographic record. The variety and complexity of human societies being what it is, all that can be done in what is already bound to be the longest chapter in this volume is to examine as briefly as practicable some of the societies which I have already cited together with a very few others in order to see how well the theory explains their evolution from one mode or sub-type of the distribution of power to the next. In no sense, therefore, is this Chapter an attempt at *Weltgeschichte*. But even if the examples which are chosen in what follows are the right ones for my purpose and the theory is at least provisionally validated by being tested against them, a great deal of further elaboration and refinement will still be called for. However persuasive the arguments of this Chapter may be, the potential volume of both theoretical and empirical literature to which they could give rise is – as the volume of literature on the theory of natural selection already suggests – awesome.

REGRESSIONS AND CATASTROPHES

§7. It is a familiar objection to theories of social evolution that even if they do not presuppose a beneficent progress towards a predetermined end-state they are contradicted by the numerous examples of regression, decline and collapse in the historical and ethnographic record. But the objection is easily met. Change to an earlier mode or sub-type of the distribution of power is to be explained no differently from change to a novel one: the answer lies, as always, in the reasons for which competitive advantage attaches to different roles and systacts and different practices become the objects of selection. If, according to your values, evolution in reverse is to be deplored as a relapse into barbarism, degeneracy and an inferior (as well as simpler) level of organization, that is up to you. But it is evolution all the same. No more than cycles of the kind discussed in Section 16 of Chapter 3 are regressions or even catastrophes evidence against the theory of social evolution just outlined.

Catastrophes, indeed, are as a rule of less theoretical interest than regressions. Puzzling as they may be, resolution of the puzzle is likely to be more in the nature of, so to speak, a detective story than a crucial experiment. As with the extinction of a species, the destruction of a society can come about from a variety of reasons which pose no theoretical difficulty in themselves: invasions, plagues, famines and earthquakes are, where they occur, all too straightforward in their effects. The difficulty is apt to be to settle which of several possible causes, each of which would have been sufficient by itself, was in fact decisive, and the most intriguing examples are those where, like the prehistoric cities of the Indus Valley or the palaces of Minoan Crete or the ceremonial precincts of Mayan Mesoamerica, the inferences on which the hypotheses to be tested are based are archaeological rather than sociological. It is (I hasten to add) no less of an achievement to settle the question whether it was earthquake or invasion which destroyed the Cretan palaces of the period known as Middle Minoan IIB than to settle which of the practices of the Karāva explains their rise to, and retention of, their élite location in the Sri Lankan social structure. But only the second, not the first, raises questions which can test and extend the theory of social evolution through the competitive selection of practices.

The qualification needs, however, to be added that in cases of catastrophe it may be the relation of natural to social causes which needs elucidation. Thus, the sudden collapse of Mayan civilization in the ninth century A.D. has been held by some specialists to have resulted from a revolt of peasant commoners against the monument-producing élite (Hamblin and Pitcher 1980). Given the food shortage which can be semi-deductively inferred from the evidence of malnutrition in the skeletons of the Late Classic period, such a revolt would have accelerated the rapid depopulation of the ceremonial centres for which the archaeological evidence is conclusive. But although a definitive explanation of the collapse has both to establish the correct temporal sequence and to assign the correct causal priority to soil-erosion, epidemic disease, hyper-exploitative extraction of tribute, unproductive temple-building, internal conflicts over land, and military intrusion from (perhaps) Yucatan, to achieve one will not necessarily advance our understanding of how societies evolve from one mode or sub-type of the distribution of power to another.

No doubt the Mayan collapse was in part the consequence of practices which had been adaptive for the élite during the evolution of the society to its 'classic' form, when a sharply stratified structure was dominated by a hereditary élite, but which ceased to be so as the environment changed. But catastrophic changes are, by definition, those that overwhelm the total set of a society's practices and institutions, even if some members of the population survive to restore them or to establish new ones. No role or systact emerges as winner when the whole society has been pushed over the brink of collapse. It is true that, as I emphasized in Section 18 of Chapter 3, there are practices and therefore roles which can be identified and reported even under conditions amounting to anarchy or chaos. But when an entire population has fled, its armies have disintegrated, its food supplies have been exhausted and its temples and their precincts have been left for the jungle to overgrow them, social evolution has not so much been arrested as obliterated. The pioneers who moved down from the North and created the institutions of the 'Postclassic' Mayan era may have brought with them practices transmitted to them by survivors of the collapse. But they were not returning to the society which had collapsed: the roles which had defined it had ceased to exist.

To test and extend the theory of competitive selection of practices, it is the steady regressions and slow declines whose study is more rewarding. Two kinds need broadly to be distinguished. In the first, evolution is regressive in the sense that a dominant systact surrenders its location under pressure and the mode of the distribution of power reverts to what it was before: these are the cases of what in one context can be labelled 'refeudalization' and in another 'rebeduinization'. In the second, evolution is regressive in the sense that a dominant systact still holds its location, but only by adopting practices and thereby institutions whose effect is to reverse the evolution of the mode through which its dominance was established in the first place. The two are by no means exclusive. Indeed, the collapse of the Maya may be a case in point if the explanation lies in the combination of peasant rebellion and self-defeating extraction of a diminishing economic surplus by an élite determined at all costs to preserve the ceremonial status on which its legitimacy rested. But the distinction is an important one. Where the decisive competitive advantage attaches to practices of which subordinate roles and systacts are the carriers, the course of the society's evolution will be very different from where the advantage attaches to practices which are initially adaptive for the élite.

§8. This distinction once made, it may be instructive to look a little more closely at post-Carolingian Europe. For the reasons summarized in Section 20 of Chapter 3, it seems agreed among specialists that a regression to a larger number of smaller and weaker patrimonial societies was inevitable. Indeed, quite apart from the difficulties posed by poor communications, limited productivity, the lack of trained and reliable administrators and the pressure from Magyars, Saracens and Vikings, the patrimonial empire which Charlemagne had created would in any case have been divided on his death if all his sons had survived. But how in fact did the structure of the West Frankish kingdom evolve as central authority devolved on the nobility of the increasingly independent territorial principalities? The first point to notice is that it was not a usurpation of power so much as a devolution to the incumbents of magnate roles of practices previously attaching to the monarchical role itself. Some practices, admittedly, were usurped rather than conceded. There is, for example, no evidence of Carolingian kings ever deliberately giving away the rights of moneying (McKitterick 1983, p. 335). But the counties and principalities which emerged as autonomous patrimonial proto-states under the later Carolingians did so not under upwardly mobile *caudillos* but under established counts or *marchiones* who, as royal power weakened, subordinated the *missi* to themselves, administered their own justice, built their own castles, and ceased to seek even nominal confirmation by the king of their own grants of lands and immunities to their own *fideles* or their own monasteries and churches (*ibid.*, p. 329).

Given the level of resources available, these practices and roles were the only ones which could so function as to preserve states of any kind in being; and even then, rulers could dominate only a modest geographical area. Hugh Capet and Robert the Pious did not even dominate all the magnates whose territories lay within the boundaries of their diminutive kingdom. The outcome of the dissolution of Charlemagne's empire was thus a recreation across a range of now separate societies of the same problems, on a smaller scale, as he and his successors had faced. But there was one critical difference. The role of vassal, which had been intended to tie both magnates and subordinate office-holders to a thereby more powerful monarchy, now functioned to transfer power over the dependent cultivators on whom the possibility of an economic surplus depended downwards to the viscounts and castellans who thereby, often with the help of marriage into the Carolingian aristocracy (Bouchard 1981), formed the 'new nobility' of France.

The contrasting evolution of post-Carolingian France, Germany and Italy has been intensively studied by specialists in each area.* In Germany, the emergence of 'feudal' institutions on the model of North-west France was (it seems agreed) delayed by the brief success of the Ottonian and Salian monarchs in maintaining a strong central authority. They were, for an initial period, able to sustain the power attaching to their roles through successful military leadership, personal charisma, reliance on the church at local level, the use of non-aristocratic *ministeriales*, the consolidation of royal lands, and the 'steady flow' of disposable wealth from the Harz mines (Leyser 1981, p. 752). But this left magnates and lesser allodialists unsubordinated to the monarchy. There were neither the inducements nor the sanctions which would modify their roles in the direction of personal fealty or salaried or beneficed officialdom, and there were not the potential recruits among lesser administrators or service tenants who might have functioned as analogues to the Russian *pomeshchiks*. As soon, therefore, as the Investiture Contest afforded them the opportunity for a 'deft

* Catalonia is yet another variant sub-type, where after the anarchy of the decades prior to about 1060, the counts of Barcelona were able to impose the role of vassal on both aristocratic lineages and their castle-holding subtenants who now held their lands as fiefs and exercised on the count's behalf rights of *seigneurie banale* over the dependent cultivators (cf. Bonnassie 1975–6, II, p. 780 on the counts' '*utilisation délibérée du système féodo-vassalique comme mode de gouvernement*').

exploitation of the bonds of feudalism' (Barraclough 1972, p. 135), they took it.

In Italy, by contrast, the decentralization of the means of coercion evolved in a quite different direction and with a quite different outcome. The institutional context was one of dispersed landholdings, towns, pervasive commercial roles and the practice of leasing in preference to conditional benefices. It was, therefore, not just that urban élites (including bishops) rather than rural magnates became the carriers of political practices which now devolved on them, thus opening the way for the emergence of the communes and the evolution to a citizen mode of the distribution of power. It was also that 'feudal' tenure gave significant power to lesser landowners. As the public obligations of free men to the state were eroded, the private relations of patronage which increasingly replaced them did not involve the same military roles as in Germany or France (or England). Instead, offices and benefices became the 'unconditional property of individual families' (Wickham 1981, p. 144).

The regional diversity of Italy is such that any generalization has to be carefully qualified. The 'feudalism' which evolved in the Papal States was as different from that imposed by the Normans to the South as from that which emerged in the aftermath of Carolingian domination in the North, where patron and client roles were pervasive and the dominant systacts were the incumbents of whatever roles, ecclesiastical or lay, carried the '*segni tangibili di prevalenza territoriale*' (Tabacco 1980, p. 219). But this very diversity offers scope for quasi-experimental comparisons. In Latium, the fusion of benefice and vassalage came about only *after* the concentration of hitherto dispersed settlements through the process of '*incastellamento*' (Toubert 1973, II, p. 1107), and then at the level of the *boni homines* who held the *castra* from great ecclesiastical landowners like the abbots of the monastery of Farfa (*ibid.*, p. 1124). In a context where population was rising, land-clearance had extended into increasingly mountainous districts, there were no strong cities other than Rome itself, monasteries were being progressively enriched by pious donations, and the land-hunger ('*ingens cupiditas terrarum*') of the lay nobility was making necessary both compact, defensible holdings and reliable military clientèles, the practices of feudalism in its narrower sense were just as adaptive for the ecclesiastical

* Like vassalage, immunity could also function differently according to the pre-existing distribution of power: as observed of post-Carolingian Italy by Drew (1962, p. 196), the roles of lesser immunists did, as intended, function to strengthen the power of the state, but greater immunists became in effect independent rulers themselves.

landowners as they had ever been for Frankish, or were to be for Norman, kings.

The comparative analysis of 'feudalism' has an extensive literature of its own, and the variation in the practices which defined the pervasive roles and central institutions of different 'feudal' societies* in Europe and elsewhere is a topic to which I shall return in more detail in Section 22. But for the understanding of social evolution, the contrast between the subsequent histories of Italy, Germany and France is at least as instructive as the contrast between them in the ninth and tenth centuries. After all, neither Italy nor Germany were reunited into a single society until the nineteenth century, whereas the French kings, improbable as it would have seemed at the time of Hugh Capet's coronation in 987, gradually extended their power over an increasingly (although never completely) integrated nation-state to the point that it became in due course an absolutism to which the other monarchs of Europe all looked as a paradigm. In part, this was achieved by the help of the Church, whose corporate interest lay in the assertion of central authority as against that of local *advocati*, and which underwrote an ideology of royal legitimacy which even magnates who ruled their territories in total independence did not refuse to acknowledge.* But it depended also on the continuance of practices which functioned to strengthen the monarchical role more effectively than many contemporaries (and some later historians) appear to have recognized.

The earlier Capetians were totally dependent on their *fideles* to enforce their writ even in the counties where their legitimacy was unquestioned. But these *fideles* owed the power which attached to their roles directly to the kings: their rank was 'secondary' in the technical sense. The pacts (*convenientiae*) to which the Carolingian kings had been prepared to subscribe were at the same time reaffirmations of the duties owed to them by the *fideles*, including the preservation of the *potestas regia* (Magnou-Nortier 1979, pp. 548–50). Moreover, the roles to which secondary rank attached were for precisely that reason well adapted to re-establishing local control in an area in which the resources available were increasing through population growth and rising agricultural productivity. The role of the *prévot*, in particular, which in some ways anticipates that of the *baillis* to whose importance in the reign of Philippe Auguste I have drawn attention already, had '*quelquechose de bien adapté à la nouvelle conjoncture*' (Lemarignier 1980, p. 242). It would be an

* Cf. Petit-Dutaillis (1936, pp. 8–10) on the strength of local and popular tradition: royal legitimacy was not just a 'myth fostered in the minds of the king, his ministers and a few churchmen'.

exaggeration to suggest that the evolution of the early French monarchy was a case of *reculer pour mieux sauter*. The advantages which it drew from its apparent weakness were more like the case of tenth-century China, which I cited in Section 10 of Chapter 2, where the relatively greater ease with which the Sung were able to re-establish a system of local prefectures after 960 was due in part to the extreme degree of political fragmentation which had followed the fall of the T'ang. But the point to be made is that this sort of resumption of power *can* happen. Practices which devolve upon hitherto subordinate local roles *can* thereby be preserved to the subsequent advantage of central roles which become once again their carriers.

§9. Regression of the other kind, where the same systact or stratum remains dominant, could in theory come about as a conscious choice on the part of its members. Might not an aristocratic warrior élite deliberately disarm and merge with the dependent cultivators from whom its members have previously exacted tribute or plunder, or an absolutist monarch decide that the society over which he or she rules should revert to a feudal or patrimonial mode, or the electors in a liberal-democratic industrial society vote into office a government pledged to dismantle its existing institutions in favour of a loose-knit federation of semi-states economically based on agriculture and local craft production? But no such case is anywhere to be found in the historical or ethnographic (or archaeological) record. The reported cases which need to be explained are where a dominant systact becomes steadily less powerful as a result of its failure to modify the society's practices and institutions in a way which can be seen with hindsight to be necessary to preserve the mode of the distribution of power unchanged. Such regression is no more a refutation of the theory of competitive selection of practices than regression through inability to contain subordinate roles and systacts within the existing structure and culture. But to demonstrate why it is not, let me analyze in a little more detail two examples which have been touched on already: Sparta and Venice.

Sparta's uniquely distinctive sub-type of the 'citizen' mode of the distribution of power did, as I remarked in Section 4 of Chapter 3, break down in the end. But this was not because of a usurpation of Spartiate power by hitherto subordinate *perioikoi* or Helots. Nor was it for the reasons (to be discussed in more detail in Section 12) for which the Greek *polis* turned out, in any and all of its variant forms, to be an evolutionary dead-end. Indeed, Sparta's 'decline' was, if anything, a failure on the part of its rulers to make it the dead-end they wanted it to be. Following the defeat of Athens in the Peloponnesian War and the consequent involvement of Spartiates outside Sparta in the novel role of foreign military governor of 'harmost', Spartan society became exposed to the pressure of just such alien institutions as the makers of its constitution had sought to keep at bay. To contemporary observers like Xenophon, the story was one of moral decay, the wilful neglect of the Lycurgan ideal and the corrupting effects of a new-found love of money. But this is no less misleading than the moralizing account which Sallust and other contemporaries gave of the 'decline' of the Roman Republic. It is true that immediately after the defeat of Athens, the inequalities within the dominant stratum of 'Peers' began to widen. But it was not this in itself which led to its loss of power. There was no Helot uprising – the Messenians seceded only after the Spartan defeat by Thebes at Leuctra in 371 B.C.; and the one attempt at rebellion reported in the sources (Xenophon, *Hellenica* III. 3; cf. Aristotle, *Politics* 1306b) was a failure.

The critical change was, as I briefly mentioned in Section 15 of Chapter 3, demographic. Between the Battle of Plataea and the Battle of Leuctra, the number of Spartiates who could be put into the field had shrunk from 5,000 to 1,000. Aristotle appears to attribute the decline to a law permitting individual estates (*klēroi*) to be given or bequeathed away from natural heirs – a law which, if not spurious, has to be dated somewhere between 404 B.C. and 371 B.C. (Christien 1974). But the shortage of Spartiate manpower had already become critical a generation earlier, as can be semi-deductively inferred both from the heightened concern with which Spartiate casualties in battle were regarded and from the intensified moral pressure brought to bear on those of an age to have children to do so whether within or without marriage. Replenishment of their numbers could only be by birth. No outsiders were admitted, and upward mobility by Helots who had distinguished themselves in battle into the category of *neodamodeis* still fell short of full membership of the dominant élite.

It was because (and only because) of this constraint on numbers that increasing differentiation within the Spartiate stratum was bound to recreate the type of structure which 'Lycurgus' had deliberately abolished. There re-emerged out of the *damos* an aristocratic systact for whom the mutation of practices which followed the defeat of Athens was adaptive at the expense of their fellow 'Peers'. Relaxation or evasion of both the traditional prohibition on the use of money and the traditional rule of inheritance combined to concentrate landholding among fewer families and increase the number of *hypomeiones* unable to pay their dues to the common messes (*syssitia*) (Oliva 1977, p. 177).* It still could not be said that the Spartiates lost power through surrendering it to hitherto subordinate systacts. Nor, despite the defeat at Leuctra, did Sparta cease to be an independent citizen-state. But by the Hellenistic period, the internal structure of the dominant élite had evolved so far in the same direction that there remained, according to Plutarch (*Agis* v.5), only 700 Spartiates of whom 600 had no more than the bare minimum of land enabling them to keep up their *syssitia* dues.† The subsequent attempts by Cleomenes III and Nabis to restore the Lycurgan system required, as they recognized, not merely redistribution of land into equal *klēroi* but the enfranchisement of enough *perioikoi* or Helots to occupy them. Their attempts failed for reasons which had more to do with the pattern of inter-societal relations than with any internal contradiction which doomed them in advance to failure. But even if they had succeeded, it would not have been a recreation of the Lycurgan system in its traditional form. By now, the crucial difference was that the rigorous separation of dominant 'Peers' from subordinate cultivators off whose produce they lived had been comprehensively breached. The practices, ritual or otherwise, which had kept the Helots in subjection could not have been restored, however determined an attempt had been made to do so.

The parallel to the Venetian nobility in the seventeenth and eighteenth centuries is strikingly close. Here, likewise, there was no surrender of power to previously subordinate roles or systacts but only a similar (if not quite so drastic) decline in the number of nobles and a similar reluctance to admit into the dominant élite anyone other than members by birth. The result was that, as with the Spartiates, its capacity to perform its traditional functions was significantly impaired;‡

* It is plausibly conjectured by Christien (1974, p. 217) that the accumulation of land in the hands of the rich came about through the practice of *donatio mortis causa* as a means of extinguishing debt. Cartledge (1979, p. 318) is sceptical about debt but does accept the fact of downward mobility by poorer Spartiates to the role of *hypomeiones* (*ibid.*, p. 316). It may also be that the *hypomeiones* included younger sons who had not inherited a *klēros* (Hooker 1980, p. 117).

† These figures have, no doubt, to be viewed as sceptically as all statistics for societies of the Ancient World drawn from literary sources. But even if Plutarch's 700 is seriously at variance with whatever figure the recording angel would confirm, there is no reason to question the significance of the relative decline.

‡ Georgelin (1978, p. 802) makes the point that '*le lien entre le nombre total des nobles et le déclin politique n'apparaît pas évident*', and it is of course true that the number of officials is not critical in the same way as the number of hoplites. But James C. Davis is surely right to see it as a weakness that 'the core of the ruling class, able and public-spirited nobles who served year-in, year-out in the most important offices, decreased rapidly so that direction of government affairs was no longer always in the hands of experienced and respected statesmen' (1962, p. 104).

and although the system was then overturned from without, not within, it is at least arguable not only that Venice would have put up a much more effective resistance if its nobility had been replenished by capable 'new men' but also that it would, if left to itself, have in due course evolved backwards, so to speak, towards what Weber (1956, II, p. 766) called the '*durchaus stadtkönigliche patrimoniale Charakter*' of the original *Dogenherrschaft*.

Thanks to the 'Golden Book', the numerical decline can be traced with precision. The number of nobles of office-holding age declined from 2,500 in the late fifteenth century to 1,300 in the late eighteenth, despite some emergency recruitment at the time of the Cretan and Morean wars which was done more to raise cash than to replenish noble manpower. The danger which this posed was recognized and deplored by numerous contemporaries. It was not just that ill-qualified incumbents were having to fill important governmental roles, but that the Great Council itself was becoming too small for its disinterested members to hold the constitutional balance between the Council of Ten, the *Quarantie* and the Senate, whose power was therefore becoming dangerously oligarchic. As with Sparta and Rome, there is always the possibility that contemporary observers may be more concerned to evaluate than to explain; and the hypothesis that, value-judgements apart, the decline in numbers of nobles would have weakened the political system of the Republic to the point that the mode of the distribution of power would have become unworkable cannot be validated or falsified since Napoleon took the matter into his own hands in 1797. But the loss of power which did undoubtedly follow to some degree from the loss of numbers is enough, as in the Spartan case, to pose the question: how, when power does not pass to a hitherto subordinate systact which is the carrier of mutant or recombinant practices which function to its advantage, is that loss of power to be explained in terms of the theory of competitive selection?

The answer is that the mutation and recombination of practices which took place *was* to the competitive advantage of the dominant systact in relation to the rest of Venetian society. The decline in its numbers meant a decline both in its own absolute level of resources and in the relative power of the society as a whole in competition with others. But it was not a decline in the sense of a radical compression of social distance between the dominant systact and the rest. Four responses to their changed environment (apart from their increasing unwillingness to accept unremunerative governmental roles) contributed to the fall in the absolute level of the nobles' power: their shift from entrepreneurial to rentier roles;* the increasing tendency for noble sons to enter the Church; their frequent restriction of the marriage of more than one son per generation; and their increasing adoption of the *fideicommissum*. But precisely because of the loss of competitive advantage which Venice had, for other reasons, suffered in inter-societal relations, all four of these responses were adaptive for them. There no longer existed the same opportunities which there had been for noble careers. Riches now depended on conserving family fortunes over successive generations; prestige was now more readily attainable in the Church than through politics for the sons of families not at the very centre of the institutions of government; and the conquest of territory overseas was no longer feasible. As in the Spartan case, the practices selected were those which were advantageous for the roles to which there continued to attach preponderant power, whatever might be the further consequences in terms of resistance to a Theban army under Epaminondas or a French army under Napoleon. The moral to be drawn, therefore, is not that a theory of competitive selection of practices cannot account for regression of this kind just as well as it can for a zero-sum transfer of power to the incumbents of hitherto subordinate roles or systacts. It is that the explanation of the regression is here, as always, to be found in the answer to the question: what is it that the practices seen to emerge and survive are being selected *for*? And in the Venetian case, as in the Spartan, the answer is that practices can be selected for the competitive advantage they confer on a dominant stratum even if they function to the competitive *dis*advantage of the society as a whole at the level of competition with others.

DEAD-ENDS AND TURNING-POINTS

§10. If evolution in reverse poses a problem – but a soluble one – for the theory of competitive selection of practices, so likewise do cases where a society either fails to evolve into a different mode of the distribution of power despite apparent pressure (or opportunity) for it to do so, or does evolve into a different mode despite an apparent lack of the relevant practices or the carriers for them. A *dead-end* is not a symbiotic equilibrium in which, as with nomadic pastoralists who draw as necessary on the output of sedentary agriculturalists, the environment and the existing set of the society's institutions are mutually sustaining;

* This should not be assumed automatically to involve a reduction in income: increasing returns from agricultural investment in the territories of the mainland offset the decline of manufacturing even if, as Georgelin concedes (1978, p. 14), productivity per head was below that of England or Flanders.

it is the continuance of a set of existing institutions within the same mode or sub-type when the environment is changing in a way which, if those institutions do not change too, will cause the society in question to lose so much power relative to others that they cease to be workable. Equally, a *turning-point* is not a mutation or recombination of practices which is adaptive for the dominant élite at the expense of the competitve advantage of the society as a whole; it is a critical transition to a novel mode which significantly augments the total amount of power available to it.

For example: when Winter (1958, p. 165), in contrasting the Amba with the Nuer as extreme sub-types of segmentary systems, says that 'By contrast the Amba system seems to have reached the end of a blind alley', he means that it lacks the potential for the degree not only of political centralization but also of political integration achieved by the Nuer. Where a Nuer tribe might contain up to 45,000 people, in Bwamba the largest group of allied villages seems never to have contained more than 2,000 (*ibid.*, p. 164). Winter's explanation is that the Amba system is constrained by a lineage ideology which not only prohibits the feud within villages which are organized around eponymous maximal lineages but also enjoins exogamy. Among the Nuer, on the other hand, although lineages are likewise exogamous, villages contain members of unrelated lineages. The result is that a dominant lineage within a Nuer village is integrated into a wider political structure and, conversely, that the outbreak of feud is possible within the same segment – which in turn explains why blood payment and the role of the leopard-skin chief are found among the Nuer but have no analogue (and still less a homologue) among the Amba.

The constraint on the Amba system can equally well (in accordance with the argument of Section 15 of Chapter 3) be viewed as a contradiction – Winter, indeed, is prepared to call it a 'fundamental' one (*ibid.*, p. 151) – between the need for allies and the need for wives. But from an evolutionary perspective, the conjunction of practices is not one which makes it impossible for reproduction of the existing institutions to continue for successive generations, but one which makes it impossible for them to adapt to a requirement, if and when there is one, for the greater degree of centralization and integration exemplified by the Nuer. It is a dead-end – or, if you prefer, a 'blind alley' – not because its evolution has, for the moment, come to a halt, but because it cannot be restarted, even under pressure, without 'radical new principles of organization' (*ibid.*, p. 165).

Similarly, 'turning-points' occur when a mutation or recombination of practices which under other initial conditions might have no effect on the society's transition from one mode or sub-type of the distribution of power to another turns out, in the particular context, to be decisive. I discussed in Chapter 3 of Volume 1 the decisive effect of the introduction of European firearms into nineteenth-century Madagascar (Maurice Bloch 1977). Given the initial conditions, it enabled the ruler of one particular semi-state to effect the transition to statehood and the unification of the whole geographical territory into a single kingdom. But there are any number of cases where firearms, although they have modified a society's practices and roles to some degree, have neither altered its mode of the distribution of power nor given it a decisive competitive advantage against the neighbouring societies with which it is, or has been, at war. True, the example of Madagascar can be paralleled in this respect from West Africa (Kea 1971, p. 201; Wilks 1975, p. 110) or Fiji (Ward 1972, pp. 110–11). But there are other cases where the introduction of firearms merely re-establishes an equilibrium between the contestants. Artillery, for example, although it was decisive in augmenting the power of European societies over those of Asia, did not constitute a turning-point in the competition of the European societies with one another. 'It helped to raise the price of warfare and the efficiency of the state, and certainly entrepreneurs' profits' (Braudel 1973, p. 294); but it cannot be said to have accelerated more than marginally the evolution of the societies of Europe in the direction of industrial capitalism, towards which they were, unbeknownst to any of their members, already on the way.

There is, perhaps, a sense in which turning-points are more easily explained than dead-ends. I have cited already a number of examples where mutant practices have an importance for the subsequent evolution of the society in question out of all proportion to their first, immediate effect; and the carriers are easy enough to identify with hindsight, whether in the field of production and trade, of secular or religious ideology, or of political or military institutions and roles. But even with hindsight, it is likely to be harder to see why something didn't happen than why it did. If, despite the pressures (or opportunities) for change, no change occurs, it must be because retention of the existing set of practices functions to the advantage of the incumbents of those roles to which there attaches the preponderance of power in the relevant dimension. If, as in Southern Italy, *latifundia* continue to be unproductively worked by impoverished, sharecropping tenants on very short leases, it must be because these practices sustain the location of dominant landlords; if, as in Ming China, intellectual and scientific enquiry is stultified despite there being a clerisy willing and able to pursue it, it must be because the ideological hegemony of the dominant status-group is threatened by it; if, as in Mamluk Egypt, military tactics and techniques are reproduced without modification in the face of superior tactics and techniques which have evolved elsewhere, it must be because the ruling élite would risk loss of control of the means of coercion by adopting them. But such claims have to be demonstrated, not assumed. It has to be shown *why* the competitive advantage of the dominant systact would have been diminished if practices for which carriers were at hand and which would have functioned to the competitive advantage of the society as a whole had not been deliberately inhibited by those in a position to do so.

The examples examined in more detail in the following Sections have, accordingly, been chosen for the difficulties which they pose; but the difficulties are of different kinds. As examples of dead-ends I have chosen, first, the Melanesian 'big-men' and second, the Classical Greek *poleis*. As examples of turning-points I have chosen, first, the formation of states in Archaic Greece and second, the evolution of industrial capitalism in England. The first two are difficult because it is impossible to demonstrate conclusively that an evolution which fails to happen was, given the initial conditions, literally impossible. The second two are difficult because it is impossible conclusively to assign relative importance to different practices all of which contributed to an eventual outcome which their carriers neither intended nor foresaw. But all four are consistent with the theory of competitive selection of practices; none invalidates it; and such quasi-experimental contrasts as they permit support it.

§11. I have already, in Sections 9 and 19 of Chapter 3, discussed the difference between the role of the big-man, whose location depends on a continuing exercise of personal prowess, and that of a chief, to which there attaches power independently of the energy, skill or generosity of the particular incumbent. But even within Melanesia the range of variation is wider than the ideal-typical account would suggest. The practices which define the big-man's role do indeed impose the constraint – or contradiction – that the more he accumulates, the more he must give away and therefore the more he is at risk of alienating the followers on whom his power depends if he fails to do so. But there are, despite this, wider political functions which incumbents of the role can sometimes perform. Healey (1978, pp. 203, 206) argues that through their participation in ceremonial exchange cycles big-men both convey messages about the relative military strength of different groups and stabilize political relations over a wider geographical area than any single man or group could influence, let alone control. Moreover, successful big-men can gain resources for expansion from external partners (Strathern 1971, pp. 223–4). The question why big-man roles cannot be adapted to perform functions which would permit an evolution to the institutions of a proto-state is not fully answered just by pointing to the practice of institutionalized generosity and consequent dissipation of power.

The critical determinants have, as always, to be sought in the pre-existing institutional (and ecological) context and the selective pressures thereby brought to bear. The constraints acting on these societies are, as is to be expected, of all three kinds. Economically, the accumulation of a surplus in other than ceremonial goods depends principally on the productive capacities of wives or other dependents working in the big-man's gardens. Coercively, power depends on the capacity to organize fighting groups of relatives or clients and to retain their loyalty by individual display in battle. Ideologically, the egalitarianism already implied by these social relations is reinforced by a mythology which is at once conservative and consensual.* Moreover where, as among the South Fore, the 'parish' (in which co-residence is symbolized by fictive descent) is characterized by high turnover of membership through geographical mobility, the big-man is even less powerful than in other parts of the New Guinea Highlands (Glasse and Lindenbaum 1971, p. 376). Nor, under these conditions, does incumbency of a big-man role carry more than minimal institutional entitlement either to transmit such power as attaches to it or to determine the selection of the next incumbent: the necessary monopoly of sufficient means of production, persuasion or coercion is simply not there. Although there is in practice a good deal of succession from fathers to sons (Strathern 1979, p. xvii), it is far from an institutional rule.† Indeed, the big-man's own career may well not last his own lifetime: Meggitt (1974, p. 201) estimates that Mae Enga big-men are effective for no more than about a decade before they run up against the ecological and demographic constraints on the extent to which they can exploit their roles through shrewd political judgement and management of wealth produced by (or flowing through) their clans.

* Lawrence (1971, p. 16) argues that New Guinea big-men generally have 'limited policy-making roles' because 'most activities are culturally prescribed. Mythological validation not only places New Guinea societies within the conceived cosmic order but also reflects the regular cycle of annual events made inevitable by the subsistence economy and, by the same token, the consensual ideology of the people.'

† Cf. Salisbury (1970, p. 329) on Vunamami: '...although many pre-1870 clan *lualua* did owe their positions to heredity, most of the big men had achieved that position through demonstrating political and business skills, and had subsequently consolidated their position by becoming clan *lualua*'.

A good test of the constraints which prevent big-man roles from being adapted to proto-statehood is furnished by those cases where either the practices which constitute the role come closest to chieftainship 'properly so-called' or the individual big-man is of such outstanding ability as to be able, if anyone can, to turn his role into that of a despot or tyrant. Among the Lakalai, there is the very chief-like role of the '*valipoi*', who is elected by general agreement of all the other big-men (which here means the members of the *suara* wristband society associated with leadership in war) and is thereby empowered 'to make ultimate decisions regarding war and peace, the settlement of internal disputes, and other matters directly affecting the collective safety and welfare of the village's members' (Chowning and Goodenough 1971, p. 136). But this still leaves him no nearer rulership than an Archaic Greek *basileus* or an early Sumerian *lugal*; and all he can do to hand on the succession when approaching death is to designate a favoured son or sibmate by giving him a special belt, which by no means guarantees the recipient the role unless or until he has proved himself in his turn (*ibid*., p. 162). Likewise, even where an exceptional big-man like the Tairora Matotu acquires an unusual degree of power, he still cannot translate his domination of his followers into a paramount chiefdom.* Matotu – so far as his career can accurately be reported by inference from later oral testimony – was an astute politician who occupied 'a role well transcending that of the "hot" killer' (Watson 1971, p. 241). But even so, the 'maximum expression of military authority and central leadership' possible for him was to arrange for groups of his clients to fight abroad and to receive emissaries who came to him for help; and his economic resources still depended on accumulating wealth through taking productive women as wives (*ibid*., p. 265).

Further confirmation – if needed – is provided by the reports of what happened in these societies when a change in the mode of the distribution of power was imposed from without by the Australian government. Predictably, the individual traits which proved advantageous to the incumbents of big-man roles 'have been highly adaptive under modern conditions requiring change' (Valentine 1973, p. 228, quoted by Chowning 1979, p. 84). In other words, given the constraints on the practices constitutive of big-man roles, no mutation or recombination could bring about an institutional change from within. Selective pressure, therefore, came to bear at the level of competition between individual incumbents of those roles, and when the time came that the institutions of these societies had to evolve under exogenous

* Cf. Strathern (1971, pp. 225–7) for the inability even of 'major big-men' in the Mount Hagen area to act autocratically without forfeiting support.

pressure it was these same individual traits of the successful big-men which fitted them for incumbency of now drastically modified political, entrepreneurial and (particularly in the case of cargo cults) religious roles.

But is there, it might be asked, no evolutionary way forward at all for societies of the Melanesian sub-type without the exogenous influence of an alien power? The answer is evidently 'no' so far as the question is directed to the practices constitutive of the big-man role itself. But the interesting suggestion has been made by Allen (1984) that the decisive constraint is the need for the big-man to preserve legitimacy in the face of competition from others who seek prominence through cultural innovation (p. 36). It is, accordingly, arguable that the institutional potential for adaptation should, if anywhere, be sought in the strongly matrilineal and patrivirilocal communities of North Vanuatu, since matriliny functions to define descent-group membership but at the same time divorce it from the context of warfare and property ownership. The result is that the secret graded societies, which are particularly prolific in the Towers and Banks Islands, provide greater institutional support and legitimation than big-men could otherwise command. An able and ambitious man who rose to the top of one of these elaborate ritual hierarchies could then command not merely the symbolic paraphernalia attaching to the role but also the cooperation of young men willing to exercise coercive sanctions on his behalf. The resulting formation of political ties independent of kinship is, on this view, an evolutionary response to the contradiction between 'the indispensable flexibility of political processes and the relative inflexibility of matrilineal affiliation' (*ibid.*, p. 78), and it can, therefore, provide the means to transform a 'status into a power [i.e., an ideological into a coercive] hierarchy' (*ibid.*, p. 36). This hypothesis does not make 'classic' big-man societies of the Melanesian sub-type any less of an evolutionary dead-end than they have been shown to be. But if it is valid, it both points to a distinctive evolutionary by-way down which societies at this modest level of free-floating resources might make the transition to proto-statehood and also illustrates strikingly well how randomly mutant or recombinant practices are selected for their advantages to carriers who have no idea of the signficance of the institutional changes to which their performance of their roles is going to lead.

§12. When we turn from Melanesia to Classical Greece, it might be objected that without the irruption of an unexpectedly powerful monarchical *ethnos* from the fringes of the Hellenic world, the *poleis* – or at least one of them – might have succeeded in adapting to the ecological and sociological environment of the late fourth century B.C. But although it happened to be Macedon which destroyed the *poleis*, it would be rash to hypothesize that they would otherwise have survived. Philip of Macedon was only one of a number of 'monarchs or semi-monarchs' who 'used the techniques pioneered by Dionysius to move opportunistically into the gaps left by the interaction, spoiling and internal contradictions of the major powers (including Persia) and to create principalities for themselves' (J. K. Davies 1978, p. 228). What Philip's and Alexander's achievements showed was that monarchical practices and roles, even if patrimonial rather than absolutist, now gave a society at a similar level of technology and resources to the *poleis* a decisive competitive advantage over them. The *poleis* were stuck fast in all three dimensions: coercively, they were restricted by their failure to extend citizen roles to aliens (as Rome was later to succeed in doing); economically, they were restricted by their failure to expand beyond small-scale trade and commerce (as Venice was later to succeed in doing); and ideologically, they were restricted by their failure to formulate an ideology of legitimacy going beyond local particularism and communal self-defence (as Byzantium was later to succeed in doing).

This is, however, not to say that it was *stasis* which explains their incapacity to evolve. Internal dissension, however extreme, does not of itself either forbid or require the society in which it occurs to evolve into a different mode of the distribution of power. We have seen already in societies as different as Haiti and Korea that rapid and violent turnover in the incumbency of highly located roles can sustain rather than undermine the existing mode; and even where rival factions are divided not merely by competition for incumbency of the available governmental roles but by differences in wealth and doctrinal persuasion, there may be nothing about the practices of which they are the carriers which is in contradiction with the existing mode. The most extreme instance of *stasis* reported in the literary sources for the period between the end of the Peloponnesian War and the victory of Macedon is Argos in 370 B.C., when 'club-law' (*skytalismos*) got so far out of hand that, according to Diodorus (XV. 57–8), a thousand people, including some of the demagogues who had started it, were killed before the people 'recovered their senses'. But no change of institutions or practices resulted from it.

It may be that episodes of this kind were commoner in the fourth century B.C. than they had been in the fifth.* Moreover, the sense of relative deprivation among poorer citizens does seem to have intensified as the distance widened between their richer fellow-citizens and themselves; and it is plausible to suppose that relative deprivation of this kind increased the likelihood of tyranny, as in the medieval North Italian cities it increased the likelihood of a *signoria*. But the two obvious cases where societies belonging to the 'citizen' mode of the distribution of power *did* adapt their institutions in a way that the *poleis* did not – Rome and Venice – both continued to be riven by *stasis*. Rome, as I have remarked already, was pervaded by practices resting on the sanction of force; and Venice, although by comparison less violent, was a great deal more so than its economists liked to pretend. The murder of Tiberius Gracchus as he tried to escape from the forum in 133 B.C. is, in this respect, strikingly paralleled by the murder of Doge Vitale II Michiel in the doorway of the church of San Zaccaria in 1172, and the feuds between Caloprini and Morosini in Venice were just as intractable as those between the followers of Clodius and the followers of Milo in Rome.

It is true that the expansion of Rome led in the end to its evolution to absolutism, so that it could to that extent be claimed that the political institutions of the citizen mode worked to the advantage of the first 'monarch or quasi-monarch' able and fortunate enough to exploit them for his own ends. But the fact remains that (for reasons to be considered in more detail in Section 37) Rome reproduced the institutions of a citizen mode over several generations despite a massive increase in wealth and territory alike. The practice which critically differentiated it from the Greek *poleis* was the extension of the role of citizen to selected inhabitants of conquered territories. Rome was already distinctive in the precocious legal practices codified in the so-called 'Twelve Tables' of the mid fifth century B.C., and its governing élite appears to have realized from the very beginning of its expansion by force of arms that there were advantages in adding to citizen numbers both by the enfranchisement of selected citizens of conquered territories and by the manumission of selected slaves captured in the process of conquest. The institutions thereby created functioned not only to provide manpower

* Fuks (1974, p. 59) finds only six cases of 'revolution' in the Classical period as against 'about 70' from the societies of the fourth century to the middle of the second; but Lintott (1982, p. 253) aruges that the reports of *stasis* in the 4th-century sources are no evidence for its not having been equally prevalent for several generations already.

which helped Rome to avoid the 'oligandry' which weakened Sparta, but also to integrate the roles of potential rebels into the political structure of Rome itself. In diametric constrast to Sparta, Rome adapted its institutions to the pressures and opportunities of conquest without, until much later and through other causes, its mode of the distribution of power being changed.*

In the Venetian case, evolution from a citizen to a bourgeois mode was not only swifter but more predictable than Rome's to an absolutist one. But the critical difference was in economic rather than coercive practices. As in the other North Italian cities, and unlike either the *poleis* or Rome, commercial roles carried both political influence and social prestige. There therefore evolved in Venice a systact of resident merchants who, in contrast to either Athenian metics or Roman freedmen, performed their economic functions as fully integrated members of the citizen body. This contrast is, admittedly, not to be pressed too far: a Roman senator, no less than a Venetian doge, would have money out on loan for commercial purposes; the line between piracy and trade was often as blurred in the Middle Ages as it had been in Antiquity; Greek and Roman gentlemen could be no less eager for profit than their Venetian, Florentine or Genoese counterparts;† and even in Classical Athens (as in France under the *ancien régime*) it was the role of retail trader (*kapēlos*) rather than that of merchant (*emporos*) which was looked down on (Ehrenberg 1943, p. 90). This said, however, it is inconceivable that there should be reported of Rome or a Greek *polis* the incumbency by a person of noble status of the role of *consul mercatorum*, as happened in late twelfth-century Florence and Modena (Waley 1969, p. 24), or that the topmost role should be occupied, as in Venice after Vitale II Michiel's assassination, by a merchant whose enormous fortune has been built up by foreign trade and investment in commercial ventures as well as loans secured on landed property.

The environment in which the institutions of Venice evolved was one in which commercial practices were both ecologically and sociologically favoured. Ecologically, the lagoons which preserved its isolation also

* On the symptomatic reluctance to substitute taxation for liturgy, cf. Nicolet (1980, p. 343): '... the close and fundamental solidarity between the citizen and the City appears clearly from the fact that taxes were refunded when possible and ceased to be levied for more than a century after Rome's wars became victorious'.

† Plutarch, who is the source for Cato's involvement (through an agent) in maritime loans as well as Crassus's in the rebuilding of collapsed houses for profit, also reports that Pericles used to market the surplus produce of his estate (*Pericles* XVI.4); and Livy's remark (XXXI.63) that the *patres* despised profit is flatly contradicted by the agricultural treatises of Cato, Columella and Varro.

gave it both its need and its opportunity for sea-borne trade. The often-quoted annotator of the eleventh-century document known as the *Honorantiae Civitatis Papiae* who remarked of the Venetians that they neither ploughed nor sowed nor grew vines ('*illa gens non arat*, *non seminat*, *non vindemiat*') may have been underestimating the connections which already existed between Venice and the mainland, but he was quite right in the exceptional priority given to maritime commerce from its very beginnings. Sociologically, the consequence was both political independence and, even under the patrimonial rule of the earlier doges, a nobility already commercially minded (and ideologically attached to the cult of Saint Mark, which remained the symbol and focus of Venetian unity for as long as the Republic lasted). Once communal institutions were established in the mid eleventh century, naval imperialism and commercial expansion could be successfully combined without reversion to monarchy or subordination to, let alone absorption by, another society.

By about 1400, this combination in its turn favoured the carriers of practices whose emergence and selection brought about the evolution of citizen into bourgeois institutions: liturgy was giving way to tax, merchants had become more rentiers than pirates, mercenaries on shipboard were replacing the citizen sailors who had provided their own arms and armour, and a proletarianization of both seamen and (some) smaller artisans had begun. But for some 200 years, from the restriction of the doge's power by a council of *sapientes* in the mid twelfth century to the explicit differentiation of the *cittadini* as a middle class (and status-group) in the mid fifteenth century, Venice maintained the institutions of a citizen mode. Moreover, it did so without the inflexibility of practices and the loss of power relative to other societies which would have caused it to suffer at the hands of a patrimonial or absolutist monarchy what Athens suffered at the hands of Macedon. Geography helped, to be sure. But it was the competitive advantage attaching to commercial practices which was decisive.

Directly to juxtapose Athens and Venice is to invite the supplementary question why Athens as the dominant naval power in Greece could not have evolved within the citizen mode just as Venice did. But the juxtaposition only highlights the interrelated coercive, economic and ideological constraints which made Athens, no less than Sparta or any other of the variant *poleis*, an institutional dead-end. Like Venice, Athens grew rich on trade as well as tribute, and depended on imported grain; and like Venice, its population included both sailors and craftsmen who were each as important to the maintenance of its power as the other. But the relevant resemblances end there. The pervasive roles and central institutions of Athenian society were political; and although it would be an exaggeration to say that those of Venice were economic, even after 1400 – they were, rather, a fusion of the two – the critical difference is between societies like the *poleis* where 'there simply cannot be any question of industry or commerce being "rational" in character, least of all in Athens where economic development had reached a fairly high level' (Austin and Vidal-Naquet 1977, pp. 113–14) and a society like Venice where 'government was frankly and efficiently capitalistic in the fourteenth and fifteenth centuries in the sense that its decisions were aimed at enabling Venetians to make profits by commercial investments' (F. C. Lane 1973, p. 144). The difference cannot be explained simply by pointing out, true though it is, that it did not occur to the Athenian élite to adopt the practices later pursued by their Venetian counterparts.* This lacuna has itself to be accounted for; and the answer is that whereas Athens (like the other *poleis*) had evolved in competition with other societies of the same mode, the evolution of Venice (like the other North Italian cities) had been made possible by an inter-societal vacuum of power which could be filled by citizen societies because and only because their dominant systacts fused their political and economic roles as they did.

§13. This stagnation, as it were, of the institutions of the *polis* at the close of its heyday makes all the more striking the orginality and vigour of its emergence. Post-Mycenaean Greece might seem, at first sight, a singularly unpromising environment for the evolution of citizen-states in any of their sub-typical forms. The memory of the patrimonial monarchies now known to us through the decipherment of the Linear B tablets had been all but obliterated; population was scattered and small; the art of writing had been lost; raiding and brigandage were endemic; the terrain was harsh and unproductive; and there was no tradition of royal legitimacy on which an ideology of statehood could be rebuilt. Yet during the course of the eighth century B.C., there evolved a whole set of societies whose constituent roles included those by which the transition from semi- to proto-statehood is defined. The *basileis* became magistrates or tyrants; the people became citizens or subjects; warfare ceased to be a series of 'Homeric' contests between heroic leaders and

* The conclusive text is Xenophon's *Ways and Means* (*Poroi*), which shows an explicit awareness of the value of the revenues accruing to Athens from trade conducted through the Peiraeus but assumes thoughout that it will always be aliens or metics, not citizens, who practise it.

their attendant hosts and became battle between close-formed armies of shield-bearing hoplites; laws began to be promulgated and set down in writing; economic surpluses were applied not merely to individual dedication of trophies but to monumental building of temples of patron deities of the community as a whole; and male household heads came to be assigned locations in a systactic structure of roles rather than a purely individual ranking.

The process is impossible to document as thoroughly as one would wish. But in the case of Greece, as opposed to those of Mesoamerica, or Egypt, or North India, or North China, or Mesopotamia, or Peru, we have the advantage of literary as well as archaeological evidence. This carries the attendant risk of anachronism and bias.* But it makes it possible to reconstruct with a high degree of plausibility the accumulation of resources of all three kinds which together generated a selective pressure in favour of permanent, centralized,† governmental roles transcending the limits of actual or fictive kinship. Economically, such evidence as there is points not only to a shift from pastoralism to arable farming but also to a major increase in wealth in the form of metals, as attested by a sudden and substantial upsurge in metallic dedications (Snodgrass 1980, p. 53). Ideologically, the emergence of the new civic consciousness is attested by the number of places of worship – over 70 known sites by 700 B.C. of which over half have temples (Coldstream 1977, p. 317). Coercively, the change in the form and scale of warfare seems to have come about by the time of the so-called 'Lelantine War' fought sometime before 700 B.C. between Chalcis and Eretria and their respective allies which, to judge from an inscription at a neighbouring shrine later noticed by the geographer Strabo (X.1), involved a degree of organization far beyond anything in Homer or Hesiod (whose *Works and Days* depicts Boeotia at about the same date as still consisting of *poleis* which, although they fight one another, have not yet evolved beyond semi-states ruled by local *basileis*). By then, accordingly, there was in at least some of the autonomous and mutually competitive societies‡ of the Hellenic world an accretion of

* Even in the writings of Thucydides: his report of the 'synoecism' of Athens (II.15) is couched in terms of institutions and roles which can have evolved only after it had happened, and his report of the institutions of the Aetolians (III.94) is transparently biassed in favour of what he (and as far as we know all Greek intellectuals) regarded as the superior virtues of *poleis* as opposed to *ethnē*.

† Including sometimes federal roles in semi-centralized *ethnē* (and, as Larsen (1968, p. 4) points out, all federal states were classified as *ethnē* in Greek usage).

‡ Formalization of inter-societal relations brought into being the role of 'consul' (*proxenos*), as attested in an inscription from Corcyra dated by Meiggs and Lewis

power sufficient for would be-rulers not to have, in Sahlins's phrase, to 'personally construct their power over others' but to be able to 'come to power' instead.

Urbanization in the form of 'synoecism' between hitherto separate villages and households was an important part of this process. But it was neither a necessary nor a sufficient condition of statehood. Residential concentrations surrounded by a defensive wall are found as early as the ninth century B.C., but they were settlements or trading-posts, not *poleis* in the sociological sense, whereas Sparta, which *was* a *polis*, did not become urbanized in the geographical sense until long after (and states of the *ethnos* sub-type did not necessarily do so at all). The most that can be said is that urbanization will have tended to favour the emergence and reproduction of governmental roles. At a slightly later stage, when juridically autonomous *poleis* were visible as models for others to follow, synoecism might be part of a conscious evolution from semi- to proto-statehood, and a lawgiver (*nomothetēs*) might be called in, as was Philolaus of Corinth by Thebes in the last quarter of the eighth century B.C. (Aristotle, *Politics* 127b), to codify rules laid down by the incumbents of new governmental roles. But the initial transition had first to have come about whereby, in Corinth's case, there was a 'president' (*prytanis*) and a 'general' (*polemarchos*) as well as a *basileus* who together 'could operate the state continuously as a political unity' (Roebuck 1972, p. 126).

Two further conditions, both negative, were necessary to this process over and above the accumulation of economic, ideological and coercive resources: absence of large-scale dispersal on the one hand and of external conquest on the other. Clearly, the evolution from semi- to proto-statehood will not come about if the prospective incumbents of citizen or subject roles simply remove themselves, together with their families, chattels and dependent servants, to another territory, like the disgruntled followers of a Baluchi *sardar*. Nor will it come about if the accumulation of resources merely encourages alien predators to annex or overrun the territories over which *basileis* are coming to exercise their new roles as generals, lawmakers, magistrates, dictators or tyrants. But both conditions were fulfilled. Although piracy continued (cf. Thucydides I.7), the large-scale depredations of the immediate post-Mycenaean period came to an end; and Greece (unlike Africa) was an area of sharp 'ecotones' (M. Harris 1979, pp. 101–2) – that is, geographical bound-

(1969, p. 5) to the last quarter of the seventh century B.C. which, as they say, 'has a fascinating tension between its Homeric echoes and the political circumstances of a new age'.

aries beyond which emigrants will find their economic circumstances less advantageous, even if to remain where they are involves a loss of independence.

In this environment, population growth will have been strongly favoured by the combination of relative political tranquillity and the shift from pastoralism to agriculture; and although that growth, and consequent land-hunger, provoked the sudden wave of colonization which started around 735 B.C, it was by then an organized dispersal from communities of origin in which governmental roles had evolved sufficiently for an 'oecist' to be appointed,* a suitable body of citizens conscripted, and a formula laid down in advance for the allocation of land in the territory to be settled. By now, moreover, the differentiation of economic roles had reached the point that dependent household servants were giving way to serfs or slaves or debt-bondsmen categorically distinguished from free, arms-bearing citizens. Difficult as it is precisely to reconstruct the practices which defined their roles, not only the Spartan Helots but the Thessalian '*penestai*', the Cretan '*klarotai*', the Locrian '*woikiatai*', the Miletan '*gergithes*', the Sicilian '*killyrioi*' and the indigenous Maryandynians at Heraclea Pontica or Bythynians at the mouth of the Hellespont were all forced down to a systactic location where they were denied the control of the allocation of the product of their labour and even (in some cases) were liable to be bought and sold.

The best documented, although (or perhaps because) least typical, *poleis* are Athens and Sparta. But the different circumstances which led the former to evolve uniquely democratic, and the latter uniquely oligarchic, political institutions within the common framework of a citizen mode are less germane to the argument of this Section than the different circumstances in which they evolved into statehood. Athens, according to the literary tradition, was synoecized under the legendary Cecrops (Strabo IX.1; cf. Jacoby 1949, p. 126), but even if such an event ever took place, it will not have marked the decisive transition to proto-statehood. What was decisive was an alliance between the *basileis* of East Attica and the rulers of the Acropolis, whose obvious importance as a military stronghold was further enhanced by its importance as a ritual centre. It was a form of, so to speak, aristocratic centralization (Alföldy 1969, p. 14) which favoured the practices defining the roles of archon and then of polemarch, with life-tenure of a by then purely ritual *basileia*

* Like Battus, the seventh-century founder of Cyrene, whose role is designated by Herodotus (IV.153) as *hēgemōn* as well as *basileus* and by a surviving inscription (Meiggs and Lewis 1969, pp. 6–9) as *archagetēs* as well as *basileus*.

being subsequently abolished (Hignett 1952, pp. 41–3); and the incumbents of these roles were drawn from the Attic nobility (*eupatrides*) as a whole. Once political unification had been achieved in this way, the defensibility of the Attic peninsula made possible a residential *de*centralization by the nobility out into the Attic countryside (Coldstream 1977, p. 133). The subsequent political history of Athens from the attempted *coup d'état* of Cylon in the second half of the seventh century through Solon's celebrated reforms in 589 B.C. and the Peisistratid tyranny to the institution of democracy by Cleisthenes in 508 B.C. was a series of contingent variations within a structure and culture in which permanent, central governmental roles might be either seized or peacefully inherited from one incumbent – tyrannical, oligarchic or democratic – by another.

In Sparta, by contrast, the transition to statehood was triggered by an offensive war. Relative overpopulation in the Eurotas valley may possibly have been its cause (Cartledge 1979, p. 115). But whatever started it, the four (or perhaps more) villages jointly ruled by two *basileis* which conquered the exceptionally fertile territory of Messenia between about 731 B.C. and 715 B.C. were thereby enabled to extract an economic surplus from subordinate Helots and legitimate the status of the Spartiates as a self-reproducing systact of warrior-citizens. Thereafter, there emerged the role of the 'ephors', who were specialized officers empowered to enforce laws approved by the citizen body and to check any excessive accretion of personal power to the *basileis* – to the point, in due course, that the then ephors even arrested Pausanias, the victor of Plataea (Thucydides I.131). In a very different way, therefore, but to the same effect, rising population and a mutually reinforcing accretion of economic, ideological and coercive resources created an environment in which practices constitutive of permanent, centralized, non-kin-based governmental roles gave their carriers a critical competitive advantage.

Even if the tyrannies and the *ethnē* are both left out of account, the states which took the form of *poleis* exhibit a wide range of variation in structure and culture alike.* But the selective pressures which favoured the practices defining governmental roles can be identified readily enough. First, increasing population per unit of territory in a context of increasing resources created a need and an opportunity for political-cum-administrative organization on a scale transcending the family or

* There are also, as might be expected, intermediate sub-types such as the Locrians, whose unification under a 'magistrate' (*archos*) and an assembly in a form somewhere in between the ideal types of *ethnos* and *polis* is attested in a long and in some ways puzzling inscription (Meiggs and Lewis 1969, pp. 340–50) of the early fifth century B.C.

village community or extended household (*oikos*). Second, the maintenance of political independence against adjacent communities similarly evolving from semi- to proto-statehood created a need and an opportunity for political-cum-military organization on a scale commensurate with the new style of hoplite warfare – which, as we have seen, strongly favoured the role of soldier-cum-citizen in contrast to the noble warrior and his attendant following. It did not happen overnight. Indeed, many archaic practices survived into the Classical period (cf. I. Morris 1985 on gift-exchange). But except in the poorest and most mountainous districts, where pastoralism and dispersed village communities remained normal, these selective pressures worked strongly in favour of statehood, with consequences which were to give Greece its distinctive places in the cultural history of the West. Turning-point as it was, it did not generate a continuing accretion of resources capable of taking the mode of the distribution of power on to a further evolutionary stage. On the contrary, the *polis*, as we have just seen, turned out to be a dead-end. But only by comparison with the enormous increase in resources brought about by the evolution to industrial capitalism does the transformation of the institutions of Homer's into those of Pericles's Greece look small.

§14. The evolution of industrial capitalism in England is a topic both so complex and so intensively studied that simply to invoke the notion of competitive selection of practices might be thought to add little or nothing to the large literature already directed to explaining it. But although the relative causal importance of the many different conditions necessary and sufficient for it to come about cannot be any better disentangled thereby, the structural and cultural changes which it involved do illustrate very clearly the way in which novel practices were adopted to the advantage of their carriers with consequences out of all proportion to either the intentions or the expectations of the incumbents of the relevant roles. The turning-point came when capitalist relations of production – the roles, that is, not only of entrepreneur and wage-worker but of banker (especially small, country banker), middleman, broker and salesman – started to pervade the particular sectors of the economy (and geographical regions) most favourable to them and to the new industrial technology. It was not a sudden, single, random mutation of practices which brought it about. But the speed of both structural and cultural change, the degree to which the advantages accruing to the carriers of the novel practices reinforced one another, and the magnitude of the increase in the society's resources which resulted from it make it a paradigm example of a turning-point as defined in Section 10.

The institutional context which made it possible (and to which I shall return in Section 32) is also a paradigm example of the mutual interrelation (but irreducibility) of the economic, ideological and coercive dimensions of power. Specialists are agreed on the importance, even if not on the relative importance, of an available supply of wage-labourers, an ideology favourable both to trade and to technical innovation, and a form of government which had already proved itself capable of controlling private violence without inhibiting private pursuit of wealth. It is true that the availability of labour was not, as Marx believed, the result of ruthless enclosure of agricultural land by capitalist proprietors and the consequent migration of impoverished smallholders and rural proletarians to the towns: quantitatively, the migration from country to town was much later, and the spread of enclosure much earlier, than is consistent with that now radically modified view (Chambers 1952–3; Wordie 1983). But Marx was right about the effect of the availability of wage-labourers (particularly women and children) in ensuring that real wages were so low that 'the reward for successful innovation was largely shared between the investor and the consumer' (Deane 1979, p. 144).

This was not by itself a guarantee of success. Many incumbents of the expanding number of entrepreneurial roles did not, in fact, succeed. But given the potential afforded by the markets available, both domestic and foreign, and a technology by which output per head could be spectacularly increased, the competitive advantage accruing in aggregate to the emerging systact of industrial capitalists was irresistible. It might still not have been enough to effect an irreversible change in the mode of production if either the prestige attaching to entrepreneurial roles had been too low or the restraints imposed on them by the incumbents of governmental roles too severe – as they were in some other societies where the practice of wage-labour was by no means unknown and the geographical, demographic and technological conditions not self-evidently prohibitive. It was not, as we have seen already, as if Roman senators, Chinese entrepreneurs or Islamic merchants were hostile to the pursuit of profit.* But only in North-west Europe, and there only

* Or, for that matter, Louis XIV himself, who was perfectly well aware that France needed to be rich if his wars were to be paid for, but for whom, whenever it came to a conflict of priorities, 'profit was sacrificed to prestige and order' (Grassby 1960–1, p. 37).

in late eighteenth-century England, was there an environment in which profit could be pursued with such unforeseen but far-reaching effects.

But what exactly were the selective pressures which, given the environment, acted on the practices constitutive of entrepreneurial roles? They can be said to have originated in the first place from an increase in population from just over five million in 1701 to just under ten million in 1811, with a decrease only in the exceptional decade of the 1720s and a marked acceleration in the rate of increase from the middle of the century onwards (Wrigley and Schofield 1981, p. 578). But this would not have had any major effect on the evolution of the society's institutions if its increasingly numerous members had not enjoyed sufficient purchasing power in their roles as consumers to generate a growing aggregate demand for what the new techniques of manufacturing could provide.* Behind the eighteenth-century upsurge in population lay the seventeenth-century growth in *small*-scale industry. At this stage, the pervasive practice in the country towns and often infertile uplands was that of putting-out, and it was the payment to underemployed families of wages related to marginal costs which furthered, and was furthered by, population increase. This by itself was not unique to England (cf. Pollard 1981, p. 66, on the Sambre-Meuse area). But in the conditions unique to England, the mutation of putting-out into full-time factory wage-labour gave the industrial capitalist a competitive advantage which in due course displaced the putting-out system, with its inherent restrictions on productivity per worker, entirely. This took some time.† Adult male factory-workers, whose number was 'insignificant' at the end of the eighteenth century (Rule 1981, p. 30), were to remain a minority of the employed population for many decades to come. But it did happen with remarkable speed in the region and industry where selective pressure and opportunity came most strongly to bear and the conditions unique to England were most favourable: Lancashire cotton.

* Britain's dominance of international trade in the emerging world economy, although it helped to sustain the momentum of industrialization, was not decisive in setting it off, simply because the volume of such trade was relatively so small.

† Landes (1969, p. 119): '...the putting-out system proved hardier than might have been expected. It dragged on unconscionably in those trades where the technology advantage of power machinery was still small (as in weaving) or where the home artisan could build himself a rudimentary power device (as in nail-making and other light metalwork). And it often survived in symbiosis with the factory; many manufacturers found it profitable to install only so much machinery as would supply a conservatively estimated normal demand, relying on a reserve pool of dispersed labour for additional output in time of prosperity.'

The story has often been narrated, and it is a no less arresting one from the standpoint of descriptive or evaluative than of explanatory theory. But whatever it may have been like for the first generation of resentful, bewildered and demoralized entrants into roles for which nothing in their previous lives had prepared them, and however deplorable it may be that the initial gains to the investor and consumer should have been at the expense of plantation slaves in the American South and overworked, ill-housed and undernourished women and children in North-west England, the causes and consequences of the changes which transformed the cotton industry between 1770 and 1850 are now fairly well agreed. The technical inventions (of which the first were, as it happened, achieved with wool rather than cotton in mind) turned out in combination to be peculiarly suitable for cotton. But without the demand for the product and the supply of cheap material and cheap capital* as well as cheap labour, they could not have had the dramatic effect which they did. It was this combination which gave such a powerful competitive advantage to the capitalist manufacturers of Lancashire. By the time that their rivals in other places or with other products were in a position to encroach on their market, their high profits and consequent high rates of reinvestment, coupled as by then they were with the introduction of steam power and the consequent further profitability of a factory system, had brought a new mode of production into being: 'The new prevailed over the old. Capital accumulated within industry replaced the mortgages of farms and the savings of innkeepers, engineers the inventive weavers-cum-carpenters, power-looms the hand-weavers, and a factory proletariat the combination of a few mechanized establishments with a mass of dependent domestic workers' (Hobsbawm 1968, p. 47). The question 'what were the novel practices selected *for*?' can thus be answered correctly enough by saying 'profit'. But it was because and only because profit on such a scale and over such a period was available in a few particular sectors of the economy of which the cotton industry was the foremost that there came to attach to the role of capitalist manufacturer enough power to make its incumbents the dominant systact in the economy as a whole.

This power was, to be sure, deliberately pursued, and a considerable

* A qualification may be necessary here. It is not always the cost of capital which is decisive in motivating entrepreneurs, but rather its availability; and access to bank credit for working capital was at least as important as access to equity investment for fixed assets, which in eighteenth-century England were a remarkably small proportion of total assets even in the most capital-intensive business (Mathias 1979, p. 94).

increase in individual intra-generational mobility resulted from its pursuit. But its longer-term consequences were neither intended nor foreseen. The process has therefore to be treated as random not only in the sense in which all mutations and recombinations of practices have to be treated as random but in two further senses: first, the juxtaposition of the several initial conditions which were jointly necessary was entirely fortuitous; and second, since the transformation of the mode of production was the first of its kind, there was no goal which the agents who created it could have in view to aim at. As always, the initial distribution of power was critical, and about this there could be little doubt in the minds of the incumbents of either capitalist or proletarian roles. But the scale and degree of exploitation which this made possible was a function of initial conditions of which contemporaries were well aware but whose potential for institutional transformation they realized only as it happened around them.

REBELLIONS, REFORMS AND REVOLUTIONS

§15. Thus far in this Chapter, I have emphasized the unpredictability of social evolution and the unlikelihood that evolution from one mode or sub-type of the distribution of power to another will have been either intended or foreseen by the persons whose joint and several actions have brought it about. But, as I also stressed earlier, there are few if any societies in which there is not someone consciously attempting to alter the existing distribution of power, and many where some person, group or category of persons is seeking consciously to engineer or promote a change of mode; and they sometimes succeed. Their success is, it is true, likely to lead to further consequences which they neither intended nor foresaw, and might well have deplored. What would Cleisthenes have thought of Cleon, Muhammad of al-Mansur, Louis XIV of Louis-Philippe, Bolivar of Perón, or Lenin of Brezhnev? But changes which are the successful outcome of plans carefully laid and skilfully implemented are self-evidently different from changes resulting from mutations and recombinations of practices of which nobody was aware at the time.

The distinction between rebellions, reforms and revolutions needs, accordingly, to be drawn within the terms set out in this volume. From this standpoint, it can be put by saying that in *rebellions*, the agents' aim is to change the structure, not the culture; in *reforms*, it is to change the culture, not the structure; and only in *revolutions* is it to change both. It follows that whereas 'revolutions from above' should strictly be classed as reforms, 'real' revolutions are brought about only from below. But there is the difference from rebellions that those who plan them (if not always those who execute them) are inspired by some sort of vision of a new social order.* These are, of course, ideal types, and simply to define them does nothing to explain any particular case. Changes forced from below are, as we have seen, not always easy to distinguish from changes conceded from above; reformers who change their society from above may effect changes of structure along with changes of culture, particularly when they need to recruit *ministeriales*, *radcnihts*, *pomeshchiks*, *baillis*, *administradores*, Janissaries, apparatchiks and their like from subordinate systacts of origin; and rebellious *frondeurs* may be the carriers of practices with novel cultural content as well as the promoters of upward and downward individual and collective mobility. But however confused the patterns of structural or cultural change and therewith of individual or collective mobility observed in any given case, it is only in relation to these distinctions that the outcome can be given an explanation adequately grounded in the theory of competitive selection of practices. It is perhaps worth re-emphasizing, obvious as it may be, that the fundamental concept underlying all these distinctions is that of power. Institutional change is brought about only by the incumbents of roles to which there attaches by definition enough power for the purpose, and the critical question to be answered is what mutant or recombinant practices have conferred it on them. Changes which the existing incumbents of dominant roles are already in a position to effect have to be distinguished not only from those which require new incumbents to displace them but also from those where those roles themselves have instead (or as well) to be stripped of the power which hitherto attached to them.

In changes which count ('only') as reforms, there is the further difficulty that the term is often used to carry an implied presupposition that the change is for the better. But for the purpose of explaining it, any such implication has to be just as firmly repudiated as where a change is implied to be an instance of 'progress'. Neither description of what it felt like nor evaluation of its outcome is of any relevance to the framing and testing of hypotheses which will explain why the practices of which the reformers were the carriers were sufficiently favoured by the processes of social selection for a change in the society's institutions to

* And (mere) *revolts*? The answer is largely a matter of terminological convention, but for the purposes of this Chapter revolts are best defined as attempts by the agents concerned either to redress a grievance within the society's existing structure and culture or to express a merely symbolic repudiation of them.

follow. Consider again the example of the purchase of army commissions in England, which I cited in Section 2 of Chapter 3 as both an analogue of Greek and Republican Rome liturgies and a homologue of the French *paulette*. Both the reformers who introduced it and the reformers who subsequently abolished it thought of themselves as making a deliberate change for the better, and in the eyes of some (but by no means all) of those affected, they were. But their success is explicable only by reference to the selective pressures at work in the given institutional context. In the first case, purchase was favoured because it kept access to the means of coercion in the hands of men of property who had no ambitions to constitute a standing army which might function as a tool of monarchical absolutism. But in the second, abolition was favoured because that risk was by now negligible in a society which was more firmly than ever entrenched in a bourgeois rather than an absolutist mode, and had come increasingly to confer selective advantage on professional roles for the performance of political and administrative functions.

In changes which count as rebellions, on the other hand, the difficulty is that the term is often used to carry an implied presupposition that the change is not as revolutionary as it ought to be. But again, it is as irrelevant to deplore rebellions as lacking revolutionary content as it is to welcome them as functioning to preserve rather than to undermine the existing mode of the distribution of power. The question to be answered is whether or not practices of which the rebels are the carriers are such as to be selected for advantages which will, if sustained, modify the culture as well as the structure of the society concerned. In 'Zulu-type states' (Gluckman 1963, p. 22), where rebellions are led by members of a royal family contending for the succession, the outcome may be either fission or reunification, but in neither case will the mode or even sub-type of the distribution of power be changed. In the kind of *stasis* of which I have cited Korea and Haiti as examples, the rebels are seeking only to occupy roles whose defining practices they have no intention of changing except to the extent that a replacement of one incumbent by another involves a change in the criteria for individual social mobility. In societies like pre-industrial England and France, where rebellion commonly takes the form of riots over food prices or (more in France than in England) taxation, the rioters may be concerned purely with the redress of an immediate grievance and the enforcement of standards 'determined by tradition, consumer need and basic notions of equity' (Malcolmson 1981, p. 118). But in other contexts, rebels may be consciously seeking to reverse a reform imprudently imposed from above,* or even be the carriers of revolutionary doctrines to which the immediate grievance gives an added impetus.† Where no revolutionary ideology exists at all, as in the slave rebellions of the Roman world or the peasant rebellions of China, then cultural change is, at least in the short term, not an option. But there is always the possibility of a mutation of ideological practices which will then confer selective advantage on the incumbents of revolutionary roles. In China, this is what differentiates the Taiping from earlier rebellions – so much so, indeed, that it has been suggested that the influence of Christian doctrine makes it a more convincing example of the 'Weber thesis' than any of the others, Calvinism included, which Weber discussed (Lockwood 1982, pp. 115–18).‡

These criteria may seem straightforward enough. But once again, there are in practice all sorts of borderline cases which cannot be theory-neutrally categorized. There is not merely the problem of articulation – the problem, that is, of relating changes in different geographical and/or institutional areas to one another. There is also the problem of distinguishing endogenous pressure for the selection of mutant or recombinant practices from the exogenous influences which have time and again been necessary and even sufficient for revolutionary changes of mode; and there are the contingent shifts of strategy and alliance which can alter the conscious purposes of leaders and spokesmen from one day to the next. In consequence, there are not only changes in the mode of the distribution of power which are at the same time part-rebellions, part-reforms and part-revolutions. There are also rebellions which evolve into revolutions and revolutions which evolve into

* As, for example, when in 1763–4 the French Government took the decision radically to liberalize the grain trade following three good harvests (Kaplan 1976, I, pp. 144–5) only to revert to 'apprehensive paternalism' a few years later in the face of popular unrest, obstruction by (some) provincial *parlements*, and a run of bad harvests.

† Cause and effect are notoriously difficult to disentangle here: but there seems no doubt that in the case of the German *Bauernkrieg* of 1525 the authors of the 'Twelve Articles' were able at the same time to articulate the immediate discontents of the peasantry and to infuse them with a radical theological-cum-political ideology (Blickle 1975, p. 74; cf. 1981, pp. 117–18).

‡ Weber himself was well aware of the difficulty of estimating this influence at all precisely, particularly since the missionaries on whose accounts subsequent researchers are dependent were likely to exaggerate it; but E. P. Boardman (1952), although emphasizing that 'central features of Christian belief were absent in the religious ideology described by the Taiping rebels' (p. 116), and that 'as an instrument of persuasion the Christian component of the ideology was a failure' (p. 123), also allows that 'The conclusion is inescapable that the Biblical content was an effective instrument of mass control and an important factor in Taiping military success' (p. 121).

rebellions. Of the first of these, a particularly instructive example is the 'Revolt of the Netherlands', and of the second, the Bolivian Revolution of 1953.

The sequence of events from the promulgation of the 'Compromise' of 1566 to the Truce of 1609 which effectively conceded independence to the Dutch Republic is, on any theory, full of might-have-beens.* If Philip II had been more conciliatory at the outset, if the 'Sea Beggars' had not captured Brill and Flushing in 1572, if the Spanish monarchy had not been forced to declare bankruptcy in 1575, if the Armada sent against England in 1588 had succeeded, if William of Orange had been assassinated in 1580 instead of 1584, or if his son Maurice had failed to capture Breda in 1590, the evolution of Holland into a prosperous, independent, bourgeois republic might never have occurred. But, however improbably, the events of these years had the effect of conferring on the carriers of the practices which were to constitute this novel mode a greater degree of advantage than any of them realized at the time. We have seen already how, once the process was well under way, these practices reinforced one another within a set of institutions in which the pursuit of profit, the repudiation of the legitimacy of an alien monarchy and religion, and the exercise of political control through a federal but not wholly decentralized constitution combined to give the emergent republic power out of all apparent proportion to its size. Yet its evolution was marked at each stage by a positive reluctance on the part of its agents to hasten it in the direction in which they saw it being driven by the insensitivity and brutality of Spain.

To be sure, the Calvinist militants were actively bent on the extirpation of Catholicism and the establishment of radical communal governments in the towns. But the revolutionary practices of which they were such zealous carriers did not, and never could have, enabled them to sustain the rebellion by themselves (G. Parker 1977, pp. 14–15). They were part of a vertical coalition of minor nobles, urban merchants and artisans, and sailors and fishermen, and this coalition was headed by a Protestant prince as unsympathetic to Calvinist as to Catholic bigotry, who continued to maintain that his role as stadholder in the States of Holland derived its legitimacy from the Spanish Crown. Even after the formal Deposition of Philip II in 1581, the States General turned first to the French and then to the English monarchy before they finally founded the Dutch Republic. The evolution to a novel mode of the

* Among which geography was as important as personalities and policies: for Geyl (1964, p. 9), the outcome is 'the sudden, catastrophic result of military operations conditioned by the geographical configuration of the country'.

distribution of power can fairly be called revolutionary, but only if the qualification is added that it was rebels and not revolutionaries who brought it about.

Bolivia, by constrast, offers the example of a revolution which conforms almost exactly to the ideal type but which nevertheless, even before the further evolution to an authoritarian mode in 1964, turned out to have effected changes which were much more structural than cultural. The events of 1953 followed the classic model of the overthrow by violence of the government in power by a coalition of middle-class radicals and proletarian workers with peasant support under the leadership of a self-consciously revolutionary party – the *Movimiento Nacionalista Revolucionario* (M.N.R.). The army was purged; the peasantry were enfranchised; civilian militias took over the means of coercion; the big mining companies were nationalized and the mines jointly administered with workers' representatives; *hacienda* lands were handed over to communal peasant ownership; and devaluation of the currency effectively wiped out the value of urban property in the hands of the middle class. Yet the location of the mineworkers did not significantly or lastingly improve; the government accepted the terms of aid from the International Monetary Fund; the army was rebuilt; and the peasantry reduced the volume of agricultural output to the cities so far that large-scale food imports became called for.

As so often, inter-societal influence is part of the story, here compounded by the irony that the United States, which had initially misinterpreted the ideology of the M.N.R. and was concerned to support it out of fear that Bolivia might otherwise go Communist, was paying directly for one-third of the Bolivian budget by 1958 (H. S. Klein 1982, p. 238). But it is in the countryside that the transition from revolution to rebellion is most striking. The practices of patronage previously carried by the *hacienda*-owners now passed to the syndicates, while particular functions required for commercial agriculture were performed by the ex-*hacendados* who had mostly remained where they were (Heath 1973, pp. 80, 87).* The peasantry were concerned above all with possession of titles to the land which they held to be theirs. The mode of production was neither fully commercialized nor fully

* Conditions naturally varied widely from region to region; but the pre-revolutionary pattern persisted equally in the *altiplano* (where most of the arable land was already unequally distributed between different classes of tenants), the cash-crop valleys (where abundance of land had already created relative social fluidity), and the Quechua-speaking highlands (where sub-tenants and landless dependents remained as insecure as before): see Heyduk (1974), who concludes (p. 79) that agrarian reform was most successful where already foreshadowed under the *haciendas*.

socialized, and the role of syndicate boss simply replaced, at the same location, that of *hacendado*. It was only the systactic origin of the incumbents of the dominant local roles which had been radically changed.

Holland from 1566 to 1609 and Bolivia from 1953 to 1964 are both extreme cases, chosen as such. But apart from clarifying the distinctions between types of change and the apparent paradoxes generated by them, they also confirm that the practices which social selection selects are often other than those deliberately being furthered even by the incumbents of powerful roles who have clear and explicit policies in view. To say this is not to dismiss these policies as irrelevant. But it is to say that for the purpose of explaining, as opposed to describing or evaluating, social evolution, they need to be viewed as one among many random influences whereby selective pressures are brought to bear which may or may not, in the given institutional context, favour the practices of which rebels, reformers or revolutionaries are the relatively deprived and collectively conscious carriers and advocates.

§16. Of all the numerous rebellions reported in the historical or ethnographic record, perhaps the nearest to the ideal type is the *Fronde*, which may conventionally be taken to cover the sequence of events from the Decree of Union proclaimed by the *Parlement* of Paris in May 1648 to the re-entry of the young Louis XIV into Paris in October 1652. There can be no doubt of the strength of the feelings of relative deprivation which animated it or of the breadth of support on which it drew (including on occasion the urban poor). The grievances of the *frondeurs* were corporate as well as systactic. The judges, firmly attached by their interests and beliefs to roles of which they were proprietors by purchase, were no less outraged by what they saw as arbitrary abuse of royal power than were the *grands*, whose privileges were likewise threatened by a centralizing monarchy which denied their right to participate directly in the government of the realm and operated instead through *intendants* and tax-farmers. Anne of Austria, in the role of regent, and Cardinal Mazarin, in the role of prime minister, had no doubt that the declaration of the *Chambre Saint Louis* which they were compelled to accept in the autumn of 1648 was a blow directly aimed at the foundations of monarchical absolutism. But was it? Pamphleteering apart, what more were the judges seeking than the preservation of the power traditionally attaching to their roles, including the right of judicial review of royal decrees and freedom from arbitrary arrest? What more would Condé have done if his terms had been conceded in 1650 than evict Mazarin from the prime ministerial role in favour of himself and replace Mazarin's partisans and clients with his own? The *Fronde* was undoubtedly more than a mere conjunction of revolts against fiscal oppression and forcible suppression of dissent. But, in the words of one of its recent historians, 'what it did not and probably could not do was break with absolute monarchy, question the social structure, or develop an ideological alternative to existing beliefs' (Moote 1978, p. 148).

In other words, the *frondeurs*, whether venal office-holders and their associates or high-born magnates and theirs, were not the carriers of any mutant or recombinant practices, whether ideological, coercive or economic, by which the existing mode of the distribution of power could have been overturned.* This conclusion, moreover, is strongly reinforced by the two most obvious quasi-experimental constrasts: the same society at a different time (France in 1789), and a different society at the same time (England in 1648). In both cases, the practices which define the constitutive roles of a 'bourgeois' society were by those dates far more pervasive and the competitive advantages accruing to their carriers far more apparent. The *parlementaires* of mid seventeenth-century Paris were no more a mid seventeenth-century English Parliament than they were either a homologue or an analogue of the Estates-General as convened under outdated rules and with, therefore, a systactically based revolutionary potential in 1789.†

If Mazarin and the regent had genuinely conceded the demands imposed on them in October 1648, then no doubt the resulting changes would to some degree have been cultural as well as structural: the role of *intendant* would have been abolished altogether rather than filled by other incumbents, new rules would have restricted the ability of the Crown to create venal offices at will, and the burden of taxation on the countryside would have been lightened. But the critical difference from England in 1648 or France in 1789 is that, even though the incumbent monarchs may have been unable and unwilling to recognize it, the prior selection of non-, if not anti-, monarchical practices had gone so far that in those two societies absolutism had already lost its competitive

* Mousnier (1970b, p. 282) is prepared to call the attitude of the *Parlement* revolutionary on the grounds that it was a '*bouleversement, une séparation par la pensée de deux éléments en réalité unis inséparables et indispensables*: *Roi et Royaume, Souverain et Nation, un seul être*'. But he qualifies this immediately with the observation that '*cette révolution était par ailleurs profondément conservatrice*'.

† It is arguable that the *Parlement's* 'long political tradition had been boosted during the preceding century by the decline of the Estates-General whose role it had to some extent adopted' (Shennan 1968, p. 265); but 'it was not asserting any right of representation but only its ancient due to preserve and defend the rights and privileges of the various elements in the state' (*ibid*., p. 270).

advantage. For all the might-have-beens by which Charles I and Louis XVI could have kept their heads on their shoulders, the institutional distribution of power was by then such that no amount of ingenuity and luck on the part of their counsellors or themselves could have arrested their societies' continuing evolution away from an absolutist mode. But in mid seventeenth-century France, competitive advantage lay in the hands of the incumbents of the centralizing roles. The opposition which they faced, however determined, had nothing to offer except local resistance to the encroachment of a monarchy from which, nevertheless, the legitimacy of both noble and official roles derived.

To cite the *frondeurs* as the ideal-typical rebels might perhaps be held to be taking a too Europocentric view. Are there not (it could plausibly be asked) as good or better examples to be drawn from Islamic societies, where time and again discontented tribesmen from the peripheries of weakly centralized states have displaced the urban incumbents of governmental roles only to recreate the same institutions and practices in their turn? But there is a difference. Muhammad's own career was, after all, 'the classic one of a revolutionary leader' (Mortimer 1982, p. 39), and the replacement of an ungodly regime by a godly one is likely to require a more radical change than the mere replacement of impious incumbents of political and military roles by pious ones. Debatable as it may be how far the Abbasid caliphate was heterodox, there can be no question that the Abbasids were not only successful revolutionaries but the carriers of practices which enabled them to construct what was, while it lasted, the most powerful Islamic abolutism before the evolution of Ottoman Turkey. Likewise, the overthrow of the second Pahlevi Shah of Iran in 1980 was much more than the replacement of a secularizing monarch by a *mujtahid* committed to governing in conformity with Islamic law; it was a revolution carried by an alliance of clerical and popular interests with (as I speculated in Section 31 of Chapter 3) the potential to evolve into a wholly distinctive and not nessarily unstable mode of the distribution of power. The relative prevalence of rebellions in Islamic societies is not an argument for saying that Islam tends to select out the carriers of reformist and revolutionary practices in favour of purely structural change. Rather, Islam creates an ideological context within which selective pressure sometimes favours cyclical change on the model of Ibn Khaldun, sometimes favours millennarian movements reminiscent of certain forms of Protestant Christian sectarianism, sometimes favours rebellions which turn into revolutions, and sometimes (as we shall see in the following Section) revolutions which turn into reforms.

The same qualification has to be made about the other form of rebellion which might be claimed to be as close to the ideal type as the *Fronde* – Latin American *caudillaje*, where the successful leader seeks only to exploit the weakness of the central government for the benefit of his followers and himself. But consider the career of one of the near-proverbial examples of a violent and perhaps even pathological '*caudillo barbaro*' (Arguédas Díaz 1929, pp. 24ff.) who was as indifferent to ideology as he was independent of organized systactic support: Mariano Melgaréjo, who ruled Bolivia from 1864 to 1870. He had previously been involved in a series of military revolts before usurping control of the government in (allegedly but improbably) a personal shoot-out (*ibid.*, p. 56). But thereafter, he did not merely exercise his role for his own enrichment; he mounted 'the first serious attack on the land question since the early days of the republic' and 'also attempted some fundamental reforms' in the economy and currency (H. S. Klein 1982, pp. 136, 139). Anyone less of a reformer in the dictionary sense of a person motivated by an ethical desire to bring about an institutional amelioration would be hard to conceive. But the question to be asked is why he then acted as though he were; and the answer is to be found in the pressures to which Bolivia's economic institutions were subjected. In a context of inter-societal competition with Chile and Peru, the active intrusion of foreign capital and critical shortage of ready money, no incumbent of the role of dominant *caudillo* could do other than favour the silver-mining interest, negotiate extensive foreign concessions in return for short-term funding, devalue the currency and compulsorily liberalize the communal landholdings of the Indian peasantry. His only alternative would have been to abandon his role and leave the central government to fend for itself. Whether these 'reforms' were good or bad is up to you. But they demonstrate how even where a successful rebel is indifferent to cultural change as such, structural change can never be divorced from cultural. Competitive selection of practices is always at work.

§17. If the *Fronde* is the near ideal-typical model of a rebellion, then the near ideal-typical model of a reform must be the Meiji Restoration in Japan. But I defer further analysis of its causes and consequences until later in this Chapter because the application of the theory of competitive selection of practices to changes of the kind which count as reforms can be better tested against the example of a society where not only was the plan less thoroughly premeditated but the systactic opposition more formidable.

From this perspective, a particularly instructive case is the evolution of an absolutist mode in Safavid Iran over the period from the occupation of Tabriz by the young Ismail in the summer of 1501 to the establishment of the capital at Isfahan by the young Abbās in 1598. In one dimension – the ideological – the Safavids were just as deliberate reformers as the Meiji were. Ismail and his successors were seeking not merely to strengthen the power attaching to their roles but also to use it to impose 'Twelver' Shiism on a society hitherto dominated by more or less orthodox Sunnism. But they were not seeking to impose a preconceived set of economic, social-cum-ideological and political-cum-military institutions deliberately adopted from more powerful alien societies for the purpose of competing with them. The achievement was personal, haphazard, improbable and eclectic. How, then, can it be explained by a hypothesis derived from the theory of competitive selection of practices?

The first point to notice is that the transition to absolutism did not come about, as in Western Europe, from a feudal mode. Ismail's initial success was charismatic. His legitimacy rested on his composite role as both a religious leader regarded by many of his followers as harbinger of the Hidden Imam and a military leader not only formidable in battle but generous with booty. The early Safavid state was patrimonial, administered by the personal representatives of a ruler who was both an 'emperor' (*padishah*) and a Sufi 'grand master' (*murshid-i kamil*). When, therefore, his invincibility was shattered by the Ottoman victory at Chaldiran in 1514 and, ten years later, he died leaving an heir only ten years old, the likelihood was that his empire would not survive him. Either it would break up through fission into rival warrior-states, or it would regress to a feudal monarchy in which the ruler had no effective control of his own troops and taxes but served merely as the symbolic focus of Iranian unity for autonomous magnates seeking to exploit his role for the benefit of their own tribal followings. In the event, Tahmasp succeeded in holding his inheritance together as, for the time being, an emirate writ large. Under him, Iran was a warrior society dependent on the collective loyalty of Quizilbash tribesmen. The 'lords of the pen' were subordinate to the 'lords of the sword' and the succession to the topmost role was (as became clear when Tahmasp fell ill) by no means assured to his chosen heir. It is true that some of the institutional reforms carried through subsequently by Shah Abbās were foreshadowed in practices initiated by Ismail and Tahmasp, particularly the recruitment from outside of 'new Muslims' loyal only to the dynasty (Hodgson 1974, III, p. 32) and the admission to high military roles of

Iranian notables who had traditionally staffed only the civilian administration (Roemer 1986, p. 230). But nothing could have seemed more implausible during Tahmasp's lifetime than that Iranian society was about to evolve Meiji-style, as it were, into an absolutist mode.

The state of the society over which Abbās's father handed him control was accordingly such that the random accidents of temperament and personality were just as important to his early successes as they had been to the early successes of Ismail. If Abbās had not been the man he was, and if he had not managed as soon as he did to deal with the external threat posed by both Ottomans and Oxbegs, the possibility of creating a Safavid absolutism would not have arisen. But once it did, the institutional context was sufficiently favourable, as it had not been in 1501, to the practices constitutive of an absolutist mode. Abbās was able to effect changes which never occurred to Ismail or Tahmasp and would not have been capable of implementation if they had. Abbās's legitimacy was not charismatic in the way that Ismail's had been: he did not present himself to his people in the role of 'shadow of God upon the earth' or even of Sufi 'master' owed allegiance by his subjects as disciples. But he was, nevertheless, the beneficiary of what was by now a Shiite orthodoxy as strongly established in the cities as among the tribes. At the same time, and thanks in the same way to his predecessors, he was able to place in high administrative roles recruits who were neither of Turkish nor of Persian origin. Militarily, he formed his own corps of royal troops paid directly in cash. Economically, he converted 'state' (*mamalik*) into 'crown' (*khassa*) lands by forced purchase and increasingly restricted the fief-like *tiyūls* to clerical holders or required their non-clerical holders to pay substantial taxes. The traditional systactic division in Islamic 'warrior' societies between the incumbents of military roles entitled to receipt of the economic surplus and the subordinate cultivators required to produce it was maintained, but under a civilian administration no longer controlled by the emirs.

The reforms by which the evolution to an absolutist mode was carried through can, accordingly, be said – by then – to be deliberate. But the institutions which emerged could not have done so without the prior accumulation of sufficient resources, economic, ideological and coercive alike. Only then could Safavid Iran become a society which belongs, for all the cultural differences between them, to virtually the same sub-type of the absolutist mode as imperial Rome. In both, the ruler could rely on administrators (including eunuchs) whose loyalty was effectively pledged to himself; in both, successful military careers of gifted commanders worked to strengthen, not weaken the central government;

in both, the *res privata* (controlled under Abbās by the incumbent of the newly created role of *mustaufi-yi-khassa* which equates precisely to that of the Roman *magister rei privatae*) was a major source of revenue entirely within the ruler's control; in both, taxes were regularly and systematically levied and, where farmed, effectively supervised (with the difference that in Iran the volume of trade was higher and the revenue from port and highway tolls to that extent more valuable); in both, the ruler's immediate subordinates included not merely patrimonial household servants but a professional secretariat; and in both, the ruler's legitimacy was no longer seriously open to question, even in the event of military or diplomatic reversals. In both, it is true, the personal characteristics of the ruler could materially affect the stability of the system: the later Safavids, like some of the later Roman emperors (and some of the later Ottoman sultans), allowed their power to be usurped not only by local magnates but also by ambitious members of their own households. But these attendant dangers serve to reinforce the explanation of how Abbās, like Augustus, came to be able to effect the institutional reforms which he did – however regressive the subsequent evolution of Iranian society under his successors. It was because and only because a set of mutant or recombinant practices could be selected by conscious design in a context in which, for independent sociological reasons, they had come to carry a decisive competitive advantage.

§18. To cite Shah Abbās of Iran as the paradigm of a 'reformer' may seen rather far-fetched to English readers for whom there are other and more obvious paradigms nearer to home. Descriptively, indeed, the ideal-typical picture conjured up by the term 'reform' is for them – or perhaps I should say, us – likely to be the Gladstonian heyday of mid-Victorian liberalism, when abolition of privilege, repudiation of militarism, free trade, sound finance, extension of the franchise, systematic education and the opening of careers to talent formed a practical programme rationalized by a coherent ideology. Yet the institutional changes which successive British governments conceived and implemented at that time were both symptoms and causes of an evolution which was as much structural as cultural. They cannot be explained simply as mutations of practices whereby the incumbents of existing roles adapted them to their changing environment without the occurrence of collective, as well as individual, mobility.

For a start, reforms of this nature required a 'large, educated, energetic middle class with enough money' such as had existed in England for a century already (N. Stone 1983, p. 18). The practices which it carried had earlier been selected for the advantages they conferred on a systact whose members were already upwardly mobile within their roles, not out of them, like the 'attorneys' turned 'solicitors' whom I cited in Section 1 of Chapter 3. The new professionals, administrators, educators and entrepreneurs were not the creation of the governments by which their interests were served. Their roles were not homologues of these of the demilitarized samurai whom the Meiji reformers recruited sideways into the performance of analogous functions. Their own experience as conceptualized by themselves was (as often) at best partial and at worst seriously misleading as an explanation of how it had come about. To many of 'them', it was a crusade against the 'Old Corruption', a high-minded campaign for peace and retrenchment, and the removal of outdated impediments to the allocation of prestige according to merit rather then birth. But it was also, and from the perspective of social evolution more importantly, a structural change in favour of the relatively deprived members of a rising systact who were not only collectively conscious of their interests but also the carriers of practices to which there now attached a decisive competitive advantage. To stress their success is not to deny that their traditional superiors were, on the whole, remarkably skilful in adapting to the 'reformed' institutional context. But the new 'middle-class' élite of civil servants, manufacturers, parliamentarians, intellectuals and the rest were arrogating power to themselves at their traditional superiors' expense.* They were – however indignant they might have been to be thought so – a little more revolutionary than they appeared; and this explains why, both in England and elsewhere, there was a subsequent reaction *against* Liberalism. This reaction was not confined to an increasingly well-organized and collectively conscious working class. It found expression also among conservative politicians who saw in the economic difficulties of the late nineteenth century the opportunity to reaffirm the power of the state – that is, of their own roles and those of the traditional élite of which they were the leaders and spokesmen.

Can there, then, ever be 'reforms from below'? Or do they have to be explained as a kind of revolution (albeit a non-violent one) in the same way that 'revolutions from above' have to be explained as a kind of reform? To the question so put, the answer must be that ideal-typical reforms can, indeed, only be from above. But the cases from the

* Cf. Torrance (1978, p. 80) on the 'invigorated consciousness of the upper-middle class' at the end of the eighteenth century and the sense of relative deprivation of status among provincial notables whose wealth and prestige had not yet been translated into influence at national level.

historical and ethnographic record which call to be explored are not ideal types. In practice, as I have insisted throughout, changes of culture can never be entirely divorced from changes of structure. The usefulness of the notion of 'reform from below' is that it brings out the contrast between changes which involve the members of subordinate systacts in individual mobility out of their roles into roles in the governing élite and those which, on the contrary, involve them in remaining in their existing roles and exerting counter-cultural pressure from there. These roles will, to be sure, rise relative to those of the governing elite; but they will not displace them. The difference can therefore be put by saying that the successful leader of a movement for reform 'from below', whether in the role of radical priest, trade union official, ex-soldier turned outlaw, rent-strike organizer, or dissident intellectual, effects the maximum of cultural for the minimum of structural change: institutional abuses (as they are then regarded as being) are remedied and the mode and distribution of power altered to that extent, but no downward mobility, either individual or collective, is imposed on the dominant systact or stratum. On the other hand, the successful rebel, whether in the role of aspiring *caudillo*, 'club-law' demogogue, provincial separatist, dissident colonel, or noble *frondeur*, effects the maximum of structural for the minimum of cultural change: inadequate incumbents (as they are then regarded as being) of dominant roles are replaced, but no attempt is made to modify the power attaching to the roles themselves beyond altering the criteria of entry into them.

In many societies, particularly rapid evolution from one mode or sub-type of the distribution of power to another is carried through by a threefold combination of reform, rebellion and revolution. The difficult question is then to settle which mattered most – whether, that is, it was the reformers, the rebels or the revolutionaries who were the carriers of the practices which, in a shifting institutional context, conferred the decisive competitive advantage on the roles and systacts to which they severally attached. But the answer may well be that all three were necessary and their combination contingently sufficient. In the English Civil War, the institutional changes which occurred (only to be subsequently reversed) were caused by some of each, and this is not the least of the reasons for which its interpretation is so controversial among specialists. Only thereafter, when the risk of civil war had abated, did English society become, as it was to remain, remarkable for the predominance of reform over rebellion or revolution. This was not because of the desires, and still less the virtues, of its rulers. It was because of the advantages to reformers at all locations of practices which functioned to maintain the existing structure almost unchanged even when the culture was changing, and changing fast.

I commented in the opening Section of this Chapter on the way in which the First Reform Bill of 1832 was enacted not just out of fear of revolution but through a systactic coalition for which there was a joint advantage in so redistributing parliamentary representation as to strengthen simultaneously the landowning interest in the counties and the middle-class interest in the big towns. Within the set of institutions which had evolved by then, 'reformers from below' saw their aims as likelier to be realized by endorsing practices which left the dominant roles, economic, ideological and political alike, where they were. The working-class activists of Victorian England perceived that their systactic interest could best be served by seeking a modest degree of collective mobility, not 'circulation' or 'exchange' mobility of the kind which follows from revolution:* 'the whole inheritance of constitutionality, rule of law and political freedom, profoundly flawed as it was by class privilege, prejudice and gross inequalities of power, provided footholds and leverage for organised groups among the working class, provided they showed no intention of using them to overturn the social system' (Fox 1985, p. 230). That this was their response was a matter of puzzlement to many contemporaries (and some later historians). But, as we shall see in greater detail in Volume III, it ceases to be so once it is recognized just how strong were the selective pressures favouring the practices and roles of a liberal-democratic-capitalist mode of the distribution of power.

§19. A revolution, then, is a change of culture effected by practices whose carriers are structurally located below the hitherto dominant systact which they replace. But even when a revolution, so defined, has unmistakably occurred, it must not be assumed without further argument that its occurrence explains the society's subsequent evolution from one mode of the distribution of power to the next. There are two alternative possibilities. In the first, the revolutionaries who overthrow the existing regime are supplanted in turn by reformers who institutionalize the practices by which a new mode then comes to be defined. In the second, the revolutionaries themselves are indeed the carriers of the practices by which the new mode comes to be defined, but the evolution to that mode has already been initiated by selective

* For Scotland, cf. Smout (1986, pp. 248–9): 'The Scottish artisan believed in thrift, sobriety and education not because he was brainwashed by the upper classes but because these beliefs were functional in his life.'

pressures for whose effects the revolution was neither sufficient nor necessary. The paradigm example of the first is Mexico after 1910, and of the second France after 1789.

In the Mexican case, the starting-point is Francisco Madero's Declaration of San Luis Potosí and the forced resignation and exile of Porfirio Díaz. The institutions of the 'Porfiriato' were such as unequivocally to assign it to an authoritarian mode which, under Díaz, had evolved out of a *caudillo* sub-type of feudalism characterized by the inability of successive post-colonial governments to dominate the peripheries of a society still economically undeveloped, politically uncontrolled and ideologically disunited.* It seems plausible to suppose that if Madero had succeeded in establishing a stable regime, it would have been of a broadly liberal-democratic-capitalist kind. But in the event, his revolution and subsequent assassination were the prelude to an extended period of anarchy and civil war from which the Constitutionalists under Carranza and Obregón emerged dominant only after they had in turn defeated the Zapatistas and Villistas whose coalition had defeated the counter-revolutionary government of General Victoriano Huerta. It is no wonder, then, that the 'Mexican Revolution' has been interpreted by different specialists as a peasants' revolt, a bourgeois revolution, a civil war between rival *caudillos*, and an authoritarian recentralization along the lines laid down by Díaz. For different periods and from different aspects, it was all of these. But the process by which Mexican society finally evolved into a new and stable sub-type of the authoritarian mode was one of reform, not revolution. The institutions which the victorious Constitutionalists imposed from above involved the creation or reinforcement of practices which, while different from those for which their opponents were ostensibly fighting, were different also from those which a restored Porfirian dictatorship under General Huerta would have sought to preserve. But individual mobility apart, their selection left the systactic structure more or less intact.

To explain this outcome, therefore, requires (as always) an answer both to the question: what were these practices selected *for*?, and to the question: who carried them? The losers – the Zapatistas in the South and the Villistas in the North – were not only, after their initial successes, military losers. They were also losers in the sense that the

* There was, however, no question of fission, any more than in a feudal European monarchy like the Polish: the continuing sense of national solidarity is strikingly illustrated by the willingness of even the Zapatistas to support the Constitutionalist government under Carranza in 1919 when armed intervention by the United States appeared imminent (Womack 1969, pp. 347–52).

practices of which they were both carriers and advocates lacked the competitive advantages which might have enabled them to change the institutions of Mexican society as a whole. This lack was, indeed, all too apparent when their initial military victories put them in control of Mexico City at the end of 1914. Zapata's aims were clear enough: to regain for the villagers of Morelos the control of the means of agricultural production which their counterparts in some other parts of Southern Mexico had not yet lost. But partly for that reason, agrarian reform of the kind he sought commanded no support elsewhere except among some dissident intellectuals (Waterbury 1975, p. 440), and offered no solution to the pressure for increased productivity which had led to the encroachment on communal village lands in the first place. Similarly, Villa's aims were restricted to enlarging and preserving an autonomous fiefdom whose economic surplus could be used to reward his own followers and assure the supply of weapons from the United States. Zapata was a classic 'reformer from below': although ready and willing to take up arms, he had no wish to displace rulers who once conceded to him and his followers what they held to be their traditional rights. Villa, by contrast, was a classic rebel: although he was prepared to support expropriation of *haciendas* for his own limited purposes,* he and his generals merely replaced the *hacendados* in their roles.

The changes which the Constitutionalists implemented were by no means unopposed, and the opposition was by no means only that of local *caudillos* or *caciques* who saw themselves about to be displaced by members of a rival faction. But their success was not simply the result of their defeat of their opponents on the battlefield. It was also the result of their ability to construct a programme with appeal across a broad range of systactic interests. In part, this was through a combination of good luck and good management. The Sonoran 'Jacobins' (B. Carr 1972–3, p. 333) who injected much of the ideological radicalism into the Constitutionalist programme turned out to be particularly good at pretending a revolution had taken place when it hadn't (*ibid*., p. 346). Obregón recognized the need not only to offer some prospect of agrarian reform but also to cooperate with organized labour, which he succeeded in doing in 1915 despite the fact that the *Casa del Obrero Mundial* had originally been founded by anarchists (Cockcroft 1968, p. 223).† Salvador Alvarado, the most effective of all the Carrancista

* It is possible that Villa would have wanted (like Augustus) to make extensive distributions of land to his own veterans, but that he deliberately did not do so while the fighting continued for fear of thereby undermining their willingness to fight (Katz 1980, p. 75).

† Cf. Knight (1984, p. 57) on the 'perceived identity of interest between urban bourgeoisie and working class'.

'proconsuls' (Knight 1980, p. 54), introduced education and labour reforms in Yucatan as well as abolishing debt peonage. Further, the Constitutionalists' articulate nationalism enabled them, as we just have seen, to draw even on Zapatista support when American intervention was in prospect. But opportunism apart, the roles to which the Constitutionalists' reforms were principally addressed were those to whose defining practices competitive advantage attached much more than to those of either the villagers and *rancheros* of Morelos or the freebooting cowboys and pioneers of Chihuahua. The defeat of Villa by Carranza at Celaya was not the defeat of one *caudillo* by another; it was the defeat of the old feudal *caudillaje* by a 'modernizing' coalition based economically on captalist relations of production, ideologically on nationalism (as opposed to either clericalism* or regionalism), and politically and militarily on control of the means of coercion by a central government bureaucratically staffed.

Homologous patron–client relations persisted under the new regime; but their function had changed. As I remarked in Section 30 of Chapter 3, vertical ties are a functional requirement of any of the variant sub-types of the authoritarian mode, and in the Mexican case this involved the integration of regional networks of patronage, whether corporate† or associational, into a set of national institutions controlled from the centre. In this process, the local *caciques* ceased to be autonomous power-brokers negotiating the transactions between centre and periphery. The difference from the old *caudillaje* is vividly illustrated in the careers alike of those who fought against and those who accommodated to the change. Saturnino Cedillo in San Luis Potosí, who had sided with Villa in 1914 and with Obregón in 1920, rebelled against Cárdenas in the hope of supplanting him, but his supporters were easily overwhelmed by the federal troops sent against them and he himself was hunted down and killed. By contrast, members of the younger generation of the Figueroa family in Guerrero, whose head had rebelled unsuccessfully against Obregón in 1924, successfully occupied orthodox political roles at local and national level. The power now attaching to the

* It was the anti-clericalism of the Constitutionalists which provoked the so-called *Cristero* revolt of the 1920s which had much in common with Zapatism.

† The colonial social structure had been pervaded by corporate roles (Wolf 1971, pp. 5–6), and the 1917 Constitution still referred to the communal villages as 'corporations' (F. Chevalier 1967, p. 166 n. 15); from the perspective of this contrast, therefore, the success of Carranza and his successors can be said to have been achieved by 'mobilising support on a mass, apersonal, national, associational basis' (Knight 1980, p. 57).

roles of the central government* was so much greater than it had been under Díaz that no local *caudillo* could hope to extend his base sufficiently to mobilize a coalition capable of toppling the regime: revolt and assassination were not enough.† Economically, the state's control of markets and credit was decisive alike for industries and regions;‡ ideologically, the propagation of nationalist-cum-revolutionary rhetoric and the suppression-cum-conciliation of the Church legitimated the status of the government and the P.R.I.;§ politically, central control of the means of coercion was supplemented by party patronage.‖ As the balance of rural and urban interests shifted in favour of the latter, industrialization and the investment necessary to promote it took place within the institutions of a capitalist but single-party state.

It could perhaps be argued that the Presidency of Cárdenas from 1934 to 1940 was revolutionary and not merely reformist: the vigorous impetus which he gave to agrarian reform and nationalization of the oil companies were measures far more radical than any taken by his predecessors. But neither was symptomatic of an evolution in the direction of socialism. Cárdenas himself was at pains to reassure both domestic and foreign opinion to that effect,¶ and his encouragement of private industry was matched by his establisment of an *Oficina de Pequeña Propriedad* to represent private landowners threatened with, or

* Which did not have to be concentrated in the President's role: after 1930, Calles's role was institutionalized as '*jefe nato*', and commissions called on him first and the President afterwards (Bazant 1977, p. 175).

† It is an unanswerable question how far the events of 1910–20 were necessary to bring this about. But the fact that they had occurred meant that, as it is put by L. Meyer (1982–3, p. 194) the Revolution '*occupo todo el espacio politico disponible*': rival factions or parties were faced with the choice of being coopted or repressed.

‡ Cf. Eisenstadt and Roniger (1980, p. 59): 'It is the combination of potentially open access to the markets with continuous semi-institutionalized attempts to limit free access that is the crux of the clientelist model.'

§ 'Mexicanization' did not only help to legitimate the government, but also provided openings for 'aggressive and competent individuals to acquire power, wealth and prestige within the system' (Anderson and Cockcroft 1966, p. 15) rather than nurture a sense of relative deprivation from a location where dissent might lead to rebellion.

‖ Casanova (1970, pp. 34–5) points the contrast with the relations of Díaz to his *caciques* by saying that the new 'revolutionary, anti-clerical and agrarian *cacique*... is still a *cacique*, and he calls himself a revolutionist. The difference is that he now belongs to the rural upper bourgeoisie'.

¶ In his own words, as quoted from a speech of 1940 by Michaels (1970, p. 78): 'There is not a communist government in Mexico. Our constitution is democratic and liberal. True, it has some moderately socialistic features such as those concerning national territory and relations between capital and labour, yet they are no more radical than those of other democratic countries and of some which retain monarchical institutions.' No doubt the speech was intended to disarm his liberal critics, but it cannot be discounted entirely even so.

already the victims of, unauthorized expropriation. The *ejidos* were not intended to become the central institutions of the Mexican economy, or even of its agricultural sector, but only to accommodate and control a still too numerous smallholding peasantry of whom many continued to depend on seasonal wage-labour or temporary migration to the United States. Nor were they organized as collectives on the Soviet model: they coexisted with much more productive and capital-intensive farming by private landowners of the better-irrigated land.* Internally, they were differentiated much as the traditional pueblos had been, and were often dominated by *caciques* to whom Communism was anathema (Friedrich 1965, p. 205). Likewise, the nationalization of the oil companies was neither a part of nor a prelude to the expropriation of domestic capitalists or the transfer of control of the means of production into the hands of the state. Redistribution of private property, not abolition, was the aim in view (Córdova 1977, pp. 17–18). However striking as a change of policy, Cárdenas' measures were conceived and effected within the same mode and sub-type of the distribution of power.

On the other hand, the institutions established and sustained after 1920 were not simply a recreation of Porfirismo under a different and purely simulated revolutionary rhetoric. Two institutions had lost the power they once had and did not recover it: the *haciendas* and the Church. Although many former *hacendados* might move into roles not much less advantageously located in commerce, politics or smaller-scale farming, they no longer dominated the countryside, and the ecclesiastical institutions to which many *hacendados* had themselves been in debt were no longer there at all. Just as the political integration of Mexican society was achieved by adapting the practices of clientelism and *cacicazgo* to the institutions of a one-party state, so was its ideological integration achieved by substituting the nation for the Church as the symbol of legitimacy, and its economic integration achieved by the simultaneous pursuit of growth by capitalist means and modest redistribution of land. If the Meiji Restoration effected a change of mode through reform without needing a revolution either to start or to finish it, and the Russian Revolution effected a change of mode through a revolution from below followed by another from above, Mexico offers the example of a revolution which led to a reform which effected a restoration of the pre-revolutionary mode in a different sub-type. That the majority of Mexicans regarded this as an improvement from their own point of view

* In 1940 over 87% of registered *ejidatorios* were farming holdings of less than 10 hectares (F. Chevalier 1967, p. 178).

(albeit at the cost of a million dead) seems beyond doubt. Whether they were right to think so is, as always, up to you.

§20. In the case of France after 1789, we are again dealing with the consequences of a series of events which unambiguously fits the definition of a 'revolution'. But it was a revolution which came about only through a wholly unpredictable sequence of coincidences, and which if anything retarded rather than advanced the evolution of French society to a capitalist-liberal-democratic mode. The institutions of the *ancien régime* could not have continued to reproduce themselves unchanged into the nineteenth century, as Calonne, who had succeeded Necker in charge of finance in 1783, came to realize by the time he submitted his proposals for reform in 1786. But there was nothing inevitable about a *révolte nobiliaire* against despotism which then, contrary to the intentions of those who started it, undermined their own ability to alter the existing institutions on their own terms* or about the response of the National Assembly to a breakdown of order in the countryside caused by the fear, anger, frustration and distress of a peasantry whose aims were no more than relief from fiscal exactions and secure possession of their plots.† The vote to abolish 'feudal' privileges on 10 June 1789 was a response not to a contradiction of which only one resolution was possible, but to a purely contingent combination of the 'counter-offensive of the Ancien Régime and anti-privilege pressure from below' (Lucas 1976, p. 139).

It was without doubt a 'bourgeois' revolution in the sense that the systactic interest which it served was that of the possessors of property and/or marketable professional skills. But it was not a pre-existing 'bourgeois' systact whose members carried the practices which were to pervade the structure of nineteenth-century France. In the first place, the carriers and advocates of the new of modified economic, ideological and coercive practices were as likely to be noble as not; and in the second, the pre-Revolutionary 'bourgeoisie', such as it was, consisted of traders, landowners, rentiers and officials, not bankers, industrialists, joint-stock promoters or entrepreneurs. On no interpretation can the Second and Third Estates by viewed as distinctive and antagonistic classes: as with the nobles and *equites* of late Republican Rome, the

* Cf. Lefebvre (1954, p. 248): '*La Révolution a été déclenchée par ceux qu'elle devait anéantir, non par ceux qui en ont profité.*'

† In this, they resembled alike the Mexican peasantry of Morelos and elsewhere in 1910 and the Bolivian peasantry in 1953, but with the difference that in Bolivia peasant revolution depended on urban revolution (Malloy 1970, p. 334), in Mexico urban revolution depended on peasant revolutiuon, and in France it was the combination of the two which caused the governing élite to lose its nerve.

division between the two was much more a matter of social status than of relation to the means of production. Not only can the *cahiers* of the Third Estate not be construed as anticipating the programme later formulated by the Constituent Assembly, but the *cahiers* of the Second Estate can be argued to be, if anything, more innovative (Chaussinand-Nogaret 1976, p. 183; G. V. Taylor 1972). The sense of relative deprivation articulated by the representatives of the Third Estate in 1789 was directed against their exclusion from privileges, or potential access to privileges, still restricted to the nobility as juridically defined rather than against a superior class in opposition to which they identified their economic interests with the propertyless members of their order.

The sequence of events which culminated in the decisions taken by the Assembly on the night of 10 August has been recounted many times by narrators whose presuppositions range all the way from strictly 'orthodox', according to which the Revolution is to be explained as the achievement of a bourgeois class '*parvenue à sa maturité*', to the radically 'revisionist', according to which it is to be explained as the result of a failure of strategy by a regime still perfectly capable of maintaining itself in power if its policy-makers had played their cards right. But there is no disagreement that, to quote again from Lefebvre (1954, p. 247), '*la Révolution de 1789, comme fait spécifique, a nécessité un concours vraiment extraordinaire et imprévisible de causes immédiates*'. If the bankruptcy of the government had not coincided with a disastrously poor harvest, if the Bastille had not fallen,* if Louis XVI had been of the character of Henri IV or even (Lefebvre 1939, p. 29) Louis XIV, or if the *Parlement* of Paris had not thoughtlessly insisted that the Estates-General must meet in accordance with the forms of 1614,† the whole subsequent history of France (and not only France) could have been different. Yet it is just such haphazard and paradoxical sequences which time and again set the context within which competition for power is acted out under selective pressures of which neither the winners nor the losers are more than dimly aware. With hindsight, what is remarkable is not the unpredictability of the events

* That it might well not have fallen is conceded even by the 'orthodox' school: according to Godechot's detailed account (1965, p. 271), '*Un chef résolu aurait donc pu facilement résister à une attaque.*'

† Doyle (1980, p. 140): 'There is no evidence that the magistrates had thought at all deeply about the implications of this, or even that all of them knew for certain what the forms of 1614 were.'

of 1788–9, or even of the subsequent sequence from the fall of the monarchy and the declaration of war through the Convention, the Terror, the fall of Robespierre, the Directory, the rise and fall of Napoleon and the restoration of Louis XVIII. It is that the evolution of French society from an absolutist to a 'bourgeois' mode of the distribution of power should have been so little influenced by it one way or the other.

To speak of *la France bourgeoise* is to invite the objection that not only is the term notoriously ambiguous (whether explanatorily, descriptively or evaluatively used), but that under any definition it covers a category of roles many of which were much more in conflict than in cooperation. But both points can readily be conceded without there having to be modified the claim that the central institutions of nineteenth-century France were such as both to reflect and to promote the common systactic interest of the owners of property and/or marketable professional skills. Some of these were, by social origin, noble; some were upwardly mobile from the tenant or smallholding peasantry; some moved over no great social distance into the new or expanding roles of doctors, lawyers, teachers and local officials; some (and their origins were very diverse) more or less created their own roles as industrial capitalists.* That they differed among themselves in wealth, social standing and political influence and that their interests and the ideologies through which they were articulated were often opposed to one another is clear from any social history of the period. But they had in common not only a similar relation to the means of production but a similar commitment to representative institutions and to *les carrières ouvertes aux talents*; and it is even arguable that the fragmentation of their individual interests within their large common area of social space made it easier for them to continue to dominate the roles beneath them (Zeldin 1973, I, p. 13). This systactic structure was the creation of the Revolution in one sense only: individual (but not collective)† mobility had been dramatically accelerated, and the experience of the Revolution created an 'enormous gap' (Higonnet 1981, p. 263) in the lives of those who lived

* Cf. Lefebvre (1955, p. 343): '*les révolutionnaires ne pouvaient soupçonner le progrès que la concentration capitaliste a réalisé après eux*'.

† It is not as if the Revolution had, as Michelet mistakenly believed, brought into being a whole new class of independent peasant proprietors. Lefebvre (1954, p. 263) is explicit that '*on ne peut donc pas dire que la Révolution ait diverti le cours de l'histoire agraire de la France*', and Marc Bloch had already pointed out in his agrarian history of France (1931, p. 147) that '*La Révolution, par la vente des biens nationaux, a changé beaucoup de propriétés de mains, mais elle ne les a qu'assez faiblement morcelées.*'

through it. But the selective pressures in response to which the structure evolved were neither created nor even significantly reinforced by the actions of those who abolished the *ancien régime*.

The principal institutional changes which the Revolutionaries did effect can be summarized readily enough: abolition of the vestiges of seigneurial rights in the countryside; removal of the corporate autonomy of the Church; discontinuance of sale of offices; greater centralization of government; removal of internal tariffs; rationalization of law (including denial of special privilege); abolition of guilds; and opening of recruitment to higher political and military roles. But they would have come about in any case. The selective pressure in their favour was already there, and so were the carriers of the mutant practices which they required. No significant structural change was necessary to effect them or, for that matter, followed from them. It was industrialization, with the concomitant commercialization of the countryside and gradual transformation of 'peasants into Frenchmen' (E. Weber 1977), which changed the social structure of nineteenth-century France; and to this, the Revolution contributed nothing. The dispute among specialists is not about whether it advanced industrialization, but about how far it retarded it (Trebilcock 1981, Ch. 3).

In the towns, the small merchants and shopkeepers were hardly less hampered by restrictions after the Revolution than before (Zeldin 1973, I, pp. 108–9), and the industrial workers were organized only through *compagnonnages* which did nothing (and perhaps less than nothing) to fuse them into a working class collectively conscious of a common systactic interest (Bergier 1973, p. 421). In the countryside, as we have seen already, individual redistribution of ownership did nothing to alter the collective location of the peasantry. Nor was any significant change made to either the number or the market- and work-situation of the million-strong class of resident domestic servants. Only very much later in the century did there emerge a class-conscious proletariat organized through trade unions, and the political interests articulated through the ballot-box come to reflect national rather than regional dispositions and antagonisms. Even the criteria of social prestige remained much what they had been. Nobles whose ancestors had had the right to ride in the King's carriage now graced the boards of the newly incorporated railway companies (Brogan 1961, p. 126), and 'Both before and after the Revolution, the social values of the old *élite* dominated the status-conscious men and women of the wealthy third estate' (G. V. Taylor 1967, p. 497). Where major institutional changes, as opposed to changes of personnel, are in question, the most that can be argued is that the

Revolution accelerated them though a '*passage au plan juridique*' of what was already in prospect (Chaunu 1966, p. 344).

The only possible objection which could be raised against this conclusion is that if the Revolution had not taken place, the institutions of the *ancien régime* would have continued to reproduce themselves intact. But this was out of the question. The selective pressures already acting on the systactic structure were too great. This is nowhere more clearly visible than in the breakdown of the royal finances which, in the words of Furet and Richet (1965, p. 59), '*noue l'ensemble des contradictions sociales de l'Ancien Régime*'. It is not that bankruptcy, or an inability to raise loans in the market, need have proved fatal in itself. But 'by the 1780s, the crisis of the system had become at the same time a crisis of the position of the nobility within it' (Runciman 1983, p. 305). The difficulty was not just that noble incomes, even though they did not escape tax altogether (Behrens 1963), were much more lightly taxed than non-noble (Cavanaugh 1974). More seriously, the fiscal system itself was controlled by roles whose noble incumbents could neither, on the one hand, be curbed by a *chambre de justice* nor, on the other, be replaced by salaried officials. The result was that the govenment was unable to increase its tax revenue, and depended therefore on credit. But credit depended on the roles of the private financiers whose profits came from lending the government's own monies back to itself; and these roles, however undesirable, could not be abolished without depriving the government of its ability to borrow at all. Well before the events of 1788 brought matters to a head, the government was inextricably constrained by the contradiction that until its fiscal institutions had been reformed its financial resources could not be augmented to cover its needs, but until its resources had been augmented its fiscal institutions could not be reformed (Bosher 1970, p. 306).

One way of viewing this contradiction is as a symptom of the failure of the French monarchy to create a service nobility on the Russian or Prussian model. By relying on venality of office and the domestication of the *noblesse d'épée* at Versailles, Louis XIV did, as we saw in Section 25 of Chapter 3, succeed in averting any possible future threat to the monarchy from noble *frondeurs*. But the unintended consequence was a weakening of the joint power of the monarchy and the nobility in the face of concerted resistance from below. Nobles occupied all the important governmental roles (Necker being the exception that proves the rule); but they no longer had the direct control of the means of coercion which had enabled their predecessors to wage civil war. The monarchy no longer risked provoking the nobility to civil war, but it had now to rely on an apparatus of repression which, while adequate to put down local riots, could not be guaranteed to hold firm in the face of a generalized breakdown of order on the scale of 1789. By the 1780s, the political power of the nobility was enough to paralyse the workings of monarchical institutions regarded as 'despotic', but not enough to impose an alternative on its own terms.

At the same time, the traditional ideology which had legitimated noble privilege had come under steadily increasing strain. It was not that the monarchy itself, unpopular as it may have become after 1785, had lost its legitimacy; nor had the philosphers and pamphleteers of the Enlightenment converted more than a handful of their readers to Freemasonry or Republicanism. But as a criterion of deference, birth was inevitably giving way to function, with a consequently explicit identification of rank with money (McManners 1967). The *grand fermiers*, not the *rustres blasonnés*, were the status-equals of the blue-blooded *noblesse d'épée* (Chaussinand-Nogaret 1976, p. 95). The criterion of merit rather than birth is increasingly visible in the preambles to *lettres d'anoblissement* after 1760 (*ibid*., pp. 53–5). Noble life-styles continued to be emulated by those who could afford them, and individual nobles continued to exact the deference which they held to be their due. But although it was only nobles who could be carriers of the practices by which institutional reforms could come about, it was not because of deference to birth that they would succeed. On the contrary: it was the lack of agreement among themselves on the justification for their own traditional privileges which, when they came under pressure from below, further weakened the regime which had accorded them.

A change in the mode of the distribution of power was, therefore, inevitable; and the institutional context of the second half of the eighteenth century was such that without some random external event to prevent it, the change was bound to be such as to favour 'bourgeois' practices and roles. A theoretical possibility, for which the Napoleonic interlude might seem to offer an argument, is that the transition could have been made to an authoritarian rather than a liberal-democratic mode. Might not French society have evolved the institutions of a single mass party, state-controlled trade unions and a corporate capitalist economy legitimated by an ideology of nationalism and militarism? And does not the regime of Napoleon III, which was ended by defeat in war, not by internal revolution, give further support to the hypothesis? But the *révolte nobiliaire* which initiated the French Revolution was precisely a revolt against 'despotism', and it was only because it was, indeed, a revolution which that revolt unintentionally initiated that Napoleon emerged as its heir. The selective pressures at work in the 1770s and '80s were pressures favouring the institutions of representative government (in whatever form) as well as private ownership of the means of production and careers open to merit. If the crisis of 1788–9, when it came, had been differently handled, *la France bourgeoise* could quite well have evolved through reform not revolution. The outcome would have been the same. Only the contingent route to it (and thereby the gains and losses to different groups and categories of individuals) would have been different. In the event, a coalition of the people of Paris and the exasperated peasantry was able to prevent any regression from revolution to reform. But for the sociological theorist, as opposed to the historian, the interest of the French Revolution is not in the might-have-beens which could have kept it a reform but in the irrelevance of the revolutionary sequence which in fact occurred to the society's evolution in a direction which it was following in any case.

TEST CASES (1)

§21. In announcing that the examples of social evolution to be discussed in this and the next two groups of Sections are 'test' cases, I do not imply that those discussed hitherto have been no more than self-confirming illustrations pre-emptively immunized against awkward evidence. But the cases which will most rigorously test and most constructively extend the theory of competitive selection of practices need to be chosen with that purpose in mind. In principle, the theory can be put to the test as well at one stage of social evolution as at another. But in practice, it is at the later stages that the combination of reliable, detailed reportage with illuminating quasi-experimental contrasts is most likely to be found. In this group of Sections, therefore, I revert to the societies which not only in Europe but elsewhere fit the definition of 'feudalism' in what I have called its broader sense; I then go on to compare the evolution of selected 'absolutist' societies; and I end by contrasting the evolution of the industrial societies of different modes and sub-types whose workings were briefly analyzed in Sections 28 to 31 of Chapter 3.

This choice inevitably accords the institutions and practices of the societies of Europe a privileged position, not in the sense that they are presupposed to carry some invincible competitive advantage but only in the sense that their dominance over the period from roughly the fifteenth century A.D. to the present is an unarguable social fact which has therefore to be explained. This 'old question', as Weber called it, can only be answered by way of quasi-experimental contrasts between the institutions of European and non-European societies on the one hand and of earlier and later European societies on the other. It is not a question to which this volume is directly addressed. But it does underlie the comparisons which most obviously present themselves in the search for cases with which to put the theory of competitive selection of practices to the test. Why, at an approximate common level of total available resources, do some societies evolve a set of practices and roles, and a consequent systactic structure, which turn out to carry a significant advantage at the level of inter-societal competition?

In contrasting the evolution of different feudal societies, therefore, I have in mind not only the different selective pressures which may have favoured the practices constitutive of feudal roles, but also the differences of context which have meant that for some but not other feudal societies the combination of tied agricultural labour, decentralized control of the means of coercion and an ideology of qualified national legitimacy could only be a transitional stage. Two necessary conditions are worth re-emphasizing. First, there has to be *a* central state, residual as it may be, which the magnates recognize. Second, although the roles of the dependent cultivators from whom a disposable surplus is extraced can take a range of juridical forms, they have to be dependent in the strong sense that they are not merely subordinate but denied freedom of social and geographical mobility except on terms which accord with the magnates' interests. Inter-societal comparisons, accordingly, have to be made in terms of a systactic location of magnate roles which can vary in both their political relations to the state and their economic (and juridical) relations to the dependent cultivators. But the two do not vary independently of one another. It is not simply a matter of chance that we do not find, for example, a society in which the practices of vassalage at the one level are combined with those of debt-peonage at the other. Once the selective pressures at work have been identified, it is possible to see not only what the mutant or recombinant practices were selected for, but also why certain theoretically possible institutional combinations were never, and could never have been, in prospect.

At the same time, there is an implicit quasi-experimental contrast with those other societies which might have evolved into a feudal mode but didn't. Africa apart, there has to be some sociological reason for which there did not evolve in Mamluk Egypt or Sung China or Anglo-Saxon England or Inca Peru or post-Mauryan India a landed aristocracy acknowledging the legitimacy of a central monarchy but controlling its own means of coercion and appropriating the economic surplus by way of corvée or rent; and in each case, there is. The Mamluks did not evolve a hereditary class of landed magnates because theirs was an Islamic warrior-state in which Mamluk roles could not be transmitted to children* and political power was centred not in the countryside but in Cairo and the garrison towns (Irwin 1986, p. 8). Sung China did not evolve a feudal structure because the new dynasty was determined not to decentralize the means of coercion, taxation was centrally levied in an increasingly commercialized enconomy, and the scholar-gentry acted as the local bureaucratic agents of the central power. In Anglo-Saxon England, as in Hammurapi's Babylonia, there never ceased to attach to the monarchical role the power to levy troops on a national basis and the large manorial or quasi-manorial landowners never wrested (or were conceded) juridical independence amounting to local or regional autonomy. In Inca Peru, the claim of the Crown (or the centrally controlled cult of the Sun) to all land was enforced by integration of local élites backed by the threat of military intervention or deportation. In post-Mauryan India, the central institutions of *jāti* and *jajmani* and the ideology of Hinduism underlying them gave no scope for local landholders to establish the necessary domination over dependent free cultivators;† although some patrimonial kingdoms might be so much more effective than others in extending their institutional catchment areas as to count as a different sub-type of their common mode,‡ no intermediate structure was possible between domination of village communities and their surroundings countryside by anointed kings and the domination of such kings at a higher level by an imperial state. No doubt in all these societies, landholders would have liked there to attach to their roles power equivalent to those of the Polish *szlachta* in relation both to the central government and to the peasantry from whom they could extract a disposable surplus at will. But the practices through which they would have had to do so were not those which, in these

* Sons of Mamluks (*awlad al-nas*) were largely employed in an auxiliary militia created for the purpose: 'The whole Mamluk system was predicated on the importation of new men in each generation to take the highest positions of the state' (Lapidus 1984, p. 116).

† Cf. Baechler (1986, pp. 45–6), who stresses the lack not only of a territorial nobility ('*Il n'y a pas d'aristocrates en Inde, sinon localement comme les Mahrattes qui sont une résurgence tribale ou chez les tribus Nair, Coorg et Tulu de la côte du Malabar*') but also of a household-based peasantry on the European (or Japanese) model.

‡ Thus, 'The Vijayanagara State differed from the Chola with respect to its greater coercive capacity, its deeper penetration into local situations, and the changed character of the agrarian and commerical base of the society it governed' (Stein 1985, p. 80).

altogether different institutional contexts, competitive selection could ever select.

§22. From a purely 'Linnaean' perspective, early Capetian France can quite well be taken as the model of a feudal society, both in the magnates' relation to the Crown and in their exercise of *seigneurie banale* over the dependent cultivators working on their demesnes or holding land from them in tenancy. Once fiefs had become heritable, the state had lost its monopoly of the means of coercion to mounted, castle-holding warriors, and dependent cultivators had no choice but to subordinate their persons and/or their lands to a local lay or ecclesiastical lord in return for his protection, the institutions of Northern France offer a paradigm against which the range of variant practices can be assessed both in other societies and in other regions of France. Yet from a 'Darwinian' perspective, the evolution of Northern France is a transitional case. Its period of feudalism is merely a relatively short and idiosyncratic interlude between the decline of central authority (and control of land) about which Charlemagne had explicitly complained in his own lifetime* and its re-establishment in a context where, as I remarked in Section 17 of Chapter 3, there was no alternative between recentralization and fission.

Once relative peace and prosperity had been restored, the magnates were confronted with a monarchy not only militarily and economically secure but recognized as legitimate and therefore as the source from which their own prestige derived. It was not just that the roles of *prévôt* and *bailli* were there, as we have seen, to be adapted under the *nouvelle conjoncture* to the interests of the monarchy. It was also that the inheritors of the autonomous principalities and counties who lacked the resources to maintain their autonomy against a reconstituted central government faced the same contradiction which was later to frustrate the *frondeurs*. How could they overturn a mode of the distribution of power from which their own structural location derived? A feudal society in the narrow sense, where the magnates held their land and offices as vassals of the Crown, could no longer reproduce itself as a feudal society in the broader sense: the selective pressures which

* In cc. 6 and 7 of the Nijmegen Capitulary of March, 806 (Borétius 1883, p. 131): '*Auditum habemus qualiter et comites et alii homines qui nostra beneficia habere videntur comparant sibi proprietates de ipso nostro beneficio et faciant servire ad ipsas proprietates servientes nostros de eorum beneficio... Audivimus quod aliqui reddunt beneficium nostrum ad alios homines in proprietatem et in ipso placito dato pretio comparant ipsas res iterum sibi in alodem...*'

encouraged the retention of these practices gave competitive advantage to the monarch's rather than the magnates' role. Paradoxical as it may seem, the practice of vassalage was very much *shorter*-lived in Poland, where there evolved the structure and culture nearest to the ideal type of feudalism in the broader sense.

The quasi-experimental contrast between France and Northern Italy brings out a number of well-studied institutional differences which I have already discussed in broad outline in Section 8 of this Chapter. But what was it about the persistence of urban roles, the tradition of written law, the dispersion of landholding and use of money which explains why, in Italy, the collapse of the state led neither to a self-reproducing feudalism in the broader sense nor to a reconstitution of the monarchy on the narrower foundation of a fusion of benefice and vassalage? After the reign of Louis II, royal power was dissipated under the same pressures as in France. Support for the Crown depended on concessions to magnates whose loyalty became increasingly tenuous once the concessions had been made. Under Berengar I and his successors, control of the means of coercion passed to private military clientèles and the holders of fortified *castelli*; the capacity to raise public taxes lapsed after its final exercise by Berengar II in the year 947; and the loss of royal prestige was compounded by Berengar I's own failings as a military leader against the Hungarians. A degree of 'feudalization' of social relations ensued, both on the ground (as we saw in the case of tenth-century Latium) and in the codifications of the *Libri Feudorum* at a time when a strong German emperor furnished the role to which the chain of vassalage could be re-attached. But in the Italian context, an indigenous monarchy could no longer hope to reconstitute the necessary prestige, military following and territorial control. Ironically, it was in the *more* 'feudalized' world of tenth-century France that the king was better placed. In Italy, where the magnates did *not* hold their land from him, ties of purely personal loyalty dissolved as soon as they came under strain (Wickham 1981, p. 179).

There might have been expected to follow a permanent decentralization of sovereignty into the hands of the rising local magnates. But it is here that the relation of the towns to the countryside was decisive. Initially, power devolved on the role of the bishops, rather as it had done in Merovingian Gaul; and this had, for the kings, the twofold advantage that bishops could be played off against counts and that bishops, unlike counts, could not transmit their roles to their heirs. There were, to be sure, a few families which built up their power, including the exercise of local jurisdiction, on the basis of large rural landholdings. But the towns remained the administrative centres, and despite the decline in the number of *arimanni* with no lord but the king, the ideology of free men's rights survived. The role to which competitive advantage attached after the collapse of the central state was, therefore, that of the urban citizen, and its emergence can conveniently be dated between the first surviving charter of liberties granted to a citizen body (in Genoa) in 958 and the burning of the palace at Pavia by its citizens in 1024. The 'Darwinian' path to the evolution of a 'citizen' mode was now open. Indeed, there is a parallel to be drawn between the war between Chalcis and Eretria in Archaic Greece and the war between Pisa and Lucca in 1004; and just as in the seventh century B.C. the leading male household heads of the emerging Greek proto-states became Athenians, Corinthians, Thebans and so forth with their own hoplite militias, their own subordinate rural hinterlands and their own patriotic ideologies symbolized in their cults, coins and temples, so did the *cives* of North Italy in the eleventh century A.D. become Pisans, Mantuans, Veronese and so forth with their own militias, their own *contadi* and their own patriotic ideologies of which the new cathedral in Pisa is as striking an expression as the new temple of Apollo in Corinth.

In the German case, the broad contrast was likewise outlined in Section 8 of this Chapter. The later decentralization of the means of coercion favoured the emergence of separate territorial principalities, and despite the continuing personification of the imperial ideology by Frederick Barbarossa, there was not the institutional basis for a monarchy sufficiently powerful to reverse the trend to fission. 'In these states', as Marc Bloch put it, 'what survived of vassalage was turned to the advantage of their rulers and even the Church was obedient. Politically speaking, there was no longer a Germany; but, as they said in France, "the Germanies"' (1961, p. 429). But as in Italy, it is necessary to ask just why the retarded evolution of Germany made recentralization on the French model more difficult rather than less. Why was it that 'feudal' practices conferred competitive advantage on seceding magnates rather than on centralizing monarchs?

In historical terms, there are numerous might-have-beens by which the German monarchs could, perhaps, have established a lasting dominance. It must be possible that if the Papacy had been (from this point of view) less intransigent, or if Sicily had not been part of the empire at all, or even if (like Berengar I in Italy) Frederick II had been a better general than he was (Van Cleeve 1972, p. 535), an imperial absolutism, or at least a more stable patrimonial empire, might have evolved. But once Henry IV had failed to create the strong German state which, without the Investiture Contest, he might have done, later emperors lacked the economic and coercive resources with which to attempt it. Nor, despite the ideological legitimacy of the imperial role itself, could they assure the succession to it. The interests of those to whose roles local power had been delegated in return for their support came, therefore, to lie more in securing or augmenting that power than in maintaining loyalty to a central monarchy which had no more effective inducements to offer or sanctions to impose. After 1245, this was as evident to the *ministeriales*, for whom upward mobility into the expanding systact of petty nobles was now visibly possible, as to the princes and bishops. The practices of delegated authority and the roles defined thereby favoured local magnates to the point that they had no motive whatever to surrender the autonomy they now enjoyed. Indeed, given the weakness of the emperors relative to the Papacy and the other societies of Europe (including the emergent communes), they were more likely to lose that autonomy by remaining within the emperor's institutional catchment area than by risking a fission which he was, by the mid thirteenth century, powerless to prevent.

These contrasts make it all the more readily understandable (in the secondary, explanatory sense) why it was in Poland, above all, that ideal-typically 'feudal' practices and roles so functioned that its institutions could remain stable until competitive pressure shifted from the intra- to the inter-societal level. The reason for which the Polish *szlachta* had come to acquire so much power relative to the monarchy is simple enough. In the absence of a native dynasty, they were strong enough to bargain for it with foreign aspirants to the role. The monarchs, from Louis of Anjou in 1374 to Henry of Anjou in 1573, depended not only for military support but for the choice of their own successors on the consent of the members of a systact which was both an order and an estate. This systact controlled the Church as well as the peasantry; and since, unlike Italy, there were no urban centres of power, its members granted their consent entirely on their own terms. Unlike Germany, on the other hand, fission was not an option for them. By this time, inter-societal pressure required a militarily centralized nation-state.

The powers successively conceded to the Polish nobility were not 'feudal' in the narrower sense (N. Davies 1981, I, p. 214). Noble land was allodially held; the obligation of military service was directly to the Crown; the Crown never surrendered the right to levy tax directly; and the topmost political roles were (until the seventeenth century) filled at the Crown's discretion. But in the broader sense, the roles of the noble systact were defined by practices as advantageous to their interests as it is possible to conceive. Quite apart from their political privileges, their ability to extract economic surpluses from their dependent cultivators was strengthened by the growth of grain exports. Even nobles of moderate means could take part, and only the few peasants able to buy their freedom and employ wage-labourers in their turn could hope to compete with them on the open market. Nor, given the fiscal and juridical concessions already made by the monarchy, could the revenues from the grain trade be channelled to any material degree in its direction. The incumbents of noble roles thus came to enjoy the double advantage of, on the one hand, economic and juridical domination of those who worked the land and, on the other, the capacity to resist any attempt by the monarchy to increase its power at their expense. Ideologically, too, they were able to develop a collective systactic consciousness which based the privileges of their order on (often fictitious) descent and thus justified the categorical exclusion of peasants, townsmen and Jews. In Poland, unlike any of the societies of Western Europe, there were (as I argued in Section 23 of Chapter 3) no internal contradictions to prevent a feudal mode of the distribution of power from reproducing itself indefinitely. The competitive pressures which rendered it unviable were exogenous. Its downfall began because, and only because, it succumbed to 'two fatal geopolitical flaws' (Anderson 1974, p. 288): inadequate defence on the northern Baltic front and overextension on the southern front into the Ukraine.

§23. That Japan was by the fifteenth century, at any rate, a 'feudal' society in both senses seems agreed by specialists of all schools. Not merely does it exemplify a decentralization of the means of coercion into the hands of local magnates dominating their own dependent cultivators while still acknowledging the legitimacy of a national monarch; it was also pervaded by a set of practices similar, although not identical, to the benefices and vassalages of Western Europe. But the critical difference is in the practices defining the monarchical role. Once the emperor had abdicated *de facto* sovereignty in favour of successive shoguns, the ties between ruler and subjects in the ideological dimension ran separately from those in the coercive dimension of power. Whereas the slow evolution of a strong central state in France rested partly on the success with which the sacral character of the monarchical role was exploited by its incumbents, in Japan it rested on the political and military success of the incumbent of a role which was never intended to displace that of the monarch. It is not the only difference, or even the most important difference: the absence of manorialism,* the difference in the practices by which the respective roles of lord and vassal were defined, the different functions performed by religious and monastic institutions (including the performance of military roles by Buddhist monks up to their forcible suppression by Odo Nobunaga), and the persistence of peasant communities which did not 'belong' to local magnates but merely paid taxes (i.e., protection-rents) to whichever was strongest, all mark off Japanese society as a distinctive sub-type of the feudal mode. But if its evolution is to be explained, it is the way in which selective pressures acted on the roles of the shogun and local magnates respectively which needs to be elucidated in more detail.

Under the Ashikaga Shogunate, power was decentralized further than it had ever been under the Kamakura Shogunate, whose institutions had been conceived as supplementing, not replacing, the imperial administration. But the power attaching to the role of *shugo* was still constrained. Not only were the *shugos'* landholdings dispersed, but they needed to spend time in the capital and had therefore no choice but to rely on local families. Furthermore, the succession to their own roles was often in dispute. They were accordingly displaced from below, as we saw in Section 23 of Chapter 3, by the new *daimyō* who emerged from the Ōnin War.† At that point, the parallel is closest to the practices of European feudalism in the narrower sense: the relation of the different categories of *daimyō* to the shogun was that of vassals holding fiefs (*chigyōs*). But this relation was essentially unstable for the single and sufficient reason that the role of the shogun itself was seizable by force. By the mid sixteenth century, many *daimyō* were nurturing ambitions of conquest outside their own domains. The similarity which now suggests itself is less to the Capetian monarchy than to *caudillaje* on the Latin American model. It is not altogether fanciful to suggest a parallel between Tokugawa Ieyasu in Japan and Mariano Melgaréjo in Bolivia or (had he won) Pancho Villa in Mexico. An institutional context which favours the role of the magnates at the expense of the power of the central government can hardly fail to suggest to the more ambitious and

* To the extent that there *was*, given the exigencies of riziculture, a form of landholding homologous to manorial *seigneurie* on the European model, it can even by argued to have retarded rather than advanced the evolution of feudalism (Joüon des Longrais 1958, p. 142): *shiki* practices, by which rights to a share of the 'manor's' output could be both divided and transferred, functioned for that reason to weaken vertical social ties.

† The change is directly reflected in the vernacular term for the role – *sengoku-daimyō* ('daimyō of the period of warring provinces') as opposed to *shugo-daimyō* (Varley 1967, pp. 204–5).

powerful magnates the idea of not simply controlling their own domains but seizing (or creating) a role to which there can attach control of the means of coercion over the society as a whole.

Fission, however, was never an option. No Japanese magnate ever repudiated allegiance to the emperor or sought to establish an autonomous principality of his own. Although the Taihō reforms had failed to create an absolutism on the Chinese model under the imperial family, they did bequeath an ideological legacy not only of national unity but of Confucian norms.* It is plausible to suppose that geographical isolation was a necessary condition. But whatever the relative importance of geographical as opposed to ideological influences, the imperial line remained sacrosanct. Nor was there sufficient social space for autonomous city-states† to evolve in the interstices between the geographical and institutional catchment areas of rival magnates. When, therefore, the emperor and court progressively lost such coercive power as they had had, the system which evolved placed the means of coercion in the hands of the shoguns while leaving the emperor secure in the topmost ideological role. In the countryside, economic relations were articulated between extraction of the surplus for the benefit of absentee court landlords through the traditional practices and imposition of dues and taxes by new governors and stewards established by the shogun. Yoritomo's *shugos* initially functioned much like Charlemagne's *missi*, and his *gokenin* much like Charlemagne's *vassi*. But since it was at the topmost military, not ideological, role that the ties of vassalage culminated, the further decentralization of the means of coercion involved little further diminution of the power of the emperor than had taken place already. The shoguns were doubly at risk: not only might they be displaced from the role by a rival aspirant, but they might also be compelled to concede more power than they wished to magnates whom they could not fully control. But the emperor's role would remain

* Norms, that is, of government: it would be a misdescription to imply that Japanese society in all periods and milieux was even metaphorically 'Confucian'. See Morishima (1982, p. 44): 'We may say in general that, even after the impact of Westernisation, Confucianism still prevails in the government, Shintoism in the imperial family, and Buddhism among the populace.'

† Sakai, the port of modern Osaka, evolved through overseas trade and the provisioning of rival armies to the point that 'its citizens were to some extent self-governing and enjoyed a certain degree of judicial autonomy; and since many of them were *rōnin* (masterless samurai) they knew how to defend themselves against aggressors' (Sansom 1931, p. 349). But fully independent statehood on the Venetian model was out of the question: Hideyoshi simply had Sakai's protective moats filled in and encouraged its merchants to move to Osaka.

intact in either event. It was as inconceivable for even the most ambitious *daimyō* to aspire to independent kingship as to attempt to usurp the monarchical role for himself.

The near-anarchy of the late fifteenth century is thus explicable as a response to selective pressure which conferred decisive advantage on local samurai whose new, fief-like rights (*chigyōken*) over portions of *shōen* were effectively proprietorial. This enabled them not only to extract surplus produce (and corvée labour) from the dependent cultivators, but also to extend the linkage of land grants to military service down to subordinate retainers or family members of their own (J. W. Hall 1962, p. 42). The relevant practices were, so to speak, lying waiting for selection. The strong vertical ties of kinship which had permeated the social structure since before the Taihō reforms could readily be adapted to the relations between lords and vassals, and by comparison with the homologous roles in the West European sub-type of the feudal mode, the vernacular terms in which they were symbolized were much more explicitly familial. As samurai attached themselves to local magnates, they could be rewarded with *shiki* rights to the income from the *shōen* now controlled by the magnates within a relationship much more heavily weighted towards the obedience due from sons to their fathers than the reciprocal obligations due in theory, at least, from European lords to their vassals. As warfare became steadily more specialized and professional, the samurai evolved into an increasingly clearly differentiated systact with its own ideology and life-style inculcated within 'military houses' (*buke*). The Ashikaga shoguns could no more resist the decentralization of the means of both coercion and production than could the later Carolingians. The autonomous territorial units which emerged during the sixteenth century were not, as the territories assigned to the *shugo* by the shoguns had been, separate jurisdictional units, but compact domains held by a new generation of *daimyō* whose enfeoffed vassals directly supervised the village communities within them. Of these developments, the emperor and court were no more than the unchallenged but impotent spectators.

Yet this system reproduced itself only for some two generations before Odo Nobunaga's victory over the Takeda in 1575 initiated the unification completed by Tokugawa Ieyasu. In Western Europe, the feudal mode was inherently unstable because, broadly put, monarchies had either to succeed or to fail. In Japan, by contrast, the feudal mode was inherently unstable because the shogun's (or *kampaku*'s) role was still there to be filled. It could only last – and only did – for as long as there was a meta-stable equilibrium between *daimyō* none of whom commanded sufficient force to control the central territories.* The practices constitutive of 'feudal' roles functioned, as in Western Europe, to the advantage rather than the disadvantage of central governmental roles from the moment that sufficient economic, ideological and coercive resources could be reconstituted by a sufficiently skilful or fortunate aspirant. But the earlier decentralization of power was, all the same, a necessary antecedent condition. By no sequence of historical contingencies, however improbable, could the Tokugawa system have evolved directly out of the Taihō system: it was only a sub-type of absolutism on the Chinese model which might conceivably have evolved if a mandarinate could somehow have been recruited and empowered to administer it – which it could not. Once the Taihō system had failed, and armed retainers begun to attach themselves to local magnates who controlled the means of production directly, decentralization of power accelerated to the point that the *daimyō* could be misreported by visiting Europeans as 'kings'. But precisely because they weren't (but the emperor still was, ideologically speaking), evolution to another mode was sooner or later inevitable even in the absence of exogenous pressure.

§24. The role of the *caudillos* of Latin America in the decade following independence from Spain functioned analogously to those of the magnates of societies of other sub-types of the feudal mode. But their relations to state and peasantry were not homologous with that of any other. The *caudillos* were not a landed nobility on either the European or the Japanese mopel; and the more powerful an individual *caudillo* became, the *less* likely he was to be able to transmit his role to a chosen heir (J. J. Johnson 1964, p. 56). Their military followers were not vassals, or hired professionals, or (except incidentally) kinsmen or quasi-kinsmen. They followed them '*por cariño*' and in hope of reward conditional on their success. Like the *daimyō*, the *caudillos* might see control of the means of coercion on a national scale as within their grasp. But there was no role of shogun waiting for them to fill. They were not tax-farmers exploiting their revenues, or emirs exploiting their control of urban garrisons, or castellans exploiting their control of territories entrusted to them as fiefs. They owed their systactic location to the

* As we have seen, the period of meta-stability was shortened, in the Japanese context, by the introduction of firearms. But this was only because the systactic structure was such as to favour the first *daimyō* to use them effectively: in Ottoman Turkey, as we shall see in a moment, introduction of muskets hastened a *de*centralization of the means of coercion.

vacuum of central power after 1823 and to their local domination of dependent cultivators from whom they were, in addition, for the most part ethnically distinct.

In generalizing about 'Latin America', I am well aware of the regional diversities which make it in some ways as much of an oversimplification as to generalize about 'Europe'. Brazil has at once to be excluded from remarks about colonial independence after 1823; the history of nineteenth-century Mexico is quite unlike the rest, and that not only because of proximity to the United States; and Chile stands out from any summary account of *caudillaje* through its early establishment of a greater degree of civilian control of the means of coercion. But for the purposes of discussion of the evolution of different modes and sub-types of the distribution of power, the resemblances are more important than the differences. Not only did the sudden withdrawal of a long-established central authority generate in all of them selective pressures favouring the practices of which oligarchic landowners were the carriers, but these same pressures were to constrain their future evolution in the direction of an authoritarian rather than a liberal-democratic or socialist mode once industrialization was under way and power had begun to be transferred from the countryside to the towns.

In the colonial period itself, the power of the Spanish Crown had already been much decentralized. Indeed, it could hardly be otherwise, given the size of the continent, the slowness of communications, the development of the indigenous economy, the relative weakness of Spain itself under pressure of inter-societal competition, and the consequent pervasiveness at all levels of government of 'venality, graft, peculation and personal use of public funds' (Gibson 1966, p. 107). The institution of the *encomienda*, although it survived in legal form until the eighteenth century, had already by the end of the sixteenth 'ceased to exercise any vital function in colonial life' (Simpson 1950, p. xii). Large landholders, whether ecclesiastical or lay, could hardly fail to gain increasing autonomy, even to the point that a *hacendado* might be able to obtain a writ from the Viceroy forbidding visits by officials (F. Chevalier 1963, p. 296, on Mexico). In this context, the decision of the Spanish government to admit creoles to the role of officer in the Spanish army and the privileges attaching to it was tantamount to the recruitment of a generation of prospective *caudillos* (of whom Bolivar himself was one*). When independence came, the vacuum of power was ideological

* Not that Bolivar was a 'real' *caudillo*: he was a high-minded professional soldier who sought neither to consolidate his dictatorial role by becoming emperor nor even to use it to build up a personal fortune (Brading 1983, pp. 14–15). But the fission of the

as well as political: once the legitimacy of a monarch sanctified by the Church had been explicitly repudiated, power passed to those most capable of sustaining their roles by force independently either of political doctrine or of their own systactic origin. In the 1820s that was not, and could not be, a 'bourgeois' systact of notaries, merchants and officials.

Independence thus altered the modes of both coercion and persuasion. But the mode of production remained unchanged. In no Latin American society was there a significant vertical redistribution of landed property. The *caudillos* continued to extract the surpluses created by the dependent cultivators as before. There were, as there had been in the colonial period, marked variations both within and between different societies and regions, and rural social relations were seldom exclusively 'feudal', if by that is meant that the cultivators were tied to the soil by peonage in a precise analogue of European serfdom. As I noted in passing in Section 18 of Chapter 2, *hacendados* could be in debt to peons rather than the other way round and the practice of credit could be an inducement as much as a sanction.* But the *brazos* from whose labour the productivity of the land principally derived were still in a dependent role. They remained a subordinate and, indeed, exploited systact, whether willingly attracted by the advancement of wages offered by middlemen for seasonal employment† or coerced into near-servile debt-bondage as on the henequen plantations of Yucatan or rubber plantations of the Amazon headwaters. Only in the north of Mexico by the late nineteenth century did the possibility of alternative employment, the scarcity of labour, and the intrusion of the capitalist practices and roles from the United States create a genuine labour market and generate a sense of relative deprivation by comparison with American wages.

Elsewhere, over virtually the whole of the continent, employers were in a position to adapt their practices according to their perceived requirement for labour. Wage-labour on the capitalist model was seldom

Colombian republic which he had created demonstrates only too well the strength of the pressures for decentralization of the means of coercion of which he himself was fully aware.

* The topic of debt is controversial among specialists if only because of the almost inevitable intrusion of evaluative presuppositions. For the purposes of this volume, however, the moral to be drawn is that, as with sharecropping, the same practices can fulfil different functions in different contexts depending on the relative power of the systacts whose constituent roles they define.

† The value of debt to the employers can be quasi-deductively inferred from the prices at which debts changed hands – sometimes two or three times face-value (McCreery 1983, p. 750, on Guatemala).

an option for the simple reason that there were not yet the consumer goods on which workers could be motivated to spend the higher wages which higher productivity would earn. Tribute, fees and forced purchase of merchandise were practices consciously intended to heighten their perceived needs in a 'pre-consumer' context (Bauer 1979, p. 55). Although they were, in a few regions, formally tied to their particular employer's land, from the employers' point of view they did not need to be. Employers' interests were as well or better served by short-term employment and deliberate choice between relatively more and less unatttractive alternatives. Often, indeed, where they *were* tied in practice, it was because the demand for land had been so far heightened by population increase that neither debt nor coercion were necessary to retain them. This was a very different system from feudalism on the North European model. But it was feudalism all the same. Local magnates were both politically independent of central government and economically dominant over dependent cultivators within societies whose national unity they needed to preserve for their own interests. It made – for the moment – no difference that the magnates did not concede legitimacy to the embryonic urban élites who would in due course succeed in undermining the power attaching to their roles.

This sub-type of the feudal mode could thus be stable for as long as two conditions held: first – as with all feudal societies – the economy of the area had to remain dependent on agriculture (supplemented by mining); second, the balance of military power within each more or less well-defined society had to be such that no lasting monopoly of the means of coercion could be won and held. A successful *caudillo* like Melgaréjo might, it is true, transform his role into that of a short-term dictator. But the institutional basis for a stable authoritarian mode had yet to evolve underneath him. The practices did not yet exist from which there could be constructed a mass party, a centralized army and police, and an economy whose surpluses could be taxed directly for the purposes of the state. Even Porfirio Díaz, who appeared to have effected the transition in Mexico, turned out to be unable to retain his role and designate his chosen successor: as we saw in Section 19, *caudillaje* was not tamed until a recentralization was achieved within a 'modernized' sub-type of the authoritarian mode. *Caudillaje*, therefore, was not simply an ephemeral variant thrown up by the sudden withdrawal of colonial authority. It was, if you will, transitional, but no more so than the North European sub-type whose defining practices of benefice and vassalage ceased to function in the interests of magnates, as against monarchs, as soon as relative peace and prosperity had been restored. Its evolution was the product of a uniquely destructive conquest on a continental scale and a uniquely dramatic withdrawal some three centuries later of an authority which, remote as it had become, had created a set of institutions whose legitimacy was by then accepted as traditional. Once this had happened, it was inevitable that the practices to which competitive advantage attached should create a systactic structure and mode of the distribution of power which was as clearly 'feudal' in the broader sense as it was clearly a distinctive sub-type within that mode.

§25. To bring the evolution of Islamic agricultural societies into comparison with the evolution of post-Carolingian Europe, post-colonial Hispanic America, and pre-Tokugawa Japan is to introduce the complication that Islam creates a context much less favourable to a stable decentralization of the means of coercion to local landowners than to an alternation between patrimonial empires and their fission into a greater or lesser number of petty kingdoms or warrior emirates. It is not as if feudalism in the broader sense had been unknown to *pre*-Islamic Arabia. In the tribal kingdom of Saba, expansion by conquest created a structure in which power passed from the king and popular assembly to privileged clans controlling their own separate territories and dealing individually and directly with the king. But the king remained the ideological symbol of unity, and the prestige attaching to his role was sufficient to bring the separate tribes together in times of emergency and for communal irrigation works which they could not carry out by themselves. It is, therefore, perfectly valid to speak of a '*véritable féodalité*' (Ryckmans 1951, p. 331) as having evolved in Southern Arabia during the four or five centuries before Muhammad. After Muhammad, the difficulty in the way of a similar evolution was not ecological but ideological. To what quasi-monarchical role could legitimacy now attach if control of the means of coercion had once been decentralized?

The legitimacy of Muhammad's own role was, and could not have been other than, charismatic. It rested on the credibility of his mission and its success, and its survival after his death was due to a whole series of unpredictable contingencies of which the luck and skill of Abu Bakr in averting immediate fission is perhaps the most remarkable. Thereafter, the initial basis of legitimacy could never be recreated, however effective the ideology of the *jihād* in uniting the faithful in common opposition to the infidels. For the subsequent rulers of Islamic societies to claim to have realized upon earth the ideals of the Quran was to invite rebellion, if not indeed revolution, on the part of subjects very well aware that the claim could not seriously be upheld. Rulers could, and usually did, claim to be following the *Sharīʿa*. But their roles depended on coercive, not ideological, sanctions. None of the societies which emerged out of the collapse of the Abbasid caliphate, whether dominated by rulers who taxed the surpluses produced by the dependent cultivators in order to purchase the services of imported *ghilmān* or by rulers whose nomadic followers extracted the surpluses themselves in the form of protection-rent, denied ideological allegiance to *a* caliph (even if not the same one). But none acknowledged a political superior unless compelled by force of arms. The warrior mode therefore became, as we have seen, the norm* until the evolution of the Ottoman, Safavid and Mughal absolutisms. It was only under a very unusual combination of selective pressures that a mutation or recombination of the practices and roles constitutive of agricultural Islamic societies could generate a stable, self-reproducing feudal mode.

When the Buyids took over Baghdad in the mid tenth century A.D., there was waiting for one of them to fill the role of *amīr-al-umara* or 'commander-in-chief' which had been created earlier for the former governor of Wāsit (Kennedy 1986, pp. 197, 218); and this might appear to suggest the possibility of an evolution parallel to that of the Japanese shogunate in which a military ruler would exercise coercive sanctions in the name of the incumbent of the topmost ideological role. But an Islamic caliph whose role was purely ideological was not a Japanese *tennō* to whom national as well as religious loyalty was due. He was no more than the symbol of the idea of the caliphate. A local emir or king (*mālik*) might have the name of the current caliph mentioned at his Friday prayers or on his coinage (Mottahedeh 1980, p. 18), but only as a figurehead. Evolution to a feudal mode was ruled out for the simple reason that decentralization of the means of coercion was, in this institutional context, tantamount to fission. Within the territories which they controlled, the Buyids operated a system of the patrimonial-cum-federal sub-type presided over by a *shāhanshāh* whose role, despite its high-sounding title, was much closer to that of a Thessalian *tagos* than

* There is also reported in Bahrein an interesting Ismaili variant which appears to have evolved in the direction of a citizen rather than a warrior mode. The Carmathians (Qarāmita) of the tenth century A.D. were reported in the following century as a body of some 20,000 arms-bearing citizens governed by a council which owned the 30,000 slaves who did agricultural labour (B. Lewis 1970, pp. 110–11). But an earlier reference by the geographer Ibn Hawqal (Kramers and Wiet 1964, II pp. 289–90) suggests a government more like that of a warrior-state dependent on tolls forcibly levied on pilgrimage and commerce.

a feudal, and still less an absolutist, monarch. The role rested on a mixture of practices including ties of kinship, patronage of Daylamite troops, and the granting of *iqtas* (with the attendant risk of weakening the *shāhanshāh*'s subsequent ability to channel agricultural surpluses to the benefit of the state). Outside of this limited institutional catchment area, the decentralization of power into the hands of emirs appointed to support their own troops out of the revenues of tax-farming made them into independent rulers: purely formal legitimacy was subsequently bestowed on them by the caliph in Baghdad in return for their own purely formal submission.

It was, accordingly, only because of a particular combination of accidental circumstances that, as I briefly mentioned in Section 23 of Chapter 3, an Islamic feudalism evolved in fourteenth-century Iran between the Mongols and the Safavids. The institution of the *suyūrghāl* involved a significantly further decentralization of power than the *iqta* because and only because the rulers were now too dependent on Türkmen and their tribal followers to be able to refuse them heritable grants both of revenue from substantial territories and of exemption from taxation. Some of these territories were very large indeed, and a local emir might control the reserves of whole towns. But the reason for which they did not evolve into independent societies was straightforwardly military. In the dangerously fragmented political conditions of a period which permitted the spectacular conquests of Timur, 'whole political federations' like the adjoining Qarā Quyūnlū and Aq Quyūnlū (Fragner 1986, p. 507) could count on the military support of local commanders even though (or because) they could not deprive them of the tax revenues granted to them in return for it. Only when, as we have seen, Shah Abbās succeeded in recreating an Iranian monarchy in which the state had its own tax revenues, its own armies and its own Shiite devotees were the *suyūrghāls* suspended, or their holders removed, or local governorships granted in the form of non-heritable *tiyūls*.

This period of Iranian feudalism was, it could be said, no more than an interlude which without the Mongol invasion would not have occurred at all. But Islam does offer another very different example of the evolution of a feudal mode, which in this case emerged directly out of an absolutism that had been more successful than any other in resolving the ideological contradiction facing all Islamic states. The Ottoman sultans had achieved, as we saw in Section 25 of Chapter 3, a 'tacit concordat' in which the role of Sunni *mufti* functioned more like that of a Christian prelate in a West European monarchy than any other analogous role in any other Islamic society. The decline in the power of the sultan's role which followed the failure to carry the *jihād* further West or East did not, therefore, result either in a revolution like that which overwhelmed the Umayyads or a fission like that which followed the collapse of the Abbasids. The power of the central government weakened dramatically from the end of the sixteenth century onwards, but there was no openly acknowledged dilution of the sultan's institutional monopoly of the means of production, persuasion and coercion alike. The critical change was from the holding of *timars* by *sipahis* to the holding of tax-farms (*iltizams*) by local notables (*ayāns*) who thereby came to form a 'semi-feudal landed aristocracy in the provinces' (Inalcik 1964, p. 45). Under pressure from the introduction and spread of firearms and the shifting pattern of international trade and currency movements, the government came to depend on the tax-farmers for the reserves with which to employ paid companies of musketeers, while the Janissaries were now allowed both to enter civilian roles in the towns where they were stationed and to transmit their roles to their sons. The *ayāns*, accordingly, were authorized to enrol musketeers locally, whether for the sultan's army or for themselves (Inalcik 1975, p. 201); and even local courts came to be leased out to substitutes for the collection of dues in the judge's name (Inalcik 1972, pp. 341–2).

Hitherto, the *timars*, like the traditional *iqta* or the Mughal *jagir*, had been held on conditional tenure at the ruler's discretion. But now, leases of state land to notables were lifetime and even hereditary. '*Vakf*' estates, although nominally religious endowments, passed increasingly under the control of secular magnates who operated them commercially. The labour for these estates came either from slaves or from hired *reaya* faced with the choice between falling into debt with local moneylenders, from which (at rates of up to 50%) they were unlikely ever to free themselves, and attaching themselves to a large estate where, although protected from freelance bandits or regular soldiers requisitioning their surpluses by force, they were equally unlikely to regain their independence. By the eighteenth century, therefore, Ottoman society had evolved into a sub-type of the feudal mode whose institutions, while markedly different from those of Europe, Hispanic America or Japan, still functioned as a self-reproducing system almost as close, in its way, as Poland to the ideal type of feudalism in the broader sense. The local magnates enjoyed both political-cum-military independence from the central government and virtually complete economic and juridical domination of the dependent cultivators. But they did so within a set of ideological institutions which still gave unchallenged legitimacy to a monarchical ruler supported by a '*seyhülislam*' whose authority to interpret the *Shari'a*, while enabling him to oppose any challenge to Sunni orthodoxy, gave no licence to would-be theocratic interference with the 'ruling institution' itself.

The introduction of Islamic societies into comparison of the evolution of different societies within the feudal mode does not, accordingly, provide a negative control group so much as an alternative 'Darwinian' sequence from which, despite pressure more favourable to a patrimonial, warrior or even absolutist mode, a distinctively Islamic sub-type of feudalism could nevertheless evolve. The practices defining it are strikingly different from the West European fusion of benefice and vassalage. Indeed, the Ottoman institution most closely homologous to the fief – the *timar* – functioned to strengthen rather than weaken the sultan's control over mounted 'knights' supported from the revenues of dependent cultivators assigned to them in benefice. When power subsequently devolved from the sultan to the new systact of *ayāns*, it was, in complete contrast to Western Europe, in a context of infantry rather than cavalry warfare and commercialization of the economy rather than manorial autarky. Yet the practices to which the sultans had no choice but to consent were decisively advantageous to magnates who, in the absolutist period, had been at most tolerated intermediaries between the central government and the tax-paying *reaya*. Once the cycle of conquest and taxation carried out by servile functionaries had been broken by exogenous pressure, neither a service nobility nor a secularly educated mandarinate (and still less a bourgeoisie ready to purchase office as a means of upward mobility) was available to the sultans. Delegation of their notionally absolute control of the means of both production and coercion was the only practical alternative. But the resulting mode of the distribution of power was stable, however much weaker it left Ottoman society as a whole relative to the Christian societies of Europe. Only later again, when exogenous pressure had been renewed in other forms, did the *ayāns* evolve into *pashas* powerful enough to remove their provinces altogether from the institutional catchment area of the 'Sublime Porte'.

TEST CASES (2)

§26. There is no one case of the evolution of a society from either a feudal or a citizen (or any other) mode to an absolutist one which should be taken as the model with which all the rest are to be contrasted. But there are two reasons for going back initially to Japan: first, because far from exemplifying an ideal type it only barely, although decisively, qualifies; and second, because the selective pressures which determined the sub-type into which it evolved were decisive also in determining its subsequent evolution into an authoritarian rather than either a socialist or a liberal-democratic mode.

Tokugawa Japan was, as it can be put, '*à la fois centralisé et décentralisé*' (Mutel 1986, p. 60). But the same could no less accurately be said of Louis XIV's France. There too, the strengthening of royal authority was achieved as much by concessions of local autonomy as by the deployment of troops. A *pays d'état* like Brittany could well enjoy a similar relative autonomy to that enjoyed by the *han* of an 'outside' *daimyō* like Chōshū, and the Catholic Church remained far stronger in *ancien régime* France than the Buddhist orders in Tokugawa Japan, which after their virtual destruction by Odo Nobunaga were reinstated largely as an ideological counterweight to Christianity. It can fairly be said that the Tokugawa shoguns 'supervised' rather than 'administered' the *han* (A. Lewis 1974, pp. 75–6). But could the same not be said of the eighteenth-century kings of France and their provinces? The role of 'inspector-general' (*ometsuke*), although less power attached to it than to that of a French *intendant*, performed an analogous function, and Tokugawa law, although there was much less of it than French, applied equally across the society as a whole: the shogunate required its own example to be followed (*ibid.*). All sub-types of the absolutist mode depend on some degree of indirect rule. The corporate privileges which survived in eighteenth-century France were just as much of an impediment to the exercise of the king's nominally unlimited power as the privileges of the *daimyō* to the exercise of the shogun's.

The critical practices were those which ensured that even the most recalcitrant *daimyō* could no longer, any more than the most powerful regional magnates of eighteenth-century France, perform the role of *frondeur*. It was not only that a national army could be put in the field stronger than any alliance of magnates could mobilize, but that the magnates' own roles were now tied to the central government, in Japan as in France. The *diamyō* were vassals of the shogun; and although their tenure of their domains became, in due course, transmissible to their chosen heirs, in 1650 very few *daimyō* families were occuping the same territories as in 1600 (Duus 1969, p. 91). Moreover, as we saw in Section 24 of Chapter 3, periods of enforced residence in the capital by the *daimyō* (and the leaving of their families there as hostages) functioned as did the French nobility's periods of residence at Versailles. A monopoly of coinage, the disarmament of all commoners, a corps of salaried officials, and a network of police and informers extending over the whole of the country tightened the hold of the shoguns over the regions to a degree fully comparable to that achieved by Louis XIV in France or Catherine the Great in Russia or even Frederick the Great in Prussia, where the relative autonomy of noble landowners within their own manors* did not make them any better able to challenge the central government directly.

Given the almost total isolation of Japanese society from exogenous pressures, its evolution from a feudal to an absolutist mode was as near to inevitable as any such shift can be. When and how it might actually happen was contingent partly on military technology and tactics and partly on the competition at an individual level between rival *daimyō* of differing abilities and strengths. It might have taken longer than it did if a different *daimyō* had managed to usurp the shogun's role without then nullifying, as Tokugawa did, the threat still posed by aspiring rivals. But although this would have prolonged for a time the autonomy of the outlying *han*, it would have continued to be to each *daimyō*'s interest to occupy and strengthen the role of shogun for himself. It was not possible for them to create a 'nobles' paradise' on the Polish model where the landholding magnates are at peace with one another but serve together in the army of the king against external enemies. Nor was there the pressure (or opportunity) for an evolution from a feudal into a bourgeois mode. The carriers of commercial practices were there, to be sure; and those practices, or their mutants, were to enrich the systact of *chōnin* during the long Tokugawa peace. But the magnates had no interest in adopting commercial careers themselves, and the merchant class, such as it was, had neither the influence nor the prestige (nor the sense of relative deprivation) to make the transition from systactic identity to collective action.

The *chōnin* were not even legally permitted to buy agricultural land. Their importance to the economy, and with it their personal wealth, increased steadily over the course of the seventeenth century: they did not only market the agricultural surpluses and provide banking and loan facilities for the *daimyō* and the shogunate, but engaged in building, manufacturing and coastal shipping. But they had no effective legal

* The degree of their autonomy, and in particular the power of the *Landrat*, is disputed among specialists. But however unsatisfactory from Frederick's point of view some individual incumbents of the *Landrat*'s role, a *Landrat* was not merely the creature of the fellow-landowners who had (in some but not all cases) nominated him: 'All his functions, in so far as he discharged them, limited the sovereignty of the *Gutsherr* over his estate' (Behrens 1985, p. 144).

protection in their performance of their roles. To an even greater degree than their Islamic or early European or Sung Chinese or nineteenth-century West African counterparts, they were defenceless against arbitrary levies or repudiations of debt tantamount to outright confiscation.* Ideologically, they ranked below not only warriors but cultivators; and the geographical bases of their operations were no longer towns enjoying even a minimal degree of municipal autonomy, but either cities controlled by the shogunate directly or towns subordinated to the castles of the local *daimyō*. Far from standing in the way of consolidation of absolutism, the Japanese merchant class if anything facilitated it.

This still leaves unanswered the question what particular practices were selected which effected the transition to a stable, and not merely transient or experimental, absolutist mode; and the answer is that the decisive practice, or set of practices, was the mutation which turned the role of the *bushi* from that of armed retainer into that of salaried official. Specialists seem agreed that 'the fundamental current of change in sixteenth-century Japan was the one which drew the samurai off the land and left the peasantry in place within the newly defined village communities' (J. W. Hall 1974, p. 44). When, in 1585, Toyotomi Hideyoshi instituted a systematic land survey, a systactic division between cultivators (*hyakushō*) and *bushi* registered as stipendiaries of the local *daimyō* was effectively formalized. Although a nostalgic vision of a reunion of the two in which frugal warriors would exercise paternal supervision over contented peasants now released from burdensome taxation persisted throughout the Tokugawa period (J. W. Hall 1970, p. 205), it was no more than a myth. At first, the *bushi* continued in their role of armed retainers congregated in the *daimyōs*' castle-towns. But their duties gradually shifted to finance and administration, and their remuneration to stipends paid in rice.

These trends were simultaneously accompanied by an ideological shift from military to intellectual skills as the legitimation of the social location of the *bushi* – a shift reinforced by a selective but convenient version of Confucian moral principles. Status remained hereditary. There was no scope for upward mobility into samurai roles by able and ambitious sons of peasants, artisans or merchants. But specialization of function within what was by now a salaried (and overstaffed) bureaucracy developed to the point of a complex intra-corporate

* It is true that there were only two general cancellations of debt (*kien*) during the Tokugawa period; but there were no less than sixteen forced loans (*goyō-kin*) to the shogunate (Sheldon 1958, pp. 119, 166).

hierarchy, and in the eighteenth century the shogunate instituted for its officials a practice of incremental stipends whereby abler but lower-ranking samurai could move into more responsible roles. Internal peace and the demilitarization of the samurai role were mutually reinforcing. The *han* and the shogunate were administered by a self-reproducing systact comprising perhaps 7% of the total population whose members were increasingly well educated and whose ties to their superiors were increasingly impersonal.

The system was by no means free of conflicts and contradictions. There were sporadic, small-scale peasant revolts and sporadic outbreaks of samurai violence; the periods of residence by the *daimyō* in the captial involved very large outlays of unproductive expenditure which required them both to raise taxes on the rice surpluses from their domains and to borrow heavily from the urban merchants; commercial expansion was constrained not only by the ban on foreign trade but by the lack of a unified national market; the administration of the shogunate and the *han* alike was cumbersome and inflexible; rising population was not matched by rising productivity; technology was static; and the coinage was regularly devalued throughout the eighteenth century. But a stable absolutism had evolved, and it had evolved in a form which, when a change of mode came about under exogenous pressure, determined what the direction of that change would be.

§27. The evolution of a stable absolutist mode in China constrasts with the Japanese sub-type not only in the difference between the practices carried by a systact of mandarins rather than samurai, but also in the length of the antecedent history during which those practices, although institutionally established, were not yet pervasive. The test case is the transition from the T'ang system to the Sung. It is true that centuries before the reign of the 'Grand Progenitor' of the Sung Dynasty, Chao K'uang-yin, there had been rulers of more or less extensive areas who for shorter or longer periods had succeeded in curbing the power of the regional magnates, maintaining standing armies, extracting for their own governmental purposes the agricultural surpluses from the dependent cultivators, and retaining the services of a permanent administrative staff. Even the testing of civil service candidates for ability is attested as far back as 140 B.C. (Loewe 1966, p. 131), and in the late fifth century A.D. the advisers to the Northern Wei empress-dowager Wen-ming devised a whole set of institutions deliberately intended to strengthen the central government, including the conversion of large private landholdings to benefices conditional on the occupancy of an official role and payment of salaries to officials (Elvin 1973, p. 48). Earlier still, indeed, the Ch'in state of the third century B.C. had replaced the archaic monarchy with a legalistic, anti-autocratic, centralized system resting on the twin principles of 'enriching the state' (*fu-kuo*) and 'strengthening the armies' (*ch'iang ping*) in accordance with objective criteria (J. Gernet 1982, pp. 79, 82). But these were no more than short-lived precursors of the distinctive sub-type of absolutism into which Chinese society only much later evolved in a stable form; and it did so not, as in Japan, through a sequence from patrimonial monarchy to feudalization to civil war to recentralization, but out of a series of cycles of imperial advances and retreats, aristocratic or dynastic rebellions, usurpations of local power by magnates, wars between states created by fission, and periods of anarchy in which there emerged 'great companies' both homologous and analogous to those of medieval Europe which I cited in Section 22 of Chapter 3.

It is true that, under the T'ang, China was not only a unified state but one whose influence and prestige extended far beyond its borders. But in this, it is more reminiscent of the reign of Charlemagne than the reign of Louis XIV. Although the success of the T'ang did not rest to the same degree on the personal qualities of a single patrimonial ruler, the system did similarly depend on a form of political-cum-military organization in which the price of expansion and conquest was the devolution of power from the central government to the provincial and frontier generals.* Like the Carolingian counts, the T'ang 'commissioners' (*chieh-tu-shih*) became effectively autonomous rulers of the military districts assigned to them. The central government was powerless to prevent the designation by the current incumbent of his own chosen successor to the role. Despite the attempts at reform following the rebellion of An Lu-shan, the provinces of Hopei and Shantung passed entirely out of the emperor's control, and the simplification of the system of tax assessment and collection after 779 involved its delegation to provincial prefects who drew their own revenues from it. The income derived from the state monopoly of salt, substantial as it was, was not substantial enough, and its collection functioned likewise to increase the power of the merchants to whom it was entrusted as agents. At the same time, the roles of the central bureaucracy were being undermined in favour of the court eunuchs. It

* It is worth noting that in the absence of the practice of vassalage, social relations among provincial rebels were cemented by adoptions and oaths (J. Gernet 1982, p. 270) in a manner very reminiscent of the warrior emirates which emerged after the collapse of the Abbasid caliphate.

is hardly surprising that many of the institutional innovations of Chao K'uang-yin were motivated by an explicit intention to strengthen the civil service and to ensure that the provinicial generals could no longer usurp local control – which he did by keeping the best of his troops in the capital and replacing the old military governors by civilian officials. This concern with internal order had, as I have already remarked, the unintended consequence of weakening the society's capacity to resist the Jürchen and subsequently the Mongols. But the transition to a self-reproducing absolutist mode had been achieved.

The context in which the transition took place did not favour only those practices which functioned to centralize control of the means of coercion. The modes of production and persuasion changed too. Chinese society under the T'ang had been dominated by families of horse-breeding warrior magnates who were only conditionally loyal to the current incumbent of the imperial role and whose estates with their own mills, parks, orchards, oil-presses and workshops were, by the end of the eighth century, encroaching increasingly on the lands of the free cultivators. Indeed, these estates are strikingly reminiscent of the sort of manorial autarky depicted in the Carolingian capitulary *De villis*. The institutions of the Sung, although they did not significantly alter the structural location of the dependent cultivators, required nonetheless a whole range of novel roles. Culturally, demilitarization and commercialization between them brought into being a world of rentiers, industrialists, stewards, middlemen, brokers, agents, managers, overseas traders, civilian advisers, literati, entertainers and shopkeepers* protected by a mercenary army and legitimated by a neo-Confucian ideology. The pressures which gave rise to it were, moreover, strongly reinforced by a geographical shift to the South, where population growth, intensive rice cultivation, foreign trade and the increasing sophistication of money and credit created an environment overwhelmingly favourable to the spread of commercial practices.

In the economy, too, many of the practices which came to pervade the institutions of the Sung can be traced back to the T'ang, notably the use of state monopolies to raise government revenue and the shift from persons to land as the tax base. Furthermore, the salt monopoly, as I have remarked, had been (if no more) a useful source of revenue, and the assessment of tax on household property was not only more equitable

* The guilds, which under the T'ang had been no more than officially sanctioned quarters consisting of merchants and shopkeepers in the same trade (compare the Roman *collegia*), now evolved into something approaching autonomous trade associations (Shiba 1970, p. 1).

but more productive than assessment on persons once the *chün-t'ien-fa* system had ceased to function. But these mutations could not, in the context in which they first emerged, generate a qualitative change in the mode of production. It was only when, after the recentralization of government and the establishment of internal peace, a mutually reinforcing cycle of increasing population and increasing productivity was under way, that increasing volumes of both internal and external trade, improved communications, a massive expansion in the output of copper cash, and the use of bills of exchange and paper money led to a pervasive commercialization of Chinese society. The heightening of agricultural output by the use of new fertilizers, new strains of rice-seed, and new techniques of irrigation was supplemented by a rapid – indeed spectacular – rise in coke-fired iron output. The greater wealth of the society as a whole did not, to be sure, improve the well-being of all classes: as in the societies of Early Modern Europe, the problem of poverty in the expanding cities was exacerbated by the influx of country dwellers from regions where an adverse ecology and climate prevented productivity (or the opening-up of new lands) from keeping pace with the increase in population (Scogin 1978, p. 37). But this too was a symptom of the spread of market practices and the evolution of a commercial mode of production. The difference from T'ang China is perhaps most succinctly illustrated by the observation which I quoted from McKnight (1971, p. 6) in Section 11 of Chapter 3: under the Sung, local élites were simply 'the rich'.

In this new culture and structure, however, the dominant systact was from the beginning the mandarinate. Here again, the process at work was the adaptation of practices initially introduced under the T'ang; and again, it was partly the pursuit of a deliberate policy – including the design of a *cursus honorum* for bureaucratic careers – and partly the product of chance improvisation.* But the critical mutation was from the practice of selection of incumbents by ascriptive criteria to selection by merit, whether through examination or sponsorship or a mixture of both. To avoid favouritism, the emperor himself took part in the examination of candidates for the topmost administrative roles, and the principle of anonymity in written examinations was taken so seriously that a Board of Copyists was established to eliminate the risk that an examiner would recognize a favoured candidate's handwriting. These

* Kracke (1953, p. 54): '...the new devices came about almost by accident, incidental to the solution of some immediate and perhaps minor problem. The long range utility of a device commonly appeared only after it had been tried, and the improvised scheme was then shaped into a conscious procedure.'

practices functioned to the advantage of the imperial role and the mandarin systact alike. Not only did they increase the power of civilian relative to military roles, but they substituted for the influence of court favourites the influence of professional civil servants. The Draconian injunctions of the T'ang law code, whose articles are reminiscent in both their priorities and their penalties of the laws of the Anglo-Saxon kings, were replaced by Confucian norms of obedience and right conduct by which local sub-prefects and the populations in their care were (in theory) guided. Nor was there any risk that the mandarins would evolve into a systact of landholding magnates capable of usurping the power of the central government. True, they used their wealth to acquire land; but they had little if any control of the means of coercion, their systematic rotation over the course of their careers from region to region prevented them from building up enduring local clientèles, and their ambitions for their sons were for success in the examinations whereby they could follow their fathers into mandarin roles.

The system was not without its conflicts, quite apart from its failure to make its large and expensive mercenary army strong enough to resist invasion from the North. The rise and subsequent fall of the reforming minister Wang An-Shih in the late eleventh century illustrates both the need for further fiscal and administrative measures and the difficulty of implementing them. The Sung mandarins could not abolish inflation, factionalism, corruption, banditry, urban overpopulation and peasant indebtedness; the influence of the court eunuchs increased again after Wang An-Shih's death; and although the Mongols and subsequently the Ming did not abolish the civil service entirely, it never regained quite the dominant location which it had held under the Sung. Yet China was not again subjected to fission into separate dynasties and kingdoms. Nor did it either regress to a patrimonial monarchy or evolve into a sub-type of absolutism dependent on a systact of venal office-holders, or servile functionaries, or service nobles. Nor, finally, did it evolve from an absolutist into a bourgeois mode. To raise this even as a possibility is to invite counterfactual speculation of the kind for which there is no possibility of conclusive test. But the quasi-experimental contrast is worth drawing because the shift to a commercial mode of production within a stable absolutism invites the obvious question why selective pressure did not favour the practices of which the commercial systact was the carrier sufficiently to raise its political as well as its economic location. What was it about the context in which commercialization took place which constrained Chinese society within its distinctive sub-type of absolutism? The question cannot be answered simply by saying that China failed to make the transition to industrialization, since evolution to a bourgeois mode might in any case have released new forces of production in much the same way as happened in eighteenth-century England. But what were the pressures which could have brought it about? It was the systactic power of the mandarinate which preserved the absolutist mode, even when the Chinese merchants and industrialists as a class were at their richest and most influential; and the practices which enabled it to do so were ideological as well as political.*

Politically, the mandarins were no less determined to curb overmighty entrepreneurs than overmighty generals, and their determination was both inspired and reinforced by a Confucian ideology which, while not actively inimical to the pursuit of private profit, held in low esteem both the means by which it was pursued and the ends to which it was applied. Conspicuous flaunting of control of the means of production was no less distasteful than of control of the means of coercion. The response of Chinese officials to the rapid expansion of any sector of industry and commerce was either to curb it or to absorb it within the direct control of the state. Regulation, taxation, proscription and expropriation of entrepreneurs was, as I remarked in Section 26, by no means unique to China. But China was unique in the degree to which 'official ideology and popular psychology ... coincided to reinforce the advantage officials had in any and every encounter with merely private men of wealth' (McNeill 1983, p. 50). Whatever the relative strength of ideological and coercive pressures, the contrast with the commercialization of English society is unarguable. The members of the Chinese merchant and entrepreneurial class carried out the same commercial practices, and enriched themselves through the performance of the same commercial roles, as their English counterparts. But there is not a single ancillary competitive advantage which they shared with them. Unpredictable as historical contingencies are, it is difficult if not outright impossible to conceive of a sequence of events whereby the commercialization of the Chinese economy which accompanied its reunification under the Sung could have led to the evolution of a parliamentary monarchy unsupported by a standing army, an autonomous capitalist class, and an ideology which encouraged nobility and gentry alike to invest directly in industry.

* Schurmann (1956, p. 507) says likewise of the 'oppressive and restrictive forces' which accompanied the increasing alienability of the means of production from the T'ang onwards that they 'have a social and religious, and not an economic base'.

§28. The evolution of an absolutist mode in Islamic societies is constrained by the same familiar problem of legitimacy confronting all Islamic rulers since Muhammad himself. But it is at the same time facilitated by the almost uniquely Islamic use of not only freedmen and clients but slaves for military and administrative roles* and dependent but formally free peasants for the production of economic surpluses – an institutional variant which one specialist attributes to the same inescapable problem of ideological legitimation.† The potential advantage to the would-be absolutist ruler of servile soldiers and functionaries is, as I have remarked already, clear enough, provided that a sufficient supply of suitable recruits is available for the reproduction of the system. There are, at the same time, the two concomitant risks of what might be called the 'Mamluk effect' (the servile soldiery usurp the power of their masters) and the 'Janissary effect' (they use their power to obtain civilian privileges for themselves and their successors); and it was the first of these which undermined the power of the Abbasid caliphs, just as it was the second which undermined the power of the Ottoman sultans. But if the risks turned out to lead to a regression to a warrior mode in the first case and a feudal mode in the second, it was still the competitive advantages conferred by the practice which enabled these two societies to evolve into reproducible absolutist modes in the first place.

The Abbasids and Ottomans are not, to be sure, the only Islamic absolutisms in the historical record. I have discussed already as an example of a successful reform of pre-existing institutions the achievement of Shah Abbās in Iran in fostering practices constitutive of an absolutist mode with a minimal disturbance to the structure; and there is also the Mughal sub-type briefly cited in Section 25 of Chapter 3, in which a homologue of the European fief (the *jagir*), together with rotation of office-holders and a well-staffed bureaucracy, prevented the decentralization of power to the local *mansabdars*. But the Abbasids and Ottomans provide a more instructive quasi-experimental contrast. The use of servile soldiers and administrators was central to both. But whereas the Abbasids came to power through the failure of the

* The Christian society of Georgia is an exception which might be said to prove the rule; the Byzantine army did include a special corps of Turkish children brought up as Christians, but they were not servile.

† Pipes (1981, p. 59) argues that military slavery is not 'Islamic' in the sense that 'it has no religious sanction and it is not even unambiguously legal', but 'Islamicate' in the sense that 'As a result of the unattainable nature of Islamic public ideals, Muslim subjects in premodern times relinquished their political and military power' (p. 70), particularly when military service involved fighting fellow-Muslims (p. 71).

Umayyads to break out of the constraints of a warrior mode, the Ottomans evolved their novel institutions in the course of an expansion by conquest in the name of the faith no less successful than that of the Umayyads had been.

The Umayyad caliphate, having at once usurped and preserved the early Islamic State, remained a society in the warrior mode, despite the undoubted success of Abd al-Malik in introducing some monarchical practices into the role of caliph. It would be an oversimplification to report the systactic structure of Umayyad society in terms of a clear-cut division between dominant Arabs, intermediate *mawālī*, and subordinate *dhimmī* not converted to Islam. But the warriors whose salaries were paid out of the agricultural surpluses of conquered territories were overwhelmingly Arab, and the majority of *mawālī* were, although exempt from the poll-tax levied on non-Muslims, still liable to land-tax as well as the *zakat* for the benefit of the poor. Nor were the revenues of the caliphate derived to any significant extent from industry or trade. On the contrary, 'even the merchant class of Mecca with some exceptions seems to have abandoned its former vocation for the role of a warrior aristocracy' (B. Lewis 1970, p. 69). The precarious unity of the Umayyad state was, moreover, threatened not only by systactic conflicts between Arabs and Islamicized non-Arabs but by threats of rebellion or fission on the part of one or another tribal or regional Arab group. The maintenance and reproduction of a unified Islamic society depended, therefore, both on integrating the *mawālī* and on keeping the warrior Arabs loyal to a caliph whose legitimacy derived from his leadership of the *jihād* and his appointment through a quasi-elective process in which personal prestige was more important than descent.

The collapse of this system, when it came, was through a revolution effected by a coalition in which non-Arab warriors and Arab non-warriors, both of whose anomalous locations generated a mounting sense of relative deprivation, alike played a significant part. But they themselves were not the carriers of the practices which were to define the Abbasid system: no sooner had the revolution succeeded than the leading revolutionaries were executed, their doctrines discarded and their soldiery displaced. Thereafter, however, the new dynasty was able to establish itself in an environment more favourable to an absolutist mode in all three dimensions. The yield of the mines of the Hindu Kush and fertile heartlands of Iraq, together with a rapid expansion of commerce, generated an economic surplus adequate to support a cosmopolitan bureaucracy and an army no longer predominantly Arab. With that army, the legitimacy of a caliph who proclaimed himself the

'Shadow of God upon the Earth' could be forcibly, and indeed ruthlessly, sustained. The Umayyad garrison towns became market centres; the military *corps d'élite* came increasingly to consist of Turkish slaves; and the disenchanted ulemate were left with no choice between sectarian apostasy and a tacit acquiescence in a Persian-style monarchy of whose theocratic trappings they wholeheartedly disapproved. All these practices, to be sure, had consequences which were later to weaken the dynasty rather than strengthen it. Excessive exploitation of agriculture in Iraq, coupled with an adverse change in ecology and climate (Waines 1977), made it increasingly less able to sustain what had become, because of loss of territory elsewhere, an increasingly heavy burden of taxation; the Mamluks in Baghdad remained loyal only as long as they could be kept internally divided among themselves; and the caliphs were continually faced with dissident religious movements whose followers were ready for armed revolt (or revolution) in the cause of a purer Islam. But the Abbasids had by then transformed the warrior mode of the Umayyads into a monarchical absolutism well able to reproduce itself without dependence on either the charismatic qualities of the individual incumbent of the caliph's role or the purely conditional support of warriors liable to secede at will.

The Ottoman Turks, by contrast, created an Islamic absolutism not by abandoning the *jihād* in order to consolidate an empire already won but, on the contrary, by using it to create a set of institutions in which its continuance reinforced, and was reinforced by, absolutist practices. We have seen, in Section 25, how the failure to carry the war against the infidel further East or West led to an evolution – or regression – to a feudal mode of the distribution of power. But in the fifteenth century, after they had recovered from defeat by Timur in 1402, the Ottomans were able, by means of a set of mutually reinforcing economic, ideological and coercive practices, to channel the resources generated by conquest into further expansion without in the process undermining the power of the central state. As in the expansion of the first Islamic state, it was the triple attraction to converted warriors of booty, status and a military career in the service of their victorious conquerors which simultaneously solved the problems of military recruitment and regional (or tribal) loyalty. But the distinctive Ottoman combination of a servile military and administrative élite with provincial timariots whose share of tax revenue was conditional on cavalry service made it possible for territorial conquest simultaneously to function as the agent of institutional absorption – supplemented as necessary by forced deportations reminiscent of the Mongols and Inca.

The pre-existing administrative boundaries were, as a rule, preserved. The Ottoman sources show that 'not only many Ottoman *beys* in the government of the provinces but also a considerable number of timariots in the main Ottoman army during the fifteenth century were direct descendants of the pre-Ottoman local military classes or nobility' (Inalcik 1954, p. 113). There were, as is to be expected, considerable variations in the system from one part of the empire to another: thus there are reported Muslim children in Bosnia being taken for the *devshirme*, Christian timariots in Albania who once they have shown themselves loyal to the sultan are not required to convert to Islam, and in Cyprus an explicit policy of conciliating the dependent cultivators hitherto liable to forced labour on the demesnes of their Venetian landlords. But the standard procedure was to conduct a survey of the taxable resources of a newly conquered territory and to entrust it to one or more *beys*, who were then responsible both for the leadership of the timariots under them and for the implementation of the legal decisions of the judges (*kadis*). The *devshirme* was, it would seem, much disliked by the Christian families in the European and Near Eastern provinces who were subject to it (Vryonis 1956, p. 441). But the burden of taxation was probably no greater than under the 'Franks', and except in the more remote and mountainous areas, resistance appears to have been minimal. Both the landholding élites and the indigenous peasantry were, accordingly, absorbed into the institutions of a society both Islamic and absolutist whose continuing expansion under the ideology of the *jihād* functioned to the advantage alike of timariots, Janissaries, Turkish settlers in the conquered territories, and the sultanate itself.

That the Ottomans should succeed in evolving through expansion by conquest into a absolutist mode whereas the Umayyads should fail is, accordingly, another of those apparent paradoxes which dissolves as soon as the selective pressures at work are more closely examined. The geographical, as well as the sociological, context of the Ottoman expansion was critically different. Like the Arabs, the Turcoman pastoralists were at once nomadic and warlike. But where Umayyad expansion made it progressively more difficult for the caliphs to adapt the traditional practices of Arabian politics to Syrian domination from Damascus (Donner 1981, pp. 276–7), Ottoman pressure on the frontiers of the Byzantine empire continually reinforced the crusading zeal of successive immigrants seeking booty, land and the further western extension of the *dar-al-Islam*. Meanwhile, the urban artisans, merchants and clerisy, whose sense of relative deprivation under the Umayyads had made them so receptive to heterodox ideology, found under the

Ottomans ample opportunities to pursue their interests in the commercial centres of an expanding empire ideologically unified by orthodox Sunnism. An analogous mutation had enabled the Abbasids to integrate the commercial systact within an Islamic absolutism, but only after abandoning the political institutions of the Islamic state for those of the traditional Iranian monarchy. This was not (as it has sometimes been misreported) a displacement of Arabs by Iranians: Iranian scribes and administrators had served the Umayyads as well as the Abbasids. But it was a displacement of Arab by Iranian practices. Arab roles and institutions could be adapted, under Islam, to function with remarkable efficiency as instruments of conquest, but not as instruments of empire.

§29. What then about Europe, both Western and Eastern? France is, as it has been treated throughout this volume, the obvious model. This is not only because of the success of Louis XIV after the *Fronde* in establishing control of the means of coercion through a regular army, control of the means of production through effective taxation* of the agricultural surplus, and control of the means of persuasion through an ideology of monarchy sanctioned by the Church. It is also because of the overwhelming impression which his success made on his contemporaries elsewhere. But (as I have also emphasized) French society of the late seventeenth century was not as free from internal contradictions as it was made to appear. By the mid eighteenth century, the systactic structure seemed stable, for all the inadequacies of the fiscal system and strains imposed by war. Yet only a generation later, by the time that Calonne reported to Louis XVI that France was effectively bankrupt, that structure was fragile beyond the possibility of avoiding either revolution or major reform. Why then, it might fairly be asked, take France as a model at all?

But it can equally pertinently be pointed out that Russia, too, succumbed to revolution in 1917, and that Prussia, having survived only by a hairsbreadth in 1762–3, went down before Napoleon in 1806. The relevant comparison lies not in the institutional weaknesses which

* The importance of tax-collection has been sufficiently stressed already, but is perhaps best illustrated by the example of Spain, where the monarchy's inability to tax Aragon as it could Castile was a double source of weakness. Aragon continued to enjoy a dangerous degree of political autonomy, whilst despite the inflow of American silver the excessive economic demands imposed by Castile undermined what would otherwise have been an opportunity for possible expansion. Hence Spain's 'decline' – or failure to reach a level of resources from which to do so (Elliott 1961; Kamen 1978).

subsequent pressures were to expose, but in the different practices by which (in contrast to Poland or, for that matter, the Habsburg empire) different absolutist regimes did manage to secure effective domination over their landed magnates. We have seen that by comparison with France, Prussia's economic institutions were relatively more efficient, and that by comparison with Russia, its political institutions were better able to extend the reach of governmental ordinances down to regional and local level. But in what most directly affected the stability of the systactic structure, all three were alike. In all three, monarchy and magnates together were well capable of holding the dependent cultivators under control. If they are contrasted as they were on the eve of the French Revolution, it can no doubt be debated among specialists in which of the three the condition of the peasantry was least favourable and their potential sense of relative deprivation as an exploited class most acute. But although peasant discontent was, as it turned out, critical for the course of events in France in 1789, this was only in the context of a previous *révolte nobiliaire*. Whatever the structural weaknesses which were then disclosed, the earlier contrast to be explored is that between the practices which determined the distinctive evolution of the roles of the three different nobilities and their common subordination to monarchies with whom they cooperated, against the interests of the dependent cultivators, in the service of the state.

In Prussia, the task of the monarchy was, as we have seen, made easier by the relative poverty of the nobles. It was not just that they did not have alternative careers open to them and that they were, no less than their counterparts in France, *nés pour le mestier de la guerre*. It was also that in Prussia the military virtues 'were rated more highly than in France, notwithstanding the honour there paid to them' (Behrens 1985, p. 67). It is more than simply a descriptive gloss to say that the style deliberately cultivated by the Hohenzollerns was professional rather than aristocratic. The officer corps was directly under the control of kings who not only led their armies into battle but exercised a continuing direction over all aspects of military organization in peace as well as in war. Furthermore, there was no competing bourgeois systact with a separate interest, whether in the sense that individual bourgeois were aware that they could acquire noble status by purchase of office or in the sense that they were collectively conscious, as a class, of controlling a significant proportion of the means of production. Sale of offices was limited to judicial roles by Frederick William I, and repudiated altogether by Frederick the Great. Although both drew on persons of non-noble systactic origins for administrative (and, as we have seen, *some* military) roles, this created no conflict of interest within the nobility such as that which intermittently broke out between the *noblesse d'epée* and *noblesse de robe* in France. Mercantile roles had of course to be performed, and the Hohenzollerns were at least as well aware as Colbert that wars have to be paid for. But because there was no previous history of urbanization, commerce, as it expanded, was in the hands of noble landowners exploiting their fiscal privileges to the disadvantage of the towns (Kamen 1984, pp. 142–3). The deliberate efforts of the Hohenzollerns to make Prussia militarily powerful and, therefore, economically prosperous enough for military purposes were made in an institutional context which tied the interests of the nobility directly to those of the monarchy. The novel roles which emerged as the relatively primitive institutions of the time of the Great Elector evolved, under the pressure of inter-societal competition, into those of the later years of Frederick the Great, were filled by incumbents with neither the opportunity nor the motive to use them against the Crown.

The evolution of Prussian absolutism can from one point of view be narrated in terms of the individual policies and preferences of the 'Great Elector', Frederick William I (the 'Sergeant King') and Frederick the Great, who successively recruited, restrained and indulged the nobility in the service of the state. But these policies were not just matters of whim, or even of a conscious attempt to create a more efficient absolutism than either the French or the Russian. They were direct responses to the competitive pressures under which the three rulers were successively acting. The Elector's immediate need was to find both troops and taxes, and these twin aims were jointly realized by the terms of the Recess of 1653 which voted a subsidy sufficient for an army whose functions were then extended, as we saw in Section 25 of Chapter 3, to include control of tax, municipal government, trade, manufacturing and the guilds. Once this had been achieved, the national political roles of the nobility were effectively curtailed at the same time that their local administrative roles were left intact. Under Frederick William I, therefore, 'the Dynasty still maintained steady pressure on the nobility, but the estates had, by then, grown accustomed to registering merely formal protests and, for the most part, the nobles offered only passive resistance to such legislative innovations as threatened their interests' (Goodwin 1967, p. 85).

It was because and only because of this earlier history that Frederick the Great could favour the nobility as he did. By then, the practices defining their roles not only limited their scope for independent opposition but channelled them into the performance of economic, as well as administrative, functions within the institutions of the state. It is true that by the end of his reign, some of these practices were no longer adaptive for the interests of their carriers. He had sought, in effect, to turn the nobility into a caste; but despite his efforts to preserve their monopoly of the means of agricultural production and their concomitant status as 'feudal' lords, many estates were mortgaged, many non-noble purchasers acquired 'noble' land, and the salaries of junior army officers and incumbents of the lower bureaucratic roles were far from adequate to support their families in the appropriate life-style. By the early nineteenth century, endogenous and exogenous pressures of a kind of which Frederick the Great had had no inkling were combining to force the reforms which broke down the systactic barriers between noble and bourgeois and integrated the two into a new, capitalist mode of production. But none of this modifies the explanation of Prussia's evolution to the position it enjoyed in Europe in the 1780s. The competitive pressures then operating selected practices which turned its landowning magnates from a recalcitrant provincial estate into a service nobility uniquely effective as the servant of a bureaucratic, militaristic and mercantilist monarchy which, although it claimed no sacral legitimacy, incarnated the interests of the state at least as effectively as the king whose apocryphal maxim was '*l'état, c'est moi*'.

The evolution of Russian absolutism followed an analogous path to Prussia's, despite the different origins of its service nobility. The critical mutation, as we briefly saw in Section 2 of this Chapter and Section 5 of Chapter 3, was the *pomestye* grant which made possible the displacement of the stratum of *boyars* by service nobles of lower systactic origin and a coalition, as in Prussia, between government and landowners to whose joint advantage it was to tie the cultivators to the soil. As in Prussia, the roles and their defining practices which in English are subsumed under the term 'serf' varied widely, and by comparison with Prussia the problems of flight and rebellion were altogether more serious. But the systactic structure rested in both cases on local control of the means of coercion under a monarchy whose legitimacy was never challenged. The difference was in the relations between the nobility and the Crown. It was not just that the Prussian service nobles were more professional, but that they were less divided by conflicts of interest than their counterparts in Russia. The obliteration in the mid seventeenth century of the distinction between *votchina* and *pomestye* estates neither overcame the resistance of the nobility to compulsory service nor narrowed the social distance between large landowners and small. The tsars had therefore to uphold the power attaching to their role as much by exploiting differences among the nobility as by imposing uniform conditions of service on them. But in this they succeeded. There can be no doubt that 'The Russian State remained an autocracy, and the successive interventions of the nobles were confined to the use of the Guards regiments to depose an unpopular autocrat, or to influence the order of succession' (Beloff 1967, p. 177). Catherine the Great did not, any more than Louis XIV or Frederick the Great, anticipate the ways in which the institutions over which she reigned might come to be subjected to pressures of an altogether different kind. But the stability of Russian absolutism was not in doubt at any stage of her reign.

§30. To contrast the evolution of the different European sub-types of absolutism is to raise all the more insistently the question why England never evolved into an absolutist mode at all. Henry VIII, after all, was to all appearances as powerful a monarch as any of his European contemporaries or, to draw the more distant parallel, Tokugawa after he had completed the unification of Japan. Yet on no theory can it be disputed that in England, monarchical absolutism failed (Mousnier 1970a, p. 104). It was not for want of trying. The Civil War of the mid seventeenth century was at least as much the defeat of a monarchical revolution from above as it was the victory of a bourgeois reform from below. But, like France's evolution to a bourgeois mode after a genuine revolution, English society by 1700 would have been one sub-type or another of the bourgeois mode with or without it. It was not that the weakness of the monarchy was the consequence of successful resistance by a united magnate systact relatively deprived of what it saw as its collective entitlement to power. It was, on the contrary, because neither monarchy nor magnates were dominant within the systactic structure that selective advantage accrued to practices constitutive of a bourgeois mode. Regional *frondeurs* (even in Scotland) no longer posed a threat to the central government; they neither commanded their own armed retinues on a sufficient scale nor disposed of dependent cultivators who were 'theirs' in an East European sense. But nor did the monarchy control sufficient means of coercion to be able to intervene directly to more than an extremely limited degree in regional and local government. Quite apart from the lack of a standing army and civil service of any size, its control of taxation was conditional on parliamentary consent, and its own revenues were far less than they might have been had the proceeds of the sale of monastic lands not been spent by Henry VIII as they were. Elizabeth's England was, in Braudel's vivid description (1966, II, p. 47) '*pugnace et rayonnante*'. But although its resources were sufficient for it to hold its own in inter-societal competition, control of those resources was far from centralized. The monarchical role inherited by James I was secure against both native rebellion and foreign invasion. But the means of production, persuasion or coercion which could be deployed by the exercise of power attaching directly to it were very much less than both he and many others supposed.

In this context, intra-societal competition for power not only favoured local and commercial interests but worked to the disadvantage of any of the alternative practices which might have functioned analogously to further the evolution of one or another sub-type of absolutism. In the absence of a service nobility or a salaried (or venal) bureaucracy,* political power at local level attached to the roles of unpaid officers recruited from among men of relative wealth and prestige who mediated between royal authority and neighbourhood interests. The role of 'Justice of the Peace' has often been cited as distinctive in the evolution of English institutions. But hardly less important were the village constables, whose role involved considerably more than amateur police duty (Kent 1985). These officials could be not merely indifferent but actively obstructive to royal demands; and the government's difficulty in mobilizing local support was compounded by the many roles of a semi-professional kind – from university fellow, army officer or clergyman to steward, preceptor or beadle – whose incumbents regarded them as freehold property and which, for the most part, carried a parliamentary vote (Plumb 1967, pp. 26–7). Governments could win compliance only by very occasional use of troops, inspection and sometimes replacement of local officials, insistence by the Privy Council on measures of poor relief and social discipline, and legislation which (like the dooms of the Anglo-Saxon kings) was sometimes more symbolic of good intentions than expressive of reliable coercive sanctions (Wrightson 1982, p. 151). Meanwhile, capitalist practices were increasingly pervading both the agricultural and the nascent industrial sector of the economy, and this process both encouraged and was encouraged by local independence from central governmental control. The rising productivity of the economy over the seventeenth century could not but reinforce the independence of an emerging 'bourgeois' systact whose profits could not be taxed or expropriated at will for the simple reason that the monarchy lacked the power to do so.

* Sale of offices (and also titles) was quite extensively practised for a period by Charles I (Aylmer 1969, pp. 225–39); but it merely antagonized the gentry without significantly strengthening the Crown.

How, therefore, even given the ablest incumbent of the monarchical role, could England possibly have evolved into an absolutist mode? Perhaps there are might-have-beens whereby Henry VIII, had he refrained from futile and costly military intervention across the Channel, could have built up a strong standing army, freed himself from dependence on parliamentary consent for the raising of tax, and enlisted the nobility and gentry directly into the service of the Crown. But even successful foreign wars would not have given him an army available for domestic repression, least of all in a society primarily dependent for its defence on an adequate navy. Nor were there any inducements or sanctions available to him either to deprive Parliament of its existing prerogatives or to draw into bureaucratic roles in the royal service the merchants and landowning gentry who were the prosperous and increasingly intransigent carriers of capitalistic practices.

In any event, by 1600 the systactic structure of English society offered almost no competitive advantages to any of the alternative practices from which the economic, ideological and coercive institutions of an absolutist mode could be deployed. The English monarchy, it is true, was not wholly without expedients. There were judges, bishops and courtiers whose roles functioned in its support (or whose incumbents could be replaced if they did not); there were methods (most famously, ship money) by which revenue could be raised without recourse to parliament; and there were favours which could be doled out at discretion on a patron-to-client basis – a pension here, a reversion of an office there, a share in a monopoly or a grant of Crown land somewhere else. But nothing could now bridge the divide between Court and Country; Puritan hostility to the Established Church had undermined the ideological hegemony of both bishops and king; a House of Commons which 'lay open to men of property in money or land' (Keir 1953, p. 141) could no longer be controlled by even the most skilful royal manipulation of threats and patronage; and the upwardly mobile who felt relatively deprived of the prestige attaching to birth could achieve recognition of gentility by adopting the appropriate life-style independently of entry to a role bestowed by the Crown. There had evolved an institutional context in which the dominant systact would be a landed and commercial class (which was also a status-group) whose rival factions competed directly with one another for incumbency of the topmost political roles. They did so under a monarchy whose legitimacy they willingly acknowledged, but whose control of the means of coercion was restricted to such informal influence as its incumbents might be able to exercise over the political office-holders of the day.

§31. The final test case of evolution to an absolutist mode is Rome, whose distinctively oligarchic sub-type of the citizen mode enabled it (as we have seen) to expand in a way that the *poleis* could not, but thereby generated contradictions which its traditional institutions were unable to resolve. In Section 28 of Chapter 3, I likened the abruptness of its transition from republic to monarchy in 27 B.C. to that of the transition of Western and Eastern Germany from an authoritarian to a liberal-democratic and socialist mode respectively in 1945. But two qualifications are needed: first, Rome's transition to absolutism was the result of endogenous pressures, whereas that of Germany in 1945 was the result of defeat in war; second, the lasting restoration of order by Augustus was the culmination of a series of internal conflicts going back to the era of the Gracchi, so that his emergence in the role of absolute monarch is more like the victory of Tokugawa after the Ōnin Wars than like a sudden seizure of power by an ambitious Greek magistrate who succeeds in turning his role into that of tyrant more or less overnight.

In Section 2, I briefly suggested that expansion by conquest impelled Rome to make the transition to absolutism because the practices which defined the relation of discharged veterans to their commanders became critical. But for that hypothesis to be adequately grounded, it needs further to be explained why it was the mode of coercion rather than the mode of production which generated the critical practices whose carriers brought the Republic down. The first great outbreak of civil war – the 'Social' War which broke out in the autumn of 91 B.C. – was, as I stressed in Section 21 of Chapter 3, motivated by a sense of relative deprivation over citizenship, not class. But that is not to say that there was no hostility or conflict of class within the citizen body, or that the *assidui* who had served with the legions felt that they had been adequately remunerated for their services to the Roman *patria*. By no stretch could their pay as soldiers be regarded as adequate compensation for their absence from their homes and farms. Opportunities for booty on any substantial scale were relatively rare in the East, and almost non-existent in the West. The support which the Gracchi undoubtedly enjoyed – Plutarch reports that after their deaths the *plebs* treated the places where they had been killed as sacred shrines – and the popularity of any proposal for cancellation of debts, redistribution of land or the issue of free or subsidized corn to the city poor are ample evidence from which to infer a conflict between rich senatorial landowners and dispossessed peasantry based on economic interests. But however intense the sense of relative deprivation among the dispossessed, it did not make of them a class '*für sich*'. As I emphasized in Section 16 of

Chapter 2, it was only at the top of the Roman social structure that shared class interests created more than a minimal systactic identity. This, as we saw, is partly explained by the common relation to the means of production of free wage-workers and slaves who, even though the chattels of their masters, could well be permitted to keep their earnings in order to purchase their freedom; and the population of freedmen was further supplemented by manumissions deliberately performed so that advantage could be taken of the corn dole.* But it was also because of the pervasiveness of coercive rather than economic or ideological sanctions, and the related functions of practices of patronage and clientship.

The role of 'client' had a long history in Rome, and in theory, at least, *clientela* was transmitted in perpetuity from father to son once a person had entrusted himself to the *fides* of another. By the time of the late Republic, these ties were no longer what they had traditionally been: Pompey's clients in Picenum, whom he had inherited from his father, soon 'melted away' (Hopkins 1978, p. 49 n. 68; cf. Brunt 1962, p. 77) when it came to his confrontation with Julius Caesar. But like the *mawla* in early Islamic societies, the client who abandoned his patron needed then to find another. It is not a universal rule that patron–client relations inhibit the formation of classes collectively conscious of a common interest and ready to take action in pursuit of it.† But in the Roman context, the competitive advantage of clientship far outweighed any that would have accrued to the free but humble citizen from cooperation with others similarly located in the social structure. The hope of reward and protection alike depended on the support of a powerful patron, whether this involved military or para-military service or merely attendance and escort. As we have seen, Roman law did not of itself provide protection or redress against coercion by the stronger party. Since, accordingly, intimidation, assault or even illegal enslavement was a chronic risk, and gangs and bodyguards were readily available for cash, practices which might in other contexts have promoted systactic solidarity among the economically disadvantaged conferred no competitive advantage at all.

Such vertical ties between patrons – in particular, generals – and armed clients or followers, many of whom were discharged veterans with experience of combat, were fatal to the domination of the Senate

* According to Dionysius of Halicarnassus (LV.24.5); the same was also done later to take advantage of cash hand-outs (*congiaria*) by the emperors (Suetonius, *Divus Augustus* XLII).

† For an example from Spain, see Gilmore (1977).

once no institutional means existed for requiring commands to be punctually terminated and troops promptly discharged. But the traditional practices of which the rival 'optimate' and 'popular' senatorial factions were alike the inheritors had initially evolved as an adaptation to the pressures acting on a small, militaristic citizen-state almost continuously at war. Early Roman society had been dominated, after the overthrow of an elective monarchy, by male lineage heads of whom the most ambitious occupied the topmost political-cum-military roles in succession. They did so, moreover, under the guidance and control of a Senate whose members had lifelong tenure. There was, it is true, the role of 'dictator'. But it had been created to deal with extreme emergencies: its tenure never exceeded six months. The unprecedented re-elections of Marius, a *novus homo*, to the consulship in the closing years of the second century B.C. were a response to the military threat posed by the German tribes, and it seems that he himself had no conception of the possible implications of either the break with constitutional legality involved or the enrolment of the propertyless *capite censi* into the legions (Brunt 1971b, p. 406).

It is therefore a testimony to the stability of the institutions of the Republic and the power of the ideology which underpinned them that it was not until Julius Caesar that a monarchical role was recreated. Even Pompey, who was no less motivated than his rival by overweening ambition,* seems not to have aspired to autocracy, but rather to being the person to whom the Senate and people of Rome had to turn in times of crisis: this caused him, perhaps, to provoke such crises to suit himself (Seager 1979, p. 188), but not out of a conscious intention to overturn the constitution. That Octavian-turned-Augustus was the final victor was a matter of contingency. But that Rome should evolve into absolutism was not – or not once ambitious generals could no longer be prevented from overstepping the limits of the constitution and could count on retaining the allegiance of their soldiers when they did so. The relevance of economic conditions to this process was, to be sure, more than marginal: if the discharged veterans and impoverished city-dwellers could all have returned to prosperous or at least viable family farms, the great majority would no doubt have preferred this to continuous street-fighting, rural gangsterism, or civil war. But because (and only because) of the mutation and recombination of coercive practices, the choice was no longer open.

* It was not that the nobility of the first century B.C. had somehow been infused with a stronger desire for *dignitas* than their fourth-century predecessors, but that the scope for it was now so much greater (Brunt 1968, p. 230).

The further question can still be asked what exactly it was about the wars of conquest which at the same time weakened the unity of the dominant stratum and conferred a decisive competitive advantage on the carriers of the coercive practices. The answer is twofold. First, the defeat of Rome's enemies did require prolongation of commands, whether the Senate liked it or not. Second, however, the successful outcome of these prolongations made Rome not merely a victorious citizen-state but a world power without any competitors whatever (Ungern-Sternberg 1982, p. 256), so that the sense of solidarity against an external enemy could never be recreated thereafter. Marius may not have seen his victories over the Germans, or Pompey his over the pirates, or even Caesar his over the Gauls as stepping-stones leading to a monarchical role. But victories of this nature left the victors threatened not by enemies abroad, but by enemies in Rome itself. The Senate could not control them; their rivals feared them; and their troops were still available to them.* A return to the role of private citizen, like that of Cincinnatus to his plough, was not only unappealing but dangerous: they risked proscription, exile or assassination if they failed to convert generalship into autocracy. Caesar's decision to cross the Rubicon was a response to the very same pressures, now further intensified, as had led to the death of Tiberius Gracchus at the hands of his cousin Scipio Nasica and a mob of cudgel-wielding senators.

The assassination of Julius Caesar delayed, but could not reverse, the evolution to absolutism. Augustus, as Dio Cassius put it (LIII.16), was bound to become a monarch (*autarchēsein*) once he was master of both the money and the soldiers, and the account which Tacitus gives (*Annals* I.2) of the motives which led to the general acquiescence in his role, rhetorical as it may be, is entirely plausible. No serious uprising was attempted against him; recollection of what had followed the assassination of Caesar was still fresh; the senatorial nobility, however much they might hanker after their former *libertas*, could not seriously expect that another civil war would do more than replace one monarch with another; and once adequate provision had been made for discharged veterans, there was no enthusiasm among the war-weary soldiery and *plebs* for a renewal of civil war.† The selective pressures

* The augmented power now attaching to the roles of the 'military dynasts' can be semi-deductively inferred from the coins struck to celebrate them, the cults devoted to them, the portraits of them worn by their supporters and the links with tutelary deities claimed by them (Crawford 1978, pp. 176–8).

† Cf. Dio's account (LX.15.3) of the refusal of support to a rebel governor of Dalmatia in 42 A.D. by his troops who feared it would merely lead to a renewal of *stasis*, and Josephus's remark (*Jewish Antiquities* XIX.228) that popular support for Claudius was

which had rendered unworkable the institutions of an expansionist 'citizen' society pervaded by coercive practices worked no less powerfully to preserve an absolutist mode once it had evolved. By the time of Pompey and Caesar, the careers of the ablest incumbents of the highest political-cum-military roles no longer ended with a consulship held as one of two, and only for a single year (followed, at most, by a censorship to which there attached ideological but not coercive power). They could now become not magistrates in the service of the state, but *caudillos* exploiting it; and (as elsewhere) the competition between rival *caudillos* could end only when one of them acquired a monopoly of the means of coercion at the societal – which in Rome's case was the global – level.

TEST CASES (3)

§32. Once social evolution is at the brink of the 'modern' world of industrial nation-states, the society which calls to be considered first is England simply because it was the first to reach that stage. We have seen already the selective pressures which worked to the competitive advantage of 'bourgeois' practices, and the consequent disadvantage of monarchical absolutism. But the process did not end there. England (unlike Holland) went on to be the first industrial society; and although this raises issues which are not the concern of this volume – 'industrialism' not being a mode of the distribution of power as such – the structural and cultural changes which made it possible have to be related to the functions of the practices selected in the course of them. In Section 14, I cited the dramatic expansion of the Lancashire cotton industry as an example of a 'turning-point' whose evolutionary importance the entrepreneurs who profited from it could not possibly perceive at the time. But however unpredictably, it arose (as I also emphasized) in an institutional context which was itself the product of a long and complex anterior evolution. The ecological and technological conditions have to be taken as given – utilizable land, cheap coal, low-grade iron ore, a navigable coastline, easy internal communications, wind- and water-power, and so forth. But with these, and a unified society long immune from foreign invasion, what were the practices selected, and what for?

Institutionally, much of England's evolution from the Middle Ages onward was common to the other societies of Western Europe. All were affected by the failure of Habsburg (or Valois) imperialism, the

out of fear of *stasis* of the kind which had occurred in Pompey's time (a reference which I owe to de Ste Croix 1981, p. 362).

continuing ideological (but not political) hegemony of Christianity, and the relative autonomy of urban centres of manufacture and commerce. But England alone evolved from a patrimonial to a bourgeois monarchy – an evolution in which, despite the 'baronial gangsterism' of the Wars of the Roses, there was no genuinely feudal stage any more than there was ever a genuine absolutism. Its systactic structure was characterized by relatively easy individual mobility,* as well as by relatively modest means of coercion at the disposal of either monarchy or magnates (let alone the 'able-bodied poor'†). There was, to be sure, some collective mobility, too: not only did some individual yeomen rise into the ranks of the gentry and some individual gentry into the ranks of the nobility, but in some regions the gentry collectively gained power at the nobility's expense (Mingay 1976, p. 58). But there was no rising bourgeois systact '*parvenu à sa maturité*' carrying practices which, as it came to dominate a declining aristocracy, transformed the mode of the distribution of power in consequence. The model of a 'capitalist' class displacing a 'feudal' one by buying up its estates and then hiring as wage-workers a peasantry displaced by the enclosure of common land is not merely exaggerated but almost totally misleading. The distinctive characteristic of 'pre-industrial' English society was rather the extent to which commerical practices were carried by *all* systacts.

No doubt there was class conflict at all levels. But roles could be progressively commercialized in the way they were only because of the lack of strict systactic demarcation. This lack was apparent not only at the top of the structure, where aristrocracy and bourgeoisie interpenetrated (and intermarried), but also lower down, where 'the proliferation of clergymen, notaries, attorneys, schoolmasters after 1540 merged with and created an increasingly unified middle order out of the yeomanry and well-to-do farmers and merchants, middlemen and artisans in trade' (Holderness 1976, p. 35). The English 'peasantry', far from conforming to the ideal type of self-reproducing extended families on smallholdings or dependent tenancies producing only marginally for

* L. Stone (1966) offers a general conspectus, including the importance of the increase in the total numbers in certain categories of roles (p. 29) which, as discussed already, generates 'structural' separately from 'exchange' mobility. But regional variation is important too. Apart from the concentration of 'professional' roles (other than the clergy) in London and certain provincial towns, mobility into the gentry was much lower in some counties such as Kent (except for the part nearest London) than in others such as Northamptonshire (Everitt 1966).

† Whose sense of relative deprivation was in any case inhibited by their not knowing of any other country where living standards were notably higher (K. Thomas 1971, p. 17).

sale, might be short-term farm servants, seasonal wage-earners, out-working textile-workers, improving leaseholders, shepherds, market gardeners, cottage-weavers or nailers, yeoman-tanners or blacksmiths, part-time miners or industrial workers. Practices which defined 'bourgeois' roles conferred advantages on their carriers thoughout the whole society, and its continuing evolution towards an industrial capitalist-liberal-democratic mode was, if anything, overdetermined in all three dimensions of structure.

For all the disputes among specialists over the details of the economic history of the period from 1450 to 1750, and for all the differences, both ecological and sociological, between one part of England and another, by the end of that period the pervasive roles in the agricultural sector of the economy were those of the rentier landlord and the commercial tenant. The practice of leasing for money rents could not but suit landlords neither able nor willing to work their own estates directly; and the tenants to whose advantage it worked were those best able to generate profit from the landlord's investment in fixed, and their own in working, capital. The selective pressures favouring this type of farming were strongest in the grain-growing areas. Marketable surpluses could be generated without, however, any individual producer being able to control either prices or rents (Coleman 1977, p. 123). There were few smallholdings in these areas, and they could not in any case be made to yield comparable returns. But nor, on the other hand, could landlords raise rents too high without the risk that their tenants would either make too little profit to be able to pay them or else move elsewhere. Low grain prices and rising costs (including, after 1693, the land tax) encouraged both the trend to larger and more compact estates and the search for improved techniques. This virtuous circle of rising production and rising profit did not (it hardly needs saying) arise because the incumbents of landlord roles were any less strongly motivated to pursue their economic interests than either their English predecessors or their foreign contemporaries. It arose because the changed institutional context no longer permitted, let alone encouraged, landlords to pursue their interests by more labour-intensive cultivation and/or exploitation of the land-hunger of a settled but over-populous smallholding peasantry.

Of the features of the changed institutional context which were peculiar to English society, geographical as well as, and often combined with, social mobility was one. But it in turn reinforced the selective pressure which favoured the spread of market practices (wage-labour included). Many of the areas into which migrants moved were areas which combined some form of industrial with agricultural employment. Indeed, this was often the result of direct encouragement by putting-out merchants anxious to circumvent the restrictions on production imposed in the towns by the traditional craft-based guilds. The resulting increase in earnings from wages, coupled with a growth in the size of towns outside of London, generated an increased demand for agricultural and other produce which in turn encouraged an increasing trend towards market specialization. In this, the roles of broker and middleman were hardly less important than those of capitalist landlord, improving tenant, newly affluent professional, yeoman turned entrepreneur, and part-time wage-worker (and his family).

Precise delineation of the systactic structure is not possible. But some quasi-deductive inferences can be drawn by starting from the figures reported by Gregory King, for whose *Scheme of Income and Expense in the Several Families of England*, whatever its imperfections, no student of seventeenth-century English society can (as I said in Section 13 of Chapter 1) be other than grateful. If these are compared with those which can be derived from Joseph Massie's *Computation of the Money that hath been Exorbitantly Raised upon the People of Great Britain by the Sugar Planters*... of 1760 (Mathias 1957), then it seems clear that the two generations after 1680 witnessed a marked, even precipitate, decline in the number of households engaged either wholly or partly in agriculture.* By then, if not before, a 'consumer' society thoroughly permeated by commercial practices and attitudes had evolved.

The part played in all this by ideological rather than economic pressures is, if anything, still more controversial among specialists. But there was, without doubt, an evolution of practices and doctrines which was not wholly reducible to economic interests and did independently augment the competitive advantages accruing to 'bourgeois' roles. This was not because of the elective affinity between the 'Protestant ethic' and the 'spirit of capitalism': the most that Protestantism can be claimed to have done is to help the members of some marginal groups engaged in the pursuit of profit to legitimate that pursuit to themselves. It was, rather, because of a more general diffusion of secular values. Respectability and prestige now attached to the roles not merely of financial or industrial capitalist but also of inventor, experimenter and

* The necessary qualifications are fully spelt out by Mathias, including the neglect of the unpaid contributions of housewives and farmers' wives (p. 41). Holderness (1976, p. 48) regards King's and Massie's data as showing that the number of families *identifiably* engaged in agriculture fell from three-fifths to a little over half of all families; Perkin (1969, pp. 124–5) regards them as showing that the number of families *primarily* engaged in agriculture fell from two-thirds to one-third.

technician. The Calvinist ethic was, in this context, one variant of a more general application of new criteria of rationality to the conduct of daily life (Landes 1969, pp. 23–4). But these new criteria were themselves reinforced by a general repudiation of the values and life-styles of the courts of James I and Charles I. The execution of Charles I did not undermine the legitimacy of monarchy as such. But it did undermine the legitimacy of the sacral form of it which the Stuart kings, and their bishops and courtiers, had sought to uphold. Pedigree remained a criterion of status, but it was no longer the dominant one. Whatever the qualifications which have had to be made to the 'Weber thesis' (cf. Marshall 1980), it is still, at the very least, safe to conclude that an ideological mutation which was not simply a function of mutations in economic practices functioned to the further advantage of 'bourgeois' roles.

In any case, the evolution of a 'bourgeois' monarchy had a history going back to the distinctive aspects of the Anglo-Norman distribution of power between a patrimonial monarch with considerable patronage at his disposal and magnates who were neither service nobility nor *frondeurs*. Magnates did, to be sure, dispute the distribution of the means of coercion not only with the monarchy but among themselves. Yet their relations with the monarchy and its servants were, from the days of Henry I (Hollister 1986, p. 188), more cooperative than otherwise: 'growing monarchical power reflected growing aristocratic cohesion' (Brenner 1985, p. 256). This had the twofold consequence that the magnates retained, through the institution of Parliament, considerable political independence from the Crown while at the same time retaining economic domination over the cultivators on their lands. After the failure of their successive forays on the Continent and their subsequent mutual debilitation in the Wars of the Roses, they no longer commanded the resources to act the role of *caudillo*. But they did, as subsequent events were to show, retain resources sufficient to resist the forcible imposition of monarchical absolutism. By that time, the increasingly complex pattern of loyalty and antagonism to the Stuart kings precluded any clear-cut systactic conflict between royalist magnates and bourgeois parliamentarians; and whatever the disputes among specialists over the causes of the Civil War, its outcome ruled out any possibility of evolution to either a feudal or an absolutist mode of the distribution of power.

The interaction of all these economic, ideological and coercive pressures is impossible to disentangle precisely. But merely to list them is enough to account for the evolution of a culture and structure which could not be other than commercialized in mode of production, secularized (albeit nominally Christian) in mode of persuasion, and decentralized in mode of coercion. There was no way in which landowners could revert to the extraction of the agricultural surplus from dependent cultivators through rent or corvée; but nor was there any way in which they could be recruited into the full-time military, administrative and ritual service of a sacral monarchy, and the cultivators taxed by its agents for their benefit as office-holders. As early as 1700, the distribution of power favoured the carriers of the practices which were to turn an eighteenth-century commercial, aristocratic and oligarchic society into the capitalist, industrial, liberal and increasingly democratic one which evolved over the course of the nineteenth century. But – contrary to what Marx believed at the time he published the first volume of *Capital* – that evolution was not the paradigm which other societies were destined to follow. The selective pressures which explain it were unique to England; and, as we now know, liberal-democratic capitalism is only one of several possible modes of the distribution of power into which industrial societies can evolve. In Marx's day, there was no relevant quasi-experimental contrast yet to be drawn. But we can compare England directly with societies which evolved in one case through an authoritarian and in the other through a socialist mode into 'modern' industrialized nation-states without ever passing through a 'bourgeois' stage.

§33. It is difficult to think of hypothetical conditions under which Japanese society could have evolved in the course of industrialization into either a liberal or a socialist mode. It is true that by the mid nineteenth century the samurai had long been demilitarized, a land market had begun to develop, some large merchant fortunes had been accumulated, wage-labour was on the increase, and the role of rural smallholder was increasingly evolving into that of commercial tenant. But the systactic structure within which the Meiji reformers sought to raise the economic and military resources of Japan to the level enjoyed by the industrial societies of the West favoured practices which worked overwhelmingly to the advantage of authoritarian roles. It was not simply that when mutant practices were deliberately fostered in the cause of 'modernization', the commercial class was weak in political influence and social prestige: as we have just seen, capitalistic practices can be carried by members of other systacts of origin who thereby create, or move into, 'bourgeois' roles. The more important constraints were, first, the deliberate intention of the governing élite to introduce the practices which they saw as necessary for 'modernization' with as few ancillary concessions to Western institutions as possible; and second, an initial distribution of the means of production, persuasion and coercion so rigid as well as unequal that mutations and recombinations of practices which might otherwise have generated significant collective mobility merely altered the roles of subordinate systacts without altering their location.

Throughout the Tokugawa period, the mode of production remained part-'feudal' in the sense that the agricultural surpluses were extracted from the dependent cultivators in a form half way between rent and tax. The share of the rice crop surrendered, with the cooperation of the village headmen, to the local officials functioned partly as a payment to the *daimyō* (or shogun) as landlord and partly as a contribution to the expenses of the Shogunate as central goverment. But as commercial practices began to pervade the economy, social relations in the countryside evolved not towards wage-labour but towards tenancy. Family farms were cultivated by geographically immobile villagers, who were often ex-smallholders who had gradually to sell their plots under pressure of debt and had virtually no chance of being able to repurchase them subsequently. The Meiji reformers abolished 'feudal' ties and institutionalized unconditional private property in land. But this led to more intensive cultivation and an increasing polarization between rich and poor rather than to either the entrenchment of customary holdings or a large-scale exodus from the land. The techniques of riziculture and the steady pressure of population in a country where cultivable land was in restricted supply made it more advantageous to the landlords to extract rents of which, as yields grew, a diminishing proportion had to be passed on to the government in payment of the Land Tax. To introduce the practice of wage-labour would have reduced profits rather than increased them. It was not that large-scale farming on Western lines was unknown. On the contrary, deliberate attempts to introduce it were made. But in the ecological, demographic and institutional context of Meiji Japan, the competitive advantage lay in commercial tenancy.*

In a similar way, although for different reasons, the introduction of capitalistic practices into the expanding industrial sector of the economy functioned to the advantage neither of a rising entrepreneurial class nor

* Dore (1984, p. 18): 'There *were* many 19th-century experiments in large-scale farming by enthusiastic ex-samurai newly returned from the West; but they mostly failed... There may be situations, such as England of the enclosures period or the United States today, in which the marxian theory of the inevitable economic advantage of large-scale over small-scale production, in agriculture as well as in industry, holds good. But 19th-century Japan was not one of them.'

of an organized working class on the West European model. The large-scale, technologically sophisticated industries were closely tied to the state, and their senior managers were ex-samurai rather than ex-*chōnin*; the smaller plants were organized on artisan lines and often dependent on part-time and family labour; and the new recruits into the role of industrial wage-worker, of whom many were women,* had no tradition of systactic consciousness or collective organization. What is more, workers in these new proletarian roles were subordinated to labour 'bosses' who functioned partly as middlemen, partly as supervisors, and partly as concessionaires. Industrialists did, it is true, lobby governments in their systactic interest as employers, in pursuit not only of stricter labour discipline but also of cheaper rice and lower taxes; and skilled manual workers did adopt trade union practices, if only as a means of maintaining the location of their roles in a labour market strongly favourable to employers. But employers and unionists alike conformed to the hierarchical, factional, leader–follower norm of social relations; and lifetime employment patterns, which preceded industrialization, made enterprise unions the 'natural form of organization' (Dore 1974, p. 415). Employers were, therefore, in a position to dispense favours at their discretion to worker-leaders 'to achieve harmony, dilute militancy, and abet cleavages' (Scalapino 1983, p. 254). There is no question that the mode of production was capitalist: workers sold their labour-power to the owners of the means of production, and even though enterprises might initially have been financed by the state they were handed over to private companies or combines. But these practices functioned within an institutional context which conferred advantages on neither liberal-minded industrialists nor socialist-minded workers. There *was* a Liberal Party as well as a General Labour Federation. But both failed.

Their failure must in part, at least, be attributed to the independent effect of ideological inducements and sanctions and the control by the Meiji reformers and their successors of the means of persuasion. The unchallenged legitimacy of the emperor, the lack of an alternative creed, the long tradition of deference to inherited rank, and the reinforcement of an already deeply felt patriotism by intense xenophobia strongly favoured practices and doctrines which could plausibly be reconciled with traditional values. The Japanese version of the Confucian ethic was suitably interpreted 'to make all little loyalties lead up to one great loyalty to the Emperor' (T. C. Smith 1959, p. 205), and this loyalty

* Large (1981, p. 16) remarks that not only were women workers difficult for trade union organizers to reach, but even if reached they only wanted to return home to their villages.

extended down through the ex-samurai and smaller property owners to the leaders of organized labour and even to the majority of union members, who 'wanted to accommodate the unions to the status quo' (Large 1981, p. 4). No doubt much of the rhetoric of the 'Japanese Peasant Soul', the 'Great Spirit of the Emperor', and the 'Glorious History of our National Development' was no more than an attempt to legitimate a pattern of roles whose stability owed at least as much to economic and coercive sanctions as to the independent effects of a hegemonic ideology. But it would be even more implausible to suppose that the hegemonic ideology had no independent effect at all.

The conditions experienced by both rural tenants and urban wage-workers were such as could be held to justify no less intense a sense of relative deprivation than that which underlay the systactic consciousness of their counterparts in the industrial societies of Western Europe. But the virtual absence of revolutionary, or even radically reformist, 'proletarian' attitudes is attested all the way from the Meiji period to the aftermath of the Second World War even in the cities (Dore 1958, pp. 217–21). Family and local ties were stronger than any sense of systactic identity, and consciousness of rank was in any case defined in terms of status-groups rather than classes. Government propaganda consistently stressed the value of conformity in an ideological context which combined long-established differences in ascribed social prestige with an equally long-established tradition of national loyalty. Any attempt to provoke systactic conflict was therefore held to be both mischievous and unpatriotic. The esteem by which conformity was rewarded and the disgrace by which deviance was punished far outweighed the potential gain from self-definition of subordinate roles in terms of an alternative social doctrine.*

This combination acted likewise on the evolution of Japan's political institutions to constrain any incipient tendency towards domination through parliament by a faction representing either 'proletarian' or 'bourgeois' interests. The Constitution inaugurated by the Meiji reformers did have 'some of the outward trappings of parliamentary democracy' (Moore 1967, p. 291); but its practical effect was that it 'froze the ideas of absolutism in new and more impervious forms' (Scalapino 1953, p. 245). The suffrage was extremely restricted, and even when it was broadened by the Universal Manhood Suffrage Act of 1925, elections to the Diet still resulted in 'smashing majorities for the candidates of the rural elite' (*ibid.*, p. 311). Coercive power was firmly

* Recourse to religious movements with their own theodicy by which inequality may be rationalized is another matter, as I hinted already in Section 31 of Chapter 3.

in the hands of the army and police, and as, between the First and Second World Wars, Japan responded to economic recession by military aggression, the popularity of the army increased. In the countryside, 'there was no longer any question of the peasant being alienated from the goals and symbols of the nation, or of tenant resentment against the landlords turning into resentment against authority as a whole' (Dore 1984, p. 105). There had never been carriers of either liberal or socialist practices with the systactic potential to reverse this trend; and to the extent that they existed, successive governments were able and willing to bring overwhelming coercive sanctions to bear against them. The Meiji reformers had hesitated before introducing military conscription for fear that the arming of peasant recruits might be turned against them.* But in the event, their loyalty was never in question. The army offered the opportunity of a career to young villagers well aware of the constraints on their prospects if they stayed where they were. Military roles functioned both to siphon off some surplus rural manpower and to identify the interests of the peasantry with those of the governing élite.

Mobility in general was, as we have already seen, remarkably low, whether 'structural' or 'exchange'. It was not so low, either inter- or intra-generationally, as to make the systactic structure a structure of castes, except for the *burakumin* at the bottom of it. Not only did novel 'white collar' roles have to be filled by recruits who were often not of samurai origin, but many ex-samurai 'skidded' downwards as they failed to adapt to industrialization and the loss of their traditional stipends.† But neither the upwardly nor the downwardly mobile were carriers of practices subversive of the mode of the distribution of power. It was only the rural ex-smallholders whose collective consciousness found expression in the formation of a national Peasant Union in 1922, and it was weakened from the outset by both factional and doctrinal differences.‡ Indeed, it is plausible to suggest that rates of social

* This was not merely fanciful for those who remembered the defeat of a central army by a newly raised Chōshū army in 1866; but that would not have happened without Western intervention and the import of rifles (Craig 1961, p. 371).

† When stipends, whose payment had at first been taken from the *daimyō* by the central government, were abolished in 1876, bonds were issued to the samurai in their stead; but 'many of them who started enterprises with this as capital failed in their endeavours and eventually became members of the proletariat' (Morishima 1982, p. 75).

‡ Dore (1984, p. 79): 'The situation of the tenant was different from that of the industrial worker and much less conducive to the development of consciousness of class': there was no sharp definition between tenants and landlords but a gradation; neighbourhood ties outweighed class ties in long-settled, close-knit communities; and

mobility were such as to keep the sense of relative deprivation among subordinate systacts to a minimum. If solid but not impermeable barriers between systacts (or ranks) create less dissatisfaction than either a system of orders or castes on the one hand or a system of formally free competition for privileged roles on the other, then Meiji Japan is a case which fits the model well. There was no longer a hereditary nobility; a few peasants could and did become landlords; a few peasant sons could and did make careers in industry and commerce;* a few of the peasant recruits into the army could and did achieve promotion to higher rank within it; and even a few *burakumin* could (since physically indistinguishable from other Japanese) successfully 'pass' as born outside their ghettoes. The ambitious minority could, therefore, succeed at the level of individual competition, while the majority's collective systactic location remained what it had been.

It might perhaps be objected that hindsight makes it too easy to view the pervasive roles and central institutions of Meiji Japan as leading inescapably to the evolution of an authoritarian mode. Not only was this by no means obvious to rival observers at the time, but the flexibility with which the practices defining those roles and institutions were adapted to a liberal-democratic-capitalist mode after 1945 may suggest that some random mutation or recombination might have diverted Japanese society in that direction under purely endogenous pressure. But in the event, it was only after defeat and occupation that the shift of mode was effected, and then only on the direct instructions of the victors. The fact that hopes (or fears) of a trend towards either liberalism or socialism had occasionally been voiced by observers of different persuasions is no more evidence that their predictions were adequately grounded here than in any other of the by now numerous cases where we have seen that the competitive selection of practices can be explained only in retrospect.

§34. The near-simultaneous 'modernization' of Russia was, as I have remarked already, brought about no less by a 'revolution from above' than in the case of Japan. But in Russia, it was preceded by a revolution from below. This revolution was itself caused by defeat in war: the governing élite lost its control of the means of coercion as demobilized

individual tenants always had the chance, if lucky and hardworking, of one day owning their own land.

* They were likely to be those who might otherwise have been participants in or leaders of protest movements – an effect on which I have commented earlier when looking at societies as different as Republican Rome and (with its Black population in mind) the United States in the twentieth century.

and demoralized soldiers took the side of the peasantry from whom they had themselves been recruited. It is plausible to suggest that if Germany had been defeated in 1914–15 and Tsar Nicholas II led his triumphant army into Berlin as Alexander I had led his into Paris a hundred years before, Russia, like Japan, would have evolved from an absolutist into an authoritarian mode. But for the purpose of this volume, the Bolshevik seizure of power has, like the Meiji Restoration, to be taken as given; and the question which this Section has then to address is what selective pressures caused Russian society to evolve after that improbable but irreversible event into its distinctive sub-type of a socialist mode.

Post-Revolutionary Russia, like Meiji Japan, was a society with a small urban proletariat and a weak bourgeoisie. But social relations in the countryside were very different in the two cases. Not only was there a significantly greater potential for increased productivity in Japan, but the practices by which the roles of landlord and village headman were defined made it very much easier to realize it. In Russia, by constrast, the internal systactic structure of the villages was such as at the same time to constrain the production of large marketable surpluses and to strengthen the institutions of communal self-government. The attempted reforms of 1906–10 had failed to bring about a significant shift to capitalist farming and enclosure of common lands. Periodic repartition, complex cycles of household mobility,* and a tradition of decision-making by consensus within the *obshchina* conferred little or no competitive advantage on practices carried by an incipient systact of enterprising 'yeomen': the minority of so-called 'kulaks' were richer than their neighbours not through hiring wage-labour but through more extensive cultivation. After 1917, arable land was in the hands of small or at most medium-sized producers many of whom were too close to subsistence to be able, even if willing, to offer surpluses onto the market.† Once in possession of their plots, they reacted much as their counterparts were to do in Bolivia in 1953. The Bolsheviks were therefore confronted with a dilemma. There was no possibility of recreating the large estates by which marketable surpluses had been generated before, even if there had been the landlords to repossess them. There were only two choices: economic inducements to the small

* Shanin (1972, Pt 2) shows how these functioned to level out inequalities of wealth observable at any one time and to inhibit class conflict between richer and poorer peasants.

† Skocpol (1979, p. 221) underlines the twofold contrast with France: not only were French peasants much more involved in market exchanges before 1789 than their Russian counterparts before 1914, but the French Revolution actively encouraged the trend to 'individualistic farming'.

proprietors to produce more, or coercive sanctions to extract from them more of what they did.

Specialists continue to disagree over the extent to which the evolution of Soviet society towards a totalitarian sub-type of the socialist mode was a direct consequence of the personality and policies of Stalin. But whatever the answer, the selective pressures by then at work in Russian society offered as little advantage to capitalist as to authoritarian roles. Industrialization could not but require a more intensive exploitation of the labour of a still predominantly peasant economy, and it was not by a reversion to market practices that it could be brought about. Between the period of 'War Communism' and the period of forced collectivization – that is, during the so-called 'New Economic Policy' – the relation between the peasantry and a Bolshevik Party based almost exclusively in the cities was 'an uneasy truce' (Shanin 1972, p. 198). Abandonment of the practice of compulsory requisition (*Prodrazvertska*) solved the problem of peasant revolt, but it did not solve the problem of agricultural production. In 1927, the amount of grain put onto the market was less than half what it had been in 1913 (Lewin 1965, p. 164), and even grain production per head was less by 100 kg in 1928–9 than it had been in 1914 (Lewin 1968, p. 174). It is sometimes argued that if the Soviet government had been prepared to lower livestock prices so that peasants would sell the grain with which to pay for goods in which the villages were no longer self-sufficient, the resources necessary for investment in industry could have been raised by taxation rather than requisition.* But this would still have been a variation within a socialist mode of the distribution of power. The Bolsheviks were committed to central direction of the economy not simply because they wished to remain faithful to the teachings of Marx and Lenin. They were afraid, and rightly so, of the effect of any relaxation of coercive sanctions on the power attaching to their own roles. There was no question for either 'Left' or 'Right' of allowing the distribution of resources to be determined purely by the market. The concessions granted under the New Economic Policy were not a response to selective pressures in favour of capitalist practice. They were a tactical means to the strategic aim of collective ownership and central control of the means of agricultural production and exchange.

The irony that one autocracy should turn out to be replaced by another has been pointed out often enough. But it makes the Russian case all the more interesting as a quasi-experimental example of

* See the exchange between Millar and Nove (1976), which goes back to the argument of Nove (1962).

unintended consequences: what were the selective pressures which led to the emergence of pervasive roles whose functions directly contradicted the declared ideals of those who had overturned the previous mode of the distribution of power? In the immediate aftermath of the October Revolution, the answer was clear enough. The survival of the regime depended on creating an army sufficiently strong and united to penetrate those geographical and institutional areas where the incumbents of roles on whose functions the regime depended were indifferent if not actively hostile. Once the war had been won, the legitimacy of the party vindicated, and the economy restarted on a peacetime footing, recourse to the means of coercion was much less obviously necessary. But necessary it still was. Whatever the hopes and ideals of those who had brought the Revolution about, they had no escape from the selective pressures now working in favour of a centralized Party and its police.

The 'uneasy truce' with the peasantry led to an eventual and inescapable confrontation during which the extent of recourse to the means of coercion is now amply documented. Earlier, Trotsky's success in building up the Red Army had likewise depended on the recruitment of former Tsarist officers and non-commissioned officers whose questionable loyalty was secured not only by the sanction of capital punishment but by the treatment of their families as hostages (Fainsod 1963, p. 468). But the domination of the Party did not rest only on the direct application of force. It rested also on the roles of propagandists, informers and apparatchiks whose functions were, so to speak, coercive at one remove. In the early years, the Bolsheviks' control of the means of persuasion was as precarious as their control of the means of coercion. They could rely on a minority of committed and even fanatical supporters in the urban proletariat, the army and the clerical-cum-intellectual middle class. But they depended on the continued performance of their roles by civil servants whose loyalty was at least as lukewarm as that of the former Tsarist officers (Edeen 1960, p. 284). As economic conditions worsened, the conditional legitimacy accorded to the regime was progressively dissipated. The pressure towards 'centralism' and discipline within the Party was as strong as that towards the use of the *Vecheka* and subsequently the O.G.P.U. to imprison, banish or kill alleged opponents of the regime, whether on the 'counter-revolutionary' Right or the 'political' Left. Control over the army was exercised through the role of political commissar, and control over the courts through the role of state procurator – a system originally instituted by Peter the Great and revived in 1922 on the initiative of Lenin himself (Schapiro 1970, p. 269).

In industry, the trade unions performed a similar function as agents of control over the workers in the name of the revolutionary dictatorship of the proletariat. The 'Workers' Opposition' Faction was condemned at the Tenth Party Congress as a syndicalist deviation from Communism. By the mid 1920s, the organization of the unions was fully integrated into that of the Party. Under Stalin, all these institutions were deliberately adapted to the forced collectivization of agriculture. Steeply unequal material incentives and overt coercion were used to promote the rapid expansion of heavy industry. Dissidents within the Party were exiled, imprisoned or killed, and all intellectual activity was subordinated to an ideology formulated by Stalin himself and imposed by the secret police. But the practices and roles which made this possible were already in place by the time that he rose to the topmost role. Stalinism was a sub-type of a socialist mode whose evolution had already been favoured (if not determined) by the pressures of civil war, worker and peasant revolts, and the decisive competitive advantage attaching to the roles through which the means of coercion could be controlled.

The recourse to these practices and roles led inescapably to the domination of Russian society by a corporation at once internally stratified and exercising a total monopoly of the means of coercion, persuasion and – because of the nature of the ideology in whose name the revolution had been carried out – production.* The Communist Party of the Soviet Union was not, like corporations under an absolutist mode, one of several whose economic, ideological and/or coercive resources were retained at the expense of those controlled by the monarchy. Whoever controlled the Party could control the army as well as the bureaucracy and the secret police, partly by institutionalized relationships of command and partly by playing off one against another.† Admission into and expulsion from its ranks came itself to be an important instrument of policy, and careers within it to offer an attractive channel of individual mobility for the ambitious. The

* During the period of the New Economic Policy, private ownership of shops was permitted and even encouraged to the point that in 1924 there were reported to be 420,366 of them (Farbman 1924, p. 134, quoted by Fainsod 1963, p. 430); but those proprietors who did not succeed in moving undetected into other occupational roles and passing as proletarians were thereafter liable to arrest and confiscation of all their assets.

† The career of Marshal Zhukov affords something of a quasi-experimental test. His 'commanding role and exceptional position vis-à-vis Stalin' during the Second World War is reported in contemporary memoirs (Ulam 1973, p. 555), but effectively guaranteed his demotion after victory (*ibid.*, p. 702). After Stalin's death, he rose to be Minister of Defence and member of the Party Presidium only to be dismissed by Khrushchev who then re-established Party control of the army.

expanding bureaucracy of members who occupied full-time administrative roles came to enjoy a progressively greater competitive advantage over members employed in other white- or blue-collar occupations. Various structural changes were made during the years between the death of Sverdlov in 1929 and the reorganization by Stalin in 1934. But every change was at once a response to the pressures in favour of centralization and a further reinforcement of them. None of it had been either intended or foreseen in 1917 by Lenin or anybody else. But even if Lenin had lived, and even if he had succeeded (as he appears to have wished) in enlarging peasant and proletarian representation at the higher levels of the Party and diluting the influence of the bureaucrats, there was no conceivable means by which he could reverse the concentration of power which he had set in train.

The same cannot as confidently be said of the course deliberately pursued by Stalin after 1934. There is no evidence that his position was seriously threatened, and no grounds for supposing that it was necessary for the continuance of the Party's domination of Soviet society for it to be believed that it was. He may genuinely have feared for his new role if his enemies both actual and potential were not destroyed. But whatever the psychological explanation for his actions, the sociological theorist has to take them as given and use them as a quasi-experimental test of the adaptability of the institutions which he now controlled to the conscious creation of a totalitarian sub-type of socialism. From this viewpoint, nothing is more striking about the history of Russia between 1934 and 1941 than the ease with which Stalin succeeded in his aims. There was no area of social space within which organized systactic opposition could form. Agriculture had been collectivized. The new generation of urban proletarians, vividly described by Deutscher (1967, p. 48) as 'uprooted villagers, town dwellers against their will, desperate, anarchic and helpless', faced the double sanction of arrest by the secret police and deprivation of their livelihoods by the factory administration (which the Party controlled). The trade unions, as we have seen, functioned not as channels for the expression of workers' sense of relative deprivation but as agents for discipline and exhortation. The civil service was by now staffed by incumbents of relatively privileged roles who owed their careers to the system they were administering. The purges at the higher levels of the Party created vacancies which there was never any shortage of aspirants to fill. Exogenous pressure was non-existent. The Party's control of the means of persuasion could be used to reinforce stories of internal conspiracies with allegations of attempts at counter-revolutionary penetration by agents of the capitalist powers. The army was now largely staffed by officers who owed their promotion to the regime, and its senior commanders had no inkling that after the purge of the Party Stalin would next turn on them. Some members of the Central Committee may have tried to halt or moderate the recourse to terror; but they had no means of undermining Stalin's control over the N.K.V.D., and they were in any case already compromised by their acquiescence in his previous use of it. There is no reason to suppose that every society which evolves into a socialist mode of the distribution of power will, even for a limited period, pass through a totalitarian phase. But it is an option – which it could never be under even the most determinedly oppressive of absolutist modes. No Tsar, no Sapa Inca, no Ming or Roman emperor could ever wield the power that Stalin did.

§35. England, Japan and Russia can be taken as paradigm cases of societies which, once the contingencies of their earlier histories are taken as given, were overwhelmingly likely to industrialize within a liberal, an authoritarian and a socialist mode respectively. But the institutional context was at least as favourable to the practices of liberal democracy in the United States as it ever was in England. It so happened that it was England and not the United States (or Holland*) which industrialized first. But once the precedent was there for other societies to follow, the United States was even more unlikely to industrialize within either an authoritarian or a socialist mode than England. Indeed, its structure and culture were both such as to make it likely to evolve into a sub-type more liberal and more democratic as well as more capitalist. The property-owning oligarchy of the Eastern seaboard had already lost its dominant location by the 1830s, as westward migration brought into being an electorate of small property-owners with no tradition of deference to patrons and a strong distrust of intervention by central government in local affairs. Within this electorate, cooperation was much more coalitional than systactic. Interests were articulated in terms of shared individual aspirations or grievances rather than a collective sense of relative deprivation; but in a context of local autonomy and near-universal white male suffrage, it was (as I remarked in Section 26 of Chapter 3) by direct democracy rather than through roles of client and patron that those interests were pursued. By the time that the spread of

* Holland, after all, was no more constrained than England by the institutions of monarchical absolutism. But not only had it 'lost its grip on European commerce' (Coleman 1977, p. 199) under the pressure of inter-societal competition; it had also, as Adam Smith saw (endorsed by Wrigley 1972–3, p. 247), already realized its maximum potential in terms of real income per head within the constraints of its resources and population, not least because it depended for energy on peat and not coal (de Zeeuw 1978).

wage-labour and the concentration of population in cities had brought into being an industrial proletariat steadily enlarged by European immigration, democratic political institutions* and a strongly held ideology of free enterprise offered as little competitive advantage to the carriers of authoritarian as of socialist practices and doctrines.

Post-colonial South America, by constrast, differed in four important respects from the United States. First, there was not the same geographical mobility towards a continuously advancing frontier; second, there were standing armies with their own corporate interests; third, substantial minorities of the population in a number of countries (or regions, such as Southern as opposed to Northern and Western Brazil) were settled in cities well before industrialization; and fourth, the institutions of central government inherited from the colonial period offered careers to the incumbents of numerous clerical, professional and administrative roles. The several societies which divided the continent between them differed widely in their degree of 'modernization', with perhaps Bolivia or Paraguay at the lower extreme and Argentina or Chile at the upper. But in none of them could the domination of a bourgeois commercial and administrative systact operating an oligarchic parliamentary system – Weber's *Honoratiorenverwaltung* – be more than a transitional phase. It was adequate to overcome the *caudillaje* (in Brazil, *coronelismo*) of local magnates still controlling their own dependent cultivators and possessing their own means of coercion, against whom the interests of urban élites and national armies were, for the moment, the same. But it could not survive the pressures which came to bear as industrialization began to create an organized working class, populist ideologies began to seem increasingly persuasive, and those who controlled the means of coercion began to use their power to influence the form of economic as well as political institutions. In South, as opposed to North, America, the institutional and geographical context alike favoured the selection of practices defining clientelistic roles and relations of vertical incorporation. This still permitted, as we saw in Section 30 of Chapter 3, a diversity of sub-types of authoritarian institutions. The controllers of the means of coercion might or might not occupy governmental as well as military roles; the interests of the owners of the means of production might or might not be upheld at the expense of those of urban or rural proletariat; and the means of

* That these often took the form of 'machine' or 'Tammany Hall' politics in which the practice of patronage re-emerged at ward level did not undermine free competition for votes between rival parties at national level (except in the South after the Civil War).

persuasion might or might not be used to promote a 'right-wing' rather than a 'left-wing' ideology by which to legitimate the regime. But the organized working class had no more chance of forming a political party which would alternate in office with its competitors for votes on the liberal-democratic model than it had of mounting a revolution which would replace the governing élite with another ostensibly, at least, committed to its interests as defined by a socialist ideology.

If a single South American society is to be taken as a test case, Argentina is the obvious choice. Not only was it rich in both resources and manpower, but after an electoral reform in 1910 which established universal male suffrage and the secret ballot the institutions of liberal parliamentary democracy were at least ostensibly in place. It is true that the geographical territory ruled from Buenos Aires from 1820 onwards 'had none of the distinguishing marks of a nation, let alone a state' (Halperin-Donghi 1975, p. 377), that the Argentine economy remained exceptionally fragmented both regionally and sectorally (Germani 1971), and that the large numbers of immigrants from the 1880s – who by 1895 amounted to a quarter of the total population – were very imperfectly assimilated within Argentina's political institutions (Cornblit 1967). But the same could just as plausibly be said of the United States. The evolution of Argentine society into an authoritarian mode – or rather, into a succession of sub-types of it – has to be explained not by invoking features common to at least one other society which did not, but by identifying the practices selected by the institutional context at the expense of those defining the roles and thereby institutions of liberal democracy.

The dominant systact in the decades after 1880, when Buenos Aires became the capital city, was a landowning oligarchy of predominantly creole origins whose wealth was highly concentrated in very few hands and whose roles were increasingly those of rentiers dependent on the export of primary products from their large estates. There was no significant systact of smallholding homesteaders. The urban middle class was not an industrial bourgeoisie, but an administrative service class of professionals and government servants. The immigrants who gravitated increasingly to the cities formed the nucleus of a proletariat employed mostly in small, technologically simple firms (or in larger enterprises owned by foreign rather than domestic capitalists). Political power attached to the role of the president rather than the members of congress, and the choice of incumbent effectively rested with provincial governors operating through a network of *caciques* who could guarantee to deliver the necessary votes. Immigrants did not as a rule become citizens. The urban middle class did not develop a systactic consciousness directed against the élite to which their interests were largely tied, and the élite welcomed the influx of immigrants as providing cheap labour. But because (unlike the United States) the élite did not control the market for urban jobs which might have been used to establish political leadership over them, 'Argentina's political system became biased towards restriction, repression and oligarchy. There was no means of controlling the immigrants within the political system, and it was therefore deemed advisable to keep them out of it as far as possible' (Rock 1975, p. 17).

In the period between the electoral reforms of 1912 and the military *coup* of 1930, elections, even if fraudulent, did to some degree reflect the opinions of the electors. But, as in Japan, behind the outward forms of parliamentary democracy, selective pressures continued to favour practices which defined political relations in terms of patron and client roles. The Radical party, which succeeded to the Presidency in 1916, incorporated the urban middle class into the political process, but it did so not by formulating a programme directed to middle-class interests but by patronage: 'Between 1919 and 1922 the use of government offices for political purposes developed into the principal nexus linking the government with the middle class groups' (*ibid.*, p. 110). The mode of production reproduced itself undisturbed, and proletarian interests continued not to be represented. Political influence was extended downwards through ward bosses (*caudillos de barrio*) and party committees, and industrial unrest was repressed by recourse to laws under which strikers could be deported or imprisoned. In the absence of any articulated programme of reform, legitimacy was sought by plebiscitarian appeals to the charisma of the leader. There was therefore as little prospect for two or more democratic parties representing rival systactic interests to succeed each other in office as there was for a largely immigrant proletariat lacking significant means of coercion to mount a revolutionary seizure of power. At the local as well as the national level, the pressure on the incumbents of executive roles was to eliminate the opposition (Potter 1981, pp. 101, 105) and to balance the conflicting interests of the higher-located systacts, which were at the same time classes and status-groups, within a single party.

The *coup* of 1930, when it came, was precipitated by a number of contingent events about whose relative importance specialists inevitably differ. But from the perspective of this volume, the more important point is that it might just as well have happened in 1919. The army had been waiting in the wings since 1890. It was a corporation held firmly together by its own ties of patronage. Its own strong ideology of nationalism was preserved and transmitted through secret military 'lodges' (Goldwert 1972, p. 12; cf. Ciria 1974, p. 207); and its near-monopoly of the means of coercion enabled it to present a government threatened from below with the alternatives of either applying force by its own decision or being overturned itself. In 1919, faced with a general strike, the government chose the former. But by doing so it only averted direct intervention for another decade. By now, the officer corps had largely ceased to be recruited from the families of the old landed oligarchy. It was younger, more middle-class, and more professional. The selective pressure which had originally required it to adapt itself to the need to control regional *caudillos* left it with both a heightened 'corporate consciousness' (Goldwert 1972, p. 9) and an internal structure within which promotion was achieved by adherence to its own sub-cultural norms. It is true that there were rivalries and antagonisms within it which subsequently crystallized in the division between interventionist 'reds' (*colorados*) and constitutionally minded 'blues' (*azules*). But both reds and blues shared an equal commitment to an ideology which, however alien to those of liberal or socialist persuasions, enabled them to see themselves as representing a national interest above class and party. Moreover, this ideology enjoyed considerable support in the Catholic Church and was by no means repudiated by the associations of organized labour (Rouquié 1978, p. 733). In due course, after the Second World War, the then dominant faction redefined it in terms of the Cold War, and its leaders accordingly became 'ardent anti-Cuba crusaders, combining fanatical anti-communism with faith in technocratic rationality, professional autocracy, and Western Christian values' (Mouzelis 1986, p. 156).

By that time, Perón had risen and fallen, and left behind him in the historical record a distinctive sub-type of the authoritarian mode in which the organized working class was incorporated alongside the army and the two played off against one another.* Like Stalin, Perón raises the unanswerable question whether his own personality and policies were either a necessary or a sufficient condition of the evolution of his society into its particular sub-type. But just as, from the perspective of this volume, the moral pointed by Stalinism is the adaptability of socialist practices and roles to totalitarian institutions, so is the moral

* Perón threatened more than once that he might open the arsenals to the urban proletariat. But in the view of one specialist at least, he preferred near-certain defeat to 'trying to gain a victory aided by armed workers, for such an event might have signalled the advent of real power for the working class' (Spalding 1977, p. 177).

pointed by Peronism the adaptability of authoritarian practices and roles to institutions which extend relations of patronage down to the urban working class in a by now predominantly industrial rather than agricultural economy.

Perón was able to offer measures directly favourable to working-class interests* in a way that the existing trade unions, whether socialist- or communist-controlled, could not; and he was able to call on economic, ideological and coercive resources as the tactics of the occasion might require. At the same time that union members increased enormously in numbers (from half a million to two and a half million between 1946 and 1951), they were bureaucratically organized to respond to direction from above, and internal opposition was neutralized by direct recourse to coercion of non-Peronist leaders. The government granted individual unions covering different industries legal status only if they conformed to its requirements. Rival unions simply lost their negotiating rights, while members of Peronist unions enjoyed the benefits of wage increases, pensions, holidays and protection from victimization by employers. The corresponding practices did not, however, work as well when applied to military roles. Selected officers were promoted, pay was raised, internal rivalries were deliberately fomented, and non-commissioned officers were used as Peronist spies (Goldwert 1972, p. 104). But the army as such was never incorporated as a subordinate institution within the state, and Perón's attempts at *adoctrinamiento* were, like his anti-clericalism, counterproductive (Potash 1980, pp. 167–9, 178). The outcome was that the military were able to depose Perón in 1955, but were then equally unable to incorporate the now large, well-organized, and politically articulate labour movement. Perón continued to dominate it in exile, and Peronism even widened its influence among intellectuals and in rural areas (Ranis 1966, pp. 117–18, 124). No compromise was possible.† As in 1930, the competition for power was for exclusive domination of the areas of social space within which the society's central

* The hypothesis that he owed his power purely to 'charismatic' manipulation is as implausible as that he owed it to immigrant rather than established working-class support: his appeal was to the whole industrial proletariat (not least women, whose rights he championed), and the trade union leaders recognized it (Munck 1987, pp. 121–3).

† Cf. Wynia (1978, p. 250): 'The labor movement could not be held down indefinitely, even by governments as strong as Ongania's. Sooner or later it retaliated, and when it did, it undermined not only the goverment's policy but also its claim to legitimacy on the basis of its ability to maintain public order'; but democratically minded presidents equally failed to realize that they could not 'treat laborers like unorganized voters who could be won over through favorable policies and conventional election rhetoric'.

institutions now functioned. The role of leader, or even member, of a loyal opposition did not exist.

Argentina accordingly presents the comparative social theorist with the intriguing variant of a mode of the distribution of power in which the practices conferring competitive advantage are carried by roles which function within two separate, internally differentiated, and mutually antagonistic corporations. There is nothing anomalous or aberrant about the evolution which brought this about. It would be quite mistaken to hypothesize that because Argentina was richer, more populous and more 'modern' than Bolivia, it was therefore more likely to evolve into a liberal-democratic-capitalist mode.* An authoritarian mode need not, as we have seen already, be merely transitional or incapable of reproducing itself beyond a period of emergency or crisis. But nor can there be ruled out the possibility of an evolution to either a socialist or a liberal-democratic mode, particularly if some unexpected exogenous pressure is brought to bear. The military government was overturned in 1983 in consequence of a war over the Falkland/Malvinas Islands whose occurrence was even less predictable in advance than its outcome, and alternative practices were certainly present in Argentinian society which, relatively powerless as the roles carrying them had hitherto been, might turn out to confer an advantage far greater than either their incumbents or any outside observer could have imagined in the immediate aftermath of the military *coup* of 24 March 1976.

HEGEMONY AND DECLINE

§36. Where selective pressure bears most strongly at the level of competition amounting to warfare between one society and another, the outcome is at the same time more and less interesting to the sociological theorist than where it bears most strongly at the inter-systactic, intra-societal level. It is more interesting because wars and battles are not only dramatic in themselves, but can divert the whole course of human

* The same could equally well be said of the newly independent societies of post-colonial Africa, where 'pious hopes for Democracy' (Lonsdale 1981, p. 43) soon lost their supposed rationale. The obvious test case here would be Ghana, where early independence under a charismatic leader and dominant faction (Runciman 1963) led to a weakening economy and successive crises of legitimacy; although the incumbent of the topmost role still enjoyed control of the means of coercion, increasing numbers of citizens were withdrawing from participation in the official economy into smuggling, the parallel economy, emigration, or resettlement in the countryside (Azanya and Chazan 1987). But it is too soon for comparative analysis to be possible in depth.

history from one direction to another. But it is less interesting because their outcome is so often a matter of chance: the accidents of fortune which have time and again determined who loses and who wins have to be accepted as a given part of the context within which the institutions of both winners and losers continue to evolve thereafter. Consider the twentieth century itself. There are any number of fortuitous and unpredictable occurrences but for which the Second World War might never have broken out at all or, once it had, might have left the world divided between German, Russian and Japanese zones of geographical and institutional hegemony. But it didn't. Tocqueville's prophecy that America and Russia were 'marked out by the will of Heaven to sway the destinies of half the globe' was a good guess; it was not, and could not have been, a prediction grounded in a well-tested substantive theory. Battles are won or lost, and societies conquer or are conquered by others, for reasons which sometimes can, but very often cannot, be grounded in an evolutionary theory concerned only with the sociological causes of differences in modes and sub-types of the distribution of the means of production, persuasion and coercion.

Yet there are, all the same, cases where the domination of one society by another can be traced directly to practices to which there attaches a significant competitive advantage in the given context and which can, therefore, be hypothesized to be 'the' cause of the subordinate (and sometimes also the dominant) society's transition from one to another mode. The relation of the particular hypothesis to the underlying theory is then much the same as where the competition is intra-societal only and the vicissitudes of warfare irrelevant. The only difference is that the familiar difficulty in assessing the evolutionary significance of different mutations of practices is now compounded by the difficulty of assigning relative importance to the pressures on their carriers which are inter-societal and those which derive from the continuing intra-societal competition between different systacts and roles.

It is in the nature of inter-societal competition that the carriers of the practices which it selects are carriers in a geographical as well as a sociological sense. The Macedonians who founded Alexandria Eschatē, the Roman legionaries guarding Hadrian's Wall, the Vikings raiding and trading their way down the waterways of Kievan Russia, the Spanish and Portuguese priests bringing literacy and baptism to the South American Indians, the district commissioners dispensing British justice to the villagers of Nigeria and the Gold Coast, or General MacArthur in his quasi-shogunal role in Japan after 1945 are all, as it were, the physical propagators of social change exogenously driven. But this is a necessary, not a sufficient, condition of the modification of roles and institutions in the society at the receiving end. Interference of this kind does not always succeed. In the longer term, no doubt, the alien practices will be selected (or not) for the advantages they confer on the roles by which the recipient society is defined, whether the advantage is in inter- or intra-societal competition. But where both are simultaneously at work, the competitive pressure may operate to different effect at the two different levels.

This aspect of the process of social evolution is implicit already in the four separate models of 'colonization' discussed in Section 33 of Chapter 3. Selective pressure is at work at both levels in all four of them. In the 'minimalist' model, institutional changes are dictated by relations not only between colonists and indigenes on one side and colonists and their society of origin on the other but also among the colonists themselves. In 'planter' societies, as both the Jamaican and the Rhodesian examples exemplify equally well, the pattern of both relations between colonists and indigenes and relations among the colonists (and successive immigrants joining them) was critically influenced by the shifting balance of interests between the 'plantocracy' and London. Where the model is that of 'indirect rule', the indigenous élite continues to dominate a systactic structure which can respond only at second hand to pressures originating from the colonizing society; but equally, relations between colonizers and the indigenous élite evolve according to a balance of advantage determined by competition between themselves. And in the 'vice-regal' model, where an apparatus of government controlled from the colonizing society is fused with the institutions of the society colonized, selective pressure still continues to operate on the relations of that apparatus to the indigenous population even where it is itself responding directly to pressures brought to bear as a result of a systactic conflict internal to the colonizing society: to give a biographical illustration, the career of Warren Hastings is explicable only by reference to the relation between his Indian and his English roles.

Out of these complex interactions of selective pressure, there can emerge changes of extraordinary rapidity and violence. I have already cited as an example of catastrophic evolution the impact of the European fur-traders on the indigenous Indian societies of North-eastern America. But even where there is a much less obvious imbalance of power, a collapse of one to the advantage of the other can come about almost overnight if the contigencies of battle coincide with a demonstrable but not otherwise decisive difference in practices and roles. Visigothic Spain fell down like the proverbial house of cards under the impact of Arab conquest; and although it is unwarranted to fall back on explanations simply in terms of 'decay, decadence and demoralization' (Collins 1980, p. 189), there seems no dispute among specialists that previous inter-systactic conflict within a once relatively stable society functioned to give the practices of the invaders a competitive advantage out of all proportion to their apparent strength.

Likewise, even where a society declines from a position of hegemony relative to others without the accident of a catastrophic defeat, the decline can be remarkably rapid if inter- and intra-societal pressures coincide. I have earlier discussed the 'decline' of Venice with reference to the shift from entrepreneurial to rentier roles and the lack of upward social mobility into the ranks of a rigidly stratified governing élite. But these changes were at the same time a response to the pressures of inter-societal competition. As we saw, there was no consequential effect on the still remarkable stability of Venetian society: unlike Visigothic Spain, no internal breakdown of its institutions preceded loss of independence to an alien invader. But the changes in systactic structure, adaptive as they were for the roles of the governing élite within it, were adaptations to an inter-societal context in which the hegemony of Venice as the dominant imperial power in the Eastern Mediterranean was no longer tenable.

The choice of examples for more detailed analysis is, accordingly, complicated not only by the extent to which inter-societal hegemony or decline may be the result of contingencies which the sociological theorist has to treat as random, but also by the extent to which over-determination can be compounded by the mutual reinforcement of pressures at both levels. But to explain just why that reinforcement can be so very effective, the most illuminating cases are those where (as so often) the beginnings of the change can be traced to the selection of practices, whether economic, ideological or coercive, whose advantages to their carriers were almost completely unrecognized at the time. There is no objective criterion against which to measure the relative unexpectedness of the expansion to 'world-power' status of Republican Rome, early Islam, and Portugal after the defeat of the Castilians in 1385 and the capture of Ceuta from the Moors in 1415. But the conclusion which follows from comparison of the three is twofold: first, that very different combinations of economic, social-cum-ideological and political-cum-military institutions can function equally effectively in inter-societal competition if the context favours the practices which define their constituent roles; and second, that the competitive advantages conferred by mutant or recombinant practices perform the same function for their carriers whatever the relative strength of inter- and intra-societal pressure.

§37. Rome is the most spectacular case. Not only did it succeed in extending its domination over the whole *orbis terrarum*, but it did so within the institutions of a citizen mode which did not evolve until later and for other reasons into an absolutist one. The motives behind Rome's expansion are much debated among specialists: was it offensive or merely pre-emptive? were the ambitions of the victorious commanders economic as well as political? were all groups and categories of citizens in favour of war or only some of them? was territory sought for its own sake or merely to enable surplus citizens to be settled on it? were mercantile interests involved significantly or even at all? But whatever the right answers to these questions, there can be no doubt that expansion *was*, as Polybius evidently believed, actively pursued from the earliest period of the Republic.* Even though direct reportage for that period of Roman history is meagre if not non-existent, the literary and epigraphic evidence from later periods strongly supports the inference that the pursuit of *laus* and *gloria* was pervasive among the nobility, plebeian as well as patrician, from the beginning, and that victory in war was the means of achieving it.† The financial gains accruing to the state or to individual commanders may or may not have been sought for their own sake. But the near-continuous campaigns waged from the Samnite wars onward were actively welcomed by those who fought them. Even if there were a few exceptions, it was (as always) those who *did* seek power, whether in the form of booty, fame or the attainment of high political-cum-military office, whose actions determined the form which the institutions of Roman society were to take.

It may be, as argued by Badian (1968), that annexation in the Eastern Mediterranean, at any rate, was avoided where possible. Alternatively, it may be that expansion was merely deferred because of what were seen as the difficulties of making it effective. But either way, there can be no doubt of the superiority in means of coercion which Rome enjoyed. I have already quoted the maxim that refusal to annex should not be

* See particularly 1.6.3, where he says that the Romans 'got, as it were, a start to their expansion (*synauxēsis*)' after the recovery of the city from the Gauls, and 'made war against their neighbours from then on'.

† W. V. Harris (1979, pp. 10ff.). Not until 151 B.C. is there any evidence of serious reluctance on the part of individual nobles to go to war (sources cited *ibid.*, p. 36 n. 5).

confused with reluctance to control. Nor, by this stage, can it be claimed that expansionist policy was a function of a perceived threat to Roman society itself. Clemenceau's dictum that nobody has ever accused the Belgians of invading Germany in 1914 can no less aptly be applied to Rome. Campaigning was carried on well beyond its own borders; and it was directed against societies whose rulers had no intention whatever of even attempting to do what the Gauls had done to Rome in 390 B.C.

The systactic structure of Roman society during its expansion furnished a context more favourable to the practices sustaining it than is reported for any other citizen-state in the historical record. Whatever the previous history which had led to the conflict between the patrician and plebeian orders and the immiseration (to the point of debt-bondage) of numbers of poorer plebeians, reform in and after 367 B.C. was 'organically and inseparably connected with the process of expansion' (Alföldy 1985, p. 26). Competition both among and between patrician and plebeian families was intense. Both vied for the enrichment, glory and political influence symbolized in the distinctively Roman custom of the triumph which, in due course, the Senate was ready to award to victorious plebeian as well as patrician commanders. At the same time, successful wars gave poorer plebeians and younger sons their own chance for the acquisition of land; and the spread of slavery had the consequence that the interest of the large landowners no longer lay in reducing plebeians to debt-bondage (Ferenczy 1976, pp. 63–4), but in using plebeians to fight the wars which provided them with slaves with which their estates could be worked more easily. The army which fought these wars, and with increasing regularity won them, was a citizen militia whose equipment and tactics were the result of a 'hoplite revolution' similar in these respects to that which had taken place earlier in mainland Greece. But – unlike any Greek *polis* – it was supported by a twofold process of colonization by citizens who remained politically and militarily available to Rome* and incorporation of the citizens of other Latin and Italian communities who, by adding significantly to Roman manpower, furthered *synauxēsis* yet again.

This practice of extending citizenship to vanquished enemies (or to turncoats who had already transferred their allegiance to Rome) was, as I have suggested already, the critical one. It was not unknown to the *poleis* of Greece: distinguished foreigners who had rendered signal

* The size of the colonies was deliberately limited so that they were too small to form independent citizen-states (Sherwin-White 1973, p. 77).

services might be rewarded by citizenship, as might non-citizen members of the *polis* itself who served with particular gallantry in war. But its deliberate employment as an adjunct to military victory was uniquely Roman. It took a variety of forms, and was itself subject to continuing mutations by which the roles of the new and sometimes 'second-class' citizens were modified. But its function remained the same. The variant of *civitas sine suffragio* created a lower-ranking systact of 'Romans' who could marry and contract with other Romans, paid Roman taxes and fought in Roman wars but were denied the right to vote (or to hold political office) in Rome. But this generated a collective sense of relative deprivation only later, as the increasing power of Rome made municipal autonomy less attractive to local notables; at first, it was a relationship between near-equals exchanging reciprocal rights. In some cases, such as the Sabines, a grant of *ius suffragii* and enrolment in a voting tribe came within a generation; in others, such as the Volscians, it only came very much later; in the case of the Latin allies, as we have seen already, a war had to be fought before they were admitted to citizenship; and the inhabitants of Cisalpine Gaul were only enfranchised by Julius Caesar. But the diffusion of citizenship by a simultaneous migration of Romans into Latin and Italian territory and absorption of these territories into the institutional catchment area of Rome worked to the advantage of grantors and grantees alike.

It is, as so often in the study of social evolution, difficult to discover how far the Romans consciously planned the results which they achieved and how far a random mutation of practices was only subsequently turned into a deliberate instrument of policy. Although we are told by Livy (VI.4.4) that as early as 389 B.C., citizenship (and land) had been granted to Etruscans who had joined the Roman side, his account of the grant of citizenship to several Latin communities in 338 still implies that 'the boldness of the new move was appreciated' (Sherwin-White 1973, p. 59). But perhaps the most significant single episode was the 'new and momentous' (Alföldi 1965, p. 383) annexation of Tusculum in 381. It was significant not only because a people hitherto quite distinct were thereby assigned roles as full members of Roman society, but also because of the effect on the local Tusculan aristocracy. Despite a chequered history of relations with Rome, the opening of political-cum-military roles in Rome to Tusculan notables gave Rome its first Tusculan consul in 322; and this recruitment of local élites into the Roman magistracy is hardly less important to the integration of the whole Italian peninsula under Roman hegemony than the extension of the role of citizen itself.

The rate of upward mobility which resulted was not large. Quite apart from the lack of motivation on the part of those who preferred to remain larger fish in smaller pools, the topmost roles remained until the end of the Republic much more difficult to enter for so-called *inquilini*. For the great majority of 'new men', a praetor's role was a major achievement and a consulship 'the height of felicity' (Wiseman 1971, p. 155). The more important effect was that those who *were* motivated to seek Roman magistracies might otherwise have been motivated to support movements of rebellion or would-be fission. As we have seen more than once elsewhere, individual mobility of this kind can have the double effect of depriving those left behind of their potential leaders and diminishing the concern of the members of the dominant systact about the potential threat to themselves. The loyalty of the Latin and Italian allies, strained as it was by the demands which the Romans made on them, could not have been secured nearly so effectively without it. By the time of the 'Social' War, when those still excluded from citizenship were driven to fight for it, their leaders no longer had any option between absorption and fission; and if they had succeeded in the latter, the institutions and practices of the rival Italian state which they hoped to create would have been indistinguishably Roman.

These practices were, therefore, selected twice over. It was not simply that the other societies of Italy (and later beyond) came to accept, or to have forced on them, Roman practices at the expense of their own. It was also that these practices conferred a competitive advantage on all the citizens of Rome, noble or plebeian, rich or poor, as a response to the pressure of inter-societal competition. In their composite roles of citizens and militiamen, they were encouraged by each success against their opponents to continue the process within the same set of institutions. The stability of these institutions was not threatened by intra-societal competition until the Gracchi, and even then the system survived unchanged. It is true that the pattern of roles was by then very different from what it had been at the time of the First Punic War: the number of slaves had increased enormously, the number of available *assidui* had declined, and the formally free but economically dependent proletariat in the city of Rome itself had been enlarged by persistent migration from the countryside and the influx of freedmen. 'Bread and circuses' were, so to speak, around the corner. But Roman society was still a society within the citizen mode; and the roles and practices constitutive of that mode now pervaded *tota Italia*.

§38. Hardly less spectacular than the expansion of Rome is that of

Islam. But once Arabia itself could be unified,* advance beyond its borders was into something close to a vacuum of power. Rome and Sasanian Persia had fought each other to a standstill in unawareness of the onslaught impending from a group of peoples whose limited resources, as they saw them, they sought merely to neutralize to the detriment of one another. No doubt the ability to take advantage of this state of affairs was contingent on the political skill of Abu Bakr and the generalship of Khalid b. al Walid: only after their initial success did the way into Iraq and beyond lie open. But the practices which conferred decisive advantage on the armies of the caliph were very different from the practices carried, with equal success, by the Roman legions. First, it was not the acquisition of land as such which either served or was thought to serve the interests of the conquerors; second, the decisive advantage was as much ideological as either economic or coercive.

Specialists disagree over the extent to which the conquests were impelled by the pressure of population on the means of production in the Arabian peninsula. But whatever their motives, few of the nomadic tribesmen moving northwards in search of subsistence were intending to settle as peasant farmers. Conquered territories were, to be sure, distributed in due course as portions of booty (*nasib*). But they did not have to be worked full-time, or indeed at all, by the warriors to whom they were assigned. The central institution of the conquered territories was the garrison town where the warriors were quartered: productive land was taxed for their benefit rather than granted to them to own and farm like Roman *assidui*. Muhammad himself, who evidently shared much of the townsman's traditional disdain for the nomads, wanted to see them settled, but in the role not of producers so much as of pensioners of the Islamic state. The difference from the institutions of the Roman conquest is nicely captured in the dictum that the provinces controlled from the garrison-cities of Kufa and Basra were, in an already traditional phrase, 'a garden protected by our spears' – which Peter Brown (1971a, p. 196) calls 'an exact description of the Near East in the seventh and eighth centuries'.

Specialists also disagree over the significance of the doctrines of Muhammad as motives of conquest independent of the traditional aims of conquest and booty (and, for the merchant class, opportunities for trade). It is impossible to discover how important to the psychology of a soldier like Khalid, or even of the caliphs themselves, was the sense of

* A process which was complementary, rather than preliminary, to expansion into Iraq, Syria and Egypt: the 'two conquests... were simultaneous and interlinked, not successive' (B. Lewis 1970, p. 52; cf. Watt 1961, p. 222).

a mission divinely inspired, and there is no quasi-experimental contrast to which to appeal in order to hypothesize what might have been the success or otherwise of a conquest which was not also a *jihād*. But the novel mode of persuasion and novel distinctions of prestige which it engendered not only gave the conquests a legitimation which they would otherwise have lacked, but also gave the structure of the composite (and often divided) élite a stability and coherence without which fission into rival tribes would have been unavoidable. The three categories of Muhammad's supporters with their own systactic interests were, first, the 'emigrants' (*muharijun*) who had left Mecca in his company, second, the Medinese 'helpers' (*ansar*) who had sided with him, and third, his fellow-Quraysh who, once persuaded of his mission, claimed the traditional privilege of kinship. Feelings of relative deprivation of the higher rank in relation to the others which each felt they should enjoy might find expression from time to time in open hostility. But the criteria not merely of faith in, and kinship with, the Prophet, but also of *sabiqa* – priority in allegiance to Islam – made it possible to draw the peoples of the Arabian peninsula into a single institutional catchment area in a way that mutant economic and military practices could never have done by themselves.

These distinctive characteristics of the Islamic conquests both conferred advantages on their carriers which derive from the structure and culture of pre-Islamic Arabia. The exaction of booty or protection-rent (*khuwwa*) from settled cultivators by warrior nomads was a normal practice; and although many nomads were occassionally or partially settled, they continued to dominate the fully settled populations of the villages and oases, and they continued to look down on farming as an occupation unworthy of respect. At the same time, their relations with one another were articulated predominantly according to criteria of lineage (*nasab*) and *sharaf* (which some specialists translate 'honour' and others 'nobility'). *Sharaf* was, to be sure, acquired by military prowess as well as by ascription or personal recognition for religious or secular charisma. But the tribes and the lineages within them were ranked as status-groups between which social distance was precisely graded by blood-price for men and marriage-price for women. Further, high status was accorded to the role of head (*mansab*) of a cult centre (*haram*) whose functions included the adjudication of disputes and the maintenance of an enclave where violence was forbidden, and this role too tended to be transmitted from fathers to sons.

The pre-existing institutional context was, accordingly, favourable not only to Muhammad's self-chosen role of arbitrator-cum-prophet but also to that of any successor who, although his role could not be more than that of caliph or 'deputy', was able to inspire the Islamic community – the *umma* – with belief in the continuation of his mission. That this depended on military success and the booty which it yielded is beyond dispute. But it is equally beyond dispute that the means of persuasion were at least as important as the means of production and coercion. In this new context, the critical practice was the payment of the warriors out of the proceeds of conquest on a scale determined by *sabiqa*. The Sasanian army had likewise been paid by a redistribution of tax revenue. But there is no evidence that the Sasanian military register was ever, like the Islamic *diwan*, deliberately employed as an instrument of social control (Morony 1984, p. 58). The function of the Islamic practice was threefold: it integrated the warriors now garrisoned in Kufa or Basra, including those who had earlier sought to defect,* into a salaried body organized by tribes and rewarded by loyalty; it marked that body off as a systact distinct from the dependent cultivators at once exploited and protected by it; and by encouraging the nomads of the Arabian peninsula to emigrate in order to share in the fruits of conquest as salaried pensioners of the Islamic state, it secured the new composite élite in their roles.†

This triumphant expansion from Arabia into Syria, Iraq, Egypt and, in due course, beyond carried into territories hitherto dominated by Rome or Iran the practices of the Islamic state. In doing so, it transformed it from a patrimonial proto-state legitimated by the charisma of the Prophet into the first of many Islamic societies whose pervasive roles and central institutions were such as to assign it to a 'warrior' mode of the distribution of power. Its further evolution into an absolutist monarchy and regression thereafter into the emirates and sultanates of the Buyid period have been discussed already. But its unpredictable emergence from an initial context at least as unpromising as that of the Gallic sack of Rome is almost a paradigm example of the effects which can follow from a mutation of practices and consequent appearance of novel roles whose long-term effects not only on the society of origin but on a whole range of other and ostensibly more powerful societies no contemporary could possibly have foreseen.

* Shortage of manpower had compelled the caliph Umar to relax the rule that men who joined the 'apostasy' (*Ridda*) after Muhammad's death could not share in the conquests (Kennedy 1986, p. 67).

† A minor but not insignificant aspect of the process was the function of the role of 'distributor of surplus' in increasing the status of the *ashraf* who occupied it and at the same time increasing their control over their tribal warriors to whom the distribution was made (Donner 1981, p. 262).

§39. If the practices critical to the expansion of Rome were more coercive than economic or ideological, and those critical to the expansion of Islam more ideological than economic or coercive, it can equally plausibly be argued that those central to the expansion of Portugal (and the other maritime societies of Europe) were more economic than coercive or ideological. But as always, all three were present, and all three had to reinforce the selective advantages conferred by the others on their carriers for the evolutionary outcome to be what it so surprisingly became. The story of the hegemony of Western Europe is at the same time the story of the diffusion of capitalism. But there is no necessary connection. Its leaders were not members of a bourgeois systact who had already brought about a transition to a capitalist mode of production at home. The selection of capitalist practices did, to be sure, require a contingent conjunction of geographical and institutional conditions; but these conditions were independent of the systactic structure out of which the initial expansion had emerged.

It is usual to contrast the expansion of the maritime societies of Europe with the relative stagnation of the land-based empires in terms of the private enterprise characteristic of the first and the centralized bureaucratic control characteristic of the second. Nor is the contrast misplaced. It was not a matter of technological backwardness, as amply demonstrated by the 'amazing' voyages (Braudel 1973, p. 303) of the Chinese eunuch admiral Cheng Ho in the early fifteenth century. The Ming emperors were simply not interested in (or, in the view of some specialists, actively disapproved of) the potential rewards of voyages of discovery. But it would be a mistake to suppose that the rulers of the maritime states merely responded to a series of initiatives independently conceived by freebooting buccaneers and merchant adventurers. Queen Elizabeth I not only actively encouraged ventures like Sir Francis Drake's circumnavigation of the globe, but profited directly from investments on her own account in privateering. Nor would it be correct to see the carriers of these practices as members of groups or categories marginal to the systactic structure. It is true that from earliest times much financial and commercial activity has been carried on by resident aliens or ethnic or religious minorities. But the expansion of Portugal, Holland and England was the outcome of sustained cooperation between rulers of strong states commanding substantial means of coercion with entrepreneurs drawn frequently (though far from always) from privileged systactic origins.

That Portugal should have been the spearhead of European hegemony is the more remarkable because it was not, sociologically speaking, a maritime society at all. Only a very small fraction of its population was, or ever had been, engaged in fishing (Boxer 1969, p. 14). There was no surplus of trained seamen seeking employment: on the contrary, throughout the period of expansion Portugal was chronically short of them. Nor was there an established bourgeoisie capable, even if its members had so wished, of organizing the pursuit of profit overseas. The merchant communities of Lisbon and Oporto were almost entirely concerned with trading in the agricultural products from which Portugal's limited wealth was overwhelmingly derived, and it was Italian rather than Portuguese capital which financed the voyages of discovery. It might, perhaps, be argued that the successful Reconquest had created the opportunity as well as the motive for an extended crusade directed to the forcible conversion of Saracens, pagans and unbelievers (as explicitly envisaged by the Papal Bull *Romanus Pontifex* of 1455). But retrospective legitimation is not to be confused with an initial impulse to trade and raid.* The quest for booty may indeed have been combined in the minds of the pioneers with the service of God. But – in contrast to the expansion of Islam – the ideological practices of Portuguese Christianity conferred no particular competitive advantage on their carriers in this context. The rulers of Portugal were Christian kings; but there was no fusion of political with religious institutions on the Islamic model. Portuguese expansion was driven by a coalition of political-cum-military and mercantile, not ecclesiastical, interests.

The Reconquest, and its further continuance into Morocco, was of course a necessary prelude to expansion in Africa, the Indies and Brazil. It not only created a unified nation-state, but brought into being a systact of *nobres* and *cavaleiros* who, although they soon became a class of manorial landlords rather than a warrior aristocracy, had sons who could be recruited for conquest abroad rather than battle against the Moors (or each other) at home. But expansion needed the fortuitous conjunction not merely of 'guns and sails' but also of winds and currents, compasses and astrolabes, and sailing directions and charts. And it needed the Atlantic Islands to be there to be exploited first for grain and then for sugar (Serrâo 1954), before the African coast could then be exploited for gold, ivory and slaves. Prince Henry the Navigator may have been motivated by both scientific curiosity and religious zeal, but he was in debt throughout his lifetime (Boxer 1969, p. 24) and directly interested in the profit to be derived from the voyages which he financed. Once

* This conclusion is reinforced by the argument of Malowist (1962) that there were similar pressures elsewhere in Europe for emigration and conquest to which kings and nobles responded as circumstances allowed them.

they were under way (and once, in particular, the dreaded Cape Bojador had been rounded in 1434), the process was self-reinforcing. The merchants of Lisbon and Oporto now became ready participants; *cavaleiros* directed their knightly careers to expeditions against defenceless West African villages; trading-posts (*feitorias*) were established successively further down the African coast; and royal patronage promoted the more ambitious voyages of discovery which led round the Cape of Good Hope and on to India. The institutions and practices thereby diffused were perhaps marginally furthered by the missionaries who followed literally in the merchants' wake. But their influence was never more than marginal, and it was in any case very sporadic prior to the arrival of the Jesuits in Goa in 1542. The voyages of discovery raised Portugal to a position of inter-societal hegemony only because they served its economic interests so spectacularly well; and they served its economic interests so spectacularly well only because the societies on the receiving end lacked the means of coercion necessary to prevent it.

It thus so happened, unlikely as it may have been, that the 'expansion of Europe' was initiated by a patrimonial monarchy rather than by a society which had evolved into a 'bourgeois' mode. But that partly explains in its turn why, by the end of the eighteenth century, Portugal had declined to a position of negligible importance in inter-societal competition. By then, hegemony had passed to two societies which, as we have seen, had evolved into their respective sub-types of a mode in which the interests of a dominant commercial systact were paramount. The displacement of the Portuguese from the oceans of the world by the Dutch, and the displacement of the Dutch by the English (and to some degree the French), is a story which revolves in part around the vicissitudes of diplomatic and military relations among the different societies of Europe and in part around the shifting balance of technological, commercial and military advantage in the East. But on no plausible counterfactual supposition could Portuguese hegemony have been sustained. Portugal simply did not have the power. 'Guns and sails' had created for the Portuguese the opportunity to cut into the African spice trades and to extract tolls and fees from the other users of the sea lanes. But they could not hope to extend their domination into the interior of the Indian sub-continent or mainland China; they could not enforce a permanent blockade of the Persian Gulf; their entrepreneurs progressively withdrew their capital as the Cape route declined in importance and Portuguese ships in the Indian Ocean became increasingly liable to seizure; their overseas agents introduced no new commerical practices into the Asian economy,* from which they profited more in the role of middlemen than of principals; and their settlers overseas came increasingly to see themselves as enclaves belonging to the institutional catchment area of the societies of Asia rather than as colonists on a 'planter', let alone a 'vice-regal', model. The seventeenth and eighteenth centuries belonged in this respect to colonial institutions of a different kind. Only societies which had evolved significantly further towards a capitalist mode of production could extend European domination into the systactic structure of the traditional societies of Africa, Asia and the Americas and draw literally millions of their members into the catchment area of a global market.

By the end of the nineteenth century, when capitalist practices had penetrated the furthest corners of the globe, the societies whose merchants, manufacturers, financiers and entrepreneurs had brought it about had lost their successive hegemony and the United States was emerging as the foremost liberal-democratic-capitalist society in the world. It was not an 'imperialist' society, if by that is meant that its dominant systact directed its policies to the forcible annexation of territory. Its ideology was overtly anti-colonial; its domination was exercised principally through economic institutions sustained by the mutual reinforcement of financial and industrial, rather than agricultural and commercial, practices; and although the Monroe Doctrine of 1823 proclaimed Central and South America to be within the catchment area of its political-cum-military institutions, it was a repudiation of European influence rather than an assertion of pan-American fusion. Yet the diffusion of capitalist and liberal-democratic practices and roles was reinforced by unhesitating recourse to the means of coercion, whether in Mexico, Hawaii, the Philippines or the Caribbean. The Civil War, although from one point of view a violent hiccup in the evolution of the United States as a whole to an industrial capitalist mode of production with a liberal ideology and a democratic (not to say populist) polity, was from another a major step forward in the industrialization of the means of coercion. Deliberate demilitarization after 1865 concealed for a while the implications for the inter-societal distribution of power. But by the time that intervention in the First World War in 1917 had

* The only partial exception is their influence on the production of pepper (Wallerstein 1974, p. 331, citing Godinho 1969). But as Wallerstein points out, again following Godinho, the technology of pepper is so simple that mass production required only a relatively modest input of additional labour.

tipped the scales decisively against Germany, the United States not only was, but could be seen to be, the most powerful society in the world. No doubt this might, as I have hinted already, have been a short-lived hegemony if the Second World War had taken a different course. But in the event, the outcome left the two societies which had industrialized within an authoritarian mode unconditionally defeated, and – just as Tocqueville had appeared to predict – capitalist America and socialist Russia sharing hegemony of the world with consequences which hindsight does not yet allow us to explain.

This last rather breathless paragraph brings, so to speak, up to date the whole long process of social evolution which started with the transition from nature to culture. Is there then a general conclusion to be drawn? In one sense, the answer must be yes, of course: social evolution is the outcome of a process of selection whose object is the functionally defined units of reciprocal action through which the incumbents of the roles by which societies are defined bring institutional inducements and sanctions to bear on one another. But in another sense, it is no: or rather, it is that there is no general conclusion of the kind which evolutionary theorists have hitherto presupposed. Social evolution is just as susceptible to scientific explanation as biological evolution. But the form which that explanation must take is such as to bury beyond hope of resurrection any and every teleological account of human history. There is no one mode of the distribution of power predetermined to inherit the earth; no nation, race or empire has a manifest destiny; there is no valid interpretation of the history of human societies in terms of progress towards a goal; there is no inexorable sequence from one mode of production, persuasion or coercion to the next; there is no process of cumulative rationalization at work in either a formal or a substantive sense; there is no dialectic by which opposing tendencies are reconciled at a higher level; there is no will of God being acted out; there is no master plan being followed, whether consciously or not. There are only people in their roles, linked within institutional catchment areas by relations of both domination and cooperation and competing with one another for economic, ideological and coercive power, as they will continue to do for as long as the human species may survive.

CONCLUSION

§40. The theory of social selection advanced in these pages cannot be claimed to be firmly grounded for as long as it lacks not only much of the necessary historical detail but also a much more nearly adequate understanding of human psychology than we yet possess. Yet in this, it is no differently placed from the theory of natural selection in the lifetime of Darwin, who similarly lamented the lack of an adequate fossil record while holding a view of genetics which turned out to be not merely superficial but incorrect. However much further elaboration and refinement is called for, the fundamental idea that the evolution of human societies and their constituent roles and institutions proceeds through a continuing struggle for power whose outcome is determined by the competitive selection of practices in the three mutually irreducible dimensions of social structure is – or so I believe – no less demonstrably superior to its rivals than Darwin's was. Like Darwin's, it has been anticipated in many of its insights by earlier authors without whose writings no general synthesis would yet be feasible; and like Darwin's it will continue to be attacked by those whose strongly held philosophical presuppositions are incompatible with it. But the study of human societies has at all events progressed far enough for it to be possible to formulate a general evolutionary theory whose acceptance or rejection is not a matter of philosophical preference, but of its success – or not – when tested against evidence which all rival observers can check for themselves.

There is a further parallel with Darwin, too. All readers of *The Origin of Species* will recall its concluding paragraph, in which Darwin observes how 'from the war of nature, from famine and death, the most exalted object which we are capable of conceiving, namely the production of the higher animals, directly follows'. Likewise, nobody who has studied in any depth the evidence of the historical and ethnographic record can fail to be struck by the way in which the most elaborate forms of culture and the most complex patterns of structure are the product of an intense, unremitting, and all too often violent competition for power between rival armies, classes and creeds. That this sequence is, no less than natural selection, both random in its origins and indeterminate in its outcome is something which cannot but be distressing to those who would like to believe that there is some millennial goal which mankind is destined to reach and by which all the sufferings endured on the way to it will be vindicated. But as Carlyle said of the lady who told him that she accepted the universe, 'By God, she'd better!' The crimes, follies and vices of mankind – if that is what, according to your values, they are – arise out of the same irreversible yet unforeseeable process of social evolution as the most splendid manifestations of benevolence, wisdom and courage. Which is the more encouraging, or dismaying, or paradoxical, or ironic is up to you. But not the least remarkable of the 'objects which follow', in Darwin's phrase, is the academic study of the process itself, and the roles and institutions which sustain and perpetuate it – by, among other things, putting this volume into your hands.

References

Abrams, Philip (1978) 'Towns and Economic Growth: some Theories and Problems', in Philip Abrams and E. A. Wrigley, eds., *Towns in Societies* (Cambridge).

Adam, Heribert (1971) *Modernizing Racial Domination: South Africa's Political Dynamics* (Berkeley, Calif.).

Alavi, Haniza (1973) 'Peasant Classes and Primordial Loyalties', *Journal of Peasant Studies* I.

Alföldi, A. (1965) *Early Rome and the Latins* (Ann Arbor, Mich.).

Alföldy, Géza (1969) 'Der attische Synoikismos und die Entstehung der athenischen Adels', *Revue Belge de Philogie et d'Histoire* LXVII.

(1985) *The Social History of Rome* (Eng. trans., London).

Allen, Michael (1984) 'Elders, Chiefs and Big Men: Authority Legitimation and Political Conflict in Melanesia', *American Ethnologist* XI.

Ammianus Marcellinus, *Roman History*.

Ancey, G. *et al.* (1974) *L'économie de l'espace rural de la région de Bouaké* (Paris).

Andaya, Leonard Y. (1975) *The Kingdom of Johor 1641–1728: Economic and Political Developments* (Oxford).

Anderson, Bo and Cockcroft, James D. (1966) 'Control and Cooptation in Mexican Politics', *International Journal of Comparative Sociology* VII.

Anderson, Perry (1974) *Lineages of the Absolutist State* (London).

Angold, Michael (1984) *The Byzantine Empire 1025–1204: a Political History* (London).

Annan, Noël (1984) *Leslie Stephen: the Godless Victorian* (London).

Appian, *History*.

Arguédas Díaz, Alcides (1929) *Los Caudillos Barbaros* (Barcelona).

Aristotle, *Politics*.

Arjomand, Said Amir (1979) 'Religion, Political Action and Legitimate Domination in Shiite Iran: Fourteenth to Eighteenth Centuries A.D.', *Archives Européennes de Sociologie* XX.

Ashburner, Walter (1910, 1912) 'The Farmer's Law', *Journal of Hellenic Studies* XXX & XXXII.

Aston, T. H. (1958) 'The Origins of the Manor in England', *Transactions of the Royal Historical Society* 5th ser., VIII.

Auerbach, Erich (1957) *Mimesis* (Eng. trans., New York).

Austin, M. M. and Vidal-Naquet, P. (1977) *Economic and Social History of Ancient Greece: an Introduction* (London).

Ayalon, David (1975) 'Preliminary Remarks on the *Mamluk* Military Institution in Islam', in V. J. Parry and M. E. Yapp, eds., *War, Technology and Society in the Middle East* (London).

Aylmer, G. E. (1969) *The King's Servants: the Civil Service of Charles I* (London).
Azanya, Victor and Chazan, Naomi (1987) 'Disengagement from the State in Africa: Reflections on the Experience of Ghana and Guinea', *Comparative Studies in Society and History* XXXIX.
Badian, E. (1968) *Roman Imperialism in the Late Republic*² (Oxford).
Baechler, Jean (1986) 'Aux origines de la modernité: castes et féodalités (Europe, Inde, Japon)', *Archives Européennes de Sociologie* XXVII.
Baily, Susan (1983) 'The History of Caste in South Asia', *Modern Asian Studies* XVII.
Baldwin, J. W. (1970) *Masters, Princes and Merchants* (2 vols., Princeton, N.J.).
Barber, Benjamin (1974) *The Death of Communal Liberty: a History of Freedom in a Swiss Mountain Canton* (Princeton, N.J.).
Barraclough, Geoffrey (1972) *The Origins of Modern Germany*² (Oxford).
Barton, Allen (1963) *Social Organisation under Stress: a Sociological Review of Disaster Studies* (Washington, D.C.).
Bar-Yosef, R. (1959) 'The Pattern of Early Socialization in the Collective Settlements in Israel', *Human Relations* XII.
Bauer, Arnold W. (1979) 'Rural Workers in Spanish America: Problems of Peonage and Oppression', *Hispanic American Historical Review* LXIII.
Bazant, Jan (1977) *A Concise History of Mexico from Hidalgo to Cardenas 1805–1940* (Cambridge).
Bede, *Ecclesiastical History*.
Behrens, C. B. A. (1963) 'Nobles, Privileges and Taxes in France at the End of the Ancien Régime', *Economic History Review* 2nd ser., XV.
(1985) *Society, Government and the Enlightenment: the Experiences of Eighteenth-century France and Prussia* (London).
Beik, William H. (1974) 'Magistrates and Popular Uprisings in France before the Fronde: the Case of Toulouse', *Journal of Modern History* XLVI.
Beldiceanu, Niccara (1980) 'Le timar dans l'Etat ottoman (XIVᵉ–XVᵉ siècles)', in Ecole Française de Rome, *Structures féodales et féodalisme dans l'occident méditerranéen (Xᵉ–XIIIᵉ siècles)* (Rome).
Beloff, Max (1967) 'Russia', in A. Goodwin, ed., *The European Nobility in the Eighteenth Century*² (London).
Bercé, Y.-M. (1974) *Histoire des Croquants: étude des soulèvements populaires au XVIIᵉ siècle dans le sud-ouest de la France* (2 vols. Geneva).
Bergier, J.-F. (1973) 'The Industrial Bourgeoisie and the Rise of the Working Class 1700–1914', in Carlo M. Cipolla, ed., *The Fontana Economic History of Europe* III: *The Industrial Revolution* (London).
Bernard, A. and Bruel, A., eds. (1880) *Receuil des chartes de l'abbaye de Cluny II* (Paris).
Beyerle, F. (1947) *Leges Langobardorum* (Witzenhausen).
Blake, Robert (1966) *Disraeli* (London).
(1977) *A History of Rhodesia* (London).
Blickle, Peter (1975) 'The Economic, Social and Political Background of the Twelve Articles', *Journal of Peasant Studies* III.
(1981) *Deutsche Untertanen. Ein Widerspruch* (Munich).
Bliss, C. J. and Stern, N. H. (1982) *Palanpur: the Economy of an Indian Village* (Oxford).
Bloch, Marc (1924) *Les rois thaumaturges* (Strasbourg).
(1931) *Les caractères originaux de l'histoire rurale française* (Oslo).

(1961) *Feudal Society* (Eng. trans., London).
(1966) *French Rural History: an Essay on its Basic Characteristics* (Eng. trans., London).
Bloch, Maurice (1977) 'The Disconnection between Power and Rank as a Process: an Outline of the Development of Kingdoms in Central Madagascar', *Archives Européennes de Sociologie* XVIII.
Blum, Jerome (1961) *Lord and Peasant in Russia from the Ninth to the Nineteenth Century* (Princeton, N.J.).
(1978) *The End of the Old Order in Rural Europe* (Princeton, N.J.).
Blumer, Herbert J. (1965) 'Industrialisation and Race Relations', in Guy Hunter, ed., *Industrialisation and Race Relations* (London).
Boardman, E. P. (1952) *Christian Influence upon the Ideology of the Taiping Rebellion, 1851–1864* (Madison, Wis.).
Boardman, John (1980) *The Greeks Overseas: their Early Colonies and Trade* (London).
Bogardus, Emory (1925) 'Measuring Social Distance', *Sociology and Social Research* IX.
Boissevain, Jeremy (1977) 'When the Saints Go Marching Out: Reflecting on the Decline of Patronage in Malta', in Ernest Gellner and John Waterbury, eds., *Patrons and Clients in Mediterranean Societies* (London).
Bonnassie, Pierre (1975–6) *La Catalogue du milieu du Xe à la fin du XIe siècle: croissance et mutations d'une société* (2 vols., Toulouse).
Bopegamage, A. and Kulahalli, R. N. (1971). '"Sanskritization" and Social Change', *Archives Européennes de Sociologie* XII.
Borétius, A., ed. (1883) *Monumenta Germaniae Historica. Legum Sectio II. Capitularia Regum Francorum* I (Hanover).
Bosher, J. F. (1970) *French Finances 1770–1795: from Business to Bureaucracy* (Cambridge).
Boswell, John (1977) *The Royal Treasure: Muslim Communities under the Crown of Aragon in the Fourteenth Century* (New Haven, Conn.).
Bottéro, J., ed. (1954) *Le problème des Hapiru* (Paris).
Bouchard, Constance B. (1981) 'The Origins of the French Nobility: a Reassessment', *American Historical Review* LXXXVI.
Boudon, Raymond (1973) *Education, Opportunity and Social Inequality: Changing Prospects in Western Society* (New York).
(1977) 'La logique de la frustration relative', *Archives Européennes de Sociologie* XVIII.
Boutruche, Robert (1959) *Seigneurie et féodalité* I (Paris).
Boxer, C. R. (1969) *The Portuguese Seaborne Empire 1415–1825* (London).
Boyd, R. and Richerson, P. J. (1982) 'Cultural Transmission and the Evolution of Cooperative Behaviour', *Human Ecology* X.
Bradbury, R. E. (1969) 'Patrimonialism and Gerontocracy in Benin Political Culture', in Mary Douglas and Phyllis M. Kaberry, eds., *Man in Africa* (London).
Brading, D. A. (1978) *Haciendas and Ranchos in the Mexican Bajio: Léon 1700–1860* (Cambridge).
(1983) *Classical Republicanism and Creole Patriotism: Simon Bolivar (1783–1820) and the Spanish Revolution* (Cambridge).
Braudel, Fernand (1966) *La Méditerranée et le monde méditerranéen à l'époque de Philippe II²* (2 vols., Paris).
(1973) *Capitalism and Material Life 1400–1800* (Eng. trans., London).

Brenner, Robert (1985) 'The Agrarian Roots of European Capitalism', in T. H. Aston and C. H. E. Philpin, eds., *The Brenner Debate: Agrarian Class Structure and Economic Development in Pre-industrial Europe* (Cambridge).

Bresc, Henri (1980) 'Féodalité coloniale en terre d'Islam. La Sicile (1070–1240)', in Ecole Française de Rome, *Structures féodales et féodalisme dans l'occident méditerranéen (Xᵉ–XIIIᵉ siècles)* (Rome).

Brewer, John (1982) 'Commercialization and Politics', in Neil McKendrick *et al.*, *The Birth of a Consumer Society. The Commercialization of Eighteenth-century England* (London).

Brogan, D. W. (1961) *The French Nation: from Napoléon to Pétain 1814–1940* (London).

Brown, Peter (1971*a*) *The World of Late Antiquity* (London).

(1971*b*) *Relics and Social Status in the Age of Gregory of Tours* (Reading).

Brumfiel, Elizabeth M. (1983) 'Aztec State Making: Ecology, Structure and the Origins of the State', *American Anthropologist* LXXXV.

Brunt, P. A. (1962) 'The Army and the Land in the Roman Revolution', *Journal of Roman Studies* LII.

(1968) Review of Meier, *Res Publica Amissa*, *Journal of Roman Studies* LVIII.

(1971*a*) *Social Conflicts in the Roman Republic* (London).

(1971*b*) *Italian Manpower 225 B.C.–A.D. 14* (Oxford).

(1982) '*Nobilitas* and *Novitas*', *Journal of Roman Studies* LXXII.

Bryce, Lord (1910) *The American Commonwealth*² (2 vols., London).

Bullogh, D. A. (1970) '*Europae Pater*. Charlemagne and his Achievement in the Light of Recent Scholarship', *English Historical Review* LXXXV.

Burke, Peter (1974) *Venice and Amsterdam: a Study of Seventeenth-century Elites* (London).

Burleigh, Michael (1984) *Prussian Society and the German Order: an Aristocratic Corporation in Crisis* c. *1410–1466* (Cambridge).

Butterfield, Fox (1981) *Alive in the Bitter Sea* (New York).

Buve, Raymond (1980) 'State Governors and Peasant Mobilization in Tlaxcala', in D. A. Brading, ed. *Caudillo and Peasant in the Mexican Revolution* (Cambridge).

Buxton, Jean (1958) 'The Mandari of the Southern Sudan', in John Middleton and David Tait, eds., *Tribes Without Rulers: Studies in African Segmentary Systems* (London).

Cahen, Claude (1963) 'Points de vue sur la "Révolution" abbâside', *Revue Historique* CCXXIX.

Cameron, Alan (1976) *Circus Factions: Blues and Greens at Rome and Byzantium* (Oxford).

Cammack, Paul (1982) 'Bureaucratic Authoritarianism and Brazil: a Dissenting Note', *Politics* II.

Campbell, Mildred (1942) *The English Yeoman under Elizabeth and the Early Stuarts* (New Haven, Conn.).

Canetti, Elias (1962) *Crowds and Power* (Eng. trans., London).

Carr, Barry (1972–3) 'Las peculiaridades del Norte Mexicano, 1880–1927: ensayo de interpretación', *Historia Mexicana* XXII.

Carr, E. H. (1971) *Foundations of a Planned Economy 1926–1929* II (London).

Carr, Raymond (1982) *Spain 1808–1975*² (Oxford).

and Fusi, Juan Pablo (1979) *Spain: Dictatorship to Democracy* (London).

Carrasco, Pedro (1959) *Land and Policy in Tibet* (Seattle, Wash.).
Carré, H. (1920) *La noblesse de France et l'opinion publique au XVIIIe siècle* (Paris).
Carr-Saunders, A. M. (1922) *The Population Problem: a Study in Human Evolution* (Oxford).
Carsten, F. L. (1953) *The Origins of Prussia* (Oxford).
Cartledge, Paul (1977) 'Hoplites and Heroes: Sparta's Contribution to the Technique of Ancient Warfare', *Journal of Hellenic Studies* XCVII.
(1979) *Sparta and Lakonia: a Regional History 1300–362 B.C.* (London).
Casanova, Pablo Gonzalez (1970) *Democracy in Mexico* (Eng. trans., New York).
Cash, W. J. (1960) *The Mind of the South*[2] (New York).
Cavanaugh, G. J. (1974) 'Nobles, Privileges and Taxes in France. A Revision Reviewed', *French Historical Studies* VIII.
Chagnon, N. A. (1968) *Yanomamo: the Fierce People* (New York).
Chambers, J. D. (1952–3) 'Enclosure and Labour Supply in the Industrial Revolution', *Economic History Review* 2nd ser., V.
Chandavarkar, Rajnarayan (1981) 'Workers' Politics and the Mill Districts in Bombay between the Wars', *Modern Asian Studies* XV.
Chaunu, Pierre (1966) *La civilisation de l'Europe classique* (Paris).
Chaussinand-Nogaret, Guy (1976) *La noblesse au XVIIIe siècle: de la féodalité aux lumières* (Paris).
Chevalier, Bernard (1983) *Les bonnes villes de France du XIVe au XVIe siècle* (Paris).
Chevalier, François (1963) *Land and Society in Colonial Mexico: the Great Hacienda* (Eng. trans., Berkeley, Calif.).
(1966) '"Ejido" et stabilité au Mexique', *Revue Française de Science Politique* XVI.
(1967) 'The *Ejido* and Political Stability in Mexico', in Claudio Veliz, ed., *The Politics of Conformity in Latin America* (London).
Chitty, Derwas J. (1966) *The Desert a City* (Oxford).
Chowning, Ann (1979) 'Leadership in Melanesia', *Journal of Pacific History* XIV.
and Goodenough, Ward H. (1971) 'Lakalai Political Organization', in R. M. Berndt and Peter Lawrence, eds., *Politics in New Guinea* (Nedlands).
Christiansen, Eric (1980) *The Northern Crusades. The Baltic and the Catholic Frontier 1100–1525* (London).
Christie, Ian R. (1985) *Stress and Stability in Late Eighteenth-century Britain: Reflections on the British Avoidance of Revolution* (Oxford).
Christien, Jacqueline (1974) 'La Loi d'Epitadéus: un aspect de l'histoire économique et social à Sparte', *Revue Historique de Droit Français et Étranger* 4e série, LII.
Cicero, *Letters to Atticus.*
Pro Flacco.
Pro Murena.
Cipolla, Carlo M. (1965) *Guns and Sails in the Early Phase of European Expansion, 1400–1700* (London).
Ciria, Alberto (1974) *Politics and Power in Modern Argentina (1930–1946)* (Eng. trans., Albany, N.Y.).
Clarke, David L. (1978) *Analytical Archaeology*[2] (London).
Clastres, Pierre (1977) *Society against the State* (Eng. trans., Oxford).
Clay, C. G. A. (1984) *Economic Expansion and Social Change: England 1500–1700* II*: Industry, Trade and Government* (Cambridge).

Coats, A. W. (1976) 'The Relief of Poverty, Attitudes to Labour and Economic Change in England, 1660–1782', *International Review of Social History* XXI.

Cobban, Alfred (1964) *The Social Interpretation of the French Revolution* (Cambridge).

Cockcroft, James D. (1968) *Intellectual Precursors of the Mexican Revolution 1900–1913* (Austin, Texas).

Codere, Helen (1962) 'Power in Ruanda', *Anthropologica* IV.

Cohen, Ronald (1970) 'Social Stratification in Bornu', in Arthur Tuden and Leonard Plotnicov, eds., *Social Stratification in Africa* (New York).

(1978) 'State Origins: a Reappraisal' in Henri J. M. Claessen and Peter Skalnik, eds., *The Early State* (The Hague).

Coldstream, J. N. (1977) *Geometric Greece* (London).

Cole, Robert E. (1979) *Work, Mobility and Participation: a Comparative Study of American and Japanese Industry* (Berkeley, Calif.).

Coleman, D. C. (1977) *The Economy of England 1450–1750* (Oxford).

Coleman, James S. (1960) 'The Mathematical Study of Small Groups', in Herbert Solomon, ed., *Mathematical Thinking in the Measurement of Behavior* (Glencoe, Ill.).

Collins, Roger (1980) 'Mérida and Toledo: 550–585', in Edward James, ed., *Visigothic Spain: New Approaches* (Oxford).

Connor, Walter D. (1972) *Deviance in Soviet Society: Crime, Delinquency and Alcoholism* (New York).

Contamine, Philippe (1984) *War in the Middle Ages* (Eng. trans., Oxford).

Cooper, Frederick (1981) 'Islam and Cultural Hegemony: the Ideology of Slaveowners on the East African Coast', in Paul E. Lovejoy, ed., *The Ideology of Slavery in Africa* (Beverly Hills, Calif.).

Córdova, Arnaldo (1977) *La Formación del Poder Político en México*[5] (Mexico City).

Cornblit, Oscar (1967) 'European Immigrants in Argentine Industry and Politics', in Claudio Veliz, ed., *The Politics of Conformity in Latin America* (London).

Craig, Albert M. (1961) *Chōshū in the Meiji Restoration* (Cambridge, Mass.).

Crawcour, Sydney (1961) 'The Development of a Credit System in Seventeenth-century Japan', *Journal of Economic History* XXI.

(1974) 'The Tokugawa Period and Japan's Preparation for Modern Economic Growth', *Journal of Japanese Studies* I.

Crawford, Michael (1978) *The Roman Republic* (London).

Crone, Patricia (1980) *Slaves on Horseback: the Evolution of the Islamic Polity* (Cambridge).

Crook, John (1967) *Law and Life of Rome* (Ithaca, N.Y.).

Crossick, Geoffrey (1977) 'The Emergence of the Lower Middle Class in Britain: a Discussion', in Geoffrey Crossick, ed., *The Lower Middle Class in Britain 1870–1924* (London).

Dahl, Gudrun (1979) 'Ecology and Equality: the Boran Case', in L'Equipe écologie et anthropologie des sociétés pastorales, ed., *Pastoral Production and Society* (Paris).

Dahrendorf, Ralf (1959) *Class and Class Conflict in Industrial Society* (Stanford, Calif.).

Darwin, Charles (1866) *On the Origin of Species by Means of Natural Selection*[4] (London).

Das, G. K. (1977) *E. M. Forster's India* (London).

Davies, J. K. (1978) *Democracy and Classical Greece* (Brighton).

Davies, K. G. (1952) 'The Origins of the Commission System in the West India Trade', *Transactions of the Royal Historical Society* 5th ser., II.

Davies, Norman (1981) *God's Playground. A History of Poland* (2 vols., Oxford).

Davis, James C. (1962) *The Decline of the Venetian Nobility as a Ruling Class* (Baltimore, Md.).

Davis, Robert L. (1954) 'Structures of Dominance Relations', *Bulletin of Mathematical Biophysics* XVI.

Dawkins, Richard (1976) *The Selfish Gene* (Oxford).

Dawson, Raymond (1972) *Imperial China* (London).

Deane, Phyllis (1979) *The First Industrial Revolution*[2] (Cambridge).

Dekmejian, Richard H. and Wirszomski, Margaret J. (1972) 'Charismatic Leadership in Islam: the Madhi of the Sudan', *Comparative Studies in Society and History* XIV.

de Madariaga, Isabel (1981) *Russia in the Age of Catherine the Great* (London).

Demos, John (1970) *A Little Commonwealth: Family Life in Plymouth Colony* (New York).

Dessert, David and Journet, Jean-Louis (1975) 'Le lobby Colbert: un royaume ou une affaire de famille?', *Annales* XXX.

de Ste Croix, G. E. M. (1981) *The Class Struggle in the Ancient Greek World* (London).

Deutscher, Isaac (1967) *The Unfinished Revolution: Russia 1917–1967* (London).

de Zeeuw, J. W. (1978) 'Peat and the Dutch Golden Age. The Historical Meaning of Energy-attainability', *A.A.G. Bijdragen* XXI.

Diakonoff, I. M. (1982) 'The Structure of Near-Eastern Society before the Middle of the 2nd Millennium B.C.', *Oikumene* III.

Dickson, P. G. M. (1967) *The Financial Revolution in England* (London).

Dio Cassius, *Roman History*.

Dionysius of Halicarnassus, *Roman Antiquities*.

Diodorus Siculus, *History*.

Divale, William T. (1972–3) 'Systemic Population Control in the Middle and Upper Palaeolithic: Inferences Based on Contemporary Hunter-gatherers', *World Archaeology* VI.

Dollinger, Phillippe (1970) *The German Hansa* (Eng. trans., London).

Donner, Fred M. (1981) *The Early Islamic Conquests* (Princeton, N.J.).

Dore, R. P. (1958) *City Life in Japan: a Study of a Tokyo Ward* (London).

(1962) 'Talent and the Social Order in Tokugawa Japan', *Past & Present* XXI.

(1974) *British Factory – Japanese Factory: the Origins of National Diversity in Industrial Relations* (London).

(1984) *Land Reform in Japan*[2] (London).

Douglas, D. C. (1967) 'Les réussites Normandes, 1050–1100', *Revue Historique* CCXXXVII.

Douglas, Mary (1974) 'Matriliny and Pawnship in Central Africa', *Africa* XXXIV.

Doyle, William (1980) *Origins of the French Revolution* (Oxford).

Drew, Katherine F. (1962) 'The Immunity in Carolingian Italy', *Speculum* XXXVII.

Driver, G. R. and Miles, John C. (1952) *The Babylonian Laws* I (London).

Duby, Georges (1973) *Guerriers et paysans VII-XIIe siècle. Premier essor de l'économie européenne* (Paris).

(1984) *Hommes et structures du moyen âge*[2] (Paris).

Ducat, J. (1971) 'Le mépris des Hilotes', *Annales* XXIX.

Dukes, Paul (1967) *Catherine the Great and the Russian Nobility* (Cambridge).

Dumont, Louis (1970) *Homo Hierarchicus: the Caste System and its Implications* (Eng. trans., London).

Duncan, O. D. (1966) 'Methodological Issues in the Analysis of Social Mobility', in N. J. Smelser and S. M. Lipset, eds., *Social Structure and Mobility in Economic Development* (London).

Dunning, E. (1971–2) 'Dynamics of Racial Stratification: some Preliminary Hypotheses', *Race* XIII.

Dunstheimer, Guillaume (1972) 'Some Religious Aspects of Secret Societies', in Jean Chesneaux, ed., *Popular Movements and Secret Societies in China 1840–1950* (Stanford, Calif.).

Duus, Peter (1969) *Feudalism in Japan* (New York).

Dworzaczek, Wlodzimierz (1977) 'La mobilité sociale de la noblesse polonaise aux XVIe et XVIIe siècles', *Acta Poloniae Historica* XXXVI.

Dyer, Christopher (1968) 'A Redistribution of Incomes in Fifteenth-Century England?', *Past & Present* XXXIX.

Dyson-Hudson, N. (1966) *Karimojong Politics* (Oxford).

Earle, Timothy K. (1978) *Economic and Social Organization of a Complex Chiefdom: the Halelea District, Kaua'i, Hawaii* (Ann Arbor, Mich.).

Eberhard, Wolfram (1957) 'Wang Ko: an Early Industrialist', *Oriens* X.

Edeen, Alf (1960) 'The Civil Service: its Composition and Status', in Cyril E. Black, ed., *The Transformation of Russian Society* (Cambridge, Mass.).

Eggan, Fred (1966) *The American Indian: Perspectives for the Study of Social Change* (Chicago, Ill.).

Ehrenberg, Victor (1943) *The People of Aristophanes: a Sociology of Old Attic Comedy* (Oxford).

Eisenstadt, S. N. (1969) *The Political Systems of Empires: the Rise and Fall of the Historical Bureaucratic Societies* (New York).

(1981) 'Cultural Traditions and Political Dynamics', *British Journal of Sociology* XXXII.

and Roniger, Louis (1980) 'Patron–Client Relations as a Model of Structuring Social Exchange', *Comparative Studies in Society and History* XXII.

Eliade, Mircea (1970) *Shamanism: Archaic Techniques of Ecstasy*[2] (Eng. trans., Princeton, N.J.).

Elliott, J. H. (1961) 'The Decline of Spain', *Past & Present* XX.

(1969) *Europe Divided 1559–1598* (London).

Elvin, Mark (1973) *The Pattern of the Chinese Past* (London).

Epstein, S. T. (1967) 'Productive Efficiency and Customary Systems of Reward in Rural South India', in R. Firth, ed., *Themes in Economic Anthropology* (London).

Erikson, Robert *et al.* (1979) 'Intergenerational Class Mobility in Three Western European Societies', *British Journal of Sociology* XXX.

(1982) 'Social Fluidity in Industrial Nations: England, France and Sweden', *ibid.* XXXIII.

(1983) 'Intergenerational Class Mobility and the Convergence Thesis', *ibid.* XXXIV.

Esper, Thomas (1981) 'The Incomes of Russian Serf Ironworkers in the Nineteenth Century', *Past & Present* XCIII.

Evans-Pritchard, E. E. (1962) 'The Divine Kingship of the Shilluk of the Nilotic Sudan', in his *Essays in Social Anthropology* (London).

Everitt, Alan (1966) 'Social Mobility in Early Modern England', *Past & Present* XXXIII.

Fainsod, Merle (1963) *How Russia is Ruled*[2] (Cambridge, Mass.).

Fallers, Lloyd A. (1965) *Bantu Bureaucracy*[2] (Chicago, Ill.).

Farbman, Michael S. (1924) *After Lenin: the New Phase in Russia* (London).

Farriss, Nancy M. (1984) *Maya Society under Colonial Rule: the Collective Enterprise of Survival* (Princeton, N.J.).

Fehér, Ferenc, *et al.* (1983) *Dictatorship over Needs* (Oxford).

Ferenczy, Endre (1976) *From the Patrician State to the Patricio-Plebeian State* (Eng. trans., Amsterdam).

Finberg, H. P. R. (1974) *The Formation of England* (London).

Finley, M. I. (1956) *The World of Odysseus* (London).

(1968) *Ancient Sicily* (London).

(1973) *The Ancient Economy* (London).

(1975) 'Sparta', in his *The Use and Abuse of History* (London).

(1983) *Politics in the Ancient World* (Cambridge).

Florescano, Enrique (1971) *Estructuras y Problemas Agrarias de Mexico, 1500–1621* (Mexico City).

Foote, P. G. and Wilson, D. M. (1970) *The Viking Achievement* (London).

Fox, Alan (1985) *History and Heritage* (Oxford).

Fragner, Bert (1986) 'Social and Internal Economic Affairs', in Peter Jackson, ed., *The Cambridge History of Iran* VI (Cambridge).

Frank, André Gunder (1978) *World Accumulation, 1492–1789* (London).

Franklin, John Hope (1967) *From Slavery to Freedom: a History of the Negro Americans*[3] (New York).

Frazer, J. G. (1914) *The Scapegoat* (London).

Freyre, Gilberto (1963) *The Masters and the Slaves: a Study in the Development of Brazilian Civilization*[2] (Eng. trans., New York).

Fried, Morton H. (1967) *The Evolution of Political Society: an Essay in Political Anthropology* (New York).

Friedman, Jonathan (1975) 'Tribes, States and Transformations', in Maurice Bloch, ed., *Marxist Analyses and Social Anthropology* (London).

Friedrich, Paul (1965) 'A Mexican Cacicazgo', *Ethnology* IV.

Friedrichs, Christopher R. (1978) 'Capitalism, Mobility and Class Formation in the Early Modern German City', in Philip Abrams and E. A. Wrigley, eds., *Towns in Societies* (Cambridge).

Fuks, Alexander (1974) 'Patterns and Types of Social-economic Revolution in Greece from the Fourth to the Second Century B.C.', *Ancient Society* V.

Fürer-Haimendorf, Christoph von (1967) *Morals and Merit. A Study of Values and Social Controls in South Asian Societies* (London).

Furet, François and Richet, Denis (1965) *La Révolution française* (2 vols., Paris).

Galenson, Walter and Odaka, Konosuke (1976) 'The Japanese Labor Market', in H. Patrick and H. Rosovsky, eds., *Asia's New Giant* (Washington, D.C.).

Gallagher, John (1982) 'The Decline, Revival and Fall of the British Empire', in his *The Decline, Revival and Fall of the British Empire: The Ford Lectures and Other Essays*, ed. A. Seal (Cambridge).

and Robinson, Ronald (1982) 'The Imperialism of Free Trade', *ibid.*
Gallie, Duncan (1978) *In Search of the New Working Class* (Cambridge).
(1983) *Social Inequality and Class Radicalism in France and Britain* (Cambridge).
Ganshof, F. L. (1952) *Feudalism*[3] (Eng. trans., London).
Garnsey, Peter (1970) *Social Status and Legal Privilege in the Roman Empire* (Oxford).
Gelb, I. J. (1972) 'The Arua Institution', *Revue d'Assyriologie et d'Archéologie Orientale* LXVI.
Georgelin, Jean (1978) *Venise au siècle des lumières* (The Hague).
Germani, Gino (1971) 'Stratificazione sociale e sua evoluzione storica in Argentina', *Sociologica* V.
(1978) *Authoritarianism, Fascism and National Populism* (New Brunswick, N.J.).
Gernet, Jacques (1982) *A History of Chinese Civilization* (Eng. trans., Cambridge).
Gernet, Louis (1968) *Anthropologie de la Grèce antique* (Paris).
Geuss, Raymond (1981) *The Idea of a Critical Theory: Habermas and the Frankfurt School* (Cambridge).
Geyl, Pieter (1964) *History of the Low Countries: Episodes and Problems* (London).
Gibb, H. A. R. and Bowen, Harold (1957) *Islamic Society and the West. A Study of the Impact of Western Civilization on Moslem Culture in the Near East* (London).
Gibson, Charles (1966) *Spain in America* (New York).
Gill, Colin (1983–4) 'Swedish Wage-earner Funds: the Road to Economoic Democracy', *Journal of General Management* IX.
Gilmore, David (1977) 'Patronage and Class Conflict in Southern Spain', *Man* n.s. XII.
Glasse, Robert and Lindenbaum, Shirley (1971) 'South Fore Politics', in Ronald M. Berndt and Peter Lawrence, eds., *Politics in New Guinea* (Nedlands).
Gluckman, Max (1960) 'The Rise of a Zulu Empire', *Scientific American* CCII.
(1963) *Order and Rebellion in Tribal Africa* (London).
(1965) *Politics, Law and Ritual in Tribal Society* (Oxford).
Godechot, J. (1965) *La prise de la Bastille, 14 juillet 1789* (Paris).
Godinho, Vitorino Magalhès (1969) *L'économie de l'empire portugais au XVe et XVIe siècles* (Paris).
Goffart, W. (1982) 'Old and New in Merovingian Taxation', *Past & Present* XCVI.
Goffman, Erving (1961) *Asylums: Essays on the Social Situation of Mental Patients and other Inmates* (Chicago, Ill.).
Golas, Peter J. (1980) 'Rural China in the Song', *Journal of Asian Studies* XXXIX.
Goldwert, M. (1972) *Democracy, Militarism and Nationalism in Argentina 1930–1966: an Interpretation* (Austin, Texas).
Goodwin, A. (1967) 'Prussia', in A. Goodwin, ed., *The European Nobility in the Eighteenth Century*[2] (London).
Goody, Jack (1962) *Death, Property and the Ancestors* (Stanford, Calif.).
(1971) *Technology, Tradition and the State in Africa* (London).
(1976) *Production and Reproduction: a Comparative Study of the Domestic Domain* (Cambridge).
Graham, Robert (1978) *Iran: the Illusion of Power* (London).
Grassby, R. B. (1960–1) 'Social Status and Commercial Enterprise under Louis XIV', *Economic History Review* XIII.
Gregory of Tours, *History of the Franks.*

Greishaber, Erwin P. (1980) 'Survival of Indian Communities in Nineteenth-Century Bolivia: a Regional Comparison', *Journal of Latin American Studies* XII.

Gschnitzer, Fritz (1955) 'Stammes und Ortsnamen im Alten Griechenland', *Wiener Studien* LXVIII.

Gulliver, P. H. (1953) 'The Age-set Organization of the Jie Tribe', *Journal of the Royal Anthropological Institute* LXXXIII.

Habicht, Chr. (1958) 'Die Herrschende Gesellschaft in den Hellenistischen Monarchien', *Vierteljahrschrift für Soziologie und Wirtschaftsgeschichte* XLV.

Hall, John A. (1985) *Powers and Liberties. The Causes and Consequences of the Rise of the West* (Oxford).

Hall, John W. (1962) 'Feudalism in Japan – A Reassessment', *Comparative Studies in Society and History* V.

(1970) *Japan from Prehistory to Modern Times* (London).

(1974) 'Rule by Status in Tokugawa Japan', *Journal of Japaneses Studies* I.

Halperin-Donghi, Julio (1975) *Politics, Economics and Society in Argentina in the Revolutionary Period* (Eng. trans., Cambridge).

Hamblin, Robert L. and Pitcher, Brian L. (1980) 'The Classic Maya Collapse: Testing Class Conflict Hypotheses', *American Antiquity* XLV.

Hane, Mikiso (1982) *Peasants, Rebels and Outcastes: the Underside of Modern Japan* (New York).

Harris, Marvin (1971) *Culture, Man and Nature: Introduction to General Anthropology* (New York).

(1979) *Cultural Materialism. The Struggle for a Science of Culture* (New York).

Harris, R. (1963) 'The Organization and Administration of the Cloister in Ancient Babylonia', *Journal of the Economic and Social History of the Orient* VI.

Harris, William V. (1979) *War and Imperialism in Republican Rome 327–70 B.C.* (Oxford).

Harrison, Royden and Zeitlin, Jonathan, eds. (1985) *Divisions of Labour: Skilled Workers and Technological Change in Nineteenth Century Britain* (Brighton).

Harvey, Sally P. J. (1983) 'The Extent and Profitability of Demesne Agriculture in England in the Later Eleventh Century', in T. H. Aston *et al.*, eds., *Social Relations and Ideas: Essays in Honour of R. H. Hilton* (Cambridge).

Hassell, James (1970) 'The Implementation of the Russian Table of Ranks during the Eighteenth Century', *Slavic Review* XXIX.

Hatcher, John (1981) 'English Serfdom and Villeinage: Towards a Reassessment', *Past & Present* XC.

Healey, Christopher J. (1978) 'The Adaptive Significance of Systems of Ceremonial Exchange and Trade in the New Guinea Highlands', *Mankind* XI.

Heath, Dwight B. (1973) 'New Patrons for Old: Changing Patron–Client Relationships in the Bolivian Yungas', *Ethnology* XII.

Hellie, R. H. (1971) *Enserfment and Military Change in Muscovy* (Chicago, Ill.).

(1982) *Slavery in Russia* (Chicago, Ill.).

Henderson, Gregory (1968) *Korea: the Politics of the Vortex* (Cambridge, Mass.).

Herlihy, D. (1972–3) 'Three Patterns of Social Mobility in Medieval History', *Journal of Interdisciplinary History* III.

Herodotus, *History*.

Herrin, Judith (1975) 'Realities of Byzantine Provincial Government: Hellas and Peloponnesos, 1180–1205', *Dumbarton Oaks Papers* XXIX.

Herskovits, M. (1938) *Dahomey: an Ancient West African Kingdom* (Locust Valley, N.Y.).

Hesiod, *Works and Days*.

Heyduk, Daniel (1974) 'The Hacienda System and Agrarian Reform in Highland Bolivia: a Re-evaluation', *Ethnology* XIII.

Hignett, C. (1952) *History of the Athenian Constitution* (Oxford).

Higonnet, Patrice (1981) *Ideology and the Rights of Nobles in the French Revolution* (Oxford).

Hill, Polly (1976) 'From Slavery to Freedom: the Case of Farm-slavery in Nigerian Hausaland', *Comparative Studies in Society and History* XVIII.

Hilton, R. H. (1975) 'Social Structure of Warwickshire in the Middle Ages', in his *The English Peasantry in the Later Middle Ages* (Oxford).

Himmelstrand, Ulf *et al.* (1982) *Beyond Welfare Capitalism* (London).

Hoben, A. (1973) *Land Tenure among the Amhara of Ethiopia* (Chicago, Ill.).

Hobsbawm, E. J. (1968) *Industry and Empire: an Economic History of Britain since 1750* (London).

Hodgson, Marshall G. S. (1974) *The Venture of Islam* (3 vols., Chicago, Ill.).

Hofstadter, Richard (1948) *The American Political Tradition* (New York).

Holderness, B. A. (1975–6) 'Credit in English Rural Society before the Nineteenth Century, with Special Reference to the Period 1650–1720', *Agricultural History Review* XXIV.

(1976) *Pre-industrial England: Economy and Society 1500–1750* (London).

Hollister, C. Warren (1986) *Monarchy, Magnates and Institutions in the Anglo-Norman World* (London).

Holmes, Geoffrey (1982) *Augustan England: Professions, State and Society 1680–1730* (London).

Homer, *Iliad*.

Odyssey.

Hooker, J. T. (1977) *Mycenaean Greece* (London).

(1980) *The Ancient Spartans* (London).

Hopkins, Keith (1978) *Conquerors and Slaves: Sociological Studies in Roman History* I (Cambridge).

(1983) *Death and Renewal: Sociological Studies in Roman History* II (Cambridge).

Howell, P. P. (1952) 'Observations on the Shilluk of the Upper Nile. The Laws of Homicide and the Legal Functions of the Reth', *Africa* XXII.

Huizer, Gerritt and Stavenhagen, Rodolfo (1974) 'Peasant Unrest: Themes and Variations', in H. A. Landsberger, ed., *Rural Protest: Peasant Movements and Social Change* (London).

Humphreys, S. C. (1978) *Anthropology and the Greeks* (London).

Hunt, A. S. and Edgar, C. C. (1934) *Select Papyri* II: *Official Documents* (London).

Hutt, M. G. (1957) 'The Curés and the Third Estate: the Ideas of Reform in the Pamphlets of the French Lower Clergy in the Period 1787–1789', *Journal of Ecclesiastical History* VIII.

Hyams, Paul R. (1970) 'The Origins of a Peasant Land Market in England', *Economic History Review* 2nd ser., XXIII.

Hyde, J. K. (1973) *Society and Politics in Medieval Italy: the Evolution of the Civil Life, 1000–1350* (London).

Iliffe, John (1983) *The Emergence of African Capitalism* (London).

Inalcik, Halil (1954) 'Ottoman Methods of Conquest', *Studia Islamica* II.

(1964) 'The Nature of Traditional Society: Turkey', in Robert E. Ward and Dankwart A. Rostow, eds., *Political Modernization in Japan and Turkey* (Princeton, N.J.).

(1972) 'The Ottoman Decline and its Effects upon the *Reaya*', in H. Birnbaum and S. Vryonis Jr., eds., *Aspects of the Balkans: Continuity and Change* (The Hague).

(1973) *The Ottoman Empire* (London).

(1975) 'The Socio-Political Effects of the Diffusion of Firearms in the Middle East', in V. J. Parry and M. E. Yapp, eds., *War, Technology and Society in the Middle East* (London).

Ingham, Geoffrey K. (1974) *Strikes and Industrial Conflict: Britain and Scandinavia* (London).

Irwin, Robert (1986) *The Middle East in the Middle Ages: the Early Mamluk Sultanate 1250–1382* (London).

Ishino, Iwao (1953) 'The *Oyabun-Koyabun*: a Japanese Ritual Kinship Institution', *American Anthropologist* LV.

Jackson, Michael (1977) 'Sacrifice and Social Structure among the Kuranko: Parts I and II', *Africa* XLVII.

Jackson, Peter and Sisson, Keith (1976) 'Employer's Confederations in Sweden and the U.K. and the Significance of Industrial Infrastructure', *British Journal of Industrial Relations* XIV.

Jacobsen, Th. (1957) 'Early Political Development in Mesopotamia', *Zeitschrift für Assyriologie* n.f., LII.

Jacoby, F. (1949) *Atthis* (Oxford).

James, Edward (1982) *The Origins of France. From Clovis to the Capetians 500–1000* (London).

Jeffrey, L. H. (1973–4) 'Demiourgoi in the Archaic Period', *Archaeologica Classica* XXV–XXVI.

John, E. (1982) 'The Age of Edgar', in J. Campbell *et al.*, eds., *The Anglo-Saxons* (Oxford).

Johnson, Dale L. (1982) 'The Social Unity and Fractionalization of the Middle Class', in Dale L. Johnson, ed., *Class and Social Development: a New Theory of the Middle Class* (Beverly Hills, Calif.).

Johnson, John J. (1964) *The Military and Society in Latin America* (Stanford, Calif.).

Johnson, Michael (1977) 'Political Bosses and their Gangs: *zu'ama* and *qabadayat* in the Sunni Muslim Quarters of Beirut', in Ernest Gellner and John Waterbury, eds., *Patrons and Clients in Mediterranean Societies* (London).

Jones, A. H. M. (1964) *The Later Roman Empire 284–602* (3 vols., Oxford).

Jones, P. J. (1965) 'Communes and Despots: the City State in Late-Medieval Italy', *Transactions of the Royal Historical Society* 5th ser., XV.

Josephus, *Jewish Antiquities*.

Joüon des Longrais, F. (1958) *L'est et l'ouest: Institutions du Japan et de l'Orient comparées* (Paris).

Kakar, Hasan Kawun (1979) *Government and Society in Afghanistan: the Reign of Amir 'Abd al-Rahman Khan* (Austin, Texas).

Kamen, Henry (1978) 'The Decline of Spain: a Historical Myth?' *Past & Present* LXXXI.

(1984) *European Society 1500–1700* (London).

Kaplan, S. L. (1976) *Bread, Politics and Political Economy in the Reign of Louis XV* (2 vols., The Hague).

Katz, Friedrich (1974) 'Labor Conditions on Haciendas in Porfirian Mexico: some Trends and Tendencies', *Hispanic American Historical Review* LIV.

(1980) 'Pancho Villa, Peasant Movements and Agrarian Reform in Northern Mexico', in D. A. Brading, ed., *Caudillo and Peasant in the Mexican Revolution* (Cambridge).

Kawai, Masao (1965) 'On the System of Social Ranks of a Troop of Japanese Monkeys: (1) Basic Rank and Dependent Rank', in Stuart A. Altmann, ed., *Japanese Monkeys* (Edmonton).

Kea, R. A. (1971) 'Firearms and Warfare on the Gold and Slave Coasts from the Sixteenth to the Nineteenth Centuries', *Journal of African History* XII.

Keir, D. L. (1953) *The Constitutional History of Modern Britain, 1485–1951*[5] (London).

Kelly, J. M. (1966) *Roman Litigation* (Oxford).

Kemp, Barry J. (1983) 'Old Kingdom, Middle Kingdom and Second Intermediate Period *c.* 2686–1552 BC', in B. G. Trigger *et al.*, *Ancient Egypt: a Social History* (Cambridge).

Kennedy, Hugh (1986) *The Prophet and the Age of the Caliphates: the Islamic Near East from the Sixth to the Eleventh Century* (London).

Kent, Joan R. (1985) *The English Village Constable 1580–1642: a Social and Administrative Study* (Oxford).

Khazanov, A. M. (1984) *Nomads and the Outside World* (Eng. trans., Cambridge).

Kirby, D. P. (1967) *The Making of Early England* (London).

Kitahara, Taisaku (1974) *Senmin no Koei* [A Descendant of the Pariahs] (Tokyo).

Kitcher, Philip (1982) 'Genes', *British Journal for the Philosophy of Science* XXXIII.

Kitching, Gavin (1980) *Class and Economic Change in Kenya: the Making of an African Petite Bourgeoisie 1905–1970* (New Haven, Conn.).

Kitson Clark, G. S. R. (1977) ed. G. M. Young, *Victorian England* (Cambridge).

Klein, Herbert S. (1982) *Bolivia: the Evolution of a Multi-ethnic Society* (Oxford).

Klein, Martin A. (1978) Review Article, 'The Study of Slavery in Africa', *Journal of African History* XIX.

Klengel, Horst (1973) 'Die Geschäfte des Babyloniers Balmunamche', *Das Altertum* XIX.

Knight, Alan (1980) 'Peasant and Caudillo in Revolutionary Mexico 1910–17', in D. A. Brading, ed., *Caudillo and Peasant in the Mexican Revolution* (Cambridge).

(1984) 'The Working Class and the Mexican Revolution, c. 1900–1920', *Journal of Latin American Studies* XVI.

Kolosi, Tamás and Wnuk-Lipínski, Edmund, eds. (1983) *Equality and Inequality under Socialism: Poland and Hungary Compared* (Beverly Hills, Calif.).

Korpi, Walter (1983) *The Democratic Class Struggle* (London).

Kosminsky, E. A. (1956) *Studies in the Agrarian History of England in the Thirteenth Century* (Oxford).

Kracke, Edward A. Jr (1953) *Civil Service in Early Sung China, 960–1067* (Cambridge, Mass.).

Krader, Lawrence (1978) 'The Origin of the State among the Nomads of Asia', in Henri J. M. Claessen and Peter Skalnik, eds., *The Early State* (The Hague).

Kramers, J. H. and Wiet, G., eds. (1964) Ibn Hauqal, *Configuration de la Terre* (2 vols., Paris).

Kula, Witold (1976) *An Economic Theory of the Feudal System: Towards a Model of the Polish Economy 1500–1800* (Eng. trans., London).

Kumar, Krishan (1983) 'Class and Political Action in Nineteenth-century England', *Archives Européennes de Sociologie* XXIV.

Lacarra, J. M. (1963) 'Les villes-frontières dans l'Espagne des XIe et XIIe siècles', *Le Moyen Age* XVI.

Lancaster, Lorraine (1958) 'Kinship in Anglo-Saxon Society', *British Journal of Sociology* IX.

Landes, David S. (1969) *The Unbound Prometheus: Technological Change and Industrial Development in Western Europe from 1750 to the Present* (Cambridge).

Landsberger, Benno (1955) 'Remarks on the Archive of the Soldier Ubarrum', *Journal of Cuneiform Studies* IX.

Landtman, Gunnar (1938) *The Origin of the Inequality of the Social Classes* (London).

Lane, Christel (1981) *The Rites of Rulers: Ritual in Industrial Society – the Soviet Case* (Cambridge).

Lane, David (1976) *The Socialist Industrial State: Towards a Political Sociology of State Socialism* (London).

Lane, Frederic C. (1973) *Venice: a Maritime Republic* (Baltimore, Md.).

Lang, James (1975) *Conquest and Commerce: Spain and England in the Americas* (New York).

Langness, L. L. (1977) 'Ritual, Power and Male Dominance in the New Guinea Highlands', in Raymond D. Fogelson and Richard N. Adams, eds., *The Anthropology of Power* (New York).

Lankaster, William (1981) *The Rwala Bedouin Today* (Cambridge).

Lapidus, Ira M. (1975) 'Hierarchies and Networks: a Comparison of Chinese and Islamic Societies', in Frederic Wakeman Jr and Carolyn Grant, eds., *Conflict and Control in Late Imperial China* (Berkeley, Calif.).

(1984) *Muslim Cities in the Later Middle Ages*[2] (Cambridge).

Lapière, R. T. (1934) 'Attitudes vs. Action', *Social Forces* XIII.

Large, Stephen S. (1981) *Organized Workers and Socialist Politics in Interwar Japan* (Cambridge).

Larsen, J. A. O. (1968) *Greek Federal States* (Oxford).

Lash, Scott (1984) *The Militant Worker: Class and Radicalism in France and America* (London).

(1985) 'The End of Neo-corporatism?: the Breakdown of Centralised Bargaining in Sweden', *British Journal of Industrial Relations* XXIII.

Law, Robin (1977) *The Oyo Empire* c. *1600*–c. *1836* (Oxford).

Lawrence, Peter (1971) 'Introduction', in R. M. Berndt and Peter Lawrence, eds., *Politics in New Guinea* (Nedlands).

Leach, E. R. (1961) *Rethinking Anthropology* (London).

Leacock, Eleanor and Lee, Richard (1982) 'Introduction', in Eleanor Leacock and Richard Lee, eds., *Politics and History in Band Societies* (Cambridge).

Lee, Richard B. (1979) *The !Kung San: Men, Women and Work in a Foraging Society* (Cambridge).

Leemans, W. F. (1950) *The Old Babylonian Merchant* (Leiden).

Lefébure, Claude, (1979) 'Introduction: the Specificity of Nomadic Pastoral Societies', in L'Equipe écologie et anthropologie des sociétés pastorales, ed., *Pastoral Production and Society* (Paris).

Lefebvre, Georges (1939) *Quatre-vingt-neuf* (Paris).
(1954) 'La Révolution française et les paysans', in his *Etudes sur la Révolution française* (Paris).
(1955) 'Le mythe de la Révolution française', *Annales Historiques de la Révolution Française* XXVII.
Lemarignier, Jean-François (1980) 'Autour des premiers Capétiens (987–1108). D'un réseau d'encadrement à un embryon d'administration locale', in W. Paravicini and Karl F. Werner, eds., *Histoire comparée de l'administration (IVe–XVIIIe siècles)* (Munich).
Lennard, Reginald (1959) *Rural England 1086–1135* (Oxford).
Levy, Reuben (1962) *The Social Structure of Islam* (Cambridge).
Lewin, M. (1965) 'The Immediate Background to Soviet Collectivization', *Soviet Studies* XVII.
(1968) *Russian Peasants and Soviet Power: a Study of Collectivization* (Eng. trans., London).
Lewis, Archibald (1974) *Knights and Samurai: Feudalism in Northern France and Japan* (London).
Lewis, Bernard (1970) *The Arabs in History*[5] (London).
Lewis, Gavin (1978) 'The Peasantry, Rural Change and Conservative Agrarianism: Lower Austria at the Turn of the Century', *Past & Present* LXXXI.
Lewis, Naphtali (1983) *Life in Egypt under Roman Rule* (Oxford).
Leyser, Karl (1968) 'The German Aristocracy from the Ninth to the Early Twelfth Century', *Past & Present* XLI.
(1981) 'Ottonian Government', *English Historical Review* CCCLXXXI.
Liebermann, F., ed. (1903–16) *Die Gesetze der Angelsachsen* (3 vols., Halle).
Lindholm, Charles (1982) *Generosity and Jealousy. The Swat Pukhtun of Northern Pakistan* (New York).
Lintott, A. W. (1968) *Violence in Republican Rome* (Oxford).
(1982) *Violence, Civil Strife and Revolution in the Classical City* (London).
Linz, Juan (1970) 'An Authoritarian Regime: Spain', in Erik Allardt and Stein Rokkan, eds., *Mass Politics* (New York).
(1973) 'The Future of an Authoritarian Situation or the Institutionalization of an Authoritarian Regime: the Case of Brazil', in Alfred Stepan, ed., *Authoritarian Brazil: Origins, Policies, and Future* (New Haven, Conn.).
Livy, *History of Rome*.
Lloyd, Peter (1965) 'The Political Structure of African Kingdoms: an Exploratory Model', in Michael Banton, ed., *Political Systems and the Distribution of Power*, ASA Monograph 2 (London).
(1966) 'Introduction', in Peter Lloyd, ed., *The New Elites of Tropical Africa* (London).
Lo, Jung-Pang (1969) 'Maritime Commerce and its Relation to the Sung Navy', *Journal of the Economic and Social History of the Orient* XXII.
Lockwood, David (1958) *The Blackcoated Worker: a Study in Class Consciousness* (London).
(1982) 'Fatalism: Durkheim's Hidden Theory of Order', in Anthony Giddens and Gavin Mackenzie, eds., *Social Class and the Division of Labour* (Cambridge).
Loewe, Michael (1966) *Imperial China: the Historical Background to the Modern Age* (London).

Long, Edward (1774) *History of Jamaica* (London).

Lonsdale, John (1981) 'States and Social Processes in Africa: a Historiographical Survey', *African Studies Review* XXIV.

Lopez, Robert S. (1953) 'An Aristocracy of Money in the Early Middle Ages', *Speculum* XXVIII.

Lourie, Elena (1966) 'A Society Organized for War: Medieval Spain', *Past & Present* XXXV.

Lovejoy, Paul E. (1978) 'Plantations in the Economy of the Sokoto Caliphate', *Journal of African History* XIX.

(1983) *Transformations in Slavery. A History of Slavery in Africa* (Cambridge).

Low-Beer, John R. (1978) *Protest and Participation: the New Working Class in Italy*. (Cambridge).

Loyn, H. R. (1962) *Anglo-Saxon England and the Norman Conquest* (London).

Lucas, Colin (1976) 'Nobles, Bourgeois and the Origins of the French Revolution' in Douglas Johnson, ed., *French Society and the Revolution* (Cambridge).

Luhmann, Niklas (1970) *Soziologische Aufklärung: Aufsätze zur Theorie Sozialer Systeme* (Cologne).

Lukic, R. V. (1965) 'L'influence de l'autogestion ouvrière sur la structure de classe de la société Yugoslave', *Cahiers Internationaux de Sociologie* XXXVIII.

Mack Smith, Denis (1968) *Medieval Sicily 800–1713* (London).

MacLeod, Murdo (1973) *Spanish Central America: a Socioeconomic History 1520–1720* (Berkeley, Calif.).

MacMullen, Ramsay (1980) 'How Many Romans Voted?', *Athenaeum* n.s. LVIII.

Macpherson, C. B. (1962) *The Political Theory of Possessive Individualism: Hobbes to Locke* (Oxford).

Magnou-Nortier, Elizabeth (1979) 'Nouveaux propos sur "Foi et Fidélité"', *Francia* VII.

Maier, Charles S. (1978) 'The Politics of Inflation in the Twentieth Century', in Fred Hirsch and John H. Goldthorpe, eds., *The Political Economy of Inflation* (London).

Main, Jackson T. (1967) 'The Class Structure of Revolutionary America', in S. M. Lipset and R. Bendix, eds., *Class, Status and Power*[2] (London).

Malcolmson, Robert W. (1981) *Life and Labour in England 1700–1780* (London).

Malettke, Klaus (1980) 'Ämterkauflichkeit und Soziale Mobilität', in Adolf M. Birke *et al.*, eds., *Ämterkauflichkeit: Aspekte Sozialer Mobilität in Europäischen Vergleich (17 und 18 Jahrhundert)* (Berlin).

Malinowski, Bronislaw (1922) *Argonauts of the Western Pacific* (London).

Mallett, Michael (1974) *Mercenaries and their Masters: Warfare in Renaissance Italy* (London).

Malloy, J. M. (1970) *Bolivia: the Uncompleted Revolution* (Pittsburgh, Pa.).

Malowist, Marian (1962) 'Un essai d'histoire comparée: les mouvements d'expansion en Europe au XVe et XVIe siècles', *Annales* XVII.

Mandelbaum, David G. (1955) 'The World and the World View of the *Kota*', *American Anthropologist* Memoir 83.

Mann, Michael (1986) *The Sources of Social Power* I: *A History of Power from the Beginning to A.D. 1760* (Cambridge).

Maquet, Jacques J. (1961) *The Premise of Inequality in Ruanda: a Study of Political Relations in a Central African Kingdom* (London).

Maravall, José (1978) *Dictatorship and Political Dissent. Workers and Students in Franco's Spain* (London).

Marsh, Robert M. (1961) *The Mandarins: the Circulation of Elites in China, 1600–1900* (New York).

Marshall, Gordon (1980) *In Search of the Spirit of Capitalism: an Essay on Max Weber's Protestant Ethic Thesis* (London).

Martin, Calvin (1979) *Keepers of the Game: Indian–Animal Relations and the Fur Trade* (Berkeley, Calif.).

Martins, Herminio (1971) 'Portugal', in Margaret S. Archer and Salvador Giner, eds., *Contemporary Europe: Class, Status and Power* (London).

Marx, Karl (1964) *Pre-Capitalist Economic Formations* (Eng. trans. (ed. E. J. Hobsbawm), London).

Mathias, Peter (1957) 'The Social Structure of the Eighteenth Century: a Calculation by Joseph Massie', *Economic History Review* 2nd ser., x.

(1979) *The Transformation of England: Essays in the Economic and Social History of England in the Eighteenth Century* (London).

Mayer, Kurt B. (1967) 'Social Stratification in Two Equalitarian Societies: Australia and the United States', in S. M. Lipset and R. Bendix, eds., *Class, Status and Power*[2] (London).

Mazrui, Ali A. (1977) *Africa's International Relations: the Diplomacy of Dependency and Change* (London).

McBride, George M. (1923) *The Land Systems of Mexico* (New York).

McCreery, David (1983) 'Debt Service in Rural Guatemala, 1876–1936', *Hispanic American Historical Review* LXIII.

McFarlane, K. B. (1963) 'A Business Partnership in War and Administration 1421–1445', *English Historical Review* LXXVIII.

McKendrick, Neil (1982) 'Commercialization and the Economy', in Neil McKendrick *et al.*, *The Birth of a Consumer Society. The Commercialization of Eighteenth-century England* (London).

McKitterick, Rosamond (1983) *The Frankish Kingdoms under the Carolingians 751–987* (London).

McKnight, Brian E. (1971) *Village and Bureaucracy in Southern Sung China* (Chicago, Ill.).

McManners, John (1967) 'France', in A. Goodwin, ed., *The European Nobility in the Eighteenth Century*[2] (London).

McNeill, William H. (1983) *The Pursuit of Power: Technology, Armed Force and Society since A.D. 1000* (Oxford).

McSheffrey, Gerald M. (1983) 'Slavery, Indentured Servitude, Legitimate Trade and the Impact of Abolition in the Gold Coast, 1874–1901: a Reappraisal', *Journal of African History* XXIV.

Meggitt, M. J. (1971) 'The Pattern of Leadership among the Mae Enga of New Guinea', in R. M. Berndt and Peter Lawrence, eds., *Politics in New Guinea* (Nedlands).

(1974) '"Pigs are in our hearts!": the *Te* Exchange Cycle among the Mae Enga of New Guinea', *Oceania* XLIV.

Meiggs, Russell and Lewis, David (1969) *A Selection of Greek Historical Inscriptions to the End of the Fifth Century B.C.* (Oxford).

Meillassoux, Claude (1981) *Maidens, Meal and Money: Capitalism and the Domestic Economy* (Eng. trans., Cambridge).

Merton, Robert K. (1957) *Social Theory and Social Structure*[2] (Glencoe, Ill.).

Metcalf, George (1965) *Royal Government and Political Conflict in Jamaica 1729–83* (London).

Meyer, Jean (1970) 'Les ouvriers dans la révolution mexicaine: les bataillons rouges', *Annales* XXV.

Meyer, Lorenzo (1982–3) 'La Revolución Mexicana y sus elecciones presidenciales: una interpretación (1910–1940)', *Historia Mexicana* XXXII.

Michaels, A. L. (1970) 'The Crisis of Cardenismo', *Journal of Latin American Studies* II.

Millar, Fergus (1977) *The Emperor in the Roman World (31 BC–AD 337)* (London).

Millar, James R. (1976) 'A Debate on Collectivization: Was Stalin Really Necessary?', *Problems of Communism* (July–August).

Mingay, G. E. (1963) *English Landed Society in the Eighteenth Century* (London).

(1976) *The Gentry. The Rise and Fall of a Ruling Class* (London).

Momigliano, Arnoldo (1975) 'The Origins of the Roman Republic', *Quinto contributo alla storia delli studi classici e del mondo antico* (Rome).

Moore, Barrington Jr (1967) *Social Origins of Dictatorship and Democracy* (London).

Moote, A. Lloyd (1978) 'The Preconditions of Revolution in Early Modern Europe: did they Really Exist?', in Geoffrey Parker and Lesley M. Smith, eds., *The General Crisis of the Seventeenth Century* (London).

Morishima, Michio (1982) *Why has Japan 'Succeeded'? Western Technology and the Japanese Ethos* (Cambridge).

Mörner, Magnus (1953) *The Political and Economic Activities of the Jesuits in the La Plata Region: the Hapsburg Era* (Stockholm).

(1973) 'The Spanish American Hacienda: a Survey of Recent Research and Development', *Hispanic American Historical Review* LIII.

Morony, Michael G. (1984) *Iraq after the Muslim Conquest* (Princeton, N.J.).

Morris, H. S. (1980) 'Slaves, Aristocrats and Export of Sago in Sarawak', in James L. Watson, ed., *Asian and African Systems of Slavery* (Oxford).

Morris, Ian (1985) 'Gift and Commodity in Archaic Greece', *Man* n.s. XXI.

Mortimer, Edward (1982) *Faith and Power: the Politics of Islam* (London).

Mottahedeh, Roy P. (1980) *Loyalty and Leadership in an Early Islamic Society* (Princeton, N.J.).

Mousnier, Roland (1945) *La vénalité des offices sous Henri IV et Louis XIII* (Rouen).

(1970*a*) 'The Exponents and Critics of Absolutism', in J. P. Cooper, ed., *The New Cambridge Modern History* IV (Cambridge).

(1970*b*) 'Quelques raisons de la Fronde: les causes des journées révolutionnaires parisiennes de 1648', in *La plume, la faucille et le marteau: institutions et société en France du Moyen Age à la Révolution* (Paris).

(1979) *The Institutions of France under the Absolute Monarchy 1598–1789: Society and the State* (Eng. trans., Chicago).

Mouzelis, Nicos P. (1986) *Politics in the Semi-periphery: Early Parliamentarism and Late Industrialisation in the Balkans and Latin America* (London).

Munck, Ronaldo (1987) *Argentina: from Anarchism to Peronism: Workers, Unions and Politics, 1855–1985* (London).

Murakawa, Kentaro (1959) 'Demiurgos', *Historia* VI.

Murra, John V. (1980) *The Economic Organization of the Inca State* (Greenwich, Conn.).

Murray, Alexander (1978) *Reason and Society in the Middle Ages* (Oxford).

Musset, Lucien (1951) *Les peuples scandinaves au Moyen Age* (Paris).

(1959) 'A-t-il existé en Normandie au XIe siècle une aristocratie d'argent?', *Annales de Normandie* IX.

Mutel, Jacques (1986) 'La modernisation du Japon', *Archives Européennes de Sociologie* XXVII.

Myrdal, Gunnar (1944) *An American Dilemma: the Negro Problem and Modern Democracy* (New York).

Myrdal, H.-G. (1980) 'The Swedish Model – Will it Survive?', *British Journal of Industrial Relations* XVI.

Myrdal, Jan and Kessle, Gun (1971) *China: the Revolution Continued* (Eng. trans., London).

Nakane, Chie (1970) *Japanese Society* (London).

Nehru, Jawaharlal (1958) *Towards Freedom* (Boston, Mass.).

Neumann, Franz (1942) *Behemoth. The Structure and Practice of National Socialism* (London).

Nicholls, David (1979) *From Dessalines to Duvalier: Race, Colour and National Independence in Haiti* (Cambridge).

Nicolet, C. (1980) *The World of the Citizen in Republican Rome* (Eng. trans., London).

Norbeck, Edward (1970) 'Continuities in Japanese Social Stratification', in Leonard Plotnicov and Arthur Tuden, eds., *Essays in Comparative Social Stratification* (Pittsburgh, Pa.).

Norman, A. F. (1958) 'Gradations in Later Municipal Society', *Journal of Roman Studies* XLVIII.

Nove, Alec (1962) 'Was Stalin Really Necessary?', *Encounter* CIII.

(1976) 'A Debate on Collectivization: Was Stalin Really Necessary?', *Problems of Communism* (July–August).

(1983) *The Economics of Feasible Socialism* (London).

Oates, Joan (1979) *Babylon* (London).

O'Brien, Patrick (1984) 'Europe in the World Economy', in Hedley Bull and Adam Watson, eds., *The Expansion of International Society* (Oxford).

O'Connor, David (1983) 'New Kingdom and Third Intermediate Period 1552–664 B.C.', in B. G. Trigger *et al.*, *Ancient Egypt: a Social History* (Cambridge).

O'Donnell, Guillermo A. (1976) 'Modernization and Military Coups: Theory, Comparisons and the Argentine Case', in Abraham F. Lowenthal, ed., *Armies and Politics in Latin America* (New York).

Oksenberg, Michel (1970) 'Getting Ahead and Along in Communist China: the Ladder of Success on the Eve of the Cultural Revolution', in J. W. Lewis, ed., *Party Leadership and Revolutionary Power in China* (Cambridge).

Oliva, Pavel (1977) *Sparta and her Social Problems* (The Hague).

O'Meara, Dan (1983) *Volkscapitalisme. Class, Capital and Ideology in the Development of Afrikaner Nationalism 1934–1948* (Cambridge).

O'Neil, J. L. (1981) 'How Democratic was Hellenistic Rhodes?', *Athenaeum* n.s. LIX.

Oppenheim, A. Leo (1977) *Ancient Mesopotamia: Portrait of a Dead Civilization*[2] (Chicago).

Origo, Iris (1963) *The Merchant of Prato*[2] (London).

Osamu, Wakita (1982) 'The Emergence of the State in Sixteenth-century Japan: from Oda to Tokugawa', *Journal of Japanese Studies* VIII.

Ossowski, Stanislav (1956) *Class Structure in the Social Consciousness* (Eng. trans., London).

Ostrogorsky, George (1968) *History of the Byzantine State* (Eng. trans., Oxford).
Paige, Jeffery M. (1975) *Agrarian Revolution: Social Movements and Export Agriculture in the Underdeveloped World* (New York).
Pares, Richard (1960) *Merchants and Planters* (Cambridge).
Parker, David (1983) *The Making of French Absolutism* (London).
Parker, Geoffrey (1974) 'The Emergence of Modern Finance in Europe 1500–1730', in Carlo M. Cipolla, ed., *The Fontana Economic History of Europe* II: *The Sixteenth and Seventeenth Centuries* (London).
(1977) *The Dutch Revolt* (London).
Parkin, Frank (1972) 'System Contradiction and Political Transformation', *Archives Européennes de Sociologie* XIII.
Patlagean, Evelyne (1975) 'Economie paysanne et "féodalité byzantine"', *Annales* XXX.
Patterson, Orlando (1982) *Slavery and Social Death: a Comparative Study* (Cambridge, Mass.).
Paul the Deacon, *History of the Lombards.*
Peel, J. D. Y. (1971) *Herbert Spencer: the Evolution of a Sociologist* (London).
(1983) *Ijeshas and Nigerians: the Incorporation of a Yoruba Kingdom, 1890s–1970s* (Cambridge).
Peristiany, J. G., ed. (1965) *Honour and Shame: the Values of Mediterranean Society* (London).
Perkin, Harold (1969) *The Origins of Modern English Society 1780–1880* (London).
Perlman, Melvin L. (1970) 'The Traditional Systems of Stratification among the Ganda and the Nyoro of Uganda', in Arthur Tuden and Leonard Plotnicov, eds., *Social Stratification in Africa* (New York).
Pessen, Edward (1980) 'How Different from Each Other Were the Antebellum North and South?', *American Historical Review* LXXXV.
Petit-Dutaillis, Ch. (1936) *The Feudal Monarchy in France and England: from the Tenth to the Thirteenth Century* (Eng. trans., London).
Petronius, *Satyricon.*
Philip, George (1978) *The Rise and Fall of the Peruvian Military Radicals 1968–76* (London).
(1984) 'Military-Authoritarianism in South America: Brazil, Chile, Uruguay and Argentina', *Political Studies* XXXII.
Pinkney, David H. (1972) *The French Revolution of 1830* (Princeton, N.J.).
Pipes, Daniel (1981) *Slave Soldiers and Islam. The Genesis of a Military System* (New Haven, Conn).
Plato, *Republic.*
Plumb, J. H. (1967) *The Growth of Political Stability in England 1675–1725* (London).
Plutarch, *Agis.*
Crassus.
Pericles.
Poitras, G. E. (1973) 'Welfare Bureaucracy and Clientelistic Politics in Mexico', *Administrative Science Quarterly* XVIII.
Pollard, Sidney (1981) *Peaceful Conquest: the Industrialization of Europe 1760–1970* (Oxford).
Polybius, *History.*
Porter, John (1969) *The Vertical Mosaic. An Analysis of Social Class and Power in Canada* (Toronto).

Porter, Roy (1982) *English Society in the Eighteenth Century* (Harmondsworth).
Pospisil, Leopold (1963) *The Kapauku Papuans of West New Guinea* (New York).
Postan, M. M. (1972) *The Medieval Economy and Society: an Economic History of Britain in the Middle Ages* (Harmondsworth).
Potash, R. (1980) *The Army and Politics in Argentina 1945–62* (London).
Potter, Anne (1981) 'The Failure of Democracy in Argentina 1916–1930: an Institutional Perspective', *Journal of Latin American Studies* XIII.
Powell, M. A. Jr (1978) 'Götter, Könige und "Kapitalisten" im Mesopotamien des 3. Jahrtausends v.u.Z.', *Oikumene* II.
Prawer, Joshua (1980) *Crusader Institutions* (Oxford).
Price, John (1966) 'A History of the Outcaste: Untouchability in Japan', in George de Vos and Hiroshi Wagatsuma, eds., *Japan's Invisible Race: Caste in Culture and Personality* (Berkeley, Calif.).
Price, Richard N. (1977) 'Society, Status and Jingoism: the Social Roots of Lower Middle Class Patriotism, 1870–1900', in Geoffrey Crossick, ed., *The Lower Middle Class in Britain 1870–1914* (London).
Procopius, *Gothic Wars*.
Pulleyblank, E. G. (1958) 'The Origins and Nature of Chattel Slavery in China', *Journal of the Economic and Social History of the Orient* I.
Quiller, Bjørn (1980) 'Prologomena to a Study of the Homeric *Demiurgoi* (Murakawa's Theory Re-examined)', *Symbolae Osloenses* LV.
Quirk, Robert E. (1960) *The Mexican Revolution 1914–1915: the Convention of Aguascalientes* (Bloomington, Ind.).
Raeff, Mark (1983) *The Well-ordered Police State: Social Institutional Change through Law in the Germanies and Russia, 1600–1800* (New Haven, Conn.).
Ranis, P. (1966) 'Peronismo without Peron: the Years after the Fall 1955–65', *Journal of Inter-American Studies* VIII.
Ranum, O. (1968) *Paris in the Age of Absolutism* (New York).
Rattray, R. S. (1923) *Ashanti* (London).
Reichel-Dolmatoff, Gerhardo and Alicia (1961) *The People of Aritama. The Cultural Personality of a Colombian Mestizo Village* (London).
Reinhold, Meyer (1971) 'Usurpation of Status and Status Symbols in the Roman Empire', *Historia* XX.
Renfrew, Colin (1972) *The Emergence of Civilisation: the Cyclades and the Aegean in the Third Millennium B.C.* (London).
Rey, P.-P. (1975) 'L'esclavage lignager chez les Tsangui, Punu et les Kuni du Congo-Brazzaville', in Claude Meillassoux, ed., *L'esclavage en Afrique précoloniale* (Paris).
Richerson, P. J. and Boyd, R. (1978) 'A Dual Inheritance Model of Human Evolutionary Process. Basic Postulates and a Simple Model', *Journal of Social and Biological Structures* I.
Robben, Antonius C. G. M. (1982) 'Stratification, Scale and Ranking: Social Change in Two Brazilian Fishing Communities', *Ethnology* XXI.
Roberts, Michael (1968) *The Early Vasas: a History of Sweden, 1523–1611* (Cambridge).
Roberts, Michael (1982) *Caste Conflict and Elite Formation* (Cambridge).
(1985) 'From Empiricist Conflation to Distortion', *Modern Asian Studies* XIX.
Roberts, Richard and Klein, Martin A. (1980) 'The Banamba Slave Exodus of 1905 and the Decline of Slavery in the Western Sudan', *Journal of African History* XXI.

Robertson, A. F. (1980) 'On Sharecropping', *Man* n.s. XV.
Robson, Robert (1959) *The Attorney in Eighteenth-century England* (Cambridge).
Rock, David (1975) *Politics in Argentina 1890–1930. The Rise and Fall of Radicalism* (Cambridge).
Roebuck, Carl (1972) 'Urbanization in Corinth', *Hesperia* XLI.
Roemer, H. R. (1986) 'The Safavid Period', in Peter Jackson, ed., *The Cambridge History of Iran* VI (Cambridge).
Rosenberg, Hans (1958) *Bureaucracy, Aristocracy and Autocracy: the Prussian Experience 1660–1815* (Cambridge, Mass.).
Rouquié, Alain (1978) *Pouvoir militaire et société politique en la République Argentine* (Paris).
Roussel, Denis (1976) *Tribu et cité* (Paris).
Rudé, George (1964) *The Crowd in History: a Study of Population Disturbances in France and England 1730–1848* (New York).
Rule, John (1981) *The Experience of Labour in Eighteenth-century Industry* (London).
Runciman, W. G. (1963) 'Charismatic Legitimacy and One-party Rule in Ghana', *Archives Européennes de Sociologie* IV.
(1966) *Relative Deprivation and Social Justice: a Study of Attitudes to Social Inequality in Twentieth-century England* (London).
(1971–2) 'Race and Social Stratification', *Race* XIII.
(1982) 'Origins of States: the Case of Archaic Greece', *Comparative Studies in Society and History* XXIV.
(1983) 'Unnecessary Revolution: the Case of France', *Archives Européennes de Sociologie* XXIV.
(1984) 'Accelerating Social Mobility: the Case of Anglo-Saxon England', *Past & Present* CIV.
(1985) 'Contradictions of State Socialism: the Case of Poland', *Sociological Review* XXXIII.
Russell, Bertrand (1938) *Power* (London).
Ruyle, E. E. (1973) 'Genetic and Cultural Pools: some Suggestions for a Unified Theory of Biocultural Evolution', *Human Ecology* I.
Ryckmans, Jacques (1951) *L'institution monarchique en Arabie Méridionale avant l'Islam (Ma'in et Saba)* (Louvain).
Sahlins, Marshall D. (1962–3) 'Poor Man, Rich Man, Big-Man, Chief: Political Types in Melanesia and Polynesia', *Comparative Studies in Society and History* V.
(1965) 'On the Sociology of Primitive Exchange', in Michael Banton, ed., *The Relevance of Models for Social Anthropology* (ASA Monograph 1, London).
(1974) *Stone Age Economics* (London).
Salisbury, Richard F. (1970) *Vunamami: Economic Transformation of a Traditional Society* (Berkeley, Calif.).
Salmon, John (1977). 'Political Hoplites?', *Journal of Hellenic Studies* XCVII.
Salvian, *De Gubernatore Dei*.
Salzman, Philip C. (1978) 'The Proto-state in Iranian Baluchistan', in Ronald Cohen and Elman R. Service, eds., *Origins of the State: the Anthropology of Political Evolution* (Philadelphia, Pa.).
Sansom, G. B. (1931) *Japan* (London).
Sant Cassia, Paul (1983) 'Patterns of Covert Politics in Post-independence Cyprus', *Archives Européennes de Sociologie* XXIV.

Sautel, Gérard (1955) 'Les villes du Midi méditerranéen au moyen âge', *Receuils de la Société Jean Bodin* VII.

Sawyer, P. H. (1965) 'The Wealth of England in the Eleventh Century', *Transactions of the Royal Historical Society* 4th ser., XV.

Scalapino, Robert A. (1953) *Democracy and the Party Movement in Prewar Japan: the Failure of the First Attempt* (Berkeley, Calif.).

(1983) *The Early Japanese Labor Movement: Labor and Politics in a Developing Society* (Berkeley, Calif.).

Scase, Richard (1977) *Social Democracy in Capitalist Society. Working-class Politics in Britain and Sweden* (London).

Schaedel, Richard P. (1978) 'Early State of the Incas', in Henri J. M. Claessen and Peter Skalnik, eds., *The Early State* (The Hague).

Schapera, I. (1956) *Government and Politics in Tribal Societies* (London).

Schapiro, Leonard (1970) *The Communist Party of the Soviet Union*[2] (London).

Schram, Stuart R. (1984) 'Classes, Old and New, in Mao Zedong's Thought, 1949–1976', in James L. Watson, ed., *Class and Social Stratification in Post-revolutionary China* (Cambridge).

Schurmann, H. F. (1956) 'Traditional Property Concepts in China', *Far Eastern Quarterly* XV.

(1968) *Ideology and Organization in Communist China*[2] (Berkeley, Calif.).

Scogin, Hugh (1978) 'Poor Relief in Northern Sung China', *Oriens Extremus* XXVI.

Seager, Robin (1979) *Pompey: a Political Biography* (Oxford).

Serrâo, Joël (1954) 'Le blé des îles Atlantiques: Madère et Açores aux XVe et XVIe siècles', *Annales* IX.

Shahrani, M. Nazif (1978) 'The Retention of Pastoralism among the Kirghiz of the Afghan Pamirs', in James F. Fisher, ed., *Himalayan Anthropology: the Indo-Tibetan Interface* (The Hague).

Shanin, Teodor (1972) *The Awkward Class. Political Sociology of Peasantry in a Developing Society: Russia 1910–1925* (London).

Sheldon, C. D. (1958) *The Rise of the Merchant Class in Tokugawa Japan 1600–1868: an Introductory Survey* (New York).

Shennan, J. G. (1968) *The Parlement of Paris* (London).

(1974) *The Origins of the Modern European State* (London).

Shepherd, Gill (1980) 'The Comorians and the East African Slave Trade', in James L. Watson, ed., *Asian and African Systems of Slavery* (Oxford).

Sherwin-White, A. N. (1973) *The Roman Citizenship*[2] (Oxford).

Shiba, Yoshinobu (1970) *Commerce and Society in Sung China* (Eng. trans., Ann Arbor, Mich.).

Shils, Edward (1968) 'Deference', in J. A. Jackson, ed., *Social Stratification* (Sociological Studies I, Cambridge).

Shirk, Susan L. (1984) 'The Decline of Virtuocracy in China', in James L. Watson, ed., *Class and Social Stratification in Post-revolutionary China* (Cambridge).

Sidonius Apollinaris, *Letters*.

Silvert, K. H. (1968) 'Caudillismo', *International Encyclopedia of the Social Sciences* (New York).

Simpson, L. B. (1950) *The Encomienda in New Spain* (Berkeley, Calif.).

Skinner, G. William and Winckler, Edward A. (1969) 'Compliance Successions in Rural Communist China: a Cyclical Theory', in A. Etzioni, ed., *A Sociological Reader on Complex Organizations*[2] (New York).

Skocpol, Theda (1979) *States and Social Revolutions: a Comparative Analysis of France, Russia and China* (Cambridge).

Smith, Adam (1776) *The Wealth of Nations* (London).

Smith, D. S. (1977) 'A Homeostatic Demographic Regime: Patterns in West European Family Reconstitution Studies', in R. D. Lee, ed., *Population Patterns in the Past* (New York).

Smith, M. G. (1965) *The Plural Society in the British West Indies* (Berkeley, Calif.).

(1971) 'Pluralism in Precolonial African Societies', in Leo Kuper and M. G. Smith, eds., *Pluralism in Africa* (Berkeley, Calif.).

Smith, T. C. (1959) *Agrarian Origins of Modern Japan* (Stanford, Calif.).

Smout, T. C. (1969) *A History of the Scottish People 1560–1850* (Glasgow).

(1986) *A Century of the Scottish People 1850–1950* (London).

Snodgrass, Anthony (1980) *Archaic Greece* (London).

Southall, Aidan W. (1957) *Alur Society* (Cambridge).

(1970) 'Rank and Stratification among the Alur and other Nilotic Peoples', in Arthur Tuden and Leonard Plotnicov, eds., *Social Stratification in Africa* (New York).

Spalding, H. (1977) *Organized Labor in Latin America* (New York).

Speck, W. A. (1977) *Stability and Strife: England 1714–1760* (London).

Speiser, E. A. (1958) 'The Muskênum', *Orientalia* XXVII.

Spencer, Paul (1965) *The Samburu: a Study of Gerontocracy in a Nomadic Tribe* (London).

Srinivas, M. N. (1952) *Religion and Society among the Coorgs of South India* (Oxford).

Stambouli, F. and Zghal, A. (1976) 'Urban Life in Pre-colonial North Africa', *British Journal of Sociology* XXVII.

Stavrianos, L. S. (1981) *Global Rift: the Third World Comes of Age* (New York).

Stein, Burton (1985) 'Politics, Peasants and the Deconstruction of Feudalism in Medieval India', *Journal of Peasant Studies* XII.

Steinberg, Jonathan (1976) *Why Switzerland?* (Cambridge).

Steinhart, Edward I. (1967) 'Vassal and Fief in Three Lacustrine Kingdoms', *Cahiers d'Etudes Africaines* VII.

(1978) 'Ankole: Pastoral Hegemony', in Henri J. M. Claessen and Peter Skalnik, eds., *The Early State* (The Hague).

Steven, Rob (1983) *Classes in Contemporary Japan* (Cambridge).

Steward, Julian H., ed. (1949) *Handbook of South American Indians* V (Washington, D.C.).

Stewart, A. *et al.* (1980) *Social Stratification and Occupations* (London).

Stone, Elizabeth C. (1982) 'The Social Role of the Naditu Women in Old Babylonian Nippur', *Journal of the Economic and Social History of the Orient* XXV.

Stone, Lawrence (1966) 'Social Mobility in England, 1500–1700', *Past & Present* XXXIII.

(1972) *The Causes of the English Revolution 1529–1642* (London).

Stone, Norman (1983) *Europe Transformed 1878–1919* (London).

Stouffer, Samuel *et al.* (1949) *The American Soldier* I: *Adjustment during Army Life* (Princeton, N.J.).

Strabo, *Geography*.

Strathern, Andrew J. (1971) *The Rope of Moka: Big-men and Ceremonial Exchange in Mount Hagen, New Guinea* (Cambridge).

(1979) *Ongka: a Self-account by a New Guinea Big-man* (London).

Strauss, Gerald (1976) *Nuremberg in the Sixteenth Century. City Politics and Life between Middle Ages and Modern Times* (Bloomington, Ind.).

Suetonius, *Divus Augustus*.

Svalastoga, Kaare (1965) *Social Differentiation* (New York).

Svoronos, N. (1966) 'Société et organisation intérieure dans l'empire byzantin au XIe siècle: les principaux problèmes', *Proceedings of the XIIIth International Conference of Byzantine Studies* (Oxford).

Syme, Ronald (1939) *The Roman Revolution* (Oxford).

Tabacco, Giovanni (1980) 'Gli orientamenti feudali dell'impero in Italia', in Ecole Française de Rome, *Structures féodales et féodalisme dans l'Occident méditerranéen X^e^–XIIIe siècles* (Rome).

Tacitus, *Annals*.

Germania.

Taguchi, Fukuji (1968) 'Pressure Groups in Japanese Politics', in Hajime Shinohara, ed., *The Developing Economies* VI (Tokyo).

Taylor, B. K. (1962) *The Western Lacustrine Bantu* (London).

Taylor, George V. (1967) 'Noncapitalist Wealth and the Origins of the French Revolution', *American Historical Review* LXXII.

(1972) 'Revolutionary and Nonrevolutionary Content in the *Cahiers* of 1789: an Interim Report', *French Historical Studies* VII.

Taylor, Lily Ross (1949) *Party Politics in the Age of Caesar* (Berkeley, Calif.).

Thirsk, Joan (1978) *Economic Policy and Projects: the Development of a Consumer Society in Early Modern England* (Oxford).

Thirsk, Joan and Cooper, J. P., eds. (1972) *Seventeenth-century Economic Documents* (Oxford).

Thistlethwaite, Frank (1955) *The Great Experiment: an Introduction to the History of the American People* (Cambridge).

Thomas, E. M. (1959) *The Harmless People* (New York).

Thomas, Keith (1971) *Religion and the Decline of Magic* (London).

Thompson, E. A. (1963–4) 'The Barbarian Kingdoms in Gaul and Spain', *Nottingham Mediaeval Studies* VII.

(1965) *The Early Germans* (Oxford).

Thucydides, *History*.

Tlou, Thomas (1977) 'Servility and Political Control: Botlhanka among the BaTawana of Northwestern Botswana, ca. 1750–1906', in Suzanne Miers and Igor Kopytoff, eds., *Slavery in Africa: Historical and Anthropological Perspectives* (Madison, Wis.).

Tocqueville, Alexis de (1889) *Democracy in America*² (2 vols., Eng. trans., London).

Torrance, John (1978) 'Social Class and Bureaucratic Innovation: the Commissioners for Examining the Public Accounts 1780–1787', *Past & Present* LXXVIII.

Toubert, Pierre (1973) *Les structures du Latium médiéval* (2 vols., Rome).

Touraine, Alain (1965) *Sociologie de l'action* (Paris).

Trebilcock, Clive (1981) *The Industrialization of the Continental Powers 1780–1914* (London).

Treggiari, Susan (1969) *Roman Freedmen during the Late Republic* (Oxford).

Turnbull, Colin M. (1965) 'The Mbuti Pygmies of the Congo', in James L. Gibbs, ed., *Peoples of Africa* (New York).

(1972) *The Mountain People* (New York).

Turner, Mary (1982) *Slaves and Missionaries: the Disintegration of Jamaican Slave Society 1787–1834* (Urbana, Ill.).

Twitchett, Denis and Wright, Arthur F. (1973) 'Introduction', in Arthur F. Wright and Denis Twitchett, eds., *Perspectives on the T'ang* (New Haven, Conn.).

Udovitch, Abraham (1970) 'Introductory Remarks', in M. A. Cook, ed., *Studies in the Economic History of the Middle East* (New York).

Ulam, Adam B. (1973) *Stalin: the Man and his Era* (New York).

Ungern-Sternberg, Jürgen von (1982) 'Weltreich und Krise: Äussere Bedingungen für die Niedergang der Römischen Republik', *Museum Helveticum* XXXIX.

Urban, William (1973) 'The Organisation of the Defence of the Livonian Frontier in the Thirteenth Century', *Speculum* XLVIII.

Valentine, Charles A. (1973) 'Changing Indigenous Societies and Culture', in Ian Hogbin, ed., *Anthropology in Papua New Guinea* (Melbourne).

Van Cleeve, T. C. (1972) *The Emperor Frederick II of Hohenstaufen* (Oxford).

van den Bergh, Pierre L. (1965) *South Africa: a Study in Conflict* (Middletown, Conn.).

Vansina, Jan (1978) 'The Kuba State', in Henri J. M. Claessen and Peter Skalnik, eds., *The Early State* (The Hague).

Van Young, Eric (1981) *Hacienda and Market in Eighteenth-century Mexico: the Rural Economy of the Guadalajara Region, 1675–1820* (Berkeley, Calif.).

Varley, Herbert P. (1967) *The Onin War* (New York).

Vaughan, James H. Jr (1970) 'Caste Systems in the Western Sudan', in Arthur Tuden and Leonard Plotnicov, eds., *Social Stratification in Africa* (New York).

Verlinden, Ch. (1977) *L'esclavage dans l'Europe méditerranéen* II (Ghent).

Voeltzel, R. F. (1936) *Jean Domat* (Paris).

Vorren, Ornulv and Manker, Ernst (1962) *Lapp Life and Customs: a Survey* (London).

Vryonis, Speros Jr (1956) 'Isidore Glabas and the Turkish Devshirme', *Speculum* XXXI.

(1959) 'Byzantium: the Social Basis of Decline in the Eleventh Century', *Greek, Roman and Byzantine Studies* II.

Waines, David (1977) 'The Third Century Internal Crisis of the Abbasids', *Journal of the Economic and Social History of the Orient* XX.

Waitz, G., ed. (1912) *Scriptores Rerum Germanicarum* LIV (Hanover).

Walbank, F. W. (1981) *The Hellenistic World* (London).

Waley, Daniel (1969) *The Italian City-Republics* (London).

Wallace-Hadrill, J. M. (1971) *Early Germanic Kingship in England and on the Continent* (Oxford).

Wallerstein, Immanuel (1974) *The Modern World-system: Capitalist Agriculture and the Origins of the European World-economy in the Sixteenth Century* (New York).

(1980) *The Modern World-system* II: *Mercantilism and the Consolidation of the European World-economy 1600–1750* (New York).

Ward, R. Gerald (1972) 'The Pacific Bêche-de-mer Trade with Special Reference to Fiji', in his *Man in the Pacific* (Oxford).

Watanabe, Hiroshi (1972) 'The Ainu', in M. G. Bichieri, ed., *Hunters and Gatherers Today* (New York).

Waterbury, Ronald (1975) 'Non-revolutionary Peasants: Oaxaca compared to Morelos in the Mexican Revolution', *Comparative Studies in Society and History* XVII.

Watson, James B. (1971) 'Tairora: the Politics of Despotism in a Small Society', in R. M. Berndt and Peter Lawrence, eds., *Politics in New Guinea* (Nedlands).

Watt, W. Montgomery (1961) *Muhammad: Prophet and Statesman* (Oxford).

Weber, Eugen (1977) *Peasants into Frenchmen. The Modernization of Rural France 1870–1914* (London).

Weber, Max (1922) *Gesammelte Aufsätze zur Religionssoziologie*[2] (3 vols., Tübingen).

(1956) *Wirtschaft und Gesellshaft*[4] (2 vols., Tübingen).

Westergaard, John and Resler, Henrietta (1975) *Class in a Capitalist Society: a Study of Contemporary Britain* (London).

Westrich, S. (1979) *The Ormée of Bordeaux: a Revolution during the Fronde* (Baltimore, Md.).

White, G. H. (1948) 'The Household of the Norman Kings', *Transactions of the Royal Historical Society* 4th ser., XXX.

Whitehead, Laurence (1981) 'Miners as Voters: the Electoral Process in Bolivia's Mining Camps', *Journal of Latin American Studies* XIII.

Whitelock, Dorothy, ed. (1930) *Anglo-Saxon Wills* (London).

ed. (1979) *English Historical Documents* I[2] (London).

Wickham, Chris (1981) *Early Medieval Italy. Central Power and Local Society 400–1000* (London).

(1984) 'The Other Transition: from the Ancient World to Feudalism', *Past & Present* CIII.

Wiessner, Polly (1982) 'Risk, Reciprocity and Social Influences on !Kung San Economies', in Eleanor Leacock and Richard Lee, eds., *Politics and History in Band Societies* (Cambridge).

Wilensky, Harold and Edwards, Hugh (1959) 'The Skidder: Ideological Adjustment of Downwardly Mobile Workers', *American Sociological Review* XXIV.

Wilks, Ivor (1975) *Asante in the Nineteenth Century: the Structure and Evolution of a Political Order* (Oxford).

Wilson, C. H. (1968) *The Dutch Republic and the Civilization of the Seventeenth Century* (London).

Wilson, Edward O. (1975) *Sociobiology: the New Synthesis* (Cambridge, Mass.).

Wilson, Godfrey (1937) 'Introduction to Nyakusa Law', *Africa* X.

Winans, E. V. (1962) *Shabala: the Constitution of a Traditional State* (London).

Winter, Edward (1958) 'The Aboriginal Political Structure of Bwamba', in John Middleton and David Tait, eds., *Tribes without Rulers. Studies in African Segmentary Systems* (London).

Wiseman, T. P. (1971) *New Men in the Roman Senate 139 B.C.–A.D. 14* (Oxford).

Wolf, Eric R. (1971) *Peasant Wars of the Twentieth Century* (London).

(1982) *Europe and the People without History* (Berkeley, Calif.).

Wolpert, Stanley (1977) *A New History of India* (New York).

Womack, John (1969) *Zapata and the Mexican Revolution* (New York).

Wood, Ian (1977) 'Kings, Kingdoms and Consent', in P. H. Sawyer and I. N. Wood, eds., *Early Medieval Kingship* (Leeds).

Woodall, Jean (1982) *The Socialist Corporation and Technocratic Power: the Polish United Workers' Party, Industrial Organisation and Workforce Control 1958–80* (Cambridge).

Wordie, J. R. (1983) 'The Chronology of English Enclosure, 1500–1900', *Economic History Review* 2nd ser., XXXVI.

Wright Erik O. (1985) *Classes* (London).

Wrightson, Keith (1982) *English Society 1580–1680* (London).

Wrigley, E. A. (1972–3) 'The Process of Modernization and the Industrial Revolution in England', *Journal of Interdisciplinary History* III.

and Schofield, R. S. (1981) *The Population History of England 1541–1871: a Reconstruction* (London).

Wyatt-Brown, Bertram (1982) *Southern Honor: Ethics and Behavior in the Old South* (New York).

Wynia, Gary W. (1978) *Argentina in the Post-war Era: Politics and Economic Policy Making in a Divided Society* (Albuquerque, New Mexico).

Xenophon, *Hellenica*.

Ways & Means.

Yalman, Nur (1960) 'The Flexibility of Caste Principles in a Kandyan Community', in E. R. Leach, ed., *Aspects of Caste in South India, Ceylon and North-West Pakistan* (Cambridge).

Yavetz, Z. (1965) 'Plebs Sordida', *Athenaeum* n.s. XLIII.

Young, Michael and Willmott, Peter (1956) 'Social Grading by Manual Workers', *British Journal of Sociology* VII.

Zeldin, Theodore (1973) *France 1848–1945* I: *Ambition, Love and Politics* (Oxford).

Index

Entries in **bold** type indicate references to the definition or interpretation of a technical or semi-technical term.

Abbās, 350–2, 396
Abbasids, 82, 156, 158, 203, 227, 348, 383, 391n, 396, 398
Abd al-Malik, 397
'Abd al-Rahman Khan, Amir of Afghanistan, 231
absolutism, 158, 159, 197, 211, 212n, 214, 218–31, 293, 294, 296, 347, 351, 363, 372, 383, 386–411, 419, 425, 427n
absorption, 7, 208, 271, 272, 440
Abu Bakr, 382, 441
acasillados, 103
'acephalous consociation', 280
achikunda, 128
Acre, 205
Acropolis, 334
administradores, 83
Adrastus, 192
advocati, 315
Aetolians, 332n
Afghanistan, 231
Africa, 50, 51n, 110, 113, 193, 202n, 216–17, 267, 333, 433n
Afrikaners, 264n, 265
Agathocles, 51, 62n
age-grading, 73, 94
age-set(s), 24, 59, 94, 100 101n, 109, 151, 188–9, 202, 235n
Ainu, 150n
aisymnētēs, 68
Alamanni, 195
Albania, 399
Alevas the Red, 196
Alexander I, of Russia, 422
Alexander the Great, 275, 286, 327
Alexandria, 271
Alexandria Eschatē, 434
al-Ghazali, 132
allod(s), allodialists, 19, 100, 211, 216, 240, 300, 313, 370n
al-Mansur, 220, 340
al-Saffah, 220
Alur, 153
aluzinnū, 163
Alvarado, Salvador, 357
Amalfi, 204n
Amba, 321
American Independence, War of, 129n
Amhara, 305
amīr-al-umara, 383
Amsterdam, 236, 237
analogue(s), 11, 119, 120, 121, 127, 182, 198, 213, 217, 220, 222, 227, 239, 242, 255, 264, 282, 321, 347
Andalusia, 21
Andaman Islands, 150
Anglo-Saxons, 107, 162, 189, 239ff., 369, 394
Ankole, 192n
An Lu-Shan, 157, 391
Anne of Austria, 346
ansar, 442
anthropology, xi, 40, 60
Antioch, 88n
Antwerp, 236
Anuak, 79
Apa Tani, 151n
apprenticeship, 73
Arab(s), Arabia, 23, 83n, 183, 382, 397, 400, 436, 441, 443
Aragon, 400n
arat, 206
archagetēs, 334n
Ardeshir, 91
Argentina, 255, 256, 428, 429–33
Argos, 327
arimanni, 372
aristocracy, 24n, 33n, 59, 102, 118, 202, 206, 229, 238, 298, 300, 334, 385
'aristocracy of labour', 290
army, armies, 39, 56, 58, 59, 66, 69, 71, 83, 157, 207–8, 212n, 221, 255, 257, 397, 420, 428, 430–1, 449
Aro, 98, 156n
artillery, 180, 271, 322

artisans, 26, 105, 109, 144, 199n, 211, 234n, 239, 245n, 290, 308n, 309, 355n, 389, 418
Ashanti, 90n
Ashikaga Shogunate, 183, 213, 375, 377
Ashoka, 50, 195
ashraf, 443n
association(s), 3, 19, 22, 109, 250, 279, 358
Ataturk, 263
Athelstan, 241
Athens, 20, 72, 77, 89, 99n, 128, 129, 192, 198, 199, 330–1 334–5
Augustus, 156, 292, 293, 352, 357n, 407, 409
Australia, 246
Austria, 111n
Austro-Hungarian Empire, 83
Authari, 197
authoritarianism, 165–6, 214, 255–8, 356, 381, 428–33
Avars, 195
awilū, 20, 162, 240, 246
ayan, 208n, 211, 385
ayatollah, 262, 270
ayllu, 55–6

baba kekere, 51n
Babylon, Babylonia, 20, 76, 161, 239ff., 369
Bacchiads, 298
Baghdad, 82, 227, 383, 384, 398
Bahrein, 383n
bailli(s), 23, 83, 214, 286, 315, 341, 370
ba-irū, 240
bakungu, 197n
Balmunamche, 242
Baltic, 58, 272, 374
Baluchistan, 151, 186
Bank of England, 234
Banks Islands, 326
baraka, 33
Barcelona, 313n
Barnave, 53
barshchina, 223
Basil II, of Byzantium, 216, 300
basileus (*eis*), 79, 153, 179, 185, 193, 196, 202, 205, 298, 325, 331ff.
Basra, 441, 443
Bastille, 362
batongole, 50–1
Bauernkrieg, 343n
Bedouin, 23, 64, 151, 153, 286
behetria, 204
Benedictines, 84
Benin, 72n, 188
Berengar I, king of Italy, 371, 372
Berengar II, king of Italy, 371
Bergdama, 71
beys, 399
Beza, 288
'big-men', 78–9, 141, 150, 153, 179, 185–6, 323–6
biology, 7, 38, 46, 47, 297, 448
bishops, 182n, 194, 239, 241n, 371, 406, 415
Bismarck, 69
Boeotia, 298, 332
Bogardus scale, 90
Bolivar, 340, 379n
Bolivia, 131n, 267n, 345, 349, 361n, 375, 422, 428, 433
Bolsheviks, 422–3
Bombay, 80
bondi, 199
Borana, 79, 80, 141, 153, 186
Bosnia, 399
'boss (ed)', 121, 264, 418
Boswell, James, 302
botlhanka, 217n
bourgeois, bourgeoisie, 107, 111, 115, 159, 181, 204, 220, 232, 237, 244, 245n, 253, 257, 264, 290, 357n, 361, 404, 413–14, 428, 446
boyars, 140–1, 220, 293, 403
Brasidas, 27
Brazil, 84, 120, 140n, 256, 379, 428, 445
Breda, 344
Brezhnev, Leonid, 340
bridewealth, 110, 287
Brill, 344
Britain, 49, 54, 57, 107, 268
Brittany, 387
brotherhood-in-arms, 65
Bryan, Sir Francis, 169
Bryce, Lord, 169
bucellarii, 223
Buddhism, 82n, 132n, 376n, 387
Buenos Aires, 271, 429
Bulgars, 21
buraku, *burakumin*, 95n, 125, 144n, 260, 420, 421
bureaucracy, 58, 73n, 80, 113, 139, 153, 156–7, 158, 160, 207, 218, 223, 225, 226, 239, 250, 358, 389, 391, 426
Burgundy, 50
Burma, 176
bushi, 21, 286, 389
Buyids, 383, 443
Bythynians, 334
Byzantium, 88, 158, 210, 216, 299–301, 327

caballeros, 204–5
cacique(*s*), 111, 121, 257, 357, 358, 359n, 360, 429
Cairo, 53n, 369
Calicut, 280
Calonne, 361, 400
Caloprini, 328
Calvin, Calvinism, 237, 288, 344, 415
Canada, 109
Canton, 274
Cape Bojador, 446

Capetians, 192, 370, 375
capitalist(s), capitalism, 57, 67, 106, 148, 164–5, 181, 198, 239, 240, 244, 246, 247–8, 260, 264, 268–9, 301, 336–40, 363, 380, 405, 406, 412, 416, 417–18, 422, 427, 429, 444, 447
Cárdenas, 256, 359–60
career(s), 72, 75, 95, 203, 308n, 420, 425, 428
Carlyle, Thomas, 449
Carmathians, 383n
Carnegie, Andrew, 147
Carranza, 356, 358
Carthage, 233, 299n
Casa del Obrero Mundial, 357
caste, 19, 20, 23, 24, 43, 59, 67, 74, 94, 116, 154, 421
Castile, 204, 400n, 436
'Catalan Company', 207
Catalonia, 183, 313n
Catherine the Great, 223, 224, 388
Catiline, 106n, 292
Cato, 329n
caudillo(s), *caudillaje*, *caudillismo*, 84, 111, 120–1, 210, 211, 213, 214–15, 221, 312, 349, 354, 356, 357–9, 375, 378–82, 411, 415, 428
caudillos de barrio, 430
cavaleiros, 445–6
Cecrops, 334
Cedillo, Saturnino, 358
Celaya, Battle of, 358
ceorl(s), 21, 107, 146, 162, 241
Ceuta, 436
Chalcis, 332, 372
Chaldiran, Battle of, 350
Chao K'uang-yin, 390, 392
chapelains ducaux, 308n
charisma, 59, 153, 255, 313, 430, 432n, 433n, 442, 443
Charlemagne, 21, 50, 82, 195, 312, 370, 376, 391
Charles I, of England, 405n, 415
Charles V, of Spain, 277
Charles XI, of Sweden, 222n
Charles the Bald, of France, 50
Chatti, 202
Chenchu, 71
chengfen, 252
Cheng Ho, 444
Chesterton, G. K., 108
Cheyenne, 187
chief(s), chiefdom, 59, 74, 78, 127n, 153, 154, 155, 217, 267, 303
chieh-tu-shih, 391
Chihuahua, 215
childhood, children, 17, 29n
Chile, 255, 349, 379, 428
Chilperic I, king of the Franks, 194
Ch'in, 391
China, Chinese, 34, 42, 58, 67, 69, 73n, 75, 84n, 98, 137, 139n, 157, 158, 160, 171, 176, 225–6, 249n, 252–4, 272, 274, 315, 322, 369, 390–5
Chinghis Khan, 206
Chola, 369
chōnin, 21, 388, 418
Chōshū, 387, 420n
Church (Roman Catholic), 5, 37, 82, 84, 113, 133, 144, 194, 210, 219, 257, 270, 277, 308, 315, 320, 359, 360, 364, 372, 373, 387, 431
Church of England, 236, 406
Cicero, 50, 118n, 199n
Cincinnatus, 96, 156, 410
Cineas, 196
Cisalpine Gaul, 439
cittadini, 237, 330
civitas sine suffragio, 439
civitates, 193, 194
clan(s), 103, 175, 185, 299, 303
clase media, 92, 107, 108
clases acomodadas, 107
classe(es), 20, 23, 25, 56, 101n, 105, 110, 209, 220, 222, 231, 269, 395, 406, 412, 420n, 449
Cleisthenes, 335, 340
Cleisthenes of Sicyon, 192
Clemenceau, Georges, 438
Cleomenes III, 318
Cleon, 340
clergy, 108n, 154, 210, 230, 412
clerk(s), 72, 112, 276, 428
client(s), clientage, clientelism, 52, 83, 102, 105, 106, 190, 199, 200, 201, 227, 246, 257, 258, 289, 290, 325, 359n, 408, 428
Clodius, 328
Cluny, 34n
Cnut, 239n
coalition(s), 105–6, 108n, 109, 189, 195, 210, 211, 248n, 257n, 358, 427, 445
Colbert, Jean Baptiste, 221
collatio lustralis, 228n
collegia, 105, 392n
Colombia, 16
coloni, 106n, 229
colonialism, colonies, colonists, 101, 184, 265, 273ff., 334, 435, 438, 447
Columella, 329n
comitatus, 192, 202
commensalism, 26, 35, 88
Communist Party (of the Soviet Union), 250–1, 425–7
Comneni, 300
compagnonnages, 364
compression, 8, 138–48
Comte, Auguste, 168
Condé, prince de, 288–9
Condé, prince de, ('*le grand Condé*'), 346

condottiere, 148n
Confucianism, 69, 132n, 170, 171, 226, 376, 389, 392, 418
Congo, 26
conquistadores, 277
Conrad, Joseph, 35
consorterie, 199
conspiracy(ies), 66n, 106, 426
constables, 405
Constantine, 228n
Constantinople, 65, 158
Constituent Assembly, 362
Constitutionalists (Mexican), 214n, 215, 356ff.
cooperation, 3, 5, 6, 18, 25, 65, 97, 100, 127, 232, 241, 267, 271, 280, 290, 415, 444
Coorgs, 369n
Corcyra, 129n, 332n
Corinth, 298, 333, 372
coronelismo, 428
corporation(s), 3, 19, 75, 83, 84ff., 109, 111, 250, 279, 358, 387, 389, 425, 428, 431, 433
corregidores, 278
Cortes, Hernando, 277
corvée labour, 54ff., 74, 180, 212, 230, 377, 416
cottagers, *cottars, cottarii*, 21, 53, 208n
Courçon, Robert de, 34
Cremona, 155
Crete, 187, 310, 334
Cristeros, 358n
Crusaders, 53, 158
cubicularii, 230
Culloden, Battle of, 302
'Cultural Revolution', 67, 252, 253n
culture, 1, 8, 11, 17n, 18, 20, 25, 26, 68, 125–6, 139–40, 148, 214, 309, 341, 448, 449
curacas, 42
cursus honorum, 73, 393
custom(s), 9, 16n, 25, 41
Cylon, 335
Cyprus, 399
Cyrene, 334n
Czechoslovakia, 271

Daflas, 151
Dahomey, 64
daimyō, 21, 121, 211, 213–14, 219, 375, 378, 387ff., 417
Damascus, 399
Dandalo, Enrico, 51
Darien, 274
Darwin, Charles, xii, 8n, 47, 449
Datini, Francesco di Marco, 199n
dauphin, 73, 79
defensor pacis, 50
deference, 13, 71, 303
Defoe, Daniel, 117
Dega Darnot, 305n
Deioces, 152
Delphic oracle, 81
dēmiourgos, 54, 68
Deng Xiaoping, 253
Denmark, 44n, 205
devshirme, 128, 228, 399
Dewas Senior, 275–6
dhāmma-mahāmāttas, 50, 121
dhimmī, 397
Díaz, Porfirio, 103, 214, 356, 359, 381
dictator, 96, 381, 409
Diocletian, 218, 229
Dionysius, 327
Disraeli, Benjamin, 22, 290
division of labour, 77, 95, 269, 285
diwan, 227, 443
doge, 136, 319, 329
Domat, 53
dominance structures, 9n
domination, 3, 5, 6, 9, 12, 18, 25, 61, 66, 100ff., 267, 272, 280, 369, 415, 448
Drake, Sir Francis, 444
Dreros, 187
Durkheim, Emile, 168
Dutch Republic, 232n, 236–7, 344
Dutch East India Company, 236
dynatoi, 211

East Africa, 79, 128, 134n, 189
Ebo, Archbishop of Rheims, 82
Edgar, king of England, 242, 243n
edion, 72n
education, 14, 112n, 143, 166
Edward I, king of England, 218
Edward the Confessor, 161, 163, 239
Egypt, Egyptian(s), 19, 55, 80n, 83, 84, 128n, 191, 193, 271, 273–4, 275, 441n, 443
ejidos, 131n, 166, 360
elders, 72, 152, 187, 188, 193
élite(s), 27, 108, 133n, 145, 202, 203, 226, 232–3, 237, 243, 250, 259, 273, 274, 275, 278, 294, 311, 354, 369, 381, 393, 416, 428, 430, 439, 442, 443
Elizabeth I of England, 5, 404, 444
emir(s), 154, 198, 203, 204, 206, 351, 383
en, 193
encomienda, encomenderos, 277, 379
endogamy, 26, 100, 110, 260
Engels, Friedrich, 47
England, 5, 21, 43, 50, 52, 75, 84, 92, 95, 99, 107, 109, 111, 121, 130n, 145–6, 159, 161, 183, 211, 218–19, 233–6, 247, 273, 279–80, 287, 294, 314, 336–40, 342, 347, 352–3, 395, 404–6, 411–16, 427
entrepreneur(s), 62, 77, 186n, 226, 231n, 234, 263, 337, 414, 444, 446, 447
Epaminondas, 320
ephebes, 72
epistratēgos, 128n

equites, 10–11, 19, 105, 233, 362
Eretria, 332, 372
estate(s), 20, 23, 92, 211, 224
Estates-General, 220, 347
Eta, 95
Ethiopia, 21, 305
ethnē, 85, 327, 332n
ethnicity, 19, 59, 73, 109, 144n, 166, 167, 264n, 282
Etruscans, 439
eunuchs, 82, 157, 219, 227, 230, 351, 391
eupatrides, 335
exogamy, 151n, 321

faction(s), 24, 56, 105, 111, 140n, 220, 233, 259, 262, 263, 290, 292, 431, 433n
Falange, 165
Falier, Doge Marino, 136
Farfa, 314
'Farmer's Law', 300n
feitorias, 446
Ferguson, Adam, 77n
fermiers-généraux, 220
feud(s), 101, 103, 151, 176, 328
feudalism, 51, 148, 158–9, 180, 202, 208–17, 294, 313–14, 356, 367–86
fideicommissum, 320
fief(s), 203, 218, 293, 375, 396
Fiji, 322
fission, 7, 83, 84, 138n, 179, 196, 280, 301ff., 372, 376, 440, 442
Florence, 329
Flushing, 344
France, French, 21, 22n, 23, 32, 33n, 37, 53, 64, 66, 67n, 94, 102, 144, 173, 180, 191, 214, 235n, 270, 273, 287, 288–9, 313, 342, 343n, 361–7, 370–1, 387, 401
Franco, Francisco, 165, 256
Frankfurt School, 132n
Frederick Barbarossa, 372
Frederick II Hohenstaufen, 372
Frederick the Great, 224, 401–3
Frederick William I, of Prussia, 223, 224, 401, 402
freedmen, 19, 74, 82, 90, 105, 219, 329, 440
Freemasonry, 97n, 108n, 366
French Revolution, 108, 169, 253, 361–7, 422n
friendly societies, 65
Fronde, 221, 346–8
Fulani, 92
fur trade, 295–6, 435
Furnivall, J. S., 65n
fusion, 7, 280, 435, 447
futuwwah, 263

Galbert de Bruges, 50
Ganda, 50
Gaul, 50, 184, 193, 216, 223, 300n, 321
geburs, 21, 242
geneats, 21, 242
Geniza, 53
Genoa, 201
genocide, 63
'gentility', 'gentleman', 90n, 124, 199, 222, 329
Georgia, 396n
gergithes, 334
Germany, German(s), 27, 66n, 69, 75, 99–100, 165, 195, 218n, 255, 273, 313, 372–3, 448
Ghana, 433n
ghilmān, 227, 383
Gierek, 177
gift-exchange, 70, 336
Gilbert, Sir Humphrey, 274n
Gini coefficient, 90
Gladstone, W. E., 34, 352
Goa, 446
godi, 80
gokenin, 376
'Golden Book', 237
Golden Horde, 207
Gomulka, Wladyslaw, 177
Gonja, 156
Gordon riots, 130n
Grand Master, 206
'Grand Pensionary', 160, 237
Grand Vizier, 228
'Great Elector', 402
Greece, Greek(s), 19, 57, 65, 68, 81, 85, 102, 133, 191, 202, 255, 273, 275, 298, 325, 336
Gregory of Tours, 194
Grey, Earl, 89
Guadalajara, 101n
Guarané, 107n
Guatemala, 380n
Guerrero, Vincente, 215
guilds, 105, 224, 364, 392n, 414
gumlao, 176
gumsa, 176
gurush, 242
Gustavus Vasa, 82
Gutsherr, 388n

hacienda, *hacendado(s)*, 101, 113, 114–15, 208n, 215, 223, 269, 307, 345–6, 357
Haiti, 137, 327, 342
hakom, 186
Hammurapi, 20, 81, 161, 239–40, 241, 242, 369
Hansa, 160, 283
hapirū, 162
Harijan, 95, 144n, 162
'harmost', 316
Harun-al-Rashid, 227
Harz mines, 313
Hastings, Battle of, 243

Hastings, Warren, 435
Hawaii, 110n, 153, 179, 280, 447
headman(men), 150, 154n, 417, 422
hēgemōn, 334n
helot(s), 21, 27, 92, 106, 155, 198, 316–17, 334
Henri IV, of France, 362
Henry I, of England, 218n, 415
Henry II, of Germany, 182n
Henry IV, of Germany, 373
Henry VIII, of England, 169, 404
Henry of Anjou, 373
Henry the Navigator, 445
Heraclea Pontica, 334
Heraclius, 299
hetaireia, 65, 66
hidalgo(s), 21, 93, 204
Hidden Imam, 262, 350
hierocracy, 262
Hinduism, 16, 20, 74, 82n, 369
Hindu Kush, 397
Hitler, Adolf, 165, 256
Holland, 236, 237, 287–8, 344, 411, 427
'holy man (men)', 68, 84, 194
homologue(s), 11, 80n, 119, 120, 121, 127, 182, 190, 198, 203, 213, 222, 239, 246, 247, 249, 264, 275, 282, 321, 347, 353, 396
honestiores, 21, 201n
Honorantiae Civitatis Papiae, 330
Hopei, 391
'hoplite revolution', 142, 289, 298–9, 304, 438
Hottentots, 263
Huerta, General Victoriano, 356
Hugh Capet, 313, 315
Huguenots, 221, 289
humiliores, 21, 201n
Hungary, 271
hunter-gatherers, 5, 31, 40, 58, 78, 101, 149–50, 178, 268, 297
Huron, 295
Hutu, 106
hxaro, 64
hyakusho, 389
hypomeiones, 27, 317

Ibn Hawqal, 383n
Ibn Khaldun, 175, 348
Iceland, 80, 198, 199, 201
'ideological hegemony', 132
Ijeshaland, 217n
Ik, 127
ilkumahum, 163
iltizams, 385
immunities, 314n
imperialism, 272, 278
Incas, 55, 85, 189, 190, 369, 398
incastellamento, 314
incest, 5n
India, 20, 23, 74, 94, 116, 169, 195, 270, 273, 276, 305n, 369, 446
Indus Valley, 310
industrialism, 'Industrial Revolution', 39, 244, 250, 258, 278, 411ff., 447
Ine, 92, 107, 241
infanticide, 179
inquilini, 440
institution(s), 2 and *passim.*
'institutional catchment area(s)', 5, 8, 16, 18, 45, 182, 238, 296, 373, 439, 447, 448
intendant(s), 195, 220–1, 239, 387
International Monetary Fund, 345
interest(s), 3, 4, 97–8, 112, 209, 286–7
Investiture Contest, 313, 373
iqta, 203f., 210, 212n, 220, 293, 384, 385
Iran, 158, 212n, 216, 263, 269, 348, 350–2, 384, 443
Iraq, 397, 398, 441n, 443
Iroquois, 295
ishakkū, 242
Islam, 19, 82n, 83, 85, 97, 98n, 134n, 156, 166–7, 175, 202–3, 206, 210, 227–8, 262–3, 270, 337, 348, 369, 382–6, 396–400, 436, 441–3
Ismail, 350–1
Israel, 102
istina, 227
Italy, Italian(s), 23, 68, 84, 115, 197, 204n, 255, 286, 313–15, 322, 371–2
Ithaca, 79
ius suffragii, 439
Ivan IV, of Russia, 140, 141
Ivory Coast, 287

Jackson, Andrew, 238
jacquerie, 120
jagir(s), 230, 293, 385
Jahiz of Basra, 91n
jajmani, 116–17, 369
Jamaica, 134n, 276–7, 435
James I, king of England (James VI of Scotland), 303, 405, 415
Janissaries, 128, 228, 341, 385, 396
Japan, 21, 23, 26, 52, 54, 57, 73n, 95, 125, 165, 210, 212–14, 215, 219, 246–7, 259–60, 286, 294, 296, 374–8, 386–90, 391, 416–21, 430
Jaruzelski, General, 177
jāti, 74, 75, 94, 124, 369
Jean d'Ibelin, 53
Jena, Battle of, 224
Jesuits, 107n, 138n, 205, 275, 446
Jews, 374
Jie, 189
'jingoism', 112
John Lydus, 80n
Johnson, Samuel, 302
Johor, 231, 280

Julius Caesar, 51, 408–11, 439
Junkers, 224
Jürchen, 225
justice(s) of the peace, 235, 405
justicia, 50

kabaka, 50–1
Kachin, 175–6, 178
kadis, 399
Kalahari Desert, 150
Kamakura Shogunate, 213
kampaku, 158, 377
Kao-tsung, 69n, 226
Kapauku, 71
Karāva, 43, 310
Karimojong, 189
Kenya, 173
Khalid b. al Walid, 441
khums, 167
khuwwa, 442
kibbutzim, 102
killyrioi, 334
king(s), kingship, 51–2, 59, 81, 84, 96, 121, 153, 155, 192, 193, 195, 198, 239–40, 312
King, Gregory, 53, 91n, 414
kinship, 11, 14, 18n, 19, 43, 57, 101–3, 113, 150n, 153, 187, 190, 217, 225, 241, 295, 332, 377, 378, 442
Kirghiz, 151, 187
klarotai, 334
knes, 205
Korea, Koreans, 124, 260, 327, 342
kosmos, 187
Kota, 18
kotsetlas, 242
Kshatriya, 154
Kuba, 192
Kufa, 441, 443
kulaks, 422
!Kung, 64, 127n, 187
kuttāb, 227

laboureurs, 144
Laertes, 79
Lakalai, 325
Lancashire, 339, 411
Landrat, 388
land, landholding, land-tenure, 14, 90n, 101, 116, 158, 162, 210, 225, 242–3, 305, 308, 317, 369, 379, 413
Lapps, 187n
latifundia, 149, 166, 292, 304, 322
Latins, 201, 438, 439
Latium, 314, 371
law(s), 9, 16n, 25, 71, 81, 202, 206, 218, 387, 394, 408
leadership, 64, 70
Lebanon, 52
leilendingr, 199
'Lelantine' War, 332
Lenin, V. I., 166, 340, 423, 426
leopard-skin chief, 321
Leovigild, 62
Lepidus, 292n
Leuctra, Battle of, 317, 318
Libanius, 88n
Liberia, 283
Lisle, Lord, 169
liturgy(ies), 81, 127, 156, 199, 329n, 330
Livonia, 206
Lloyd George, David, 164
Locke, John, 34
Locrians, 334, 335
Lombards, 81, 92, 102, 158, 195, 196–7, 216
London, 50, 99, 277, 435
Losung, 199
Louis II, king of Italy, 371
Louis XIV, king of France, 51, 64, 157, 218, 219, 220, 224, 340, 346, 362, 365, 387, 388, 391, 400
Louis XVI, king of France, 362, 400
Louis XVIII, king of France, 363
Louis the Pious, king of France, 195
Louis of Anjou, 373
Louis-Philippe, king of France, 340
Loyseau, 53
lualua, 324
Lucca, 155, 372
lugal, 14, 325
Lycurgus, 317, 318

MacArthur, General, 434
Macedon, Macedonians, 193, 327, 330, 434
Madagascar, 153, 179, 189, 322
Madero, Francisco, 356
Mae Enga, 324
Mafia, *mafiosi*, 113, 257
Maghreb, 160
magister rei privatae, 352
magnati, 199
Magyars, 180, 312
Mahdi, 262n, 270
Mahrattas, 369n
Maitland, F. W., 218
Malaysia, 306
Malta, 52
Mamluks, 83, 271, 369, 396, 398
mana, 186
mancipi, 230
Mandari, 150
Mandelstam, Nadezhda, 169
manor, manorialism, 84, 115n, 180, 208n, 209, 212, 241, 242, 375, 388, 392, 445
manumission, 129, 146, 241n
mansab(s), *mansabdar(s)*, 230, 396
Mao Zedong, 34, 67, 252–3
Mar, 150
marchiones, 312

Marghi, 76
Marienburg, 206
mari-i-taqlid, 263
Marius, 292, 409, 410
Maroboduus, 152
Marx, Karl, 12n, 36n, 38, 47, 48, 77n, 106, 287, 289, 337, 416, 423
Marxism, 132n, 148, 172, 181
Marxism-Leninism, 171
Maryandynians, 334
Massie, Joseph, 414
Matotu, 325
matriliny, 5, 113–14, 326
mawlā, *mawāli*, 83, 204, 227, 397, 408
Maya, 267, 311–12
Mayflower, 272
Mayhew, Henry, 50
Mazarin, Cardinal, 346–7
Mbutu, 26, 34, 64
Mehmet the Conqueror, 228
'Meidner proposals', 166, 261
Meiji Restoration, 125, 126n, 286, 349, 360, 422
Mekong delta, 306
Melanesia, 79, 80, 150, 186, 326
Melanippus, 192
Melgaréjo, Mariano, 349, 375, 381
mercenaries, 44n, 104, 154, 155, 232, 237, 330, 392
merchant(s), 5, 22n, 26, 75, 85, 109n, 154, 161, 163, 199n, 204, 207, 210, 226, 242, 243, 273, 329, 388–9, 390, 395, 397, 412, 441, 446, 447
Merovingian(s), 50, 51, 194, 216n
Mesopotamia, 80n, 134, 162
Messenia, 335
mestizos, 16
metics, 155, 200, 329
Mexican Revolution, 103, 356, 359n
Mexico, 101, 103, 114, 131n, 166, 214–15, 256, 269, 307, 356–61, 375, 379, 381, 447
Mexico City, 85, 357
Micmac, 295n
'middle class', 10, 108, 111, 117, 255, 265, 353, 424, 429–30
Milan, 201
militia, 59, 155, 159, 174, 222n, 372, 438
Milo, 328
Minamoto-no-Yoritomo, 213
ministeriales, 82, 83, 154, 157, 219, 313, 341, 373
mir, 223, 225
missi dominici, 50, 121, 195
Mittelstand, 92, 108
M.N.R. (*Movimiento Nacionalista Revolucionario*), 345
Modena, 329
monarch(s), monarchy, 30, 61, 69, 74, 94, 98, 106, 134, 159, 190, 209, 218, 222, 226, 243n, 289, 327, 372, 373, 406, 415
monasteries, 84, 300, 314
moneyers, 98n
moneylenders, 385
moneying, 312
Mongols, 78, 85, 156, 206–7, 212n, 225, 384, 398
Montpellier, 200
Morelos, 215, 357, 361n
Morocco, 33, 445
Monroe Doctrine, 447
Morosini, 328
Moscow, 83
mothakes, 21, 27
Mozambique, 94
Mudéjares, 104
mufti, 270, 384
Mugabe, 192
Mughals, 230, 396
Muhammad, 23, 203, 204, 286, 340, 348, 382, 396, 441–2, 443n
muharijun, 442
mujtahid, 348
mullahs, 166, 263
murshid-i kamil, 350
mushkēnū, 20, 163, 190, 240, 242
mustaufi-yi-khassa, 392

Nabis, 318
naditum, 76, 163
Napier, General Sir Charles, 273
Naples, 137n
Napoleon I, 136, 224, 319, 320, 363, 367, 400
Napoleon III, 366
nasab, 442
National Debt, 234
natural selection, 44n, 45, 46, 449
Naucratis, 273
Necker, 361, 365
Nehru, Jawaharlal, 270, 276
neodamodeis, 27, 317
Neolithic Revolution, 39
Nepal, 21
'New Economic Policy', 423, 425n
New England, 106
New Guinea, 77, 135, 324
New York, 283
Ngura, 88
Nicholas II, of Russia, 422
Nilotes, 188
Nippur, 76n
niyabat-i-'amma, 262
N.K.V.D., 427
noble(s), nobility, 10, 22n, 26, 33, 48, 67n, 74–5, 91n, 93, 95, 106, 117n, 120, 162, 212, 220, 224, 234, 288, 289, 293, 294, 313, 318–19, 362, 364, 365–6, 373–4, 399, 402–3, 409n, 445
noblesse d'épée, 21, 221, 365, 366
noblesse de robe, 21, 222, 223
nomenklatura, 249

nomothetēs, 333
North Vanuatu, 326
Norway, 283
Nuer, 151, 321
Nuremberg, 199n
Nyakusa, 187n
Nyoro, 191, 192

oba, 188, 217n
Obregón, 356, 357, 358
obrok, 233
obschina, 422
odnodvortsy, 222n
Odo Nobunaga, 158, 214, 377, 387
Odysseus, 79
oey, 187
officiers, 220–1
O.G.P.U., 424
okonko, 98
omadhes, 97
ometsuke, 387
Ongania, 432
orang kaya, 231
orang laut, 231
order(s), 20, 23, 92, 138n, 421
Ormists, 173
Osaka, 376n
Oswine of Northumbria, 153
Ottoman(s), 21, 175, 210, 216, 227–8, 271, 350, 384–6, 396, 398–400
Ottonians, 121, 182, 313
outcaste(s), 63, 95, 98
Oxbegs, 351
oyabun-koyabun, 246
Oyo, 51n, 217

Pachacuti, 220
padishah, 350
Papacy, 372, 373, 445
Papal States, 314
Paraguay, 96, 107n, 138n, 205, 275, 428
'paramount', chiefs, 185, 186, 325
Paris, 34
parlement(s), 173, 221, 343n, 346, 362
pashas, 386
Pasion, 129n
'passing', 19, 61, 95, 112n, 144n, 421, 425n
pastoralism, 141n, 150–1, 152, 187, 188–9, 190, 207, 334
patrimonialism, 155, 156, 190–1, 193, 194–6, 206, 213, 227, 231, 237, 312, 372, 391, 443, 446
patrocinium, 215
patron(s), patronage, 52, 83, 102, 105, 140n, 200, 204, 257, 258, 289, 305, 358, 359, 406, 408
Paul the Deacon, 196–7
paulette, 127, 230, 342
Pausanias, 335
Pavia, 372
pawnship, 113–14, 116n
peasant(s), peasantry, 22, 58, 95, 101, 111, 120, 174, 203, 206, 212, 215, 223, 253n, 276, 294, 300, 306–7, 349, 361n, 363n, 364, 369, 373, 399, 412–13, 423
Peiraeus, 331n
Peisistratus, 192
Peloponnesian War, 27, 129, 316, 327
penestai, 196, 334
peonage, peons, 59, 114, 305, 358, 368, 380
peones acasillados, 307
Pepin, king of the Franks, 50, 154
Periander of Corinth, 130, 192
Pericles, 329n
perioikoi, 155, 198, 200, 316, 318
Perón, 256, 340, 431–2
Perry, Commodore, 294
Persia, 203, 307, 421
Peru, 42, 55, 58, 189, 256, 349, 369
Peter the Great, of Russia, 99, 220, 423
pharaoh, 193
Philip II, king of Spain, 344
Philip of Macedon, 327
Philippe Auguste, 23, 286, 315
Philippines, 447
Philolaus of Corinth, 333
Picenum, 408
Pilaga, 127n
Pisa, 155, 198, 372
Pitt, William (the Younger), 235
Pizarro, Francisco, 277
Place, Francis, 89
planters, 276–7
plebeians, 75, 142n, 437, 438
Pliny the Younger, 118
'plural' societies, 65n
Plymouth, Massachusetts, 201
podestà, 68
Poland, 93, 95, 158, 176–7, 181, 212, 213, 251n, 356n, 369, 373–4, 385, 388
polarization, 8, 138–48, 181
polemarchos, 333
polis, *poleis*, 5, 57, 58, 128, 133, 155, 175, 197, 198, 199, 202, 280, 299, 327–31, 438–9
Polybius, 437
polygyny, 143n
pomeshchik(s), 140–1, 220, 222, 293, 313, 341, 403
Pompey, 409, 410, 411
popolo, 199
population, 31, 41n, 176, 242, 263, 281, 285, 300, 304, 308, 314, 338, 417, 441
Portugal, 132n, 255, 271, 436, 444ff.
poverty, 35n
power, 2, and *passim*.
practice(s), 41 and *passim*.
'prebendalism', 220
prédroit, 14, 81
prestanza, 199n

prestige, 12, 13, 18, 30, 31, 33, 57, 59, 62, 63, 74, 110, 118, 151n, 163, 188, 204, 254, 277, 298, 337n, 364, 419
prévot(s), 214, 315, 370
priest(s), 77, 109, 132, 193, 222n, 240, 289, 434
primogeniture, 143n, 235
prodrazvertska, 423
proletarii, 174
pronoia, 216, 293, 300
propinacja, 212
proskynesis, 163
Protestantism, 288–9, 348, 414
proto-state(s), 152–3, 155, 194, 195, 217, 298, 308, 312, 326, 443
proxenos, 50, 280, 332n
Prussia, 126n, 222, 223–4, 281, 400–3
prytanis, 333
psychology, 7, 32–3, 38, 46, 126, 281, 426, 441, 449
publicani, 207, 233
Pukhtun, 68n
putting-out, 54, 337, 414

Qays, 204n
Querini, Marco, 136
Quizilbash, 350

radcniht(s), 83, 146, 341
Raetia, 201
Ragyappo, 95
rank(s), rank-order, 9, 16, 17, 20, 29, 70n, 83, 86ff., 107, 169, 245, 279, 421, 442
reaya, 208n, 386
rebellion(s), 13, 111, 154, 215, 217, 317, 340ff.,
Reconquest, 104, 204–5, 445
Rectitudines Singularum Personarum, 53, 242
Red Army, 178, 424
reddingsdaad, 264n
redū, 240
Reform Bill (1832), 89, 290, 355
reform(s), 340ff., 352ff., 367
'relative deprivation', 36, 37, 97, 99, 101, 103, 111, 112, 113, 130, 184, 201, 225n, 236, 243, 244, 247, 260, 262, 286, 290, 296, 298, 307, 353n, 380, 388, 397, 399, 401, 407, 419, 426, 427, 439, 442
religion, 14, 57, 116, 132n, 161, 198, 259, 262, 285, 344, 398, 419n
rent, 61, 156, 159, 180, 203–4, 208, 216, 416
reproduction, 8, 138–48, 185, 253
'reproduction ratio', 139, 143, 144–5, 147, 210, 211, 225, 250, 308
reth, 81, 150
retrait lignager, 143n
revolution(s), 30, 106, 146, 154, 184, 260, 290, 328n, 340ff., 355ff., 360, 361n
Reza Shah, of Iran, 269
Rhodes, 130
Rhodesia, 272–3, 435
ritual(s), 13, 18, 35, 59, 61, 62, 77, 102, 150, 198, 295, 416
Robert the Pious, 313
Robespierre, 363
Roger II, king of Sicily, 121, 218
role(s), 3 and *passim*.
role-reversal, 67
Rome, Roman(s), 10–11, 19, 21, 24n, 33, 50, 58, 65n, 74, 80n, 88, 89, 90, 91n, 95, 105–6, 115, 128, 129, 133, 169, 174, 183, 199, 200–1, 228–30, 232–4, 244, 272, 287, 291–3, 299, 327, 351–2, 362, 407–11, 436, 437–40, 443
rōnin, 376n
Rousseau, Jean-Jacques, 15
Russell, Bertrand, 2, 4
Russia, Russian(s), 58, 76, 99, 140–1, 165, 183, 207, 221ff., 246, 293–4, 421–7, 434, 448
Russian Revolution, 94, 126n, 360, 424
Rwanda, 51, 106, 107

Saba, 382
Sabines, 439
sabiqa, 442, 443
Safavids, 212n
Saint-Simon, Duc de, 53
Sakaki, 376n
Salazar, 256n
Sallust, 317
Salvian, 216
Samburu, 188–9
Samnites, 437
samurai, 26, 125, 294, 353, 377, 389, 419, 420n
'Sanskritisation', 124, 126, 144n
sanyasi, 16
Sapa Inca, 21, 427
Saracens, 180, 312, 445
Sarawak, 33
Sarbadar, 262n
sardar, 151, 186, 333
Satsuma Rebellion, 125
Saxons, Saxony, 195, 222n
scapegoat(ing), 66–7
Scipio Nasica, 410
Scotland, 21, 266, 274, 302–3, 355n, 404
'Sea Beggars', 344
'secondary' rank, 29, 83, 106, 110
secret societies, 97, 98n, 326
seigneur(s), 144, 173
seigneurie banale, 213, 300, 313n, 370
Seljuks, 212n
semi-states, 153, 189, 193, 195, 197, 205, 295, 308
serf(s), serfdom, 53, 58, 95, 141, 196, 222–3, 294, 334, 380, 403
service nobility, 141, 157, 218, 220ff., 230, 365, 403

Servius Tullius, 142n
seyhülislam, 385
shahanshah, 383, 384
shaman(s), shamanism, 62
Shantung, 391
sharaf, 442
sharecropping, 58, 114, 148–9, 304–7, 322
Sharente, 127n
Sharī'a, 262, 383, 386
sheikh(s), 153, 179
Shiism, 245n, 262, 270, 350, 351
shiki, 375n, 377
Shilluk, 81, 150
Shintoism, 376n
shōen, 213, 377
shogun, 158, 213–14, 387ff., 417
shugo, 213, 375
Sicily, 51, 121, 191, 218–19, 299n, 372
Sidonius Apollinaris, 194n
Siena, 155
Sigehard of Burghausen, 97n
signore, *signoria*, 68, 191, 328
Sind, 273
Sippar, 76n
'skidders', 103, 420
slave(s), slavery, 11, 19, 48, 59, 63, 74, 92, 94, 96, 97, 98, 106n, 113, 115–16, 118, 124n, 133–4, 155, 205, 207, 217, 219, 227–8, 240–1, 242, 267, 268, 277, 301–2, 334, 385, 396n, 408, 438, 445
smallholers, 112n, 174, 199, 222n, 235, 242, 287, 363, 413, 417
Smith, Adam, 31, 73, 77n, 427n
social mobility, 25, 26, 27–37, 28, 82, 105, 110, 123ff., 138–48, 151, 203, 220, 234n, 235, 237, 243, 244, 254, 269, 289, 290, 308, 309, 317, 352, 355, 363, 389, 412, 413, 425, 440
'Social' War, 201, 407, 440
socialism, 164, 177, 181, 238, 249–55, 359, 422, 423, 448
Soga, 197n
Sokoto Caliphate, 156
Solon, 20, 99n, 335
sosloviye, 24
South Africa, 164, 167, 263–5
South Fore, 324
Soviet Union, 82, 92, 169, 171, 177, 178, 181, 250–1, 272, 281
Spain, Spanish, 34, 107, 165, 204–5, 255, 256, 267, 277–8, 287, 344, 379, 400n, 408n, 435, 436
Sparta, 21, 27, 92, 106, 136, 198, 199, 316–18
Spartacus, 128, 129
Spartiates, 21, 27, 92, 106, 136, 155, 173, 198, 199, 316–18
Spencer, Herbert, 38, 168
spice trade, 236, 446
sredniak, 22
Sri Lanka, 43
stadholder, 237
Stalin, 126n, 165, 169, 250, 270, 423, 425, 426–7, 431
stasis, 124n, 129n, 299n, 327–8, 342, 410n
status-group(s), 17n, 18, 23–4, 26, 56, 59, 63, 67, 98n, 105, 110, 112n, 220, 222, 231, 253, 406, 442
Stephen, king of England, 183, 218
stock-friends, 65
stratum, strata, 20, 24, 105, 110, 151, 209, 320
Stroessner, General, 96
structure, 8–9, 11, 12–20, 25, 26, 67, 125–6, 148, 214, 309, 341, 449
Sudan, 76, 130, 150
Sufism, 228, 350, 351
Sulla, 292
Sumer, Sumerians, 189, 193, 273, 325
Sunnism, 228, 245n, 270, 350
suyūrghāl, 212n, 384
Sverdlov, 426
Swat, 68n
Sweden, 44n, 54, 57, 82, 145–6, 164, 248, 260–2
Switzerland, 100, 155, 201
Symmachus, 229
sympoliteiai, 280
synoecism, 332n, 333
Syracuse, 299n
Syria, 273, 441n, 443
syssitia, 198, 317–18
'systact(s)', 20 and *passim*.
szlachta, 93, 214, 223, 369, 373

'Table of Ranks', 99
Tabriz, 350
tagos, 121, 196, 383
Tahiti, 280
Tahmasp, 350–1
Tahuantinsuyu, 55–6, 220, 230, 231
taille, 221
Taiping Rebellion, 343
Tairora, 325
Takeda, 214
Tallensi, 21
tamkarum, 163n
'Tammany Hall', 428
tax(es), taxation, 42, 61, 79, 80–1, 95, 109, 118, 128, 156, 159, 186, 197, 203–4, 207, 216, 218, 219, 222, 235, 240, 245, 329n, 330, 365, 373, 392, 397, 400, 417, 439
tax-farmers, 154, 207, 219–20, 288, 385
Telemachus, 79
tenancy, tenants, 30, 58, 84, 101, 149, 154, 155n, 209n, 242, 243, 266, 305, 413, 417
tennō, 52, 121, 383
Teutonic Knights, 58, 156, 160, 198, 205–6, 207, 222n
Thebes, 333
thegn(s), 21, 146, 239, 240, 243

theow(s), 21, 161
Thessaly, 121, 196, 334
Thrasybulus of Miletus, 130
Tiberius Gracchus, 174, 292, 328, 410
Tibet, 95, 158
Tichbourne, Chidiock, 5
Tiepolo, Bajamonte, 136
timar, timariot(s), 210, 230, 293, 385
'Time of Troubles', 183
Timur, 207, 384, 398
Tito, 251, 252
tiyūls, 351, 384
Tocqueville, 37, 168, 238n, 434, 448
Todar Mal, 230
Tokugawa Ieyasu, 158, 220, 375, 377, 404, 407
Toltec, 189
Toro, 141
'total' institutions, 84, 103
totalitarianism, 66n, 165, 423, 426, 431
Totila, 129n
Towers Islands, 326
Toyotomi Hideyoshi, 158, 214, 376n, 389
trade unions, 22, 166, 245, 246, 256, 257, 261, 282, 290, 425, 426, 432
tresantes, 27
trésoriers épiscopaux, 308n
tribunus plebis, 65n, 299
tribute, 61, 79, 153, 156, 190, 202, 203–4, 207, 381
Trobriand Islanders, 55
Trotsky, 423
tsar(s), tsardom, 94n, 223, 228, 293–4, 403–4, 427
Tullianus, 129n
Tulu, 369
Tupino, 127n
Turkana, 189
Turkey, 58, 119, 263, 281, 282, 348, 378n
turuq, 97
Tusculum, 439
Tutsi, 106
'Twelve Articles', 343n
'Twelve Tables', 328
tyrant(s), tyranny, 66n, 130, 155, 187, 191, 192, 193n, 199, 299

ubuhake, 51
Ukraine, 374
ulemate (*ulama*), 98n, 204, 228
Umar, 443n
Umayyads, 397–8, 399
umma, 167, 443
'underclass', 27, 108, 245, 250n
United Privinces, 160
United States of America, 34, 36n, 54, 57, 64, 160, 169, 238–9, 245–6, 269, 270, 273, 280, 281, 301–2, 345, 356n, 357, 360, 380, 427–8, 429, 447–8

urbanization, 85–6, 210, 333

Vakf, 385
vakil, 230
valipoi, 325
Varro, 329n
vassal(s), vassalage, 50–1, 121, 154, 158, 184, 195, 212, 213–14, 217, 227, 313n, 314n, 368, 370–1, 375, 377, 387
vavasour(s), 22
Vecheka, 424
Venice, 51, 136, 237, 318–20, 327, 328, 376n, 436
verkrampte, 265
Verlager, *Verlagssystem*, 99–100
verligte, 265
Versailles, 387
Vietnam, 306
Vijayanagara, 369n
Vikings, 21, 180, 312, 434
Villa, Pancho (Villistas), 85, 214n, 215, 356–7, 375
villani, 240
Visigoths, 62
Vitale II Michiel, Doge of Venice, 328, 329
Volscians, 439
votchina, 222, 293, 403
Vunamami, 324n

wage-labour, 59, 62, 98, 99, 114, 117, 134, 208n, 233, 235, 244, 287, 302, 337, 360, 374, 380, 408, 413, 417, 428
wahil tujjar, 49
wanax, 14
Wang An-Shih, 394
Wang Ko, 62
wardū, 20, 161
Washington, George, 303
Weber, Max, 12n, 23, 47, 48, 83, 155, 167, 168, 191, 194n, 220, 343, 368, 415, 428
Wen-ming, 390
Werner of Urslingen, 84, 207
Wessex, 92, 107
West Africa, 102, 322, 389, 446
wilayat al-faqih, 263
Wilkes, John, 108n
William I, king of England, 121, 218
William of Orange, 344
Wilson, Sir Thomas, 91n
Wisselbank, 236
woikiatai, 334
women, 29, 67–8, 73, 90n, 106, 110, 125, 235, 246, 260, 263, 287, 418, 442
'working class', 108, 181, 245, 256, 290, 353, 355, 357n, 418, 428, 429, 431n

Xenophon, 316, 331n

yanaconas, 190
yanas, 42

Yanomamo, 39
yeomen, 21, 124, 160, 235, 412, 414, 422
Young, G. M., 34n
Yucatan, 267, 311, 358, 380
Yugoslavia, 251–2

zaibatsu, 259
za'im, 52
zakat, 167, 397
Zapata, Zapatistas, 356–7
Zhukov, Marshal, 425n.